Programming ADO.NET

Programming ADO.NET

Richard Hundhausen
Steven Borg

Gearhead Press™

Wiley Computer Publishing

John Wiley & Sons, Inc.

Publisher: Robert Ipsen
Editor: Theresa Hudsen
Consulting Editor: Donis Marshall
Managing Editor: Angela Smith
New Media Editor: Brian Snapp
Text Design & Composition: John Wiley Composition Services

This book is printed on acid-free paper. ♾

Published by John Wiley & Sons, Inc., New York

Published simultaneously in Canada.

Library of Congress Cataloging-in-Publication Data:

ISBN: 0-471-20187-1

Printed in the United States of America.

10 9 8 7 6 5 4 3 2 1

To all of the developers and IT professionals who lost their lives during the September 11 tragedy, and for their family members who continue on.

A Note from Gearhead Press

Gearhead Press is dedicated to publishing technical books for experienced Information Technology professionals—network engineers, developers, system administrators, and others—who need to update their skills, learn how to use technology more effectively, or simply want a quality reference to the latest technology. Gearhead Press emerged from my experience with professional trainers of engineers and developers: people who truly understand first-hand the needs of working professionals. Gearhead Press authors are the crème de la crème of industry trainers, working at the companies that define the technology revolution. For this reason, Gearhead Press authors are regularly in the trenches with the developers and engineers that have changed the world through innovative products. Drawing from this experience in IT training, our books deliver superior technical content with a unique perspective that is based on real-world experience.

Now, as an imprint of John Wiley & Sons, Inc., Gearhead Press will continue to bring you, the reader, the level of quality that Wiley has delivered consistently for nearly 200 years.

Thank you.

Donis Marshall
Founder, Gearhead Press
Consulting Editor, Wiley Computer Publishing

Gearhead Press Books in Print

(For complete information about current and upcoming titles, go to www.wiley.com/compbooks/)

Books in the Gearhead Press *Point to Point* Series
Migrating to Microsoft Exchange 2000 by Stan Reimer
ISBN: 0-471-06116-6

Installing and Configuring Web Servers Using Apache by Melanie Hoag
ISBN: 0-471-07155-2

VoiceXML: 10 Projects to Voice Enable Your Website by Mark Miller
ISBN: 0-471-20737-3

Books in the Gearhead Press *In the Trenches* Series
Windows 2000 Automated Deployment by Ted Malone and Rolly Perraux
ISBN: 0-471-06114-X

Robust Linux: Assuring High Availability by Iain Campbell
ISBN: 0-471-07040-8

Programming Directory Services for Windows 2000 by Donis Marshall
ISBN: 0-471-15216-1

Programming ADO.NET by Richard Hundhausen and Steven Borg
ISBN: 0-471-20187-1

Designing .NET Web Services Using ADO.NET and XML by Richard Hundhausen and Steven Borg
ISBN: 0-471-20186-3

Making Win32 Applications Mobile: Porting to Windows CE by Nancy Nicolaisen
ISBN: 0-471-21618-6

Programming Windows CE Wireless Applications by Barry Shilmover and Derek Ball
ISBN: 0-471-21469-8

Mastering SQL Server 2002 Security by Mike Young and Curtis Young
ISBN: 0-471-21970-3

Microsoft.NET Security Programming by Donis Marshall
ISBN: 0-471-22285-2

Contents

About the Authors

RICHARD HUNDHAUSEN is a software architect, author and Microsoft Certified Trainer specializing in constructing useful Windows and Web-based applications using Microsoft products and technologies. His background is in leading development of distributed object systems in the agricultural, engineering, medical, telecommunications, and military sectors. Richard holds a B.S. degree in Computer and Information Science from the University of Maryland, is an MCSD, MCDBA, and is co-author of the *MCSD Training Guide: Visual Basic 6 Exams* (New Riders) and several industry articles. Richard lives in Boise, Idaho, with his wife Kristen. When he is not in front of the computer, deciphering MSDN and sipping Macallan, you'll find him on the soccer field, hacking away as left fullback.

STEVEN BORG is a software architect and developer, specializing in XML and .NET development for Windows and the Web. He's an independent consultant, trainer, and author with a passion for theory. His background is in mathematical modeling, operations research, non-linear dynamics, economics, and philosophy. He spends far more time in front of the computer than he should, but loves programming, learning, and CNN.com. Steve hasn't put down roots anywhere since leaving Germany, but is currently sleeping in Boise, Idaho. When he's not programming, he's admiring the non-linear dynamics of his five ant colonies.

Preface

We wrote this book to assist you in developing ADO.NET applications. Whether you're a veteran ActiveX Data Objects programmer or new to the idea of accessing data via an object model, you will share the same predicament: ADO.NET is radically different than previous versions of ADO. As intimidating as that sounds, consider it an opportunity for you to master what Microsoft has finally perfected!

After so many versions of Microsoft's Data Access Components (MDAC), XML integration and the disconnected capabilities of classic ADO still felt like an afterthought. ADO.NET was engineered with these two principals at its core. XML integration is automatic with the DataSet class, allowing a developer to read from a traditional data source and write to an XML source, or vice versa by simply calling a method. The disconnected personality of ADO.NET is apparent when you realize that you can create and persist an entire database in memory, including all tables, relationships, and all schema information. We believe that Microsoft got it right this time, the first time with ADO.NET.

Our book serves three purposes:

First, our book will be your scythe, allowing you to cut through the thick tangle of "marketecture" (architecture as explained by marketing folks) that exists in the world right now. Who hasn't read a product review or article and been lead to believe that .NET will cure world hunger or become the platform of choice for the Matrix? In the first two chapters we explain, in clear terms, what .NET and ADO.NET are and are not. In fairness to the technology, ADO.NET is not simply the latest version of ADO, but rather the collective term for the data access services found in the .NET Framework. Yes, its texture and taste are vaguely familiar to that of the ADO that you found in MDAC, but ADO.NET adheres to the strict principals of the .NET Framework. Yahoo!

Second, our book will be your comprehensive reference guide, providing you with a thorough and detailed reference to everything that's ADO.NET. This was no small undertaking. The ADO.NET section of the .NET Framework, which you will come to know as System.Data and its related namespaces, delivers over 200 classes, structures, and enumerations, each containing between 5 to 50 members. Chapters 4 through 9 cover System.Data, System.Data.Common, Microsoft.Data.Odbc, System.Data.OleDb, System.Data.SqlClient, and System.Data.SqlTypes, respectively.

No, our reference section is not simply a regurgitation of Microsoft's MSDN. It is, in fact, a complete rewrite of the ADO.NET documentation, in our own unambiguous words, using our own simple code samples. In addition, we have added many notes about what doesn't work in ADO.NET as advertised, and we point out the work-arounds and shortcuts that MSDN has missed.

Finally, our book will *teach* you how to use ADO.NET. Chapter 3 takes the initial steps in this direction by showing you how easy it is to build ADO.NET applications within the Visual Studio .NET IDE. We review the Server Explorer and introduce you to Data Adapter objects and how to configure them with the configuration wizard and preview the data at Design Time. We will also show how DataSets, the cornerstone of ADO.NET, can be generated from within the IDE and their XML schema definition (XSD) viewed and edited. Conversely, we will show how easy it is to create XML documents and schemas and then generate the associated DataSets. These demonstrations are intended to make you comfortable with the concept that ADO.NET DataSets are XML documents and vice versa.

Our tutorial section also includes three chapters at the end of the book, which demonstrate the primary areas of functionality with ADO.NET. Chapter 10 shows how to access data sources using one of the three managed providers. We'll look at System.Odbc, System.OleDb, and System.SqlClient here, and show you how to establish a connection and retrieve data either to a DataReader object for a quick scan, or to a DataSet object for a thorough walkthrough. We will explore Connection, Transaction, Command, Parameter, and Error/Exception objects here—all familiar topics to a seasoned ADO developer. Chapter 11 will continue the tutorial, showing you how to manipulate data after it has been accessed. This chapter is not provider specific, meaning that we look at the core objects, such as the DataTable, DataRow, and DataSet, as well as the level of functionality provided by each. What you learn in this chapter will be usable in your ODBC, OLEDB, or SQL Server applications. Finally, in Chapter 12, you will see the full power of the DataSet control as we demonstrate the various XML integration mechanisms.

Although you could read this book from cover to cover, provided you have a serious cup of coffee to get you through the reference section, we recommend that you take a more tactical approach:

- If you are new to .NET, you will want to read Chapter 1.
- If you are new to ADO.NET, you will want to read Chapters 2, 10, 11, and 12.
- If you are planning on building data-centric applications with Visual Studio .NET, you will want to read Chapter 3.
- Once you begin writing ADO.NET code, you will want to refer to the appropriate reference sections and, possibly, the tutorial sections again.
- Once you become a skilled ADO.NET developer, you will probably only need to refer to the reference section.

Remember that ADO.NET is nothing more than a conduit for your data to reach your users. We recommend that readers of this book should have an understanding of Structured Query Language (SQL) and experience working with relational databases or XML files, as these represent the data sources that you will be working with.

Acknowledgments

Thanks to the hardworking people at Wiley Computer Publishing and Gearhead Press for their efforts on constructing this reference book—especially Kathryn Malm, Terri Hudson, and Trudy Neuhaus. We bent a few of their rules to get this epic reference guide produced and, hopefully, they'll have us back to do another one soon. The .NET Framework, much like central Idaho, has many areas yet to be documented.

This wouldn't be possible without the direct members of our virtual team (only some of whom I've met face to face): Donis Marshall for being the publishing visionary that he is and for cracking that whip across our collective spine, Carl Prothman (www.able-consulting.com) for being an ADO guru and Visual Basic MVP thus keeping our material accurate, Jon Beck for providing us with a strategist's insight and a screamin' fast server to host our projects, and David Jordan for swapping me a faster laptop for my Klein mountain bike. A large thanks also to the folks at MSN, specifically those who built MSN Messenger, without which we could not have collaborated so closely with (most) of our team. Donis, are you reading this?

My wife Kristen was my principal sponsor during this writing effort, mostly for supporting me throughout those marathon writing sessions, but also for understanding the commitment and not seeking out one of those 24-hour divorce courts.

Finally, I must thank my co-author Steven Borg who convinced me that we could do it. I knew from the day I met him that we could accomplish anything that we put our minds to. This book proves my point. If he hadn't mentioned this crazy notion of sailing the Wings of Morning, we'd still be in Stuttgart building COM objects and disrupting John's desktop.

—Richard Hundhausen

Ditto on Rich's acknowledgements. So many people, so much help. MSN Messenger truly was a help. Without it, I'd have been stranded in a remote Alaskan village for much of this book's writing, without the nearly constant reassurance of having Rich only a mouse click away. A final plea as this book goes to press—"Donis, get on Messenger!"

A huge thanks to all the people who've housed me during my global wandering this past year. Thanks for the couches, sleeping bags, meals, and internet connections that allowed me to keep writing this book. (Oh, and for putting up with "homeless and unemployed" jokes—writing a book isn't real "employment," is it?)

I would be remiss if I didn't thank the one person most responsible for this book, Rich Hundhausen. I've never met a more productive or professional programmer. He's at least three times as fast at developing solid production code as any other programmer I've ever met. He's also a master salesman. First, he convinced me I should get my MCSD. Then, why not an MCT? There's good money in training, and it's fun. And finally, why not be an independent? Give up your high-paying job in Europe and give up the security of having a constant paycheck. Thanks, Rich, I couldn't be happier.

—Steven Borg

PART One

Introduction

This section introduces you to .NET, ADO.NET, and Visual Studio .NET. You have probably been introduced to .NET by now, and, given the number of marketing channels available to Microsoft, we're fairly sure you have. Since Microsoft is branding nearly all of its products as .NET products, we want to ensure that you understand .NET as it pertains to software development. Since we are programmers and not marketing suits, we will define the ubiquitous .NET term in a *what can it do for you as a programmer* context.

It is also important to bring you up-to-date on ADO. We will explain the history of ActiveX Data Objects and how the many version upgrades through the years have lead to such a strong XML presence and disconnected nature in the current version of ADO. We will also explain how these behaviors were inherited and improved upon in ADO.NET. You should understand the difference between the ADO that you receive in the Microsoft Data Access Components (MDAC) download, and ADO.NET which is part of the .NET Framework. In communicating with other firms and software developers, we found that a percentage of new .NET applications will continue to use classic ADO from within their .NET applications. We show you how and when to interoperate with classic ADO.

Finally, if you'll forgive us, we blatantly devote a whole chapter to all of the bells and whistles in Visual Studio .NET that pertain to generating ADO.NET code. As with classic ADO, ADO.NET is free and doesn't require Visual Studio .NET. It is part of the .Net Framework and will be downloaded and installed accordingly. That having been said, if you happen to own Visual Studio .NET, we'll show you how quickly you can generate most of the primary objects and accompanying source code—to get your data-intensive projects under way.

CHAPTER

1

Introduction to .NET

"If you don't make your own products obsolete, the competition will do it for you."
Akio Morita, President of Sony

We're lucky to live in such a thrilling age. With Microsoft's release of the .NET Framework, we are on the cusp of a revolution that will forever change life as we know it. No longer will people be tied to their desks. People will remain wired, even on the beach, where they will gather daily for frolics in the sand and sun. The programmer's Nirvana has arrived, world peace is near at hand, and pestilence and disease will finally be conquered, once and for all. Soon battalions of programmers and Internet surfers will be solving the great problems that beset humanity. With computer languages interoperating with ease, even inheriting functionality from one another, it cannot be long before even death itself is conquered.

Or so say the marketing materials and press releases we've read lately.

Of course, the future may not be so rosy after all. Some say the unveiling of .NET portends the dawning of an evil age. Microsoft will finally eliminate all remaining competition, spreading its monopolistic tentacles into every facet of our private lives. From bedroom to boardroom, our every move will be tracked. Enormous databases to track our preferences will record our every purchase, flooding us with bulk-mail that promises to cater to our deepest and most embarrassing secret desires. Once Microsoft has bought all the world's other corporations, it will squeeze us into a life of antlike servitude, serving only our corporate masters. This, of course, may take a while, but we'll see foreshadowing of what's to come with the downfall of first Sun, then IBM. The world's open source programmers, disillusioned by Sun's handling of Java, will be wooed by the platform and language independence of .NET, abandon their principles, and begin enriching the coffers of the Evil Empire.

Or so say the discussion threads on Slashdot.

The .NET Framework is good, very good. But it's not as good as its proponents claim. It could give Microsoft a formidable advantage to wield against competitors. It, however, will neither cure disease nor allow Microsoft to dominate the planet Earth.

As programmers, we've seen the hype and experienced the reality of countless software releases. In very few cases does software live up to the hype its proponents hope for or cause the worldwide devastation its detractors fear. Software just is. Some software is useful and becomes part of our toolkit; other software becomes obsolete and gets left to the side.

The .NET Framework and its associated technologies are tools, and some of the most useful at our disposal as programmers, but they remain only that—a toolkit. Like object-oriented programming or relational databases, it will cause a major shift in the way we design, write, and even think about software. Our productivity will rise, our earning potential will increase, but we'll still work hard to design good software. We may get to inherit more functionality, but we'll still have to assemble useful and usable applications. .NET assemblies may eliminate "DLL Hell," but users will still screw up installations of their software.

All pleasantries and introductions aside, this chapter is about .NET—what it is and what it *actually* will do for you. So let's get down to business.

First, the marketing department has made a muddle of the term ".NET." It's being slapped onto every new software release out of Redmond. SQL Server 2000 is one of the new .NET Servers, even though it is still based on COM architecture and has to have its arm twisted (though only just a bit) to kick out reasonable XML. BizTalk Server 2000 and Application Center 2000 have the .NET logo slapped onto their marketing, almost as an afterthought, despite being firmly footed in Windows DNA (Distributed iNternet Architecture). We believe all three of these will become very important tools for .NET applications; however, that's down the road. Right now, anything that can speak a little XML is being touted as .NET. To be fair, Microsoft calls these the ".NET Enterprise Servers," and, if you read it the right way, that can imply that they help serve .NET applications, but are not actually built to use any of the .NET technologies. It's as if Microsoft prefixed its SQL Server 6.5 release with the word "Internet" just because the database could be used to provide data for Web servers.

For the purposes of this book (and for reasons of common sense), we'll define .NET a bit more specifically. For us, .NET will be composed of the .NET Framework itself and applications that compile to the Microsoft Intermediate Language (MSIL) and are run using the Common Language Runtime. Microsoft calls this managed code (more on all these things in just a moment).

.NET applications are those that have three key attributes:

- They use a common set of services that can be accessed from a large number of programming languages.
- They are compiled to an intermediate code that is independent of the machine architecture.
- They operate within a machine-specific runtime that manages resources and execution.

We'll forgive you if the first thing that springs to your mind is Java. Except for the first attribute, this all sounds suspiciously like Java. In fact, there are so many parallels it would be unreasonable to believe that a great deal of the inspiration for the .NET architecture did not come from Java.

Code, written in one (or more) supported .NET languages, is compiled into a platform-independent intermediate language called the Microsoft Intermediate Language (MSIL for short or IL for shorter). This code can then be run on any machine that sports a common language runtime, which is a machine-specific interface that translates the MSIL into the machine-specific code needed to run on the underlying architecture. If you're familiar with Java, the MSIL equates roughly to Java byte code, and the common language runtime compares to the Java Virtual Machine (JVM). There are many other similarities with Java and other technologies, but .NET takes them much further. In many cases, Microsoft has advanced the state-of-the art considerably. In other cases, it has made a few mistakes and left inconsistencies that distract from the beauty, but not the function, of .NET as a programming environment.

All in all, the .NET Framework is an incredible technological achievement. Yes, Microsoft has stood on the shoulders of giants, but taking the state of the art in so many fields and combining it into a single, coherent framework is an amazing achievement for any single project.

Microsoft: .NET or Bust

One of the most troubling aspects of programming is ensuring that applications will behave similarly across platforms. The dominance of the Windows platform across the industry was a remarkable boon to programmers. They could program to one platform that had broad acceptance throughout the industry. This simplified development greatly. But the problems weren't completely solved. Trouble existed even between versions of Windows. (Anybody remember the Win32s debacle?) Programs that ran just fine under Windows NT raised unexpected errors when installed on a Windows 98 platform. NT platforms without SP4 crashed when running software designed on a box with SP4. No matter how carefully you wrote code, you couldn't be sure that your application would perform the same way on another version (and sometimes even another install) of Windows without deploying it for testing on that platform.

The "Write Once, Run Anywhere" Java tagline didn't even exist as "Write Once, Run Anywhere There's Windows." Sun upped the bar when it produced Java and the first commercially successful virtual machine. Suddenly, programmers could code against a common interface and expect it to work anywhere there was a JVM. Microsoft reacted very strongly to this threat, and for good business reasons. If programmers could create a single program that could run anywhere, the key benefit of using the Windows operating system would disappear. Why buy Windows when any OS, even a free one, could be used to run all applications? .NET is Microsoft's latest response. Instead of the heavy-handed, some say anti-competitive, measures Microsoft has used in the past, .NET is an "if you can't beat 'em, join 'em" response. Microsoft has seen the future, and it is betting its future profitability, if not survival, on .NET. To see why, let's take a short walk down memory lane.

In the beginning, programmers wrote code specifically for a single chip. Usually written in machine language, or a bit later, assembly, these programs could run on only one type of machine. The code interacted directly with the chip, making it completely unreadable by any other processor. Later came higher-level languages, like Fortran and COBOL, which allowed programmers to write code in a language and, within some fairly strict limits, compile that code to different processors. At the time, this made financial sense—computer processor time was drastically more expensive than programmer time.

As computers got cheaper and technology improved, operating systems became more advanced. Operating systems provided a standard interface that could be programmed against. For instance, programmers could write software for Windows NT that could run on machines using both Intel x86 or Alpha chips. This came at a performance cost, it but simplified development—a reasonable trade-off now that processing time was beginning to cost much less than developer time. But it also signaled a major change in the computer industry. This departure made computer chips a commodity. No longer were programmers tied specifically to a brand of chip; they instead began to program in chosen languages or to a particular operating system. This meant chip manufacturers had to compete solely on speed, features, and price and not rely on having a large programmer base that coded to their instruction set. Microsoft benefitted greatly from this move, dominating the desktop operating system market. It was natural to have a dominant operating system. As more programmers developed programs for Windows, it became more attractive for buyers to choose Windows. More users of Windows, more programmers building Windows applications. More users = more programmers = more users = ...

NOTE This spiraling of increased use is called a virtuous cycle. (Unless, of course, you're Apple, in which case it's called a vicious circle.)

We're in the beginnings of another major shift. Introduced from two directions, almost simultaneously, both involve a further layer of abstraction on top of the operating system. These were the browser, popularized by Netscape, and the virtual machine, popularized by Sun. As a program written for an operating system could run on different computer chips, so programs written for a browser or the Java Virtual Machine could run on different operating systems. Although the browser and the virtual machine are two separate technologies, they both seek to do one thing—diminish the importance of the operating system. This threatened Microsoft's very existence as the market leader in operating systems. If it didn't matter what OS was running under the hood, why spend money for Windows when Linux was free? Microsoft fought both of these technologies aggressively and, for the most part, successfully. But it saw the writing on the wall. The browser API didn't have very many or very useful features, and the JVM was slow. Still, how long would it be before someone created a layer with enough features to make the OS obsolete? With computer speed increasing every day and costs for hardware plummeting, the day would soon come when writing specifically to the Windows API to optimize speed would become unnecessary. Microsoft is betting the bank on .NET—not because it wants to, but because it must. The operating system will soon become a commodity. Someone will be providing the next layer; it's only a question of who. Following its own corporate culture (and in the footsteps of Intel and Sony), Microsoft is making its own OS obsolete... before someone else does.

Microsoft is pouring hundreds of millions of dollars into .NET. It portrays its move to .NET as a shift to software services and mobile code. Yes, that's true; however, this is the marketing, not the underlying reality. .NET is there because, without it, Microsoft is in big trouble.

Microsoft is betting the bank on .NET. Where does that leave you and me? Learning to use .NET! Microsoft is currently the dominant company in the computer industry. If anyone can make a technology stick, especially a revolutionary one, it's Microsoft. And, with luck, .NET will attract programmers, who will attract users, who will attract programmers, who will attract users... Welcome once again to the virtuous cycle!

The Cure for the Common Code

Microsoft is going for .NET full speed ahead. How will it disconnect the development environment from the operating system? The .NET Framework is the first step, and the key components that work together are the MSIL and the common language runtime, coupled with large amounts of meta data, in the form of XML.

As explained previously, the MSIL is the platform-independent intermediate code that is compiled for execution on the platform-specific Common Language Runtime engine. The common language runtime takes the intermediate code and creates machine instructions optimized for the individual platform being used. There are two main Just-In-Time (JIT) compilers included in the Windows-based common language runtime. One of them is a very fast compiler that converts MSIL code into unoptimized machine code for executing code that will likely be run only once. For code that has a reasonably good chance of being executed often, the other major JIT compiler creates well-optimized code, which is kept in cache for reuse. (More JIT compilers are arriving all the time as well, to take advantage of scenarios falling between these two extremes.) In .NET all code is compiled, which includes the scripting languages supported by ASP.NET (JScript, VBScript). It's just that if a script is used, it is compiled to MSIL in the background, further compiled to native code, and cached. Because ASP.NET supports the use of compiled code at design time (through Visual Basic, C#, and others), we recommend you start weaning yourself from scripting languages and get into one of the powerful new languages available for ASP.NET design.

In addition to carrying out the compilation to native code at runtime, the common language runtime handles memory management, thread management, code security access, exception handling, and the execution of managed code. (Managed code is special code that is run completely internal to the common language runtime.) It provides a common type system that provides a standard set of types shared by all users of the common language runtime, thus ensuring that types are standard across all .NET languages and platforms. (This means that an Integer type will behave the same in VB, C#, and any other .NET language.) It handles the extensive meta data used by .NET to ensure that the user of the code has the proper permissions, that the code has passed a level of trust (to minimize malicious code), and that the versioning of all components is correct. The memory management internal to the common language runtime provides it with one of its largest benefits when compared with traditional programming—automatic garbage collection. Just as Java simplified coding compared to C++ by providing automatic reclamation of memory, so the .NET framework provides garbage collection for all .NET managed code. The Common Type System (CTS) not only provides for a series of basic types, but also enforces requirements for self-describing meta data for all managed code.

The management of code security and trust in the common language runtime deserves special mention. Applications and users of .NET can set varying levels of trust that they are willing to grant to individual pieces of code. This means that "Write Once, Run Anywhere" isn't *technically* true—but for good reason. When the code is run, the common language runtime takes into consideration a number of factors when determining the level of trust for a piece of code. Signed code from trusted sources gets more trust than unsigned code. Code installed from a CD gets more trust than that downloaded from the Internet. All in all, some pieces of code might not run if the user settings and common language runtime determine that the code lacks a level of trust to perform a particular action.

We've seen some of the wonderful features of the common language runtime. Now enter a strong dose of reality. .NET is new, and although people are working on implementations for other platforms, right now you've got one—and that's the one that runs on Windows. That's not necessarily a bad thing... yet. Sun didn't have implementations for more than a handful of operating systems when it released Java. It will take at least one more platform before people begin taking the platform independence of .NET seriously. Microsoft has opened the .NET Framework up to development by other firms and developers. A successful port to Linux or FreeBSD would significantly boost Microsoft's reputation among open-source advocates. Microsoft now owns a 25 percent nonvoting stake in Corel, a company with a strong reputation in the Linux community. Corel is currently porting its office suite to .NET, and it isn't unreasonable to assume a port of .NET to Linux is a strong possibility. In addition, there is a major open-source port to Linux in progress. The Mono Project, by Ximian Software, is attempting to clone the .NET common language runtime for the Linux OS using open source. If it succeeds, it will open to Linux all of the XML Web services and other .NET code that was built for the Windows common language runtime. In addition, it will provide a development platform for Linux users that will allow them to create software that will run seamlessly on Windows machines, without being limited to Java. Still, neither of these ports yet exists, but we can continue to hold out hope.

Namespaces and Base Classes

Though the Common Language Runtime is one of the main foundations of .NET, it is not the whole enchilada. In fact, as programmers, we'll likely interact far more with another rather foundational aspect of .NET—the Base Class Library (BCL). The BCL sits atop the common language runtime and provides programmers with a standard set of classes that can be used to support their own development, regardless of the programming language used. To say "set of classes" really is an understatement. We should probably say horde, bevy, multitude, host, or swarm and prefix that with an adjective like huge, enormous, uncountable, infinite, or unreasonably large. In all seriousness, the number of classes provided by .NET, in its current release, is absolutely huge—over 9,000. There is everything you've come to expect from a serious object-oriented language: all manner of collections, sophisticated IO classes, and a whole family of exceptions. In addition, there are the very powerful XML classes, the reflection and serialization classes, and even classes that assist in the automatic generation of code. The BCL replaces the reliance on native APIs and preserves platform independence by abstracting threading and other important system calls.

But that's not all. Because the .NET Framework is fully object oriented, you can inherit from prebuilt objects, adding your own functionality as required. Or you can implement a provided interface, ensuring that your objects can interact freely with the hundreds or thousands of other objects in the framework that accept implementations of the interface you used. These features are cool, very cool. If you're a Java programmer, my excitement may sound a bit excessive because you've had access to much of this functionality already. But many of you may have come from a background in Visual Basic or C++. For VB programmers, inheriting functionality has always been a colossal pain in the rump. Not only did you need to provide your custom functionality, you needed to provide your own signature for every single overridden method and property in the base object. This cluttered your code and was error prone. For C++ programmers coming to .NET, the ability to inherit was taken for granted. But you couldn't inherit easily from prebuilt objects without dealing in depth with COM interfaces, IUnknown, and other hassles. The BCL is inheritable from all languages. Even custom classes designed in a different .NET language can be seamlessly derived from. We can't possibly express our excitement sufficiently. We'd love to write several chapters on the possibilities this opens up for the developer. Unfortunately, this book isn't an OOP tutorial, and this chapter isn't an introduction to the wonders of inheritance and polymorphism. So, we must continue. (But mark my words, if you haven't been exposed to a fully object-oriented language, you're in for the ride of your life! Once you make the move to a fully OOP language, your view of software development is forever changed. You can never go back—it's a blue pill/red pill decision.)

Getting access to all these wonderful classes could be difficult if they were all jumbled up in one location. To solve this problem, and to ensure that class, method, and property names would remain unique, Microsoft has organized the BCL into a group of namespaces. A namespace is simply a logical grouping of related classes, interfaces, enumerations, and other namespaces. This is a large improvement over Java, where the namespaces are collected as a physical mapping on the hard disk. The BCL consists of a root namespace called System. Included in the System namespace is a collection of other major namespaces, such as IO, Security, and our favorite, Data. To see a listing of the top-level namespaces, take a look at Figure 1.1. We've also expanded the Data namespace, so you can see how the lower-level namespaces are organized.

The System namespace contains all of the basic types used by the .NET Framework, such as Byte, String, and the ubiquitous Object class. All objects in .NET implicitly derive from the Object class and can be assigned to an Object object. This even includes all of the primitive types such as Integer, Double, and Char. This is distinctly different from Java. In Java, the value types exist both as primitives and as reference types, a break from pure object orientation due to performance concerns. Microsoft, however, chose to implement all types, even the foundational ones, as objects.

NOTE To increase performance in .NET, Microsoft introduced a concept called "boxing" that allows primitives to be treated as objects, even though under the covers they are actually implemented as primitives.

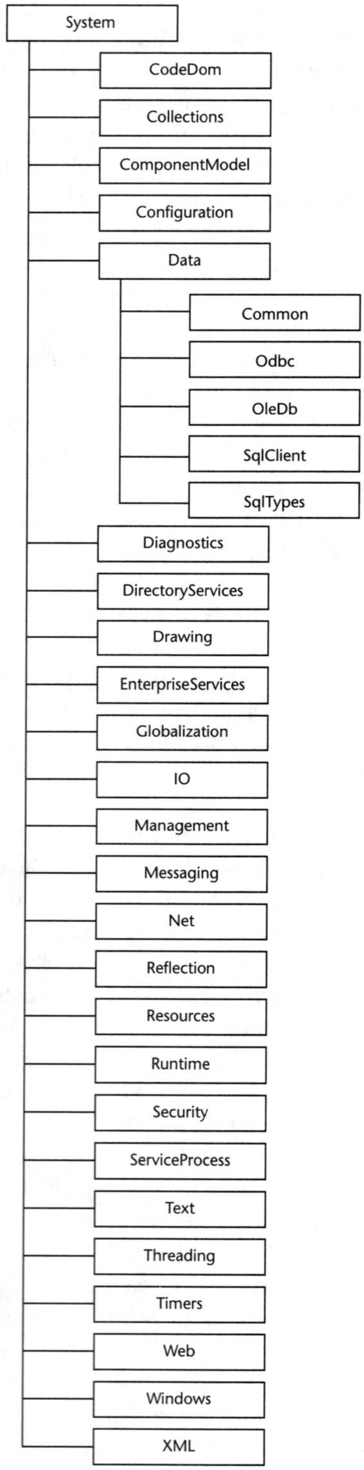

Figure 1.1 Namespace listing.

There are actually two namespaces tucked under System that handle retrieval and updating of data: System.Data and System.Xml. The System.Data namespace is used by ADO.NET, and the XML namespace handles, you guessed it, XML data sources. We'll be looking at the System.Data namespace in detail throughout this book, woven in with some examples of how to use the XML namespace as well.

.NET—The Debabelizer

Now the final act, the big show, the fat lady singing—multilanguage support. One of the largest advances in the .NET release is the support for a vast array of languages. OK, maybe it's not so vast, as yet, but it's growing fast! Even T-SQL, the high-performance SQL Server scripting language, is slated to be ported to .NET. Eiffel, COBOL, and Perl are on their way. Rumors have flown for ages that Java will be ported by Rational, makers of the famous Rational Rose, or by Borland, language gurus extraordinaire. And Microsoft itself has come out with J#, a language with a syntax very similar to that of Java.

NOTE It's interesting to note that C#, in contrast to Java, has been released to the European Computer Manufacturers Association (ECMA) for standardization. Microsoft has let it go, whereas Sun, while proclaiming its dedication to openness, has kept Java under copyright to "protect it from contamination."

There are a set of open guidelines for porting a language to .NET, and even for porting it to run under the Visual Studio environment. These guidelines, the Common Language Specification, allow language developers to port or develop new languages that will compile flawlessly into MSIL code for running on the common language runtime. The benefit to the programmer of all these languages running in the common language runtime is that, through the common interfaces supported by the CLR, we're able to use code developed in any other .NET language. Not only can we call such code from within our programs (we've been able to do that with COM), but our classes can inherit from a class written in an entirely different language. This is an advance of staggering proportions. Although there are still good reasons for a team to use a single language, multilanguage projects are now practical. Companies can more fully use their programmer talent. Because multilanguage support has been so hyped, we're not telling you anything new here. I'll keep this section short, but there are a couple of thoughts I'd like to share.

The importance of the multilanguage support isn't really so much in the common language runtime or in the MSIL code that's generated. Sure, it's convenient, but it's not everything. The biggest impacts, both good and bad, are in the BCL. Every object in the framework is available, in a standard hierarchy of namespaces, to any .NET language. This means learning a new language is simply a matter of learning a new syntax, but not a new object model. For example, all .NET languages use a common set of objects for dealing with XML. Moving to a new language is now drastically simpler. But all is not rosy—there are some serious implications.

A language is not only its syntax, as we have hinted. It is also the objects it uses, the frameworks it runs against, the tips and tricks programmers have learned to tweak performance, and even the workarounds required to get out of problems. It is the set of useful design patterns and even a culture that its users share. Sharing a common intermediate language and a set of objects does not mean the language has been ported, merely its syntax. A concrete example is Java.

Let's say Java does get ported soon. What will that mean? Will Java programmers be able to jump to the .NET Framework and be as productive as they were with the Sun implementation? Not even close. The .NET Java "Hello World" will look identical to the Sun implementation (see System.HelloWorld). But any serious programming will be drastically different:

- Database access will be done through the System.Data classes in the .NET implementation of Java, instead of through the entirely different JDBC classes. The code won't even look similar.
- The Java design patterns that speed up garbage collection are useless—a different model is used in .NET.
- The Enterprise Java Beans you've written won't port to .NET—there's no framework for them to run in.
- Java Server Pages will be useless to port. ASP.NET is entirely different from JSP.

The syntax will look similar, but a Sun Java programmer will be lost in the .NET Java world, and vice-versa. Other languages suffer other problems. Only a small class of programming languages is object oriented, even though they are used in the vast majority of programming. Still, porting a non-OOP language to .NET has fewer benefits than might be assumed. Languages like Perl and Lisp, though no doubt portable, may see a loss of performance if forced to use the common classes for string processing.

Overall, we give the multilanguage support two thumbs up. It's a powerful feature that will save programmers more hassle than they can imagine. (It's one of the best things to come across our desks in a while.) But don't expect programmers to come rushing into the .NET fold, just because their syntax is there. Billions of dollars and thousands of programmer hours have been spent on Java. That won't go away overnight, nor will Java programmers happily leave the well-developed frameworks they've worked within for so long, abandoning their trainings, certifications, and respect.

NOTE There is a major open source initiative to convert MSIL code to run on the JVM. This may be an interesting development, but we fear it will suffer the same problems as we've discussed previously.

The Sizzle, Not the Steak

In sales, you are taught to sell the "sizzle, not the steak"—customers don't care about the product features. They care about what the product will do for them. Being convertible doesn't sell cars; the image of driving down the road at 55 miles per hour (the author would *never* suggest speeding in a brand new sports car) with wind blowing through your hair sells convertibles.

In that spirit, what will .NET do for you? What do you get out of your effort in learning .NET, and learning ADO.NET in particular? Quite a lot, actually! Here are a few of the features and benefits you'll derive.

No More Windows OS Programming

The extra layer of indirection between you and the operating system allows you to program to the .NET Framework, instead of Windows. This means higher productivity. You no longer have to wonder if you're working within Win32, COM, or DCOM. You don't have to think about the registry, HRESULTs, IUnknown, AddRef, and Release. And it's not because .NET has hidden them from you. It's because they're gone! All of those things are handled by the common language runtime. This also means that you'll be able to sell your code to users of other platforms as soon as a common language runtime is available for their machine.

Hate determining what types of errors to trap or how to trap them? No longer. The entire error-handling framework has been reworked and simplified. .NET errors are all reported through exceptions. All of them! Period. No more trapping errors, checking an HRESULT, looking for Win32 error codes, and listening for exceptions. In .NET, you have to catch only exceptions. That's it.

Banish DLL Hell

In .NET, if you can install it successfully once, that's it; it'll continue running. .NET applications run with the components they were built and tested with. New components can run side by side with the old, with applications calling the proper one. Another vendor won't inadvertently overwrite your DLL with its "new, improved" one, breaking your code.

Remember installing programs with XCOPY? If so, you're either a Unix type or a programmer who's been around since the DOS days. Welcome home! Goodbye, expensive installation software! Goodbye, registry! Goodbye, littered hard drive! .NET components aren't listed in the registry, and you don't have to use a fancy installation script. Copy the files to a directory and "Presto"! Need to run an application from a CD? Go ahead, no installation required! Oh, and uninstalling? Right-click, Delete.

Design Once for Multiple Platforms

Build your application once, and run it on a number of different platforms. Right now it'll only run on newer Windows platforms, but even that's a relief! Several versions of Windows are still in common use today. We brainstormed seven different Windows versions that are in common use today, not including Windows 3.1 or the service packs that make them different. Code developed on the .NET platform will run on any 32-bit Windows platform (with the exception of Windows 95). This greatly simplifies development for an enterprise.

There is also a side benefit to the MSIL code being compiled to machine code on the target machine. Currently, running managed code is a bit slower than code compiled directly to the machine code of a specific platform. But maybe not so in the future.

Standard compilers must make several assumptions about the computer being compiled to. They normally will compile for Pentium chips, but Pentium III chips have optimizations that Pentium II chips don't. Standard compilers can't take advantage of those. A JIT compiler, because it is running on the end machine, knows exactly what type of processor is being used, how much cache is available, what registers can be used, and other machine-specific information. This information can then be used for further optimization. Down the road, this may mean faster and faster execution, quite possibly exceeding execution speeds of precompiled programs.

Debug across Languages

A great deal of bug handling and debugging is provided by the .NET Framework. This introduces the possibility of debugging across language barriers, as well as a shorter learning curve when forced to debug a program in a different language. Exceptions are handled uniformly across languages, and the stack trace is always available to assist in tracking down hard-to-find bugs. Since the debug engine is actually contained in the common language runtime, you can even debug across different languages!

Run Code with Confidence

You can force your application to run only trusted code. Multiple levels of code permissions are provided, and more can be created. You have the control. Back when everything was installed from a CD or purchased disks, there was no need to deal with these issues. Now, with code being run from all over the Internet, people want more control. .NET gives it to them.

NOTE Digital signatures will become more important as .NET code becomes more common. We trust code signed by Microsoft. With its signature attached, we'll both allow our computers to run it without question. Same with code we've created ourselves.

.NET—The Future

The .NET Framework is an evolutionary improvement over several existing technologies designed to minimize the importance of the operating system as a platform. It introduces few new technologies, but it combines several of the latest and most important technologies and standards into a single coherent framework. As a unified whole, the .NET Framework is more than the sum of its parts—and greater than any of the competing programming environments.

.NET allows several languages to be compiled to the Microsoft Intermediate Language (MSIL) that can be run on any machine that has a Common Language Runtime. At first, common language runtimes will be available only for Windows machines, but that will change in the near future, we hope. The Base Class Library (BCL) provides a standard class library that spans all .NET languages. This ensures a short learning curve when using a new language, and it allows different languages to work together seamlessly. These advances provide the programmer with simplified development, simplified deployment, more code security, and other major benefits.

CHAPTER

2

Introduction to ADO.NET

So, what is ADO.NET? Just the thought that Microsoft has released a new Data Access API makes us shudder. Lately, our lives have been spent healing the cuts endured on this bleeding edge of APIs. It seems like just yesterday, we started getting the hang of Remote Data Objects (RDO) and were enjoying ODBC productivity when ActiveX Data Objects (ADO) made the scene. Forced to board this new flagship, we experimented and learned all about COM and OLE DB as it pertained to data access. Amazed at how many ways we could now retrieve a list of customer phone numbers from a database, we settled in for a long season of version episodes on our all-ADO channel. After the many seasons of the other channels, namely DAO, RDO, ODBC API, DB Library, and OLE DB, our expectations were high!

The first season, which aired in 1996, contained the pilot episode of ADO, which we will call the 1.0 show. This version of the Microsoft Data Access Components (MDAC) included ODBC drivers for Access/Jet, SQL Server, and, for the first time, Oracle. As for OLE DB providers, the first and only one introduced this season was the OLE DB provider for ODBC drivers. We will inevitably see more OLE DB providers on the show in the episodes to come. Unfortunately, 1996 was also known as the *stealth* season of ADO, as it wasn't distributed in a very consistent manner and therefore was not enjoyed by too many viewers.

The second season, which began August 1997, saw an increase in functionality and stability of ADO in version 1.5 and thus a more solid distribution plan for the MDAC 1.5 stack. For the first time, Microsoft allowed the MDAC to be downloaded and installed as a standalone package. This new version was also distributed through the Windows NT 4.0 Option Pack, Internet Explorer 4.0, and Windows 98. MDAC 1.5 contained ODBC 3.5, OLE DB 1.5, Remote Data Services (RDS) 1.5, and ADO 1.5. The standard was now established that the version of the MDAC would be synonymous with the version of ADO contained within. There were four additional releases of ADO 1.5 that were referred to as ADO 1.5a through 1.5d.

In the third season, things started to get interesting as the long 2.0 story line began. This season also began a bit earlier than the usual fall lineup. It was in July 1998 that MDAC 2.0 was first distributed in the MDAC 2.0 SDK as a cool 40 MB download. More viewers were able to catch the show when it was distributed with the rollout of Visual Studio 6.0 later that fall. In addition to the OLE DB and ODBC support for Access/Jet, SQL Server, and Oracle, MDAC 2.0 included a FoxPro ODBC driver that, before then, had to be downloaded separately. For the first time, ADO 2.0 allowed the developer to persist the data to disk in an Advanced Data Table Gram (ADTG) format. ADO 2.1 was generally considered the most stable API to date, and many successful database applications were developed and deployed on version 2.1. ADO 2.1 added XML persistence support, albeit a limited implementation referred to variously as "Microsoft XML-Data Schema format," "XML Reduced Data Schema," or just "Reduced Data."

ADO 2.5, which arrived with Windows 2000, offered persistence to any object that supported the IStream interface, such as the ADO Stream object, the IIS 5.0 Response and Request objects, and the XML DOM Document object. Plus the RDS DataControl's "URL" property was added, which allows one to bypass the security-prone RDS DataFactory and its Default Handler INI file and to use ASP Web pages to pass back and forth ADO Recordsets, saved as XML Streams. The writing was definitely on the wall with regard to XML support. ADO 2.5 was also extended to support semi-structured data, such as hierarchical data stores (file systems, directory services, etc.) and direct binding to objects via URLs. MDAC 2.5 was released as part of Windows 2000, early in 2000. Two MDAC 2.5 SP1 and SP2 service packs were made available via the Windows 2000 SP1 and SP2 service packs. (Note that you must install these to get the MDAC service packs installed also. You will not be able to install MDAC 2.5 SP1 or SP2 directly because they are considered part of the OS.)

ADO 2.6, which was introduced with SQL Server 2000 in the fall of 2000, further extended OLE DB and ADO to expose SQL Server 2000's XML features, including the ability to catch results or specify a command object with Streams. Improved error reporting, singleton SELECT statements, and retrieval of schema objects by ADO Multidimensional (ADO MD) were included in ADO 2.6. This release also began excluding the Microsoft Jet, Jet OLE DB Provider, Visual FoxPro, or the other ODBC desktop database drivers. These are still available as a separate download.

ADO 2.7, which includes support for 64-bit systems, was released in the fall of 2001 with Windows XP. In addition, 2.7 fixed some other bugs. You can view the complete manifest by clicking the MDAC 2.7 link from the following page: www.microsoft.com/data.

NOTE As of this writing, Microsoft is no longer supporting MDAC 1.5, 2.0, or 2.1. Support will continue, however, for MDAC 2.5, 2.6, and 2.7.

Now that ADO has enjoyed a dozen or so major and minor releases, it's time to learn a new object model. The fourth season, which begins at the end of 2001, shall see a spin-off program to be known as ADO.NET.

ETIQUETTE **Don't refer to ADO.NET as "ActiveX Data Objects.NET" because ActiveX implies using the COM framework, which is now deprecated with the .NET Framework. ADO.NET is 100 percent .NET Framework managed code and should be called "ADO.NET." Just never mind what the ADO stands for.**

ADO.NET was developed in preparation for the next phase of Internet development, which will see processing functionality scattered across the globe and made available through HTTP via XML Web services. Classic ADO (MDAC) required COM marshalling to transmit data from component to component, and because of this, every component that handled data had to be a COM component. This may have been a nonissue for some because of the presence of a homogenous architecture at every tier. For developers hoping to target consumers or providers that do not exist in COM-friendly environments, ADO.NET's ability to natively read/write XML is here to save the day. Software designers or integrators must simply agree on a common XML schema.

OUR TERM **We will refer to the traditional, COM-based ADO as *MDAC ADO*, to differentiate it from ADO.NET. The industry may also refer to it as *ADOc*, where the small c stands for COM (or "classic," as we'd like to think of it). Some folks at Microsoft refer to it as "classic ADO," which begs the question if it will be returning some day!**

ADO.NET Defined

You can define ADO.NET a few different ways:

Logically. The suite of data access services within the .NET Framework.

Conceptually. System.Data, Microsoft.Data, and related namespaces and classes.

Physically. System.Data.Dll.

ADO.NET is an important assembly within Microsoft's .NET Framework. Because the common language runtime is such a "code Utopia" where everything is created equal and runs in a common environment, porting MDAC ADO directly to the .NET Framework was impossible. MDAC ADO, which had holdovers from RDO, DAO, and other APIs, would have broken many of the design patterns and behaviors of the .NET Framework. Another problem was the major differences in the .NET Framework's Common Type System (CTS) and MDAC ADO's data types. Every bit of managed code in the framework (more than 9,000 classes) utilizes a common type system, security mechanism, design patterns, and naming conventions.

Remember that the .NET Framework was built on a series of standards, including Extensible Markup Language (XML), Simple Object Access Protocol (SOAP), and Web Service Description Language (WSDL); therefore, all of the classes in the Base Class Library (BCL) must be built on these same standards.

OPINION **The .NET Framework is strong and will be successful because of its uniformity. You just need to overlook a few warts here and there, such as class members listed but not implemented, naming convention violations, and some classes in the wrong namespace.**

Because of this strong integration, ADO.NET can leverage the .NET Framework's implementation of XML directly. This becomes most apparent, as you will see, in the DataSet class, which can read and write XML (data *and* XSD schema) using streams, files, or other types of readers and writers. By working with the XML in an XMLDocument or XMLDataDocument, you'll use the same XML methods and commands when working with data from ADO.NET that you'd use with any other XML application that you cook up.

In addition to running under the .NET Framework, ADO.NET is a prime choice for Web development in that it has been heavily engineered to assist the disconnected world of Web development. Data can now be passed through a firewall as simple XML text. This capability was introduced in MDAC ADO 2.1 and polished in 2.5, but it is perfected in ADO.NET.

ADO.NET applications that leverage the disconnected benefits of the DataSet class, with the ability to maintain an entire database or subset of a database in memory, will realize a new level of scalability. Database connections, considered one of the most precious of system resources, are opened and closed only during the initial population of the DataSet and then later when the updates are flushed back to the data source. In-between calls, the database connections remain idle to serve other clients. Sounds like custom solutions some of us have coded in the past—now performed graciously for you by ADO.NET!

And, let's not forget that nearly everything in the .NET Framework is a class. This means that if you don't like the factory-installed functionality, just inherit from it and extend it yourself. This idea of "inherit and improve" should quickly populate the database programming market with useful classes and solutions to very specific problems. No longer will you need to wait for your vendor to catch up or a service pack to update the functionality. If you need a new ADO.NET data provider, just inherit and improve. For example, if you want your updates to be applied to two databases simultaneously, for mirroring or auditing, you could just inherit the appropriate DataAdapter class and override the functionality of the Update method. Nearly everything in the .NET Framework can be customized in this way.

ADO.NET for Web Development

The Internet has become a patchwork of different types of Web and database servers. With the possibility of so many volatile links, sluggish routes, and rickety hardware between your database and your client, you could easily classify the whole contraption as unstable. Your data, however, still needs to be shared and processed—sometimes at each tier of the application. The modern distributed application cannot bask in the safety that current hardware and Microsoft products will be running on each tier. Reality brings the realization that there may be as many platforms and vendor software as there are tiers in your application. Threading your data through this heterogeneous haystack requires a standard that transcends a Microsoft technology. We call it XML for short.

ADO.NET is built on an XML foundation. ADO.NET enjoys a solid disconnected behavior by being able to persist data to XML as a stream or file and then deserialize it into meaningful objects on the receiving end. Because the intermediate form is XML, any client or technology that understands XML can transform it into a number of meaningful structures. Since the XML blitz of the last few years, it is safe to assume that an XML parser is available for just about any platform.

As expected, ADO.NET supports traditional connected scenarios as well. ADO.NET can easily handle single-tier or two-tier .NET database applications, mating Visual Basic windows client applications or C# ASP.NET Web applications with data that lives in Access, SQL Server, Oracle, or any other ODBC or OLE DB data providers. ADO.NET will continue to serve the needs of any LAN or WAN .NET applications, which benefit from a persistent connection to their data source, just as MDAC ADO has done in the past.

ADO.NET shines, however, when it comes to allowing data to be manipulated when it is not permanently connected to a data source. MDAC ADO has supported disconnected recordsets in the past, but ADO.NET has achieved enlightenment. If ADO.NET had a charter or a list of design goals, they would include data sharing, standardization, performance, scalability, and readability.

Comparing MDAC ADO and ADO.NET

ADO.NET is only loosely based on MDAC ADO. Tables 2.1 and 2.2 compare the features and classes of MDAC ADO and ADO.NET. Only a few of the new classes will look and feel familiar. For example, connection strings, the bane of any ADO programmer's existence, haven't changed too drastically. They are still a pain in the asterisk!

If you are building .NET applications, then take what you know about the MDAC ADO object model and discard it. Rip it from your memory, like a picture from a book. That is, unless your clients are expecting you to complete an existing MDAC ADO project in the near future.

Sure, with ADO.NET we're still talking about tables, columns and rows, properties, methods, and events, but the object model is completely different. Where MDAC ADO had just three primary objects (Connection, Command, and Recordset), ADO.NET offers five primary objects (Connection, Command, DataAdapter, DataSet, and DataReader).

ADO.NET has taken the attitude that classes should be more specific to the task at hand, rather than loaded down with switches and modes to handle every situation. For example, how many times did you fumble with the CursorType, CursorLocation, and LockType properties on an MDAC ADO Recordset to get the exact behavior you wanted? How long did it take you to figure out which combination would give you an accurate RecordCount? Or did you just settle for a RecordCount of -1 and loop through the data counting it manually? Go on, you can admit it. It will start the healing process. We've all done some creative coding around MDAC ADO's bulkiness. ADO.NET now delivers classes specific to the type of operation you want to perform.

Table 2.1 Comparing Features of MDAC ADO and ADO.NET

FEATURE	MDAC ADO	ADO.NET
.NET integration	Only via COM Interop. Services	Managed common language runtime assembly code
Firewall requirements	Port 135 (DCOM), Port 80 (HTTP, but limited)	Port 80 (HTTP)
Data providers	OLE DB	OLE DB, ODBC, SQL Server, Oracle
Persistence format	ADTG, XML (limited)	XML, XSD
Data Source Query language	SQL	SQL
Results delivery format	Record or Recordset	DataSet, DataReader, XML
Scrollable server-side cursors	Via ADO Recordset	Not supported in initial release
Transfer format	ADTG, XML (limited)	XML
XML support	Limited XML supported ADO	Fully supports XML

With ADO.NET, your first choice is which .NET data provider to use, not just which OLE DB provider. If possible, you should select the .NET data provider built specifically for the data source. For SQL Server 7.0 or 2000, for example, you should use the SQL Server managed provider (System.Data.SqlClient). We have heard these providers referred to as "pure," "targeted," "custom," or "bridged." Next, you should decide if you want fast, read-only access to the data to popular a static control or generate a report. If so, then you should focus your attention on the DataReader class. If you want to perform flexible updates to the data you retrieve, then you should be looking at the Command/DataAdapter classes. If you want to interact with XML directly or store a whole database in memory, then you should be looking at the DataSet class.

Table 2.2 Comparing Classes of MDAC ADO and ADO.NET

MDAC ADO	ADO.NET
Connection	Connection
Command	Command
Error	Error
Field	DataColumn

MDAC ADO	ADO.NET
Parameter	Parameter
Property	Property
Record	DataRow
Recordset (complex/ updates/disconnected)	DataTable
Recordset (server-side, forward-only, read-only)	DataReader
Recordsets (client-side, static, batch optimistic lock)	DataSet
Stream	(Supported via .NET reader and writer classes)

Using MDAC ADO from within .NET

Microsoft has worked hard to provide a set of tools to assist in making COM components compatible with the .NET Framework. This means all of your old MDAC ADO and other COM data access APIs can be made compatible with your .NET projects. This compatibility is provided by the suite of classes known as the COM Interoperability Services (a.k.a. COM Interop).

This compatibility means a protection of your investment in ADO code and knowledge. Compatibility, however, comes at a price. The Framework must type-match and marshal all data from the common language runtime (managed code) to the COM process (unmanaged code) and back again. Repetitive calls can induce a performance hit on your application. Future compatibility problems may also arise.

OVERHEAD Microsoft has announced that there is an overhead of approximately 50 additional instructions per method call from a .NET client to a COM server.

We hope that your legacy ADO code is buried in compiled COM+ components and that you won't have to convert your MSADO15.dll file to .NET and reference MDAC ADO code within your managed code project. Although this would be a nice crutch to get you started on your .NET software development, it could also be a painful process, and you might miss out on the new features of ADO.NET. The better, but not best, approach would be to have your MDAC ADO code intertwined with your business objects in custom COM+ components. Then you can simply import those components into your .NET application and make method calls to your business objects. Your .NET application doesn't have to know anything directly about MDAC ADO.

If you are porting your legacy applications over to run on .NET, then you should consider retooling your applications using pure ADO.NET code. A multitiered application with hundreds, maybe thousands, of lines of code makes it difficult, if not impossible, to port everything at one time. It would be much more prudent to port individual components, test, and then port more code. That having been said, with

COM Interop you may continue to use MDAC ADO in your .NET applications. You will be instantiating and calling the same familiar classes and methods that you've been doing in the past. The .NET Framework is able to create and manipulate COM objects as long as there is sufficient meta data describing the COM types. Incidentally, if this meta data does not sufficiently describe the parameters or return type, you can use the *MarshalAsAttribute* class. This meta data can be retrieved from existing COM type libraries.

COOL The System.Data.OleDb.OleDbDataAdapter class implements two overloaded Fill methods specifically for copying MDAC ADO Recordset or Record object data. These are one-way operations, however, that support only the filling of data from MDAC ADO.

Microsoft provides several ways to generate the meta data required by .NET to use a COM component. From the command line, you can convert any COM or COM+ component (.TLB, .DLL, .ODL, .OCX, .EXE) using the Type Library Importer (Tlbimp.exe) utility. This will create a meta data assembly (a .NET wrapper class) around the component's interfaces and coclasses. Tlbimp.exe will also create an assembly and namespace for the type information automatically. Optional switches allow you to specify the namespace, assembly version, and key information to sign your code. After running Tlbimp.exe, any .NET client can create instances of the COM component and access its methods or properties.

Migrating MDAC ADO to Run under .NET

Follow these steps to manually generate the meta data required by .NET, using the command line utility and then reference that inside Visual Studio .NET.

1. Install the MDAC of your choice, preferably the latest version and preferably using Microsoft's setup program mdac_typ.exe.
2. Locate the ADO component. Typically, it is found here:

   ```
   C:\Program Files\Common Files\System\ado\msado15.dll
   ```

   Note: Never mind the "15" version in the filename; even the 2.x versions use this DLL.
3. From the command line, change over to the appropriate directory, and run the Tlbimp utility on the component. Tblimp.exe may not be in your path, so be prepared to look for it in your Microsoft.NET folder; if you have Visual Studio .NET installed, you can also launch the "Visual Studio .NET Command Prompt," which will have the path already properly established.

   ```
   TlbImp msado15.dll /out: msado15net.dll
   ```

4. Copy the new meta data assembly to a folder where it will be easily accessible both at compile time and at runtime.

5. Inside your Visual Studio .NET project, select Add Reference under the Project menu.
6. On the .NET tab, click the Browse button, and locate the new DLL (msado15net.dll) that you generated.
7. Click OK to select the component. Visual Studio will add the appropriate references to your project.
8. You may now reference the namespace and use the components like any other .NET class.

```
Imports msado15net

Dim myMDACConnection As New msado15net.Connection()
myMDACConnection.ConnectionString = "Provider=SQLOLEDB; " & _
   "Data Source=Morpheus;User ID=sa;Password=;"
myMDACConnection.Open()
```

Using Visual Studio .NET to Migrate MDAC ADO to Run under .NET

Follow these steps to have Visual Studio .NET import the MDAC ADO library and create the meta data automatically. This demonstrates Visual Studio .NET's usefulness in building interop applications.

1. Install the MDAC of your choice, preferably the latest version and preferably using Microsoft's setup program mdac_typ.exe.
2. Launch Visual Studio .NET, and create a new project, appropriate for data access.
3. Select Add Reference under the Project menu.
4. On the COM tab, locate and double-click the appropriate MDAC ADO library in the Component Name listing. For example, you might select "Microsoft ActiveX Data Objects 2.7 Library." The component will now appear in the small list at the bottom.
5. Click OK to return to your project. Visual Studio .NET will add the appropriate references to your project.
6. You may now reference the namespace and use the components like any other .NET class.

```
Imports ADODB

Dim myMDACConnection As New msado15net.Connection()
myMDACConnection.ConnectionString = "Provider=SQLOLEDB; " & _
   "Data Source=Morpheus;User ID=sa;Password=;"
myMDACConnection.Open()
```

Exploring ADO.NET

ADO.NET is spread out over several namespaces. Understanding what classes and functionality are provided by each namespace is crucial to using ADO.NET effectively. For example, it is rare that you would ever use a class from System.Data.Common directly. Rather, you would use descendants of those classes in Microsoft.Data.Odbc, System.Data.OleDb, or System.Data.SqlClient.

TERM A namespace is a logical naming scheme for group-related classes. These namespaces are typically organized hierarchically to help present the relationships to other namespaces. Namespaces also make it easier for programmers to browse and reference types in their code.

Here are the namespaces that constitute ADO.NET:

System.Data. Bulk of the ADO.NET classes and foundation functionality.

System.Data.Common. Abstract classes used to provide base functionality for all .NET data providers.

Microsoft.Data.Odbc. Classes used when working with ODBC data sources.

System.Data.OleDB. Classes used when working with OLE DB data sources.

System.Data.SqlClient. Classes used when working with SQL Server 7.0/2000 data sources.

System.Data.SqlTypes. Classes to support native SQL Server data types.

NOTE Another reason to learn the namespaces is that it will help you use Part Two of this book more effectively. Part Two is the ADO.NET reference section, and it is arranged by *namespace*, class, and member.

ADO.NET Object Model

The full ADO.NET object model is too large to depict graphically, in this book. We considered contracting with the people who put the Lord's Prayer on a single grain of rice, but even they passed. In fact, it will take several chapters in Part Two to reveal the full ADO.NET object model. The good news is that the object model is fairly consistent across the various data providers (Microsoft.Data.Odbc, System.Data.OleDb, and System.Data.SqlClient). So, if you take the time to understand one, you're already proficient with the others. "Learn one, know all."

The ADO.NET model divides neatly into two segments: the segment that deals with pure data manipulation, regardless of source, and the segment that deals directly with data sources. (See Figure 2.1.)

The first segment contains the DataSet, DataTable, and other such objects that carry no information about the source from which they came. These objects are pure .NET.

They speak only XML and can be used by any .NET language or environment. They are completely disconnected from the data source. They don't even speak SQL.

The second segment gets down-and-dirty with the data source. It has to speak not only .NET, but also the language of the data source with which it communicates. The .NET data providers live on this level. Some speak OLE DB, translating to .NET for the DataSet objects. Another speaks Tabular Data Stream (TDS), translating from SQL Server to .NET. Both of those data providers also speak SQL.

Thanks to this stratification, the data manipulation in the DataSet remains pure across all platforms and data sources, effectively shielded from the complexities of diverse data sources (including data sources that don't speak SQL at all). The .NET data providers dirty their hands in the muck of different data source protocols, retrieving data from the sources and translating it into the .NET language for use by the DataSet and DataTable objects.

Familiar ADO.NET Classes

Let's take a moment and show you a few of the classes in ADO.NET that may seem familiar to you as an MDAC ADO programmer. This should provide comfort, if you are a transitional developer.

Connection

The Connection class represents a unique connection to a data source. (See Figure 2.2.) A Connection manages all of the communication between your ADO.NET application and the data source. This can be a network connection to a remote database server or a file handle to an ISAM (Indexed Sequential Access Method) file on a local drive, such as a dBase, Paradox, Excel, or ASCII text file. Connections are opened after specifying the ConnectionString information, which includes the location of the data source, any security credentials required to open it, and possibly the name of the provider or driver to use. Connections can also manage explicit transactions.

Command

The Command class, in its various implementations throughout ADO.NET, represents a SQL statement or stored procedure to execute against a given connection. (See Figure 2.3.) The executing statement may return results to the client, or it may perform specific insert, update, or delete operations. Most ADO.NET commands support these three modes of execution:

ExecuteNonQuery. For action queries, like updates, where no results are returned.

ExecuteReader. For queries that return results for read-only, forward-only access to the data source.

ExecuteScalar. For queries that return a single value, such as an average price.

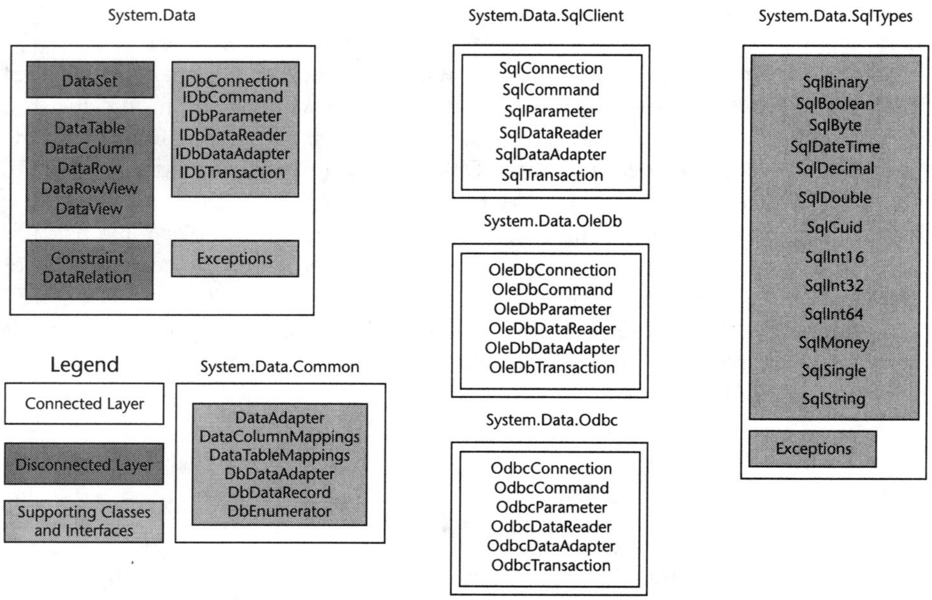

Figure 2.1 ADO.NET namespaces and layers.

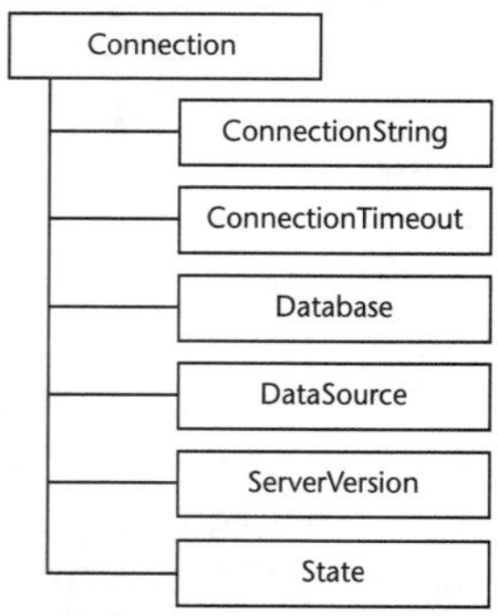

Figure 2.2 Connection object model.

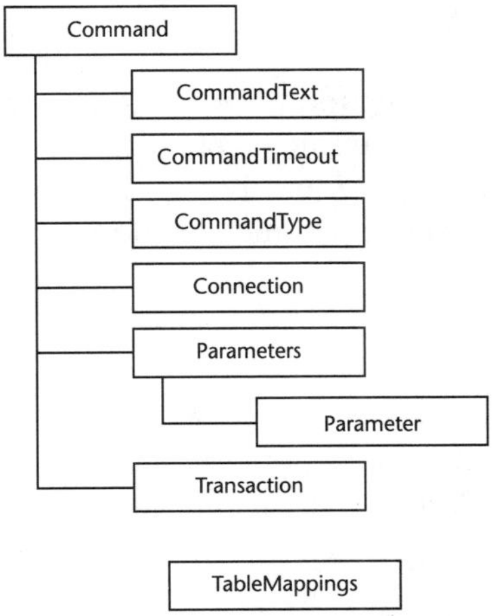

Figure 2.3 Command object model.

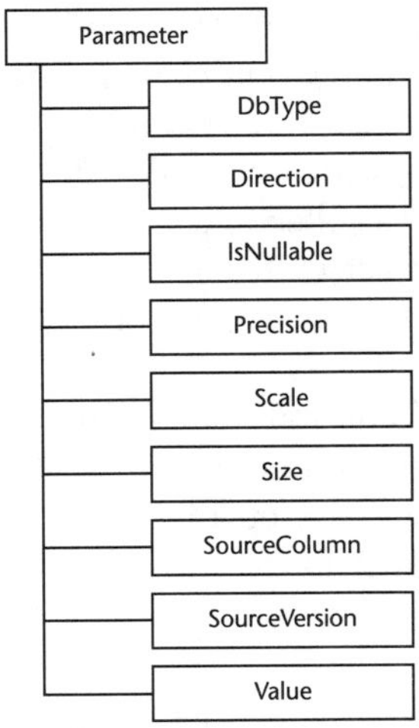

Figure 2.4 Parameter object model.

Parameter

The Parameter class, as with MDAC ADO, serves the Command object. (See Figure 2.4.) The parameters collection can contain one or more parameter objects, which match the parameters of the SQL command or stored procedure being executed. Because stored procedures can return information via output parameters and return values, the *direction* of each parameter object is important.

New ADO.NET Classes

Now for some of the new classes in the ADO.NET object model. Your brain may try to draw tangents to MDAC ADO classes, but don't let it. Some of these new classes are radically different from what you might be used to.

DataSet

Without a doubt, the flagship of ADO.NET is the DataSet. Think of a DataSet as an in-memory view of your database. The DataSet is a collection of client-side, static, batch optimistic, disconnected recordsets (known as DataTable objects in ADO.NET). But it is more than just a number of MDAC ADO recordsets. The DataSet class can contain any number of sets of data, be they from tables, stored procedures, SQL queries, SQL views, or XML documents or Streams. The DataSet can track any relationships between these tables as well as all schema information. In fact, a DataSet can represent your entire database. Because the DataSet can encapsulate so much information and persist it using XML, it becomes an ideal means of transport for an XML Web Service.

The DataSet class contains collections of DataTable and DataRelation classes. The DataTable, in turn, provides DataRow, DataColumn, and Constraint classes. With these five classes, ADO.NET provides enough information to reconstruct your database schema in memory. The DataTable class provides the Rows collection, which is a collection of DataRow objects. DataRows are where you interact with your data. In order to support conflict resolution, these DataRows are able to maintain several different versions of data: Default, Original, Current, and Proposed.

Having the DataRelations established for two or more DataTables provides referential integrity, in memory. It also enables you to use ADO.NET's programming model to navigate between related tables. Given a DataRow, you may call the GetChildRows or GetParentRow methods to return related DataRows. (See Figure 2.5.)

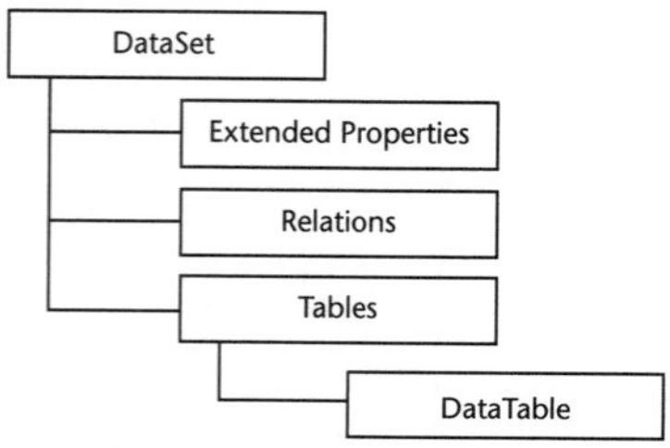

Figure 2.5 DataSet object model.

DataTable

Similar to the MDAC ADO Recordset class in functionality, the ADO.NET DataTable represents a single table of in-memory data. (See Figure 2.6.) You can create DataTables as standalone objects or refer to them as part of a robust hierarchy within a DataSet object. DataTable's beefy object model allows it to hold all its necessary schema information: columns, constraints, keys, row data, and relations.

DataAdapter

The DataAdapter provides an interface between a data source and the .NET Framework data handling objects, such as the DataSet. (See Figure 2.7.) The DataAdapter both retrieves data from a data source, populating a DataSet with data and constraints, and resolves updates, additions, and deletions back to the data source. The DataAdapter depends on a Connection object to provide the connection to the data source and Command objects to retrieve data from and resolve changes to the data source.

NOTE You can think of the DataAdapter as a proxy or broker that reconciles data between the DataTable in the DataSet and the data in the data source.

A DataAdapter abstracts the specifics of the data source from the DataSet. This abstraction means the manipulation in your application is identical regardless of the data source. You can learn one set of classes and members, regardless of the data source.

DataReader

The DataReader provides read-only, forward-only access to a data source. (See Figure 2.8.) Because it maintains only one record in memory at a time, there is minimal resource impact. Because there is no need to create a DataSet object (or other data structures found in the System.Data namespace), and because the DataReader is always fully connected to the database, it is much faster than other forms of data access. It can be an excellent choice for populating read-only controls, printing reports, or providing data for Web pages; however, be aware that once a DataReader has been opened, the connection it is using cannot be used by any other object, and the connection to the data source is maintained until the DataReader's Close method is called. While this may not impact your data source, it may force you to instantiate a second Connection object to interact with your DataReader.

NOTE Imagine the DataReader as a forward-only, read-only cursor, sometimes called a firehose.

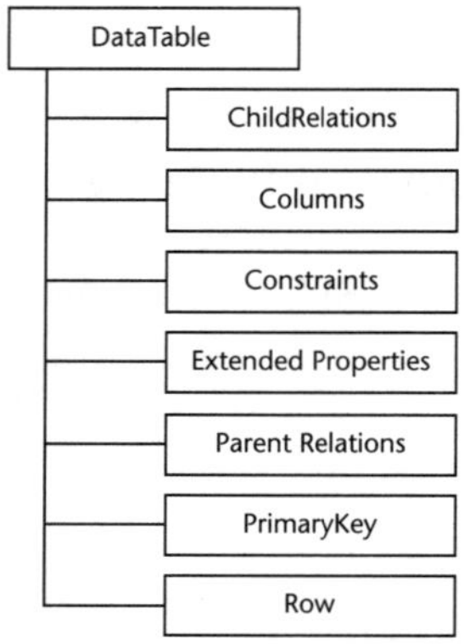

Figure 2.6 DataTable object model.

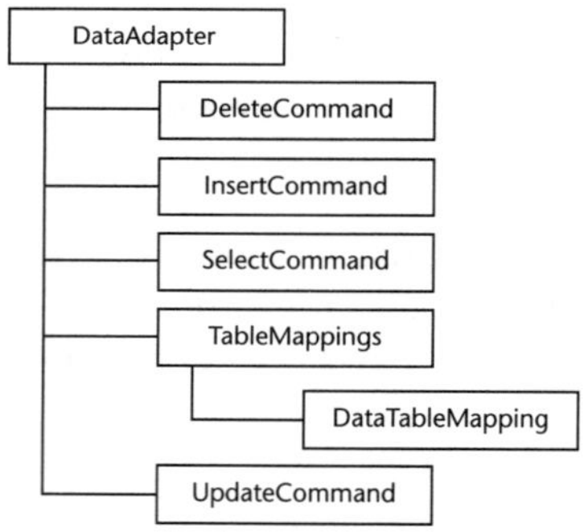

Figure 2.7 DataAdapter object model.

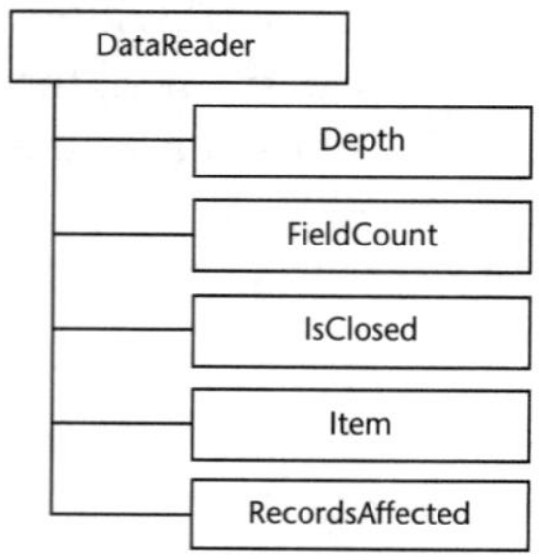

Figure 2.8 DataReader object model.

ADO.NET Data Providers

The concept of a data provider roughly translates to the idea of an OLE DB provider from the MDAC ADO world. The data provider is the collection of classes built specifically for communicating with one type of data source. With regards to System.Data.Odbc and System.Data.OleDb, these are generic mechanisms, which use COM Interop to communicate with legacy drivers and providers, respectively.

The holy grail, however, will be in using custom or "pure" data providers that *target* a specific data source, such as System.Data.SQLClient. Targeted data providers are engineered for optimal communication to a specific data source, even going so far as communicating with the server using its native protocols. Microsoft and other database vendors have agreed to provide these data providers as soon as possible.

NOTE As of this writing, we have been made aware of projects under way to develop targeted data providers for SQLXML, Access/Jet, DB2, Exchange, and Oracle. Microsoft is also considering a System.Data.Sqlserver namespace, which will greatly improve performance by executing directly inside the SQL Server's process space.

ODBC .NET Data Provider (Microsoft.Data.Odbc)

The Microsoft.Data.Odbc namespace is the recommended managed provider for accessing ODBC data sources. There are still hundreds of viable ODBC drivers in the marketplace, and thus ODBC continues to be a very popular way to access data. Although no major enhancements are planned for ODBC support, Microsoft has no plans to deprecate it either. The ODBC .NET data provider, along with others that ship after the .NET Framework is released, will be available for download from Microsoft. Microsoft may include the ODBC .NET provider with the SDK at a later time, however. The ODBC .NET data provider requires MDAC 2.6 or later to be installed. Tracing and connection pooling are handled by the ODBC Driver Manager utility, which ships with 2.6.

At the time of this writing, Microsoft has only tested the ODBC .NET provider with SQL Server, Jet, and Oracle drivers, although they claim that it is intended to support all ODBC drivers. We have tested it on most of the desktop/ISAM drivers as well, and found no problems with connecting to dBase, Paradox, or FoxPro files.

Keep in mind that ODBC drivers are not managed code. Using Microsoft.Data.Odbc requires the use of the expensive COM Interoperability Services.

TIP If you are in a tight spot and are having problems using your ODBC driver to connect to the data source, you can use a trick that we've come up with. Actually, there's no magic involved. Simply create an Access database and *link* the various ODBC data sources to it. Then, you can connect to the MDB file using OLE DB .NET data provider. It's kind of a cheesy workaround, and it adds a couple more layers, but it will get the job done.

OLE DB .NET Data Provider (System.Data.OleDb)

OLE DB is only a few years old and has already proven itself very valuable and very powerful. Microsoft and several other database vendors have provided OLE DB providers primarily because the COM interfaces allow a much richer access to their data stores than the traditional, rigid ODBC APIs allowed. Microsoft's MSDAORA provider is still a very workable way of connecting to Oracle 7 and, to some degree, Oracle 8 databases.

You may use the OLE DB .NET data provider to access SQL Server 7.0 or 2000, but life is better (and faster) if you use System.Data.SqlClient, which takes advantage of managed code and speaks directly to the server in its native tongue, which is Tabular Data Stream (TDS). TDS allows SQL Server and its clients to communicate regardless of the operating system, server release, or network protocols. If you need to communicate with SQL Server 6.5, then you will need to use System.Data.OleDb.

Keep in mind that OLE DB providers use COM and thus are not managed code. Using System.Data.OleDb requires the use of the expensive COM Interoperability Services.

Some other compatibility notes follow:

- The MSDAORA OLE DB provider has not yet been tested with Oracle 9.0.
- The OLE DB .Net data provider does not currently support the generic OLE DB provider for ODBC (MSDASQL). If you need to access ODBC data sources, you should consider using a native provider or the ODBC .Net data provider directly.
- The OLE DB .Net data provider does not currently support the OLE DB provider for Data Shaping (MSDADS). If you need to shape your data hierarchically, you should consider streaming it out to XML and transforming it appropriately.
- The OLE DB data provider does not support the OLE DB 2.5 interface. Thus you cannot use the MS OLE DB provider for Exchange, the MS OLE DB provider for Internet Publishing, or any other provider exposing the OLE DB 2.5 interface.

SQL Server .NET Data Provider (System.Data.SqlClient)

This is the only *targeted* .Net data provider available as of the RTM version of the .NET Framework. This data provider is also the only one of the three that runs 100 percent managed code, with no Interop required. System.Data.SqlClient has been customized for the extra features and idiosyncrasies of SQL Server. The primary classes, SQLDataReader, SQLDataAdapter and SQLCommand, have all been tailored to access SQL Server's formats directly.

It is also considerably faster to use this provider over one of the other two. For this reason alone, you should use the SQL Server .NET managed provider to communicate with SQL Server.

Roll Your Own .NET Data Provider

Building your own .NET data provider is beyond the scope of this book. But, before you start inheriting from the ADO.NET base classes, we would ask you to evaluate your data source and determine if it can return XML. If you can retrieve your data in XML either directly or via some intermediate layer, then you will be able to access it directly from the .NET Framework using the vast XML services. Having a schema would also be very useful. Perhaps you might be able to derive one directly from the data source or build a custom one.

If your data store has a propriety network protocol and you cannot use OLE DB or ODBC to access your data and if an XML interface is out of the question, then you should consider creating a .NET data provider.

NOTE Microsoft has promised to deliver a fully documented .NET data provider SDK.

Given how extensible the .NET Framework is, you have several options for accessing your data. Figure 2.9 shows a few of the available avenues.

Using ADO.NET

We assume that you've had some training in or exposure to writing .NET applications. The reference and tutorial sections of this book assume that you are comfortable with declaring, instantiating, and manipulating classes and objects. That's what using the Base Classes is about.

Although the .NET Framework is language agnostic, we have chosen Visual Basic .NET as our primary example language. Not only is it very popular, but the language is so noncryptic that it's actual readable—even by those programmers who don't use Visual Basic. We've included C# sample code in those places where C# offers additional ADO.NET functionality, as with operator overloading. Both Visual Basic .NET and C# are easy to read and understand. Manipulating the ADO.NET classes is nearly identical between these two languages, with just a few differences in declarations and operators.

Before we march off to learn ADO.NET, we want to stress the importance of having a solid foundation in SQL and XML.

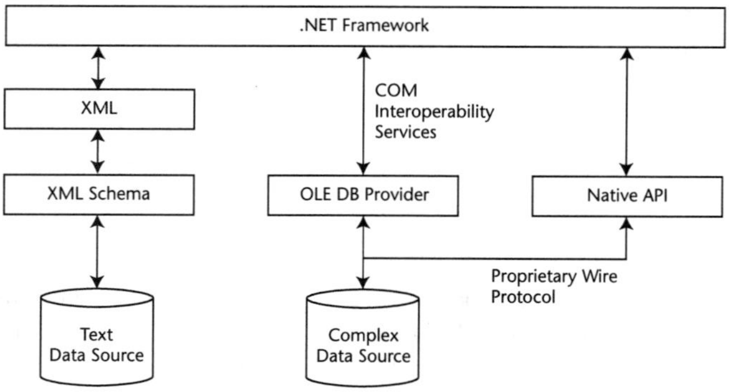

Figure 2.9 Alternate .NET data providers.

Learn Structured Query Language (SQL)

If you've been putting it off, now is the time to learn SQL. Because ADO.NET is geared toward high-performance, distributed applications, many of the traditional mechanisms of "cursors doing all the work for you" have been deprecated—they're gone! Yes, every Select, Insert, Update, and Delete operation is now performed with raw SQL. SQL that you can see and touch.

For those who saw the light early on, this has been the only way to go for building applications that needed to perform well and scale. Rather than use expensive cursors, maintain pessimistic locks, or take advantage of MDAC ADO's cursor update mechanisms, developers used the bare minimum approach (forward-only, read-only cursors) to retrieve data to the client and, when it came time to update the data, built raw SQL statements right then and there or made calls to custom stored procedures to do the work. Sure, it was more work for us programmers, but the customer could feel the payoff when the application ran and scaled efficiently.

To ease the pain of building these commands, Microsoft has included the CommandBuilder class into each of its .NET data provider namespaces. With the CommandBuilder class, the raw Insert, Update, and Delete SQL statements as well as the corresponding parameters collection are built automatically for you; but only in the case of updates dealing with a SINGLE table. You still need to learn SQL! Why? Because you can alter these (factory-built) SQL statements or even substitute stored procedures, to force the DataAdapters to update the table(s) the way you want them to. Life is good!

NOTE For a good SQL tutorial and reference guide, check out Judy Bowman's *The Practical SQL Handbook* (Addison-Wesley, 1996).

Learn Extensible Markup Language (XML)

Okay, our last thought here. We're going to go out on a limb and say that within the next two years, all Web database programmers will have to either read or write XML. Sure, the concept of XML is simple: Put some goofy tags around your data, and save it with an XML extension. Or, better yet, you could simply add the "FOR XML AUTO" clause to your SQL Server 2000 SELECT statement, and you're working with XML.

There's a big difference between looking like XML and being well-formed XML. There's even a bigger difference between being well formed and being valid, by conforming to your system's DTD or XML Schema. New standards pop up every week, it seems. Face it, you've got a lot to learn, and the classroom keeps moving. Given that the XMLDataDocument is basically a second interface to ADO.NET's DataSet class, you've got a lot of firepower at your disposal, if you just learn it.

Nah, you don't really have to learn XML to build ADO.NET applications—just as you don't really have to learn the metric system to live in the United States. If you ever travel to another country, however, such as SunLand or Linuxgrad, be ready for a heck-uva culture shock, and even a process halt, if you're not ready to translate to the local standards.

Maybe we were a bit too tongue-in-cheek in that last paragraph. Just keep in mind that XML is here to stay, and, even if you try to avoid it, it's still going to pop up from time to time, so you'd better understand it—even if just at its broadest level.

NOTE For a good XML tutorial and reference guide, check out Elliotte Rusty Harold's *XML in a Nutshell* (O'Reilly, 2001).

CHAPTER

3

Using ADO.NET from Visual Studio .NET

Sure, you can sit down to Microsoft Notepad, start a blank text file, reference the appropriate System.Data namespaces, and build that killer ADO.NET app, component, or XML Web service completely by hand. You can also memorize all of those classes, members, and syntax expressions—not just the ones in ADO.NET, but the foundation classes in the System namespace. Because Microsoft provides the Visual Basic .NET and Visual C# .NET compilers gratis, as part of the .NET Framework, you can compile your code and slay those compiler errors completely by hand, too. When it comes time to address those runtime and logic errors in your application, the manual approach provides you with a sharp stick, known as System.MessageBox, with which to defend yourself.

If the preceding paragraph describes your way of writing professional software, well, you just became our new hero. It's not that we would consider you a role model for professional software development, but we have the utmost respect for someone who is willing to sacrifice himself or herself in the name of... the name of... well, something, we suppose.

On the other end of the spectrum from our hero, you might find the novice, slothful, or extremely economical coder (depending on the project) who takes full advantage of all of the wizards, builders, assistants, drag-and-drop functionality, bound-controls, and other capabilities of a good Integrated Development Environment (IDE).

The boundary between too much control and too much productivity has been defined in the past by the folks at Microsoft, and the code (or lack thereof) generated by its Visual Studio IDE.

Books, videos, and courseware have long touted the Data Environment features of Visual Studio. While these features can empower novice programmers just embarking on data-enabled applications or provide for that "quick and dirty" application for their local sewing club, they have been notorious for hamstringing any serious database programming.

Maybe our opinions of prior versions of Visual Studio Data Environments and Data Tools are a bit too harsh. To be fair to Visual Studio .NET, these opinions have been built on prior versions of Visual Studio. It's just that we've built or been asked to rescue our fair share of "data-bound" applications in Visual Basic or their "design time control" counterpart applications in Visual Interdev, only to be found locked inside a box for the lifespan of the project.

Under Visual Studio .NET's slick UI veil, most of these elements will generate native ADO.NET code, with which you can steal, modify, and enhance your application—something that prior versions of Visual Studio promised but, only to a limited degree, delivered.

This book is an ADO.NET reference book, so we are going to spend the bulk of our pages showing you how to retrieve, manipulate, and save data via raw code. Look to Part Three of this book to demonstrate pure ADO.NET coding examples. This chapter, however, will open your eyes to a number of the user interface elements in Visual Studio .NET that pertain to manipulating data.

Server Explorer

From a data access perspective, the Server Explorer is used to create and manipulate data connections and to connect to existing servers. For that reason, it usually serves as the beginning of your project. The servers found in Server Explorer can be any server that shares resources such as event logs, message queues, performance counters, Win32 system services, and, more applicably, SQL databases and XML Web services. The Server Explorer is also your source for drag-and-drop operations with which you can create data components that reference your data. The Server Explorer subsumes the functionality of the Data View from Visual Studio 6.0, plus offers much more.

Many ADO.NET objects can be created automatically by simply dragging and dropping. Whether you use the objects or not, you can always peek at the source code that is automatically generated, to learn the language and the inner workings of ADO.NET. We define these data access objects in our reference section.

NOTE You can manually add Connections, DataAdapters, Commands, and DataSets to your project without using the Server Explorer. The Toolbox has a Data tab with all of the primary ADO.NET classes listed. When you drop one onto your designer, that component will appear in the *Component Tray*, and you will be able to configure it by hand or by answering the questions in the wizard that automatically launches. Dragging and dropping from the Server Explorer simply saves you time in setting those properties and writing that code. The Data tab is covered later in this chapter.

The Server Explorer is a TreeView control that appears as a vertical tab to the left of the main development environment area. If the tab is not visible, you can click

Server Explorer from the View menu. As with any of these elements, the Server Explorer can float or be docked to the main document window or any of the tool windows. See Figure 3.1.

Because an entire book could be devoted to Server Explorer and all of its capabilities, we will instead limit our coverage to the Data Connections part of the Explorer, which can directly assist in the development of ADO.NET projects and help you generate your data access code automatically.

Data Connections Node

By creating Data Connections in the Server Explorer, you are setting the stage to add many different ADO.NET objects easily to your project without writing any code. Not only will the Connection objects themselves be saved with your project, when you drag and drop a connection node, but any tables, columns, stored procedures, and functions will be saved as well. All of these ADO.NET objects will then persist in your project as pure ADO.NET code—code that you can change and improve at will. Also, any Data Connections that you set up on the Server Explorer tree will persist from project to project, saving you additional setup time between projects.

Before covering how to add the individual components to your project, let's discuss how to create these Data Connections both in the Server Explorer as well as in your project.

Creating Database Connections

Initially, the Data Connections node contains no connections. You must add a connection before you can begin dragging and dropping any objects onto your project.

1. Start a new project and open a blank form.
2. In the Server Explorer Window, right-click the Data Connections node and choose Add Connection. You can also click the Connect to Database toolbar button atop the Server Explorer Window.

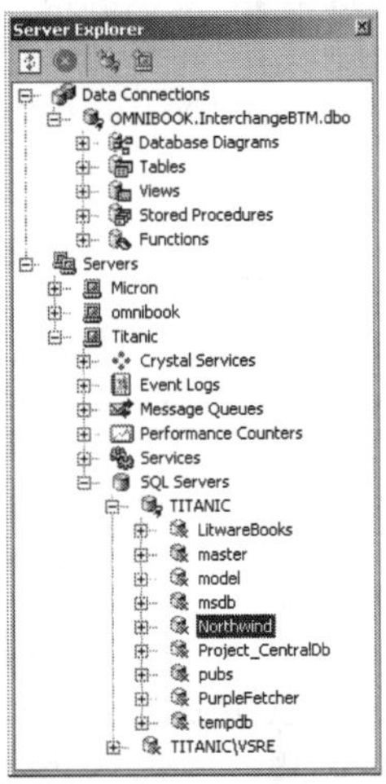

Figure 3.1 Server Explorer.

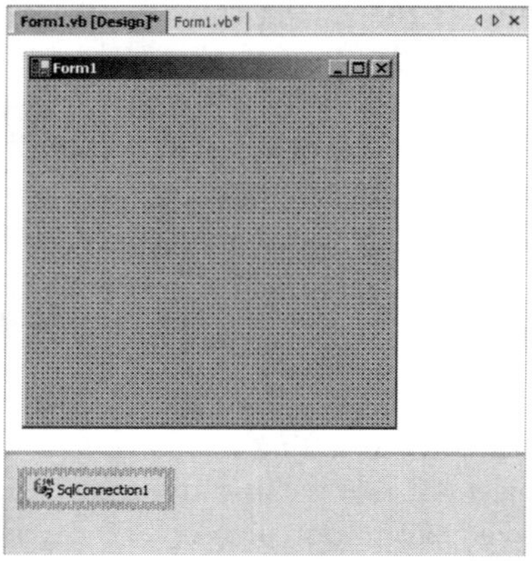

Figure 3.2 Connection object in the Component Tray.

3. The familiar Data Link Properties dialog box will appear. Using the different tabs, specify all of the connection string information, such as the provider, server, database, and security credentials to use to connect. There are some restrictions to the type of OLE DB providers you can use with ADO.NET. (See the OleDbConnection class reference in Chapter 7, "System.Data.OleDb," for more information.)
4. After testing the connection, click OK to save the connection information. At this point, you've already generated code that can be useful to your ADO.NET project. If you highlight the new connection node in the Server Explorer and then look to the Properties Window, you can see a complete ConnectionString ripe for the clipboard. Let's continue, however, and see how easy it is to build a Connection with the mouse.
5. Drag the new Data Connection to your form and drop it anywhere. At this point, your project solution will add a reference to System.Data, and a Connection object (such as SqlConnection1) will appear in the *Component Tray* below the form designer. You can see this new connection object sitting in the Component Tray in Figure 3.2.

The Component Tray is actually an instance of the Component Designer and is very handy when working with invisible controls, such as timer controls. The tray keeps these invisible controls neatly arranged, so that they are always available—without being obscured by other controls. The items in the tray also represent a single source by which you can delete a whole batch of code with minimal effort.

Once the Connection object is a part of your designer, you can view the source code and find the reference to the Connection in an expandable region marked *Windows Form Designer generated code* or *Web Form Designer Generated Code* (depending on the type of project you are building). You will notice that the connection object variable is declared using the WithEvents tag, so that you are able to add event handlers easily for the *InfoMessage* and *StateChange* events. You can do this in the Code Editor, by first selecting the object you want from the Class Name drop-down list on the left and then selecting the event you want to handle from the Method Name drop-down list on the right.

```
Public Class WebForm1
   Inherits System.Web.UI.Page
   Protected WithEvents SqlConnection1 As _
      System.Data.SqlClient.SqlConnection
#Region " Web Form Designer Generated Code "
   Me.SqlConnection1 = New System.Data.SqlClient.SqlConnection()
   '
   'SqlConnection1
   '
   Me.SqlConnection1.ConnectionString = "data source=TITANIC;" & _
      "initial catalog=Northwind;integrated security=SSPI;" & _
      "persist security info=False;workstation id=OMNIBOOK;" & _
      "packet size=4096"
#End Region
```

NOTE In Visual Studio .NET, you may only create and save OLE DB Data Connections in the Server Explorer. There is no facility to create a SqlConnection in the Server Explorer. That having been said, when you drag and drop a data connection to a SQL Server from the Server Explorer onto the designer, Visual Studio .NET will actually create a SqlConnection object, thus using the Sql Server .NET Data Provider. If you'd rather have an OLE DB connection to the SQL Server in your code, you'll need to manually update this source code.

NOTE Also, Visual Studio .NET does not synchronize changes made in the Server Explorer with the code in the form. Once you drop it, you're responsible for making updates to the ADO.NET code.

Creating DataAdapters for Tables, Views, and Columns

Once you have created a Data Connection in the Server Explorer, you may drag Tables, Views, and Columns to your form. Doing so will cause an ADO.NET DataAdapter object to be created. A DataAdapter object, as you will learn in the reference section, is the *broker* between your application and the data source. It's the DataAdapter's function to manage the retrieval and updating of data to and from the data source. The DataAdapter object will be automatically configured in code, with all of the settings necessary to SELECT, INSERT, UPDATE, and DELETE data. Don't try to drag the individual parameters or columns from a Stored Procedure, as that operation is not supported. Refer to Figure 3.3 while you read through the following steps on creating a DataAdapter.

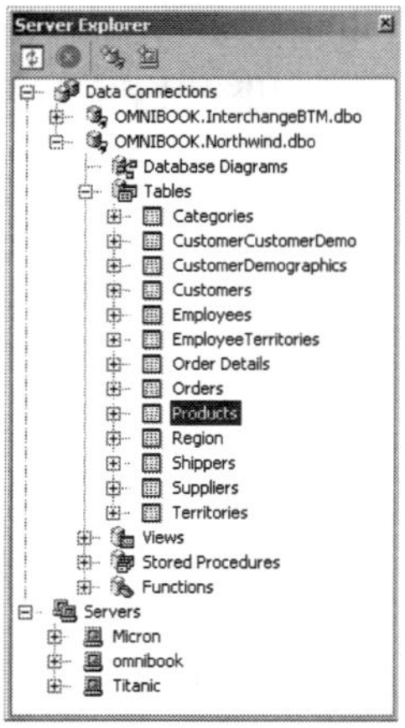

Figure 3.3 Selecting a table.

1. Expand the Data Connections node and then the appropriate Connection.
2. Locate the table, view, or column for which you want to generate an ADO.NET DataAdapter object. You can drag multiple items and combinations of items at a time. If you want to drag over all tables, for example, you can drag the Tables folder node itself and drop it on the form.
3. Drag the selection to your form, and drop it anywhere. At this point, your project solution will add a reference to System.Data, and a DataAdapter object(s) will appear in the Component Tray below the form designer (see Figure 3.4). If your form does not already have a Connection object, one will be generated automatically.

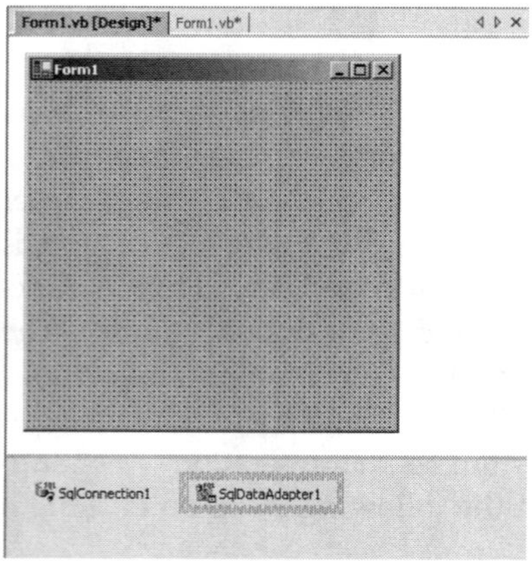

Figure 3.4 DataAdapter object in the Component Tray.

Once the DataAdapter object is a part of your form, you can view the source code and see that Visual Studio .NET has generated several additional variables.

```
Friend WithEvents SqlSelectCommand1 As System.Data.SqlClient.SqlCommand
Friend WithEvents SqlInsertCommand1 As System.Data.SqlClient.SqlCommand
Friend WithEvents SqlUpdateCommand1 As System.Data.SqlClient.SqlCommand
Friend WithEvents SqlDeleteCommand1 As System.Data.SqlClient.SqlCommand
Friend WithEvents SqlDataAdapter1 As
System.Data.SqlClient.SqlDataAdapter
```

More importantly, Visual Studio .NET configured each of the SqlCommand objects with their CommandText and Parameters collections fully and accurately populated, as well as the Table and Column mappings, based on the objects you dropped. For the Products table from Northwind, this meant that 100 lines of tedious code were generated automatically.

You may want to rename some of the objects and make any minor tweaks here and there. The great part is that you can! Visual Studio .NET doesn't keep any links to the Server Explorer. Once it's dropped, it's just code. This is, however, a double-edged sword, in that any changes you make to the data source or the Server Explorer are not automatically reflected in your code or the Properties Windows.

NOTE **If you are dragging and dropping SQL Server Views, they must have a primary key or a unique key defined in order to generate a proper UPDATE or DELETE statement. If this is not the case, then you will have to locate that section of code and update the statements manually, using your judgment on which column(s) to use for a WHERE clause. Also, the logon account must have adequate permissions to perform the operation.**

Creating Commands for Stored Procedures and Functions

You can also drag Stored Procedures and Table-valued functions from the Data Connection node to your form. Doing so will cause ADO.NET Command objects to be created. A Command object, as you will learn in the reference section, represents a SQL command or stored procedure call to the data source. These commands may or may not return data. An important member of the Command class is the Parameters collection, which Visual Studio .NET will automatically create for you. The Command object will be configured in code with a parameter collection ready to execute and process the command. See Figure 3.5 while reading the following directions on how to create a Command object for a stored procedure.

1. Expand the Data Connections node and then the appropriate connection.
2. Locate the stored procedure or function for which you want to generate an ADO.NET Command object. You can drag multiple stored procedures or functions at the same time. Visual Studio .NET will generate separate Commands for each item. You cannot, however, drag and drop scalar functions or the individual stored procedure parameters and columns.

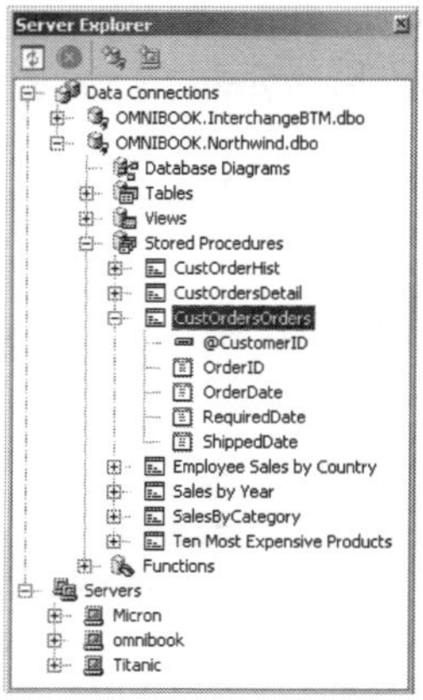

Figure 3.5 Selecting a stored procedure.

3. Drag the selection to your form, and drop it anywhere. At this point, your project solution will add a reference to System.Data, and a Command object(s) will appear in the Component Tray below the form designer (see Figure 3.6). If your form does not already have a Connection object, one will be generated automatically.
4. Once the Command object is a part of your form, you can view the source code and see that Visual Studio .NET has declared a command object and generated all the code that initializes the CommandText, CommandType, Connection, and Parameters collection.

```
Me.SqlCommand1 = New System.Data.SqlClient.SqlCommand()
'
'SqlCommand1
'
Me.SqlCommand1.CommandText = "dbo.[CustOrdersOrders]"
Me.SqlCommand1.CommandType = System.Data.CommandType.StoredProcedure
Me.SqlCommand1.Connection = Me.SqlConnection1
Me.SqlCommand1.Parameters.Add( _
   New System.Data.SqlClient.SqlParameter("@RETURN_VALUE", _
   System.Data.SqlDbType.Int, 4, _
   System.Data.ParameterDirection.ReturnValue, False, CType(10, Byte), _
   CType(0, Byte), "", System.Data.DataRowVersion.Current, Nothing))
Me.SqlCommand1.Parameters.Add( _
   New System.Data.SqlClient.SqlParameter("@CustomerID", _
   System.Data.SqlDbType.NVarChar, 5))
```

More importantly, each of the SqlCommand objects is preconfigured with its CommandText and Parameters collections fully and accurately populated, as well as defining the necessary Table and Column mappings. You may want to rename some of the objects and make some minor tweaks here and there, and you can—that's the great part.

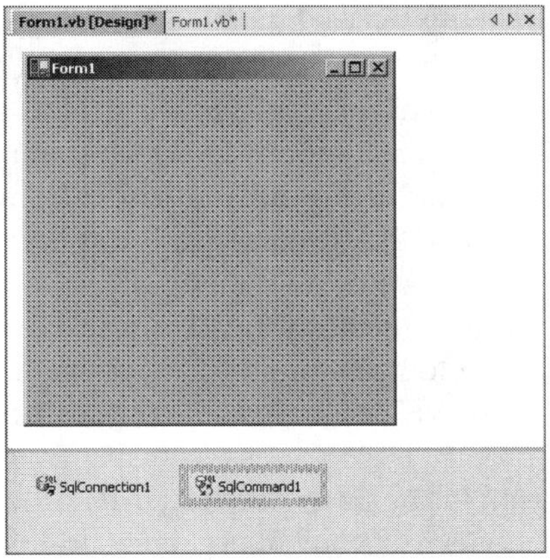

Figure 3.6 Command object in the Component Tray.

NOTE **Visual Studio .NET will not create command objects for scalar functions using this method. If you wish to call a scalar-valued user-defined function, then you must build the command manually and execute it with the ExecuteScalar method.**

It's worth mentioning that Visual Studio .NET does not use the functionality of the CommandBuilder object to generate the SQL, but rather generates the mass of code internally. The CommandBuilder class, as you will learn, is a utility that you can use programmatically to generate single-table commands used to insert, update, or delete data.

Configuring Data Adapters

Once you have a DataAdapter sitting in your Component Tray, you have a couple of options for configuring it. Our first reaction is to just open the code editor and go to work with the keyboard, updating the code that Visual Studio .NET has generated for you. Other options include making changes to the properties in the Properties Window (see Figure 3.7) or using the Data Adapter Configuration Wizard. These windows allow you to configure the important SelectCommand, InsertCommand, UpdateCommand, and DeleteCommand properties, as well as adjust the TableMappings and change the behavior of the adapter's actions.

Configuring Data Adapters with the Properties Window

Visual Studio takes a great first guess at how you would like to configure your Select, Insert, Update, and Delete Command objects, but they may not be quite how you pictured them. Also, they may not be tuned for your multiuser environment. For example, you may not want your SelectCommand to return all columns, or you may want your WHERE clauses to include more fields or a timestamp, rather than just the key fields assumed by Visual Studio .NET.

You could have curtailed the columns by not dragging the entire table over to your designer, but rather just those columns you wanted. What if you wanted to return a constant value or a computed or aggregate column? What if you wanted to add a WHERE clause to the SELECT statement? These are some situations in which you're going to have to modify the command. Our hero would bring up the source code behind the form and make the changes to the CommandText property and the Parameters collection directly, but there are a couple of easier ways to do this.

Notice that in Figure 3.7 there is an ellipsis button (...) next to the CommandText property of the SelectCommand property. Each of the four command properties has this as well. When you click this button, Visual Studio .NET's Query Builder pops up, as shown in Figure 3.8.

This Query Builder, like those you may have used in the past, possibly from other Microsoft products, provides a standard four-pane view of your query, view, in-line function, or single-statement stored procedure. You can show or hide any of the four panes.

Diagram pane. Displays the tables that you are querying, allowing you to check the selected columns.

Grid pane. A grid that allows you also to select the columns to display, select, or group.

SQL pane. A text area that shows the SQL statement being constructed; you can also edit this yourself.

Results pane. A grid showing the data returned by the query when it is run; you may make changes to the data.

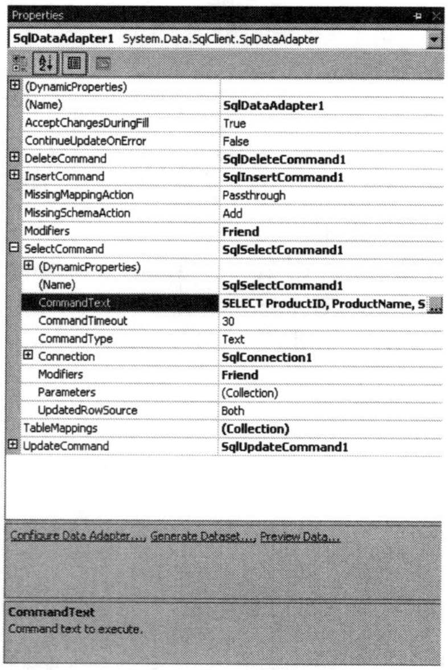

Figure 3.7 DataAdapter Properties Window.

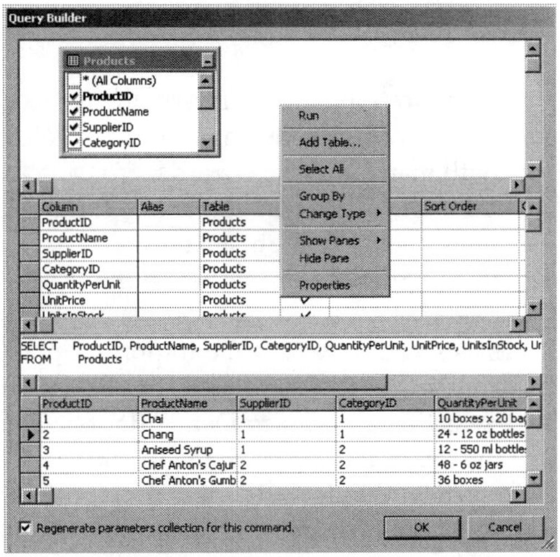

Figure 3.8 Query Builder with popup menu.

After you have made the changes to the SQL statement and clicked the OK button, the corresponding Command object will be updated with the new CommandText.

If you didn't have the Query Builder automatically generate a parameters collection for you, or if you wish to override Visual Studio .NET's "best guess," then you can click the ellipsis (...) button next to the corresponding Parameters property of the Command and use the Parameter Collection Editor, shown in Figure 3.9. Again, you can make these same changes directly in your code, but this GUI allows you to see the range of options for ADO.NET Parameter objects—something you will learn more about in the reference section.

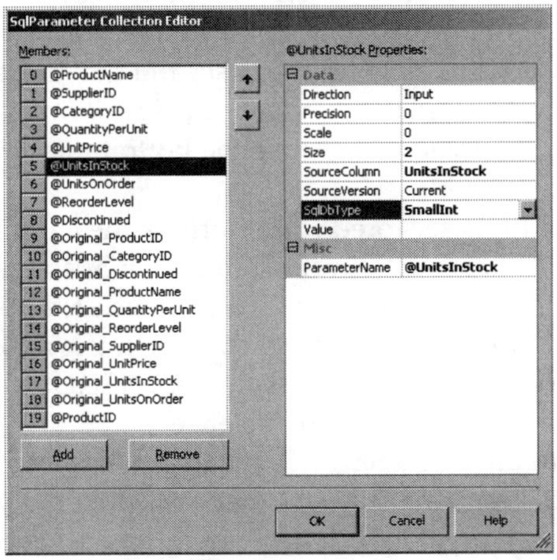

Figure 3.9 Parameter Collection Editor.

Configuring Data Adapters with the Data Adapter Configuration Wizard

Wizards offer a simple, linear approach to configuration. Their "interview" process keeps you in a sandbox, forcing you to answer the really interesting questions before continuing. Visual Studio .NET provides you with many of these wizards, typically for the more complicated objects, such as a DataAdapter, which can take many forks and sidetracks. You can always configure these components without using the wizards, either by directly manipulating the code or by changing the properties in the Properties Window.

The Data Adapter Configuration Wizard assists you in setting the important properties of a new or existing DataAdapter. You can launch the wizard by right-clicking on a DataAdapter in the Component Tray and selecting Configure Data Adapter. This option can also be set from the Data menu at the top of the screen or via the link in the *Description Pane* at the bottom of the Properties Window. If you drop a fresh DataAdapter onto your designer from the Toolbox, this wizard will run automatically.

The wizard's first prompt is for you to select or create a connection that the DataAdapter will use to communicate with the data source. If you already have connections configured in the Server Explorer, they will be listed here; otherwise, you can create a connection object on the fly. The next prompt is for you to decide which Query Type you will use to facilitate the changes made to your data source (see Figure 3.10).

This step of the wizard presents you with a crossroad of choices. Before you answer this question, you need to understand stored procedures, the security model of your SQL Server, and whether your DBA has already created stored procedures to facilitate the selecting and/or updating of your data.

The first choice, to use SQL statements, is probably the simplest, but least secure, approach, as it does not use stored procedures, but rather builds INSERT, UPDATE, and DELETE statements on the client and issues them directly against the data source. When your data source does not support stored procedures, this is the obvious choice. If you are going to use stored procedures, then you can have Visual Studio .NET create them for you, which is recommended. You've always got the option of improving the stored procedure later through SQL Server's Enterprise Manager. Just make sure that you don't alter the parameters or your ADO.NET. Assuming that you already have stored procedures in place that facilitate the updating of your database, and that these stored procedures follow the model of how DataAdapters work (by specifying a parameter for every column being updated), then you can choose the bottom option and specify your existing procedures.

One capability that you might want to add to these stored procedures is the ability to echo any changes to an auditing database. This feature is very common in business applications, where managers appreciate being able to follow the changes made to specific tables by specific individuals. You could also pull this off by using SQL triggers. Triggers, which are similar to stored procedures, execute when data in a specified table is modified. Triggers can fire in response to an Insert, Update, or Delete event.

The choice to *use SQL statements* asks you to provide a SELECT statement or launch the Query Builder to assist you. The wizard needs a SELECT statement, preferably from a single table, which supports a primary or unique key. Once it has a valid SELECT statement, corresponding INSERT, UPDATE, and DELETE statements can be created automatically.

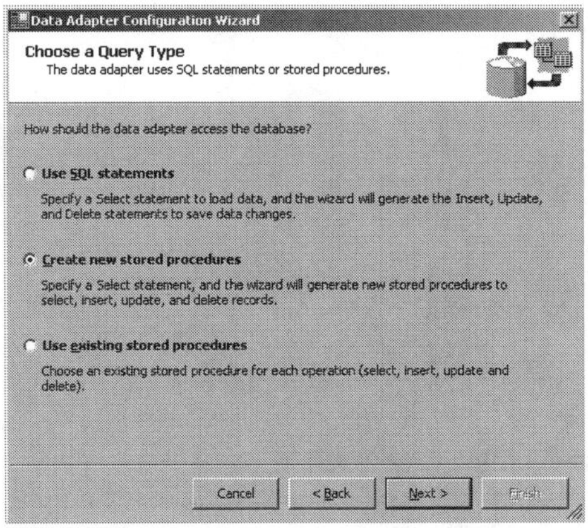

Figure 3.10 Choosing a Query Type.

The choice to *create new stored procedures* also asks you to provide a SELECT statement or launch the Query Builder to assist you. The wizard needs a SELECT statement, preferably from a single table, which supports a primary or unique key. Once it has a valid SELECT statement, it will prompt you for names of each of the stored procedures that it will build. The wizard can create the procedures immediately or allow you to save and execute the SQL script at a later time.

TIP **To secure your application tightly, you will want to use stored procedures to select your data as well as when inserting, updating, and deleting. You can then revoke direct access to the tables, forcing all traffic to use stored procedures. To have Visual Studio .NET wizard create the stored procedures for you, however, it will need access to the table at design time. Before you deploy, make sure you either revoke the access to the tables for that credential or change the connection string to a user account that cannot access the tables directly.**

Here is an example of an automatically created stored procedure to facilitate the inserting of data into the Products table.

```
IF EXISTS (SELECT * FROM sysobjects WHERE name = 'NewInsertCommand' AND
           user_name(uid) = 'dbo')
   DROP PROCEDURE [dbo].[NewInsertCommand];
GO
CREATE PROCEDURE [dbo].[NewInsertCommand]
(
   @ProductName nvarchar(40),
   @SupplierID int,
   @CategoryID int,
   @QuantityPerUnit nvarchar(20),
   @UnitPrice money,
```

```
    @UnitsInStock smallint,
    @UnitsOnOrder smallint,
    @ReorderLevel smallint,
    @Discontinued bit
)
AS
    SET NOCOUNT OFF;
    INSERT INTO Products(ProductName, SupplierID, CategoryID,
        QuantityPerUnit, UnitPrice, UnitsInStock, UnitsOnOrder,
        ReorderLevel, Discontinued) VALUES (@ProductName, @SupplierID,
        @CategoryID, @QuantityPerUnit, @UnitPrice, @UnitsInStock,
        @UnitsOnOrder, @ReorderLevel, @Discontinued);
    SELECT ProductID, ProductName, SupplierID, CategoryID, QuantityPerUnit,
        UnitPrice, UnitsInStock, UnitsOnOrder, ReorderLevel, Discontinued
    FROM Products WHERE (ProductID = @@IDENTITY);
GO
```

If you choose to *use existing stored procedures,* then you must provide the stored procedure names for each of the four operations. You must also map data columns, provided by the SELECT stored procedure, to the parameters of the Insert, Update, and Delete stored procedures. This can take some time and be tedious for wide tables, but it's important to get your mappings correct.

NOTE ADO.NET DataAdapters do not support Inserting, Updating, or Deleting to more than one table at a time. Microsoft has acknowledged this as a limitation in the technology, and it has indicated that it is looking at expanding the capability in the future. In addition to the single table limitation, the underlying table that you are updating must have a unique key defined, and your connection must have the appropriate permissions to change the data.

If you are generating SQL statements or new stored procedures, you can click the Advanced Options button and customize the creation process (see Figure 3.11).

Generate Insert, Update, and Delete statements. When your DataAdapter is to be used for read-only data, then unchecking this box will result in more efficient code, as Visual Studio .NET has to configure only the SelectCommand object.

Use optimistic concurrency. Should the wizard include code to determine if the record has changed since the last time your code read it from the database? Visual Studio .NET implements this by beefing up the WHERE clause for Updates and Deletes, to compare *all* column data, instead of just the key column(s). It's recommended to keep this one checked because, although it generates larger SQL commands or stored procedures, it helps to avoid collisions and conflicts.

Refresh the DataSet. Should the wizard include code to reread the data after you perform an update? This is recommended as well, but it could be disabled if your application is smart about refreshing its interfaces with the user's changes.

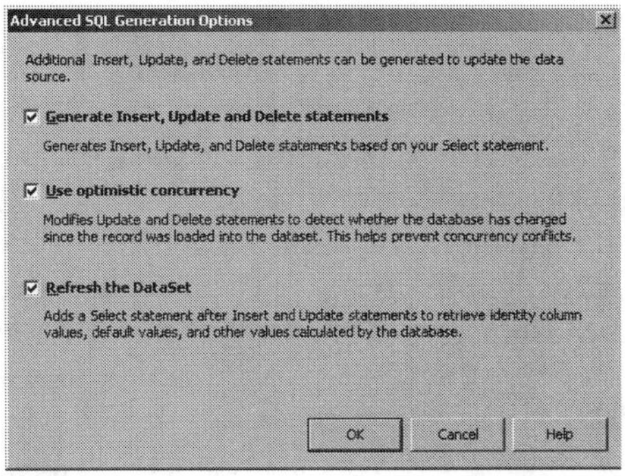

Figure 3.11 Advanced SQL generation options.

Previewing Data Adapter Data

Once you've sweated the details of configuring your Data Adapter, you should take advantage of Visual Studio .NET's ability to preview the data returned to your Data Adapter at design time. This read-only preview, shown in Figure 3.12, shows exactly how the data will be filled into a DataSet object at runtime—when an adapter's Select-Command is executed. This way, you can confirm that you are returning all the columns you need and none you don't. If your SelectCommand accepts parameters, this dialog will allow you to specify them as well.

The Data Adapter Preview can be launched by right-clicking on a Data Adapter in the Component Tray and then selecting Preview Data. You can also select this option from the Data menu at the top of the screen or via the link at the bottom of the Properties Window.

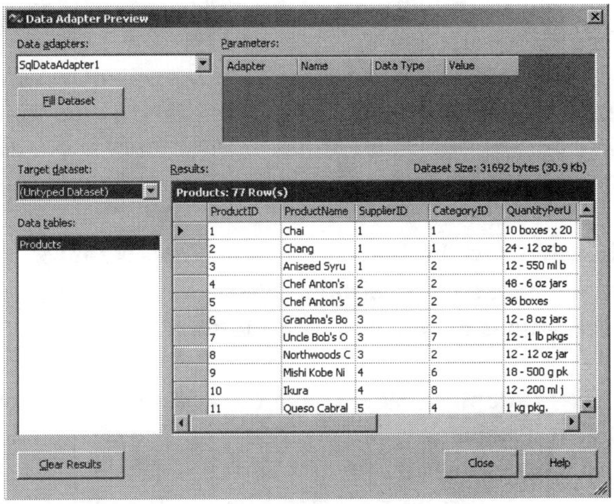

Figure 3.12 Data Adapter preview.

In the Data Adapter Preview screen, select the Data Adapter to preview and click the Fill DataSet button. The DataSet will fill with the table returned by the Data Adapter. Each time you fill the DataSet with a new DataTable, it will append the new table to the collection of data tables. You can also select <All data adapters> to fill the DataSet with data from all tables of all adapters.

Be ready for errors that may occur during the Fill method call, especially if there are data type mismatches, syntax errors in the SQL, or stored procedures being called or if the MissingMappingAction or MissingSchemaAction properties are set to *error*. You will learn more about these properties in the reference section. Just remember to use this Preview utility for what it is—a way to debug your SelectCommand.

If the SQL or stored procedure behind the SelectCommand object requires parameters before it will execute, the grid at the top of the Preview Window will allow you to specify any required values. Some of these parameters may be set to <DEFAULT> or <NULL>, depending on your stored procedure. By varying your parameters, you can test the capabilities and range of your SelectCommand.

You may also wish to choose a Target DataSet other than the untyped one used by the preview feature. The untyped DataSet does not have a schema, so it is not a very good choice to model your process. If you have added DataSet objects to your project, they will be listed in the Target DataSet pull-down list for you to choose. When you choose your DataSet, you can then choose the DataTable you wish to view.

Generating DataSets

As you will learn, the DataSet is ADO.NET's structure for storing data *and* schema information when your application is disconnected from the data source. Remember, in ADO.NET all DataSet manipulation is performed offline. A DataSet can contain all tables, constraints, keys, relationships, and data from an entire database—or two separate databases. DataSets may also be merged with other DataSets at runtime. DataSets are populated by DataAdapters, so it's important to have the corresponding DataAdapters created beforehand.

In an ADO.NET application, you will likely do most of your data manipulation using DataSets. Sophisticated, offline data-entry applications as well as applications that serialize data to and from streams or XML will do so using a DataSet object. Along with Connection and DataAdapter, the DataSet rounds out the big three of the four ADO.NET classes used in most ADO.NET applications. You will learn more about all of these objects in the reference section.

NOTE The DataReader is the fourth object, built for when you simply want to rip through the data returned from a data source, without altering or persisting it. The DataReader maintains a continuous connection with the server.

Once you have configured your DataAdapters, as we have done in the preceding pages, you can generate your DataSet or DataSets automatically, at design time. You do this by right-clicking on any DataAdapter in the Component Tray and selecting Generate DataSet. You can also select this option from the Data menu at the top of the screen or via the link at the bottom of the Properties Window in the description pane.

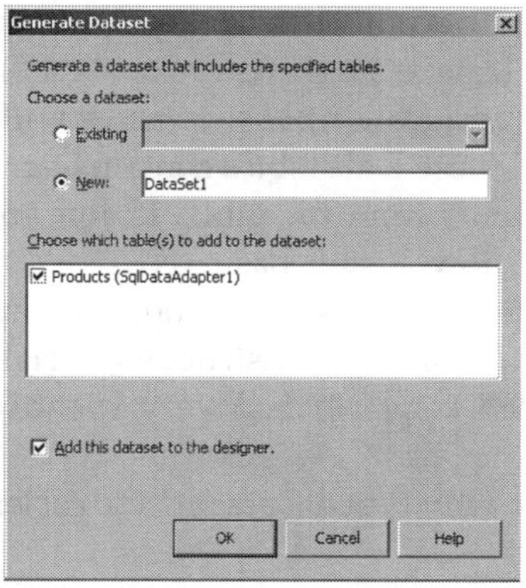

Figure 3.13 Generating DataSet.

Regardless of which DataAdapter you may have highlighted in the Component Tray, you are brought to the same standard dialog window (see Figure 3.13). This dialog lists all DataAdpaters found in the Component Tray and offers you the choice of adding any of the tables returned by any of the DataAdapters to a new or existing DataSet. If the tables listed differ from what you expected to see, you may have to tweak the TableMappings property of the suspect DataAdapter.

This dialog allows tables only to be added or updated in a DataSet. If you add a table to a DataSet that already contains that table, you are asking Visual Studio .NET to update the table schema and data. When you do this, you may be prompted with a message indicating that your class file (.vb or .cs) has been modified outside of the source editor. You should reload the file if you wish to update the DataSet class.

If you want to remove a table from a DataSet, you will need to use the XML Designer. This dialog isn't set up to remove tables. You will learn about the XML Designer later in this chapter.

The final checkbox asks if you want the DataSet to appear in the Component Tray. If you are creating this DataSet to be used elsewhere in your application (rather than on the current form) or if you simply want to generate the schema files, deselect this option. When you have finished and have clicked the Ok button, the DataSet is created. Visual Studio .NET creates a schema (.xsd) file and a corresponding class (.vb or .cs) file that implements and extends the schema information.

Typed DataSets

What's really great about these DataSet objects, compared to the ones you would create manually, is that Visual Studio .NET generates *typed* DataSets. Typed DataSets are subclasses of the DataSet class, with additional properties and overrides that customize the DataSet for the data contained within. If you look at the code generated behind your form, you'll see that your new DataSet object variable is declared as an instance of a custom class.

```
Friend WithEvents DataSet11 As MyVisualStudioNetApp.DataSet1
```

Additional investigation, using the Class View Window, will turn up an elaborate subclass of the DataSet class in the file DataSet1.vb (or DataSet1.cs if you're using C#). More importantly, within the DataSet1 class, you will find DataTable subclasses with the actual names of the tables from the data source. And these DataTables contain DataColumn properties with the actual names of the columns from the table. If you are looking for sample code to familiarize yourself with how Visual Basic .NET or C# implements OOP, this sample code is worth a look. Several new OOP concepts are demonstrated here, such as inheritance, overriding, overloading, constructors, serialization, and .NET event handlers. All of this generated code yields a very friendly class, which exactly models your data source.

Compare the following two snippets of code and see why typed DataSets are easier to use and read.

```
' Working with untyped (traditional) DataSet
Dim s As String
s = _
  Me.DataSet1.Tables("Products").Rows(0).Item("ProductName").ToString()
' Working with typed DataSets
Dim s As String
s = Me.DataSet1.Products(0).ProductName
```

Notice in the typed DataSet example that you do not need to refer to each collection and property down the hierarchy. We don't have to explicitly reference the Tables and Rows collection, nor the Item property. You can simply refer to the table by its friendly name "Products," and you can then refer to the column by its friendly name "ProductName." The zero in parentheses there indicates that you are interested in the first row in the table. Also, notice that there is no need to coerce the data type to a string. At design time, Visual Studio .NET took care of that for us in the class definition.

Did we mention Intellisense? As with any class definition, your typed DataSet is referenced by Intellisense at design time to assist you in statement and word completion (see Figure 3.14).

TIP **You can also use the XSD.EXE tool found in the .NET Framework SDK to read an XSD file and generate a strongly typed DataSet in either Visual Basic .NET or Visual C# .NET source code. Refer to the SDK for more information.**

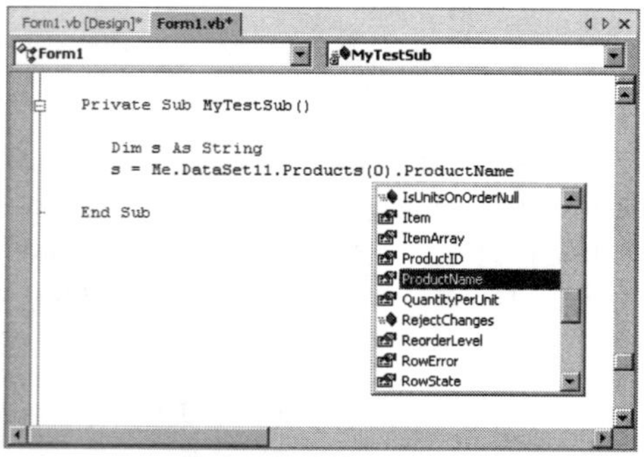

Figure 3.14 Intellisense with a typed DataSet.

Manually Adding a DataSet

When you drag and drop a DataSet object from the Toolbox onto your designer, the Add DataSet dialog box pops up (see Figure 3.15). This dialog will allow you to create the new DataSet as a Typed DataSet, based on an existing class definition. The pull-down list will contain all DataSet classes that were defined using an XML schema (.xsd file). The class could be one that you created earlier and attached to your project, or one that you are referencing from an XML Web service. If the DataSet class is not in the pull-down list, you can manually type the name of the class. Be sure that the DataSet class and schema are made available to the project before you compile your application.

If you choose to create a Typed DataSet, you are effectively creating an instance of that custom class. The name of the instance will be the name of the class plus a sequential number. For example, if the DataSet class is named DataSet1, the first instance is named DataSet11, then the second instance is DataSet12, and so on.

If you choose to create an untyped DataSet, you are essentially creating an instance of the base System.Data.DataSet class. This untyped DataSet can have its schema populated later, during design time or programmatically during runtime. See the section *Building an Untyped DataSet* in this chapter.

DataSet Properties

DataSets can get very large and complicated in a hurry. It takes only a dozen tables with a dozen relationships and two dozen constraints to turn your object into *data bouillabaisse*. You can use the Data Adapter Preview to view the data of individual tables, but that doesn't help you with the schema information. You can use the Properties Window, but that can be tedious and not reveal much about the schema itself. If you had Visual Studio .NET build you a typed DataSet, you could move through the pages of code that it generated for you, hoping for a glimpse of the forest through all of the trees.

By using the DataSet Properties dialog, however, you can get a good impression of what your DataSet looks like. All tables, columns, keys, constraints, data types, defaults, and other behaviors of the data are displayed. The dialog is hierarchical, with a TreeView control in the left pane to show you the DataSet and its tables. There is a grid in the right pane, which shows the properties of the currently selected node.

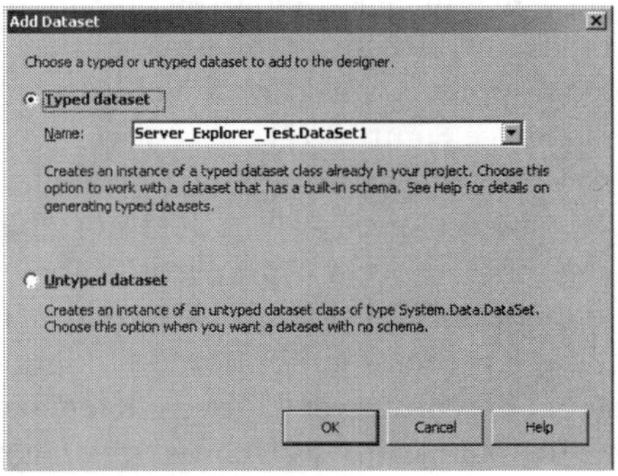

Figure 3.15 Adding a DataSet.

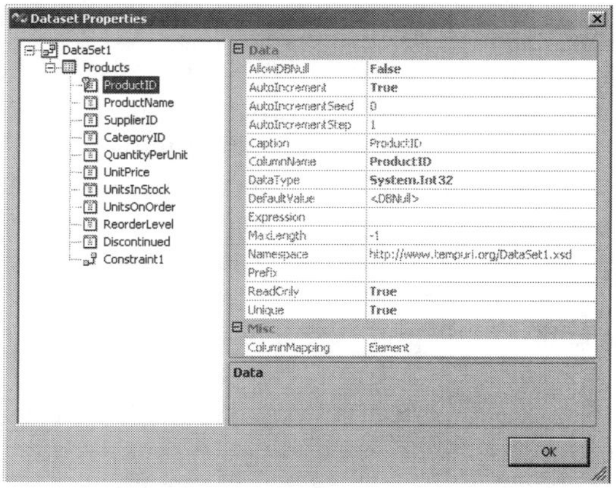

Figure 3.16 Read-only DataSet properties.

You can bring up the DataSet Properties dialog (Figure 3.16) by right-clicking on any typed DataSet in the Component Tray and selecting DataSet Properties. You can also select this option from the Data menu at the top of the screen or via the link at the bottom of the Properties Window. You can view this dialog only for typed DataSets, which are DataSets that have an accompanying schema (.xsd) file.

Building an Untyped DataSet

Just because your DataSet is untyped and wasn't created automatically for you by Visual Studio .NET doesn't mean that you're on your own to create its schema. Sure, things won't get interesting for that DataSet until it has a schema, but there are a couple of additional dialogs to help you build your DataSet. You are able to specify tables, columns, constraints, and relationships. These items don't have to exist in your data source yet, either.

By having the ability to create your DataSets (schemas) manually, you're able to model any relational data source and most hierarchical data sources that you can imagine. Your design can start right here, inside Visual Studio. Populating the DataSet and then updating a physical data source will require some actual programming. We hope that you'll be interfacing with one of the .NET Data Provider data sources or an XML file so that ADO.NET can assist you.

When you click on an untyped DataSet, you'll see that there is a Tables and Relations property in the Properties Window. These are collections, and they can be manipulated by their respective Collections Editor, which pops up when you click the ellipsis (...) button. It is best to build your Tables collection first (see Figure 3.17).

Use this dialog to add each new DataTable. You can also edit or remove DataTables. When you have your DataTable highlighted, you should specify all of the DataTable properties in the grid to the right. Probably the most important property is TableName, which you will use in code to reference this DataTable object. Next, you will probably want to specify the columns by clicking its ellipsis (...) button (see Figure 3.18). Next, you define the Primary Key by selecting the column or columns that make up the key. Finally, you should define any table constraints, such as Unique or Foreign Key constraints.

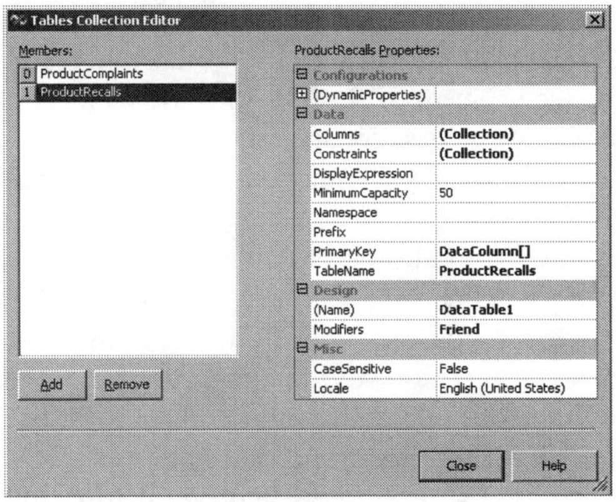

Figure 3.17 Tables Collection Editor.

If you know anything about XML schemas, either .xdr or .xsd format, these properties will look familiar. The idea of Namespace, Prefix, and Locale may be new to traditional database folks, but because DataSets are XML schemas, we all need to get used to these terms. We may not have to actually use them, just become comfortable with the concepts. You'll learn more about XML integration with ADO.NET in Chapter 12, "Integrating XML with ADO.NET."

When defining the columns in your table, be sure to give each a meaningful ColumnName. Select the appropriate DataType and MaxLength as well. Other popular properties you may want to set are the AutoIncrement (which acts like a SQL Server Identity column), DefaultValue, ReadOnly, and Unique. The Unique property will automatically create a Unique constraint.

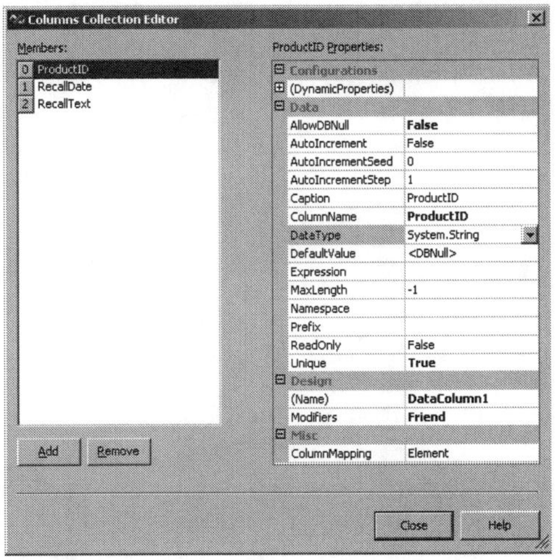

Figure 3.18 Columns Collection Editor.

After you define all of the Columns, you can establish any necessary constraints. When you return to the Tables Collection Editor, you can click on the Constraints ellipsis (...) button and work with that builder (see Figure 3.19). The current version of Visual Studio .NET supports only the creation of Unique constraints (see Figure 3.20) and Foreign Key constraints. You will have to implement Check constraints manually, in your code.

With the Constraints Collection Editor, you are not allowed to make changes to the properties in the grid directly. Instead, when you click Add or Edit, you will be taken to another dialog specific to the type of constraint you are working with. With a Foreign Key constraint, for example, you are encouraged to provide a meaningful name, specify the parent and child tables, choose the column or columns that join the two tables, and specify the referential integrity rules for updating and deleting.

After you define your tables, columns, and constraints, you may want to define some additional relationships between the tables. These relations are implemented as DataRelation objects within the DataSet. DataRelation objects are similar to Foreign Key constraints, but they provide a more evident link when viewing and querying the DataTables. Many of the referential integrity functions of a DataRelation object are duplicated in a Foreign Key constraint of the same settings.

You can launch the Relations Collection Editor shown in Figure 3.21 by clicking the ellipsis (...) button next to the Relations property in the Properties Window. The Collection Editor dialog will list all relationships in the left pane and the read-only properties in the right pane. You can add a new relation or edit an existing one. This will pop up a new window, in which you define the relation. This window is identical to the one used to create Foreign Key constraints.

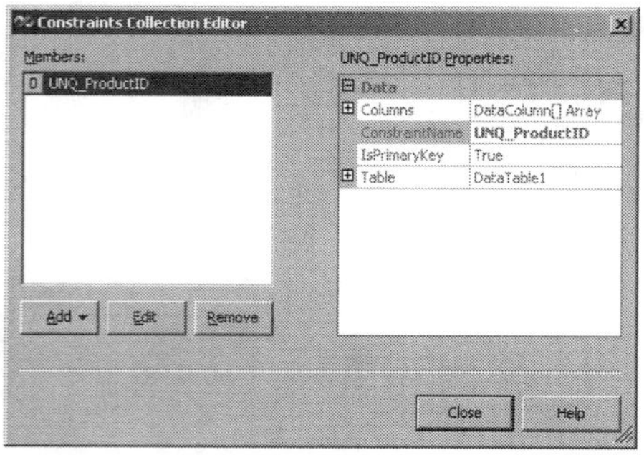

Figure 3.19 Constraints Collection Editor.

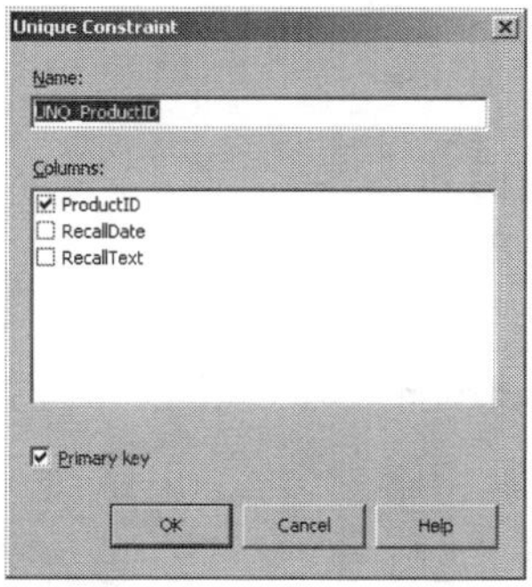

Figure 3.20 Unique constraint.

So what did all of these dialogs build for us? Because this is an untyped DataSet, we're not able to view the DataSet easily with the slick XML Designer, which you will see in the next section. We are able to see this DataSet only by using the collection builder dialogs or by looking at the generated code:

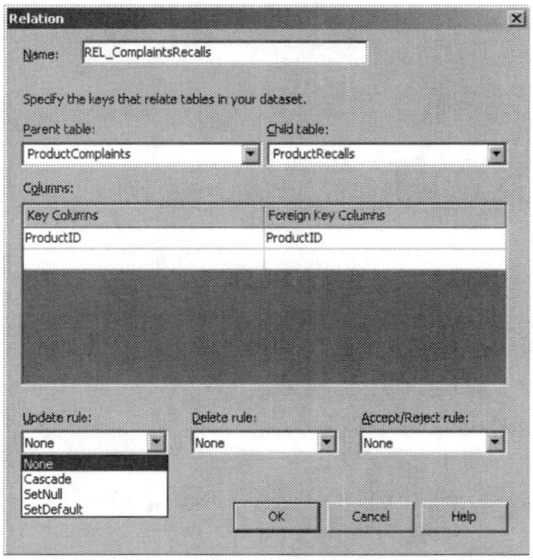

Figure 3.21 Data Relation Editor.

```
' Declare variables
Friend WithEvents MyUntypedDataSet As System.Data.DataSet
Friend WithEvents DataTable1 As System.Data.DataTable
Friend WithEvents DataTable2 As System.Data.DataTable
Friend WithEvents DataColumn1 As System.Data.DataColumn
Friend WithEvents DataColumn2 As System.Data.DataColumn
Friend WithEvents DataColumn3 As System.Data.DataColumn
Friend WithEvents DataColumn4 As System.Data.DataColumn
' Instantiate
Me.MyUntypedDataSet = New System.Data.DataSet()
Me.DataTable1 = New System.Data.DataTable()
Me.DataTable2 = New System.Data.DataTable()
Me.DataColumn1 = New System.Data.DataColumn()
Me.DataColumn2 = New System.Data.DataColumn()
Me.DataColumn3 = New System.Data.DataColumn()
Me.DataColumn4 = New System.Data.DataColumn()
' Initialize
' MyUntypedDataSet
'
Me.MyUntypedDataSet.DataSetName = "NewDataSet"
Me.MyUntypedDataSet.Locale = New System.Globalization.CultureInfo("en-US")
Me.MyUntypedDataSet.Relations.AddRange(New System.Data.DataRelation() _
   {New System.Data.DataRelation("REL_ComplaintsRecalls", _
   "ProductComplaints", "ProductRecalls", New String() {"ProductID"}, _
   New String() {"ProductID"}, False)})
Me.MyUntypedDataSet.Tables.AddRange(New System.Data.DataTable() _
   {Me.DataTable2, Me.DataTable1})
' DataTable2
'
Me.DataTable2.Columns.AddRange(New System.Data.DataColumn()  _
   {Me.DataColumn4})
Me.DataTable2.Constraints.AddRange(New System.Data.Constraint() _
   {New System.Data.UniqueConstraint("Constraint1", New String() _
   {"ProductID"}, False)})
Me.DataTable2.TableName = "ProductComplaints"
'DataTable1
'
Me.DataTable1.Columns.AddRange(New System.Data.DataColumn() _
   {Me.DataColumn1, Me.DataColumn2, Me.DataColumn3})
Me.DataTable1.Constraints.AddRange(New System.Data.Constraint() _
   {New System.Data.UniqueConstraint("UNQ_ProductID", New String() _
   {"ProductID"}, True), New
System.Data.ForeignKeyConstraint("REL_ComplaintsRecalls", _
   "ProductComplaints", New String() {"ProductID"}, New String() _
   {"ProductID"}, System.Data.AcceptRejectRule.None, _
   System.Data.Rule.None, System.Data.Rule.None)})
Me.DataTable1.PrimaryKey = New System.Data.DataColumn() {Me.DataColumn1}
Me.DataTable1.TableName = "ProductRecalls"
' DataColumn1
'
Me.DataColumn1.AllowDBNull = False
```

```
Me.DataColumn1.ColumnName = "ProductID"
' DataColumn2
'
Me.DataColumn2.ColumnName = "RecallDate"
Me.DataColumn2.DataType = GetType(System.DateTime)
' DataColumn3
'
Me.DataColumn3.ColumnName = "RecallText"
' DataColumn4
'
Me.DataColumn4.ColumnName = "ProductID"
```

Viewing Typed DataSet Schema

Typed DataSets are implemented as XML schema (.xsd) files with an accompanying class module. By viewing the XML schema, you can gain full insight into the ADO.NET—XML symmetry. The Schema View, shown in Figure 3.22, provides you with a visual representation of the elements, attributes, and data types that make up the DataSet. You can also switch the view to see the raw XML that forms the schema.

You can bring up the Schema View by right-clicking on any typed DataSet in the Component Tray and selecting View Schema. You can also select this option from the Data menu at the top of the screen or via the link at the bottom of the Properties Window. You can view this designer only for typed DataSets, which are DataSets that have an accompanying schema (.xsd) file and a class module (.vb or .cs) file. If your project contains other .xsd files, they too may be edited in the Schema designer.

Schema View is implemented using Visual Studio .NET's XML Designer. With this designer, you can work with XML Schemas (.xsd files), ADO.NET DataSets, and XML documents. The designer does not, however, support DTDs (document type definitions) or XDR (XML-Data Reduced) files.

You may make any changes to your documents graphically or via the XML code directly. You can construct schemas and DataSets by dragging XML Schema items from the Toolbox and dropping them onto the designer, or you can right-click the designer surface and select Add and then choose your item. You can add any of these items to your schema. The following are the available XML Schema items:

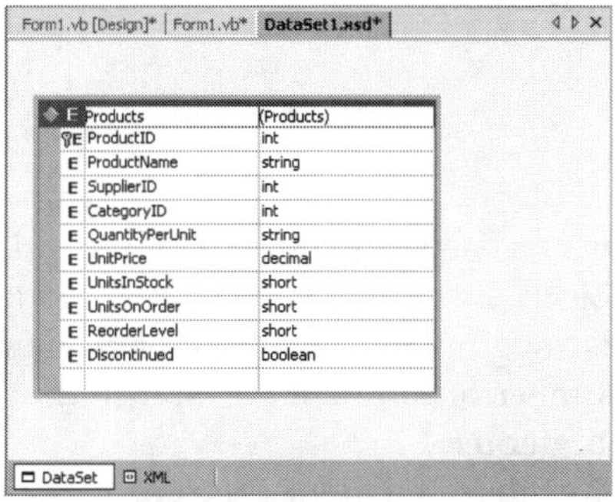

Figure 3.22 DataSet Schema View.

Element. A fundamental building block of an XML Schema or document; an element, in its simplest form, describes the data that it will contain by defining a name and a data type; elements can contain other elements; here is an example of an element:

```
<employee><name>Richard</name></employee>
```

Attribute. A fundamental building block of an XML Schema or document; an attribute is very similar in functionality to an element, in that it is defined with a name and data type; attribute data is optional, and it cannot contain other attributes; here is an example of an element:

```
<employee name="Richard"\>
```

AttributeGroup. A way to group a set of attribute items by name; this allows them to be used to build complex type definitions easily.

ComplexType. A type definition for elements; a ComplexType may contain attributes and elements; you can then define elements as being of a ComplexType.

SimpleType. A type definition for elements similar to ComplexType; SimpleTypes cannot contain elements or attributes and are derived from only the built-in data types.

Group. A way to group a set of element items by name; this allows them to be used to easily build complex type definitions.

Any. A way to enable any element from a given namespace to appear in a sequence or choice element.

AnyAttribute. A way to enable any attribute from a given namespace to appear in a ComplexType element or AttributeGroup element.

Facet. A defining aspect of a simple type, such as length, minLength, maxLength, or pattern; by defining several facets, you are essentially establishing your primitive business rules; facets are implemented as elements.

Key. A way to identify an element or attribute as being a key value; this will force the data in that element or attribute to be unique within its scope.

Relation. Allows you to create a relationship between two tables; drop the relation onto a table in the XML Designer to launch the Edit Relation dialog.

If you would prefer to see your schema in raw XML, you can right-click anywhere in the designer and select View XML Source (see Figure 3.23). You can also click the XML tab at the bottom of the designer.

The Data Tab

The Toolbox, typically found near the Server Explorer, is used as a container for a variety of items you use in your Visual Studio .NET projects. By selecting from the various tabs, scores of components are made available for dragging and dropping onto your project forms. You can customize this Toolbox a number of different ways, including parking your own code fragments and text here for later use.

With regard to ADO.NET, you should be especially interested in the *Data* tab, shown in Figure 3.24. This tab is available to most Visual Basic .NET and C# projects. From the

Figure 3.23 DataSet Schema View (XML).

Data tab, you are able to select many of the popular objects in ADO.NET and drop them onto your designer, where Visual Studio .NET will assist in their configuration.

DataSet. Adds an instance of a typed or untyped DataSet class to the Component Tray. When you drop this onto the designer, a dialog box will appear asking which type of DataSet you wish to create. As an alternative, you may wish to generate a DataSet from an existing DataAdapter, which is the only way to automatically create a typed DataSet class.

OleDbDataAdapter. Adds an instance of an OleDbDataAdapter to the Component Tray. The OleDbDataAdapter allows you to read and update data on an OleDbConnection. When you drop this onto the designer, the Data Adapter Configuration Wizard will launch.

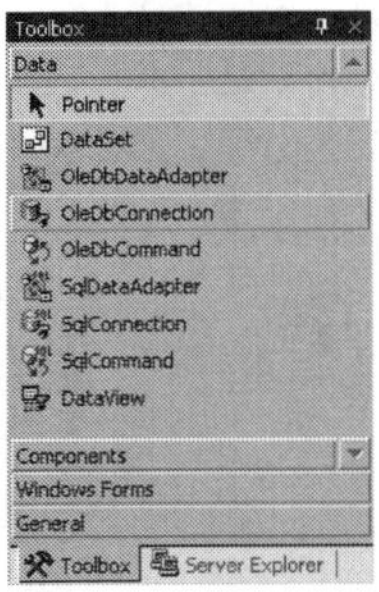

Figure 3.24 Data tab in the Toolbox.

OleDbConnection. Adds an instance of an OleDbConnection to the Component Tray. The OleDbConnection represents a connection to an OLE DB compatible data source. No dialogs or wizards pop up on drop.

OleDbCommand. Adds an instance of an OleDbCommand to the Component Tray. The OleDbCommand represents a SQL statement or stored procedure to execute on an OleDbConnection. No dialogs or wizards pop up on drop.

SqlDataAdapter. Adds an instance of a SqlDataAdapter to the Component Tray. The SqlDataAdapter allows you to read and update data on a SqlConnection. When you drop this onto the designer, the Data Adapter Configuration Wizard will launch.

SqlConnection. Adds an instance of a SqlConnection to the Component Tray. The SqlConnection represents a connection to SQL Server 7.0 or 2000. No dialogs or wizards pop up on drop.

SqlCommand. Adds an instance of a SqlCommand to the Component Tray. The SqlCommand represents a SQL statement or stored procedure to execute on a SqlConnection. No dialogs or wizards pop up on drop.

DataView. Adds an instance of a DataView class to the Component Tray. DataViews, similar to SQL views, allow you to specify a table, filter, and sort options. No dialogs or wizards pop up on drop.

Data Form Wizard

Similar to the Data Form Wizards of prior versions of Visual Studio, this workhorse will help you construct a Web Form or Windows Form with data-bound controls. These controls will display data from the specified data source—making it easy to build a simple database access application. The wizard can create a form only in an application that supports forms—typically, these are Visual Basic or Visual C# .NET Windows or ASP.NET Web applications.

Now that we have spent the better part of a chapter showing you how to build the individual components of a database access application, I'm going to show you the easy way to do it in one fell swoop. The Data Form Wizard will step you through the entire process of building a data-bound form that displays information from the DataSet you specify. Although you may not be happy with the form layout or the code generated behind it, it is code, nonetheless—a starting point from which you can delta.

Don't look for this wizard on the Data or Tools menu. To run the wizard, you need to add a new Data Form Wizard item to your project.

1. Load or create an application that supports Web or Windows Forms.
2. From the File menu, choose Add New Item.
3. Expand the Categories tree, and highlight the Data category.
4. In the Templates pane, select Data Form Wizard.
5. Change the name, and click Open.

Generating the ADO.NET Components

The first step of the wizard is to select or create the DataSet that you will be using. If you already have a typed DataSet, then most of your work is finished, as your DataSet class definition already knows its adapter, connection, tables, columns, and relationships. You can skip to the section on *Using an Existing DataSet*.

If you are creating a new DataSet, then you must select or create the Connection to your data source, choose the tables or views (see Figure 3.25), which will be available to your form, and then choose any static relationships to define. Behind the wizard, each of these steps will create ADO.NET components, either in the Component Tray of the current form or as file-based items found in your Solution Explorer. The Data Form Wizard can also connect to an XML Web service, provided that it returns a DataSet.

When your DataSet contains more than one table, you should consider creating a static relationship. Unfortunately, Visual Studio .NET does not build these for you, which we found odd, because most data sources provide this schema information. Defined relationships enable table synchronization and easier traversing of your data at runtime. When you define a relationship between two tables, the Data Form Wizard is able to derive a master-detail (parent-child) relationship and create a form with form and subform behavior (see Figure 3.26).

If you ever persist your DataSet to XML, these relationships are apparent in the schema. To see what this relationship looks like in XML, locate and double-click on your DataSet in your Solution Explorer after the wizard has finished. Next, click the XML tab at the bottom of the XML Designer to view the XSD. Using our example, you'll see that the relationship is implemented with constraints established on the ComplexType *EmployeeTerritories*.

Once your DataSet is defined, the Data Form Wizard needs to know which columns from which tables you want to appear on your form. If you choose a single table, your form will have the capability to view and manipulate only that data. If you choose two tables and have your relationship properly established, then your form will exhibit a master/detail behavior, where the detail section is implemented by a grid or table below the master section. Be sure to choose only those columns that you want to display (see Figure 3.27). Displaying meaningless IDs, especially those implemented as GUIDs, can be very distracting.

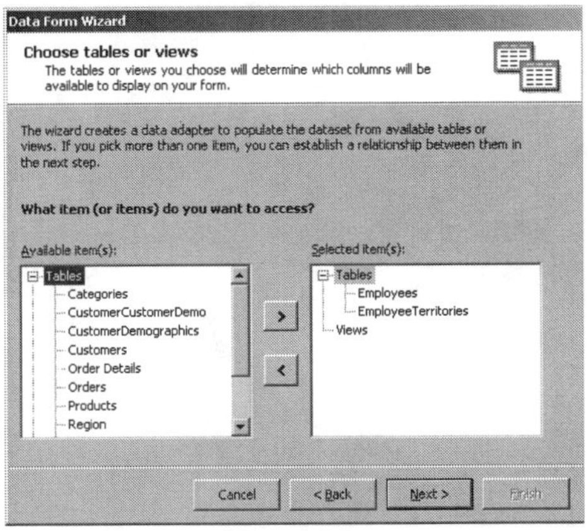

Figure 3.25 Choosing tables or views for your Data Form.

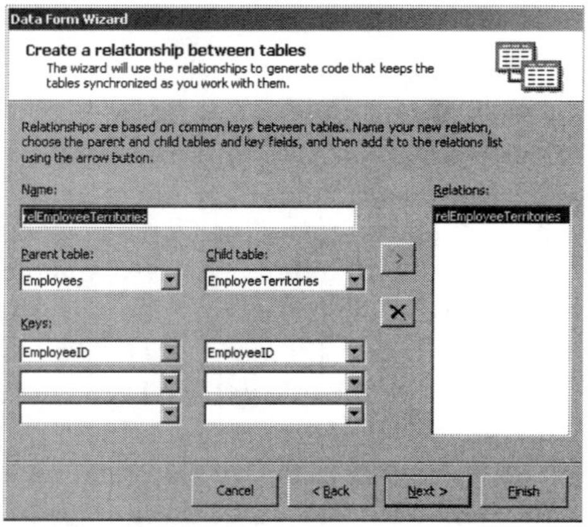

Figure 3.26 Defining a relationship.

Using an Existing DataSet

When the Data Form Wizard is creating *all* of the parts from scratch, it knows exactly how to wire the form to fill the DataSet and update the data source. When you ask the wizard to use an existing DataSet, however, you must provide these method hooks manually. You'll need to complete an extra step, to inform the wizard which method will fill the DataSet and which method will update the DataSet (see Figure 3.28). The only requirement is that these methods have to return a DataSet. You can choose the [None] option and then manually wire the methods later. The Update method applies only to Windows forms.

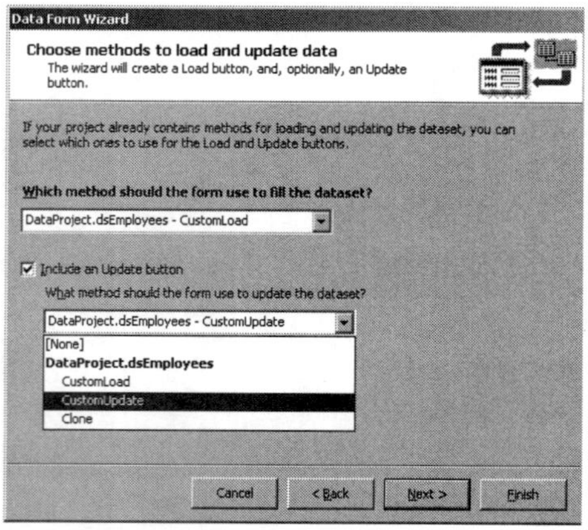

Figure 3.27 Selecting tables and columns to display.

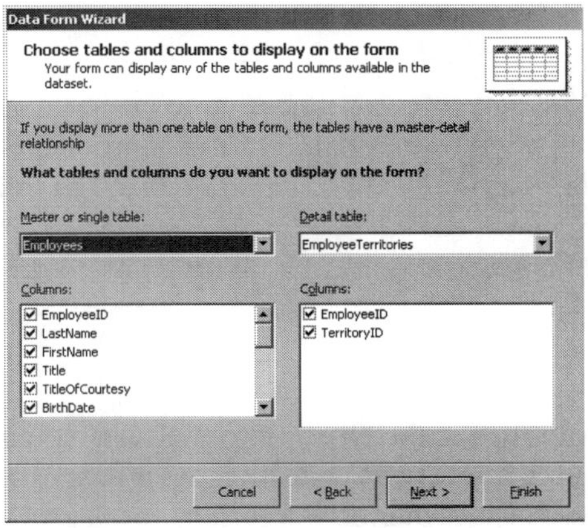

Figure 3.28 Choosing Load and Update methods.

Building Your Data Form

If you are building a Windows application, you may want to fine-tune the appearance or display style of the Data Form. Web applications, on the other hand, have a standard display style that may not be customized from within the wizard. Also, Web Forms built by the Data Form Wizard are read-only.

For Windows applications, your display choices are to display the data in a grid (which is very efficient about using screen real estate for viewing data) or to display your data in a set of individual controls, which can be very appealing for data-entry screens (see Figure 3.29). In addition, you have the ability to include or exclude certain user controls on the form. We recommend trying out various combinations of these settings for yourself on some sample forms, to see which style you like the best. We would also recommend selecting all of the possible controls to be included, as you can always remove them later manually.

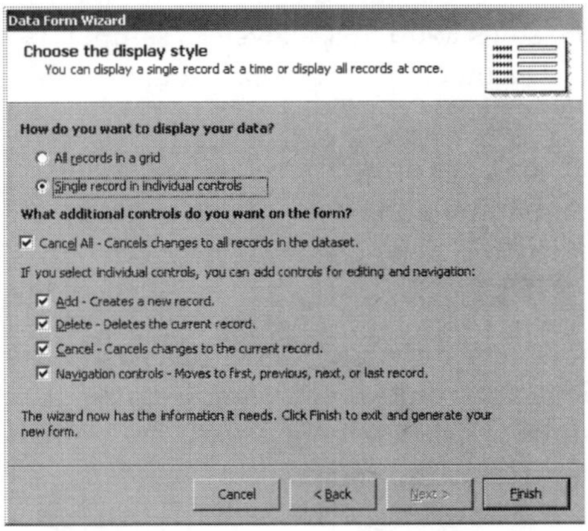

Figure 3.29 Selecting display style (windows only).

The Completed Form

When you click the Finish button, Visual Studio .NET will generate all of the necessary pieces and parts to complete the Data Form. You may have noticed, if your Designer or Solution Explorer has been visible behind the wizard, that some of the components have been built and associated with your project as you've been stepping through the wizard.

Figures 3.30 and 3.31 are samples of what Visual Studio .NET built for us as a Windows Form and again as a Web Form.

Improving Your Data Form

Once the wizard finishes, you cannot return to it to make changes to the form or its components. It's a one-way ticket—you'll need to modify the code directly or abandon the form and start over (which is sometimes easier). As mentioned earlier, you'll probably want to make aesthetic changes to the form, as well as add your business logic and any validation.

Here are a few specific changes you may want to make:

Switch to SqlClient .NET Data Provider. The Data Form Wizard will always generate OLE DB provider code. For performance and compatibility reasons, you should change all references to System.Data.OleDb namespaces and classes to System.Data.SqlClient if you're using SQL Server 7.0 or higher. This may be a substantial amount of work, as you would have to rename several objects and possibly handle the passing of parameters differently. It may save you some time to eliminate the OleDbConnection and any OleDbDataAdapter objects from the Component Tray and replace them (using drag and drop) with SqlConnection and SqlDataAdapter objects.

Merge the two DataSets. The Data Form Wizard generates two separate DataSets, which are merged during runtime. This is a safe approach that the wizard takes, as the source of the data may come from another DataSet, as with an XML Web service. XML Web services shuttle data around the web as XML documents and schema. When your application receives this data, it can receive it as an ADO.NET DataSet. The merging process allows for this. If your DataSet receives its data from a traditional data source, you should consider consolidating your code to use a single DataSet. The steps to do this, as well as sample code, can be found in Visual Studio .NET Documentation by searching for "Data Form Wizard Generated Code."

Adding update code to your Web form. The Data Form Wizard generates only read-only Web forms. The procedures for manipulating data, which could be extended to provide add and edit capability to a Web Form, will be covered in Chapter 11, "Manipulating Data in ADO.NET."

In summary, you should use the Data Form Wizard for what it is—a quick and dirty way to generate a data-bound form. This could be for a quickie application that you are using yourself or for a tutorial or refresher on how to use data-bound controls. Improving the wizard's code and adding your business rules are a must.

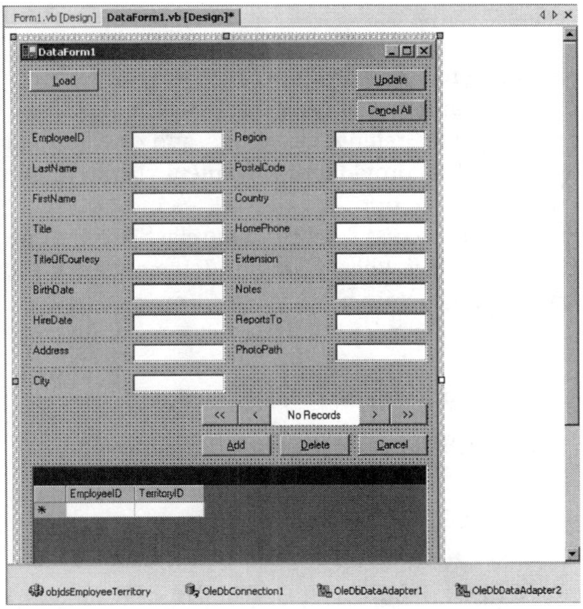

Figure 3.30 Sample Windows Data Form.

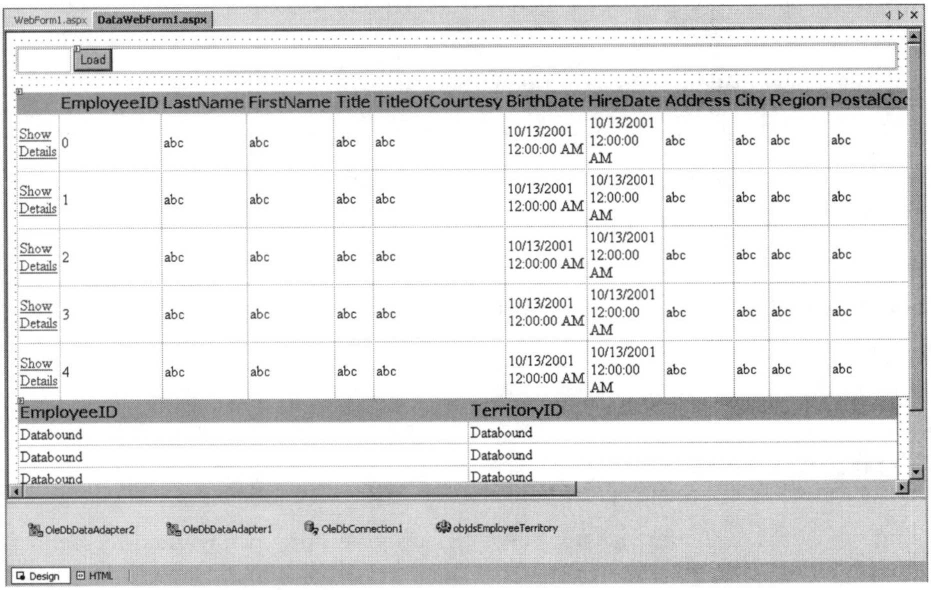

Figure 3.31 Sample Web Data Form.

Database Projects

In Visual Studio .NET, Database Projects are projects geared specifically toward manipulating database objects. While you can do a number of tasks directly with the Server Explorer, a Database Project allows you to persist references, scripts, and queries for a number of different databases to a solution. This provides a convenient way to return to the project any time and pick up where you left off.

Database Projects, however, are not database access projects in the classic sense. You should avoid the urge to start a Database Project when you want to create an ADO. NET application. A Database Project does not contain modules or forms, nor can you compile or run the project. It is simply a container for database-related maintenance tasks.

Here are some things that you can do with a Database Project:

Generate change scripts. Create and run SQL scripts that record a series of changes to database objects.

Generate create scripts. Create and run SQL scripts that create (or re-create) database objects.

Generate queries. Create and run SELECT, INSERT, UPDATE, DELETE queries.

Generate stored procedures. Create, run, and debug SQL stored procedures.

Create command files. Create and run Command (.cmd) files that can contain multiple scripts.

Save database references. Maintain static references to one or more database connections for convenience.

Save data exports. Generate table data from Server Explorer and save with the corresponding create script.

To create a new Database Project, follow these steps:

1. From the File menu, click New and then click Project.
2. In the New Project dialog box, expand Other Projects.
3. Select Database Project from the Database Projects folder.
4. Provide a name and location for the project.
5. Ensure that you close any current Solution you may have open.
6. Click OK.

Moving Forward

Although our book is a reference for ADO.NET programming, we wanted to spend a chapter showing you the data-related builders, wizards, and designers in Visual Studio .NET. More importantly, we wanted to show you when and where these time-saving features generate ADO.NET code that you can copy, paste, and improve on. All successful database developers share a common trait: *resourcefulness*.

Also, some readers and .NET tire-kickers may think that ADO.NET requires Visual Studio .NET or that you have to buy Visual Studio .NET to acquire ADO.NET. These are both false assumptions—ADO.NET comes free with the .NET Framework, which is made available as a free download from Microsoft and will ship with upcoming software packages. This is similar to Microsoft's approach to distributing MDAC ADO.

From this point on, our book focuses on 100 percent code solutions. Coding solutions by hand gives you full control over your application's behavior. Our tutorial chapters will refer back to this chapter for ways to shrink your coding time by using a drag-and-drop shortcut, but we won't spend any more time dealing specifically with the GUI builders.

PART Two

ADO.NET Reference

Every reference book covering Microsoft software development technologies must answer one question immediately: What makes it different than MSDN? We've all read "reference" books that simply regurgitated MSDN, and know how frustrating that can be. From the very beginning, we decided to focus this book on providing concrete, correct, and complete information targeted to the software developer working toward solving business problems with ADO.NET. MSDN is written by techno-geeks for other techno-geeks. There's nothing wrong with this, and I find MSDN to be a valuable resource. However, its focus is often on explaining the concept behind a technology and not how to use that technology. This reference section attempts to be complete, and to explain fully the concepts behind each method and property, as well as how to use it.

With Visual Basic .NET, the language has finally been granted structured exception handling. This is one of the greatest leaps forward for the language, and we both are thrilled by its introduction. However, to properly utilize structured exception handling, you need to know which properties and methods throw exceptions, and what exceptions they can throw. (Yes, even some properties can throw exceptions.) MSDN often lists a few exceptions that are commonly thrown, but only rarely provides a comprehensive list. We've spent hundreds of hours trying to provide a complete list of all exceptions for each and every member in ADO.NET. This alone is worth the price of the book.

NOTE **Did we get all the exceptions? Probably not. Despite all our attempts, there are surely several that we've missed. So, we ask your help in making this book even more complete. If you find an exception thrown by a method or property that we have failed to list, please email the exception and how to generate it to adobook@gearheadpress.com. We'll host it on the Web site errata, and include it in the next edition.**

This section is also helpful to the early adopters. When we began writing this book, MSDN information was virtually non-existent on the System.Data namespace. As Visual Studio .NET and the .NET Framework was released in its final form, it is much better, but still contains sparse and sometimes incorrect information on a majority of the methods and classes in System.Data and the related namespaces.

As .NET matures, MSDN will get better and more useful. But right now it's not as useful as it could be. For those programmers adopting .NET within the first year of its formal release, this section is for you!

Since the ADO.NET namespaces are organized in a hierarchical manner, this section is organized along the same lines. System.Data is covered first, consisting of all of the data source independent classes, such as the DataSet and DataTable objects. This is followed by a chapter covering System.Data.Common classes that are common to the Data Adapters. The next chapters introduce Data Adapters themselves, which are used to access data sources such as SQL Server, Access or Oracle. These are System.Data.OleDb, for accessing OLE DB compliant data sources, and System.Data.SqlClient for accessing MS SQL Server 7.0 and higher. (The Microsoft.Data.Odbc chapter is available online. As of the release of Visual Studio .NET and the .NET Framework, it was still in beta.) The section concludes with System.Data.SqlTypes, which provide a number of non-standard .NET data types that can be used to match the data types internal to MS SQL Server.

Although this is not meant to be a tutorial section, it contains numerous pieces of sample code that illuminate the use of difficult class members. In most cases the sample code for a class is listed before the first members of the class, showing how to use the class as a whole. In other cases, an individual method or property may have sample code attached if there is a difficult concept involved.

Each class, enumeration, and structure within a namespace is listed in alphabetical order. For each class the constructors and constructor parameters are provided. If the class is sufficiently complex, there is also sample code listed here. After that the members of the class (properties, fields, and methods) are listed, once again in alphabetical order. The goal was to make finding information in this book simple and fast. Some of the classes are abstract (MustInherit) classes that cannot be created as independent objects. These are listed since they provide the common behavior for the descendent classes. When examining the inheriting classes, you may see some duplication of descriptions. Trust us, this wasn't to "pad" the book. We fought tooth and nail to keep this book this length. The purpose is to prevent referencing another class that may occur in another namespace altogether. For instance, if you're looking for the System.Data.SqlClient.SqlDataAdapter.Fill method, because you're using a SQL Server database, it made no sense to us to force you to go looking at System.Data.Common.DataAdapter.Fill to find out how to use that method. The information is simply duplicated in the SqlClient and OleDb chapters.

As mentioned previously, this section is geared toward programmers developing business applications. Because of this, we've left out discussion of protected members, which are members that cannot be called by an instantiated class. They are used internally to a class, have no public use, and can only be called by members of an inheriting class. Thus, we've decided not to document these protected members.

In addition, we've left out three methods that are common to all objects, since they inherit directly from the Object class. These are GetType, which returns the Type of an object; GetHashCode, which returns a hash code for the object, and Equals, which can be used to determine equality between objects. The exception is when the method has been overridden and provides new functionality. In that case, it is documented. The determination to leave out these members was made after the book was written—they were repetitive, simple, and cluttered the book greatly.

CHAPTER

4

System.Data

System.Data is the key namespace for all of the data manipulation that occurs in ADO.NET. Classes here provide all the tools necessary to build an in-memory relational database, complete with tables, relationships, and constraints. Here is where you find the data objects that can be bound to the data-aware controls in the System.Web and System.Windows namespaces. This namespace also defines many of the interfaces used by the data providers.

The most important class is the DataSet, which provides a container for the in-memory database, as well as numerous methods to assist in integration with XML, data binding, and dealing with concurrency issues. Each DataSet can contain a number of DataTable objects, created easily from code, imported from XML data files, or read from existing databases. The DataTable objects are related to one another through DataRelation objects, and they are constrained by UniqueConstraint and ForeignKey-Constraint objects. DataTable columns, made up of DataColumn objects, can be defined to accept virtually every type of data and can contain expressions to create their value on the fly, depending on the values of other fields. Data is stored in a collection of DataRow objects, which maintain a number of different states, depending on whether they've been edited.

The ability to bind a data-aware control to a DataSet opens up a whole new field of user interface experience. Using a simple DataGrid control, users are able to conveniently drill down through parent-child tables, looking for specific data.

The data provider interfaces, included in this chapter, define the class signatures for many of the methods and properties of the SqlClient, OleDb, and Odbc data providers. These interfaces are the only contents of the System.Data namespace that deal with connected data access. At the beta 2 release of the .NET Framework, the rest of the connected classes were moved to the newly created System.Data.Common namespace, which provides many common implementations for the specific data providers. In a poor design decision or simple oversight, these supporting interfaces were not moved to the new namespace as well, leaving them awkwardly stranded in a namespace dedicated to disconnected data manipulation.

The System.Data namespace is, by far, the largest and most diverse of all the ADO.NET namespaces. It has an impressing breadth, dealing effectively with most of the difficult issues in data manipulation. This chapter is therefore quite long. Because many of the classes explained here are so crucial to data manipulation, Chapter 11, "Manipulating Data in ADO.NET," has been dedicated to providing a comprehensive tutorial. Some of the classes in the System.Data namespace do not provide sample code within this chapter. Instead, because the interplay between the classes is so critical and sample code is needed to fully explore their extensive use, the reader is urged to read Chapter 11 in its entirety for a full exploration of the key System.Data classes.

System.Data.AcceptRejectRule

The AcceptRejectRule enumeration provides the values used to determine whether to cascade the AcceptChanges or RejectChanges method to the child DataRow. If this value is set to Cascade, then when AcceptChanges is called on the parent row, AcceptChanges will also be called on the child rows. (For the ForeignKeyConstraint.AcceptRejectRule property, the default is None.)

AcceptRejectRule Enumeration

Cascade (1)	Changes are cascaded across the relationship.
None (0)	No action occurs. (Changes are *not* cascaded.)

System.Data.CommandBehavior

The CommandBehavior enumeration provides the values used to specify the effect on a data source when the ExecuteReader method is called by a class that implements the IDbCommand interface such as SqlCommand and OleDbCommand. Because this class implements the FlagsAttribute, bitwise combinations of values are allowed.

CommandBehavior Enumeration

CloseConnection (32)	After the command is executed, the connection to the data source is set to close when the DataReader closes.
Default (0)	The query may return multiple recordsets, and execution of the query may affect the data source state.

KeyInfo (4)	The query returns column and primary key information, without locking any of the selected rows.
SchemaOnly (2)	The query returns column information only and does not affect the database state.
SequentialAccess (16)	Allows the DataReader to load row data as a stream (using the GetBytes or GetChars method). This allows the DataReader to handle columns with large binary values. You need not start reading at the beginning of the stream, but you can read forward-only.
SingleResult (1)	The query returns a single result set and may affect the state of the data source.
SingleRow (8)	Requests that the data source return only a single row. This can be used to optimize queries (on some databases) that are expected to return single rows. Executing a query that returns multiple result sets will still return multiple sets, but each result set will have only a single row.

System.Data.CommandType

The CommandType enumeration provides the values used to specify how a command string is interpreted. A command string is generally assigned to the CommandText property of the various Command objects (OleDbCommand, SqlCommand, etc).

WARNING The TableDirect value is available only for the OLE DB data provider. You may use it only in conjunction with the OleDbCommand object.

CommandType Enumeration

StoredProcedure (4)	The associated command should be set to the name of the stored procedure.
TableDirect (512)	The associated command is set only to the name of a valid table or set of tables. All of the columns and rows of the designated tables are returned. (This is equivalent to the CommandType.Text with the command of "Select * from myTableName".)
Text (1)	(Default). The associated command can be any valid SQL text command.

System.Data.ConnectionState

The ConnectionState enumeration provides the values used to return the current state of a connection to a data source. They are passed with the StateChangeEventArgs in the StateChange events of the OleDbConnection and SqlConnection objects (as well as future connection objects), and they can be referenced in the State property of the preceding connection objects.

Because this class implements the FlagsAttribute, bitwise combinations of values are allowed.

ConnectionState Enumeration

Broken (16)	Not currently used. In the future this may be used because you are able to call the Close and Open methods to reinitialize a connection.
Closed (0)	The Connection object is closed.
Connecting (2)	Not currently used. In the future, this will indicate that the Connection object is connecting to the data source.
Executing (4)	Not currently used. In the future, this will indicate that the Connection object is executing a command at the data source.
Fetching (8)	Not currently used. In the future, this will indicate that the Connection object is fetching data from the data source.
Open (1)	The Connection object is open.

System.Data.Constraint

The Constraint class is an abstract (MustInherit) class that represents a rule used to maintain data integrity in a DataSet. Because it is abstract, it cannot be directly instantiated but must be used through one of its descendent classes—ForeignKeyConstraint or UniqueConstraint. The Constraint class itself implements little functionality, but it provides two properties that are common to the descending classes, ConstraintName and DataTable.

Constructors

No public constructors.

Parameters

None.

Constraint Sample Code

```
'See the sample code for the inheriting classes for examples of using
'this class.
```

Members

ConstraintName

The ConstraintName property returns or sets a String value that represents the name of the Constraint object.

Usage

```
myString = myConstraint.ConstraintName
myConstraint.ConstraintName = myString
```

Parameters

None.

Exceptions

None.

ExtendedProperties

The read-only ExtendedProperties property returns a PropertyCollection object that allows you to store custom information with the object. Although the property itself is read-only, you may add properties to the returned PropertyCollection with the Add method.

NOTE **If the ExtendedProperties collection is to be persisted as XML, then the members of the collection must be of type String.**

Usage

```
myPropertyCollection = myConstraint.ExtendedProperties
```

Parameters

None.

Exceptions

None.

Table

The read-only Table property returns the System.Data.DataTable object to which the Constraint applies.

Usage

```
myDataTable = myConstraint.Table
```

Parameters

None.

Exceptions

None.

ToString

The ToString method returns the ConstraintName as a String.

Usage

```
myString = myConstraint.ToString()
```

Parameters

None.

Exceptions

None.

System.Data.ConstraintCollection

The ConstraintCollection class is a container class that maintains a collection of Constraint objects. Because the constructor for the ConstraintCollection is private, an instance cannot be independently created. A ConstraintCollection object is accessible only from the DataTable.Constraints property.

Constructors

No public constructors.

Parameters

None.

ConstraintCollection Sample Code

```
'This function demonstrates the ConstraintCollection
'  class.  It assumes two valid DataTables are passed,
'  with Table1.Column1 being the primary key, and
'  Table2.Column1 being the foreign key.
Public Sub DemoConstraintCollection( _
         ByRef myDataTable1 As DataTable, _
         ByRef myDataTable2 As DataTable)
   Dim myUniqueConstraint As UniqueConstraint
   Dim myForeignKeyConstraint As ForeignKeyConstraint
   Dim myConstraints() As Constraint

   'create a primary key and add it to the collection
   myDataTable1.Constraints.Add("myUnique", _
      myDataTable1.Columns(0), True)

   'add a range of constraints
   myDataTable1.Constraints.AddRange(New UniqueConstraint(0) _
      {New UniqueConstraint("myUnique2", _
      myDataTable1.Columns(1))})
```

```
    'define the foreign key and add it to DataTable2
    '  Recall the FK must be assigned to thechild table
    myDataTable2.Constraints.Add("myForeignKey", _
       myDataTable1.Columns(0), myDataTable2.Columns(0))

    'copy the collection to an array
    ReDim myConstraints(myDataTable1.Constraints.Count - 1)
    myDataTable1.Constraints.CopyTo(myConstraints, 0)
    '  array can now be used...

    'remove a constraint, if it is possible
    If myDataTable1.Constraints.CanRemove( _
          myDataTable1.Constraints(0)) Then
       myDataTable1.Constraints.RemoveAt(0)
    Else
       MessageBox.Show("Cannot remove Constraint.")
    End If

End Sub
```

Members

Add

The various Add methods add a Constraint to the ConstraintCollection and return the added System.Data.Constraint object. All Add methods return the added Constraint, with the exception of the Add method that takes only a Constraint as a parameter. This method returns nothing.

Usage

```
myConstraintCollection.Add(myConstraint)
myUniqueConstraint = myConstraintCollection.Add(strName, _
     myDataColumn, boolPrimaryKey)
myUniqueConstraint = myConstraintCollection.Add(strName, _
     myDataColumnArray, boolPrimaryKey)
myForeignKeyConstraint = myConstraintCollection.Add(strName, _
     myDataColumnPrimaryKey, myDataColumnForeignKey)
myForeignKeyConstraint = myConstraintCollection.Add()
```

Parameters

`myConstraint`	Constraint object to add to the collection.
`strName`	Name to give the constraint (String).
`myDataColumn`	DataColumn to which the UniqueConstraint applies.
`boolPrimaryKey`	True if passed DataColumn or DataColumn array is a primary key, False otherwise (Boolean).

`myDataColumnPrimaryKey`	DataColumn object that represents the primary key in the ForeignKeyConstraint.
`myDataColumnForeignKey`	DataColumn object that represents the foreign key in the ForeignKeyConstraint.
`myDataColumnArray`	Array of DataColumn objects that represent the columns involved in the UniqueConstraint.
`myDataColumnPrimaryKeyArray`	Array of DataColumn objects that represent the primary keys in the ForeignKeyConstraint.
`myDataColumnForeignKeyArray`	Array of DataColumn objects that represent the foreign keys in the ForeignKeyConstraint.

Exceptions

ArgumentNullException	The constraint argument is null.
ArgumentException	1.) The Constraint already belongs to the ConstraintCollection or to another collection. 2.) The constraint is declared as a Primary Key, but the DataTable already has a primary key assigned.
DataException	The added constraint constrains the same columns as a constraint already in the collection.
DuplicateNameException	The ConstraintCollection contains a Constraint with the same name. (The comparison is not case sensitive.)
InvalidConstraintException	The ForeignKey in a ForeignKeyConstraint does not belong to the DataTable hosting this collection. (You can add a ForeignKeyConstraint only to the child table.)

AddRange

The AddRange method copies the passed array of Constraint objects to the end of the ConstraintCollection. Passing an empty array or an array set to null (`Nothing` in Visual Basic .NET) will not throw an error, but it will simply not impact the collection.

Usage

```
myConstraintCollection.AddRange(myConstraintArray)
```

Parameters

`myConstraintArray`	Array of Constraint objects to be added to the ConstraintCollection.

Exceptions

ArgumentException	1.) The Constraint already belongs to the ConstraintCollection or to another collection. 2.) The constraint is declared as a Primary Key, but the DataTable already has a primary key assigned.
DuplicateNameException	The ConstraintCollection contains a Constraint with the same name. (The comparison is not case sensitive.)
InvalidConstraintException	The ForeignKey in a ForeignKeyConstraint does not belong to the DataTable hosting this collection. (You can add a ForeignKeyConstraint only to the child table.)

CanRemove

The read-only CanRemove method returns a Boolean value that indicates whether the passed Constraint can be removed from the ConstraintCollection. Use this method to determine whether a Constraint can be removed from the collection.

WARNING The Release To Manufacturer (RTM) MSDN help on CanRemove states that it returns True if it can be removed and throws an Exception if it cannot. This is not correct.

Usage

```
myBoolean = myConstraintCollection.CanRemove(myConstraint)
```

Parameters

`myConstraint`	Constraint to be tested for removal from the ConstraintCollection.

Exceptions

NullReferenceException	The passed Constraint object is null (`Nothing` in Visual Basic .NET).

Clear

The Clear method removes all Constraint objects from the ConstraintCollection. If the removal is successful a CollectionChange event is fired. (See CollectionChanged event for more information.)

WARNING Clear will remove the constraints even if CanRemove returns False.

Usage

```
myConstraintCollection.Clear()
```

Parameters

None.

Exceptions

None.

CollectionChanged

The CollectionChanged event is fired whenever Constraints are added to or removed from the ConstraintCollection.

Usage

```
Private Sub myConstraintCollection_CollectionChanged( _
   ByVal sender As Object, _
   ByVal e As System.Data.StateChangeEventArgs) _
   Handles myConstraintCollection.CollectionChanged

End Sub
```

Parameters

`sender`	Contains a reference to the originator of the event.
`e`	Contains the System.ComponentModel.CollectionChangeEventArgs object. See the table below.

CollectionChangeEventArgs (e)

e.Action	A System.ComponentModelCollection-ChangeAction enumeration representing how the collection was changed.
e.Element	An Object that refers to the collection that has changed (the ConstraintCollection, in this case).

CollectionChangeAction Enumeration

Add (1)	An element has been added to the collection.
Remove (2)	An element has been added to the collection.
Refresh (3)	Specifies that the entire collection has changed (for instance, when the Clear method has been called).

Exceptions

None.

Contains

The Contains method returns a Boolean value that indicates whether a Constraint object with the passed name (String) exists in the ConstraintCollection. It returns True if a Constraint with the passed name exists and False otherwise.

Usage

```
myBoolean = myConstraintCollection.Contains(strName)
```

Parameters

`strName`	String defining the name of the Constraint to check for.

Exceptions

None.

CopyTo

The CopyTo method (inherited from System.Data.InternalDataCollectionBase) is used to copy the Constraint objects in the ConstraintCollection to an array. (Please see System.Data.InternalDataCollectionBase for more information.)

Usage

```
myConstraintCollection.CopyTo(myConstraintArray, myStartIndex)
```

Parameters

`myConstraintArray`	The passed buffer array to hold the Constraint objects.
`myStartIndex`	The Integer index designating the location in the passed array to begin filling with the Constraint objects.

Exceptions

ArgumentException	The passed array was not long enough to hold the passed constraints.
ArgumentNullException	The passed array is null (`Nothing` in Visual Basic .NET).
ArgumentOutOfRangeException	myStartIndex is negative or greater than the length of the array.
InvalidCastException	The object type of the collection cannot be cast automatically to the object type of the array.

Count

The read-only Count property (inherited from System.Data.InternalDataCollectionBase) returns an Int32 value specifying the number of Constraints in the ConstraintCollection.

Usage

```
myInt32 = myConstraintCollection.Count
```

Parameters

None.

Exceptions

None.

GetEnumerator

The GetEnumerator method (inherited from System.Data.InternalDataCollectionBase) returns a System.Collections.IEnumerator object that can be used to iterate over the collection. This method assists in using the For Each - Next (or equivalent statements) to iterate through a collection.

Usage

```
myIEnumerator = myConstraintCollection.GetEnumerator()
```

Parameters

None.

Exceptions

None.

IndexOf

The IndexOf() method returns an Integer specifying the zero-based location of a specified Constraint within the ConstraintCollection. Because this method is overloaded, you may pass either the Constraint object itself or a String representing the name of the Constraint. If the Constraint does not exist in the ConstraintCollection, a value of -1 is returned.

Usage

```
myInt32 = myConstraintCollection.IndexOf(myConstraint)
myInt32 = myConstraintCollection.IndexOf(strName)
```

Parameters

`myConstraint`	The Constraint for which to find the index.
`strName`	The name of the Constraint for which to find the index.

Exceptions

None.

IsReadOnly

The read-only IsReadOnly property returns a Boolean value specifying whether the ConstraintCollection is read only. This property is inherited directly from the InternalDataCollectionBase class. (Please see System.Data.InternalDataCollectionBase for more information.)

Usage

```
myBoolean = myConstraintCollection.IsReadOnly
```

Parameters
None.

Exceptions
None.

IsSynchronized

The read-only IsSynchronized property (inherited from System.Data.InternalData-CollectionBase) returns a Boolean value indicating whether the ConstraintCollection is currently synchronized. For information on synchronizing the ConstraintCollection, see the ConstraintCollection.SyncRoot property.

Usage
```
myBoolean = myConstraintCollection.IsSynchronized
```

Parameters
None.

Exceptions
None.

Item

The read-only Item property returns an indicated Constraint object from the collection. You can pass either the Integer index or String name of the desired Constraint. If you pass an invalid integer, an IndexOutOfRangeException will be thrown. If the passed name doesn't match any of the constraints, a null (`Nothing` in Visual Basic .NET) is returned, and no exception is raised.

Usage
```
myConstraint = myConstraintCollection.Item(intIndex)
myConstraint = myConstraintCollection.Item(strName)
```

Parameters

`intIndex`	Integer specifying the index of the desired Constraint.
`strName`	String specifying the name of the desired Constraint.

Exceptions

IndexOutOfRangeException	The passed integer is outside the bounds of the collection.

Remove

The Remove() method removes a specified Constraint object from the Constraint-Collection. Because this method is overloaded, you may pass either the Constraint object itself or a String representing the name of the Constraint.

Usage
```
myConstraintCollection.Remove(myConstraint)
myConstraintCollection.Remove(strName)
```

Parameters

`myConstraint`	The Constraint object to remove.
`strName`	The name of the Constraint object to remove.

Exceptions

ArgumentNullException	The constraint argument is a null reference (`Nothing` in Visual Basic).
ArgumentException	1.) The item does not belong to the collection. (Often the passed name matches none of the constraints.) 2.) Attempting to remove a constraint that does not belong to this collection. 3.) The constraint cannot be removed. (CanRemove = False)
AmbiguousMatchException	A System.Reflection exception thrown when the passed constraint is null. (It may also throw ArgumentNullException. This is a weird case. It seems that only the ArgumentNullException should be thrown.)

RemoveAt

The RemoveAt() method removes a Constraint object from the ConstraintCollection specified by the passed index of the Constraint.

Usage

```
myConstraintCollection.RemoveAt(intIndex)
```

Parameters

`intIndex`	Integer specifying the index of the Constraint to remove.

Exceptions

ArgumentException	1.) A Constraint does not exist at the desired index. 2.) The constraint cannot be removed. (CanRemove = False)

SyncRoot

The read-only SyncRoot property returns a System.Object object that can be used to Synchronize the ConstraintCollection. (Please see System.Data.InternalDataCollectionBase for more information.)

Usage

```
myObject = myConstraintCollection.SyncRoot
```

Parameters

None.

Exceptions
None.

ToString

The ToString method returns "System.Data.ConstraintCollection".

Usage
```
myString = myConstraintCollection.ToString()
```

Parameters
None.

Exceptions
None.

System.Data.ConstraintException

The ConstraintException class (descended from the DataException class) defines exceptions that are thrown when an action occurs that would violate a constraint.

Constructors

```
Dim myConstraintException As New ConstraintException()
Dim myConstraintException As New _
     ConstraintException (myString)
```

Parameters

`myString`	A String object that will initialize the Message property.

ConstraintException Sample Code

```
Dim myConstraintException As ConstraintException
myConstraintException = New _
     ConstraintException("Constraint Violated")
Throw myConstraintException
```

Members

GetBaseException

The GetBaseException method returns an Exception object containing the original exception. To return the original exception, it traverses the chain of InnerException objects. If the InnerException property of the current exception is null, GetBaseException will return a reference to the current Exception object.

To determine only the parent exception to the current exception, use the InnerException property.

Usage

```
myException = myConstraintException.GetBaseException()
```

Parameters

None.

Exceptions

None.

GetObjectData

The GetObjectData method fills the passed System.Runtime.Serialization.SerializationInfo buffer object with information about the Exception object. There is no value returned by this method. Depending on the passed System.Runtime.Serialization.StreamingContext object, this method can be used to serialize the object to a stream or read serialization from a stream.

Because it deals mainly with Serialization and not data access, further discussion of this property is beyond the scope of this book.

Usage

```
myConstraintException.GetObjectData(mySerializationInfo, _
   myStreamingContext)
```

Parameters

`mySerializationInfo`	A System.Runtime.Serialization.SerializationInfo buffer object to be filled with the exception's serialization data.
`myStreamingContext`	A System.Runtime.Serialization.StreamingContext object specifying the stream to write the serialization info to or read the information from.

Exceptions

ArgumentNullException	The passed SerializationInfo buffer object is null (`Nothing` in Visual Basic .NET).

HelpLink

The HelpLink property returns or sets a String linking to a help file associated with the ConstraintException. The HelpLink is formatted as a Uniform Resource Name (URN) or Uniform Resource Locator (URL). An example of this property that points to the MSDN help available with Visual Studio .NET would be: `ms-help://MS.VSCC/MS.MSDNVS/cpref/html/frlrfsystemexceptionclasshelplinktopic.htm`.

The HelpLink is often not set, so it is wise to verify both that the HelpLink property itself is not an empty string and that the HelpLink points to a valid help file before exposing the HelpLink to a user of your program.

Usage

```
myString = myConstraintException.HelpLink
myConstraintException.HelpLink = myString
```

Parameters
None.

InnerException

The read-only InnerException property returns the Exception object linking to a previous exception that caused the current exception to be thrown, if any, or a null value (`Nothing` in Visual Basic .NET), if not. This permits a chain of InnerException objects to be generated, allowing a program to trace the exception chain all the way to the root exception. Be aware that InnerException may be null.

To find the base exception that originally was fired, use the GetBaseException method.

Usage

```
myException = myConstraintException.InnerException
```

Parameters
None.

Message

The read-only Message property returns a String describing the first error that caused the exception. Because it provides information only from the first error, use this property cautiously when building robust error handling.

Usage

```
myString = myConstraintException.Message
```

Parameters
None.

Source

The Source property sets or returns a String containing the name of the provider that generated the first error. Because it provides information only from the first error, use this property cautiously when building robust error handling.

Usage

```
myString = myConstraintException.Source
myConstraintException.Source = myString
```

Parameters
None.

StackTrace

The read-only StackTrace property returns a String containing a textual representation of the stack trace. The stack trace reports all of the methods that are in execution at the time just prior to the execution being thrown. It is read from top to bottom with the latest method in execution at the top.

The StackTrace can be invaluable in tracing difficult-to-find bugs because it provides a way to see all of the methods that could have led up to the error.

TIP **To see the stack trace programmatically when no exception has been raised, use the Environment.StackTrace property.**

Usage

```
myString = myConstraintException.StackTrace
```

Parameters

None.

TargetSite

The read-only TargetSite property returns an object inheriting from System.Reflection.MethodBase that contains a reference to the method that caused the error to be thrown.

This property is primarily used to programmatically find information about the method that raised the exception. The returned object will provide information such as the method's parameters and return type and whether the method is virtual, a constructor, public, private, etc. Because it deals mainly with Reflection and not data access, further discussion of this property is beyond the scope of this book.

Usage

```
myMethodBase = myConstraintException.TargetSite
```

Parameters

None.

ToString

The ToString method is overridden to return information relating to the ConstraintException exception. The returned String contains the full class name and also the error message, name of the inner exception, and stack trace, if they exist.

Usage

```
myString = myConstraintException.ToString()
```

Parameters

None.

Exceptions

None.

System.Data.DataColumn

The DataColumn class represents the schema for a column in a DataTable. It is one of the fundamental classes in ADO.NET. The schema for a DataTable is built by adding DataColumn objects.

Defining a DataColumn is an excellent way to ensure data integrity because the Unique, ReadOnly, and AllowDbNull properties can be used to restrict data entry. In addition, you may constrain the data types allowed in the DataColumn, matching them to the types supported by a data source. AutoIncrement columns can be used to provide primary keys for DataTables, and DataRelation objects can be defined linking a DataColumn to a column in another DataTable, thus establishing a relationship between the two tables. DataColumn objects can also contain expressions that calculate values, filter rows, or aggregate other columns.

In short, the DataColumn is one of the most useful classes in System.Data for maintaining the integrity of your data.

NOTE Because the DataSet, DataTable, DataColumn, and DataView objects are so central to ADO.NET data manipulation, and because their methods and properties are so extensive, an entire tutorial chapter has been dedicated to their use. Duplicating the code for each object independently would not be as clear as demonstrating the use of these objects acting in concert. Thus sample code will not be provided for the majority of this object. For code examples, see Chapter 11.

Constructors

```
Dim myDataTable As New DataSet()
Dim myDataTable As New DataSet(strName)
```

Parameters

`strName`	Name of the DataTable, as a String.

DataColumn Sample Code

```
'This function demonstrates the DataColumn class.
'  This code sample is relatively short, please
'  see Chapter 11 for a more in-depth sample.
Public Sub DemoDataColumn()
   Dim myDataTable As DataTable
   Dim myDataColumn As DataColumn

   'build a DataTable
   myDataTable = New DataTable("myTable")

   'add a column to use as a primary key
   '  make it AutoIncrement
   myDataColumn = myDataTable.Columns.Add( _
         "AutoInc", GetType(Int32))
   myDataColumn.AutoIncrement = True
   myDataTable.Constraints.Add( _
         "PK", myDataColumn, True)

   myDataColumn = myDataTable.Columns.Add( _
         "Greeting", GetType(String))
   myDataColumn.DefaultValue = "myDefault"
```

```
    myDataColumn = myDataTable.Columns.Add( _
          "Country", GetType(String))
    myDataColumn = myDataTable.Columns.Add( _
          "Expression", GetType(String))
    myDataColumn.Expression = _
          "'Use ' + Greeting + ' when in ' + Country"

    'add three rows to the table
    myDataTable.Rows.Add(New Object(2) _
          {Nothing, "Hello", "USA"})
    '  add a row, resetting the AutoIncrement value
    myDataTable.Rows.Add(New Object(2) _
          {5, "Bonjour", "France"})
    '  add another row, passing a value for the column
    '     with the expression. This value will be discarded.
    myDataTable.Rows.Add(New Object(3) {Nothing, "Guten Tag", _
          "Germany", "Say Servus in Bavaria"})
    myDataTable.AcceptChanges()

    ''diplay the resulting table (if you have a DataGrid)
    'DataGrid1.DataSource = myDataTable
    'DataGrid1.Refresh()

End Sub
```

Members

AllowDBNull

The AllowDBNull property returns or sets a Boolean value indicating whether this DataColumn holds null values. If this property is set to True, a DataRow in a DataTable may contain a null value in this column. If False, then no null values are allowed.

Usage

```
myBoolean = myDataColumn.AllowDBNull
myDataColumn.AllowDBNull = myBoolean
```

Parameters

None.

Exceptions

None.

AutoIncrement

The AutoIncrement property returns or sets a Boolean value indicating whether this column increments its value automatically when new rows are added the DataTable.

To set the initial value and the step for this column, see the AutoIncrementSeed and AutoIncrementStep properties.

NOTE **When passing values to a row with an AutoIncrement column, a null value (`Nothing` in Visual Basic .NET) should be passed to the column so that the column will increment properly.**

WARNING **If a valid value is passed to this column, that value will be used in lieu of the AutoIncrement value. In addition, the next added record will increment from this new value.**

Usage

```
myBoolean = myDataColumn.AutoIncrement
myDataColumn.AutoIncrement = myBoolean
```

Parameters

None.

Exceptions

None.

AutoIncrementSeed

The AutoIncrementSeed property returns or sets a System.Int64 value that determines the first value to be used in the DataColumn when AutoIncrement is set to True.

Usage

```
myInt64 = myDataColumn.AutoIncrementSeed
myDataColumn.AutoIncrementSeed = myInt64
```

Parameters

None.

Exceptions

None.

AutoIncrementStep

The AutoIncrementStep property returns or sets a System.Int64 value that indicates the increment that the column will increase at each row addition. The default value is 1.

Usage

```
myInt64 = myDataColumn.AutoIncrementStep
myDataColumn.AutoIncrementStep = myInt64
```

Parameters

None.

Exceptions

None.

Caption

The Caption property returns or sets a String value that is the caption for this column. If this column is not set, then the ColumnName is used. This property allows you to set a friendly column caption in the place of a column name.

NOTE This caption is not necessarily used when displaying the column in data bound controls.

Usage

```
myString = myDataColumn.Caption
myDataColumn.Caption = myString
```

Parameters

None.

Exceptions

None.

ColumnMapping

The ColumnMapping property returns or sets a MappingType enumeration value that specifies how a DataColumn is mapped to an XML document. The MappingType determines how the column data and schema will be written to an XML document when the DataSet.WriteXml method is called. Depending on the MappingType the column may be exported as an element, an attribute, or a simple text node.

For instance, suppose a column named "CustomerID" is set to map as an Attribute, and a column named "CustomerName" is mapped as an element. The following XML document fragment might be output.

```
<Customer CustomerID="1">
             <CustomerName>Sedef Paulfranz</CustomerName>
</Customer>
```

Usage

```
myMappingType = myDataColumn.ColumnMapping
myDataColumn.ColumnMapping = myMappingType
```

Parameters

None.

MappingType Enumeration

Attribute (2)	The DataColumn is mapped to an XML attribute.
Element (1)	The DataColumn is mapped to an XML element.
Hidden (4)	The DataColumn is mapped to an internal structure.
SimpleContent (3)	The DataColumn is mapped to an XmlText node.

Exceptions

ArgumentException	Cannot define a column as SimpleContent if its DataTable table contains any columns expressed as Elements or contains a nested relation.

ColumnName

The ColumnName property returns or sets a String value that specifies the name of the DataColumn.

Usage

```
myString = myDataColumn.ColumnName
myDataColumn.ColumnName = myString
```

Parameters

None.

Exceptions

None.

Container

The read-only Container property returns the object implementing the System.ComponentModel.IContainer interface that contains the DataColumn. If the DataColumn is not contained, then the Container method returns a null reference (`Nothing` in Visual Basic .NET).

Usage

```
myIContainer = myDataColumn.Container
```

Parameters

None.

Exceptions

None.

DataType

The DataType property returns or sets a Type value that indicates the data type of the DataColumn.

Usage

```
myType = myDataColumn.DataType
myDataColumn.DataType = myType
```

Parameters

None.

Exceptions

None.

DefaultValue

The DefaultValue property returns or sets an Object value that is used as the default value when no value is explicitly assigned to the DataColumn. The type of the DefaultValue must match the type of the DataColumn.

NOTE When passing values to a column with a default value, a null value (`Nothing` in Visual Basic .NET) should be passed to the column to use the default value.

Usage

```
myObject = myDataColumn.DefaultValue
myDataColumn.DefaultValue = myObject
```

Parameters

None.

Exceptions

None.

DesignMode

The read-only DesignMode property (inherited from System.ComponentModel.MarshalByValueComponent) returns a Boolean value specifying whether the object is currently in design mode. If the object is not hosted in a development environment, this property will always return False.

Usage

```
myBoolean = myDataColumn.DesignMode
```

Parameters

None.

Exceptions

None.

Dispose

The Dispose method (inherited from System.ComponentModel.MarshalByValueComponent) releases all resources used by the DataColumn.

Usage

```
myDataColumn.Dispose()
```

Parameters

None.

Exceptions

None.

Disposed

The Disposed event is fired whenever the Dispose method has been called on the object.

Usage

```
Private Sub myDataColumn_Disposed(ByVal sender As Object, _
    ByVal e As System.EventArgs) _
    Handles myDataColumn.Disposed

End Sub
```

Parameters

`sender`	Contains a reference to the originator of the event.
`e`	Contains the System.EventArgs object containing no useful information.

Exceptions

None.

Expression

The Expression property returns or sets a String value that is used to filter rows, calculate values, or perform aggregation functions. When building the Expression, you must ensure that the return type of the expression matches the column's DataType.

A column may not have an Expression property if either the AutoIncrement or Unique property is set to True.

WARNING **Passing a value to a column when an Expression is set will result in the passed value being discarded.**

Usage

```
myString = myDataColumn.Expression
myDataColumn.Expression = myString
```

Parameters

None.

Exceptions

ArgumentException	The AutoIncrement or Unique property is set to True.
ArgumentOutOfRangeException	Either the start or length argument of the SUBSTRING function is out of range.
FormatException	The CONVERT function cannot convert the passed String to the requested Type.
InvalidExpressionException	The expression is invalid.
InvalidCastException	The CONVERT function cannot cast to the requested Type.
Exception	The argument passed to the LEN or TRIM functions does not evaluate to a String.
SyntaxErrorException	The Value of Expression contains a syntax error.

ExtendedProperties

The read-only ExtendedProperties property returns a PropertyCollection object that allows you to store custom information with the object. Although the property itself is read only, you may add properties to the returned PropertyCollection with the Add method. See the Sample Code for an example.

NOTE If the ExtendedProperties collection is to be persisted as XML, then the members of the collection must be of type String.

Usage

```
myPropertyCollection = myDataColumn.ExtendedProperties
```

Parameters

None.

Exceptions

None.

Sample Code

```
myDataSet.ExtendedProperties.Add("EasterEggKey", "Ctrl-Alt-Q")
```

GetService

The GetService method returns an Object that implements the IServiceProvider interface. This object is used to provide custom support to the calling object through the use of a custom-built server.

This method is almost exclusively used to support Visual Studio .NET.

Usage

```
myObject = myDataColumn.GetService(myServiceType)
```

Parameters

`myServiceType`	A System.Type that defines the requested service.

Exceptions

None.

MaxLength

The MaxLength property returns or sets an Integer specifying the maximum length, in characters, of a text column. This property is ignored for nontext columns.

Usage

```
myInt32 = myDataColumn.MaxLength
myDataColumn.MaxLength = myInt32
```

Parameters

None.

Exceptions

None.

Namespace

The Namespace property returns or sets a String value that is the namespace for the DataColumn. This property is used when writing and reading XML documents to and from a DataSet. By assigning separate namespace names to different columns, objects with the same name can still be differentiated when they are both combined into a single XML document. It also prevents namespace conflicts when reading XML documents that may contain similarly named data, but that come from a separate namespace.

For more information on namespaces, please see an XML guide or search for "Namespace" in MSDN.

Usage

```
myString = myDataColumn.Namespace
myDataColumn.Namespace = myString
```

Parameters

None.

Exceptions

None.

Ordinal

The read-only Ordinal property returns an Integer specifying the ordinal position of the DataColumn within a DataColumnCollection. (Use this ordinal for determining the position of the column in a DataRow.) If the DataColumn is not a member of a DataColumnCollection, the return value is -1.

Usage

```
myInt32 = myDataColumn.Ordinal
```

Parameters

None.

Exceptions

None.

Prefix

The Prefix property returns or sets a String value and serves as the namespace prefix that will be used throughout an output XML document. The example XML document here shows the namespace prefix "myCo" being used.

```
<myDataSet xmlns:myCo=
      "urn:schemas-myCompany-com:myCompanyData">
<myCo:myEmployee>
      <myCo:Name>John Jacob Jingleheimer Schmidt</Name>
</myCo:myEmployee>
</myDataSet>
```

Usage

```
myString = myDataColumn.Prefix
myDataColumn.Prefix = myString
```

Parameters
None.

Exceptions
None.

ReadOnly

The ReadOnly property returns or sets a Boolean value indicating whether this DataColumn can be changed once it has been added to a DataTable. If this property is set to True, changes to the DataColumn can be made only before it is added to a DataTable. If ReadOnly is set to False, then changes are allowed at any time.

Usage
```
myBoolean = myDataColumn.ReadOnly
myDataColumn.ReadOnly = myBoolean
```

Parameters
None.

Exceptions
None.

Site

The Site property returns or sets a System.ComponentModel.ISite value that specifies the site for the DataColumn. A site links a component to its container and allows for storage of information specific to the relationship, such as visual coordinates or component name. It provides a link so that containers can manage their contained components.

Generally, this property is used mainly by Visual Studio .NET and the .NET Framework in the background, and there is little reason to specifically work with this property.

Usage
```
myISite = myDataColumn.Site
myDataColumn.Site = myISite
```

Parameters
None.

Exceptions
None.

Table

The read-only Table property returns the DataTable object that contains the DataColumn.

Usage
```
myDataTable = myDataColumn.Table
```

Parameters
None.

Exceptions
None.

ToString

The ToString method is overridden to return the Expression property, if it is assigned, or the ColumnName property, if it is not.

Usage

```
myString = myDataColumn.ToString()
```

Parameters

None.

Exceptions

None.

Unique

The Unique property returns or sets a Boolean value indicating whether this DataColumn must be unique across its parent DataTable. If this property is set to True, duplicate values are not allowed to be assigned to this DataColumn. If False, then duplicate values are allowed.

When this value is changed from False to True, a UniqueConstraint is automatically generated.

Usage

```
myBoolean = myDataColumn.Unique
myDataColumn.Unique = myBoolean
```

Parameters

None.

Exceptions

None.

System.Data.DataColumnChangeEventArgs

The DataColumnChangeEventArgs class is automatically created and passed to any code handling either the DataTable.ColumnChanging or DataTable.ColumnChanged events. Objects of this class allow access to the original data in the DataColumn as well as the proposed new value. (The DataRow containing the DataColumn is also included for completeness.)

DataColumnChangeEventArgs also has a public constructor, which can be used to define and throw your own exception.

Constructors

```
Dim myDataColumnChangeEventArgs As New _
    DataColumnChangeEventArgs(myDataRow, myDataColumn, _
    myObject)
```

Parameters

`myDataRow`	DataRow whose value is being changed.
`myDataColumn`	DataColumn whose value is being changed.
`myObject`	The proposed new value for the DataColumn.

Members

Column

The read-only Column property returns the DataColumn object that is being changed (or has been changed).

Usage

```
myDataColumn = myDataColumnChangeEventArgs.Column
```

Parameters
None.

Exceptions
None.

ProposedValue

The ProposedValue property returns or sets the object to be assigned (or just assigned) to the DataColumn during the update.

Usage

```
myObject = myDataColumnChangeEventArgs.ProposedValue
myDataColumnChangeEventArgs.ProposedValue = myObject
```

Parameters
None.

Exceptions
None.

Row

The read-only Row property returns the DataRow object that contains the DataRow that is being changed (or has been changed).

Usage

```
myDataRow = myDataColumnChangeEventArgs.Row
```

Parameters
None.

Exceptions
None.

ToString

The ToString method returns "System.Data.DataColumnChangeEventArgs".

Usage

```
myString = myDataColumnChangeEventArgs.ToString()
```

Parameters

None.

Exceptions

None.

System.Data.DataColumnCollection

The DataColumnCollection class is a container class that maintains a collection of DataColumn objects. Because the constructor for the DataColumnCollection is private, an instance cannot be independently created. A DataColumnCollection object is accessible only from the DataTable.Columns property.

Constructors

No public constructors.

Parameters

None.

DataColumnCollection Sample Code

```
'See System.Data.ConstraintCollection for examples of the
'common collection members.
```

Members

Add

The various Add methods add a DataColumn to the DataColumnCollection and return the added System.Data.DataColumn object. All Add methods return the added DataColumn, with the exception of the Add method, which takes only a DataColumn as a parameter. This method returns nothing.

Usage

```
myDataColumn = myDataColumnCollection.Add()
myDataColumnCollection.Add(myDataColumn)
```

```
myDataColumn = myDataColumnCollection.Add(strName)
myDataColumn = myDataColumnCollection.Add(strName, myType)
myDataColumn = myDataColumnCollection.Add(strName, myType, _
     strExpression)
```

Parameters

`myDataColumn`	DataColumn object to add to the collection.
`strName`	Name to give the DataColumn (String).
`myType`	The DataType of the new DataColumn.
`strExpression`	String value to assign to the Expression property of the DataColumn. (Used to filter rows, provide aggregate values, or perform calculations.)

Exceptions

ArgumentNullException	The DataColumn argument is null.
ArgumentException	The DataColumn already belongs to the Data-ColumnCollection or to another collection.
DuplicateNameException	The DataColumnCollection contains a Data Column with the same name. (The comparison is not case sensitive.)
InvalidExpressionException	The passed strExpression was invalid.

AddRange

The AddRange method copies the passed array of DataColumn objects to the end of the DataColumnCollection.

Usage

```
myDataColumnCollection.AddRange(myDataColumnArray)
```

Parameters

`myDataColumnArray`	Array of DataColumn objects to be added to the DataColumnCollection.

Exceptions

ArgumentException	The DataColumn already belongs to the Data-ColumnCollection or to another collection.
DuplicateNameException	The DataColumnCollection contains a Data-Column with the same name. (The comparison is not case sensitive.)

CanRemove

The CanRemove method returns a Boolean value that indicates whether the passed DataColumn can be removed from the DataColumnCollection. Use this method to determine whether a DataColumn can be removed from the collection.

To determine whether a DataColumn can be removed, this method checks to see if the DataColumn exists, if it belongs to the DataTable, and whether the DataColumn is involved in a constraint or relation.

Usage

```
myBoolean = myDataColumnCollection.CanRemove(myDataColumn)
```

Parameters

`myDataColumn`	DataColumn to be tested for removal from the DataColumnCollection.

Exceptions

ArgumentNullException	The DataColumn argument is null.
ArgumentException	1.) The DataColumn does not belong to this collection. 2.) The DataColumn is part of a relationship. 3.) The DataColumn is part of another column's expression.

Clear

The Clear method removes all DataColumn objects from the DataColumnCollection. If the removal is successful, a CollectionChange event is fired. (See CollectionChanged event for more information.)

Usage

```
myDataColumnCollection.Clear()
```

Parameters

None.

Exceptions

None.

CollectionChanged

The CollectionChanged event is fired whenever DataColumns are added to or removed from the DataColumnCollection.

Usage

```
Private Sub myDataColumnCollection_CollectionChanged( _
   ByVal sender As Object, _
   ByVal e As System.Data.StateChangeEventArgs) _
   Handles myDataColumnCollection.CollectionChanged
```

Parameters

`sender`	Contains a reference to the originator of the event.
`e`	Contains the System.ComponentModel.Collection-ChangeEventArgs object. See the following table.

CollectionChangeEventArgs (e)

e.Action	A System.ComponentModelCollectionChange-Action enumeration representing how the collection was changed.
e.Element	An Object that refers to the collection that has changed (the DataColumnCollection, in this case).

CollectionChangeAction Enumeration

Add (1)	An element has been added to the collection.
Remove(2)	An element has been added to the collection.
Refresh (3)	Specifies that the entire collection has changed (for instance, when the Clear method has been called).

Exceptions

None.

Contains

The Contains method returns a Boolean value that indicates whether a DataColumn object with the passed name (String) exists in the DataColumnCollection. Returns True if a DataColumn with the passed name exists and False otherwise.

Usage

```
myBoolean = myDataColumnCollection.Contains(strName)
```

Parameters

`strName`	String defining the name of the DataColumn to check for.

Exceptions

None.

CopyTo

The CopyTo method (inherited from System.Data.InternalDataCollectionBase) is used to copy the DataColumn objects in the DataColumnCollection to an array. (Please see System.Data.InternalDataCollectionBase for more information.)

Usage

```
myDataColumnCollection.CopyTo(myDataColumnArray, myStartIndex)
```

Parameters

`myDataColumnArray`	The passed buffer array to hold the Data Column objects.
`myStartIndex`	The Integer index designating the location in the passed array to begin filling with the DataColumn objects.

Exceptions

ArgumentException	The passed array was not long enough to hold the passed objects.
ArgumentNullException	The passed array is null (`Nothing` in Visual Basic .NET).
ArgumentOutOfRangeException	myStartIndex is negative or greater than the length of the array.
InvalidCastException	The object type of the collection cannot be cast automatically to the object type of the array.

Count

The read-only Count property (inherited from System.Data.InternalDataCollection-Base) returns an Int32 value specifying the number of DataColumns in the Data-ColumnCollection.

Usage

```
myInt32 = myDataColumnCollection.Count
```

Parameters

None.

Exceptions

None.

GetEnumerator

The GetEnumerator method (inherited from System.Data.InternalDataCollectionBase) returns a System.Collections.IEnumerator object that can be used to iterate over the collection. This method assists in using the For Each - Next (or equivalent statements) to iterate through a collection.

Usage

```
myIEnumerator = myDataColumnCollection.GetEnumerator()
```

Parameters

None.

Exceptions

None.

IndexOf

The IndexOf() method returns an Integer specifying the zero-based location of a specified DataColumn within the DataColumnCollection. Because this method is overloaded, you may pass either the DataColumn object itself or a String representing the name of the DataColumn. If the DataColumn does not exist in the DataColumnCollection, a value of -1 is returned.

Usage

```
myInt32 = myDataColumnCollection.IndexOf(myDataColumn)
myInt32 = myDataColumnCollection.IndexOf(strName)
```

Parameters

`myDataColumn`	The DataColumn for which to find the index.
`strName`	The name of the DataColumn for which to find the index.

Exceptions

None.

IsReadOnly

The read-only IsReadOnly property returns a Boolean value specifying whether the DataColumnCollection is read only. This property is inherited directly from the InternalDataCollectionBase class. (Please see System.Data.InternalDataCollectionBase for more information.)

Usage

```
myBoolean = myDataColumnCollection.IsReadOnly
```

Parameters

None.

Exceptions

None.

IsSynchronized

The read-only IsSynchronized property (inherited from System.Data.InternalDataCollectionBase) returns a Boolean value indicating whether the DataColumnCollection is currently synchronized. For information on synchronizing the DataColumnCollection, see the DataColumnCollection.SyncRoot property.

Usage

```
myBoolean = myDataColumnCollection.IsSynchronized
```

Parameters

None.

Exceptions

None.

Item

The read-only Item property returns an indicated DataColumn object from the collection. You can pass either the Integer index or String name of the desired DataColumn. If you pass an invalid integer, an IndexOutOfRangeException will be thrown. If the passed name doesn't match any of the items, a null (`Nothing` in Visual Basic .NET) is returned, and no exception is raised.

Usage

```
myDataColumn = myDataColumnCollection.Item(intIndex)
myDataColumn = myDataColumnCollection.Item(strName)
```

Parameters

`intIndex`	Integer specifying the index of the desired DataColumn.
`strName`	String specifying the name of the desired DataColumn.

Exceptions

IndexOutOfRangeException	The passed integer is outside the bounds of the collection.

Remove

The Remove() method removes a specified DataColumn object from the DataColumn-Collection. Because this method is overloaded, you may pass either the DataColumn object itself or a String representing the name of the DataColumn.

Usage

```
myDataColumnCollection.Remove(myDataColumn)
myDataColumnCollection.Remove(strName)
```

Parameters

`myDataColumn`	The DataColumn object to remove.
`strName`	The name of the DataColumn object to remove.

Exceptions

ArgumentNullException	The DataColumn argument is a null reference (`Nothing` in Visual Basic).
ArgumentException	The DataColumn does not belong to the collection.

RemoveAt

The RemoveAt() method removes a DataColumn object from the DataColumnCollection specified by the passed index of the DataColumn.

Usage

```
myDataColumnCollection.RemoveAt(intIndex)
```

Parameters

`intIndex`	Integer specifying the index of the DataColumn to remove.

Exceptions

ArgumentException	A DataTable does not exist at the desired index.

SyncRoot

The read-only SyncRoot property returns a System.Object object that can be used to Synchronize the DataColumnCollection. (Please see System.Data.InternalDataCollectionBase for more information.)

Usage

```
myObject = myDataColumnCollection.SyncRoot
```

Parameters

None.

Exceptions

None.

ToString

The ToString method returns "System.Data.DataColumnCollection".

Usage

```
myString = myDataColumnCollection.ToString()
```

Parameters

None.

Exceptions

None.

System.Data.DataException

The DataException class defines the exceptions that are thrown by ADO.NET objects. Although it has public constructors, it is mainly used as the base class for all the other exceptions found in the System.Data namespace.

Constructors

```
Dim myDataException As New DataException()
Dim myDataException As New DataException(myString)
Dim myDataException As New DataException(myString, myException)
```

Parameters

`myString`	A String object that will initialize the Message property.
`myException`	An Exception object to use as the InnerException for the new DataException.

DataException Sample Code

```
Dim myDataException As DataException
myDataException = New DataException("Data Exception!")
Throw myDataException
```

Members

GetBaseException

The GetBaseException method returns an Exception object containing the original exception. To return the original exception, it traverses the chain of InnerException objects. If the InnerException property of the current exception is null, GetBaseException will return a reference to the current Exception object.

To determine only the parent exception to the current exception, use the InnerException property.

Usage

```
myException = myDataException.GetBaseException()
```

Parameters

None.

Exceptions

None.

GetObjectData

The GetObjectData method fills the passed System.Runtime.Serialization.SerializationInfo buffer object with information about the Exception object. There is no value returned by this method. Depending on the passed System.Runtime.Serialization.StreamingContext object, this method can be used to serialize the object to a stream or read serialization from a stream.

Because it deals mainly with Serialization and not data access, further discussion of this property is beyond the scope of this book.

Usage

```
myDataException.GetObjectData(mySerializationInfo, _
     myStreamingContext)
```

Parameters

`mySerializationInfo`	A System.Runtime.Serialization.SerializationInfo buffer object to be filled with the exception's serialization data.
`myStreamingContext`	A System.Runtime.Serialization.StreamingContext object specifying the stream to write the serialization info to or read the information from.

Exceptions

ArgumentNullException	The passed SerializationInfo buffer object is null (`Nothing` in Visual Basic .NET).

HelpLink

The HelpLink property returns or sets a String linking to a help file associated with the DataException. The HelpLink is formatted as a Uniform Resource Name (URN) or

Uniform Resource Locator (URL). An example of this property that points to the MSDN help available with Visual Studio .NET would be: `ms-help://MS.VSCC/MS.MSDNVS/cpref/html/frlrfsystemexceptionclasshelplinktopic.htm.`

The HelpLink is often not set, so it is wise to verify both that the HelpLink property itself is not an empty string and that the HelpLink points to a valid help file before exposing the HelpLink to a user of your program.

Usage

```
myString = myDataException.HelpLink
myDataException.HelpLink = myString
```

Parameters

None.

InnerException

The read-only InnerException property returns the Exception object linking to a previous exception that caused the current exception to be thrown, if any, or a null value (`Nothing` in Visual Basic .NET), if not. This permits a chain of InnerException objects to be generated, allowing a program to trace the exception chain all the way to the root exception. Be aware that InnerException may be null.

To find the base exception that originally was fired, use the GetBaseException method.

Usage

```
myException = myDataException.InnerException
```

Parameters

None.

Message

The read-only Message property returns a String describing the first error that caused the exception. Because it provides information only from the first error, use this property cautiously when building robust error handling.

Usage

```
myString = myDataException.Message
```

Parameters

None.

Source

The Source property sets or returns a String containing the name of the provider that generated the first error. Because it provides information only from the first error, use this property cautiously when building robust error handling.

Usage

```
myString = myDataException.Source
myDataException.Source = myString
```

Parameters

None.

StackTrace

The read-only StackTrace property returns a String containing a textual representation of the stack trace. The stack trace reports all of the methods that are in execution at the time just prior to the execution being thrown. It is read from top to bottom with the latest method in execution at the top.

The StackTrace can be invaluable in tracing difficult-to-find bugs because it provides a method to see all of the methods that could have led up to the error.

TIP To see the stack trace programmatically when no exception has been raised, use the Environment.StackTrace property.

Usage

```
myString = myDataException.StackTrace
```

Parameters

None.

TargetSite

The read-only TargetSite property returns an object inheriting from System.Reflection.MethodBase that contains a reference to the method that caused the error to be thrown.

This property is primarily used to programmatically find information about the method that raised the exception. The returned object will provide information such as the methods parameters and return type and whether the method is virtual, a constructor, public, private, etc. Because it deals mainly with Reflection and not data access, further discussion of this property is beyond the scope of this book.

Usage

```
myMethodBase = myDataException.TargetSite
```

Parameters

None.

ToString

The ToString method is overridden to return information relating to the DataException exception. The returned String contains the full class name and also the error message, name of the inner exception, and stack trace, if they exist.

Usage

```
myString = myDataException.ToString()
```

Parameters

None.

Exceptions

None.

System.Data.DataRelation

The DataRelation class provides a way to link two DataTable objects inside of a DataSet, defining one as the parent and one as the child. The two tables are linked by selecting columns with the same data type and establishing one as a parent and one as a child. In many ways this is similar to the creation of a UniqueConstraint on the parent DataColumn and a ForeignKeyConstraint linking it to a child DataColumn on a different table. In fact, when creating a DataRelation, you can specify that it do just that—create the constraints for you. The DataRelation, however, is a bit more flexible. You can create a relation between two tables that doesn't enforce a uniqueness constraint. This can cause difficulties when exporting to XML because there may not be a unique value in the parent table to nest the child rows under.

When constructing a DataRelation, you define a name, specify the child and parent column (or columns), and possibly pass a Boolean determining whether corresponding constraints are added to the DataTable objects participating in the DataRelation. If you do not pass the Boolean dealing with the creation of constraints, they will, by default, be created and added to the Constraints collection of each DataTable. The constraints created are a UniqueConstraint on the parent DataColumn (added to the parent DataTable) and a ForeignKeyConstraint linking the two DataColumn objects (added to the child DataTable). The creation of the corresponding constraints is fairly robust. When creating the constraints, if one already exists, it is not overwritten; only constraints not yet in existence are created. So, if the DataRelation you're building refers to a primary key column, that UniqueConstraint will not be overwritten.

There are numerous constructors for the DataRelation. In most of them, a name for the constraint is passed along with objects that act as the parents and children of the relationship. One constructor, however, takes a number of Strings and String arrays. This constructor was designed for the runtime support of Visual Studio .NET. Although it works perfectly fine, you must ensure, prior to calling the constructor, that all of the Strings refer to actual tables and rows that are currently in existence. Because the other constructors are simpler and just as powerful, we recommend that you avoid using the last constructor, unless you have a specific, well-defined need for it (such as on-the-fly generation of relations from an XML data source).

HINT When creating new relations for a DataSet, use the DataSet.Relations.Add method for convenience and speed, instead of the DataRelation constructors.

Constructors

```
Dim myDataRelation As New DataRelation(strName, _
     myDataColumnParent, myDataColumnChild)
Dim myDataRelation As New DataRelation(strName, _
     myDataColumnParentArray, myDataColumnChildArray)
Dim myDataRelation As New DataRelation(strName, _
     myDataColumnParent, myDataColumnChild, _
     boolCreateConstraints)
```

```
Dim myDataRelation As New DataRelation(strName, _
     myDataColumnParentArray, myDataColumnChildArray, _
     boolCreateConstraints)
Dim myDataRelation As New DataRelation(strName, _
     strParentTableName, strChildTableName, _
     strParentColumnNameArray, strChildColumnNameArray, _
     boolIsNested)
```

Parameters

`strName`	Name of the DataRelation, as a String.
`myDataColumnParent`	DataColumn object that is the parent.
`myDataColumnChild`	DataColumn object that is the child.
`myDataColumnParentArray`	Array of DataColumn objects that are the parents. (This array must match the size of the matched child array.)
`myDataColumnChildArray`	Array of DataColumn objects that are the children. (This array must match the size of the matched parent array.)
`boolCreateConstraints`	Boolean indicating whether to create associated constraints.
`strParentTableName`	Name of the parent DataTable, as a String.
`strChildTableName`	Name of the child DataTable, as a String.
`strParentColumnNameArray`	Array of Strings that are the names of the parent columns.
`strChildColumnNameArray`	Array of Strings that are the names of the child columns.
`boolIsNested`	Boolean indicating whether the relationships are nested.

Exceptions

ArgumentException	1.) The passed arrays are not the same length. 2.) Child table cannot be nested in more than one parent table.
ArgumentNullException	One or both of the DataColumn objects in a relationship is null (`Nothing` in Visual Basic .NET).
InvalidConstraintException	1.) DataColumn objects in a relationship have different types. 2.) A passed array is not composed of distinct DataColumn objects. 3.) The DataTable objects do not belong to the same DataSet.

DataRelation Sample Code

```
'This function demonstrates the DataRelation class
'  It assumes two valid DataTables are passed,
'  with Table1.Column1 being the parent column,
'  and Table2.Column1 being the child column, and
'  a valid DataSet containing those items.
Public Sub DemoDataRelation( _
            ByRef myDataSet As DataSet, _
            ByRef myDataTable1 As DataTable, _
            ByRef myDataTable2 As DataTable)

   Dim myDataRelation As DataRelation
   Dim myConstraint As Constraint

   'create a DataRelation between the tables
   myDataRelation = New DataRelation("myRelation", _
         myDataTable1.Columns(0), _
         myDataTable2.Columns(0), False)
   'add the DataRelation to the DataSet
   myDataSet.Relations.Add(myDataRelation)


   'get  name of unique constraint created with the Relation
   myConstraint = myDataRelation.ParentKeyConstraint
   If Not myConstraint Is Nothing Then
      MessageBox.Show(myConstraint.ConstraintName.ToString)
   End If

End Sub
```

Members

ChildColumns

The read-only ChildColumns property returns an array of DataColumn objects that are the child columns in the DataRelation.

Usage

```
myDataColumnArray = myDataRelation.ChildColumns
```

Parameters

None.

Exceptions

None.

ChildKeyConstraint

The read-only ChildKeyConstraint property returns the ForeignKeyConstraint object for this DataRelation. If no constraint exists, this property will return null (`Nothing` in

Visual Basic .NET). (This property will return a Constraint, if one exists, even when it was not created automatically by the DataRelation.)

Usage
```
myForeignKeyConstraint = myDataRelation.ChildKeyConstraint
```

Parameters
None.

Exceptions
None.

ChildTable

The read-only ChildTable property returns a DataTable object that is the child table (contains the child DataColumn objects of this relationship).

Usage
```
myDataTable = myDataRelation.ChildTable
```

Parameters
None.

Exceptions
None.

DataSet

The read-only DataSet property returns the DataSet object that contains the DataRelation.

Usage
```
myDataSet = myDataRelation.DataSet
```

Parameters
None.

Exceptions
None.

ExtendedProperties

The read-only ExtendedProperties property returns a PropertyCollection object that allows you to store custom information with the object. Although the property itself is read only, you may add properties to the returned PropertyCollection with the Add method. See the sample code for an example.

NOTE If the ExtendedProperties collection is to be persisted as XML, then the members of the collection must be of type String.

Usage
```
myPropertyCollection = myDataTable.ExtendedProperties
```

Parameters
None.

Exceptions
None.

Sample Code
```
myDataRelation.ExtendedProperties.Add("Sister", "Sandi Borg")
```

Nested

The Nested property returns or sets a Boolean value indicating whether the tables involved in a DataRelation are nested. Inside of DataSet, this value isn't of much use because the two tables are distinct objects. When the DataSet is written as XML or synchronized with an XmlDataDocument object, this property becomes critical. It determines whether the child table will be output as a child element inside of the parent table.

For example, below is the same DataSet, output twice with differing values of Nested. In the example, a relationship was defined between Column1 (parent) and ColumnA (child). As you can see, when Nested is False the DataTable objects are output separately. When Nested is True, TableA is nested inside of Table1.

Nested = False **Nested = True**
```
<myDataSet>
  <Table1>
    <Column1>1</Column1>
    <Column2>Hello</Column2>
  </Table1>
  <TableA>
    <ColumnA>1</ColumnA>
    <ColumnB>World</ColumnB>
  </TableA>
</myDataSet> <myDataSet>
  <Table1>
    <Column1>1</Column1>
    <Column2>Hello</Column2>
    <TableA>
      <ColumnA >1</ColumnA>
      <ColumnB >World</ColumnB>
    </TableA>
  </Table1>
</myDataSet>
```

Usage
```
myBoolean = myDataRelation.Nested
myDataRelation.Nested = myBoolean
```

Parameters
None.

Exceptions

Exception	Description
ArgumentException	Child table cannot be nested in more than one parent table.

ParentColumns

The read-only ParentColumns property returns an array of DataColumn objects that are the parent columns in the DataRelation.

Usage

```
myDataColumnArray = myDataRelation.ParentColumns
```

Parameters

None.

Exceptions

None.

ParentKeyConstraint

The read-only ParentKeyConstraint property returns the UniqueConstraint object for this DataRelation. If no UniqueConstraint exists, this property will return null (`Nothing` in Visual Basic .NET). (This property will return a Constraint, if one exists, even when it was not created automatically by the DataRelation.)

NOTE **Because a relationship is parent-child, the constraint on the parent is a UniqueConstraint, while the constraint returned from ChildKeyConstraint is a ForeignKeyConstraint.**

Usage

```
myUniqueConstraint = myDataRelation.ParentKeyConstraint
```

Parameters

None.

Exceptions

None.

ParentTable

The read-only ParentTable property returns a DataTable object that is the parent table (contains the parent DataColumn objects of this relationship).

Usage

```
myDataTable = myDataRelation.ParentTable
```

Parameters

None.

Exceptions

None.

RelationName

The RelationName property returns or sets a String that is the name of the DataRelation.

Usage

```
myString = myDataRelation.RelationName
myDataRelation.RelationName = myString
```

Parameters
None.

Exceptions
None.

ToString

The ToString method is overridden to return the RelationName property.

Usage
```
myString = myDataRelation.ToString()
```

Parameters
None.

Exceptions
None.

System.Data.DataRelationCollection

The DataRelationCollection class is a container class that maintains a collection of DataRelation objects. Because the constructor for the DataRelationCollection is private, an instance cannot be independently created. A DataRelationCollection object is accessible from the DateSet.Relations and DataTable.ParentRelations properties.

The DataRelationCollection is a convenient way to add rows to a DataSet. Instead of independently creating relations and adding them to the DataSet, through the three-step declare-initialize-add procedure, use the DataRelationCollection.Add method to add a DataRelation in one step.

Constructors

No public constructors.

Parameters

None.

DataRelationCollection Sample Code

```
'See System.Data.ConstraintCollection for examples of the
'common collection members.
```

Members

Add

The various Add methods add a DataRelation to the DataRelationCollection and return the added System.Data.DataRelation object. All Add methods return the added

DataRelation, with the exception of the Add method, which takes only a DataRelation as a parameter. This method returns nothing.

Usage

```
myDataRelationCollection.Add(myDataRelation)
myDataRelation = myDataRelationCollection.Add( _
    myDataColumnParent, myDataColumnChild)
myDataRelation = myDataRelationCollection.Add( _
    myDataColumnParentArray, myDataColumnChildArray)
myDataRelation = myDataRelationCollection.Add(strName, _
    myDataColumnParent, myDataColumnChild)
myDataRelation = myDataRelationCollection.Add(strName, _
    myDataColumnParentArray, myDataColumnChildArray)
myDataRelation = myDataRelationCollection.Add(strName, _
    myDataColumnParent, myDataColumnChild, _
    boolCreateConstraints)
myDataRelation = myDataRelationCollection.Add(strName, _
    myDataColumnParentArray, myDataColumnChildArray, _
    boolCreateConstraints)
```

Parameters

`myDataRelation`	DataRelation object to add to the collection.
`myDataColumnParent`	The parent DataColumn of the relation.
`myDataColumnChild`	The child DataColumn of the relation.
`myDataColumnParentArray`	An Array of parent DataColumn objects to act in the relation.
`myDataColumnChildArray`	An Array of child DataColumn objects to act in the relation.
`strName`	Name to give the DataRelation (String).
`boolCreateConstraints`	Boolean value determining whether to create associated constraints.

Exceptions

ArgumentNullException	The DataRelation argument is null.
ArgumentException	The DataRelation already belongs to the DataRelationCollection or to another collection.
DuplicateNameException	The DataRelationCollection contains a DataRelation with the same name. (The comparison is not case sensitive.)
InvalidConstraintException	The DataRelation to add has entered an invalid state.

AddRange

The AddRange method copies the passed array of DataRelation objects to the end of the DataRelationCollection.

Usage

```
myDataRelationCollection.AddRange(myDataRelationArray)
```

Parameters

`myDataRelationArray`	Array of DataRelation objects to be added to the DataRelationCollection.

Exceptions

ArgumentException	The DataRelation already belongs to the Data RelationCollection or to another collection.
DuplicateNameException	The DataRelationCollection contains a DataRelation with the same name. (The comparison is not case sensitive.)

CanRemove

The CanRemove method returns a Boolean value that indicates whether the passed DataRelation can be removed from the DataRelationCollection. Use this method to determine whether a DataRelation can be removed from the collection. CanRemove returns True if the DataRelation can be removed, False otherwise.

Usage

```
myBoolean = myDataRelationCollection.CanRemove(myDataRelation)
```

Parameters

`myDataRelation`	DataRelation to be tested for removal from the DataRelationCollection.

Exceptions

ArgumentNullException	The DataRelation argument is null.
ArgumentException	The DataRelation does not belong to this collection.

Clear

The Clear method removes all DataRelation objects from the DataRelationCollection. If the removal is successful a CollectionChange event is fired. (See CollectionChanged event for more information.)

Usage

```
myDataRelationCollection.Clear()
```

Parameters

None.

Exceptions

None.

CollectionChanged

The CollectionChanged event is fired whenever DataRelations are added to or removed from the DataRelationCollection.

Usage

```
Private Sub myDataRelationCollection_CollectionChanged( _
    ByVal sender As Object, _
    ByVal e As System.Data.StateChangeEventArgs) _
    Handles myDataRelationCollection.CollectionChanged
```

Parameters

`sender`	Contains a reference to the originator of the event.
`e`	Contains the System.ComponentModel.CollectionChangeEventArgs object. See the table below.

CollectionChangeEventArgs (e)

e.Action	A System.ComponentModelCollectionChangeAction enumeration representing how the collection was changed.
e.Element	An Object that refers to the collection that has changed (the DataRelationCollection, in this case).

CollectionChangeAction Enumeration

Add (1)	An element has been added to the collection.
Remove(2)	An element has been added to the collection.
Refresh (3)	Specifies that the entire collection has changed (for instance, when the Clear method has been called).

Exceptions

None.

Contains

The Contains method returns a Boolean value that indicates whether a DataRelation object with the passed name (String) exists in the DataRelationCollection. Returns True if a DataRelation with the passed name exists, False otherwise.

Usage

```
myBoolean = myDataRelationCollection.Contains(strName)
```

Parameters

`strName`	String defining the name of the DataRelation to check for.

Exceptions

None.

CopyTo

The CopyTo method (inherited from System.Data.InternalDataCollectionBase) is used to copy the DataRelation objects in the DataRelationCollection to an array. (Please see System.Data.InternalDataCollectionBase for more information.)

Usage

```
myDataRelationCollection.CopyTo(myDataRelationArray, _
    myStartIndex)
```

Parameters

`myDataRelationArray`	The passed buffer array to hold the DataRelation objects.
`myStartIndex`	The Integer index designating the location in the passed array to begin filling with the DataRelation objects.

Exceptions

ArgumentException	The passed array was not long enough to hold the passed objects.
ArgumentNullException	The passed array is null (`Nothing` in Visual Basic .NET).
ArgumentOutOfRangeException	myStartIndex is negative or greater than the length of the array.
InvalidCastException	The object type of the collection cannot be cast automatically to the object type of the array.

Count

The read-only Count property (inherited from System.Data.InternalDataCollectionBase) returns an Int32 value specifying the number of DataRelations in the DataRelationCollection.

Usage

```
myInt32 = myDataRelationCollection.Count
```

Parameters

None.

Exceptions

None.

GetEnumerator

The GetEnumerator method (inherited from System.Data.InternalDataCollectionBase) returns a System.Collections.IEnumerator object that can be used to iterate over the collection. This method assists in using the For Each - Next (or equivalent statements) to iterate through a collection.

Usage

```
myIEnumerator = myDataRelationCollection.GetEnumerator()
```

Parameters

None.

Exceptions

None.

IndexOf

The IndexOf() method returns an Integer specifying the zero-based location of a specified DataRelation within the DataRelationCollection. Because this method is overloaded, you may pass either the DataRelation object itself or a String representing the name of the DataRelation. If the DataRelation does not exist in the DataRelationCollection a value of -1 is returned.

Usage

```
myInt32 = myDataRelationCollection.IndexOf(myDataRelation)
myInt32 = myDataRelationCollection.IndexOf(strName)
```

Parameters

`myDataRelation`	The DataRelation for which to find the index.
`strName`	The name of the DataRelation for which to find the index.

Exceptions

None.

IsReadOnly

The read-only IsReadOnly property returns a Boolean value specifying whether the DataRelationCollection is read only. This property is inherited directly from the InternalDataCollectionBase class. (Please see System.Data.InternalDataCollectionBase for more information.)

Usage

```
myBoolean = myDataRelationCollection.IsReadOnly
```

Parameters

None.

Exceptions

None.

IsSynchronized

The read-only IsSynchronized property (inherited from System.Data.InternalDataCollectionBase) returns a Boolean value indicating whether the DataRelationCollection is currently synchronized. For information on synchronizing the DataRelationCollection, see the DataRelationCollection.SyncRoot property.

Usage

```
myBoolean = myDataRelationCollection.IsSynchronized
```

Parameters

None.

Exceptions

None.

Item

The read-only Item property returns an indicated DataRelation object from the collection. You can pass either the Integer index or String name of the desired DataRelation. If you pass an invalid integer, an IndexOutOfRangeException will be thrown. If the passed name doesn't match any of the items, a null (`Nothing` in Visual Basic .NET) is returned, and no exception is raised.

Usage

```
myDataRelation = myDataRelationCollection.Item(intIndex)
myDataRelation = myDataRelationCollection.Item(strName)
```

Parameters

`intIndex`	Integer specifying the index of the desired DataRelation.
`strName`	String specifying the name of the desired DataRelation.

Exceptions

IndexOutOfRangeException	The passed integer is outside the bounds of the collection.

Remove

The Remove() method removes a specified DataRelation object from the DataRelation-Collection. Because this method is overloaded, you may pass either the DataRelation object itself or a String representing the name of the DataRelation.

Usage

```
myDataRelationCollection.Remove(myDataRelation)
myDataRelationCollection.Remove(strName)
```

Parameters

`myDataRelation`	The DataRelation object to remove.
`strName`	The name of the DataRelation object to remove.

Exceptions

ArgumentNullException	The DataRelation argument is a null reference (`Nothing` in Visual Basic).
ArgumentException	The DataRelation does not belong to the collection.

RemoveAt

The RemoveAt() method removes a DataRelation object from the DataRelationCollection specified by the passed index of the DataRelation.

Usage

```
myDataRelationCollection.RemoveAt(intIndex)
```

Parameters

`intIndex`	Integer specifying the index of the DataRelation to remove.

Exceptions

ArgumentException	A DataTable does not exist at the desired index.

SyncRoot

The read-only SyncRoot property returns a System.Object object that can be used to Synchronize the DataRelationCollection. (Please see System.Data.InternalDataCollectionBase for more information.)

Usage
```
myObject = myDataRelationCollection.SyncRoot
```

Parameters
None.

Exceptions
None.

ToString

The ToString method returns "System.Data.DataRelationCollection".

Usage
```
myString = myDataRelationCollection.ToString()
```

Parameters
None.

Exceptions
None.

System.Data.DataRow

The DataRow class is one of the primary data manipulation classes in ADO.NET. All data in DataTables is stored in DataRow objects. DataRow objects are roughly equivalent to a record or row in a relational database. They contain a number of values of differing data type, which can be used to store data.

There are no public constructors for the DataRow class, so you must create them either through the DataTable.NewRow method or through the DataRowCollection. Add method.

HINT **When creating a new DataRow for a DataTable, use the DataTable.Rows.Add method for convenience and speed, instead of the DataRow constructors.**

Constructors

No public constructors.

Parameters

None.

DataRow Sample Code

```
'This function demonstrates the DataRow class
'  There are additional DataRow code samples in
'  Chapter 11.
Public Sub DemoDataRow()
   Dim myDataTable As DataTable
   Dim myDataColumn As DataColumn
   Dim myDataRow As DataRow

   myDataTable = New DataTable("GreetingTable")

   'build a DataTable
   myDataTable = New DataTable("GreetingTable")

   'add a column to use as a primary key
   '  make it AutoIncrement
   myDataColumn = myDataTable.Columns.Add( _
         "AutoInc", GetType(Int32))
   myDataColumn.AutoIncrement = True
   myDataTable.Constraints.Add( _
         "PK", myDataColumn, True)

   'add greeting and country columns
   myDataColumn = myDataTable.Columns.Add( _
         "Greeting", GetType(String))
   myDataColumn.AllowDBNull = False
   myDataColumn.DefaultValue = "myDefault"

   myDataColumn = myDataTable.Columns.Add( _
         "Country", GetType(String))

   'add two rows to the table
   myDataTable.Rows.Add(New Object(2) _
         {Nothing, "Hello", "USA"})
   myDataTable.Rows.Add(New Object(2) _
         {Nothing, "Guten Tag", "Germany"})
   myDataTable.AcceptChanges()

   'add a column using DataTable.NewRow
   myDataRow = myDataTable.NewRow
   myDataRow.BeginEdit()
   myDataRow.Item(1) = "Bonjour"
   myDataRow.Item(2) = "France"
   myDataRow.EndEdit()
   myDataTable.Rows.Add(myDataRow)

   'retrieve the first DataRow
   myDataRow = myDataTable.Rows(0)

   'display the State of the DataRow
```

```
    MessageBox.Show(myDataRow.RowState.ToString)

    'set an error on the row & on 2nd column
    myDataRow.RowError = "Greeting also used in Ireland"
    myDataRow.SetColumnError(1, "Hello is too formal")

    'display the error
    Dim myErrorColumns() As DataColumn = _
          myDataRow.GetColumnsInError
    MessageBox.Show("Number of Column errors: " + _
          myErrorColumns.Length.ToString)
    MessageBox.Show("Column Name: " + _
             myErrorColumns(0).ColumnName + _
          ControlChars.CrLf + "Error String: " + _
          myDataRow.GetColumnError( _
             myErrorColumns(0).ColumnName))

    'clear the error & verify all are gone
    myDataRow.ClearErrors()
    If myDataRow.HasErrors Then
       MessageBox.Show("Row still has errors!")
    End If

End Sub
```

Members

AcceptChanges

The AcceptChanges method commits all the changes to the DataRow that have been made since the last AcceptChanges method was called. Calling AcceptChanges at the DataSet forces AcceptChanges to be called at the DataTable level, which in turn causes each DataRow to call AcceptChanges. Calling AcceptChanges at the DataRow level causes the DataRow.RowState property to change as well. Added and Modified DataRow objects become Unchanged, and Deleted DataRow objects are removed from the DataTable.

If any DataRow objects are in an edit mode (BeginEdit has been called), AcceptChanges will end the edit and successfully accept all of the updates. Because DataRow objects in an edit mode do not yet verify their contents with Foreign Key constraints, calling AcceptChanges may trigger the AcceptRejectRule to be applied.

See RejectChanges to force child DataRow objects to reject changes, and roll back any changes made while still in an edit mode.

NOTE Although the AcceptChanges method occurs at a hierarchy of levels, you cannot use RejectChanges at a higher level to roll back changes accepted at a lower level. Calling AcceptChanges on a DataRow will permanently accept those changes, despite calling RejectChanges at the DataSet level.

Usage

```
myDataRow.AcceptChanges()
```

Parameters

None.

Exceptions

None.

BeginEdit

The BeginEdit method begins an edit operation on a DataRow. This method suspends all events so that edits that violate validation rules can be made. For instance, if several rows tracking percentages must sum to 100 percent, then by placing all the rows in edit mode the changes can be made. When EndEdit has been called on each of the rows, the validation rules fire.

When in the edit mode, you can retrieve the original and newly changed values of a column by passing DataRowVersion.Original or DataRowVersion.Proposed in the Item property. To determine if a row has a version, you can call the HasVersion method.

Changing a value using the Item property will automatically place the DataRow in edit mode, even if BeginEdit has not been called.

To cancel all unaccepted edits on the DataRow, call the CancelEdit method. To accept the edits, call the EndEdit method.

Usage

```
myDataRow.BeginEdit()
```

Parameters

None.

Exceptions

InRowChangingEventException	BeginEdit was called inside the RowChanging event.
DeletedRowInaccessibleException	BeginEdit was called on a deleted row.

CancelEdit

The CancelEdit method cancels an edit operation on a DataRow and takes it out of edit mode. For more information on edit mode, see BeginEdit. Calling CancelEdit on a row that is not in the edit mode will have no effect.

Usage

```
myDataRow.CancelEdit()
```

Parameters

None.

Exceptions

None.

ClearErrors

The ClearErrors method clears the errors that exist on the DataRow. This includes both errors that exist on the entire row and errors specified for individual columns.

To determine if the DataRow has errors, use the HasErrors method. To retrieve the columns that contain errors, use the GetColumnsInError method.

Usage

```
myDataRow.ClearErrors()
```

Parameters

None.

Exceptions

None.

Delete

The Delete method deletes the row from the table by setting the RowState to Deleted. The deletion can be cancelled at any time before AcceptChanges is called, by calling RejectChanges on the DataRow, parent DataTable, or parent DataSet.

Usage

```
myDataRow.Delete()
```

Parameters

None.

Exceptions

DeletedRowInaccessibleException	Delete was called on a deleted row.

EndEdit

The EndEdit method ends the edit on a DataRow and takes it out of edit mode. For more information on edit mode, see BeginEdit. Calling EndEdit on a row that is not in the edit mode will have no effect.

Usage

```
myDataRow.EndEdit()
```

Parameters

None.

Exceptions

NoInRowChangingEventException	EndEdit was called inside the RowChanging event.
ConstraintException	The performed edit violated a constraint.
ReadOnlyException	An attempt was made to change the value of a read-only column, while the row belonged to a table.
NoNullAllowedException	The edit attempted to place a null value in a column where AllowDBNull is false.

GetChildRows

The GetChildRows method returns an array of DataRow objects that are the child rows of a DataRelation, where the current row is the parent. The method accepts a parameter specifying the relation to use and, optionally, the version of the destination row to return.

If there are no child rows, an array of zero length is returned.

Usage

```
myDataRowArray = myDataRow.GetChildRows(myDataRelation)
myDataRowArray = myDataRow.GetChildRows(strRelationName)
myDataRowArray = myDataRow.GetChildRows(myDataRelation, _
     myDataRowVersion)
myDataRowArray = myDataRow.GetChildRows(strRelationName, _
     myDataRowVersion)
```

Parameters

`myDataRelation`	A DataRelation object that has the current DataRow as a parent.
`strRelationName`	A String representing the desired DataRelation.
`myDataRowVersion`	A DataRowVersion enumeration value specifying the version of the child DataRow to be returned.

Exceptions

RowNotInTableException	The DataRow does not belong to the DataTable designated in the DataRelation.
ArgumentNullException	The DataRelation is null (`Nothing` in Visual Basic .NET).
ArgumentException	The DataRelation and DataRow do not belong to the same table.
VersionNotFoundException	The child DataRow does not support the requested DataRowVersion.

GetColumnError

The GetColumnError method returns a String representing the error on the specified column.

Usage

```
myString = myDataRow.GetColumnError(myDataColumn)
myString = myDataRow.GetColumnError(intIndex)
myString = myDataRow.GetColumnError(strName)
```

Parameters

`myDataColumn`	The DataColumn object for which to return the error.
`intIndex`	The Integer index of the desired DataColumn.
`strName`	The name of the desired DataColumn as a String.

Exceptions

ArgumentException	The indicated DataColumn does not belong to the DataTable containing the DataRow object.
ArgumentNullException	Passed DataColumn is null (`Nothing` in Visual Basic .NET).
IndexOutOfRangeException	Passed index could not be found in the Column collection.

GetColumnsInError

The GetColumnsInError method returns an array of DataColumn objects that contain errors. If no columns have errors, a zero-length string is returned.

This method is used to reduce the number of columns that must be processed when dealing with errors. If you wish to cause a column to be in error, you can use the SetColumnError method.

Usage

```
myDataColumnArray = myDataRow.GetColumnsInError()
```

Parameters

None.

Exceptions

None.

GetParentRow

The GetParentRow method returns a DataRow that is the parent row in a DataRelation, where the current row is the child. The method accepts a parameter specifying the relation to use and, optionally, the version of the destination row to return.

Usage

```
myDataRow = myDataRow.GetParentRow(myDataRelation)
myDataRow = myDataRow.GetParentRow(strRelationName)
myDataRow = myDataRow.GetParentRow(myDataRelation, _
     myDataRowVersion)
myDataRow = myDataRow.GetParentRow(strRelationName, _
     myDataRowVersion)
```

Parameters

`myDataRelation`	A DataRelation object that has the current DataRow as a child.
`strRelationName`	A String representing the desired DataRelation.
`myDataRowVersion`	A DataRowVersion enumeration value specifying the version of the parent DataRow to be returned.

Exceptions

RowNotInTableException	The DataRow does not belong to the DataTable designated in the DataRelation.

ArgumentNullException	The DataRelation is null (`Nothing` in Visual Basic .NET).
ArgumentException	The DataRelation and DataRow do not belong to the same table.
VersionNotFoundException	The parent DataRow does not support the requested DataRowVersion.
InvalidConstraintException	The DataRelations object's child table isn't the DataTable to which the DataRow belongs.

GetParentRows

The GetParentRows method returns an array of DataRow objects that are the parent rows of a DataRelation, where the current row is the child. The method accepts a parameter specifying the relation to use and, optionally, the version of the destination rows to return.

If there are no child rows, an array of zero length is returned.

Usage

```
myDataRowArray = myDataRow.GetParentRows(myDataRelation)
myDataRowArray = myDataRow.GetParentRows(strRelationName)
myDataRowArray = myDataRow.GetParentRows(myDataRelation, _
     myDataRowVersion)
myDataRowArray = myDataRow.GetParentRows(strRelationName, _
     myDataRowVersion)
```

Parameters

`myDataRelation`	A DataRelation object that has the current DataRow as a child.
`strRelationName`	A String representing the desired DataRelation.
`myDataRowVersion`	A DataRowVersion enumeration value specifying the version of the parent DataRow objects to be returned.

Exceptions

RowNotInTableException	The DataRow does not belong to the DataTable designated in the DataRelation.
ArgumentNullException	The DataRelation is null (`Nothing` in Visual Basic .NET).
ArgumentException	The DataRelation and DataRow do not belong to the same table.
VersionNotFoundException	The parent DataRow does not support the requested DataRowVersion.
InvalidConstraintException	The DataRelations object's child table isn't the DataTable to which the DataRow belongs.

HasErrors

The read-only HasErrors property returns a Boolean value specifying whether any of the DataColumn objects in the DataRow contain an error. HasErrors returns True if any of the columns have an error, False otherwise.

HINT A column with an error is displayed in Red when viewed in a DataGrid control hosted on a Windows Form.

Usage

```
myBoolean = myDataRow.HasErrors
```

Parameters

None.

Exceptions

None.

HasVersion

The HasVersion method returns a Boolean value specifying whether the DataRow has a specified version. See the DataRowVersion table below for possible versions.

Usage

```
myBoolean = myDataRow.HasVersion(myDataRowVersion)
```

Parameters

`myDataRowVersion`	A System.Data.DataRowVersion enumeration value that represents the desired version.

DataRowVersion Enumeration

Current (512)	The DataRow contains current values.
Default(1536)	The DataRow contains its default values. (Note: This is a bitwise combination of Current and Proposed.)
Original(256)	The DataRow contains its original values.
Proposed(1024)	The DataRow contains a proposed value.

Exceptions

None.

IsNull

The IsNull method returns a Boolean value denoting whether the specified Data Column is null.

Usage

```
myBoolean = myDataRow.IsNull(myDataColumn)
myBoolean = myDataRow.IsNull(intIndex)
myBoolean = myDataRow.IsNull(strName)
myBoolean = myDataRow.IsNull(strName, myDataRowVersion)
```

Parameters

`myDataColumn`	The DataColumn object for which to determine nullness.
`intIndex`	The Integer index of the desired DataColumn.
`strName`	The name of the desired DataColumn as a String.
`myDataRowVersion`	A System.Data.DataRowVersion enumeration value that represents the desired version.

Exceptions

ArgumentException	The indicated DataColumn does not belong to the DataTable containing the DataRow object.
ArgumentNullException	Passed DataColumn is null (`Nothing` in Visual Basic .NET).
IndexOutOfRangeException	The specified column cannot be found.

Item

The Item property returns or sets the data stored in a designated DataColumn. If you wish to add the next step in a column with an auto increment field or default value, pass a null (`Nothing` in Visual Basic .NET) to ensure that the column is filled with the proper value.

Usage

```
myObject = myDataRow.Item(myDataColumn)
myObject = myDataRow.Item(intIndex)
myObject = myDataRow.Item(strName)
myObject = myDataRow.Item(myDataColumn, myDataRowVersion)
myObject = myDataRow.Item(intIndex, myDataRowVersion)
myObject = myDataRow.Item(strName, myDataRowVersion)

myDataRow.Item(myDataColumn) = myObject
myDataRow.Item(intIndex) = myObject
myDataRow.Item(strName) = myObject
myDataRow.Item(myDataColumn, myDataRowVersion) = myObject
myDataRow.Item(intIndex, myDataRowVersion) = myObject
myDataRow.Item(strName, myDataRowVersion) = myObject
```

Parameters

`myDataColumn`	The DataColumn object for which to return the error.
`intIndex`	The Integer index of the desired Data Column.

`strName`	The name of the desired DataColumn as a String.
`myDataRowVersion`	A System.Data.DataRowVersion enumeration value that represents the desired version.

Exceptions

ArgumentException	1.) Attempted to assign a null value to an AutoIncrement column or one with an active Expression value. 2.) The indicated DataColumn does not belong to the DataTable containing the DataRow object.
ArgumentNullException	The DataColumn is null (`Nothing` in Visual Basic .NET).
VersionNotFoundException	The parent DataRow does not support the requested DataRowVersion.
IndexOutOfRangeException	The specified column cannot be found.
InvalidCastException	The data types of the passed object and the DataColumn do not match.
DeletedRowInaccessibleException	The row was deleted.

ItemArray

The ItemArray property returns or sets an array of Object values that represent all of the columns in the DataRow. This allows you to set or retrieve all the column values in one call.

When passing the array of objects, you must ensure that each object in the array maps to the DataColumn at the same index location. If you are passing an array into a DataRow that has an auto increment field (or similar field), pass null (`Nothing` in Visual Basic .NET) to ensure that the column is filled with the proper value.

WARNING **When setting this value to an array, the array will automatically be redimensioned to the number of columns. This is true even if you pass an array with more than enough members. Thus, if a loop through an array depends on a preset array length, instead of determining the number of loops dynamically, you may get an exception when the count goes above the new dimension of the array.**

HINT **To determine the proper length of the array, you can use DataRow.Table. Columns.Count. The DataRow itself has no property that returns the number of columns.**

Usage

```
myObjectArray = myDataRow.ItemArray
myDataRow.ItemArray = myObjectArray
```

Parameters
None.

Exceptions

ArgumentException	The Array length is larger than the number of columns (occurs only when setting).
InvalidCastException	The data types of the passed object and the DataColumn do not match.
ConstraintException	The performed edit violated a constraint.
ReadOnlyException	An attempt was made to change the value of a read-only column, while the row belonged to a table.
NoNullAllowedException	The edit attempted to place a null value in a column where AllowDBNull is false.
DeletedRowInaccessibleException	The row was deleted.

RejectChanges

The RejectChanges method rolls back all the changes to the DataTable that have been made since the last AcceptChanges method was called. Calling RejectChanges at the DataSet forces RejectChanges to be called at the DataTable level, which in turn causes each DataRow to call RejectChanges. Calling RejectChanges at the DataRow level causes the DataRow.RowState property to change as well. Deleted and Modified DataRow objects become Unchanged, and Added DataRow objects are removed from the DataTable.

If any DataRow objects are in an edit mode (BeginEdit has been called), RejectChanges will end the edit and reject all of the updates.

See AcceptChanges to force child DataRow objects to accept changes, and commit any changes made while in an edit mode.

NOTE Although the RejectChanges method occurs at a hierarchy of levels, you cannot use AcceptChanges at a higher level to accept changes already rolled back at a lower level. Calling RejectChanges on a DataRow will permanently roll back those changes, despite calling AcceptChanges at the DataSet level.

Usage

```
myDataRow.RejectChanges()
```

Parameters
None.

Exceptions
None.

RowError

The RowError property returns or sets a String representing a custom error description for the DataRow.

HINT When a row has an error, it will appear with a red exclamation mark in the appropriate row of displayed System.Windows.Forms.DataGrid control. Hovering over the red exclamation mark will cause the error description to appear as a ToolTip. (Way cool—see SetColumnError for more excitement!)

Usage

```
myString = myDataRow.RowError
myDataRow.RowError = myString
```

Parameters

None.

Exceptions

None.

RowState

The read-only RowState property returns a DataRowState enumeration value specifying the edit state that the row is in. This property is queried by the GetChanges and HasChanges methods. See the DataRowState table below for possible states.

Usage

```
myDataRowState = myDataRow.RowState
```

Parameters

None.

DataRowState Enumeration

Added (4)	DataRow has been added to a DataRowCollection, and AcceptChanges has not been called.
Deleted(8)	The DataRow has been deleted using the DataRow.Delete method.
Detached(1)	The DataRow is not part of any DataRowCollection. A DataRow is in this state before it has been added to a DataTable or if it has been removed from a DataTable.
Modified(16)	The DataRow has been modified, and AcceptChanges has not been called.
Unchanged(2)	The DataRow has not changed since AcceptChanges was last called.

Exceptions

None.

SetColumnError

The SetColumnError method is used to set an error on a desired DataColumn. Simply indicate the desired DataColumn and pass a user-defined description of the error.

HINT **When a column has an error, it will appear with a red exclamation mark in the appropriate column of displayed System.Windows.Forms.DataGrid control. Hovering over the red exclamation mark will cause the error description to appear as a ToolTip. (That's so cool!)**

Usage

```
myDataRow.Item(myDataColumn, strError)
myDataRow.Item(intIndex, strError)
myDataRow.Item(strName, strError)
```

Parameters

`myDataColumn`	The DataColumn object to which the error is assigned.
`intIndex`	The Integer index of the desired Data Column.
`strName`	The name of the desired DataColumn as a String.
`strError`	A String that describes the error.

Exceptions

ArgumentException	The indicated DataColumn does not belong to the DataTable containing the DataRow object.
ArgumentNullException	The DataColumn is null (`Nothing` in Visual Basic .NET).
IndexOutOfRangeException	The specified column cannot be found.
DeletedRowInaccessibleException	The row was deleted.

SetParentRow

The SetParentRow method is used to designate a parent row for this DataRow.

Usage

```
myDataRow.SetParentRow(myDataRow)
myDataRow.SetParentRow(myDataRow, myDataRelation)
```

Parameters

`myDataRow`	The DataRow object to act as the parent for the current DataRow.
`myDataRelation`	A DataRelation object to update with the new information.

Exceptions

ArgumentNullException	The DataColumn is null (`Nothing` in Visual Basic .NET).
DeletedRowInaccessibleException	The row was deleted.

RowNotInTableException	One of the DataRow objects does not belong to a DataTable.
InvalidConstraintException	The DataRelations object's child table isn't the DataTable to which the DataRow belongs.
ArgumentException	The DataRelation and DataRow do not belong to the same table.
IndexOutOfRangeException	The passed row could not be found.

Table

The read-only Table property returns the DataTable object that contains the DataRow or, in the case of a Detached DataRow, the DataTable that was used to create the DataRow.

Usage

```
myDataTable = myDataRow.Table
```

Parameters

None.

Exceptions

None.

ToString

The ToString method returns "System.Data.DataRow".

Usage

```
myString = myDataRow.ToString()
```

Parameters

None.

Exceptions

None.

System.Data.DataRowAction

The DataRowAction enumeration provides the values that determine what action will occur during the update of a DataRow. They are used by the DataRowChangeEventArgs event passed by the DataTable.RowChanging or DataTable.RowChanged events. Setting the values during these events can impact how the DataRow is updated. (See these events for more information.)

Because this class implements the FlagsAttribute, bitwise combinations of values are allowed.

DataRowAction Enumeration

Add (16)	The DataRow has been added (or will be added) to the table.
Change (2)	The DataRow has changed (or will change).

Commit (8)	The change to the DataRow has been committed (or will be committed).
Delete (1)	The DataRow has been deleted (or will be deleted) from the table.
Nothing (0)	The DataRow has not changed (or will not change).
Rollback (4)	The change to the DataRow has been rolled back (or will be rolled back).

System.Data.DataRowBuilder

The DataRowBuilder class is generally used to support the .NET Framework and was not designed to be used with your code. It contains no public methods or properties that are not directly inherited from System.Object. Nor does it provide any public constructors.

ToString

The ToString method returns "System.Data.DataRowBuilder".

Usage

```
myString = myDataRowBuilder.ToString()
```

Parameters

None.

Exceptions

None.

System.Data.DataRowChangeEventArgs

The DataRowChangeEventArgs class is automatically created and passed to any code handling either the DataTable.RowChanging or DataTable.RowChanged events.

DataRowChangeEventArgs also has a public constructor, which can be used to define and throw your own exception.

Constructors

```
Dim myDataRowChangeEventArgs As New _
     DataRowChangeEventArgs(myDataRow, myDataRowAction)
```

Parameters

`myDataRow`	DataRow whose value is being changed.
`myDataRowAction`	A DataRowAction enumeration value.

DataRowAction Enumeration

Add (16)	The DataRow has been added to the table.
Change (2)	The DataRow has changed.
Commit (8)	The change to the DataRow has been committed.
Delete (1)	The DataRow has been deleted to the table.
Nothing (0)	The DataRow has not changed.
Rollback (4)	The change to the DataRow has been rolled back.

Members

Action

The Action property returns or sets a DataRowAction enumeration value specifying the action to be taken (or already taken) on the DataRow.

Usage

```
myDataRowAction = myDataRowChangeEventArgs.Action
```

Parameters

None.

DataRowAction Enumeration

Add (16)	The DataRow has been added to the table.
Change (2)	The DataRow has changed.
Commit (8)	The change to the DataRow has been committed.
Delete (1)	The DataRow has been deleted to the table.
Nothing (0)	The DataRow has not changed.
Rollback (4)	The change to the DataRow has been rolled back.

Exceptions

None.

Row

The read-only Row property returns the DataRow object on which the Action is being performed.

Usage

```
myDataRow = myDataRowChangeEventArgs.Row
```

Parameters

None.

Exceptions

None.

ToString

The ToString method returns "System.Data.DataRowChangeEventArgs".

Usage

```
myString = myDataRowChangeEventArgs.ToString()
```

Parameters

None.

Exceptions

None.

System.Data.DataRowCollection

The DataRowCollection class is a container class that maintains a collection of DataRow objects. Because the constructor for the DataRowCollection is private, an instance cannot be independently created. A DataRowCollection object is accessible only from the DataTable.Rows property.

The DataRowCollection is a convenient way to add rows to a DataTable. Instead of independently creating rows and adding them to the table, through the three-step declare-initialize-add procedure, use the DataRowCollection.Add method to add a DataRow in one step.

Constructors

No public constructors.

Parameters

None.

DataRowCollection Sample Code

```
'See System.Data.ConstraintCollection for examples of the
'common collection members.
```

Members

Add

The various Add methods add a DataRow to the DataRowCollection and return the added System.Data.DataRow object. The Add method taking an array of objects returns the added DataRow. When passing an array of objects, you must ensure that each object in the array maps to the DataColumn at the same index location. If you are passing an array into a DataRow that has an auto increment field (or similar field), pass a null object (`Nothing` in Visual Basic .NET) to ensure that the column is filled with the proper value. (You cannot pass DBNull.Value to achieve this result.)

Passing an array of objects to the Add method that has a length less than the number of columns will result in the DataColumn objects being filled up to the number of objects in the array. Any further DataColumn objects will be set to null, an auto increment value, or the default value. If any of these columns does not have auto increment or default values, and if AllowDbNull is False, then an exception will be raised.

The Add method that takes only a DataRow as a parameter returns nothing.

WARNING **If the DataRow being added is in edit mode, the EndEdit and AcceptChanges methods are called. Rolling back the DataRow to a previous data state is not possible. (RejectChanges on the DataTable will remove the added DataRow from the DataTable.)**

Usage

```
myDataRowCollection.Add(myDataRow)
myDataRow = myDataRowCollection.Add(myObjectArray)
```

Parameters

`myDataRow`	DataRow object to add to the collection.
`myObjectArray`	An Array of Object objects with which to fill the DataRow.

Exceptions

ArgumentNullException	The DataRow argument is null.
ArgumentException	The DataRow already belongs to the DataRowCollection or to another collection.
DuplicateNameException	The DataRowCollection contains a DataRow with the same name. (The comparison is not case sensitive.)
ConstraintException	The new DataRow conflicts with an active constraint.
NoNullAllowedException	The new DataRow attempted to place a null value in a column where AllowDBNull is false.

Clear

The Clear method removes all DataRow objects from the DataRowCollection.

Usage

```
myDataRowCollection.Clear()
```

Parameters

None.

Exceptions

None.

Contains

The Contains method returns a Boolean value that indicates whether a DataRow object in the collection contains a DataRow with a primary key equal to the passed object (or array of objects). If the collection contains a DataRow with the requested primary key, True is returned; otherwise, False is returned.

Usage

```
myBoolean = myDataRowCollection.Contains(myObject)
myBoolean = myDataRowCollection.Contains(myObjectArray)
```

Parameters

`myObject`	Object to compare to the primary key values in the DataRowCollection.
`myObjectArray`	An Array of objects to compare to the primary key values in the DataRowCollection.

Exceptions

MissingPrimaryKeyException	The DataTable containing the collection has no primary key.
FormatException	String was not properly formatted (if passing a String). (Note: This exception appears to be raised whenever you pass a string, when the primary key column is a different type.)

CopyTo

The CopyTo method (inherited from System.Data.InternalDataCollectionBase) is used to copy the DataRow objects in the DataRowCollection to an array. (Please see System.Data.InternalDataCollectionBase for more information.)

Usage

```
myDataRowCollection.CopyTo(myDataRowArray, myStartIndex)
```

Parameters

`myDataRowArray`	The passed buffer array to hold the DataRow objects.
`myStartIndex`	The Integer index designating the location in the passed array to begin filling with the DataRow objects.

Exceptions

ArgumentException	The passed array was not long enough to hold the passed objects.
ArgumentNullException	The passed array is null (`Nothing` in Visual Basic .NET).
ArgumentOutOfRangeException	myStartIndex is negative or greater than the length of the array.
InvalidCastException	The object type of the collection cannot be cast automatically to the object type of the array.

Count

The read-only Count property (inherited from System.Data.InternalDataCollection-Base) returns an Int32 value specifying the number of DataRows in the DataRow-Collection.

Usage

```
myInt32 = myDataRowCollection.Count
```

Parameters

None.

Exceptions

None.

Find

The Find method returns the DataRow value in the collection that has a primary key equal to the passed object (or array of objects).

Usage

```
myDataRow = myDataRowCollection.Find(myObject)
myDataRow = myDataRowCollection.Find(myObjectArray)
```

Parameters

`myObject`	Object to compare to the primary key values in the DataRowCollection.
`myObjectArray`	An Array of objects to compare to the primary key values in the DataRowCollection.

Exceptions

MissingPrimaryKeyException	The DataTable does not have an assigned primary key.
FormatException	String was not properly formatted (if passing a String). (Note: This exception appears to be raised whenever you pass a string, when the primary key column is a different type.)

GetEnumerator

The GetEnumerator method (inherited from System.Data.InternalDataCollectionBase) returns a System.Collections.IEnumerator object that can be used to iterate over the collection. This method assists in using the For Each - Next (or equivalent statements) to iterate through a collection.

Usage

```
myIEnumerator = myDataRowCollection.GetEnumerator()
```

Parameters

None.

Exceptions

None.

InsertAt

The InsertAt method inserts a DataRow into the collection at the specified index.

WARNING If you specify an index larger than the current count, the DataRow will be added to the collection at the end. If you later attempt to retrieve the DataRow using that index, an IndexOutOfRangeException will be thrown.

Usage

```
myDataRowCollection.InsertAt(myDataRow, intIndex)
```

Parameters

`myDataRow`	The DataRow to insert into the DataRowCollection.
`intIndex`	Integer specifying the location to add the DataRow.

Exceptions

ArgumentException	The DataRow already belongs to the DataTable.
IndexOutOfRangeException	The insert position is not valid (only negative numbers will throw this exception).

IsReadOnly

The read-only IsReadOnly property returns a Boolean value specifying whether the DataRowCollection is read only. This property is inherited directly from the Internal-DataCollectionBase class. (Please see System.Data.InternalDataCollectionBase for more information.)

Usage

```
myBoolean = myDataRowCollection.IsReadOnly
```

Parameters

None.

Exceptions

None.

IsSynchronized

The read-only IsSynchronized property (inherited from System.Data.InternalData-CollectionBase) returns a Boolean value indicating whether the DataRowCollection is currently synchronized. For information on synchronizing the DataRowCollection, see the DataRowCollection.SyncRoot property.

Usage

```
myBoolean = myDataRowCollection.IsSynchronized
```

Parameters

None.

Exceptions

None.

Item

The read-only Item property returns a DataRow object from the collection, as indicated by the passed Integer index value. (This is different from most of the collection classes, in that you cannot pass a String. This makes sense, however, because DataRow objects are unnamed.)

Usage

```
myDataRow = myDataRowCollection.Item(intIndex)
```

Parameters

`intIndex`	Integer specifying the index of the desired DataRow.

Exceptions

IndexOutOfRangeException	The passed integer is outside the bounds of the collection.

Remove

The Remove() method removes a specified DataRow object from the DataRowCollection. To remove the row you must pass the DataRow object itself.

This is somewhat similar to using the Delete method of the DataRow object. The Remove method makes the DataRow completely unavailable, whereas the Delete method marks only the DataRow for deletion. Calling Remove is equivalent to calling DataRow.Delete followed by AcceptChanges.

Usage

```
myDataRowCollection.Remove(myDataRow)
```

Parameters

`myDataRow`	The DataRow object to remove.

Exceptions

ArgumentNullException	The DataRow argument is a null reference (`Nothing` in Visual Basic).
ArgumentException	The DataRow does not belong to the collection.

RemoveAt

The RemoveAt() method removes a DataRow object from the DataRowCollection specified by the passed index of the DataRow.

This is somewhat similar to using the Delete method of the DataRow object. The RemoveAt method makes the DataRow completely unavailable, whereas the Delete method marks only the DataRow for deletion. Calling RemoveAt is equivalent to calling DataRow.Delete followed by AcceptChanges.

Usage

```
myDataRowCollection.RemoveAt(intIndex)
```

Parameters

`intIndex`	Integer specifying the index of the DataRow to remove.

Exceptions

ArgumentException	A DataTable does not exist at the desired index.

SyncRoot

The read-only SyncRoot property returns a System.Object object that can be used to Synchronize the DataRowCollection. (Please see System.Data.InternalDataCollection-Base for more information.)

Usage

```
myObject = myDataRowCollection.SyncRoot
```

Parameters

None.

Exceptions

None.

ToString

The ToString method returns "System.Data.DataRowCollection".

Usage

```
myString = myDataRowCollection.ToString()
```

Parameters

None.

Exceptions

None.

System.Data.DataRowState

The DataRowState enumeration provides the values that reflect the state of a DataRow. Use this enumeration to determine if a DataRow has been altered, deleted, or added or, in the case of the DataSet.GetChanges method, to filter the returned data.

Because this class implements the FlagsAttribute, bitwise combinations of values are allowed.

DataRowState Enumeration

Added (4)	DataRow has been added to a DataRowCollection, and AcceptChanges has not been called.
Deleted (8)	The DataRow has been deleted using the DateRow.Delete method.
Detached (1)	The DataRow is not part of any DataRowCollection. A DateRow is in this state before it has been added to a DataTable, or if it has been removed from a DataTable.

Modified(16)	The DataRow has been modified, and AcceptChanges has not been called.
Unchanged(2)	The DataRow has not changed since AcceptChanges was last called.

System.Data.DataRowVersion

The DataRowVersion enumeration provides the values that describe what versions of a DataRow exist (for instance, whether a DataRow exists in current, original, or proposed versions). This enumeration is used in the values of the DataRow.Item property or DataRow.GetChildRows method.

Because this class implements the FlagsAttribute, bitwise combinations of values are allowed.

The available versions of a DataRow change depending on the state the DataRow is currently in. The changes occur in the following manner:

Method	Result
DataRow.BeginEdit	If a value has changed, the Current and Proposed values become available.
DataRow.CancelEdit	The Proposed value is discarded.
DataRow.EndEdit	The Proposed value becomes the Current value.
DataRow.AcceptChanges	The Proposed value becomes the Current value, and the Original value remains as before the changes.
DataTable.AcceptChanges	The Original value is set to the Current (changed) value.
DataRow.RejectChanges	The Proposed value is discarded.

DataRowVersion Enumeration

Current (512)	The DataRow contains current values.
Default(1536)	The DataRow contains its default values. (Note: This is a bitwise combination of Current and Proposed.)
Original(256)	The DataRow contains its original values.
Proposed(1024)	The DataRow contains a proposed value.

System.Data.DataRowView

The DataRowView class represents a customized view of a DataRow. DataRowView objects are associated with a given DataRow object. The customized display of the DataRow is done through the DataRowView object. This is important because only one version of a DataRow can be displayed at any one time. The DataRowView can display the DataRow as one of four different states: Default, Original, Current, and Proposed.

When dealing with a DataRowView object, be aware that there is often little distinction placed between the DataRowView object and the DataRow it deals with. For instance, placing the DataRowView in edit mode also places the corresponding DataRow in edit mode as well. Likewise, retrieving or changing values for a DataRowView, using the Item property, is actually manipulating the underlying DataRow.

Constructors

No public constructors.

Parameters

None.

DataRowView Sample Code

```
'This function demonstrates the DataRowView class
'  It assumes a valid DataTable is passed.
'  The table contains two rows, the first an Int32 value,
'  the second a String.
Public Sub DemoDataRowView(ByVal myDataTable As DataTable)
   Dim myDataRowView As DataRowView
   Dim myDataView As DataView

   'add two rows to the table
   myDataTable.Rows.Add(New Object(1) {1, "Hello"})
   myDataTable.Rows.Add(New Object(1) {2, "Guten Tag"})
   myDataTable.AcceptChanges()

   'get the DataView associated with the DataTable
   myDataView = myDataTable.DefaultView

   'get the DataRowView for the first DataRow
   myDataRowView = myDataView.Item(0)

   'show some of the properties
   MessageBox.Show("Edit mode = " + _
         myDataRowView.IsEdit.ToString)
   MessageBox.Show("Newly added = " + _
         myDataRowView.IsNew.ToString)

   'demonstrate how changing a column value in the
   '  DataRowView changes the column in the DataRow
   MessageBox.Show(myDataTable.Rows(0).Item(1).ToString)
   myDataRowView.BeginEdit()
   '  shot the change in the edit mode
   MessageBox.Show("Edit mode = " + _
         myDataRowView.IsEdit.ToString)
```

```
    myDataRowView.Item(1) = "Bonjour"
    myDataRowView.EndEdit()

    MessageBox.Show(myDataTable.Rows(0).Item(1).ToString)

    'accept the changes at the DataTable, since
    '  DataRowView has no AcceptChanges method
    myDataTable.AcceptChanges()


End Sub
```

Members

BeginEdit

The BeginEdit method begins an edit operation on a DataRowView (and corresponding DataRow). This method is identical to the DataRow.BeginEdit method. It suspends all events so that edits that violate validation rules can be made. For instance, if several rows tracking percentages must sum to 100 percent, then by placing all the rows in edit mode the changes can be made. When EndEdit has been called on each of the rows, the validation rules fire.

When in the edit mode, you can retrieve the original and newly changed values of a column by passing DataRowVersion.Original or DataRowVersion.Proposed in the Item property. To determine if a row has a version, you can call the HasVersion method.

To cancel all unaccepted edits on the DataRowView, call the CancelEdit method. To accept the edits, call the EndEdit method.

Usage

```
myDataRowView.BeginEdit()
```

Parameters

None.

Exceptions

None.

CancelEdit

The CancelEdit method cancels an edit operation on a DataRowView (and corresponding DataRow) and takes it out of edit mode. For more information on edit mode, see BeginEdit.

Usage

```
myDataRowView.CancelEdit()
```

Parameters

None.

Exceptions

None.

CreateChildView

The CreateChildView method returns the DataView associated with the DataRowView object's child, given a DataRelation. Basically, if the DataRow associated with this DataRowView object is involved as a parent in a DataRelation, this method will return the DataView of the child DataTable.

This is very useful when a change in the parent view should result in a change in the view of the child as well. CreateChildView is a convenient way of eliminating multiple steps that would otherwise be required to get at the child DataView.

Usage

```
myDataView = myDataRowView.CreateChildView(myDataRelation)
myDataView = myDataRowView.CreateChildView(strRelationName)
```

Parameters

`myDataRelation`	A DataRelation object that has the DataRow associated with the current DataRowView as a parent.
`strRelationName`	A String representing the desired DataRelation.

Exceptions

RowNotInTableException	The DataRow does not belong to the DataTable designated in the DataRelation.
ArgumentNullException	The DataRelation is null (`Nothing` in Visual Basic .NET).
ArgumentException	The DataRelation and DataRow do not belong to the same table.

DataView

The read-only DataView property returns the DataView object that contains the current DataRowView.

Usage

```
myDataView = myDataRowView.DataView
```

Parameters

None.

Exceptions

None.

Delete

The Delete method deletes the row from the table by setting the RowState to Deleted. The deletion can be cancelled at any time before AcceptChanges is called, by calling RejectChanges on the DataRowView, parent DataView, or parent DataSet.

Usage

```
myDataRowView.Delete()
```

Parameters

None.

Exceptions

DeletedRowInaccessibleException	Delete was called on a deleted row.

EndEdit

The EndEdit method ends the edit on a DataRowView (and corresponding DataRow) and takes it out of edit mode. For more information on edit mode, see BeginEdit.

Usage

```
myDataRowView.EndEdit()
```

Parameters

None.

Exceptions

InRowChangingEventException	EndEdit was called inside the RowChanging event.
ConstraintException	The performed edit violated a constraint.
ReadOnlyException	An attempt was made to change the value of a read-only column, while the row belonged to a table.
NoNullAllowedException	The edit attempted to place a null value in a column where AllowDBNull is false.

IsEdit

The read-only IsEdit property returns a Boolean value specifying whether the DataRowView (and corresponding DataRow) is in edit mode. IsEdit returns True if the DataRowView is in edit mode; otherwise, it returns False.

Usage

```
myBoolean = myDataRowView.IsEdit
```

Parameters

None.

Exceptions

None.

IsNew

The read-only IsNew property returns a Boolean value specifying whether the DataRowView is new. IsNew returns True if the DataRowView is new, False otherwise.

Usage

```
myBoolean = myDataRowView.IsNew
```

Parameters

None.

Exceptions

None.

Item

The Item property returns or sets the data stored in a designated DataColumn of the related DataRow.

Usage

```
myObject = myDataRowView.Item(intIndex)
myObject = myDataRowView.Item(strName)

myDataRow.Item(intIndex) = myObject
myDataRow.Item(strName) = myObject
```

Parameters

`intIndex`	The Integer index of the desired DataColumn.
`strName`	The name of the desired DataColumn as a String.

Exceptions

IndexOutOfRangeException	The specified column cannot be found.
DeletedRowInaccessibleException	The row was deleted.

Row

The read-only Row property returns the DataRow object that is associated with this DataRowView.

Usage

```
myDataRow = myDataRowView.Row
```

Parameters

None.

Exceptions

None.

RowVersion

The read-only RowVersion property returns a DataRowVersion enumeration value that describes the current version of the DataRowView.

Usage

```
myDataRowVersion = myDataRowView.RowVersion
```

Parameters

None.

DataRowVersion Enumeration

Current (512)	The DataRowView contains current values.
Default (1536)	The DataRowView contains its default values. (Note: This is a bitwise combination of Current and Proposed.)
Original (256)	The DataRowView contains its original values.
Proposed (1024)	The DataRowView contains a proposed value.

Exceptions

None.

ToString

The ToString method returns a "System.Data.DataRowView".

Usage

```
myString = myDataRowView.ToString()
```

Parameters

None.

Exceptions

None.

System.Data.DataSet

The DataSet class is the central class for the System.Data namespace and, arguably, ADO.NET itself. It is the pure data representation, expressible in XML, and unlinked to any particular data source. The majority of data manipulation in .NET is done through the DataSet and its contained objects.

A DataSet is an in-memory representation of a relational database structure, complete with tables, relationships, and constraints. It is not tied to any one particular database implementation. A programmer can use either the object model or SQL commands to access and manipulate the stored data.

More specifically, a DataSet is a collection of DataTable objects, connected by DataRelation objects, and constrained by Constraint objects.

NOTE **Because the DataSet, DataTable, DataColumn, and DataView objects are so central to ADO.NET data manipulation, and their methods and properties are so extensive, an entire tutorial chapter has been dedicated to their use. Duplicating the code for each object independently would not be as clear as demonstrating the use of these objects acting in concert. Thus, sample code will not be provided for the majority of this object. For code examples please see Chapter 11.**

Constructors

```
Dim myDataSet As New DataSet()
Dim myDataSet As New DataSet(strName)
```

Parameters

`strName`	Name of the DataSet, as a String.

DataSet Sample Code

```
'Because the DataSet is so key to ADO.NET, sample code is
'  provided in detail in Chapter 11, a tutorial chapter.
```

Members

AcceptChanges

The AcceptChanges method commits all the changes to the DataSet that have been made since the last AcceptChanges method was called. Calling AcceptChanges at the DataSet forces AcceptChanges to be called at the DataTable level, which in turn causes each DataRow to call AcceptChanges. Calling AcceptChanges at the DataRow level causes the DataRow.RowState property to change as well. Added and Modified DataRow objects become Unchanged, and Deleted DataRow objects are removed from the DataTable.

If any DataRow objects are in an edit mode (BeginEdit has been called), AcceptChanges will end the edit and successfully accept all of the updates. Because DataRow objects in an edit mode do not yet verify their contents with Foreign Key constraints, calling AcceptChanges may trigger the AcceptRejectRule to be applied.

See RejectChanges to force child DataRow objects to reject changes, and roll back any changes made while still in an edit mode.

NOTE Although the AcceptChanges method occurs at a hierarchy of levels, you cannot use RejectChanges at a higher level to roll back changes accepted at a lower level. Calling AcceptChanges on a DataRow will permanently accept those changes, despite calling RejectChanges at the DataSet level.

Usage

```
myDataSet.AcceptChanges()
```

Parameters

None.

Exceptions

None.

BeginInit

The BeginInit method locks the DataSet object, so that it cannot be accessed until the EndInit method is called. This is mainly used by visual development environments (such as Visual Studio .NET) to ensure that the object is not used before all values have been set accurately and the object is ready for use. It has use only in a multithreaded environment, where a process could attempt to use the DataSet before it has been fully initialized.

Usage

```
myDataSet.BeginInit()
```

Parameters
None.

Exceptions
None.

CaseSensitive

The CaseSensitive property returns or sets a Boolean value indicating whether the string comparisons made within the collection of DataTable objects are case sensitive. This property affects how sorting, searching, and filtering operations are conducted. The default value for newly created DataSet objects is False.

When setting this value, by default, all of the DataTable objects in the DataSet will have their CaseSensitive properties set to the same value.

NOTE **When this value is False, string comparisons are actually conditionally case sensitive. See the System.Data.DataTable introduction for more information.**

Usage

```
myBoolean = myDataSet.CaseSensitive
myDataSet.CaseSensitive = myBoolean
```

Parameters
None.

Exceptions
None.

Clear

The Clear method removes all the DataRow objects from the DataTable objects in the DataSet, thus removing all the data from the DataSet. The schema from the DataSet is not removed, however, so all tables, relationships, and constraints remain intact.

To remove the data and schema from the DataSet, use the Reset method.

Usage

```
myDataSet.Clear()
```

Parameters
None.

Exceptions
None.

Clone

The Clone method returns a DataSet object that contains the structure, but not the data, of the cloned DataSet. The returned DataSet will have the identical schemas, relations, and constraints.

See the Copy method for information on copying both structure and data.

NOTE **Be aware that any objects (tables, constraints, etc.) will have the same names in both DataSet objects. This is not a problem because object names across DataSet objects do not have to be unique, but it can be confusing.**

Usage

```
myDataSet = myDataSet.Clone()
```

Parameters

None.

Exceptions

None.

Container

The read-only Container property returns the object implementing the System.ComponentModel.IContainer interface that contains the DataSet. If the DataSet is not contained, then the Container method returns a null reference (`Nothing` in Visual Basic .NET).

Usage

```
myIContainer = myDataSet.Container
```

Parameters

None.

Exceptions

None.

Copy

The Copy method returns a DataSet object that contains the structure and data of the copied DataSet. The returned DataSet will have the identical schemas, relations, and constraints, as well as an identical copy of the data.

See the Clone method for information on copying only the structure of the DataSet.

NOTE **Be aware that any objects (tables, constraints, etc.) will have the same names in both DataSet objects. This is not a problem because contained object names do not have to be unique across DataTable objects, but it can be confusing.**

Usage

```
myDataSet = myDataSet.Copy()
```

Parameters

None.

Exceptions

None.

DataSetName

The DataSetName property returns or sets the name of the DataSet as a String.

Usage

```
myString = myDataSet.DataSetName
myDataSet.DataSetName = myString
```

Parameters

None.

Exceptions

None.

DefaultViewManager

The read-only DefaultViewManager property returns a DataViewManager object that allows the creation of custom views for each of the contained DataTable objects. The returned DataViewManager maintains a collection of DataViewSetting objects, each of which is tied to a particular DataTable in the DataSet. This DataViewManager is automatically created with the DataSet and is modified when DataTable objects are added or removed from the DataSet.

Use the returned object to manipulate the way tables are sorted and filtered when viewed in a data-bound control. (See System.Data.DataViewSetting for more information.)

HINT **Use the returned DataViewManager object's CreateDataView method to return a DataView that inherits the sort and filter properties of the DataViewSetting object associated with a DataTable. This will work, whereas the DataTable.DefaultView method will not inherit the properties of the DataViewSetting. (See System.Data.DataTable.DefaultView for more information.)**

Usage

```
myDataViewManager = myDataSet.DefaultViewManager
```

Parameters

None.

Exceptions

None.

DesignMode

The read-only DesignMode property (inherited from System.ComponentModel.MarshalByValueComponent) returns a Boolean value specifying whether the object is currently in design mode. If the object is not hosted in a development environment, this property will always return False.

Usage

```
myBoolean = myDataSet.DesignMode
```

Parameters
None.

Exceptions
None.

Dispose

The Dispose method (inherited from System.ComponentModel.MarshalByValueComponent) releases all resources used by the DataSet.

Usage
```
myDataSet.Dispose()
```

Parameters
None.

Exceptions
None.

Disposed

The Disposed event is fired whenever the Dispose method has been called on the object.

Usage
```
Private Sub myDataSet_Disposed(ByVal sender As Object, _
    ByVal e As System.EventArgs) _
    Handles myDataSet.Disposed

End Sub
```

Parameters

`sender`	Contains a reference to the originator of the event.
`e`	Contains the System.EventArgs object containing no useful information.

Exceptions
None.

EndInit

The EndInit method unlocks the DataSet object, so that it can be accessed after the BeginEdit method has been called. This is mainly used by visual development environments (such as Visual Studio .NET) to ensure that the object is not used before all values have been set accurately and the object is ready for use. It has use only in a multi-threaded environment, where another process could attempt to use the DataSet before it has been fully initialized.

Usage
```
myDataSet.EndInit()
```

Parameters
None.

Exceptions
None.

EnforceConstraints

The EnforceConstraints property returns or sets a Boolean value specifying whether the constraint rules should be followed when attempting to update the data. The default value is True.

Usage
```
myBoolean = myDataSet.EnforceConstraints
myDataSet.EnforceConstraints = myBoolean
```

Parameters
None.

Exceptions

ConstraintException	Fired when setting EnforceConstraints to True and one or more constraints cannot be enforced.

ExtendedProperties

The read-only ExtendedProperties property returns a PropertyCollection object that allows you to store custom information with the object. Although the property itself is read-only, you may add properties to the returned PropertyCollection with the Add method. See the Sample Code for an example.

NOTE If the ExtendedProperties collection is to be persisted as XML, then the members of the collection must be of type String.

Usage
```
myPropertyCollection = myDataSet.ExtendedProperties
```

Parameters
None.

Exceptions
None.

Sample Code
```
myDataSet.ExtendedProperties.Add("EasterEggKey", "Ctrl-Alt-Q")
```

GetChanges

The GetChanges method returns a DataSet object that contains all of the changes that were made since the original DataSet was loaded or since AcceptChanges was last called. A DataRowState enumeration can be passed to limit the returned changes to specific states (such as Added or Modified DataRow objects). The DataRowState enumeration allows a bitwise combination of its values.

See HasChanges for determining whether the DataSet has unaccepted changes.

WARNING **Relationship constraints may force DataRow objects that are Unchanged to be included in the collection.**

Usage

```
myDataSet = myDataSet.GetChanges()
myDataSet = myDataSet.GetChanges(myDataRowState)
```

Parameters

`myDataRowState`	A DataRowState enumeration value.

DataRowState Enumeration

Added (4)	DataRow has been added to a DataRowCollection, and AcceptChanges has not been called.
Deleted (8)	The DataRow has been deleted using the DataRow.Delete method.
Detached (1)	The DataRow is not part of any DataRowCollection. A DataRow is in this state before it has been added to a DataTable or if it has been removed from a DataTable.
Modified (16)	The DataRow has been modified and AcceptChanges has not been called.
Unchanged (2)	The DataRow has not changed since AcceptChanges was last called.

Exceptions

None.

GetService

The GetService method returns an Object that implements the IServiceProvider interface. This object is used to provide custom support to the calling object through the use of a custom-built server.

This method is almost exclusively used to support Visual Studio .NET.

Usage

```
myObject = myDataSet.GetService(myServiceType)
```

Parameters

myServiceType	A System.Type that defines the requested service.

Exceptions

None.

GetXml

The GetXml method returns a String representing the data in the DataSet in XML. This method will not include the schema in the output string. Its output is equivalent to the WriteXml method, with the XmlWriteMode set to IgnoreSchema.

Because the output of this method is a string, it can be very convenient; however, it requires more overhead than the WriteXml method.

Chapter 12, "Integrating XML with ADO.NET," is a tutorial specifically covering ADO.NET and XML. Please see Chapter 12 for several XML examples with sample code.

Usage

```
myString = myDataSet.GetXml()
```

Parameters

None.

Exceptions

None.

GetXmlSchema

The GetXmlSchema method returns a String representing the DataSet's schema in XML in the XSD (XML Schema Definition) format. By simply creating a DataSet, a schema is defined, so this function will always return a String.

Chapter 12 is a tutorial specifically covering ADO.NET and XML. Please see Chapter 12 for several XML examples with sample code.

Usage

```
myString = myDataSet.GetXmlSchema()
```

Parameters

None.

Exceptions

None.

HasChanges

The HasChanges method returns a Boolean value indicating whether the DataSet contains changes that were made since the DataSet was loaded or since AcceptChanges was last called. A DataRowState enumeration can be passed to limit the returned changes to specific states (such as Added or Modified DataRow objects). The DataRowState enumeration allows a bitwise combination of its values.

See GetChanges for returning a DataSet object containing only the changes.

Usage

```
myDataSet = myDataSet. HasChanges()
myDataSet = myDataSet. HasChanges(myDataRowState)
```

Parameters

`myDataRowState`	A DataRowState enumeration value.

Exceptions

None.

HasErrors

The read-only HasErrors property returns a Boolean value indicating whether the DataSet contains any DataRow objects that have errors. Basically, if the DataRow.HasErrors property is true for any DataRow in any DataTable in the DataSet, the

DataSet.HasErrors property will return True. It is a good idea to check the HasErrors property and reconcile any errors before updating a data source.

See the DataTable.GetErrors method to return an array of DataRow objects that have errors.

Usage

```
myBoolean = myDataSet.HasErrors
```

Parameters

None.

Exceptions

None.

InferXmlSchema

The InferXmlSchema method infers a schema from an XML document and applies it to the current DataSet. If there is an attached or inline schema provided by the XML document, it is ignored. This method allows any number of namespaces to be ignored while inferring the schema.

If the DataSet already has a schema, the incoming schema will be merged with the current schema. Of course, if there are duplicate table names, constraints that violate current data, or any other similar problems, an exception will be raised.

The XML document is accessed by passing a Stream, file name, TextReader, or XmlReader object. You cannot simply pass a String containing the XML document.

NOTE If you do not need to ignore any namespaces and the XML document does not contain a schema, using the ReadXmlSchema method is generally simpler. It will infer the schema from the document, without the need to specify namespaces to be excluded.

Chapter 12 is a tutorial specifically covering ADO.NET and XML. Please see Chapter 12 for several XML examples with sample code.

For specific information on how the DataSet schema is actually inferred from an XML data source, search in MSDN for "Inferring DataSet Relational Structure from XML."

Usage

```
myDataSet.InferXmlSchema(myStream, strNameSpaceArray)
myDataSet.InferXmlSchema(strFileName, strNameSpaceArray)
myDataSet.InferXmlSchema(myTextReader, strNameSpaceArray)
myDataSet.InferXmlSchema(myXmlReader, strNameSpaceArray)
```

Parameters

`myStream`	The System.IO.Stream object from which to read the XML document.
`strNameSpaceArray`	An array of String objects containing the namespace URI strings to be excluded from schema.
`strFileName`	The filename (including path) of the XML document from which to infer the schema.

`myTextReader`	A System.IO.TextReader object that contains the XML document.
`myXmlReader`	A System.Xml.XmlReader object that contains the XML document.

Exceptions

System.Xml.XmlException	The incoming XML Document is not well formed or cannot be parsed.

Sample Code

```
'Code snipped (some objects need to be defined before using)
'This will exclude any elements or attibutes that are specific
'  to the officedata namespace.
myDataSet.InferXmlSchema("myXMLFile.xml", _
     New String() {"urn:schemas-microsoft-com:officedata"})

'This will infer the schema without excluding any namespace
myDataSet.InferXmlSchema("myXMLFile.xml", New String[] {""})
```

Locale

The Locale property returns or sets a System.Globalization.CultureInfo value that returns information about the locale of the user's machine. This value is used to determine how to compare strings. The default value is null (`Nothing` in Visual Basic .NET).

Usage

```
myCultureInfo = myDataSet.Locale
myDataSet.Locale = myCultureInfo
```

Parameters

None.

Exceptions

None.

Merge

The Merge method merges the current DataSet with a passed DataSet, DataTable, or DataRow object. All objects must have a similar schema in order to merge properly. This method is most often used when refreshing client data with changes that have occurred in the data source, so having a similar, if not identical, schema is likely.

Like any topic dealing with concurrency issues, merging can be an extremely complex undertaking. There are numerous issues to keep in mind and many options for changing how the merge operation takes place. We recommend a thorough understanding of the Merge method before using it willy-nilly in a production application.

To understand how merging takes place, let's look at a brief scenario. Assume we have a data source with a table that includes an auto increment field. After creating a DataSet, we are effectively disconnected from that data source. When we update the data source with newly added DataRow objects, these will be added as rows in the data source. Our DataSet will not have the proper values in the auto increment fields, however, because the DataSet cannot generate auto increment fields that are guaranteed to be unique at the data source. So after we update the data source, we need to retrieve the values of the fields that were incremented. We could do this by emptying our DataSet and reissuing the SQL command through our DataAdapter.Fill method to refill it with new data. (Indeed, this is an approach often used when connected to a data source.) This approach, though, can be very expensive. Instead, we can retrieve a DataSet with only the changes to the data source, then merge those back into our DataSet, minimizing the required amount of data that must be passed.

To control how the merging takes place, you may pass a Boolean parameter specifying whether changes to the original DataSet should be preserved when merging. The default value of this parameter is False, meaning any changes to the original DataSet will be lost. Technically, this means that the DataRow stored in the Current row state will be overwritten by the incoming data. By passing a value of True, changes to the original DataSet are preserved. Technically, this works by overwriting the Original row state of the DataRow with the merged value, while leaving the value in the Current row state in its changed value.

For an example, see the following table, which shows how the DataSet will be updated based on this setting. Assume that a data-entry specialist has downloaded the profile of one of the authors and notices that the first name is spelled incorrectly (or is using an alternate spelling not used by the author). He or she simply makes the editing change to the preferred name. Meanwhile, someone changes the data source to correct the name as well. If preserving changes, when the next AcceptChanges is called, the DataSet will change the name to "Steve". If it is not set, then the DataSet will change the name to "Steven".

	ORIGINAL DATASET	MERGING DATA	POST-MERGE WITH PRESERVE CHANGES	POST-MERGE WITHOUT PRESERVE CHANGES
Original value	"Stephen"	"Steven"	"Steven"	"Stephen"
Current value	"Steve"	*N/A*	"Steve"	"Steven"

Another parameter that impacts the way that the merge is conducted is the MissingSchemaAction parameter. This parameter specifies what to do when there are schema elements in the incoming data that are not present in the original DataSet. The values of the MissingSchemaAction enumeration allow you to specify whether the schema should be added or ignored or whether an exception should be thrown.

One final consideration when dealing with the Merge method is that the constraints on the DataSet are not enforced until after the merge is complete. Once the data has been merged, the constraints are checked against the Current values of the DataRow objects. Ensure that you are prepared to handle any of the generated exceptions that may occur if constraints have been violated.

Because of the difficulty in concisely demonstrating the many facets of the Merge method, a code sample will not be included here. Please see Chapter 11 for a complete merge example with sample code.

Usage

```
myDataSet.Merge(myDataRowArray)
myDataSet.Merge(myDataSet)
myDataSet.Merge(myDataTable)
myDataSet.Merge(myDataSet, boolPreserveChanges)
myDataSet.Merge(myDataRowArray, boolPreserveChanges, _
     myMissingSchemaAction)
myDataSet.Merge(myDataSet, boolPreserveChanges, _
     myMissingSchemaAction)
myDataSet.Merge(myDataTable, boolPreserveChanges, _
     myMissingSchemaAction)
```

Parameters

`myDataRowArray`	Array of DataRow objects containing the data to merge.
`myDataSet`	DataSet object containing the data to merge.
`myDataTable`	DataTable object containing the data to merge.
`boolPreserveChanges`	Boolean that determines whether the changes made to the original DataSet should be preserved.
`myMissingSchemaAction`	A MissingSchemaAction enumeration value determining how the merge should handle additional schema information from the incoming date.

MissingSchemaAction Enumeration

Add (1)	Adds the columns to the schema.
AddWithKey (4)	Adds the columns and primary key information to the schema.
Error (3)	Forces a System.SystemException to be thrown.
Ignore (2)	Ignores the extra columns (data will not be appended to the DataSet).

Exceptions

ConstraintException	Merged data violates one or more constraints.
ArgumentNullException	A passed DataSet, DataTable, or array of DataRow objects was null (`Nothing` in Visual Basic .NET).
SystemException	MissingSchemaAction is set to Error, and a schema was missing.

MergeFailed

The MergeFailed event is fired whenever an update occurs where the source and target DataRow objects share the same primary key value and EnforceConstraints is True. The event sends a MergeFailedEventArgs class that provides information about the event to the event handler.

Usage

```
Private Sub myDataSet_MergeFailed(ByVal sender As Object, _
        ByVal e As System.Data.MergeFailedEventArgs) _
        Handles myDataSet.MergeFailed

End Sub
```

Parameters

`sender`	Contains a reference to the originator of the event.
`e`	Contains a System.Data.MergeFailedEventArgs object containing information about the MergeFailed event.

Event Argument Data

e.Conflict	String describing the merge conflict.
e.Table	Returns the DataTable that contains the DataRow with the conflict.

Exceptions

None.

Namespace

The Namespace property returns or sets a String value that is the namespace for the DataSet. This property is used when writing and reading XML documents to and from the DataSet. By assigning separate namespace names to different DataSets, objects with the same name across two DataSet objects can still be differentiated when they are both combined into a single XML document. It also prevents namespace conflicts when reading XML documents that may contain similarly named data but come from a separate namespace.

For more information on namespaces, please see an XML guide or search for "Namespace" in MSDN.

Usage

```
myString = myDataSet.Namespace
myDataSet.Namespace = myString
```

Parameters

None.

Exceptions

None.

Prefix

The Prefix property returns or sets a String value that serves as the namespace prefix that will be used throughout an output XML document. This example XML document shows the namespace prefix "myCo" being used.

```
<myDataSet xmlns:myCo=
"urn:schemas-myCompany-com:myCompanyData">
<myCo:myEmployee>
      <myCo:Name>Sinead McGuinness</Name>
</myCo:myEmployee>
</myDataSet>
```

Usage

```
myString = myDataSet.Prefix
myDataSet.Prefix = myString
```

Parameters

None.

Exceptions

None.

ReadXml

The ReadXml method reads data and schema from an XML document and applies it to the current DataSet. If there is no attached or inline schema provided by the XML document, then the schema is inferred from the XML data itself. If the incoming schema (or inferred schema, if no attached or inline schema exists) conflicts with the existing DataSet schema, an exception is raised. Otherwise, the DataSet schema is extended.

ReadXml can understand schemas in both XDR (XML Data Reduced) and XSD (XML Schema Definition) formats (unlike most of functions in Visual Studio .NET, which interpret only the XSD format).

WARNING **Using XmlReadMode.DiffGram on an XML document that is not in DiffGram format will return an XML document with only an empty element representing the DataSet.**

If the DataSet already has a schema, the incoming schema will be merged with the current schema. Of course, if there are duplicate table names, constraints that violate current data, or any other similar problems, an exception will be raised.

Chapter 12 is a tutorial specifically covering ADO.NET and XML. Please see Chapter 12 for several XML examples with sample code.

Usage

```
myXmlReadMode = myDataSet.ReadXml(myStream)
myXmlReadMode = myDataSet.ReadXml(strFileName)
myXmlReadMode = myDataSet.ReadXml(myTextReader)
myXmlReadMode = myDataSet.ReadXml(myXmlReader)
myXmlReadMode = myDataSet.ReadXml(myStream, myXmlReadMode)
myXmlReadMode = myDataSet.ReadXml(strFileName, myXmlReadMode)
myXmlReadMode = myDataSet.ReadXml(myTextReader, myXmlReadMode)
myXmlReadMode = myDataSet.ReadXml(myXmlReader, myXmlReadMode)
```

Parameters

`myStream`	An object inheriting from the System.IO.Stream object from which to read the XML document.
`strFileName`	The filename (including path) of the XML document from which to read the data.
`myTextReader`	A System.IO.TextReader object that contains the XML document.
`myXmlReader`	A System.Xml.XmlReader object that contains the XML document.
`myXmlReadMode`	A System.Data.XmlReadMode enumeration value that determines how the XML document will be read.

XmlReadMode Enumeration

Auto (0)	(Default) Performs one of the other actions according to the following rules: 1.) If the data is a DiffGram, uses DiffGram value. 2.) If data has a schema, then uses ReadSchema value. 3.) If data does not have schema, uses InferSchema value.
DiffGram (4)	Reads the document as a DiffGram, applying changes from the DiffGram to the DataSet. The target DataSet schema must match the DiffGram schema, or the operation will fail and an exception will be thrown. (Caution: When using DiffGram, the ReadXml should generally be used with data created with WriteXml as a DiffGram.)
Fragment (5)	Reads XML documents containing inline XDR schema fragments. (Usually created when executing FOR XML queries against SQL Server.)
IgnoreSchema (2)	Ignores any inline schema and reads data into the existing DataSet schema. If any data does not match the existing schema, it is discarded. (Note: If the data is a DiffGram, IgnoreSchema is the same as DiffGram.)
InferSchema (3)	Infers schema from the data and loads the data, ignoring any inline schema information. (If the DataSet already contains a schema, the current schema is extended by adding new tables or adding columns to existing tables. An exception is thrown if the inferred table already exists but with a different namespace, or if any of the inferred columns conflict with existing columns.)

ReadSchema (1)	Reads any inline schema and loads the data. If the DataSet already contains schema, new tables are added to the schema, unless any tables in the inline schema already exist in the DataSet, in which case an exception is thrown.

Exceptions

ConstraintException	EnforceConstraints is True, and data from the incoming XML data violates one or more constraints.
System.Xml.XmlException	The incoming XML Document is not well formed or cannot be parsed.

ReadXmlSchema

The ReadXmlSchema method reads a schema from an XML document and applies it to the current DataSet. If there is no attached or inline schema provided by the XML document, then the schema is inferred from the XML data itself. ReadXmlSchema can understand schemas in both XDR (XML Data Reduced) and XSD (XML Schema Definition) formats (unlike most of functions in Visual Studio .NET, which interpret only the XSD format).

If the DataSet already has a schema, the incoming schema will be merged with the current schema. Of course, if there are duplicate table names, constraints that violate current data, or any other similar problems, an exception will be raised.

NOTE This is often the most convenient way to infer schema from an XML document that doesn't have a schema; however, there are limitations. If you need to infer a schema from an XML document and to exclude a namespace or group of namespaces, then use the InferXmlSchema method.

Chapter 12 is a tutorial specifically covering ADO.NET and XML. Please see Chapter 12 for several XML examples with sample code.

Usage

```
myDataSet.ReadXmlSchema(myStream)
myDataSet.ReadXmlSchema(strFileName)
myDataSet.ReadXmlSchema(myTextReader)
myDataSet.ReadXmlSchema(myXmlReader)
```

Parameters

`myStream`	An object inheriting from the System.IO.Stream object from which to read the XML document.
`strFileName`	The filename (including path) of the XML document from which to infer the schema.
`myTextReader`	A System.IO.TextReader object that contains the XML document.
`myXmlReader`	A System.Xml.XmlReader object that contains the XML document.

Exceptions

System.Xml.XmlException	The incoming XML Document is not well formed or cannot be parsed.

RejectChanges

The RejectChanges method rolls back all the changes to the DataSet that have been made since the last AcceptChanges method was called. Calling RejectChanges at the DataSet forces RejectChanges to be called at the DataTable level, which in turn causes each DataRow to call RejectChanges. Calling RejectChanges at the DataRow level causes the DataRow.RowState property to change as well. Deleted and Modified DataRow objects become Unchanged, and Added DataRow objects are removed from the DataTable.

If any DataRow objects are in an edit mode (BeginEdit has been called), Reject-Changes will end the edit and reject all of the updates.

See AcceptChanges to force child DataRow objects to accept changes and commit any changes made while in an edit mode.

NOTE Although the RejectChanges method occurs at a hierarchy of levels, you cannot use AcceptChanges at a higher level to accept changes already rolled back at a lower level. Calling RejectChanges on a DataRow will permanently roll back those changes, despite calling AcceptChanges at the DataSet level.

Usage

```
myDataSet.RejectChanges()
```

Parameters

None.

Exceptions

None.

Relations

The read-only Relations property returns a DataRelationCollection object containing all the DataRelation objects in the DataSet. If no DataRelation objects exist in the DataSet then a null value is returned (`Nothing` in Visual Basic .NET). The DataRelation objects link tables to one another and allow navigation between parent and child tables. (See System.Data.DataRelation for more information.)

Usage

```
myDataRelationCollection = myDataSet.Relations
```

Parameters

None.

Exceptions

None.

Reset

The Reset method clears the DataSet of all tables, relations, constraints, and data. This is similar to the Clear method, except that the schema is deleted as well as the data.

To remove only data from the DataSet, use the Clear method.

Usage

```
myDataSet.Reset()
```

Parameters

None.

Exceptions

None.

Site

The Site property returns or sets a System.ComponentModel.ISite value that specifies the site for the DataSet. A site links a component to its container and allows for storage of information specific to the relationship, such as visual coordinates or component name. It provides a link so that containers can manage their contained components.

Generally, this property is used mainly by Visual Studio .NET and the .NET Framework in the background, and there is little reason to specifically work with this property.

Usage

```
myISite = myDataSet.Site
myDataSet.Site = myISite
```

Parameters

None.

Exceptions

None.

Tables

The read-only Tables property returns a DataTableCollection object containing all the DataTable objects in the DataSet. If no DataTable objects exist in the DataSet then a null value is returned (`Nothing` in Visual Basic .NET).

Usage

```
myDataTableCollection = myDataSet.Tables
```

Parameters

None.

Exceptions

None.

ToString

The ToString method returns "System.Data.DataSet".

Usage

```
myString = myDataSet.ToString()
```

Parameters

None.

Exceptions

None.

WriteXml

The WriteXml method writes data (and possibly the schema) from the DataSet as an XML document. You have some control over how the DataSet is written to XML by passing an XmlWriteMode enumeration value.

Although ReadXml can understand schemas in both XDR (XML Data Reduced) and XSD (XML Schema Definition) formats, WriteXml supports on XSD.

HINT To further control how the XML document is output you can use the DataColumn.ColumnMapping property to specify whether the DataColumn should be output as an attribute, element, or simple text node.

Chapter 12 is a tutorial specifically covering ADO.NET and XML. Please see Chapter 12 for several XML examples with sample code.

Usage

```
myDataSet.WriteXml(myStream)
myDataSet.WriteXml(strFileName)
myDataSet.WriteXml(myTextReader)
myDataSet.WriteXml(myXmlReader)
myDataSet.WriteXml(myStream, myXmlWriteMode)
myDataSet.WriteXml(strFileName, myXmlWriteMode)
myDataSet.WriteXml(myTextWriter, myXmlWriteMode)
myDataSet.WriteXml(myXmlWriter, myXmlWriteMode)
```

Parameters

`myStream`	An object inheriting from the System.IO.Stream object to use in writing the XML document.
`strFileName`	The filename (including path) of the XML document to which to write the data.
`myTextWriter`	A System.IO.TextWriter object to receive the XML document.
`myXmlWriter`	A System.Xml.XmlWriter object to receive the XML document.
`myXmlWriteMode`	A System.Data.XmlWriteMode enumeration value that determines how the XML document will be written.

XmlWriteMode Enumeration

DiffGram (2)	Write the entire DataSet as a DiffGram, including the original and changed values. (This DiffGram can be sent directly to SQL Server 2000.) To retrieve only the changed values, use the DataSet.GetChanges method before calling the WriteXml method.

IgnoreSchema (1)	Writes the entire DataSet as an XML document without an inline schema.
WriteSchema (0)	Writes the entire DataSet as an XML document and includes the DataSet schema as an inline XDR schema. If the DataSet contains only a schema (structure) then only the schema is written. If the DataSet does not have a schema, nothing will be output.

Exceptions
None.

WriteXmlSchema

The WriteXmlSchema method writes the schema of the DataSet as an XML document.

Although ReadXmlSchema can understand schemas in both XDR (XML Data Reduced) and XSD (XML Schema Definition) formats, WriteXmlSchema supports on XSD.

Chapter 12 is a tutorial specifically covering ADO.NET and XML. Please see Chapter 12 for several XML examples with sample code.

Usage

```
myDataSet.WriteXmlSchema(myStream)
myDataSet.WriteXmlSchema(strFileName)
myDataSet.WriteXmlSchema(myTextWriter)
myDataSet.WriteXmlSchema(myXmlWriter)
```

Parameters

`myStream`	An object inheriting from the System.IO.Stream object to use in writing the XML document.
`strFileName`	The filename (including path) of the XML document to which to write the data.
`myTextWriter`	A System.IO.TextWriter object to receive the XML document.
`myXmlWriter`	A System.Xml.XmlWriter object to receive the XML document.

Exceptions
None.

System.Data.DataSysDescriptionAttribute

The DataSysDescriptionAttribute class is used to attach descriptions to properties, events, or extenders. Its primary purpose is to support visual development environments (such as Visual Studio .NET), which can display the Description property when referencing an object with this object attached.

Constructors

```
Dim myDataSysDescriptionAttribute As New _
    DataSysDescriptionAttribute(strDescription)
```

Parameters

`strDescription`	String providing the description for the DescriptionAttribute.

Members

Description

The read-only Description property returns the String value that describes the object.

Usage

```
myString = myDataSysDescriptionAttribute.Description
```

Parameters

None.

Exceptions

None.

IsDefaultAttribute

The IsDefaultAttribute method returns a Boolean specifying whether the value of this object is the default attribute. The default value is False.

Usage

```
myBoolean = myDataSysDescriptionAttribute.IsDefaultAttribute()
```

Parameters

None.

Exceptions

None.

Match

The Match method returns a Boolean indicating whether the passed Object matches the current attribute. In the default implementation, this is identical to the Equals method; however, it can be overridden to allow different comparisons. For instance, Match could be overridden to return True when one particular flag is set the same in both objects, even though all the other flags may differ.

Usage

```
myBoolean = myDataSysDescriptionAttribute.Match(myObject)
```

Parameters

`myObject`	Object to compare to the current object.

Exceptions

None	Anything can be passed to this method; if it doesn't match, False is returned, but no exception is thrown.

ToString

The ToString method returns "System.Data.DataSysDescriptionAttribute".

Usage

```
myString = myDataSysDescriptionAttribute.ToString()
```

Parameters

None.

Exceptions

None.

TypeId

The read-only TypeId property returns an Object object that is a unique identifier for this type of object. As implemented here, this value simply returns the same value as the GetType method (although it could be overridden in a descending class to provide different information).

Usage

```
myObject = myAttribute.TypeId
```

Parameters

None.

Exceptions

None.

System.Data.DataTable

The DataTable class is one of the central classes to ADO.NET. It is also one of the easiest to understand. The DataTable represents a two-dimensional table of in-memory data. It can be thought of as a recordset, very much like an ADO Recordset object (for those familiar with previous versions of ADO). Much as a dataset represents a disconnected relational database, the DataTable represents one table of that data.

By default, a DataTable is conditionally case sensitive. This means that, when comparing strings within the table, if two strings differ only by case, then the match will occur with the case matching data. For instance, if there are two values in a column, CaseSensitive and caseSensitive, a search for "CaseSensitive" will match the row containing the first value. If there is only one value, caseSensitive, then the "CaseSensitive" search will match that value, even though the cases don't match exactly. You can override this behavior by setting the CaseSensitive property to True.

NOTE **Because the DataSet, DataTable, DataColumn, and DataView objects are so central to ADO.NET data manipulation, and because their methods and properties are so extensive, an entire tutorial chapter has been dedicated to their use. Duplicating the code for each object independently would not be as clear as demonstrating the use of these objects acting in concert. Thus, sample code will not be provided for the majority of this object. For code examples, please see Chapter 11.**

Constructors

```
Dim myDataTable As New DataTable()
Dim myDataTable As New DataTable(strName)
```

Parameters

`strName` Name of the DataTable, as a String.

DataTable Sample Code

```
'Since the DataTable is so key to ADO.NET, sample code is
'  provided in detail in Chapter 11, a tutorial chapter.
```

Members

AcceptChanges

The AcceptChanges method commits all the changes to the DataTable that have been made since the last AcceptChanges method was called. Calling AcceptChanges at the DataSet forces AcceptChanges to be called at the DataTable level, which in turn causes each DataRow to call AcceptChanges. Calling AcceptChanges at the DataRow level causes the DataRow.RowState property to change as well. Added and Modified DataRow objects become Unchanged, and Deleted DataRow objects are removed from the DataTable.

If any DataRow objects are in an edit mode (BeginEdit has been called), Accept-Changes will end the edit and successfully accept all of the updates. Because DataRow objects in an edit mode do not yet verify their contents with Foreign Key constraints, calling AcceptChanges may trigger the AcceptRejectRule to be applied.

See RejectChanges to force child DataRow objects to reject changes, and roll back any changes made while still in an edit mode.

NOTE Although the AcceptChanges method occurs at a hierarchy of levels, you cannot use RejectChanges at a higher level to roll back changes accepted at a lower level. Calling AcceptChanges on a DataRow will permanently accept those changes, despite calling RejectChanges at the DataSet level.

Usage

```
myDataTable.AcceptChanges()
```

Parameters
None.

Exceptions
None.

BeginInit

The BeginInit method locks the DataTable object, so that it cannot be accessed until the EndInit method is called. This is mainly used by visual development environments (such as Visual Studio .NET) to ensure that the object is not used before all values have been set accurately and the object is ready for use. It has use only in a multithreaded environment, where a process could attempt to use the DataTable before it has been fully initialized.

Usage

```
myDataTable.BeginInit()
```

Parameters

None.

Exceptions

None.

BeginLoadData

The BeginLoadData method prevents notifications, index maintenance, and activation of constraints while data is loaded. BeginLoadData is used with LoadDataRow and EndLoadData. Use this method to ensure that your data doesn't throw exceptions and other things that might be caused by data not fully loaded. For example, if a column of percentages must add up to 100 percent, this will prevent errors from being thrown on each of the loaded rows until the total reaches 100 percent.

Usage

```
myDataTable.BeginLoadData()
```

Parameters

None.

Exceptions

None.

CaseSensitive

The CaseSensitive property returns or sets a Boolean value indicating whether the string comparisons made within the DataTable are case sensitive. This property affects how sorting, searching, and filtering operations are conducted. The default value for newly created DataTable objects is False.

NOTE **When this value is False, string comparisons are actually conditionally case sensitive. See the DataTable introduction for more information.**

Usage

```
myBoolean = myDataTable.CaseSensitive
myDataTable.CaseSensitive = myBoolean
```

Parameters

None.

Exceptions
None

ChildRelations

The read-only ChildRelations property returns a DataRelationCollection object containing all the child DataRelation objects in the DataSet that affect the DataTable. If no DataRelation objects exist in the DataSet, then null value is returned (`Nothing` in Visual Basic .NET).

The returned collection is made up of all DataRelation objects in which the current DataTable contains a column that was designated as the Parent in a relationship. Thus, the DataRelation objects returned are those that refer to other DataTables containing rows that are the children. This can sometimes be confusing; be sure you understand that the children are being returned, not the relations that exist as child columns from this table.

See ParentRelations for information or retrieving a collection of parent DataRelation objects.

Usage

```
myDataRelationCollection = myDataTable.ChildRelations
```

Parameters
None.

Exceptions
None.

Clear

The Clear method removes all the DataRow objects from the DataTable, thus removing all the data from the DataTable. The schema from the DataTable is not removed, however, so all columns, relationships, and constraints remain intact. An exception is generated if there is a column participating in an enforced relationship that would strand child rows.

To remove the data and schema from the DataTable, use the Reset method.

Usage

```
myDataTable.Clear()
```

Parameters
None.

Exceptions

InvalidConstraintException	Clear operation would strand child rows, violating a ForeignKeyConstraint.

Clone

The Clone method returns a DataTable object that contains the structure, but not the data, of the cloned DataSet. The returned DataSet will have the identical schemas, relations, and constraints.

See the Copy method for information on copying both structure and data.

NOTE **Be aware that any objects (tables, constraints, etc.) will have the same names in both DataSet objects.**

WARNING **You must rename the DataTable if you wish to add it to the same DataSet because each DataTable must have a unique name.**

Usage

```
myDataTable = myDataTable.Clone()
```

Parameters

None.

Exceptions

None.

ColumnChanged

The ColumnChanged event is fired when a value in a DataColumn of a contained DataRow has been changed. Trapping this event provides information on the column and row that were changed, including original data and the proposed changes (which are now actually changed in the DataRow, but can still be rolled back).

Usage

```
Private Sub myDataTable_ColumnChanged(ByVal sender As Object, _
    ByVal e As System.Data.DataColumnChangeEventArgs) _
    Handles myDataTable.ColumnChanged

End Sub
```

Parameters

`sender`	Contains a reference to the originator of the event.
`e`	Contains the System.Data.DataColumnChangeEventArgs object containing information dealing with the changed column.

Exceptions

None.

ColumnChanging

The ColumnChanging event is fired when a value in a DataColumn of a contained DataRow is about to be changed. Trapping this event provides information on the column and row being changed, including current data and proposed changes.

Usage

```
Private Sub myDataTable_ColumnChanging( _
    ByVal sender As Object, _
    ByVal e As System.Data.DataColumnChangeEventArgs) _
    Handles myDataTable.ColumnChanging

End Sub
```

Parameters

`sender`	Contains a reference to the originator of the event.
`e`	Contains the System.Data.DataColumnChangeEventArgs object containing information dealing with the changing column.

Exceptions

None.

Columns

The read-only Columns property returns a DataColumnCollection object containing all the DataColumn objects in the DataTable. If no DataColumn objects exist in the DataTable then a null value is returned (`Nothing` in Visual Basic .NET).

Usage

```
myDataColumnCollection = myDataTable.Columns
```

Parameters

None.

Exceptions

None.

Compute

The Compute method returns an Object that is the result of an aggregation function on a filtered DataColumn. Compute can be used only in aggregation functions and cannot contain expressions that must be evaluated. Thus, you could request the sum of a column named Profit (Sum(Profit)), but not the sum of the difference of two columns (Sum(Income-Expense)).

Usage

```
myObject = myDataTable.Compute(strExpression, strFilter)
```

Parameters

`strExpression`	An aggregate function as a String.
`strFilter`	A filter to limit the number of rows involved in the computation, as a String.

Exceptions

None.

Sample Code

```
'sets myProfit equal to the sum of the Profit column from
'  Division number 12
myProfit = myTable.Compute("Sum(Profit)", "DivID = 12")
```

Constraints

The read-only Constraints property returns a ConstraintCollection object containing all the constraints in the DataTable. If no Constraint objects exist in the DataTable, then a null value is returned (`Nothing` in Visual Basic .NET).

HINT Using the returned ConstraintCollection object's Add method is often the simplest and fastest way to create constraints. Using the Add method shortens and simplifies the constraint creation process by streamlining the declare, construct, and add process to a single method call.

For Sample Code on using this property to manipulate constraints, please see System.Data.ConstraintCollection.

Usage

```
myConstraintCollection = myDataTable.Constraints
```

Parameters

None.

Exceptions

None.

Container

The read-only Container property returns the object implementing the System.ComponentModel.IContainer interface that contains the DataTable. If the DataTable is not contained, then the Container method returns a null reference (`Nothing` in Visual Basic .NET).

Usage

```
myIContainer = myDataTable.Container
```

Parameters

None.

Exceptions

None.

Copy

The Copy method returns a DataTable object that contains the structure and data of the copied DataTable. The returned DataTable will have the identical schemas, relations, and constraints, as well as an identical copy of the data.

See the Clone method for information on copying only the structure of the DataTable.

NOTE Be aware that any objects (tables, constraints, etc.) will have the same names in both DataSet objects.

Usage

```
myDataTable = myDataTable.Copy()
```

Parameters

None.

Exceptions

None.

DataSet

The read-only DataSet property returns the DataSet that contains the current DataTable.

Usage

```
myDataSet = myDataTable.DataSet
```

Parameters

None.

Exceptions

None.

DefaultView

The read-only DefaultView property returns the DataView object that is the default DataView for the DataTable. This DataView can be used to sort and filter the table for display (or for some other purpose).

Despite common sense, this property does not return a DataView filled with properties already assigned to the DataViewSetting associated with this table. (Basically, this property does NOT return the default view.) See the sample code for a recommended work-around using the DataViewManager.CreateDataView method.

WARNING DataView objects and DataViewSetting objects are not compatible. You cannot assign a DataView as a member of a DataViewSettingCollection.

HINT See the sample code for a way to create a DataView that is filled with view options that may have already been set in the associated DataViewSetting.

Usage

```
myDataView = myDataTable.DefaultView
```

Parameters

None.

Exceptions

None.

DefaultView Sample Code

```
'This code snippet demonstrates a work-around allowing you to
'  retrieve a DataView that is already filled with the
'  properties previously set in the DataViewSetting object that
'  is associated with the current DataTable. It assumes the
'  DataTable is a member of a DataSet (otherwise no
'  DataViewSetting object is defined for it).

'This code will NOT return the default view properties
myDataView = myTable.DefaultView
```

```
'Use this code to return a DataView with the properties
'  already set in the DataViewSetting - BETTER option
myDataView =
   myTable.DataSet.DefaultViewManager.CreateDataView(myTable)
```

DesignMode

The read-only DesignMode property (inherited from System.ComponentModel.MarshalByValueComponent) returns a Boolean value specifying whether the object is currently in design mode. If the object is not hosted in a development environment, this property will always return False.

Usage

```
myBoolean = myDataTable.DesignMode
```

Parameters

None.

Exceptions

None.

DisplayExpression

The DisplayExpression property returns or sets a String value that can be used to represent the DataTable in a user interface. The DisplayExpression should be able to dynamically create a value using the current values of rows in the DataTable. For more information on creating valid expressions, see the DataColumn.Expression property. (See the warning that follows!)

WARNING We were never able to get the DisplayExpression property to properly evaluate, unlike the DataColumn.Expression property. It always returned the string assigned, instead of processing the string first. For instance, "Count(myColumn1)" did not return the number of values in myColumn1, but returned "Count(myColumn1)" instead. This is entirely unsatisfactory.

Usage

```
myString = myDataTable.DisplayExpression
myDataTable.DisplayExpression = myString
```

Parameters

None.

Exceptions

ArgumentOutOfRangeException	Either the start or length argument of the SUBSTRING function is out of range.
EvaluateException	1.) Value of DisplayExpression could not be evaluated. 2.) An invalid method call was made from within the expression.

FormatException	CONVERT function cannot convert the passed String to the requested Type.
InvalidCastException	CONVERT function cannot cast to the requested Type.
InvalidExpressionException	The expression is invalid.
SyntaxErrorException	Value of DisplayExpression contains a syntax error.
Exception	The argument passed to the LEN or TRIM functions does not evaluate to a String.

Dispose

The Dispose method (inherited from System.ComponentModel.MarshalByValue-Component) releases all resources used by the DataTable.

Usage

```
myDataTable.Dispose()
```

Parameters

None.

Exceptions

None.

Disposed

The Disposed event is fired whenever the Dispose method has been called on the object.

Usage

```
Private Sub myDataSet_Disposed(ByVal sender As Object, _
    ByVal e As System.EventArgs) _
    Handles myDataSet.Disposed

End Sub
```

Parameters

`sender`	Contains a reference to the originator of the event.
`e`	Contains the System.EventArgs object containing no useful information.

Exceptions

None.

EndInit

The EndInit method unlocks the DataTable object so that it can be accessed after the BeginEdit method had been called. This is mainly used by visual development environments (such as Visual Studio .NET) to ensure that the object is not used before all values have been set accurately and the object is ready for use. It has use only in a multithreaded environment, where a process could attempt to use the DataTable before it has been fully initialized.

Usage

```
myDataTable.EndInit()
```

Parameters

None.

Exceptions

None.

EndLoadData

The EndLoadData method releases the DataTable for notifications, index maintenance, and activation of constraints after a call to BeginLoadData. EndLoadData is used with BeginLoadData and LoadDataRow. (See BeginLoadData for more information on suspending notifications and constraints.)

Usage

```
myDataTable.EndLoadData()
```

Parameters

None.

Exceptions

None.

ExtendedProperties

The read-only ExtendedProperties property returns a PropertyCollection object that allows you to store custom information with the object. Although the property itself is read only, you may add properties to the returned PropertyCollection with the Add method. See the sample code for an example.

NOTE If the ExtendedProperties collection is to be persisted as XML, then the members of the collection must be of type String.

Usage

```
myPropertyCollection = myDataTable.ExtendedProperties
```

Parameters

None.

Exceptions

None.

Sample Code

```
myDataSet.ExtendedProperties.Add("Mother", "Alice Borg")
```

GetChanges

The GetChanges method returns a DataTable object that contains all of the changes that were made since the original DataTable was loaded or since AcceptChanges was last called. A DataRowState enumeration can be passed to limit the returned changes to specific states (such as Added or Modified DataRow objects). The DataRowState enumeration allows a bitwise combination of its values.

WARNING Relationship constraints may force DataRow objects that are unchanged to be included in the collection.

Usage

```
myDataTable = myDataTable.GetChanges()
myDataTable = myDataTable.GetChanges(myDataRowState)
```

Parameters

`myDataRowState`	A DataRowState enumeration value.

DataRowState Enumeration

Added (4)	DataRow has been added to a DataRowCollection, and AcceptChanges has not been called.
Deleted (8)	The DataRow has been deleted using the DataRow.Delete method.
Detached (1)	The DataRow is not part of any DataRowCollection. A DataRow is in this state before it has been added to a DataTable or if it has been removed from a DataTable.
Modified (16)	The DataRow has been modified, and AcceptChanges has not been called.
Unchanged (2)	The DataRow has not changed since AcceptChanges was last called.

Exceptions

None.

GetErrors

The GetErrors method returns an array of DataRow objects that contain all of the DataRow objects that contain errors. Call this method to determine which DataRow objects must be dealt with before updating the DataSet or calling AcceptChanges on the DataTable.

Usage

```
myDataRowArray = myDataTable.GetErrors()
```

Parameters

None.

Exceptions

None.

GetService

The GetService method returns an Object that implements the IServiceProvider interface. This object is used to provide custom support to the calling object through the use of a custom-built server.

This method is almost exclusively used to support Visual Studio .NET.

Usage

```
myObject = myDataTable.GetService(myServiceType)
```

Parameters

`myServiceType`	A System.Type that defines the requested service.

Exceptions

None.

HasErrors

The read-only HasErrors property returns a Boolean value indicating whether the DataTable contains any DataRow objects that have errors. Basically, if the DataRow.HasErrors property is true for any DataRow, the DataTable.HasErrors property will return True. It is a good idea to check the HasErrors property and reconcile any errors, before updating a data source or calling AcceptChanges.

Usage

```
myBoolean = myDataTable.HasErrors
```

Parameters

None.

Exceptions

None.

ImportRow

The ImportRow method imports a passed DataRow into the DataTable, maintaining all of the DataRow values, including the DataRowState, of the imported DataRow. This is different from the NewRow method, which creates a new row with the schema from the DataTable and a DataRowState of Added.

This appears, at first glance, to be a very useful method, and in some cases, it is; however, there are multiple restrictions. First, the row to be imported must come from a DataTable with the same schema as the DataTable that is importing the row. This means the column names must not only have the same data types, but must also have identical names. So, the general way of using this method is to have a clone of the DataTable or import a row from the DataTable doing the import. The second restriction, and a more severe one, is that all of the rows from the table are imported directly and with no changes. This means that if a primary key (or any uniqueness constraint) is defined on the table, a ConstraintException will be raised when the method is called. Because it is already defined as a primary key, you cannot set the value of the key column to null (`Nothing` in Visual Basic .NET) and rely on the DataColumn to provide its default value (like the DataTable.Add method). You can, however, retrieve the row, create a new primary key value, assign it to the primary key field, and then use ImportRow. Realistically, this is feasible only if the primary key value on the field is a GUID; otherwise, you run the risk of duplicating the value. (For small applications, you may be able to get by with a TUID—Town Unique IDentifier.)

Usage

```
myDataTable.ImportRow(myDataRow)
```

Parameters

`myDataRow`	DataRow to be imported into the DataTable.

Exceptions

ConstraintException	The imported row violates a constraint.

ImportRow Sample Code

```
'This function demonstrates the DataTable.ImportRow
'  method.  Many of the pitfalls are included (but
'  constraint issues aren't covered).
Public Sub DemoDataTable_ImportRow()

   Dim myDataTable1 As DataTable
   Dim myDataTable2 As DataTable
   Dim myDataTable3 As DataTable
   Dim myColumnValue As Object

   'create an initial data table
   myDataTable1 = New DataTable("myTable1")
   myDataTable1.Columns.Add("myColumn1", GetType(Int32))
   myDataTable1.Columns.Add("myColumn2", GetType(String))

   'create a new table with the same types
   myDataTable2 = New DataTable("myTable2")
   myDataTable2.Columns.Add("ColumnA", GetType(Int32))
   myDataTable2.Columns.Add("ColumnB", GetType(String))

   'create a clone of myDataTable1
   myDataTable3 = myDataTable1.Clone

   myDataTable1.Rows.Add(New Object() {1, "Hello"})
   myDataTable1.Rows.Add(New Object() {2, "Goodbye"})
   myDataTable1.AcceptChanges()

   myDataTable2.Rows.Add(New Object() {1, "World"})
   myDataTable2.Rows.Add(New Object() {2, "Cruel World"})
   myDataTable2.AcceptChanges()

   myDataTable3.Rows.Add(New Object() {1, "Wonderful World"})
   myDataTable3.Rows.Add(New Object() {2, "Evil, Evil World"})
   myDataTable3.AcceptChanges()

   'attempt to import from myDataTable2, with same
   '  types in each of the columns (but with different column
   '  names).  This will FAIL to import the row values.
   '  (If the the columns had the same names, however, then
   '  would import properly -- the schema must be the same.)
```

```
    myDataTable1.ImportRow(myDataTable2.Rows(0))
    myColumnValue = _
          myDataTable1.Rows(myDataTable1.Rows.Count - 1).Item(1)
    If myColumnValue Is DBNull.Value Then
       MessageBox.Show("Row values did not import!")
    Else
       MessageBox.Show("Value is " + myColumnValue.ToString)
    End If

    'attempt to import from myDataTable3, the clone - SUCCEEDS
    myDataTable1.ImportRow(myDataTable3.Rows(0))
    myColumnValue = _
          myDataTable1.Rows(myDataTable1.Rows.Count - 1).Item(1)
    If myColumnValue Is DBNull.Value Then
       MessageBox.Show("Row values did not import!")
    Else
       MessageBox.Show("Value is " + myColumnValue.ToString)
    End If

    'attempt to import from self - SUCCEEDS
    myDataTable1.ImportRow(myDataTable1.Rows(0))
    myColumnValue = _
          myDataTable1.Rows(myDataTable1.Rows.Count - 1).Item(1)
    If myColumnValue Is DBNull.Value Then
       MessageBox.Show("Row values did not import!")
    Else
       MessageBox.Show("Value is " + myColumnValue.ToString)
    End If

    'Note: if DataTable1 had a primary key defined, this would
    '  not have worked.
End Sub
```

LoadDataRow

The LoadDataRow method accepts an array of objects containing the data to be placed in the DataRow and returns the updated or added DataRow. In addition, you can pass a Boolean value directing the DataRow to immediately AcceptChanges. If the DataRow contains a primary key column and the corresponding object in the array matches a primary key value already in the DataTable, then that DataRow will be updated. If no matching primary key is found, then a new DataRow is created.

When passing the array of objects, you must ensure that each object in the array maps to the DataColumn at the same index location. If you are passing an array into a DataRow that has an auto increment field (or similar field), pass a null object (`Nothing` in Visual Basic .NET) to ensure that the column is filled with the proper value. (DBNull.Value will not work.)

Usage

```
myDataRow = myDataTable.LoadDataRow(myObjectArray,  _
     boolAcceptChanges)
```

Parameters

`myObjectArray`	Array of objects providing the data for each column in the DataRow.
`boolAcceptChanges`	Boolean designating whether the changes should be accepted immediately.

Exceptions

ArgumentException	The array is larger than the number of columns in the DataTable.
InvalidCastException	A passed object value does not match its respective column type.
ConstraintException	The DataRow conflicts with an active constraint.
NoNullAllowedException	The new DataRow attempted to place a null value in a column where AllowDBNull is false.

Locale

The Locale property returns or sets a System.Globalization.CultureInfo value that returns information about the locale of the user's machine. This value is used to determine how to compare strings. The default value is null (`Nothing` in Visual Basic .NET).

Usage

```
myCultureInfo = myDataTable.Locale
myDataTable.Locale = myCultureInfo
```

Parameters

None.

Exceptions

None.

MinimumCapacity

The MinimumCapacity property returns or sets an Integer value specifying the initial number of rows for which to allocate memory. This property does not need to be set, but it can increase performance when accessing large amounts of data. Simply set the value of MinimumCapacity to an approximation of the number of rows to be received (or slightly higher). Then memory doesn't need to be reallocated during the Fill process. The default value is 25.

Usage

```
myInt32 = myDataTable.MinimumCapacity
myDataTable.MinimumCapacity = myInt32
```

Parameters

None.

Exceptions

ArgumentException	Cannot be set to a negative number.

Namespace

The Namespace property returns or sets a String value that is the namespace for the DataTable. This property is used when writing and reading XML documents to and from the DataSet. By assigning separate namespace names to different tables, objects with the same name across two DataTable objects can still be differentiated when they are both combined into a single XML document. It also prevents namespace conflicts when reading XML documents that may contain similarly named data, but that come from a separate namespace.

For more information on namespaces, please see an XML guide or search for "Namespace" in MSDN.

Usage

```
myString = myDataTable.Namespace
myDataTable.Namespace = myString
```

Parameters

None.

Exceptions

None.

NewRow

The NewRow method returns a DataRow object with the same schema as the DataTable. Because DataRow does not have any public constructors, you must use this method to generate a new row. The row can then be filled with data and attached to the table with the DataTable.Rows.Add method.

Usage

```
myDataRow = myDataTable.NewRow()
```

Parameters

None.

Exceptions

None.

ParentRelations

The read-only ParentRelations property returns a DataRelationCollection object containing all the parent DataRelation objects in the DataSet that affect the DataTable. If no DataRelation objects exist in the DataSet, then a null value is returned (`Nothing` in Visual Basic .NET).

The returned collection is made up of all DataRelation objects in which the current DataTable contains a column that was designated as the child in a relationship. Thus, the DataRelation objects returned are those that refer to other DataTables containing rows that are the parents. This can sometimes be confusing; be sure you understand that the parents are being returned, not the relations that exist as parent columns from this table.

See ParentRelations for information or retrieving a collection of parent DataRelation objects.

Usage

```
myDataRelationCollection = myDataTable.ParentRelations
```

Parameters

None.

Exceptions

None.

Prefix

The Prefix property returns or sets a String value that serves as the namespace prefix that will be used throughout an output XML document. The example XML document that follows shows the namespace prefix "myCo" being used.

```
<myDataSet xmlns:myCo=
"urn:schemas-myCompany-com:myCompanyData">
<myCo:myEmployee>
     <myCo:Name>Sinead McGuinness</Name>
</myCo:myEmployee>
</myDataSet>
```

Usage

```
myString = myDataTable.Prefix
myDataTable.Prefix = myString
```

Parameters

None.

Exceptions

None.

PrimaryKey

The PrimaryKey property returns or sets an array of DataColumn objects that act as the primary key for the DataTable. The primary key for the table must uniquely identify the row in which it exists. The primary key can be made up of a number of columns; thus you pass an array of columns when defining the primary key.

WARNING **MSDN refers, incorrectly, to the columns that make up a primary key as the "Primary Keys"—plural. There is only one primary key for any table. That primary key can be made up of multiple columns, but there is only one.**

Usage

```
myDataColumnArray = myDataTable.PrimaryKey
myDataTable.PrimaryKey = myDataColumnArray
```

Parameters

None.

Exceptions

DataException The key is a foreign key in a defined relationship.

RejectChanges

The RejectChanges method rolls back all the changes to the DataTable that have been made since the last AcceptChanges method was called. Calling RejectChanges at the DataSet forces RejectChanges to be called at the DataTable level, which in turn causes each DataRow to call RejectChanges. Calling RejectChanges at the DataRow level causes the DataRow.RowState property to change as well. Deleted and Modified DataRow objects become Unchanged, and Added DataRow objects are removed from the DataTable.

If any DataRow objects are in an edit mode (BeginEdit has been called), RejectChanges will end the edit and reject all of the updates.

See AcceptChanges to force child DataRow objects to accept changes, and commit any changes made while in an edit mode.

NOTE **Although the RejectChanges method occurs at a hierarchy of levels, you cannot use AcceptChanges at a higher level to accept changes already rolled back at a lower level. Calling RejectChanges on a DataRow will permanently roll back those changes, despite calling AcceptChanges at the DataSet level.**

Usage

```
myDataTable.RejectChanges()
```

Parameters

None.

Exceptions

None.

Reset

The Reset method clears the DataTable of all columns, relations, constraints, and data. This is similar to the Clear method, except that the schema is deleted as well as the data.

To remove only data from the DataTable, use the Clear method.

Usage

```
myDataTable.Reset()
```

Parameters

None.

Exceptions

None.

RowChanged

The RowChanged event is fired when a contained DataRow has been changed. Trapping this event provides information on the row affected and the action to be used.

Usage

```
Private Sub myDataTable_RowChanged(ByVal sender As Object, _
    ByVal e As System.Data.DataRowChangeEventArgs) _
    Handles myDataTable.RowChanged

End Sub
```

Parameters

`sender`	Contains a reference to the originator of the event.
`e`	Contains the System.Data.DataRowChangeEventArgs object containing information dealing with the changed row.

Exceptions

None.

RowChanging

The RowChanging event is fired when a contained DataRow is about to be changed. Trapping this event provides information on the row affected and the action to be used.

Usage

```
Private Sub myDataTable_RowChanging(ByVal sender As Object, _
    ByVal e As System.Data.DataRowChangeEventArgs) _
    Handles myDataTable.RowChanging

End Sub
```

Parameters

`sender`	Contains a reference to the originator of the event.
`e`	Contains the System.Data.DataRowChangeEventArgs object containing information dealing with the changing row.

Exceptions

None.

RowDeleted

The RowDeleted event is fired when a contained DataRow has been deleted. Trapping this event provides information on the row affected and the action to be used.

Usage

```
Private Sub myDataTable_RowDeleted(ByVal sender As Object, _
    ByVal e As System.Data.DataRowChangeEventArgs) _
    Handles myDataTable.RowDeleted

End Sub
```

Parameters

`sender`	Contains a reference to the originator of the event.
`e`	Contains the System.Data.DataRowChangeEventArgs object containing information dealing with the deleted row.

Exceptions
None.

RowDeleting

The RowDeleting event is fired when a contained DataRow is about to be deleted. Trapping this event provides information on the row affected and the action to be used.

Usage

```
Private Sub myDataTable_RowDeleting(ByVal sender As Object, _
    ByVal e As System.Data.DataRowChangeEventArgs) _
    Handles myDataTable.RowDeleting

End Sub
```

Parameters

`sender`	Contains a reference to the originator of the event.
`e`	Contains the System.Data.DataRowChangeEventArgs object containing information dealing with the row that is about to be deleted.

Exceptions
None.

Rows

The read-only Rows property returns a DataRowCollection object containing all the DataRow objects in the DataTable. If no DataRow objects exist in the DataTable, then a null value is returned (`Nothing` in Visual Basic .NET).

To add a Row to the collection, use the DataRowCollection.Add method.

Usage

```
myDataRowCollection = myDataTable.Rows
```

Parameters
None.

Exceptions
None.

Select

The Select method returns an array of DataRow objects that, optionally, match criteria, are sorted, and are in a particular DataViewRowState. When no parameters are passed, all of the DataRow objects in the DataTable are returned. If no sort order is specified, returned rows are sorted by primary key, if one exists, or order of addition if no primary key exists. In addition, a filter expression can be passed to restrict the returned rows to only those that fit the criteria.

WARNING The array is automatically redimensioned to the number of columns. This is true even if you pass an array with more than enough members. Thus, if a loop through an array depends on a preset array length, instead of determining the number of loops dynamically, you may get an exception when the count goes above the new dimension of the array.

Usage

```
myDataRowArray = myDataTable.Select()
myDataRowArray = myDataTable.Select()
myDataRowArray = myDataTable.Select(strFilter, strSort)
myDataRowArray = myDataTable.Select(strFilter, strSort, _
     myDataViewRowState)
```

Parameters

`strFilter`	A String specifying the criteria used to filter the returned DataRow objects.
`strSort`	A String specifying the DataColumn to sort by, and the sort direction.
`myDataViewRowState`	A DataVeiwRowState enumeration value to further filter the returned DataRow objects.

DataViewRowState Enumeration

Added (4)	Show new DataRow objects.
CurrentRows (22)	Show current DataRow objects, including unchanged, new, and modified rows.
Deleted (8)	Show deleted DataRow objects.
ModifiedCurrent (16)	Show the current version, which is a modified version of original data (see ModifiedOriginal).
ModifiedOriginal (32)	Show the original versions (premodification).
None (0)	Show no DataRow objects.
OriginalRows (42)	Show original rows, including unchanged and deleted rows.
Unchanged (2)	Show unchanged DataRow objects.

Exceptions

EvaluateException	1.) Cannot find the column specified in the filter or sort. 2.) The types of the column and the filter do not match.

Select Sample Code

```
'Code snippet (variables must already be defined)
'Returns an array of DataRow objects from myDataTable
'  which have the Country column equal to Germany, are sorted
```

```
' in ascending order by the Company column, and have
' recently been deleted from the DataTable
myRowArray = myDataTable.Select("Country = 'Germany'", _
   "Company ASC", DataViewRowState.Deleted)
```

Site

The Site property returns or sets a System.ComponentModel.ISite value that specifies the site for the DataTable. A site links a component to its container, and allows for storage of information specific to the relationship, such as visual coordinates or component name. It provides a link so that containers can manage their contained components.

Generally, this property is used mainly by Visual Studio .NET and the .NET Framework in the background, and there is little reason to specifically work with this property.

Usage

```
myISite = myDataTable.Site
myDataTable.Site = myISite
```

Parameters

None.

Exceptions

None.

TableName

The TableName property returns or sets a String value that specifies the name of the DataTable.

Usage

```
myString = myDataTable.TableName
myDataTable.TableName = myString
```

Parameters

None.

Exceptions

None.

ToString

The ToString method is overridden to return a String consisting of the concatenation of the TableName and DisplayExpression properties.

Usage

```
myString = myDataTable.ToString()
```

Parameters

None.

Exceptions

None.

System.Data.DataTableCollection

The DataTableCollection class is a container class that maintains a collection of DataTable objects. This collection represents the DataTable objects that make up a DataSet. Because the constructor for the DataTableCollection is private, an instance cannot be independently created. A DataTableCollection object is accessible only from the DataSet.Tables property.

Constructors

No public constructors.

Parameters

None.

DataTableCollection Sample Code

```
'See System.Data.ConstraintCollection for examples of the
'common collection members.
```

Members

Add

The various Add methods add a DataTable to the DataTableCollection and return the added System.Data.DataTable object. All Add methods return the added DataTable, with the exception of the Add method that takes only a DataTable as a parameter. This method returns nothing.

Using the DataTableCollection.Add method with no parameters creates a DataTable with the default table name.

Usage

```
myDataTable = myDataTableCollection.Add()
myDataTableCollection.Add(myDataTable)
myDataTable = myDataTableCollection.Add(strName)
```

Parameters

`myDataTable`	DataTable object to add to the collection.
`strName`	Name to give the DataTable (String).

Exceptions

ArgumentNullException	The DataTable argument is `null`.
ArgumentException	The DataTable already belongs to the DataTable-Collection or to another collection.
DuplicateNameException	The DataTableCollection contains a DataTable with the same name. (The comparison is not case sensitive.)

AddRange

The AddRange method copies the passed array of DataTable objects to the end of the DataTableCollection.

Usage

```
myDataTableCollection.AddRange(myDataTableArray)
```

Parameters

`myDataTableArray`	Array of DataTable objects to be added to the DataTableCollection.

Exceptions

ArgumentNullException	A passed DataTable is `null`.
ArgumentException	The DataTable already belongs to the DataTable-Collection or to another collection.
DuplicateNameException	The DataTableCollection contains a DataTable with the same name. (The comparison is not case sensitive.)

CanRemove

The CanRemove method returns a Boolean value that indicates whether the passed DataTable can be removed from the DataTableCollection. Use this method to determine whether a DataTable can be removed from the collection. CanRemove returns True if the DataTable can be removed, False otherwise.

Usage

```
myBoolean = myDataTableCollection.CanRemove(myDataTable)
```

Parameters

`myDataTable`	DataTable to be tested for removal from the DataTableCollection.

Exceptions

ArgumentNullException	The DataTable argument is `null`.
ArgumentException	The DataTable does not belong to this collection.

Clear

The Clear method removes all DataTable objects from the DataTableCollection. The Clear method will not fire the CollectionChanged or CollectionChanging events.

Usage

```
myDataTableCollection.Clear()
```

Parameters

None.

Exceptions

None.

CollectionChanged

The CollectionChanged event is fired whenever DataTables are added to or removed from the DataTableCollection.

Usage

```
Private Sub myDataTableCollection_CollectionChanged( _
   ByVal sender As Object, _
   ByVal e As System.Data.StateChangeEventArgs) _
   Handles myDataTableCollection.CollectionChanged
```

Parameters

`sender`	Contains a reference to the originator of the event.
`e`	Contains the System.ComponentModel.CollectionChangeEvent-Args object. See the CollectionChageEventArgs table below.

CollectionChangeEventArgs (e)

e.Action	A System.ComponentModelCollectionChangeAction enumeration representing how the collection was changed.
e.Element	An Object that refers to the collection that has changed (the Data-TableCollection, in this case).

CollectionChangeAction Enumeration

Add (1)	An element has been added to the collection.
Remove (2)	An element has been removed from the collection.
Refresh (3)	Specifies that the entire collection has changed (for instance, when the Clear method has been called).

Exceptions

None.

CollectionChanging

The CollectionChanging event is fired whenever DataTables are about to be added to or removed from the DataTableCollection.

Usage

```
Private Sub myDataTableCollection_CollectionChanging( _
   ByVal sender As Object, _
   ByVal e As System.Data.StateChangeEventArgs) _
   Handles myDataTableCollection.CollectionChanging
```

Parameters

`sender`	Contains a reference to the originator of the event.
`e`	Contains the System.ComponentModel.CollectionChangeEvent-Args object. See the CollectionChangeEventArgs table.

CollectionChangeEventArgs (e)

e.Action	A System.ComponentModelCollectionChangeAction enumeration representing how the collection was changed.
e.Element	An Object that refers to the collection that has changed (the DataTableCollection, in this case).

CollectionChangeAction Enumeration

Add (1)	An element has been added to the collection.
Remove (2)	An element has been removed from the collection.
Refresh (3)	Specifies that the entire collection has changed (for instance, when the Clear method has been called).

Exceptions

None.

Contains

The Contains method returns a Boolean value that indicates whether a DataTable object with the passed name (String) exists in the DataTableCollection. Returns True if a DataTable with the passed name exists and False otherwise.

Usage

```
myBoolean = myDataTableCollection.Contains(strName)
```

Parameters

strName	String defining the name of the DataTable to check for.

Exceptions

None.

CopyTo

The CopyTo method (inherited from System.Data.InternalDataCollectionBase) is used to copy the DataTable objects in the DataTableCollection to an array. (Please see System.Data.InternalDataCollectionBase for more information.)

Usage

```
myDataTableCollection.CopyTo(myDataTableArray, _
     myStartIndex)
```

Parameters

`myDataTableArray`	The passed buffer array to hold the DataTable objects.
`myStartIndex`	The Integer index designating the location in the passed array to begin filling with the DataTable objects.

Exceptions

ArgumentException	The passed array was not long enough to hold the passed objects.
ArgumentNullException	The passed array is null (`Nothing` in Visual Basic .NET).
ArgumentOutOfRangeException	myStartIndex is negative or greater than the length of the array.
InvalidCastException	The object type of the collection cannot be cast automatically to the object type of the array.

Count

The read-only Count property (inherited from System.Data.InternalDataCollectionBase) returns an Int32 value specifying the number of DataTables in the DataTableCollection.

Usage

```
myInt32 = myDataTableCollection.Count
```

Parameters

None.

Exceptions

None.

GetEnumerator

The GetEnumerator method (inherited from System.Data.InternalDataCollectionBase) returns a System.Collections.IEnumerator object that can be used to iterate over the collection. This method assists in using the For Each - Next (or equivalent statements) to iterate through a collection.

Usage

```
myIEnumerator = myDataTableCollection.GetEnumerator()
```

Parameters

None.

Exceptions

None.

IndexOf

The IndexOf() method returns an Integer specifying the zero-based location of a specified DataTable within the DataTableCollection. Because this method is overloaded, you may pass either the DataTable object itself or a String representing the name of the DataTable. If the DataTable does not exist in the DataTableCollection a value of -1 is returned.

Usage

```
myInt32 = myDataTableCollection.IndexOf(myDataTable)
myInt32 = myDataTableCollection.IndexOf(strName)
```

Parameters

`myDataTable`	The DataTable for which to find the index.
`strName`	The name of the DataTable for which to find the index.

Exceptions

None.

IsReadOnly

The read-only IsReadOnly property returns a Boolean value specifying whether the DataTableCollection is read only. This property is inherited directly from the Internal-DataCollectionBase class. (Please see System.Data.InternalDataCollectionBase for more information.)

Usage

```
myBoolean = myDataTableCollection.IsReadOnly
```

Parameters

None.

Exceptions

None.

IsSynchronized

The read-only IsSynchronized property (inherited from System.Data.InternalDataCollectionBase) returns a Boolean value indicating whether the DataTableCollection is currently synchronized. For information on synchronizing the DataTableCollection, see the DataTableCollection.SyncRoot property.

Usage

```
myBoolean = myDataTableCollection.IsSynchronized
```

Parameters

None.

Exceptions

None.

Item

The read-only Item property returns an indicated DataTable object from the collection. You can pass either the Integer index or String name of the desired DataTable.

Usage

```
myDataTable = myDataTableCollection.Item(intIndex)
myDataTable = myDataTableCollection.Item(strName)
```

Parameters

`intIndex`	Integer specifying the index of the desired DataTable.
`strName`	String specifying the name of the desired DataTable.

Exceptions

IndexOutOfRangeException	The passed integer is outside the bounds of the collection.

Remove

The Remove() method removes a specified DataTable object from the DataTableCollection. Because this method is overloaded, you may pass either the DataTable object itself or a String representing the name of the DataTable.

Usage

```
myDataTableCollection.Remove(myDataTable)
myDataTableCollection.Remove(strName)
```

Parameters

`myDataTable`	The DataTable object to remove.
`strName`	The name of the DataTable object to remove.

Exceptions

ArgumentNullException	The DataTable argument is a null reference (`Nothing` in Visual Basic).
ArgumentException	The DataTable does not belong to the collection.

RemoveAt

The RemoveAt() method removes a DataTable object from the DataTableCollection specified by the passed index of the DataTable.

Usage

```
myDataTableCollection.RemoveAt(intIndex)
```

Parameters

`intIndex`	Integer specifying the index of the DataTable to remove.

Exceptions

ArgumentException	A DataTable does not exist at the desired index.

SyncRoot

The read-only SyncRoot property returns a System.Object object that can be used to Synchronize the DataTableCollection. (Please see System.Data.InternalDataCollectionBase for more information.)

Usage

```
myObject = myDataTableCollection.SyncRoot
```

Parameters

None.

Exceptions

None.

ToString

The ToString method returns "System.Data.DataTableCollection".

Usage

```
myString = myDataTableCollection.ToString()
```

Parameters

None.

Exceptions

None.

System.Data.DataView

The DataView class provides a bindable view of a linked DataTable object. This can be extremely useful when binding data to a user interface object; however, the DataView is also very useful in code manipulation as well. A DataView can be created from a DataTable and then sorted and filtered. Iterations through the DataView will present only the filtered rows, and in sorted order. This is different from the DataViewSetting class, which is a related class used for display only.

A DataView is made up of a number of DataRowView objects, which specify how a DataRow will be displayed. Each DataRowView is tied directly to its corresponding DataRow, so that any changes made to the values in a DataRowView are reflected in the DataRow. (See System.Data.DataRowView for more information.)

Creating a filtered DataView is often much more convenient than using the DataTable.Select method, which returns an array of DataRow objects. This is especially true when editing rows because a change in a DataRowView is immediately reflected in the DataTable, whereas the array of DataRow objects must be reassigned to the DataTable to update it.

NOTE **Because the DataSet, DataTable, DataColumn, and DataView objects are so central to ADO.NET data manipulation, and because their methods and properties are so extensive, an entire tutorial chapter has been dedicated to their use. Duplicating the code for each object independently would not be as clear as demonstrating the use of these objects acting in concert. Thus, sample code will not be provided for the majority of this object. For code examples please see Chapter 11.**

Constructors

```
Dim myDataViewManager As New DataViewManager()
Dim myDataViewManager As New DataViewManager(myDataSet)
```

Parameters

`myDataSet`	The DataSet to contain the DataViewManager.

Exceptions

ArgumentNullException	The DataSet is null.

DataView Sample Code

```
'Because the DataView is so key to ADO.NET, sample code is
'  provided in detail in Chapter 11, a tutorial chapter.
```

Members

AddNew

The AddNew method returns a new DataRowView to the DataView. Because DataView objects are tied so tightly to the DataTable they describe, this method also adds a new DataRow to the supported DataTable.

WARNING AddNew adds a new DataRow to the supported DataTable and returns the associated DataRowView. When you are first being introduced to views, this can be the cause of some confusion.

Usage
`myDataRowView = myDataView.AddNew()`

Parameters
None.

Exceptions
None.

AllowDelete

The AllowDelete property returns or sets a Boolean value that determines whether the associated DataTable will allow deletes. If set to True, no deletes are allowed. If False, deletes to the DataTable are allowed. The default value is True.

Usage

```
myBoolean = myDataView.AllowDelete
myDataView.AllowDelete = myBoolean
```

Parameters

None.

Exceptions

None.

AllowEdit

The AllowEdit property returns or sets a Boolean value that determines whether the associated DataTable will allow edits. If set to True, no edits are allowed. If False, edits to the DataTable are allowed. The default value is True.

Usage

```
myBoolean = myDataView.AllowEdit
myDataView.AllowEdit = myBoolean
```

Parameters

None.

Exceptions

None.

AllowNew

The AllowNew property returns or sets a Boolean value that determines whether the associated DataTable will allow new rows to be added. If set to True, no additions are allowed. If False, additions to the DataTable are allowed. The default value is True.

Usage

```
myBoolean = myDataView.AllowNew
myDataView.AllowNew = myBoolean
```

Parameters

None.

Exceptions

None.

ApplyDefaultSort

The ApplyDefaultSort property returns or sets a Boolean value indicating whether the DataView should use the default sort. The default sort is by primary key, if one exists, or in order of addition, if not. If set to True, the DataView is sorted by primary key. If False, sorting will be done using the Sort property. The default value is False. (Adding a Sort property will not automatically change the value of ApplyDefaultSort to False, if it is True.)

Usage

```
myBoolean = myDataView.ApplyDefaultSort
myDataView.ApplyDefaultSort = myBoolean
```

Parameters
None.

Exceptions
None.

BeginInit

The BeginInit method locks the DataView object (and its accompanying DataTable), so that it cannot be accessed until the EndInit method is called. This is mainly used by visual development environments (such as Visual Studio .NET) to ensure that the object is not used before all values have been set accurately and the object is ready for use. It has use only in a multithreaded environment, where a process could attempt to use the DataView before it has been fully initialized.

Usage
```
myDataView.BeginInit()
```

Parameters
None.

Exceptions
None.

Container

The read-only Container property returns the object implementing the System. ComponentModel.IContainer interface that contains the DataViewManager. If the DataViewManager is not contained, then the Container method returns a null reference (`Nothing` in Visual Basic .NET).

Usage
```
myIContainer = myDataView.Container
```

Parameters
None.

Exceptions
None.

CopyTo

The CopyTo method is used to copy the DataRowView objects in the DataView to an array. An index is passed to determine where in the array to begin copying the DataRowView objects.

NOTE MSDN states that this is to be used only for Web Form Interfaces. Although it may be useful for Web Form Interfaces, the authors found no reason to restrict its use to Web Forms.

Usage
```
myDataView.CopyTo(myDataRowViewArray, myStartIndex)
```

Parameters

`myDataRelationArray`	The passed buffer array to hold the DataRowView objects.
`myStartIndex`	The Integer index designating the location in the passed array to begin filling with the DataRowView objects.

Exceptions

IndexOutOfRangeException	Index was outside the bounds of the array.
NullReferenceException	The passed array was null.
InvalidCastException	The object type of the collection cannot be cast automatically to the object type of the array.

Count

The read-only Count property returns an Int32 value specifying the number of DataRowView objects in the DataView.

Usage

```
myInt32 = myDataView.Count
```

Parameters

None.

Exceptions

None.

DataViewManager

The read-only DataViewManager property returns the associated DataViewManager. This association goes through a very circuitous route. The DataViewManager returned is the one associated with the DataSet that is hosting the DataTable from which the DataView is derived, if the DataView was created with the DataTable.DefaultView method. Otherwise, if the DataView was created outside of a DataViewManager (using one of the constructors), then this property will return null (`Nothing` in Visual Basic .NET), even if the referenced table belongs to a DataSet.

WARNING **Depending on how this object is created, this value may return a valid DataViewManager or null (`Nothing` in Visual Basic .NET), even when based on the same DataTable. (See the sample code that follows for an example of this.)**

Usage

```
myDataViewManager = myDataView.DataViewManager
```

Parameters

None.

Exceptions

None.

Sample Code

```
Public Sub DemoDataView_DataViewManager( _
        ByVal myDataTable As DataTable)

    Dim myDataView As DataView
    Dim myDataViewManager As DataViewManager

    'will return the name of the DataSet
    '  that the DataTable belongs to.
    myDataView = myDataTable.DefaultView
    myDataViewManager = myDataView.DataViewManager
    MessageBox.Show(myDataViewManager.DataSet.DataSetName)

    'will return a null value for DataViewManager
    '  that the DataTable belongs to.
    myDataView = New DataView(myDataTable)
    myDataViewManager = myDataView.DataViewManager
    If myDataViewManager Is Nothing Then
        MessageBox.Show("DataViewManager is Null")
    End If

End Sub
```

Delete

The Delete method deletes the DataRowView (and also the associated DataRow) from the table by setting the RowState to Deleted. The deletion can be cancelled at any time before AcceptChanges is called, by calling RejectChanges on the DataRow, parent DataTable, or parent DataSet.

Usage

```
myDataView.Delete(intIndex)
```

Parameters

`intIndex`	The Integer index of the DataRow to delete.

Exceptions

IndexOutOfRangeException	There is no DataRowView at the index location. (Outside of the bounds of the collection.)

DesignMode

The read-only DesignMode property (inherited from System.ComponentModel.MarshalByValueComponent) returns a Boolean value specifying whether the object is currently in design mode. If the object is not hosted in a development environment, this property will always return False.

Usage

```
myBoolean = myDataView.DesignMode
```

Parameters

None.

Exceptions

None.

Dispose

The Dispose method (inherited from System.ComponentModel.MarshalByValueComponent) releases all resources used by the DataViewManager.

Usage

```
myDataView.Dispose()
```

Parameters

None.

Exceptions

None.

Disposed

The Disposed event is fired whenever the Dispose method has been called on the object.

Usage

```
Private Sub myDataView_Disposed(ByVal sender As Object, _
    ByVal e As System.EventArgs) _
    Handles myDataViewManager.Disposed

End Sub
```

Parameters

sender	Contains a reference to the originator of the event.
e	Contains the System.EventArgs object containing no useful information.

Exceptions

None.

EndInit

The EndInit method unlocks the DataView object (and its associated DataTable) so that it can be accessed after the BeginEdit method had been called. This is mainly used by visual development environments (such as Visual Studio .NET) to ensure that the object is not used before all values have been set accurately and the object is ready for use. It has use only in a multithreaded environment, where a process could attempt to use the DataView before it has been fully initialized.

Usage

```
myDataView.EndInit()
```

Parameters

None.

Exceptions

None.

Find

The FindRows method returns an Integer that is the index of the first DataRow in which the column value (in the sort column) matches the passed value. This method can be used only when the Sort property has been set or when ApplyDefaultSort is set to True. In addition, only the column or columns participating in the Sort are searched, and the parameters passed for the search must match the order and values of the Sort columns to return a DataRow object. In other words, if you have defined a Sort on Country and CompanyName, you must pass both a country and company name value to FindRows, in that order. If the default sort order is used, then the primary key column or columns should be passed.

To return more than one row, use the FindRows method.

Usage

```
myInt32 = myDataView.Find(myObject)
```

Parameters

`myObject`	An Object that defines the value to find. This value will be compared with the values in the defined Sort column of the DataView.
`myObjectArray`	An array of objects that define the values to match. These values will be compared with the values in the defined Sort columns of the DataView.

Exceptions

ArgumentException	Wrong number of parameters were passed. The number must equal the number of columns in the Sort property.

FindRows

The FindRows method returns an array of DataRow objects that have column values (in the sort column) that match the passed value. This method can be used only when the Sort property has been set or when ApplyDefaultSort is set to True. In addition, only the column or columns participating in the Sort are searched, and the parameters passed for the search must match the order and values of the Sort columns to return a DataRow object. In other words, if you have defined a Sort on Country and CompanyName, you must pass both a country and company name value to FindRows, in that order. If the default sort order is used, then the primary key column or columns should be passed.

To return an index of only the first element found, use the Find method.

Usage

```
myDataRowViewArray = myDataView.FindRows(myObject)
myDataRowViewArray = myDataView.FindRows(myObjectArray)
```

Parameters

`myObject`	An Object that defines the value to find. This value will be compared with the values in the defined Sort column of the DataView.

`myObjectArray`	An array of objects that define the values to match. These values will be compared with the values in the defined Sort columns of the DataView.

Exceptions

ArgumentException	The wrong number of parameters were passed. The number must equal the number of columns in the Sort property.

GetEnumerator

The GetEnumerator method (inherited from System.Data.InternalDataCollectionBase) returns a System.Collections.IEnumerator object that can be used to iterate over the collection. This method assists in using the For Each - Next (or equivalent statements) to iterate through a collection.

Usage

```
myIEnumerator = myDataView.GetEnumerator()
```

Parameters
None.

Exceptions
None.

GetService

The GetService method returns an Object that implements the IServiceProvider interface. This object is used to provide custom support to the calling object through the use of a custom-built server.

This method is almost exclusively used to support Visual Studio .NET.

Usage

```
myObject = myDataView.GetService(myServiceType)
```

Parameters

`myServiceType`	A System.Type that defines the requested service.

Exceptions
None.

Item

The read-only Item property returns or sets the DataRowView designated by the passed index of the DataRowView.

WARNING **This index is not constant across the DataView, as it is in a DataTable. Applying a filter to the DataView will rearrange the index values of each of the DataRowView objects! (This is actually one of the powers of the DataView. A DataViewSetting is unable to do this to a DataTable.)**

WARNING **MSDN states that the passed index is the index from the DataTable. This is incorrect. See the preceding warning for more information.**

Usage

```
myObject = myDataRow.Item(intIndex)
```

Parameters

`intIndex`	The Integer index of the desired DataRowView.

Exceptions

IndexOutOfRangeException	The specified column cannot be found because the index was outside the range of available DataRowView objects.

ListChanged

The ListChanged event is fired whenever one of the DataRowView objects has been added to or deleted from the DataView.

Usage

```
Private Sub myDataView_ListChanged(ByVal sender As Object, _
    ByVal e As System.ComponentModel.ListChangedEventArgs) _
    Handles myDataView.ListChanged

End Sub
```

Parameters

`sender`	Contains a reference to the originator of the event.
`e`	Contains the System.ComponentModel.List-ChangedEventArgs object containing information on the event, such as the way the list was changed, the index of added objects, or the old index of any deleted objects.

Exceptions

None.

RowFilter

The RowFilter property returns or sets a String that determines how the DataView will be filtered. Setting this row to a valid filter will cause the DataView to display a subset of the DataTable that fits the criteria in the filter.

To display only contained DataRowView objects in a particular state, use the Row-StateFilter.

Usage

```
myString = myDataView.RowFilter
myDataView.RowFilter = myString
```

Parameters

None.

Exceptions
None.

RowStateFilter

The RowStateFilter property returns or sets a String that determines which states will be displayed in the DataView. Setting this row to a valid DataViewRowState enumeration value will cause the DataView to display those DataRow objects of the DataTable that are in the desired state.

To filter the DataView object on other criteria, use the RowFilter method.

Usage

```
myDataViewRowState = myDataView.RowStateFilter
myDataView.RowStateFilter = myDataViewRowState
```

Parameters
None.

Exceptions
None.

Site

The Site property returns or sets a System.ComponentModel.ISite value that specifies the site for the DataView. A site links a component to its container and allows for storage of information specific to the relationship, such as visual coordinates or component name. It provides a link so that containers can manage their contained components.

Generally, this property is used mainly by Visual Studio .NET and the .NET Framework in the background, and there is little reason to work with this property.

Usage

```
myISite = myDataView.Site
myDataView.Site = myISite
```

Parameters
None.

Exceptions
None.

Sort

The Sort property returns or sets a String value specifying the sort columns and sort order to use when sorting the DataView. To set the property, pass a string containing the column name followed by "ASC" for ascending sorts or "DESC" for descending sorts. Because "ASC" is the default, it does not need to be included, but it does make the Sort more human-readable. Multiple sort columns can be specified in the string by separating them with a comma. See the sample code for an example.

WARNING **If an invalid sort string is specified (one with incorrect column names), no exception will be raised and the DataView will be sorted according to the default sort.**

Usage

```
myString = myDataView.Sort
myDataView.Sort = myString
```

Parameters

None.

Exceptions

None.

Sample Code

```
myDataView.Sort = "Country DESC, CompanyName ASC"
```

Table

The Table property returns or sets the DataTable object that provides the data for this DataView.

Usage

```
myDataTable = myDataView.Table
myDataView.Table = myDataTable
```

Parameters

None.

Exceptions

None.

ToString

The ToString method returns "System.Data.DataView".

Usage

```
myString = myDataView.ToString()
```

Parameters

None.

Exceptions

None.

System.Data.DataViewManager

The DataViewManager class is basically a collection class that maintains a collection of DataViewSetting objects. These objects are used to determine how DataTable objects are viewed in a user interface. (For more information, see System.Data.DataViewSetting.)

WARNING **Unlike the DataView object, the DataViewSetting objects are designed for binding to data-aware controls. If you perform a Sort operation and then iterate through the DataRow objects in a DataTable, they will not be in sorted order.**

Constructors

```
Dim myDataViewManager As New DataViewManager()
Dim myDataViewManager As New DataViewManager(myDataSet)
```

Parameters

`myDataSet`	The DataSet to contain the DataViewManager.

Exceptions

ArgumentNullException	The DataSet is null.

DataViewManager Sample Code

```
'This function demonstrates the DataViewManager class.
'  It assumes a DataSet is passed, containing
'  a DataTable with a column named Country
'  This code sample is relatively short, please
'  see Chapter 11 for how to use the DataViewManager
'  class with the other System.Data objects
Public Sub DemoDataViewManager(ByVal myDataSet As DataSet)
   Dim myDataTable As DataTable
   Dim myDataView As DataView
   Dim myDataViewManager As DataViewManager

   'use the DefaultViewManager
   myDataViewManager = myDataSet.DefaultViewManager
   myDataTable = myDataSet.Tables(0)

   'define a sort order when displayed in a control
   '  using the DataViewManager associated with the table
   myDataViewManager.DataViewSettings(myDataTable).Sort = _
         "Country ASC"
```

```
    'define a DataView based on the default
    '  the DataView can then be iterated through in
    '  the sorted order (a DataViewSetting cannot be
    '  iterated through in sorted order).
    myDataView = myDataViewManager.CreateDataView(myDataTable)

End Sub
```

Members

Container

The read-only Container property returns the object implementing the System.ComponentModel.IContainer interface that contains the DataViewManager. If the DataViewManager is not contained, then the Container method returns a null reference (`Nothing` in Visual Basic .NET).

Usage

```
myIContainer = myDataViewManager.Container
```

Parameters

None.

Exceptions

None.

CreateDataView

The CreateDataView method returns a DataView object associated with the passed DataTable. This method creates a DataView and sets its properties to those of the DataViewSetting associated with the passed DataTable. This is convenient when creating a DataView that inherits the values of the current default view.

If the passed DataTable is not a member of the DataSet (and therefore not managed by the DataViewManager), a DataView will still be returned for the DataTable. The returned DataView, however, will not have the default view values that may have been set for it.

Usage

```
myDataView = myDataViewManager.CreateDataView(myDataTable)
```

Parameters

`myDataTable`	The DataTable object for which to create the DataView.

Exceptions

DataException	The passed DataTable has not been created yet or is null (`Nothing` in Visual Basic .NET).

DataSet

The DataSet property returns or sets the DataSet to use with this DataViewManager. If you have used the DataSet.DefaultViewManager property to build the DataViewManager, that DataSet is returned.

Usage

```
myDataSet = myDataViewManager.DataSet
myDataViewManager.DataSet = myDataSet
```

Parameters

None.

Exceptions

None.

DataViewSettingCollectionString

The DataViewSettingCollectionString property returns or sets a String used for code persistence. Although this is a public method, MSDN states that users should not call this method. Instead, it is used internally to the .NET Framework.

Usage

```
myString = myDataViewManager.DataViewSettingCollectionString
myDataViewManager.DataViewSettingCollectionString = myString
```

Parameters

None.

Exceptions

None.

DataViewSettings

The read-only DataViewSettings property returns the DataViewSettingCollection object that contains the DataViewSetting objects for each of the DataTable objects in the DataSet. The returned DataViewSettingCollection can be used to modify how DataTable objects appear when they are displayed in data-bound controls.

Usage

```
myDataViewSettingCollection = _
     myDataViewManager.DataViewSettings
```

Parameters

None.

Exceptions

None.

DesignMode

The read-only DesignMode property (inherited from System.ComponentModel.MarshalByValueComponent) returns Boolean value specifying whether the object is currently in design mode. If the object is not hosted in a development environment, this property will always return False.

Usage

```
myBoolean = myDataViewManager.DesignMode
```

Parameters

None.

Exceptions

None.

Dispose

The Dispose method (inherited from System.ComponentModel.MarshalByValueComponent) releases all resources used by the DataViewManager.

Usage

```
myDataViewManager.Dispose()
```

Parameters

None.

Exceptions

None.

Disposed

The Disposed event is fired whenever the Dispose method has been called on the object.

Usage

```
Private Sub myDataViewManager_Disposed( _
    ByVal sender As Object, _
    ByVal e As System.EventArgs) _
    Handles myDataViewManager.Disposed

End Sub
```

Parameters

sender	Contains a reference to the originator of the event.
e	Contains the System.EventArgs object containing no useful information.

Exceptions

None.

GetService

The GetService method returns an Object that implements the IServiceProvider interface. This object is used to provide custom support to the calling object through the use of a custom-built server.

This method is almost exclusively used to support Visual Studio .NET.

Usage

```
myObject = myDataViewManager.GetService(myServiceType)
```

Parameters

`myServiceType`	A System.Type that defines the requested service.

Exceptions

None.

ListChanged

The ListChanged event is fired whenever a row has been added to or deleted from any of the DataView objects contained in the DataViewManager.

Usage

```
Private Sub myDataViewManager_ListChanged( _
    ByVal sender As Object, _
    ByVal e As System.ComponentModel.ListChangedEventArgs) _
    Handles myDataViewManager.ListChanged

End Sub
```

Parameters

`sender`	Contains a reference to the originator of the event.
`e`	Contains the System.ComponentModel.ListChangedEventArgs object containing information on the event, such as the way the list was changed, the index of added objects, or the old index of any deleted objects.

Exceptions

None.

Site

The Site property returns or sets a System.ComponentModel.ISite value that specifies the site for the DataViewManager. A site links a component to its container and allows for storage of information specific to the relationship, such as visual coordinates or component name. It provides a link so that containers can manage their contained components.

Generally, this property is used mainly by Visual Studio .NET and the .NET Framework in the background, and there is little reason to specifically work with this property.

Usage

```
myISite = myDataViewManager.Site
myDataViewManager.Site = myISite
```

Parameters

None.

Exceptions

None.

ToString

The ToString method returns "System.Data.DataViewManager".

Usage

```
myString = myDataViewManager.ToString()
```

Parameters

None.

Exceptions

None.

System.Data.DataViewRowState

The DataViewRowState enumeration provides the values that designate the current version of a DataRow. Use this enumeration in conjunction with the DataView.RowStateFilter property to filter the DataTable to see only newly added, unchanged, deleted, or unchanged DataRows.

Because this class implements the FlagsAttribute, bitwise combinations of values are allowed. Thus, when filtering a DataView, you can return any combination of states.

DataViewRowState Enumeration

Added (4)	Show new DataRow objects.
CurrentRows (22)	Show current DataRow objects, including unchanged, new, and modified rows.
Deleted (8)	Show deleted DataRow objects.
ModifiedCurrent (16)	Show the current version, which is a modified version of original data (see ModifiedOriginal).
ModifiedOriginal (32)	Show the original versions (premodification).
None (0)	Show no DataRow objects.
OriginalRows (42)	Show original rows, including unchanged and deleted rows.
Unchanged (2)	Show unchanged DataRow objects.

System.Data.DataViewSetting

The DataViewSetting class is a container class that holds the default view for a DataTable. The DataViewManager maintains a collection of DataViewSetting objects, one for each DataTable in the managed DataSet.

When the DataTable is bound to a data-aware user interface control, it will be displayed according to the default DataViewSetting that has been built for it. You cannot directly add or remove a DataViewSetting object from the collection because it is automatically added or removed when its associated DataTable objects are added or removed from the DataSet. The view can be manipulated, though, by editing the DataViewSetting assigned to that table.

Basically, the DataViewSetting can be thought of as a DataView-lite. Use this object to perform most of the DataView functions. The DataViewSetting is assigned to a table to provide the default view whenever the table is displayed. You cannot bind a DataViewSetting to a data-bound control; however, this is unimportant because the properties of the DataViewSetting are automatically used when the DataTable is displayed. For more information on DataView objects, see System.Data.DataView.

WARNING **Unlike the DataView object, this one is designed for binding to data-aware controls. If you perform a Sort operation and then iterate through the collection of the DataTable, they will not be in sorted order.**

WARNING **Do not try to look for a link between DataView objects and DataViewSetting objects! They are distinct. You cannot assign a DataView as a member of a DataViewSettingCollection. You can, however, create a DataView with the properties of the DataViewSetting object by using the DataViewManager.CreateDataView method. (You may think that the DataTable.DefaultView property, which returns a DataView that is the table's default view, would come with the settings of that table's DataViewSetting object, but it doesn't.)**

Constructors

No public constructors.

Parameters

None.

DataViewSetting Sample Code

```
'This function demonstrates the DataViewSetting class
'  It assumes a valid DataSet, containing a DataTable, is
'  passed.  In addition the DataTable has at least two columns,
'  named myColumn1 & myColumn2
Public Sub DemoDataViewSetting(ByVal myDataSet As DataSet)
   Dim myDataViewSetting As DataViewSetting

   'get the DataViewSetting for the first table
   '  in the DataSet
   myDataViewSetting = _
         myDataSet.DefaultViewManager.DataViewSettings(0)
```

```
    'set the sort property to sort descending by myColumn2,
    '  and myColumn1 Ascending as the minor sort.
    myDataViewSetting.ApplyDefaultSort = False
    myDataViewSetting.Sort = "myColumn2 DESC, myColumn1 ASC"

    'filter so that only recently added rows are displayed
    myDataViewSetting.RowStateFilter = DataViewRowState.Added

    'the DataTable can now be bound to a DataGrid, or some
    '  other data bound control, and only the newly Added rows
    '  will appear, sorted by the two columns.
End Sub
```

Members

ApplyDefaultSort

The ApplyDefaultSort property returns or sets a Boolean value indicating whether the DataView should use the default sort. The DefaultSort is by primary key, if one exists, or in order of addition, if not.

Usage

```
myBoolean = myDataViewSetting.ApplyDefaultSort
myDataViewSetting.ApplyDefaultSort = myBoolean
```

Parameters

None.

Exceptions

None.

DataViewManager

The read-only DataViewManager property returns the DataViewManager object that contains the current DataViewSetting.

Usage

```
myDataViewManager = myDataViewSetting.DataViewManager
```

Parameters

None.

Exceptions

None.

RowFilter

The RowFilter property returns or sets a String that determines how the DataView will be filtered. Setting this row to a valid filter will cause the DataView to display a subset of the DataTable that fits the criteria in the filter.

To display only a DataRowView object in a particular state, use the RowStateFilter.

Usage
```
myString = myDataViewSetting.RowFilter
myDataViewSetting.RowFilter = myString
```

Parameters
None.

Exceptions
None.

RowStateFilter

The RowStateFilter property returns or sets a String that determines which states will be displayed in the DataView. Setting this row to a valid DataViewRowState enumeration value will cause the DataView to display those DataRow objects of the DataTable that are in the desired state.

To filter the DataRowView object on other criteria, use the RowFilter method.

Usage
```
myDataViewRowState = myDataViewSetting.RowStateFilter
myDataViewSetting.RowStateFilter = myDataViewRowState
```

Parameters
None.

Exceptions
None.

Sort

The Sort property returns or sets a String that determines the order of the rows displayed in the DataView.

WARNING **If an invalid sort string is specified (one with incorrect column names), no exception will be raised and the DataTable will be sorted according to the default sort.**

Usage
```
myString = myDataViewSetting.Sort
myDataViewSetting.Sort = myString
```

Parameters
None.

Exceptions
None.

Sample Code
```
'to sort by Company name in descending order
myDataViewSetting.Sort = "CompanyName DESC"
'to sort by Country primarily, then Company name within country
myDataViewSetting.Sort = "Country DESC, CompanyName ASC"
```

Table

The read-only Table property returns the DataTable object to which the DataView-Setting applies.

Usage

```
myDataTable = myDataViewSetting.Table
```

Parameters

None.

Exceptions

None.

ToString

The ToString method returns "System.Data.ToString".

Usage

```
myString = myDataViewSetting.ToString()
```

Parameters

None.

Exceptions

None.

System.Data.DataViewSettingCollection

The DataViewSettingCollection class is a container class that maintains a collection of DataViewSetting objects. Each DataSet has a single DataViewSettingCollection that maintains the DataViewSetting for each of the DataTable objects in that DataSet. Because the constructor for the DataViewSettingCollection is private, an instance cannot be independently created. The DataViewSettingCollection is accessible from the DataViewManager.DataViewSettings property. Although users cannot directly add or remove a DataViewSetting object from the collection, they are automatically added or removed when their associated DataTable objects are added or removed from the DataSet.

Constructors

No public constructors.

Parameters

None.

DataViewSettingCollection Sample Code

```
'See System.Data.ConstraintCollection for examples of the
'common collection members.
```

Members

CopyTo

The CopyTo method is used to copy the DataViewSetting objects in the DataViewSettingCollection to an array.

Usage

```
myDataViewSettingCollection.CopyTo(myDataViewSettingArray, _
     myStartIndex)
```

Parameters

`myDataViewSettingArray`	The passed buffer array to hold the DataViewSetting objects.
`myStartIndex`	The Integer index designating the location in the passed array to begin filling with the DataViewSetting objects.

Exceptions

ArgumentException	The passed array was not long enough to hold the passed objects.
ArgumentNullException	The passed array is null (`Nothing` in Visual Basic .NET).
ArgumentOutOfRangeException	myStartIndex is negative or greater than the length of the array.
InvalidCastException	The object type of the collection cannot be cast automatically to the object type of the array.

Count

The read-only Count property returns an Integer value specifying the number of DataViewSettings in the DataViewSettingCollection.

Usage

```
myInt32 = myDataViewSettingCollection.Count
```

Parameters

None.

Exceptions

None.

GetEnumerator

The GetEnumerator method returns a System.Collections.IEnumerator object that can be used to iterate over the collection. This method assists in using the For Each - Next (or equivalent statements) to iterate through a collection.

Usage

```
myIEnumerator = myDataViewSettingCollection.GetEnumerator()
```

Parameters

None.

Exceptions

None.

IsReadOnly

The read-only IsReadOnly property returns a Boolean value specifying whether the DataViewSettingCollection is read only.

Usage

```
myBoolean = myDataViewSettingCollection.IsReadOnly
```

Parameters

None.

Exceptions

None.

IsSynchronized

The read-only IsSynchronized property returns a Boolean value indicating whether the DataViewSettingCollection is currently synchronized. For information on synchronizing the DataViewSettingCollection, see the DataViewSettingCollection.SyncRoot property.

Usage

```
myBoolean = myDataViewSettingCollection.IsSynchronized
```

Parameters

None.

Exceptions

None.

Item

The read-only Item property returns a DataViewSetting object associated with the specified DataTable in the collection. You can pass three different objects to this property, to specify the DataViewSetting to return: the DataTable object itself or its name as a String, which is associated with the desired DataViewSetting, or an Integer index from the DataViewSettingCollection.

Usage

```
myDataViewSetting = _
     myDataViewSettingCollection.Item(myDataTable)
```

```
myDataViewSetting = myDataViewSettingCollection.Item(strName)
myDataViewSetting = myDataViewSettingCollection.Item(intIndex)
```

Parameters

`myDataTable`	A DataTable object that is the DataTable object associated with the desired DataViewSetting.
`strName`	A String specifying the name of the DataTable object associated with the desired DataView Setting.
`intIndex`	An Integer specifying the index of the desired DataViewSetting.

Exceptions

IndexOutOfRangeException	The passed integer is outside the bounds of the collection.

SyncRoot

The read-only SyncRoot property returns a System.Object object that can be used to Synchronize the DataViewSettingCollection.

Usage

```
myObject = myDataViewSettingCollection.SyncRoot
```

Parameters

None.

Exceptions

None.

ToString

The ToString method returns "System.Data.DataViewSettingCollection".

Usage

```
myString = myDataViewSettingCollection.ToString()
```

Parameters

None.

Exceptions

None.

System.Data.DBConcurrencyException

The DBConcurrencyException class (descended from the System.Exception class) is a sealed (NotInheritable) class that defines exceptions thrown by a DataAdapter during an update operation when no records are affected. Having no records affected is often the result of a concurrency exception, but not always.

WARNING This exception is thrown when the results of an update on a DataAdapter result in exactly zero records affected. This is usually, but not always, an indication of concurrency issues.

Constructors

```
Dim myDBConcurrencyException As New _
     DBConcurrencyException(myString)
Dim myDBConcurrencyException As New _
     DBConcurrencyException(myString, myException)
```

Parameters

`myString`	A String object that will initialize the Message property.
`myException`	An Exception object to use as the InnerException.

DBConcurrencyException Sample Code

```
Dim myDBConcurrencyException As DBConcurrencyException
myDBConcurrencyException = New _
     DBConcurrencyException("No records affected!")
Throw myDBConcurrencyException
```

Members

GetBaseException

The GetBaseException method returns an Exception object containing the original exception. To return the original exception, it traverses the chain of InnerException objects. If the InnerException property of the current exception is null, GetBaseException will return a reference to the current Exception object.

To determine only the parent exception to the current exception, use the InnerException property.

Usage

```
myException = myDBConcurrencyException.GetBaseException()
```

Parameters

None.

Exceptions

None.

GetObjectData

The GetObjectData method fills the passed System.Runtime.Serialization.SerializationInfo buffer object with information about the Exception object. There is no value returned by this method. Depending on the passed System.Runtime.Serialization.StreamingContext object, this method can be used to serialize the object to a stream or read serialization from a stream.

Because it deals mainly with serialization and not data access, further discussion of this property is beyond the scope of this book.

Usage

```
myDBConcurrencyException.GetObjectData( _
     mySerializationInfo, myStreamingContext)
```

Parameters

`mySerializationInfo`	A System.Runtime.Serialization.SerializationInfo buffer object to be filled with the exception's serialization data.
`myStreamingContext`	A System.Runtime.Serialization.StreamingContext object specifying the stream to write the serialization info to or read the information from.

Exceptions

ArgumentNullException	The passed SerializationInfo buffer object is null (`Nothing` in Visual Basic .NET).

HelpLink

The HelpLink property returns or sets a String linking to a help file associated with the DBConcurrencyException. The HelpLink is formatted as a Uniform Resource Name (URN) or Uniform Resource Locator (URL). An example of this property that points to the MSDN help available with Visual Studio. NET would be: `ms-help://MS.VSCC/MS.MSDNVS/cpref/html/frlrfsystemexceptionclasshelplinktopic.htm`.

The HelpLink is often not set, so it is wise to verify both that the HelpLink property itself is not an empty string and that the HelpLink points to a valid help file before exposing the HelpLink to a user of your program.

Usage

```
myString = myDBConcurrencyException.HelpLink
myDBConcurrencyException.HelpLink = myString
```

Parameters

None.

InnerException

The read-only InnerException property returns the Exception object linking to a previous exception that caused the current exception to be thrown, if any, or a null value (`Nothing` in Visual Basic .NET), if not. This permits a chain of InnerException objects to be generated, allowing a program to trace the exception chain all the way to the root exception. Be aware that InnerException may be null.

To find the base exception that originally was fired, use the GetBaseException method.

Usage

```
myException = myDBConcurrencyException.InnerException
```

Parameters

None.

Message

The read-only Message property returns a String describing the first error that caused the exception. Because it provides information only from the first error, use this property cautiously when building robust error handling.

Usage

```
myString = myDBConcurrencyException.Message
```

Parameters

None.

Row

The Row property returns or sets the DataRow object that generated the DbConcurrencyException.

WARNING **Although the Row property is not read only, setting the Row object has no effect.**

Usage

```
myDataRow = myDBConcurrencyException.Row
myDBConcurrencyException.Row = myDataRow 'no effect
```

Parameters

None.

Exceptions

None.

Source

The Source property sets or returns a String containing the name of the provider that generated the first error. Because it provides information only from the first error, use this property cautiously when building robust error handling.

Usage

```
myString = myDBConcurrencyException.Source
myDBConcurrencyException.Source = myString
```

Parameters

None.

StackTrace

The read-only StackTrace property returns a String containing a textual representation of the stack trace. The stack trace reports all of the methods that are in execution at the time just prior to the execution being thrown. It is read from top to bottom with the latest method in execution at the top.

The StackTrace can be invaluable in tracing difficult-to-find bugs because it provides a way to see all of the methods that could have led up to the error.

TIP To see the stack trace programmatically when no exception has been raised, use the Environment.StackTrace property.

Usage

```
myString = myDBConcurrencyException.StackTrace
```

Parameters

None.

TargetSite

The read-only TargetSite property returns an object inheriting from System.Reflection.MethodBase that contains a reference to the method that caused the error to be thrown.

This property is primarily used to programmatically find information about the method that raised the exception. The returned object will provide information such as the methods parameters and return type and whether the method is virtual, a constructor, public, private, etc. Because it deals mainly with Reflection and not data access, further discussion of this property is beyond the scope of this book.

Usage

```
myMethodBase = myDBConcurrencyException.TargetSite
```

Parameters

None.

ToString

The ToString method is overridden to return information relating to the DBConcurrencyException exception. The returned String contains the full class name and also the error message, name of the inner exception, and stack trace, if they exist.

Usage

```
myString = myDBConcurrencyException.ToString()
```

Parameters

None.

Exceptions

None.

System.Data.DbType

The DbType enumeration provides the values that supply the data type for a field, property, or parameter object. Specifying the DbType of a parameter forces the conversion to that type before being passed to a .NET data provider. If the DbType is not specified, ADO.NET infers the type and performs a conversion automatically.

WARNING ADO.NET is not able to perform automatic conversion on binary data with a length greater than 8,000 bytes.

DbType Enumeration	
AnsiString	A variable-length stream of ANSI (non-Unicode) characters (up to 8,000 characters).
AnsiStringFixedLength	A fixed-length stream of ANSI characters.
Binary	A variable-length stream of binary data. (Note: If the size is greater than 8,000 bytes, ADO.NET cannot correctly infer the type. In this situation, you must explicitly specify the DbType.)
Boolean	A simple type representing Boolean values of True or False.
Byte	An 8-bit unsigned integer ranging in value from 0 to 255.
Currency	A currency value ranging from -2^{63} to 2^{63}-1 (plus or minus about 922 trillion) with accuracy to a ten-thousandth of a currency unit.
Date	Date and time data ranging in value from January 1, 1753 to December 31, 9999 to an accuracy of 3.33 milliseconds.
DateTime	A type representing a date and time value.
Decimal	A simple type representing values ranging from 1.0 x 10^{-28} to approximately 7.9 x 10^{28} with 28-29 significant digits.
Double	A floating-point type representing values ranging from approximately 5.0 x 10^{-324} to 1.7 x 10^{308} with a precision of 15-16 digits.
Guid	A globally unique identifier (or GUID).
Int16	An integral type representing signed 16-bit integers with values between -32768 and 32767.
Int32	An integral type representing signed 32-bit integers with values between -2147483648 and 2147483647.
Int64	An integral type representing signed 64-bit integers with values between -9223372036854775808 and 9223372036854775807.
Object	A general type representing any reference or value type not explicitly represented by another DbType value.
Sbyte	An integral type representing signed 8-bit integers with values between -128 and 127. (Could be thought of as an Int8.)
Single	A floating-point type representing values ranging from approximately 1.5 x 10^{-45} to 3.4 x 10^{38} with a precision of 7 digits.

String	A type representing a stream of Unicode characters.
StringFixedLength	A fixed-length stream of Unicode characters.
Time	Date and time data ranging in value from January 1, 1753 to December 31, 9999 to an accuracy of 3.33 milliseconds.
UInt16	An integral type representing unsigned 16-bit integers with values between 0 and 65535.
UInt32	An integral type representing unsigned 32-bit integers with values between 0 and 4294967295.
UInt64	An integral type representing unsigned 64-bit integers with values between 0 and 18446744073709551615.
VarNumeric	A general type representing any reference or value type not explicitly represented by another DbType numeric value.

System.Data. DeletedRowInaccessibleException

The DeletedRowInaccessibleException class (descended from the DataException class) defines exceptions that are thrown when an action occurs that refers to a DataRow that has been deleted.

Constructors

```
Dim myDeletedRowInaccessibleException As New _
     DeletedRowInaccessibleException()
Dim myDeletedRowInaccessibleException As New _
     DeletedRowInaccessibleException (myString)
```

Parameters

`myString`	A String object that will initialize the Message property.

DeletedRowInaccessibleException Sample Code

```
Dim myDeletedRowInaccessibleException As _
     DeletedRowInaccessibleException
myDeletedRowInaccessibleException = New _
     DeletedRowInaccessibleException("Row Gone!")
Throw myDeletedRowInaccessibleException
```

Members

GetBaseException

The GetBaseException method returns an Exception object containing the original exception. To return the original exception, it traverses the chain of InnerException objects. If the InnerException property of the current exception is null, GetBaseException will return a reference to the current Exception object.

To determine only the parent exception to the current exception, use the InnerException property.

Usage

```
myException = _
     myDeletedRowInaccessibleException.GetBaseException()
```

Parameters

None.

Exceptions

None.

GetObjectData

The GetObjectData method fills the passed System.Runtime.Serialization.SerializationInfo buffer object with information about the Exception object. There is no value returned by this method. Depending on the passed System.Runtime.Serialization.StreamingContext object, this method can be used to serialize the object to a stream or read serialization from a stream.

Because it deals mainly with Serialization and not data access, further discussion of this property is beyond the scope of this book.

Usage

```
myDeletedRowInaccessibleException.GetObjectData( _
     mySerializationInfo, myStreamingContext)
```

Parameters

`mySerializationInfo`	A System.Runtime.Serialization.SerializationInfo buffer object to be filled with the exception's serialization data.
`myStreamingContext`	A System.Runtime.Serialization.StreamingContext object specifying the stream to write the serialization info to or read the information from.

Exceptions

ArgumentNullException	The passed SerializationInfo buffer object is null (`Nothing` in Visual Basic .NET).

HelpLink

The HelpLink property returns or sets a String linking to a help file associated with the DeletedRowInaccessibleException. The HelpLink is formatted as a Uniform Resource

Name (URN) or Uniform Resource Locator (URL). An example of this property that points to the MSDN help available with Visual Studio .NET would be: `ms-help://MS.VSCC/MS.MSDNVS/cpref/html/frlrfsystemexceptionclasshelplinktopic.htm`.

The HelpLink is often not set, so it is wise to verify both that the HelpLink property itself is not an empty string and that the HelpLink points to a valid help file before exposing the HelpLink to a user of your program.

Usage

```
myString = myDeletedRowInaccessibleException.HelpLink
myDeletedRowInaccessibleException.HelpLink = myString
```

Parameters

None.

InnerException

The read-only InnerException property returns the Exception object linking to a previous exception that caused the current exception to be thrown, if any, or a null value (`Nothing` in Visual Basic .NET), if not. This permits a chain of InnerException objects to be generated, allowing a program to trace the exception chain all the way to the root exception. Be aware that InnerException may be null.

To find the base exception that originally was fired, use the GetBaseException method.

Usage

```
myException = myDeletedRowInaccessibleException.InnerException
```

Parameters

None.

Message

The read-only Message property returns a String describing the first error that caused the exception. Because it provides information only from the first error, use this property cautiously when building robust error handling.

Usage

```
myString = myDeletedRowInaccessibleException.Message
```

Parameters

None.

Source

The Source property sets or returns a String containing the name of the provider that generated the first error. Because it provides information only from the first error, use this property cautiously when building robust error handling.

Usage

```
myString = myDeletedRowInaccessibleException.Source
myDeletedRowInaccessibleException.Source = myString
```

Parameters

None.

StackTrace

The read-only StackTrace property returns a String containing a textual representation of the stack trace. The stack trace reports all of the methods that are in execution at the time just prior to the execution being thrown. It is read from top to bottom with the latest method in execution at the top.

The StackTrace can be invaluable in tracing difficult-to-find bugs because it provides a way to see all of the methods that could have led up to the error.

TIP To see the stack trace programmatically when no exception has been raised, use the Environment.StackTrace property.

Usage

```
myString = myDeletedRowInaccessibleException.StackTrace
```

Parameters

None.

TargetSite

The read-only TargetSite property returns an object inheriting from System.Reflection.MethodBase that contains a reference to the method that caused the error to be thrown.

This property is primarily used to programmatically find information about the method that raised the exception. The returned object will provide information such as the methods parameters and return type and whether the method is virtual, a constructor, public, private, etc. Because it deals mainly with Reflection and not data access, further discussion of this property is beyond the scope of this book.

Usage

```
myMethodBase = myDeletedRowInaccessibleException.TargetSite
```

Parameters

None.

ToString

The ToString method is overridden to return information relating to the DeletedRowInaccessibleException exception. The returned String contains the full class name, and also the error message, name of the inner exception, and stack trace, if they exist.

Usage

```
myString = myDeletedRowInaccessibleException.ToString()
```

Parameters

None.

Exceptions

None.

System.Data.DuplicateNameException

The DuplicateNameException class (descended from the DataException class) defines exceptions that are thrown when an add operation attempts to use a database object name that already exists.

Constructors

```
Dim myDuplicateNameException As New DuplicateNameException()
Dim myDuplicateNameException As New _
     DuplicateNameException(myString)
```

Parameters

`myString`	A String object that will initialize the Message property.

DuplicateNameException Sample Code

```
Dim myDuplicateNameException As DuplicateNameException
myDuplicateNameException = New _
     DuplicateNameException("Name Already Exists!")
Throw myDuplicateNameException
```

Members

GetBaseException

The GetBaseException method returns an Exception object containing the original exception. To return the original exception, it traverses the chain of InnerException objects. If the InnerException property of the current exception is null, GetBaseException will return a reference to the current Exception object.

To determine only the parent exception to the current exception, use the InnerException property.

Usage

```
myException = myDuplicateNameException.GetBaseException()
```

Parameters

None.

Exceptions

None.

GetObjectData

The GetObjectData method fills the passed System.Runtime.Serialization.SerializationInfo buffer object with information about the Exception object. There is no value returned by this method. Depending on the passed System.Runtime.Serialization.StreamingContext object, this method can be used to serialize the object to a stream or read serialization from a stream.

Because it deals mainly with Serialization and not data access, further discussion of this property is beyond the scope of this book.

Usage

```
myDuplicateNameException.GetObjectData(mySerializationInfo, _
   myStreamingContext)
```

Parameters

`mySerializationInfo`	A System.Runtime.Serialization.SerializationInfo buffer object to be filled with the exception's serialization data.
`myStreamingContext`	A System.Runtime.Serialization.StreamingContext object specifying the stream to write the serialization info to or read the information from.

Exceptions

ArgumentNullException	The passed SerializationInfo buffer object is null (`Nothing` in Visual Basic .NET).

HelpLink

The HelpLink property returns or sets a String linking to a help file associated with the DuplicateNameException. The HelpLink is formatted as a Uniform Resource Name (URN) or Uniform Resource Locator (URL). An example of this property that points to the MSDN help available with Visual Studio .NET would be: `ms-help://MS.VSCC/MS.MSDNVS/cpref/html/frlrfsystemexceptionclasshelplinktopic.htm`.

The HelpLink is often not set, so it is wise to verify both that the HelpLink property itself is not an empty string and that the HelpLink points to a valid help file before exposing the HelpLink to a user of your program.

Usage

```
myString = myDuplicateNameException.HelpLink
myDuplicateNameException.HelpLink = myString
```

Parameters

None.

InnerException

The read-only InnerException property returns the Exception object linking to a previous exception that caused the current exception to be thrown, if any, or a null value (`Nothing` in Visual Basic .NET), if not. This permits a chain of InnerException objects to be generated, allowing a program to trace the exception chain all the way to the root exception. Be aware that InnerException may be null.

To find the base exception that originally was fired, use the GetBaseException method.

Usage

```
myException = myDuplicateNameException.InnerException
```

Parameters

None.

Message

The read-only Message property returns a String describing the first error that caused the exception. Because it provides information only from the first error, use this property cautiously when building robust error handling.

Usage

```
myString = myDuplicateNameException.Message
```

Parameters

None.

Source

The Source property sets or returns a String containing the name of the provider that generated the first error. Because it provides information only from the first error, use this property cautiously when building robust error handling.

Usage

```
myString = myDuplicateNameException.Source
myDuplicateNameException.Source = myString
```

Parameters

None.

StackTrace

The read-only StackTrace property returns a String containing a textual representation of the stack trace. The stack trace reports all of the methods that are in execution at the time just prior to the execution being thrown. It is read from top to bottom with the latest method in execution at the top.

The StackTrace can be invaluable in tracing difficult-to-find bugs because it provides a method to see all of the methods that could have led up to the error.

TIP **To see the stack trace programmatically when no exception has been raised, use the Environment.StackTrace property.**

Usage

```
myString = myDuplicateNameException.StackTrace
```

Parameters

None.

TargetSite

The read-only TargetSite property returns an object inheriting from System.Reflection.MethodBase that contains a reference to the method that caused the error to be thrown.

This property is primarily used to programmatically find information about the method that raised the exception. The returned object will provide information such as the methods parameters and return type and whether the method is virtual, a constructor, public, private, etc. Because it deals mainly with Reflection and not data access, further discussion of this property is beyond the scope of this book.

Usage

```
myMethodBase = myDuplicateNameException.TargetSite
```

Parameters

None.

ToString

The ToString method is overridden to return information relating to the DuplicateNameException exception. The returned String contains the full class name, and also the error message, name of the inner exception, and stack trace, if they exist.

Usage

```
myString = myDuplicateNameException.ToString()
```

Parameters

None.

Exceptions

None.

System.Data.EvaluateException

The EvaluateException class (descended from the InvalidExpressionException class) defines exceptions that are thrown when the DataColumn.Expression property cannot be evaluated. The Expression may be properly formed but refer to another column that contains invalid information (i.e., attempting to calculate sales tax on a null value). If the Expression cannot be parsed due to a syntax error, then the SyntaxErrorException would be thrown. (See System.Data.SyntaxErrorException for more information.)

Related exceptions are the System.Data.InvalidExpressionException and System.Data.SyntaxErrorException.

Constructors

```
Dim myEvaluateException As New EvaluateException()
Dim myEvaluateException As New EvaluateException(myString)
```

Parameters

`myString`	A String object that will initialize the Message property.

EvaluateException Sample Code

```
Dim myEvaluateException As EvaluateException
myEvaluateException = New _
     EvaluateException("Can't Evaluate Expression!")
Throw myEvaluateException
```

Members

GetBaseException

The GetBaseException method returns an Exception object containing the original exception. To return the original exception, it traverses the chain of InnerException objects. If the InnerException property of the current exception is null, GetBaseException will return a reference to the current Exception object.

To determine only the parent exception to the current exception, use the InnerException property.

Usage

```
myException = myEvaluateException.GetBaseException()
```

Parameters

None.

Exceptions

None.

GetObjectData

The GetObjectData method fills the passed System.Runtime.Serialization.SerializationInfo buffer object with information about the Exception object. There is no value returned by this method. Depending on the passed System.Runtime.Serialization.StreamingContext object, this method can be used to serialize the object to a stream or read serialization from a stream.

Because it deals mainly with serialization and not data access, further discussion of this property is beyond the scope of this book.

Usage

```
myEvaluateException.GetObjectData(mySerializationInfo, _
   myStreamingContext)
```

Parameters

`mySerializationInfo`	A System.Runtime.Serialization.SerializationInfo buffer object to be filled with the exception's serialization data.
`myStreamingContext`	A System.Runtime.Serialization.StreamingContext object specifying the stream to write the serialization info to or read the information from.

Exceptions

ArgumentNullException	The passed SerializationInfo buffer object is null (`Nothing` in Visual Basic .NET).

HelpLink

The HelpLink property returns or sets a String linking to a help file associated with the EvaluateException. The HelpLink is formatted as a Uniform Resource Name (URN) or Uniform Resource Locator (URL). An example of this property that points to the MSDN help available with Visual Studio .NET would be: `ms-help://MS.VSCC/MS.MSDNVS/cpref/html/frlrfsystemexceptionclasshelplinktopic.htm`.

The HelpLink is often not set, so it is wise to verify both that the HelpLink property itself is not an empty string and that the HelpLink points to a valid help file before exposing the HelpLink to a user of your program.

Usage

```
myString = myEvaluateException.HelpLink
myEvaluateException.HelpLink = myString
```

Parameters

None.

InnerException

The read-only InnerException property returns the Exception object linking to a previous exception that caused the current exception to be thrown, if any, or a null value (`Nothing` in Visual Basic .NET), if not. This permits a chain of InnerException objects to be generated, allowing a program to trace the exception chain all the way to the root exception. Be aware that InnerException may be null.

To find the base exception that originally was fired, use the GetBaseException method.

Usage

```
myException = myEvaluateException.InnerException
```

Parameters

None.

Message

The read-only Message property returns a String describing the first error that caused the exception. Because it provides information only from the first error, use this property cautiously when building robust error handling.

Usage

```
myString = myEvaluateException.Message
```

Parameters

None.

Source

The Source property sets or returns a String containing the name of the provider that generated the first error. Because it provides information only from the first error, use this property cautiously when building robust error handling.

Usage

```
myString = myEvaluateException.Source
myEvaluateException.Source = myString
```

Parameters

None.

StackTrace

The read-only StackTrace property returns a String containing a textual representation of the stack trace. The stack trace reports all of the methods that are in execution at the time just prior to the execution being thrown. It is read from top to bottom with the latest method in execution at the top.

The StackTrace can be invaluable in tracing difficult-to-find bugs because it provides a method to see all of the methods that could have led up to the error.

TIP To see the stack trace programmatically when no exception has been raised, use the Environment.StackTrace property.

Usage

```
myString = myEvaluateException.StackTrace
```

Parameters

None.

TargetSite

The read-only TargetSite property returns an object inheriting from System.Reflection.MethodBase that contains a reference to the method that caused the error to be thrown.

This property is primarily used to programmatically find information about the method that raised the exception. The returned object will provide information such as the methods parameters and return type and whether the method is virtual, a constructor, public, private, etc. Because it deals mainly with Reflection and not data access, further discussion of this property is beyond the scope of this book.

Usage

```
myMethodBase = myEvaluateException.TargetSite
```

Parameters

None.

ToString

The ToString method is overridden to return information relating to the EvaluateException exception. The returned String contains the full class name and also the error message, name of the inner exception, and stack trace, if they exist.

Usage
```
myString = myEvaluateException.ToString()
```

Parameters
None.

Exceptions
None.

System.Data.FillErrorEventArgs

The FillErrorEventArgs class is automatically created and passed when the FillError event of the DbDataAdapter (or derived classes) is raised. It contains extended error information.

FillErrorEventArgs also has a public constructor, which can be used to define and throw your own exception.

Constructors

```
Dim myFillErrorEventArgs As New _
     FillErrorEventArgs(myDataTable, myValuesArray)
```

Parameters

`myDataTable`	DataTable object being filled with data.
`myValuesArray`	Array of Object objects that contains the values for the DataRow being added to the DataTable or updated.

Members

Continue

The Continue property returns or sets a Boolean value that determines whether the Fill operation should continue updating this DataRow, despite the error. A value of True indicates that the fill operation should continue; False terminates the Fill operation.

Usage
```
myBoolean = myFillErrorEventArgs.Continue
myFillErrorEventArgs.Continue = myBoolean
```

Parameters
None.

Exceptions
None.

DataTable

The read-only DataTable property returns the DataTable object that is being filled.

Usage
```
myDataTable = myFillErrorEventArgs.DataTable
```

Parameters
None.

Exceptions
None.

Errors

The Errors property returns or sets a System.Exception object that contains error information related to the Fill error.

Usage
```
myException = myFillErrorEventArgs.Errors
myFillErrorEventArgs.Errors = myException
```

Parameters
None.

Exceptions
None.

ToString

The ToString method returns "System.Data.FillErrorEventArgs".

Usage
```
myString = myFillErrorEventArgs.ToString()
```

Parameters
None.

Exceptions
None.

Values

The read-only Values property returns an array of Object objects that are the values for all the columns in the row that caused the fill error.

Usage
```
myObjectArray = myFillErrorEventArgs.Values
```

Parameters
None.

Exceptions
None.

System.Data.ForeignKeyConstraint

The ForeignKeyConstraint class represents a restriction imposed on a set of columns involved in a primary key/foreign key relationship when a column value or row is either updated or deleted. The action defined on a foreign key constraint can cause the child row to be deleted, or updated to either a null or default value, or defined so that an exception is raised, but the value of the child row remains unchanged.

When creating ForeignKeyConstraint objects, you may pass either a single parent column and a single child column or an array of each. If you pass arrays, the columns in both arrays must be the same length, and within each array the columns must come from the same DataTable. This ensures that a single ForeignKeyConstraint has only one parent table (RelatedTable property) and one child table (Table property).

You can add a ForeignKeyConstraint only to the Constraints collection of the child DataTable. Attempting to assign a ForeignKeyConstraint to the parent table will cause an InvalidConstraintException to be thrown.

The ForeignKeyConstraint inherits directly from the System.Data.Constraint class.

HINT When creating new constraints for a DataTable, use the DataTable.Constaints.Add method for convenience and speed, instead of the constraint constructors.

HINT When defining a UniqueConstraint and a ForeignKeyConstraint on the same parent column, you can instead define a DataRelation and pass a True in the constructors to the boolCreateConstraints parameter.

WARNING Constraints are not enforced unless the DataSet.EnforceConstraints property is set to True.

Constructors

```
Dim myForeignKeyConstraint As New _
     ForeignKeyConstraint(myDataColumnParent, _
     myDataColumnChild)
Dim myForeignKeyConstraint As New _
     ForeignKeyConstraint(myDataColumnParentArray(), _
     myDataColumnChildArray())
Dim myForeignKeyConstraint As New _
     ForeignKeyConstraint(strName, myDataColumnParent, _
     myDataColumnChild)
Dim myForeignKeyConstraint As New _
     ForeignKeyConstraint(strName, _
     myDataColumnParentArray(), myDataColumnChildArray())
Dim myForeignKeyConstraint As New _
     ForeignKeyConstraint(strName, strParentTableName, _
     strParentColumnNameArray(),strChildColumnNameArray(), _
     myAcceptRejectRule, myRuleDelete, myRuleUpdate)
```

Parameters

`myDataColumnParent`	The parent DataColumn in the constraint.
`myDataColumnChild`	The child DataColumn in the constraint.
`myDataColumnParentArray()`	The Array containing the parent Data-Column objects in the constraint.
`myDataColumnChildArray()`	The array containing the child Data-Column objects in the constraint.
`strName`	The name of the constraint as a String.
`strParentTableName`	The name of the parent DataTable that contains the DataColumn objects in the constraint.
`strParentColumnNameArray()`	The array containing the names of parent DataColumn objects in the constraint.
`strChildColumnNameArray()`	The array containing the names of child DataColumn objects in the constraint.
`myAcceptRejectRule`	A System.Data.AcceptRejectRule enumeration value (None, Cascade, and Default).
`myRuleDelete`	A System.Data.Rule enumeration value to use when a row is deleted (None, Cascade, SetNull, SetDefault, and Default). The default is Cascade.
`myRuleUpdate`	A System.Data.Rule enumeration value to use when a row is updated (None, Cascade, SetNull, SetDefault, and Default). The default is Cascade.

Exceptions

ArgumentNullException	A parameter passed is a null reference (`Nothing` in Visual Basic).
NullReferenceException	The passed DataColumn was null (`Nothing` in Visual Basic).
InvalidConstraintException	1.) The columns have different data types. 2.) The tables don't belong to the same DataSet. 3.) When passing arrays of DataColumn objects, the parent columns are not from the same table. (You cannot create a single key from parents that come from different tables.)

ForeignKeyConstraint Sample Code

```
'This function demonstrates the ForeignKeyConstraint
'  class.  It assumes two valid DataTables are passed,
'  with Table1.Column1 being the primary key, and
'  Table2.Column1 being the foreign key.
Public Sub DemoForeignKeyConstraints( _
        ByRef myDataTable1 As DataTable, _
        ByRef myDataTable2 As DataTable)

   Dim myForeignKeyConstraint As ForeignKeyConstraint
   'define the foreign key and add it to DataTable1
   myForeignKeyConstraint = New _
      ForeignKeyConstraint(myDataTable1.Columns(0), _
         myDataTable2.Columns(0))
   ''if you were to define two columns for the _
   ''  relationship, the statement below could be used.
   'myForeignKeyConstraint = New ForeignKeyConstraint( _
   '   New DataColumn(1) {myDataTable1.Columns(0), _
   '      myDataTable1.Columns(1)}, _
   '   New DataColumn(1) {myDataTable2.Columns(0), _
   '      myDataTable2.Columns(1)})

   'Get the names of the tables associated with the constraint
   MessageBox.Show("Parent table is " + _
      myForeignKeyConstraint.RelatedTable.TableName)
   MessageBox.Show("Child table is " + _
      myForeignKeyConstraint.Table.TableName)

   'set the various rule properties
   myForeignKeyConstraint.DeleteRule = Rule.Cascade
   myForeignKeyConstraint.UpdateRule = Rule.None
   myForeignKeyConstraint.AcceptRejectRule = _
      AcceptRejectRule.Cascade

   'add the key to the DataTable
   myDataTable2.Constraints.Add(myForeignKeyConstraint)

End Sub
```

Members

AcceptRejectRule

The AcceptRejectRule property returns or sets a System.Data.AcceptRejectRule enumeration value specifying the action that should be taken across this constraint when AcceptChanges is invoked. Possible values are None and Cascade. The default value is None.

Setting this method to True can ensure that cascaded changes made to child DataRow objects are accepted or rejected along with the parent row. This is useful when there are several nested AcceptChanges or RejectChanges methods being called at various levels. For instance, accepting a change at the parent row, but not cascading that to the child row, could result in an inconsistency (and an exception) if RejectChanges is called on the child row.

This means only that the AcceptChanges or RejectChanges is called on the child rows. This does not mean that the values themselves are cascaded. For setting rules on how to deal with changes in the column data when the parent is changed, see the DeleteRule and UpdateRule properties.

Usage

```
myAcceptRejectRule = myForeignKeyConstraint.AcceptRejectRule
myForeignKeyConstraint.AcceptRejectRule = myAcceptRejectRule
```

Parameters

None.

Exceptions

None.

Columns

The read-only Columns property returns an array of DataColumn objects that contains the child columns for the ForeignKeyConstraint.

Usage

```
myDataColumn[] = myForeignKeyConstraint.Columns
```

Parameters

None.

Exceptions

None.

ConstraintName

The ConstraintName property returns or sets a String value that represents the name of the ForeignKeyConstraint object.

Usage

```
myString = myForeignKeyConstraint.ConstraintName
myForeignKeyConstraint.ConstraintName = myString
```

Parameters

None.

Exceptions

None.

DeleteRule

The DeleteRule property returns or sets a System.Data.Rule enumeration value specifying the action to take in the columns of the child table(s) when a row is deleted from the parent table. Possible values are Cascade, None, SetDefault, and SetNull. This rule is invoked when the value in the parent column is deleted, unlike the AcceptRejectRule, which is called when the parent column is changed. The default value is Cascade. (See the Rule Enumeration table that follows or System.Data.Rule enumeration for more information on the behavior of the different values.)

Usage

```
myRule = myForeignKeyConstraint.DeleteRule
myForeignKeyConstraint.DeleteRule = myRule
```

Parameters

None.

Rule Enumeration

Cascade (1)	(Default) Specifies that child rows are to be deleted or child columns updated to reflect the new value.
None (0)	Does not perform any action, but throws an exception.
SetDefault (3)	Sets the child column values to their DefaultValue values.
SetNull (2)	Sets the child column values to DBNull.

Exceptions

None.

Equals

The Equals method is overridden to allow comparison of two ForeignKeyConstraint objects. The Equals method will return True if the two ForeignKeyConstraint objects constrain the same columns. (This is true even if they have different properties. For instance, if one constraint AcceptRejectRule is set to None.and the other to Cascade, they are considered equal by this method.)

You can use this method to determine equality to any of the constraints in a collection before adding a new constraint. This will prevent a DataException from being thrown.

Usage

```
myBoolean = myForeignKeyConstraint.Equals(myObject)
```

Parameters

`myObject`	The Object (likely a ForeignKeyConstraint object) to compare to myForeignKeyConstraint for equality.

Exceptions

None.

ExtendedProperties

The read-only ExtendedProperties property returns a PropertyCollection object that allows you to store custom information with the object. Although the property itself is read only, you may add properties to the returned PropertyCollection with the Add method. See the sample code for an example.

NOTE If the ExtendedProperties collection is to be persisted as XML, then the members of the collection must be of type String.

Usage

```
myPropertyCollection = _
     myForeignKeyConstraint.ExtendedProperties
```

Parameters

None.

Exceptions

None.

Sample Code

```
myForeignKeyConstraint.ExtendedProperties.Add( _
     "Father", "Elvin Borg")
```

RelatedColumns

The read-only RelatedColumns property returns an array of DataColumn objects that are the parent columns of the constraint.

Usage

```
myDataColumnArray = myForeignKeyConstraint.RelatedColumns
```

Parameters

None.

Exceptions

None.

RelatedTable

The read-only RelatedTable property returns the DataTable object that is the parent table for the constraint.

Usage

```
myDataTable = myForeignKeyConstraint.RelatedTable
```

Parameters

None.

Exceptions

None.

Table

The read-only Table property returns the DataTable object that owns this constraint. This is the child table for the constraint because a ForeignKeyConstraint can be added only to the Constraints collection of the DataTable containing the child row.

Usage

```
myDataTable = myForeignKeyConstraint.Table
```

Parameters

None.

Exceptions

None.

ToString

The ToString method returns the ConstraintName as a String.

Usage

```
myString = myForeignKeyConstraint.ToString()
```

Parameters

None.

Exceptions

None.

UpdateRule

The UpdateRule property returns or sets a System.Data.Rule enumeration value specifying the action to take in the columns of the child table(s) when a constrained column in the parent table is updated. Possible values are Cascade, None, SetDefault, and SetNull. This rule is invoked when the value in the parent column is changed, unlike the DeleteRule, which is called when the parent column is deleted. The default value is Cascade. (See the table Rule Enumeration that follows or System.Data.Rule enumeration for more information on the behavior of the different values.)

Usage

```
myRule = myForeignKeyConstraint.UpdateRule
myForeignKeyConstraint.UpdateRule = myRule
```

Parameters

None.

Rule Enumeration

Cascade (1)	(Default) Specifies that child rows are to be deleted or child columns updated to reflect the new value.
None (0)	Does not perform any action, but throws an exception.
SetDefault (3)	Sets the child column values to their DefaultValue values.
SetNull (2)	Sets the child column values to DBNull.

Exceptions

None.

System.Data.InRowChangingEventException

The InRowChangingEventException class (descended from the DataException class) defines exceptions that are thrown when the EndEdit method is called from within the DataTable.RowChanging event.

This exception should be relatively rare. The RowChanging event is fired when a row is in the process of being changed. There is no reason to place an EndEdit command within the RowChanging event. If the edit is valid, then you should wait until the RowChanged event is fired. If the edit is invalid, then the edit should be abandoned, not ended (and thereby committed).

Constructors

```
Dim myInRowChangingEventException As New _
     InRowChangingEventException()
Dim myInRowChangingEventException As New _
     InRowChangingEventException(myString)
```

Parameters

`myString` A String object that will initialize the Message property.

InRowChangingEventException Sample Code

```
Dim myInRowChangingEventException As _
     InRowChangingEventException
myInRowChangingEventException = New _
     InRowChangingEventException("Data Exception!")
Throw myInRowChangingEventException
```

Members

GetBaseException

The GetBaseException method returns an Exception object containing the original exception. To return the original exception, it traverses the chain of InnerException objects. If the InnerException property of the current exception is null, GetBaseException will return a reference to the current Exception object.

To determine only the parent exception to the current exception, use the InnerException property.

Usage

```
myException = myInRowChangingEventException.GetBaseException()
```

Parameters

None.

Exceptions

None.

GetObjectData

The GetObjectData method fills the passed System.Runtime.Serialization.SerializationInfo buffer object with information about the Exception object. There is no value returned by this method. Depending on the passed System.Runtime.Serialization.StreamingContext object, this method can be used to serialize the object to a stream or read serialization from a stream.

Because it deals mainly with Serialization and not data access, further discussion of this property is beyond the scope of this book.

Usage

```
myInRowChangingEventException.GetObjectData( _
     mySerializationInfo, myStreamingContext)
```

Parameters

`mySerializationInfo`	A System.Runtime.Serialization.SerializationInfo buffer object to be filled with the exception's serialization data.
`myStreamingContext`	A System.Runtime.Serialization.StreamingContext object specifying the stream to write the serialization info to or read the information from.

Exceptions

ArgumentNullException	The passed SerializationInfo buffer object is null (`Nothing` in Visual Basic .NET).

HelpLink

The HelpLink property returns or sets a String linking to a help file associated with the InRowChangingEventException. The HelpLink is formatted as a Uniform Resource Name (URN) or Uniform Resource Locator (URL). An example of this property that points to the MSDN help available with Visual Studio .NET would be: `ms-help://MS.VSCC/MS.MSDNVS/cpref/html/frlrfsystemexceptionclasshelplintopic.htm`.

The HelpLink is often not set, so it is wise to verify both that the HelpLink property itself is not an empty string and that the HelpLink points to a valid help file before exposing the HelpLink to a user of your program.

Usage

```
myString = myInRowChangingEventException.HelpLink
myInRowChangingEventException.HelpLink = myString
```

Parameters

None.

InnerException

The read-only InnerException property returns the Exception object linking to a previous exception that caused the current exception to be thrown, if any, or a null value (`Nothing` in Visual Basic .NET), if not. This permits a chain of InnerException objects to be generated, allowing a program to trace the exception chain all the way to the root exception. Be aware that InnerException may be null.

To find the base exception that originally was fired, use the GetBaseException method.

Usage

```
myException = myInRowChangingEventException.InnerException
```

Parameters
None.

Message

The read-only Message property returns a String describing the first error that caused the exception. Because it provides information only from the first error, use this property cautiously when building robust error handling.

Usage
```
myString = myInRowChangingEventException.Message
```

Parameters
None.

Source

The Source property sets or returns a String containing the name of the provider that generated the first error. Because it provides information only from the first error, use this property cautiously when building robust error handling.

Usage
```
myString = myInRowChangingEventException.Source
myInRowChangingEventException.Source = myString
```

Parameters
None.

StackTrace

The read-only StackTrace property returns a String containing a textual representation of the stack trace. The stack trace reports all of the methods that are in execution at the time just prior to the execution being thrown. It is read from top to bottom with the latest method in execution at the top.

The StackTrace can be invaluable in tracing difficult-to-find bugs because it provides a way to see all of the methods that could have led up to the error.

TIP **To see the stack trace programmatically when no exception has been raised, use the Environment.StackTrace property.**

Usage
```
myString = myInRowChangingEventException.StackTrace
```

Parameters
None.

TargetSite

The read-only TargetSite property returns an object inheriting from System.Reflection.MethodBase that contains a reference to the method that caused the error to be thrown.

This property is primarily used to programmatically find information about the method that raised the exception. The returned object will provide information such as the methods parameters and return type and whether the method is virtual, a constructor, public, private, etc. Because it deals mainly with Reflection and not data access, further discussion of this property is beyond the scope of this book.

Usage

```
myMethodBase = myInRowChangingEventException.TargetSite
```

Parameters

None.

ToString

The ToString method is overridden to return information relating to the InRowChangingEventException exception. The returned String contains the full class name and also the error message, name of the inner exception, and stack trace, if they exist.

Usage

```
myString = myInRowChangingEventException.ToString()
```

Parameters

None.

Exceptions

None.

System.Data.InternalDataCollectionBase

The InternalDataCollectionBase class is an ancestor class for all of the collection classes within the System.Data namespace. It provides the basic interface that is common across the classes, as well as much of the implementation.

The current classes descending from InternalDataCollectionBase are the ConstraintCollection, DataColumnCollection, DataRelationCollection, DataRowCollection, and DataTableCollection classes.

Constructors

```
Dim myInternalDataCollectionBase As New _
     InternalDataCollectionBase()
```

Parameters

None.

ConstraintCollection Sample Code

```
'See the sample code for the inheriting classes for
'examples of using this class.
```

Members

CopyTo

The CopyTo method is used to copy the member objects in the InternalDataCollection-Base (or descending classes) to an array, beginning at a specified index within the array.

Usage

```
myInternalDataCollectionBase.CopyTo(myArray, _
     myStartIndex)
```

Parameters

myArray	The passed buffer array to hold the member objects.
myStartIndex	The Integer index designating the location in the passed array to begin filling with the member objects.

Exceptions

ArgumentException	The passed array was not long enough to hold the passed objects.
ArgumentNullException	The passed array is null (`Nothing` in Visual Basic .NET).
ArgumentOutOfRangeException	myStartIndex is negative or greater than the length of the array.
InvalidCastException	The object type of the collection cannot be cast automatically to the object type of the array.

Count

The read-only Count property returns an Int32 value specifying the number of members in the collection.

Usage

```
myInt32 = myInternalDataCollectionBase.Count
```

Parameters

None.

Exceptions

None.

GetEnumerator

The GetEnumerator method returns a System.Collections.IEnumerator object that can be used to iterate over the collection. This method assists in using the For Each - Next (or equivalent statements) to iterate through a collection.

Usage

```
myIEnumerator = myInternalDataCollectionBase.GetEnumerator()
```

Parameters
None.

Exceptions
None.

IsReadOnly

The read-only IsReadOnly property returns a Boolean value specifying whether the collection is read only.

Usage
```
myBoolean = myInternalDataCollectionBase.IsReadOnly
```

Parameters
None.

Exceptions
None.

IsSynchronized

The read-only IsSynchronized property returns a Boolean value indicating whether the ConstraintCollection is currently synchronized. For information on synchronizing the collections, see the InternalDataCollectionBase.SyncRoot property.

Usage
```
myBoolean = myInternalDataCollectionBase.IsSynchronized
```

Parameters
None.

Exceptions
None.

SyncRoot

The read-only SyncRoot property returns an Object object that can be used to synchronize the collection. The returned object can be used to ensure the integrity of the collection, even when being accessed by a number of separate threads.

Usage
```
myObject = myInternalDataCollectionBase.SyncRoot
```

Parameters
None.

Exceptions
None.

ToString

The ToString method returns "System.Data.InternalDataCollectionBase", or if being called by a descendent class, the name of the calling class.

Usage
```
myString = myInternalDataCollectionBase.ToString()
```

Parameters
None.

Exceptions
None.

System.Data.InvalidConstraintException

The InvalidConstraintException class (descended from the DataException class) defines exceptions that are thrown when a relation is incorrectly created or accessed. It is thrown when incorrectly invoking the following methods:

DataRelationCollection.Add	Relation cannot be created with supplied values.
DataRowCollection.Clear	A ForeignKeyConstraint limits ability to delete a DataRow.
DataRow.GetParentRow	Columns have different data types, or tables do not belong to the same DataSet.

Constructors

```
Dim myInvalidConstraintException As New _
     InvalidConstraintException()
Dim myInvalidConstraintException As New _
     InvalidConstraintException(myString)
```

Parameters

`myString`	A String object that will initialize the Message property.

InvalidConstraintException Sample Code

```
Dim myInvalidConstraintException As _
     InvalidConstraintException
myInvalidConstraintException = New _
     InvalidConstraintException("Invalid Constraint!")
Throw myInvalidConstraintException
```

Members

GetBaseException

The GetBaseException method returns an Exception object containing the original exception. To return the original exception, it traverses the chain of InnerException objects. If the InnerException property of the current exception is null, GetBaseException will return a reference to the current Exception object.

To determine only the parent exception to the current exception, use the InnerException property.

Usage

```
myException = myInvalidConstraintException.GetBaseException()
```

Parameters

None.

Exceptions

None.

GetObjectData

The GetObjectData method fills the passed System.Runtime.Serialization.SerializationInfo buffer object with information about the Exception object. There is no value returned by this method. Depending on the passed System.Runtime.Serialization.StreamingContext object, this method can be used to serialize the object to a stream or read serialization from a stream.

Because it deals mainly with Serialization and not data access, further discussion of this property is beyond the scope of this book.

Usage

```
myInvalidConstraintException.GetObjectData( _
mySerializationInfo, myStreamingContext)
```

Parameters

`mySerializationInfo`	A System.Runtime.Serialization.SerializationInfo buffer object to be filled with the exception's serialization data.
`myStreamingContext`	A System.Runtime.Serialization.StreamingContext object specifying the stream to write the serialization info to or read the information from.

Exceptions

ArgumentNullException	The passed SerializationInfo buffer object is null (`Nothing` in Visual Basic .NET).

HelpLink

The HelpLink property returns or sets a String linking to a help file associated with the InvalidConstraintException. The HelpLink is formatted as a Uniform Resource Name (URN) or Uniform Resource Locator (URL). An example of this property that points to the MSDN help available with Visual Studio .NET would be: `ms-help://MS.VSCC/MS.MSDNVS/cpref/html/frlrfsystemexceptionclasshelplinktopic.htm`.

The HelpLink is often not set, so it is wise to verify both that the HelpLink property itself is not an empty string and that the HelpLink points to a valid help file before exposing the HelpLink to a user of your program.

Usage

```
myString = myInvalidConstraintException.HelpLink
myInvalidConstraintException.HelpLink = myString
```

Parameters
None.

InnerException

The read-only InnerException property returns the Exception object linking to a previous exception that caused the current exception to be thrown, if any, or a null value (`Nothing` in Visual Basic .NET), if not. This permits a chain of InnerException objects to be generated, allowing a program to trace the exception chain all the way to the root exception. Be aware that InnerException may be null.

To find the base exception that originally was fired, use the GetBaseException method.

Usage

```
myException = myInvalidConstraintException.InnerException
```

Parameters
None.

Message

The read-only Message property returns a String describing the first error that caused the exception. Because it provides information only from the first error, use this property cautiously when building robust error handling.

Usage

```
myString = myInvalidConstraintException.Message
```

Parameters
None.

Source

The Source property sets or returns a String containing the name of the provider that generated the first error. Because it provides information only from the first error, use this property cautiously when building robust error handling.

Usage

```
myString = myInvalidConstraintException.Source
myInvalidConstraintException.Source = myString
```

Parameters
None.

StackTrace

The read-only StackTrace property returns a String containing a textual representation of the stack trace. The stack trace reports all of the methods that are in execution at the time just prior to the execution being thrown. It is read from top to bottom with the latest method in execution at the top.

The StackTrace can be invaluable in tracing difficult-to-find bugs because it provides a way to see all of the methods that could have led up to the error.

TIP **To see the stack trace programmatically when no exception has been raised, use the Environment.StackTrace property.**

Usage

```
myString = myInvalidConstraintException.StackTrace
```

Parameters

None.

TargetSite

The read-only TargetSite property returns an object inheriting from System.Reflection.MethodBase that contains a reference to the method that caused the error to be thrown.

This property is primarily used to programmatically find information about the method that raised the exception. The returned object will provide information such as the methods parameters and return type and whether the method is virtual, a constructor, public, private, etc. Because it deals mainly with Reflection and not data access, further discussion of this property is beyond the scope of this book.

Usage

```
myMethodBase = myInvalidConstraintException.TargetSite
```

Parameters

None.

ToString

The ToString method is overridden to return information relating to the InvalidConstraintException exception. The returned String contains the full class name and also the error message, name of the inner exception, and stack trace, if they exist.

Usage

```
myString = myInvalidConstraintException.ToString()
```

Parameters

None.

Exceptions

None.

System.Data.InvalidExpressionException

The InvalidExpressionException class (descended from the DataException class) defines exceptions that are thrown when attempting to add a DataColumn to a DataColumnCollection, when the DataColumn contains an invalid DataColumn.Expression property.

The DataColumn.Expression property is a String that defines a mathematical or aggregating function for that column. (See the DataColumn.Expression property for more information.)

Related exceptions are the System.Data.EvaluateException and System.Data.SyntaxErrorException.

Constructors

```
Dim myInvalidExpressionException As New _
     InvalidExpressionException()
Dim myInvalidExpressionException As New _
     InvalidExpressionException(myString)
```

Parameters

`myString` A String object that will initialize the Message property.

InvalidExpressionException Sample Code

```
Dim myInvalidExpressionException As _
     InvalidExpressionException
myInvalidExpressionException = New _
     InvalidExpressionException("Invalid Expression!")
Throw myInvalidExpressionException
```

Members

GetBaseException

The GetBaseException method returns an Exception object containing the original exception. To return the original exception, it traverses the chain of InnerException objects. If the InnerException property of the current exception is null, GetBaseException will return a reference to the current Exception object.

To determine only the parent exception to the current exception, use the InnerException property.

Usage

```
myException = myInvalidExpressionException.GetBaseException()
```

Parameters

None.

Exceptions

None.

GetObjectData

The GetObjectData method fills the passed System.Runtime.Serialization.SerializationInfo buffer object with information about the Exception object. There is no value returned by this method. Depending on the passed System.Runtime.Serialization.StreamingContext object, this method can be used to serialize the object to a stream or read serialization from a stream.

Because it deals mainly with Serialization and not data access, further discussion of this property is beyond the scope of this book.

Usage

```
myInvalidExpressionException.GetObjectData( _
     mySerializationInfo, myStreamingContext)
```

Parameters

`mySerializationInfo`	A System.Runtime.Serialization.SerializationInfo buffer object to be filled with the exception's serialization data.
`myStreamingContext`	A System.Runtime.Serialization.StreamingContext object specifying the stream to write the serialization info to or read the information from.

Exceptions

ArgumentNullException	The passed SerializationInfo buffer object is null (`Nothing` in Visual Basic .NET).

HelpLink

The HelpLink property returns or sets a String linking to a help file associated with the InvalidExpressionException. The HelpLink is formatted as a Uniform Resource Name (URN) or Uniform Resource Locator (URL). An example of this property that points to the MSDN help available with Visual Studio .NET would be: `ms-help://MS.VSCC/MS.MSDNVS/cpref/html/frlrfsystemexceptionclasshelplinktopic.htm`.

The HelpLink is often not set, so it is wise to verify both that the HelpLink property itself is not an empty string and that the HelpLink points to a valid help file before exposing the HelpLink to a user of your program.

Usage

```
myString = myInvalidExpressionException.HelpLink
myInvalidExpressionException.HelpLink = myString
```

Parameters

None.

InnerException

The read-only InnerException property returns the Exception object linking to a previous exception that caused the current exception to be thrown, if any, or a null value (`Nothing` in Visual Basic .NET), if not. This permits a chain of InnerException objects to be generated, allowing a program to trace the exception chain all the way to the root exception. Be aware that InnerException may be null.

To find the base exception that originally was fired, use the GetBaseException method.

Usage

```
myException = myInvalidExpressionException.InnerException
```

Parameters

None.

Message

The read-only Message property returns a String describing the first error that caused the exception. Because it provides information only from the first error, use this property cautiously when building robust error handling.

Usage

```
myString = myInvalidExpressionException.Message
```

Parameters

None.

Source

The Source property sets or returns a String containing the name of the provider that generated the first error. Because it provides information only from the first error, use this property cautiously when building robust error handling.

Usage

```
myString = myInvalidExpressionException.Source
myInvalidExpressionException.Source = myString
```

Parameters

None.

StackTrace

The read-only StackTrace property returns a String containing a textual representation of the stack trace. The stack trace reports all of the methods that are in execution at the time just prior to the execution being thrown. It is read from top to bottom with the latest method in execution at the top.

The StackTrace can be invaluable in tracing difficult-to-find bugs because it provides a way to see all of the methods that could have led up to the error.

> **TIP** **To see the stack trace programmatically when no exception has been raised, use the Environment.StackTrace property.**

Usage

```
myString = myInvalidExpressionException.StackTrace
```

Parameters

None.

TargetSite

The read-only TargetSite property returns an object inheriting from System.Reflection.MethodBase that contains a reference to the method that caused the error to be thrown.

This property is primarily used to programmatically find information about the method that raised the exception. The returned object will provide information such as the methods parameters and return type and whether the method is virtual, a constructor, public, private, etc. Because it deals mainly with Reflection and not data access, further discussion of this property is beyond the scope of this book.

Usage

```
myMethodBase = myInvalidExpressionException.TargetSite
```

Parameters

None.

ToString

The ToString method is overridden to return information relating to the Invalid-ExpressionException exception. The returned String contains the full class name and also the error message, name of the inner exception, and stack trace, if they exist.

Usage

```
myString = myInvalidExpressionException.ToString()
```

Parameters

None.

Exceptions

None.

System.Data.IsolationLevel

The IsolationLevel enumeration provides the values that specify the transaction locking behavior for a connection. Once set, an IsolationLevel remains in effect until it is changed, but changes are not used until the next execution step of a transaction. If the IsolationLevel is changed during the execution of a transaction, the .NET data provider is expected to apply the new IsolationLevel to all remaining statements. Please note, however, that this is not enforced by the .NET Framework, and specific .NET data providers may not apply the new IsolationLevel until a new transaction is begun.

Because this class implements the FlagsAttribute, bitwise combinations of values are allowed.

IsolationLevel Enumeration

Chaos (16)	Any pending changes from transactions that are more highly isolated transactions cannot be overwritten. SQL Server 2000 and below do not support this isolation level.
ReadCommitted (4096)	(Default) Shared locks are held while the data is being read to avoid dirty reads, but the data can be changed before the end of the transaction, resulting in non-repeatable reads or phantom data (a.k.a. CursorStability).
ReadUncommitted (256)	No shared locks or exclusive locks are honored, so dirty reads are possible (a.k.a. Browse).

RepeatableRead (65536)	All data used in a query is locked, preventing others from updating. This prevents nonrepeatable reads, but phantom rows are still possible.
Serializable (1048576)	A range lock is placed on the data preventing other users from updating or inserting rows into the dataset until the transaction is complete (a.k.a. Isolated).
Unspecified (-1)	A different isolation level than the one specified is being used, but the level cannot be determined. (This value cannot be passed when creating a Transaction.)

System.Data.MappingType

The MappingType enumeration provides the values that specify how a DataColumn is mapped to an XML document. It is accessed through the DataColumn.ColumnMapping property. The MappingType determines how the column data and schema will be written to an XML document when the DataSet.WriteXml method is called.

NOTE A column cannot be defined as SimpleContent if the containing table has any other columns expressed as Elements or has any nested tables defined in a DataRelation.

MappingType Enumeration

Attribute (2)	The DataColumn is mapped to an XML attribute.
Element (1)	The DataColumn is mapped to an XML element.
Hidden (4)	The DataColumn is mapped to an internal structure.
SimpleContent (3)	The DataColumn is mapped to an XmlText node.

System.Data.MergeFailedEventArgs

The MergeFailedEventArgs class is automatically created and passed by the DataRow.MergeFailed event when the target and source DataRow objects have the same primary key. If you wish to replace a row, with another having the same primary key, you can set the DataSet.EnforceConstraints to False, until the DataSet has been updated, then reset it to True. Be warned, however, that this can be dangerous if other updates are taking place at the same time.

NOTE If the DataSet.EnforceConstraints is set to False, then the MergeFailed event will not be thrown.

MergeFailedEventArgs also has a public constructor, which can be used to define and throw your own exception.

Constructors

```
Dim myMergeFailedEventArgs As New _
     MergeFailedEventArgs(myDataTable, strConflict)
```

Parameters

`myDataTable`	DataTable object with DataRow being changed.
`strConflict`	A String providing a description of the conflict.

Members

Conflict

The read-only Conflict property returns a String value describing the merge conflict.

Usage

```
myString = myMergeFailedEventArgs.Conflict
```

Parameters

None.

Exceptions

None.

Table

The read-only Table property returns the DataTable object that hosts the DataRow that caused the merge conflict.

Usage

```
myDataTable = myMergeFailedEventArgs.Table
```

Parameters

None.

Exceptions

None.

ToString

The ToString method returns "System.Data.MergeFailedEventArgs".

Usage

```
myString = myMergeFailedEventArgs.ToString()
```

Parameters
None.

Exceptions
None.

System.Data.MissingMappingAction

The MissingMappingAction enumeration provides the values that determine what action will be taken when a mapping is missing from a source table or source column. The values are used as arguments in the DataColumnMappingCollection.GetColumnMappingBySchemaAction and DataTableMappingCollection.GetTableMappingBySchemaAction methods, and they can be found in the MissingMappingAction in all DataAdapter objects. Passthrough is generally used as the default value.

MissingMappingAction Enumeration

Error (3)	A System.SystemException is thrown.
Ignore (2)	Any columns or tables without mappings are ignored, returning a null reference.
Passthrough (1)	The source column or table is added to the DataSet using its original name.

System.Data.MissingPrimaryKeyException

The MissingPrimaryKeyException class (descended from the DataException class) defines exceptions that are thrown when attempting to access a row in a table with no primary key.

It is thrown by the DataRowCollection.Contains and DataRowCollection.Find methods.

Constructors

```
Dim myMissingPrimaryKeyException As New _
     MissingPrimaryKeyException()
Dim myMissingPrimaryKeyException As New _
     MissingPrimaryKeyException(myString)
```

Parameters

`myString`	A String object that will initialize the Message property.

MissingPrimaryKeyException Sample Code

```
Dim myMissingPrimaryKeyException As _
     MissingPrimaryKeyException
myMissingPrimaryKeyException = New _
     MissingPrimaryKeyException("No Primary Key!")
Throw myMissingPrimaryKeyException
```

Members

GetBaseException

The GetBaseException method returns an Exception object containing the original exception. To return the original exception, it traverses the chain of InnerException objects. If the InnerException property of the current exception is null, GetBaseException will return a reference to the current Exception object.

To determine only the parent exception to the current exception, use the InnerException property.

Usage

```
myException = myMissingPrimaryKeyException.GetBaseException()
```

Parameters

None.

Exceptions

None.

GetObjectData

The GetObjectData method fills the passed System.Runtime.Serialization.SerializationInfo buffer object with information about the Exception object. There is no value returned by this method. Depending on the passed System.Runtime.Serialization.StreamingContext object, this method can be used to serialize the object to a stream or read serialization from a stream.

Because it deals mainly with serialization and not data access, further discussion of this property is beyond the scope of this book.

Usage

```
myMissingPrimaryKeyException.GetObjectData( _
     mySerializationInfo, myStreamingContext)
```

Parameters

`mySerializationInfo`	A System.Runtime.Serialization.SerializationInfo buffer object to be filled with the exception's serialization data.
`myStreamingContext`	A System.Runtime.Serialization.StreamingContext object specifying the stream to write the serialization info to or read the information from.

Exceptions

ArgumentNullException	The passed SerializationInfo buffer object is null (`Nothing` in Visual Basic .NET).

HelpLink

The HelpLink property returns or sets a String linking to a help file associated with the MissingPrimaryKeyException. The HelpLink is formatted as a Uniform Resource Name (URN) or Uniform Resource Locator (URL). An example of this property that points to the MSDN help available with Visual Studio .NET would be: `ms-help://MS.VSCC/MS.MSDNVS/cpref/html/frlrfsystemexceptionclasshelplinktopic.htm`.

The HelpLink is often not set, so it is wise to verify both that the HelpLink property itself is not an empty string and that the HelpLink points to a valid help file before exposing the HelpLink to a user of your program.

Usage

```
myString = myMissingPrimaryKeyException.HelpLink
myMissingPrimaryKeyException.HelpLink = myString
```

Parameters

None.

InnerException

The read-only InnerException property returns the Exception object linking to a previous exception that caused the current exception to be thrown, if any, or a null value (`Nothing` in Visual Basic .NET), if not. This permits a chain of InnerException objects to be generated, allowing a program to trace the exception chain all the way to the root exception. Be aware that InnerException may be null.

To find the base exception that originally was fired, use the GetBaseException method.

Usage

```
myException = myMissingPrimaryKeyException.InnerException
```

Parameters

None.

Message

The read-only Message property returns a String describing the first error that caused the exception. Because it provides information from only the first error, use this property cautiously when building robust error handling.

Usage

```
myString = myMissingPrimaryKeyException.Message
```

Parameters

None.

Source

The Source property sets or returns a String containing the name of the provider that generated the first error. Because it provides information from only the first error, use this property cautiously when building robust error handling.

Usage

```
myString = myMissingPrimaryKeyException.Source
myMissingPrimaryKeyException.Source = myString
```

Parameters

None.

StackTrace

The read-only StackTrace property returns a String containing a textual representation of the stack trace. The stack trace reports all of the methods that are in execution at the time just prior to the execution being thrown. It is read from top to bottom with the latest method in execution at the top.

The StackTrace can be invaluable in tracing difficult-to-find bugs because it provides a way to see all of the methods that could have led up to the error.

TIP To see the stack trace programmatically when no exception has been raised, use the Environment.StackTrace property.

Usage

```
myString = myMissingPrimaryKeyException.StackTrace
```

Parameters

None.

TargetSite

The read-only TargetSite property returns an object inheriting from System.Reflection.MethodBase that contains a reference to the method that caused the error to be thrown.

This property is primarily used to programmatically find information about the method that raised the exception. The returned object will provide information such as the methods parameters and return type and whether the method is virtual, a constructor, public, private, etc. Because it deals mainly with Reflection and not data access, further discussion of this property is beyond the scope of this book.

Usage

```
myMethodBase = myMissingPrimaryKeyException.TargetSite
```

Parameters

None.

ToString

The ToString method is overridden to return information relating to the MissingPrimaryKeyException exception. The returned String contains the full class name and also the error message, name of the inner exception, and stack trace, if they exist.

Usage

```
myString = myMissingPrimaryKeyException.ToString()
```

Parameters

None.

Exceptions

None.

System.Data.MissingSchemaAction

The MissingSchemaAction enumeration provides the values that determine the action to be taken when adding data to a DataSet and the destination DataTable or DataColumn is missing. These values are used whenever there is a method that has the capability of changing the schema of a DataSet. The default value for most actions is Add.

MissingSchemaAction Enumeration

Add (1)	Adds the columns to the schema.
AddWithKey (4)	Adds the columns and primary key information to the schema.
Error (3)	Forces a System.SystemException to be thrown.
Ignore (2)	Ignores the extra columns (data will not be appended to the DataSet).

System.Data.NoNullAllowedException

The NoNullAllowedException class (descended from the DataException class) defines exceptions that are thrown when attempting to insert a null value into a column when that column's DataColumn.AllowDBNull property is set to False.

This exception is thrown by the DataRowCollection.Add, DataRow.EndEdit, DataRow.ItemArray, and DataTable.LoadDataRow methods.

Constructors

```
Dim myNoNullAllowedException As New NoNullAllowedException()
Dim myNoNullAllowedException As New _
     NoNullAllowedException(myString)
```

Parameters

`myString`	A String object that will initialize the Message property.

NoNullAllowedException Sample Code

```
Dim myNoNullAllowedException As NoNullAllowedException
myNoNullAllowedException = New _
     NoNullAllowedException("NULL not allowed!")
Throw myNoNullAllowedException
```

Members

GetBaseException

The GetBaseException method returns an Exception object containing the original exception. To return the original exception, it traverses the chain of InnerException objects. If the InnerException property of the current exception is null, GetBaseException will return a reference to the current Exception object.

To determine only the parent exception to the current exception, use the InnerException property.

Usage

```
myException = myNoNullAllowedException.GetBaseException()
```

Parameters

None.

Exceptions

None.

GetObjectData

The GetObjectData method fills the passed System.Runtime.Serialization.SerializationInfo buffer object with information about the Exception object. There is no value returned by this method. Depending on the passed System.Runtime.Serialization.StreamingContext object, this method can be used to serialize the object to a stream or read serialization from a stream.

Because it deals mainly with serialization and not data access, further discussion of this property is beyond the scope of this book.

Usage

```
myNoNullAllowedException.GetObjectData(mySerializationInfo, _
     myStreamingContext)
```

Parameters

`mySerializationInfo`	A System.Runtime.Serialization.SerializationInfo buffer object to be filled with the exception's serialization data.
`myStreamingContext`	A System.Runtime.Serialization.StreamingContext object specifying the stream to write the serialization info to or read the information from.

Exceptions

ArgumentNullException	The passed SerializationInfo buffer object is null (`Nothing` in Visual Basic .NET).

HelpLink

The HelpLink property returns or sets a String linking to a help file associated with the NoNullAllowedException. The HelpLink is formatted as a Uniform Resource Name (URN) or Uniform Resource Locator (URL). An example of this property that points to the MSDN help available with Visual Studio .NET would be: `ms-help://MS.VSCC/MS.MSDNVS/cpref/html/frlrfsystemexceptionclasshelplinktopic.htm.`

The HelpLink is often not set, so it is wise to verify both that the HelpLink property itself is not an empty string and that the HelpLink points to a valid help file before exposing the HelpLink to a user of your program.

Usage

```
myString = myNoNullAllowedException.HelpLink
myNoNullAllowedException.HelpLink = myString
```

Parameters

None.

InnerException

The read-only InnerException property returns the Exception object linking to a previous exception that caused the current exception to be thrown, if any, or a null value (`Nothing` in Visual Basic .NET), if not. This permits a chain of InnerException objects to be generated, allowing a program to trace the exception chain all the way to the root exception. Be aware that InnerException may be null.

To find the base exception that originally was fired, use the GetBaseException method.

Usage

```
myException = myNoNullAllowedException.InnerException
```

Parameters

None.

Message

The read-only Message property returns a String describing the first error that caused the exception. Because it provides information from only the first error, use this property cautiously when building robust error handling.

Usage

```
myString = myNoNullAllowedException.Message
```

Parameters

None.

Source

The Source property sets or returns a String containing the name of the provider that generated the first error. Because it provides information from only the first error, use this property cautiously when building robust error handling.

Usage

```
myString = myNoNullAllowedException.Source
myNoNullAllowedException.Source = myString
```

Parameters

None.

StackTrace

The read-only StackTrace property returns a String containing a textual representation of the stack trace. The stack trace reports all of the methods that are in execution at the time just prior to the execution being thrown. It is read from top to bottom with the latest method in execution at the top.

The StackTrace can be invaluable in tracing difficult-to-find bugs because it provides a way to see all of the methods that could have led up to the error.

TIP To see the stack trace programmatically when no exception has been raised, use the Environment.StackTrace property.

Usage

```
myString = myNoNullAllowedException.StackTrace
```

Parameters

None.

TargetSite

The read-only TargetSite property returns an object inheriting from System.Reflection.MethodBase that contains a reference to the method that caused the error to be thrown.

This property is primarily used to programmatically find information about the method that raised the exception. The returned object will provide information such as the methods parameters and return type and whether the method is virtual, a constructor, public, private, etc. Because it deals mainly with reflection and not data access, further discussion of this property is beyond the scope of this book.

Usage

```
myMethodBase = myNoNullAllowedException.TargetSite
```

Parameters

None.

ToString

The ToString method is overridden to return information relating to the NoNullAllowedException exception. The returned String contains the full class name and also the error message, name of the inner exception, and stack trace, if they exist.

Usage

```
myString = myNoNullAllowedException.ToString()
```

Parameters

None.

Exceptions

None.

System.Data.ParameterDirection

The ParameterDirection enumeration provides the values that determine the behavior of a parameter (whether it is an Input, Output, Input and Output, or a Return Value). Based on the ParameterDirection value, ADO.NET will allow or disallow certain behaviors of passing data to and receiving data from the data source via these parameters. The ParameterDirection enumeration is used by the various Parameter objects (SqlParameter, OleDbParameter, and OdbcParameter).

ParameterDirection Enumeration

Input (1)	(Default) The parameter is an input parameter only. This specifies that the parameter will provide a value to the SQL statement or stored procedure to enable it to run properly.
InputOutput (3)	The parameter serves as both an input and an output parameter. The idea here is that the stored procedure might change the value of the parameter, and you'll need to be able to receive the new value.
Output (2)	The parameter is an output parameter only. The purpose of the parameter is to receive a value back from a stored procedure. The corresponding parameter in the data source might need to be marked as OUTPUT.
ReturnValue (6)	The parameter will receive the return value.

System.Data.PropertyAttributes

The PropertyAttributes enumeration provides the values that determine the attributes of a property. They are used to specify, for instance, that a property is optional or required.

The PropertyAttributes enumeration is used in the ExtendedProperties property of the DataSet, DataTable, DataColumn, DataRelation, Constraint, UniqueConstraint, and ForeignKeyConstraint classes.

Because this class implements the FlagsAttribute, bitwise combinations of values are allowed. Be aware, though, that some combinations are nonsensical (for instance, designating a property as both optional and required).

PropertyAttributes Enumeration

NotSupported (0)	The property is not supported by the provider.
Optional (2)	The property does not need to be set.
Read (512)	The property can be read.
Required (1)	The property must be set.
Write (1024)	The property can be changed.

System.Data.PropertyCollection

The PropertyCollection class is a container class that maintains a collection of Property objects. It is directly descended from the System.Collections.Hashtable class. In fact, other than providing a Constructor, the PropertyCollection class implements no new functionality beyond the Hashtable class. (If you are unfamiliar, or a bit rusty, with HashTable and other collection objects, we recommend a quick look through MSDN or finding a good reference book on working with collections.)

The PropertyCollection is used in the DataSet, DataTable, DataColumn, DataRelation, Constraint, UniqueConstraint, and ForeignKeyConstraint classes to maintain a collection of user-defined properties that can be serialized to XML.

The sole Constructor simply creates a new PropertyCollection object, initializing all properties to their default values.

NOTE If a PropertyCollection is to be persisted as XML, then the members of the collection must be of type String.

Constructors

```
Dim myPropertyCollection As New PropertyCollection()
```

Parameters

None.

PropertyCollection Sample Code

```
'See System.Data.ConstraintCollection for examples of the
'common collection members.
```

Members

Add

The Add methods add a Property to the PropertyCollection. You pass a key and an associated value to the Add method, and the key-value pair is added to the collection.

The added key must be unique to the collection. Use this to assign custom properties to an object.

Usage

```
myPropertyCollection.Add(myObjectKey, myObjectValue)
```

Parameters

`myObjectKey`	Hashtable key, as Object.
`myObjectValue`	Value associated with the key, as Object.

Exceptions

ArgumentNullException	The Property key argument is null (`Nothing` in Visual Basic .NET).
ArgumentException	The Property key already belongs to the Property-Collection or to another collection.

Clear

The Clear method removes all Property objects from the PropertyCollection.

Usage

```
myPropertyCollection.Clear()
```

Parameters

None.

Exceptions

None.

Clone

The Clone method returns a PropertyCollection object that is a shallow copy of the current PropertyCollection.

NOTE A shallow copy implies that all of the properties are copied, but any objects referenced by those objects are not cloned. Any references in the Clone reference the same object as the original PropertyCollection.

Usage

```
myObject = myPropertyCollection.Clone()
```

Parameters

None.

Exceptions

None.

Contains

The Contains method returns a Boolean value that indicates whether the passed Property key exists in the PropertyCollection. It returns True if a Property exists and False otherwise. This is identical to the ContainsKey method.

Usage

```
myBoolean = myPropertyCollection.Contains(myObjectKey)
```

Parameters

`myObjectKey`	Object defining the Property key to check for.

Exceptions

ArgumentNullException	The Property key argument is null (`Nothing` in Visual Basic .NET).

ContainsKey

The ContainsKey method returns a Boolean value that indicates whether the passed Property key exists in the PropertyCollection. It returns True if a Property exists and False otherwise. This is identical to the Contains method.

Usage

```
myBoolean = myPropertyCollection.ContainsKey(myObjectKey)
```

Parameters

`myObjectKey`	Object defining the Property key to check for.

Exceptions

ArgumentNullException	The Property key argument is null (`Nothing` in Visual Basic .NET).

ContainsValue

The ContainsValue method returns a Boolean value that indicates whether the passed Property value exists in the PropertyCollection. It returns True if a Property exists and False otherwise.

Because a value object can be null (`Nothing` in Visual Basic .NET), an exception will not be raised if one is passed.

Usage

```
myBoolean = myPropertyCollection.ContainsValue(myObjectValue)
```

Parameters

`myObjectValue`	Object defining the Property value to check for.

Exceptions

None.

CopyTo

The CopyTo method is used to copy the Property objects in the PropertyCollection to an array.

Usage

```
myPropertyCollection.CopyTo(myPropertyArray, myStartIndex)
```

Parameters

`myPropertyArray`	The passed buffer array to hold the Property objects.
`myStartIndex`	The Integer index designating the location in the passed array to begin filling with the Property objects.

Exceptions

ArgumentException	The passed array was not long enough to hold the passed objects.
ArgumentNullException	The passed array is null (`Nothing` in Visual Basic .NET).
ArgumentOutOfRangeException	myStartIndex is negative or greater than the length of the array.
InvalidCastException	The object type of the collection cannot be cast automatically to the object type of the array.

Count

The read-only Count property returns an Int32 value specifying the number of Property objects in the PropertyCollection.

Usage

```
myInt32 = myPropertyCollection.Count
```

Parameters

None.

Exceptions

None.

GetEnumerator

The GetEnumerator method returns an object implementing the System.Collections. IDictionaryEnumerator interface that can be used to iterate over the collection. This method assists in using the For Each - Next (or equivalent statements) to iterate through a collection.

Usage

```
myIEnumerator = myPropertyCollection.GetEnumerator()
```

Parameters

None.

Exceptions

None.

GetObjectData

The GetObjectData method fills the passed System.Runtime.Serialization.SerializationInfo buffer object with information about the object. There is no value returned by this method. Depending on the passed System.Runtime.Serialization.StreamingContext object, this method can be used to serialize the object to a stream or read serialization from a stream.

Because it deals mainly with serialization and not data access, further discussion of this property is beyond the scope of this book.

Usage

```
myPropertyCollection.GetObjectData(mySerializationInfo, _
   myStreamingContext)
```

Parameters

`mySerializationInfo`	A System.Runtime.Serialization.SerializationInfo buffer object to be filled with the exception's serialization data.
`myStreamingContext`	A System.Runtime.Serialization.StreamingContext object specifying the stream to write the serialization info to or read the information from.

Exceptions

ArgumentNullException	The passed SerializationInfo buffer object is null (`Nothing` in Visual Basic .NET).

IsFixedSize

The read-only IsFixedSize property returns a Boolean value specifying whether the PropertyCollection has a fixed size.

Usage

```
myBoolean = myHashtable.IsFixedSize
```

Parameters

None.

Exceptions

None.

IsReadOnly

The read-only IsReadOnly property returns a Boolean value specifying whether the PropertyCollection is read only.

Usage

```
myBoolean = myPropertyCollection.IsReadOnly
```

Parameters

None.

Exceptions

None.

IsSynchronized

The read-only IsSynchronized property returns a Boolean value indicating whether the PropertyCollection is currently synchronized. For information on synchronizing the PropertyCollection, see the PropertyCollection.SyncRoot property.

Usage
```
myBoolean = myPropertyCollection.IsSynchronized
```

Parameters
None.

Exceptions
None.

Item

The Item property returns or sets the Property value object from the collection, as determined by the passed key. If setting this value and the key is not found, then a Property will be added to the collection with the key-value pair. If returning the value and the key is not found, a null value (`Nothing` in Visual Basic .NET) will be returned.

Usage
```
myProperty = myPropertyCollection.Item(myObjectKey)
```

Parameters

`myObjectKey` Object used as Property key to find associated value.

Exceptions
None.

Keys

The read-only Keys property returns an object implementing the ICollection interface that contains all of the keys in the PropertyCollection. Basically, all collection objects implement the ICollection interface. (See a reference for System.Collections for more information.)

Usage
```
myICollection = myHashtable.Keys
```

Parameters
None.

Exceptions
None.

OnDeserialization

The OnDeserialization method raises the Deserialization event when deserialization is complete.

Usage

```
myPropertyCollection.OnDeserialization(myObjectSender)
```

Parameters

`myObjectSender`	The source object for the deserialization event.

Exceptions

SerializationException	The System.Runtime.Serialization.SerializationInfo object that is associated with the current Property-Collection is invalid.

Remove

The Remove method removes a specified Property object from the PropertyCollection that is indicated by the passed key. If the key does not belong to the collection, nothing will happen.

Usage

```
myPropertyCollection.Remove(myObjectKey)
```

Parameters

`myObjectKey`	Object used as Property key to find associated value.

Exceptions

ArgumentNullException	The Property key is a null reference (`Nothing` in Visual Basic).

SyncRoot

The read-only SyncRoot property returns a System.Object object that can be used to Synchronize the PropertyCollection.

Usage

```
myObject = myPropertyCollection.SyncRoot
```

Parameters

None.

Exceptions

None.

ToString

The ToString method returns "System.Data.PropertyCollection".

Usage

```
myString = myPropertyCollection.ToString()
```

Parameters

None.

Exceptions

None.

Values

The read-only Values property returns an object implementing the ICollection interface that contains all of the values in the PropertyCollection. Basically, all collection objects implement the ICollection interface. (See a reference for System.Collections for more information.)

Usage

```
myICollection = myHashtable.Values
```

Parameters

None.

Exceptions

None.

System.Data.ReadOnlyException

The ReadOnlyException class (descended from the DataException class) defines exceptions that are thrown when attempting to change the value of a read-only column.

This exception is thrown by the DataRow.EndEdit and DataRow.ItemArray methods.

Constructors

```
Dim myReadOnlyException As New ReadOnlyException()
Dim myReadOnlyException As New _
     ReadOnlyException(myString)
```

Parameters

`myString`	A String object that will initialize the Message property.

ReadOnlyException Sample Code

```
Dim myReadOnlyException As ReadOnlyException
myReadOnlyException = New _
     ReadOnlyException("Column is Read Only!")
Throw myReadOnlyException
```

Members

GetBaseException

The GetBaseException method returns an Exception object containing the original exception. To return the original exception, it traverses the chain of InnerException objects. If the InnerException property of the current exception is null, GetBaseException will return a reference to the current Exception object.

To determine only the parent exception to the current exception, use the InnerException property.

Usage

```
myException = myReadOnlyException.GetBaseException()
```

Parameters

None.

Exceptions

None.

GetObjectData

The GetObjectData method fills the passed System.Runtime.Serialization.SerializationInfo buffer object with information about the Exception object. There is no value returned by this method. Depending on the passed System.Runtime.Serialization.StreamingContext object, this method can be used to serialize the object to a stream or read serialization from a stream.

Because it deals mainly with serialization and not data access, further discussion of this property is beyond the scope of this book.

Usage

```
myReadOnlyException.GetObjectData(mySerializationInfo, _
     myStreamingContext)
```

Parameters

`mySerializationInfo`	A System.Runtime.Serialization.SerializationInfo buffer object to be filled with the exception's serialization data.
`myStreamingContext`	A System.Runtime.Serialization.StreamingContext object specifying the stream to write the serialization info to or read the information from.

Exceptions

ArgumentNullException	The passed SerializationInfo buffer object is null (`Nothing` in Visual Basic .NET).

HelpLink

The HelpLink property returns or sets a String linking to a help file associated with the ReadOnlyException. The HelpLink is formatted as a Uniform Resource Name (URN) or Uniform Resource Locator (URL). An example of this property that points to the MSDN help available with Visual Studio .NET would be: `ms-help://MS.VSCC/MS.MSDNVS/cpref/html/frlrfsystemexceptionclasshelplinktopic.htm`.

The HelpLink is often not set, so it is wise to verify both that the HelpLink property itself is not an empty string and that the HelpLink points to a valid help file before exposing the HelpLink to a user of your program.

Usage

```
myString = myReadOnlyException.HelpLink
myReadOnlyException.HelpLink = myString
```

Parameters

None.

InnerException

The read-only InnerException property returns the Exception object linking to a previous exception that caused the current exception to be thrown, if any, or a null value (`Nothing` in Visual Basic .NET), if not. This permits a chain of InnerException objects to be generated, allowing a program to trace the exception chain all the way to the root exception. Be aware that InnerException may be null.

To find the base exception that originally was fired, use the GetBaseException method.

Usage

```
myException = myReadOnlyException.InnerException
```

Parameters

None.

Message

The read-only Message property returns a String describing the first error that caused the exception. Because it provides information from only the first error, use this property cautiously when building robust error handling.

Usage

```
myString = myReadOnlyException.Message
```

Parameters

None.

Source

The Source property sets or returns a String containing the name of the provider that generated the first error. Because it provides information from only the first error, use this property cautiously when building robust error handling.

Usage

```
myString = myReadOnlyException.Source
myReadOnlyException.Source = myString
```

Parameters

None.

StackTrace

The read-only StackTrace property returns a String containing a textual representation of the stack trace. The stack trace reports all of the methods that are in execution at the time just prior to the execution being thrown. It is read from top to bottom with the latest method in execution at the top.

The StackTrace can be invaluable in tracing difficult-to-find bugs because it provides a way to see all of the methods that could have led up to the error.

TIP To see the stack trace programmatically when no exception has been raised, use the Environment.StackTrace property.

Usage

```
myString = myReadOnlyException.StackTrace
```

Parameters

None.

TargetSite

The read-only TargetSite property returns an object inheriting from System.Reflection.MethodBase that contains a reference to the method that caused the error to be thrown.

This property is primarily used to programmatically find information about the method that raised the exception. The returned object will provide information such as the methods parameters and return type and whether the method is virtual, a constructor, public, private, etc. Because it deals mainly with reflection and not data access, further discussion of this property is beyond the scope of this book.

Usage

```
myMethodBase = myReadOnlyException.TargetSite
```

Parameters

None.

ToString

The ToString method is overridden to return information relating to the ReadOnlyException exception. The returned String contains the full class name and also the error message, name of the inner exception, and stack trace, if they exist.

Usage

```
myString = myReadOnlyException.ToString()
```

Parameters

None.

Exceptions

None.

System.Data.RowNotInTableException

The RowNotInTableException class (descended from the DataException class) defines exceptions that are thrown when attempting to perform an operation on a DataRow that has been deleted from, or has never been a member of, a DataTable.

This exception is thrown by the DataRow.AcceptChanges, DataRow.GetChildRows, DataRow.GerParentRow, DataRow.GetParentRows, DataRow.RejectChanges, and DataRow.SetParentRow. This is most common when the DataRow has been deleted, but it can occur when a DataRow is simply disconnected from a DataTable. Be aware of this situation when multiple threads are accessing an unsychronized DataTable.

Constructors

```
Dim myRowNotInTableException As New RowNotInTableException()
Dim myRowNotInTableException As New _
     RowNotInTableException(myString)
```

Parameters

`myString`	A String object that will initialize the Message property.

RowNotInTableException Sample Code

```
Dim myRowNotInTableException As RowNotInTableException
myRowNotInTableException = New _
     RowNotInTableException("Row not in Table!")
Throw myRowNotInTableException
```

Members

GetBaseException

The GetBaseException method returns an Exception object containing the original exception. To return the original exception, it traverses the chain of InnerException objects. If the InnerException property of the current exception is null, GetBaseException will return a reference to the current Exception object.

To determine only the parent exception to the current exception, use the InnerException property.

Usage

```
myException = myRowNotInTableException.GetBaseException()
```

Parameters

None.

Exceptions

None.

GetObjectData

The GetObjectData method fills the passed System.Runtime.Serialization.SerializationInfo buffer object with information about the Exception object. There is no value returned by this method. Depending on the passed System.Runtime.Serialization.

StreamingContext object, this method can be used to serialize the object to a stream or read serialization from a stream.

Because it deals mainly with serialization and not data access, further discussion of this property is beyond the scope of this book.

Usage

```
myRowNotInTableException.GetObjectData(mySerializationInfo, _
     myStreamingContext)
```

Parameters

`mySerializationInfo`	A System.Runtime.Serialization.SerializationInfo buffer object to be filled with the exception's serialization data.
`myStreamingContext`	A System.Runtime.Serialization.StreamingContext object specifying the stream to write the serialization info to or read the information from.

Exceptions

ArgumentNullException	The passed SerializationInfo buffer object is null (`Nothing` in Visual Basic .NET).

HelpLink

The HelpLink property returns or sets a String linking to a help file associated with the RowNotInTableException. The HelpLink is formatted as a Uniform Resource Name (URN) or Uniform Resource Locator (URL). An example of this property that points to the MSDN help available with Visual Studio .NET would be: `ms-help://MS.VSCC/MS.MSDNVS/cpref/html/frlrfsystemexceptionclasshelplinktopic.htm.`

The HelpLink is often not set, so it is wise to verify both that the HelpLink property itself is not an empty string and that the HelpLink points to a valid help file before exposing the HelpLink to a user of your program.

Usage

```
myString = myRowNotInTableException.HelpLink
myRowNotInTableException.HelpLink = myString
```

Parameters

None.

InnerException

The read-only InnerException property returns the Exception object linking to a previous exception that caused the current exception to be thrown, if any, or a null value (`Nothing` in Visual Basic .NET), if not. This permits a chain of InnerException objects to be generated, allowing a program to trace the exception chain all the way to the root exception. Be aware that InnerException may be null.

To find the base exception that originally was fired, use the GetBaseException method.

Usage

```
myException = myRowNotInTableException.InnerException
```

Parameters
None.

Message

The read-only Message property returns a String describing the first error that caused the exception. Because it only provides information from the first error, use this property cautiously when building robust error handling.

Usage
```
myString = myRowNotInTableException.Message
```

Parameters
None.

Source

The Source property sets or returns a String containing the name of the provider that generated the first error. Because it provides information from only the first error, use this property cautiously when building robust error handling.

Usage
```
myString = myRowNotInTableException.Source
myRowNotInTableException.Source = myString
```

Parameters
None.

StackTrace

The read-only StackTrace property returns a String containing a textual representation of the stack trace. The stack trace reports all of the methods that are in execution at the time just prior to the execution being thrown. It is read from top to bottom with the latest method in execution at the top.

The StackTrace can be invaluable in tracing difficult-to-find bugs because it provides a way to see all of the methods that could have led up to the error.

TIP **To see the stack trace programmatically when no exception has been raised, use the Environment.StackTrace property.**

Usage
```
myString = myRowNotInTableException.StackTrace
```

Parameters
None.

TargetSite

The read-only TargetSite property returns an object inheriting from System.Reflection.MethodBase that contains a reference to the method that caused the error to be thrown.

This property is primarily used to programmatically find information about the method that raised the exception. The returned object will provide information such as the methods parameters and return type and whether the method is virtual, a constructor, public, private, etc. Because it deals mainly with reflection and not data access, further discussion of this property is beyond the scope of this book.

Usage

```
myMethodBase = myRowNotInTableException.TargetSite
```

Parameters

None.

ToString

The ToString method is overridden to return information relating to the RowNot-InTableException exception. The returned String contains the full class name and also the error message, name of the inner exception, and stack trace, if they exist.

Usage

```
myString = myRowNotInTableException.ToString()
```

Parameters

None.

Exceptions

None.

System.Data.Rule

The Rule enumeration provides the values that indicate the action to be taken when a ForeignKeyConstraint is violated. They are set in the ForeignKeyConstraint.Update-Rule and ForeignKeyConstraint.DeleteRule properties.

After an AcceptChanges or RejectChanges method is called on the parent row, whether to cascade the AcceptChanges or RejectChanges is determined by the Accept-RejectRule enumeration. (See the System.Data.AcceptRejectRule enumeration for more information.)

WARNING **Constraints are not enforced when DataSet.EnforceConstraints is False.**

HINT **Using SetNull will result in child rows being orphaned. Be sure that you're very aware of how your relationships work before selecting this value.**

Rule Enumeration

Cascade (1)	(Default) Specifies that child rows are to be deleted or child columns updated to reflect the new value.
None (0)	Does not perform any action, but throws an exception.
SetDefault (3)	Sets the child column values to their DefaultValue values.
SetNull (2)	Sets the child column values to DBNull.

System.Data.SchemaType

The SchemaType enumeration provides the values that determine how the schema of a DataSet should change when the FillSchema method is called. Using Mapped is generally recommended because it preserves the current schema (relationships, constraints, etc.) imposed on the DataSet. Setting to Source will delete the original schema, replacing it with the incoming one.

SchemaType Enumeration

Mapped (1)	(Default) Apply existing table mappings to the incoming schema. Configure the DataSet with the newly transformed schema.
Source (0)	Ignore any table mappings on the DataAdapter. Configure the DataSet using the incoming schema without applying any transformations. (This can be dangerous if the incoming data is only slightly different from the current schema. For instance, relationships and constraints can be deleted with the old schema.)

System.Data.SqlDbType

The SqlDbType enumeration provides named constants to use when referencing the SQL Server data types. When working with objects, such as SqlParameters, you can specify the SqlDbType data type to ensure a strong data type mapping to the data source. These enumerations simplify that mapping.

The following table lists the SqlDbTypes, the numeric value of the enumeration, and the corresponding .NET data type that gets mapped.

SqlDbType Enumeration

SQLDBTYPE	.NET FRAMEWORK TYPE	DESCRIPTION
BigInt (0)	System.Int64	A 64-bit signed integer.
Binary (1)	Array of System. Byte	A fixed-length stream of binary data (up to 8,000 bytes).
Bit (2)	System.Boolean	An unsigned numeric value that can be 0, 1, or null.
Char (3)	System.String	A fixed-length stream of non-Unicode characters (up to 8,000 characters).

continues

SQLDBTYPE	.NET FRAMEWORK TYPE	DESCRIPTION
DateTime (4)	System.DateTime	Date and time data ranging from January 1, 1753 to December 31, 9999 with accuracy of 3.33 milliseconds.
Decimal (5)	System.Decimal	A fixed precision and scale numeric value between 10^{38}-1and -10^{38}.
Float (6)	System.Double	A floating-point number between -1.79E +308 through 1.79E +308.
Image (7)	Array of System.Byte	A variable-length stream of binary data ranging from 0 to 2^{31}-1 (about 2 million) bytes.
Int (8)	System.Int32	A 32-bit signed integer.
Money (9)	System.Decimal	A currency value ranging from -2^{63} to 2^{63}-1 (plus or minus about 922 trillion) with accuracy to a ten-thousandth of a currency unit.
NChar (10)	System.String	A fixed-length stream of Unicode characters ranging (up to 4,000 characters).
NText (11)	System.String	A variable-length stream of Unicode data with a maximum length of 2^{30}-1 (or 1,073,741,823) characters.
NvarChar (12)	System.String	A variable-length stream of Unicode characters (up to 4,000 characters). Note: Implicit conversion fails if the string is greater than 4,000 characters. Explicitly set the object when working with strings longer than 4,000 characters.
Real (13)	System.Single	A floating point number within the range of -3.40E +38 through 3.40E +38.
SmallDateTime (15)	System.DateTime	Date and time data between January 1, 1900 to June 6, 2079, with accuracy to one minute.
SmallInt (16)	System.Int16	A 16-bit signed integer.

SQLDBTYPE	.NET FRAMEWORK TYPE	DESCRIPTION
SmallMoney (17)	System.Decimal	A currency value ranging from -214,748.3648 to +214,748.3647 with accuracy to a ten-thousandth of a currency unit.
Text (18)	System.String	A variable-length stream of non-Unicode data with a maximum length of 2^{31} -1 (or 2,147,483,647) characters.
Timestamp (19)	System.DateTime	Data and time data in the format "yyyymmddhhmmss".
TinyInt (20)	System.Byte	An 8-bit unsigned integer.
UniqueIdentifier (14)	System.Guid	A globally unique identifier (or GUID).
VarBinary (21)	Array of type System.Byte	A variable-length stream of binary data ranging of up to 8,000 bytes. (Note: Implicit conversion fails if the byte array is greater than 8,000 bytes. Explicitly set the object when working with byte arrays larger than 8,000 bytes.)
VarChar (22)	System.String	A variable-length stream of non-Unicode characters of up to 8,000 characters.
Variant (23)	System.Object	A special data type that can contain numeric, string, binary, or date data as well as the SQL Server values Empty and Null (default).

System.Data.StateChangeEventArgs

The StateChangeEventArgs class is a sealed (NotInheritable) class that is created automatically and passed by the SqlConnection.StateChange and OleDbConnection.StateChange events (and, likely, the StateChange events of any future Data Providers). This event is raised when a connection to a database changes state (i.e., moves from Open to Closed or Closed to Open).

StateChangeEventArgs also has a public constructor, which can be used to define and throw your own exception.

Constructors

```
Dim myStateChangeEventArgs As New _
     StateChangeEventArgs(originalConnectionState, _
     currentConnectionState)
```

Parameters

`originalConnectionState`	A System.Data.ConnectionState enumeration value.
`currentConnectionState`	A System.Data.ConnectionState enumeration value.

ConnectionState Enumeration

Broken (16)	Not currently used. In the future this may be used because you are able to call the Close and Open methods to reinitialize a connection.
Closed(0)	The Connection object is closed.
Connecting(2)	Not currently used. In the future, this will indicate that the Connection object is connecting to the data source.
Executing(4)	Not currently used. In the future, this will indicate that the Connection object is executing a command at the data source.
Fetching(8)	Not currently used. In the future, this will indicate that the Connection object is fetching data from the data source.
Open(1)	The Connection object is open.

Members

CurrentState

The read-only CurrentState property returns a ConnectionState enumeration value that indicates the current (new) state of the connection. (The connection is already in the new state when the StateChange event is fired.)

Usage

```
myConnectionState = myStateChangeEventArgs.CurrentState
```

Parameters

None.

Exceptions

None.

OriginalState

The read-only OriginalState property returns a ConnectionState enumeration value that indicates the previous state of the connection. (The connection is already in the new state when the StateChange event is fired.)

Usage

```
myConnectionState = myStateChangeEventArgs.OriginalState
```

Parameters

None.

Exceptions

None.

ToString

The ToString method returns "System.Data.ToString".

Usage

```
myString = myStateChangeEventArgs.ToString()
```

Parameters

None.

Exceptions

None.

System.Data.StatementType

The StatementType enumeration provides the values for the type of SQL statement being executed by a DataAdapter or DataReader.

StatementType Enumeration

Delete (3)	A SQL DELETE statement.
Insert (1)	A SQL INSERT statement.
Select (0)	A SQL SELECT statement.
Update (2)	A SQL UPDATE statement.

System.Data.StrongTypingException

The StrongTypingException class (descended from the DataException class) defines exceptions that are thrown by a strongly typed DataSet when attempting to access a DBNull value. This exception is intended to be derived by other classes, so as to provide standard functionality for user-created, strongly typed descendents of the DataSet class. Because it is intended for use only with inherited data access classes, in-depth discussion is beyond the scope of this book.

NOTE **Unlike most descendents of System.Data.DataException, the StrongTypingException does not have a constructor with the Message property as a sole parameter. You must also pass an Exception to be used as the value for the InnerException property, although this value may be null (`Nothing` in Visual Basic .NET).**

Constructors

```
Dim myStrongTypingException As New StrongTypingException()
Dim myStrongTypingException As New _
     StrongTypingException(myString, myException)
```

Parameters

`myString`	A String object that will initialize the Message property.
`myException`	An Exception object to use as the InnerException.

StrongTypingException Sample Code

```
Dim myStrongTypingException As StrongTypingException
myStrongTypingException = New _
     StrongTypingException
Throw myStrongTypingException
```

Members

GetBaseException

The GetBaseException method returns an Exception object containing the original exception. To return the original exception, it traverses the chain of InnerException objects. If the InnerException property of the current exception is null, GetBaseException will return a reference to the current Exception object.

To determine only the parent exception to the current exception, use the InnerException property.

Usage

```
myException = myStrongTypingException.GetBaseException()
```

Parameters

None.

Exceptions

None.

GetObjectData

The GetObjectData method fills the passed System.Runtime.Serialization.SerializationInfo buffer object with information about the Exception object. There is no value returned by this method. Depending on the passed System.Runtime.Serialization.StreamingContext object, this method can be used to serialize the object to a stream or read serialization from a stream.

Because it deals mainly with serialization and not data access, further discussion of this property is beyond the scope of this book.

Usage

```
myStrongTypingException.GetObjectData(mySerializationInfo, _
     myStreamingContext)
```

Parameters

`mySerializationInfo`	A System.Runtime.Serialization.SerializationInfo buffer object to be filled with the exception's serialization data.
`myStreamingContext`	A System.Runtime.Serialization.StreamingContext object specifying the stream to write the serialization info to or read the information from.

Exceptions

ArgumentNullException	The passed SerializationInfo buffer object is null (`Nothing` in Visual Basic .NET).

HelpLink

The HelpLink property returns or sets a String linking to a help file associated with the StrongTypingException. The HelpLink is formatted as a Uniform Resource Name (URN) or Uniform Resource Locator (URL). An example of this property that points to the MSDN help available with Visual Studio .NET would be: `ms-help://MS.VSCC/MS.MSDNVS/cpref/html/frlrfsystemexceptionclasshelplinktopic.htm`.

The HelpLink is often not set, so it is wise to verify both that the HelpLink property itself is not an empty string and that the HelpLink points to a valid help file before exposing the HelpLink to a user of your program.

Usage

```
myString = myStrongTypingException.HelpLink
myStrongTypingException.HelpLink = myString
```

Parameters

None.

InnerException

The read-only InnerException property returns the Exception object linking to a previous exception that caused the current exception to be thrown, if any, or a null value (`Nothing` in Visual Basic .NET), if not. This permits a chain of InnerException objects to be generated, allowing a program to trace the exception chain all the way to the root exception. Be aware that InnerException may be null.

To find the base exception that originally was fired, use the GetBaseException method.

Usage

```
myException = myStrongTypingException.InnerException
```

Parameters

None.

Message

The read-only Message property returns a String describing the first error that caused the exception. Because it provides information from only the first error, use this property cautiously when building robust error handling.

Usage

```
myString = myStrongTypingException.Message
```

Parameters

None.

Source

The Source property sets or returns a String containing the name of the provider that generated the first error. Because it provides information from only the first error, use this property cautiously when building robust error handling.

Usage

```
myString = myStrongTypingException.Source
myStrongTypingException.Source = myString
```

Parameters

None.

StackTrace

The read-only StackTrace property returns a String containing a textual representation of the stack trace. The stack trace reports all of the methods that are in execution at the time just prior to the execution being thrown. It is read from top to bottom with the latest method in execution at the top.

The StackTrace can be invaluable in tracing difficult-to-find bugs because it provides a way to see all of the methods that could have led up to the error.

TIP To see the stack trace programmatically when no exception has been raised, use the Environment.StackTrace property.

Usage

```
myString = myStrongTypingException.StackTrace
```

Parameters

None.

TargetSite

The read-only TargetSite property returns an object inheriting from System.Reflection.MethodBase that contains a reference to the method that caused the error to be thrown.

This property is primarily used to programmatically find information about the method that raised the exception. The returned object will provide information such as the methods parameters and return type and whether the method is virtual, a constructor, public, private, etc. Because it deals mainly with reflection and not data access, further discussion of this property is beyond the scope of this book.

Usage

```
myMethodBase = myStrongTypingException.TargetSite
```

Parameters

None.

ToString

The ToString method is overridden to return information relating to the StrongTypingException exception. The returned String contains the full class name and also the error message, name of the inner exception, and stack trace, if they exist.

Usage

```
myString = myStrongTypingException.ToString()
```

Parameters

None.

Exceptions

None.

System.Data.SyntaxErrorException

The SyntaxErrorException class (descended from the InvalidExpressionException class) defines exceptions that are thrown when the DataColumn.Expression property contains a syntax error.

If the Expression is properly formed but refers to another column that contains invalid information (i.e., attempting to calculate sales tax on a null value), an EvaluateException would be thrown. (See System.Data.EvaluateException for more information.)

Related exceptions are the System.Data.InvalidExpressionException and System.Data.EvaluateException.

Constructors

```
Dim mySyntaxErrorException As New SyntaxErrorException()
Dim mySyntaxErrorException As New _
     SyntaxErrorException(myString)
```

Parameters

`myString`	A String object that will initialize the Message property.

SyntaxErrorException Sample Code

```
Dim mySyntaxErrorException As SyntaxErrorException
mySyntaxErrorException = New _
     SyntaxErrorException("Can't Evaluate Expression!")
Throw mySyntaxErrorException
```

Members

GetBaseException

The GetBaseException method returns an Exception object containing the original exception. To return the original exception, it traverses the chain of InnerException objects. If the InnerException property of the current exception is null, GetBaseException will return a reference to the current Exception object.

To determine only the parent exception to the current exception, use the InnerException property.

Usage

```
myException = mySyntaxErrorException.GetBaseException()
```

Parameters
None.

Exceptions
None.

GetObjectData

The GetObjectData method fills the passed System.Runtime.Serialization.SerializationInfo buffer object with information about the Exception object. There is no value returned by this method. Depending on the passed System.Runtime.Serialization.StreamingContext object, this method can be used to serialize the object to a stream or read serialization from a stream.

Because it deals mainly with serialization and not data access, further discussion of this property is beyond the scope of this book.

Usage

```
mySyntaxErrorException.GetObjectData(mySerializationInfo, _
   myStreamingContext)
```

Parameters

`mySerializationInfo`	A System.Runtime.Serialization.SerializationInfo buffer object to be filled with the exception's serialization data.

`myStreamingContext`	A System.Runtime.Serialization.StreamingContext object specifying the stream to write the serialization info to or read the information from.

Exceptions

ArgumentNullException	The passed SerializationInfo buffer object is null (`Nothing` in Visual Basic .NET).

HelpLink

The HelpLink property returns or sets a String linking to a help file associated with the SyntaxErrorException. The HelpLink is formatted as a Uniform Resource Name (URN) or Uniform Resource Locator (URL). An example of this property that points to the MSDN help available with Visual Studio .NET would be: `ms-help://MS.VSCC/MS.MSDNVS/cpref/html/frlrfsystemexceptionclasshelplinktopic.htm`.

The HelpLink is often not set, so it is wise to verify both that the HelpLink property itself is not an empty string and that the HelpLink points to a valid help file before exposing the HelpLink to a user of your program.

Usage

```
myString = mySyntaxErrorException.HelpLink
mySyntaxErrorException.HelpLink = myString
```

Parameters

None.

InnerException

The read-only InnerException property returns the Exception object linking to a previous exception that caused the current exception to be thrown, if any, or a null value (`Nothing` in Visual Basic .NET), if not. This permits a chain of InnerException objects to be generated, allowing a program to trace the exception chain all the way to the root exception. Be aware that InnerException may be null.

To find the base exception that originally was fired, use the GetBaseException method.

Usage

```
myException = mySyntaxErrorException.InnerException
```

Parameters

None.

Message

The read-only Message property returns a String describing the first error that caused the exception. Because it provides information from only the first error, use this property cautiously when building robust error handling.

Usage

```
myString = mySyntaxErrorException.Message
```

Parameters

None.

Source

The Source property sets or returns a String containing the name of the provider that generated the first error. Because it provides information from only the first error, use this property cautiously when building robust error handling.

Usage

```
myString = mySyntaxErrorException.Source
mySyntaxErrorException.Source = myString
```

Parameters

None.

StackTrace

The read-only StackTrace property returns a String containing a textual representation of the stack trace. The stack trace reports all of the methods that are in execution at the time just prior to the execution being thrown. It is read from top to bottom with the latest method in execution at the top.

The StackTrace can be invaluable in tracing difficult-to-find bugs because it provides a way to see all of the methods that could have led up to the error.

TIP To see the stack trace programmatically when no exception has been raised, use the Environment.StackTrace property.

Usage

```
myString = mySyntaxErrorException.StackTrace
```

Parameters

None.

TargetSite

The read-only TargetSite property returns an object inheriting from System.Reflection.MethodBase that contains a reference to the method that caused the error to be thrown.

This property is primarily used to programmatically find information about the method that raised the exception. The returned object will provide information such as the methods parameters and return type and whether the method is virtual, a constructor, public, private, etc. Because it deals mainly with reflection and not data access, further discussion of this property is beyond the scope of this book.

Usage

```
myMethodBase = mySyntaxErrorException.TargetSite
```

Parameters

None.

ToString

The ToString method is overridden to return information relating to the SyntaxErrorException exception. The returned String contains the full class name and also the error message, name of the inner exception, and stack trace, if they exist.

Usage

```
myString = mySyntaxErrorException.ToString()
```

Parameters

None.

Exceptions

None.

System.Data.TypedDataSetGenerator

The TypedDataSetGenerator class provides some functionality for creating strongly typed DataSet objects. It is not intended as a standalone class, though, but to provide inherited functionality for descendant classes. Because this deals with creating inherited classes, discussion of this class is beyond the scope of this book. Thus, only a basic overview is provided.

NOTE **This class is used by Visual Studio .NET when creating typed data sets.**

Constructors

```
Dim myTypedDataSetGenerator As New TypedDataSetGenerator()
```

Parameters

None.

Members

Generate

The Generate method generates a strongly typed DataSet. This method does not implement any functionality, but it is intended for the use of inheriting classes.

Usage

```
myTypedDataSetGenerator.Generate(myDataSet, myCodeNamespace, _
     myICodeGenerator)
```

Parameters

`myDataSet`	The source DataSet object that specifies the meta data to be used when creating a TypedDataSet object.
`myCodeNamespace`	A System.CodeDom.CodeNamespace object that defines the target namespace to use when creating the TypedDataSet.
`myICodeGenerator`	An object that implements the System.CodeDom.Compiler.ICodeGenerator interface that will be used to generate the typed DataSet.

Exceptions

None.

GenerateIdName

The GenerateIdName method takes a DataSet name and tailored ICodeGenerator object and returns a valid name for a strongly typed DataSet.

Usage

```
myString = myTypedDataSetGenerator.GenerateIdName(strName, _
     myICodeGenerator)
```

Parameters

`strName`	Source DataSet name, as a String value, that will be transformed into a valid typed DataSet name.
`myICodeGenerator`	An object that implements the System.CodeDom.Compiler.ICodeGenerator interface that will be used to generate the typed DataSet string name.

Exceptions

None.	(There are likely exceptions. None were discovered by the authors.)

ToString

The ToString method returns “System.Data.TypedDataSetGenerator”.

Usage

```
myString = myTypedDataSetGenerator.ToString()
```

Parameters

None.

Exceptions

None.

System.Data. TypedDataSetGeneratorException

The TypedDataSetGeneratorException class (descended from the DataException class) defines exceptions that are thrown when generating a strongly typed DataSet and a name conflict occurs. This exception is intended to be derived by other classes, so as to provide standard functionality for user-created, strongly typed descendents of the DataSet class. Because it is intended for use only with inherited data access classes, in-depth discussion is beyond the scope of this book.

NOTE Unlike most descendents of System.Data.DataException, the Typed-DataSetGeneratorException does not have a constructor with a Message property as a parameter. Instead, you pass a System.ArrayList object containing a dynamic list of exceptions.

Constructors

```
Dim myTypedDataSetGeneratorException As New
TypedDataSetGeneratorException()
Dim myTypedDataSetGeneratorException As New _
     TypedDataSetGeneratorException(myString, myException)
```

Parameters

`myString`	A String object that will initialize the Message property.
`myException`	An Exception object to use as the InnerException.

TypedDataSetGeneratorException Sample Code

```
Dim myArrayList As New ArrayList()
Dim myException1 As New Exception("Exception 1")
Dim myException2 As New Exception("Exception 2")
Dim myTypedDataSetGeneratorException As _
     TypedDataSetGeneratorException

myArrayList.Add(myException1)
myArrayList.Add(myException2)

myTypedDataSetGeneratorException = New _
   TypedDataSetGeneratorException(myArrayList)
Throw myTypedDataSetGeneratorException
```

Members

ErrorList

The read-only ErrorList property returns an ArrayList object that is a dynamic list of exceptions and errors. This property is generally set when the TypedDataSetGeneratorException is created.

Usage

```
myString = myTypedDataSetGeneratorException.ErrorList
```

Parameters

None.

GetBaseException

The GetBaseException method returns an Exception object containing the original exception. To return the original exception, it traverses the chain of InnerException objects. If the InnerException property of the current exception is null, GetBaseException will return a reference to the current Exception object.

To determine only the parent exception to the current exception, use the InnerException property.

Usage

```
myException = _
     myTypedDataSetGeneratorException.GetBaseException()
```

Parameters

None.

Exceptions

None.

GetObjectData

The GetObjectData method fills the passed System.Runtime.Serialization.SerializationInfo buffer object with information about the Exception object. There is no value returned by this method. Depending on the passed System.Runtime.Serialization.StreamingContext object, this method can be used to serialize the object to a stream or read serialization from a stream.

Because it deals mainly with serialization and not data access, further discussion of this property is beyond the scope of this book.

Usage

```
myTypedDataSetGeneratorException.GetObjectData( _
     mySerializationInfo, myStreamingContext)
```

Parameters

`mySerializationInfo`	A System.Runtime.Serialization.SerializationInfo buffer object to be filled with the exception's serialization data.

`myStreamingContext`	A System.Runtime.Serialization.StreamingContext object specifying the stream to write the serialization info to or read the information from.

Exceptions

ArgumentNullException	The passed SerializationInfo buffer object is null (`Nothing` in Visual Basic .NET).

HelpLink

The HelpLink property returns or sets a String linking to a help file associated with the TypedDataSetGeneratorException. The HelpLink is formatted as a Uniform Resource Name (URN) or Uniform Resource Locator (URL). An example of this property that points to the MSDN help available with Visual Studio .NET would be: `ms-help://MS.VSCC/MS.MSDNVS/cpref/html/frlrfsystemexceptionclasshelplinktopic.htm`.

The HelpLink is often not set, so it is wise to verify both that the HelpLink property itself is not an empty string and that the HelpLink points to a valid help file before exposing the HelpLink to a user of your program.

Usage

```
myString = myTypedDataSetGeneratorException.HelpLink
myTypedDataSetGeneratorException.HelpLink = myString
```

Parameters

None.

InnerException

The read-only InnerException property returns the Exception object linking to a previous exception that caused the current exception to be thrown, if any, or a null value (`Nothing` in Visual Basic .NET), if not. This permits a chain of InnerException objects to be generated, allowing a program to trace the exception chain all the way to the root exception. Be aware that InnerException may be null.

To find the base exception that originally was fired, use the GetBaseException method.

Usage

```
myException = myTypedDataSetGeneratorException.InnerException
```

Parameters

None.

Message

The read-only Message property returns a String describing the first error that caused the exception. Because it provides information from only the first error, use this property cautiously when building robust error handling.

Usage

```
myString = myTypedDataSetGeneratorException.Message
```

Parameters

None.

Source

The Source property sets or returns a String containing the name of the provider that generated the first error. Because it provides information from only the first error, use this property cautiously when building robust error handling.

Usage

```
myString = myTypedDataSetGeneratorException.Source
myTypedDataSetGeneratorException.Source = myString
```

Parameters

None.

StackTrace

The read-only StackTrace property returns a String containing a textual representation of the stack trace. The stack trace reports all of the methods that are in execution at the time just prior to the execution being thrown. It is read from top to bottom with the latest method in execution at the top.

The StackTrace can be invaluable in tracing difficult-to-find bugs because it provides a way to see all of the methods that could have led up to the error.

TIP **To see the stack trace programmatically when no exception has been raised, use the Environment.StackTrace property.**

Usage

```
myString = myTypedDataSetGeneratorException.StackTrace
```

Parameters

None.

TargetSite

The read-only TargetSite property returns an object inheriting from System.Reflection.MethodBase that contains a reference to the method that caused the error to be thrown.

This property is primarily used to programmatically find information about the method that raised the exception. The returned object will provide information such as the methods parameters and return type and whether the method is virtual, a constructor, public, private, etc. Because it deals mainly with reflection and not data access, further discussion of this property is beyond the scope of this book.

Usage

```
myMethodBase = myTypedDataSetGeneratorException.TargetSite
```

Parameters

None.

ToString

The ToString method is overridden to return information relating to the Typed-DataSetGeneratorException exception. The returned String contains the full class name and also the error message, name of the inner exception, and stack trace, if they exist.

Usage

```
myString = myTypedDataSetGeneratorException.ToString()
```

Parameters

None.

Exceptions

None.

System.Data.UniqueConstraint

The UniqueConstraint class represents a uniqueness restriction imposed on a column or group of columns. A UniqueConstraint on a DataColumn ensures that no two values in that DataColumn can contain the same value. When defining a UniqueConstraint, it is possible to declare the column or column array to be the Primary Key. Any number of columns in a DataTable may have unique constraints placed on them, but only a UniqueConstraint may be a primary key. Attempting to define two UniqueConstraint objects as primary keys will cause a System.ArgumentException to be thrown when the second one is added to the DataTable.Constraints collection.

HINT **When creating new constraints for a DataTable, use the DataTable.Constaints.Add method for convenience and speed, instead of the constraint constructors.**

HINT **When defining a UniqueConstraint and a ForeignKeyConstraint on the same parent column, you can instead define a DataRelation and pass a True in the constructors to the boolCreateConstraints parameter.**

WARNING **Constraints are not enforced unless the DataSet.EnforceConstraints property is set to True.**

Constructors

```
Dim myUniqueConstraint As New UniqueConstraint(myDataColumn)
Dim myUniqueConstraint As New _
     UniqueConstraint(myDataColumnArray)
```

```
Dim myUniqueConstraint As New _
     UniqueConstraint(myDataColumn, isPrimaryKey)
Dim myUniqueConstraint As New _
     UniqueConstraint(myDataColumnArray, isPrimaryKey)
Dim myUniqueConstraint As New UniqueConstraint(strName, _
     myDataColumn)
Dim myUniqueConstraint As New _
     UniqueConstraint(strName, myDataColumnArray)
Dim myUniqueConstraint As New UniqueConstraint(strName, _
     myDataColumn, isPrimaryKey)
Dim myUniqueConstraint As New UniqueConstraint(strName, _
     myDataColumnArray, isPrimaryKey)
Dim myUniqueConstraint As New UniqueConstraint(strName, _
     strColumnNameArray, isPrimaryKey)
```

Parameters

`myDataColumn`	The DataColumn to constrain.
`myDataColumnArray`	Array containing DataColumn objects to participate in the constraint.
`isPrimaryKey`	Boolean specifying whether this constraint is the primary key for the DataTable (True if primary key, False otherwise).
`strName`	The name of the constraint as a String.
`strColumnNameArray`	Array of String values designating the names of the DataColumn objects to participate in the constraint. (Columns of the correct name must exist when this constructor is used!)

Exceptions

ArgumentNullException	A strName or isPrimaryKey was a null reference (`Nothing` in Visual Basic).
NullReferenceException	The passed DataColumn was null (`Nothing` in Visual Basic).

UniqueConstraint Sample Code

```
'This function demonstrates the UniqueConstraint
'  class.  It assumes a valid DataTable is passed, with
'  Column1 being the primary key, and Column2 being unique.
Public Sub DemoUniqueConstraints( _
                ByRef myDataTable As DataTable)
   Dim myUniqueConstraint As UniqueConstraint
   'define a Primary Key and add it to the DataTable
   myUniqueConstraint = New UniqueConstraint("myKey", _
```

```
            myDataTable.Columns(0), True)
    myDataTable.Constraints.Add(myUniqueConstraint)

    'add a non-primary key unique constraint to the table
    '  using an overloaded Constraints.Add method
    myDataTable.Constraints.Add("myUnique", _
            myDataTable.Columns(1), False)

    'Get the name of the primary Key column (the first)
    If myUniqueConstraint.IsPrimaryKey Then
       MessageBox.Show( _
          myUniqueConstraint.Columns(0).ColumnName())
    End If

End Sub
```

Members

Columns

The read-only Columns property returns an array of DataColumn objects that contains the columns involved in the UniqueConstraint. If only one column is involved in the constraint, then the array will contain only one DataColumn object.

Usage

```
myDataColumn[] = myUniqueConstraint.Columns
```

Parameters

None.

Exceptions

None.

ConstraintName

The ConstraintName property returns or sets a String value that represents the name of the UniqueConstraint object.

Usage

```
myString = myUniqueConstraint.ConstraintName
myUniqueConstraint.ConstraintName = myString
```

Parameters

None.

Exceptions

None.

Equals

The Equals method is overridden to allow comparison of two UniqueConstraint objects. The Equals method will return True if the two UniqueConstraint objects constrain the same columns. (This is true even if they have different properties. For instance, if one constraint is a primary key and the other is merely a unique constraint, they are considered equal by this method.)

You can use this method to determine equality to any of the constraints in a collection before adding a new constraint. This will prevent a DataException from being thrown.

Usage

```
myBoolean = myUniqueConstraint.Equals(myObject)
```

Parameters

`myObject`	The Object (likely a UniqueConstraint object) to compare to myUniqueConstraint for equality.

Exceptions

None.

ExtendedProperties

The read-only ExtendedProperties property returns a PropertyCollection object that allows you to store custom information with the object. Although the property itself is read-only, you may add properties to the returned PropertyCollection with the Add method. See the sample code for an example.

NOTE **If the ExtendedProperties collection is to be persisted as XML, then the members of the collection must be of type String.**

Usage

```
myPropertyCollection = myUniqueConstraint.ExtendedProperties
```

Parameters

None.

Exceptions

None.

Sample Code

```
myUniqueConstraint.ExtendedProperties.Add( _
     "Cousins", "Dustin and Monika")
```

IsPrimaryKey

The read-only IsPrimaryKey property returns a Boolean value indicating whether the constraint is on a primary key. IsPrimaryKey returns True if the constraint is on a primary key and False otherwise.

Usage

```
myBoolean = myUniqueConstraint.IsPrimaryKey
```

Parameters

None.

Exceptions
None.

Table

The read-only Table property returns the DataTable object that is the child table for the constraint.

Usage

```
myDataTable = myUniqueConstraint.Table
```

Parameters
None.

Exceptions
None.

ToString

The ToString method returns the ConstraintName as a String.

Usage

```
myString = myUniqueConstraint.ToString()
```

Parameters
None.

Exceptions
None.

System.Data.UpdateRowSource

The UpdateRowSource enumeration provides the values that specify how a query result is applied to the DataRow being updated. They are used in the IDbCommand. UpdatedRowSource property (or from descending classes, such as SqlCommand and OleDbCommand).

In most ADO.NET objects, the default is Continue.

UpdateRowSource Enumeration

Continue (0)	Process this row, and continue processing rows.
ErrorsOccurred (1)	This update should be treated as an error. Setting this value will abort the update of this row and all remaining rows, as well as throw an Exception. To specify the Error to be thrown, add an Exception to the Errors property.
SkipAllRemainingRows (3)	Do not process this row or any remaining rows.
SkipCurrentRow (2)	Do not process this row, but continue processing rows.

System.Data.UpdateStatus

The UpdateStatus enumeration provides the values that determine the action that should be taken during an Update operation. This is used when updating to the data source using a DataAdapter, such as SqlCommand and OleDbCommand. These values can be used to terminate the update of the remaining rows, ignore the current row, throw an error, or just continue on to further rows.

In most ADO.NET objects, the default is Continue.

UpdateStatus Enumeration Values

Continue (0)	Process this row, and continue processing rows.
ErrorsOccurred (1)	This update should be treated as an error. Setting this value will abort the update of this row and all remaining rows, as well as throw an Exception. To specify the Error to be thrown add an Exception to the Errors property.
SkipAllRemainingRows (3)	Do not process this row or any remaining rows, but do not throw an exception.
SkipCurrentRow (2)	Do not process this row, but continue processing rows.

System.Data.VersionNotFoundException

The VersionNotFoundException class (descended from the DataException class) defines exceptions that are thrown when attempting to return a version of a DataRow that does not exist. The version, indicated by a DataRowVersion enumeration value, may not exist depending on the state of the DataRow. For instance, if there have been no edits to a DataRow since the last AcceptChanges was called, there is no Proposed version.

Constructors

```
Dim myVersionNotFoundException As New _
     VersionNotFoundException()
Dim myVersionNotFoundException As New _
     VersionNotFoundException(myString)
```

Parameters

`myString`	A String object that will initialize the Message property.

VersionNotFoundException Sample Code

```
Dim myVersionNotFoundException As VersionNotFoundException
myVersionNotFoundException = New _
     VersionNotFoundException("Version not found!")
Throw myVersionNotFoundException
```

Members

GetBaseException

The GetBaseException method returns an Exception object containing the original exception. To return the original exception, it traverses the chain of InnerException objects. If the InnerException property of the current exception is null, GetBaseException will return a reference to the current Exception object.

To determine only the parent exception to the current exception, use the InnerException property.

Usage

```
myException = myVersionNotFoundException.GetBaseException()
```

Parameters

None.

Exceptions

None.

GetObjectData

The GetObjectData method fills the passed System.Runtime.Serialization.SerializationInfo buffer object with information about the Exception object. There is no value returned by this method. Depending on the passed System.Runtime.Serialization.StreamingContext object, this method can be used to serialize the object to a stream or read serialization from a stream.

Because it deals mainly with serialization and not data access, further discussion of this property is beyond the scope of this book.

Usage

```
myVersionNotFoundException.GetObjectData(mySerializationInfo, _
     myStreamingContext)
```

Parameters

`mySerializationInfo`	A System.Runtime.Serialization.SerializationInfo buffer object to be filled with the exception's serialization data.
`myStreamingContext`	A System.Runtime.Serialization.StreamingContext object specifying the stream to write the serialization info to or read the information from.

Exceptions

ArgumentNullException	The passed SerializationInfo buffer object is null (`Nothing` in Visual Basic .NET).

HelpLink

The HelpLink property returns or sets a String linking to a help file associated with the VersionNotFoundException. The HelpLink is formatted as a Uniform Resource Name (URN) or Uniform Resource Locator (URL). An example of this property that points to the MSDN help available with Visual Studio .NET would be: `ms-help://MS.VSCC/MS.MSDNVS/cpref/html/frlrfsystemexceptionclasshelplinktopic.htm.`

The HelpLink is often not set, so it is wise to verify both that the HelpLink property itself is not an empty string and that the HelpLink points to a valid help file before exposing the HelpLink to a user of your program.

Usage

```
myString = myVersionNotFoundException.HelpLink
myVersionNotFoundException.HelpLink = myString
```

Parameters

None.

InnerException

The read-only InnerException property returns the Exception object linking to a previous exception that caused the current exception to be thrown, if any, or a null value (`Nothing` in Visual Basic .NET), if not. This permits a chain of InnerException objects to be generated, allowing a program to trace the exception chain all the way to the root exception. Be aware that InnerException may be null.

To find the base exception that originally was fired, use the GetBaseException method.

Usage

```
myException = myVersionNotFoundException.InnerException
```

Parameters

None.

Message

The read-only Message property returns a String describing the first error that caused the exception. Because it provides information from only the first error, use this property cautiously when building robust error handling.

Usage

```
myString = myVersionNotFoundException.Message
```

Parameters

None.

Source

The Source property sets or returns a String containing the name of the provider that generated the first error. Because it provides information from only the first error, use this property cautiously when building robust error handling.

Usage
```
myString = myVersionNotFoundException.Source
myVersionNotFoundException.Source = myString
```

Parameters
None.

StackTrace

The read-only StackTrace property returns a String containing a textual representation of the stack trace. The stack trace reports all of the methods that are in execution at the time just prior to the execution being thrown. It is read from top to bottom with the latest method in execution at the top.

The StackTrace can be invaluable in tracing difficult-to-find bugs because it provides a way to see all of the methods that could have led up to the error.

TIP **To see the stack trace programmatically when no exception has been raised, use the Environment.StackTrace property.**

Usage
```
myString = myVersionNotFoundException.StackTrace
```

Parameters
None.

TargetSite

The read-only TargetSite property returns an object inheriting from System.Reflection.MethodBase that contains a reference to the method that caused the error to be thrown.

This property is primarily used to programmatically find information about the method that raised the exception. The returned object will provide information such as the methods parameters and return type and whether the method is virtual, a constructor, public, private, etc. Because it deals mainly with reflection and not data access, further discussion of this property is beyond the scope of this book.

Usage
```
myMethodBase = myVersionNotFoundException.TargetSite
```

Parameters
None.

ToString

The ToString method is overridden to return information relating to the VersionNotFoundException exception. The returned String contains the full class name and also the error message, name of the inner exception, and stack trace, if they exist.

Usage

```
myString = myVersionNotFoundException.ToString()
```

Parameters

None.

Exceptions

None.

System.Data.XmlReadMode

The XmlReadMode enumeration provides the values that are used to determine how to fill a DataSet when the DataSet.ReadXml method is called.

The Auto value is default for the DataSet.ReadXml method.

One value bears a closer look. A DiffGram is a format to identify current and original values of data, so that any changes to the data can be compared with the original. This allows for concurrency issues to be dealt with effectively. The DiffGram is the standard format for XML Web services. In addition, the DiffGram format is understood natively by SQL Server 2000, which is able to update records based on a passed XML document in DiffGram format. (For more information see the SQL Server 2000 documentation or MSDN.)

NOTE Using Auto is most convenient when programming, but it generally causes the read to occur more slowly than by explicitly setting the XmlReadMode to one of the other values.

XmlReadMode Enumeration

Auto (0)	Performs one of the other actions according to the following rules: 1.) If the data is a DiffGram, uses DiffGram value. 2.) If data has a schema, then uses ReadSchema value. 3.) If data does not have schema, uses InferSchema value.
DiffGram (4)	Reads the document as a DiffGram, applying changes from the DiffGram to the DataSet. The target DataSet schema must match the DiffGram schema, or the operation will fail and an exception will be thrown. (Caution: When using DiffGram, the ReadXml should generally be used with data created with WriteXml as a DiffGram.)

Fragment (5)	Reads XML documents containing inline XDR schema fragments. (Usually created when executing FOR XML queries against SQL Server.)
IgnoreSchema (2)	Ignores any inline schema and reads data into the existing DataSet schema. If any data does not match the existing schema, it is discarded. (Note: If the data is a DiffGram, IgnoreSchema is the same as DiffGram.)
InferSchema (3)	Infers schema from the data and loads the data, ignoring any inline schema information. (If the DataSet already contains a schema, the current schema is extended by adding new tables or adding columns to existing tables. An exception is thrown if the inferred table already exists but with a different namespace, or if any of the inferred columns conflict with existing columns.)
ReadSchema (1)	Reads any inline schema and loads the data. If the DataSet already contains schema, new tables are added to the schema, unless any tables in the inline schema already exist in the DataSet, in which case an exception is thrown.

System.Data.XmlWriteMode

The XmlWriteMode enumeration provides the values that are used to determine how to write a DataSet to an XML document when the DataSet.WriteXml method is called. (See System.Data.XmlReadMode for more information on the DiffGram value.)

To learn more about DiffGram, see the System.Data.XmlReadMode enumeration.

XmlWriteMode Enumeration

DiffGram (2)	Writes the entire DataSet as a DiffGram, including the original and changed values. (This DiffGram can be sent directly to SQL Server 2000.) To retrieve only the changed values, use the DataSet.GetChanges method before calling the WriteXml method.
IgnoreSchema (1)	Writes the entire DataSet as an XML document without an inline schema.
WriteSchema (0)	Writes the entire DataSet as an XML document and includes the DataSet schema as an inline XDR schema. If the DataSet contains only a schema (structure) then only the schema is written. If the DataSet does not have a schema, nothing will be output.

CHAPTER 5

System.Data.Common

The System.Data.Common namespace fills the role of enabler to the .NET data providers. The entire namespace consists of classes that provide functionality for the derived data providers, such as the OLE DB data provider and the SQL Server data provider.

There are two types of classes in the Common namespace. The first type is the abstract (MustInherit) classes that cannot be independently instantiated. These are the base classes for the data source-specific classes that make up the .NET data providers. For instance, the DbDataAdapter class cannot be instantiated; however, all data providers that provide access to relational databases descend from this class and are thus provided with a bulk of the needed functionality. In addition, this ensures that a minimum number of methods are shared across all relational data providers. The other types are sealed (NotInheritable) classes that cannot be derived from. These classes ensure that there is a set of useful classes that have identical behaviors across all data providers that implement them. A DataColumnMapping object is identical regardless of whether you're using the OLE DB data provider or the SQL Server data provider.

The Common namespace is relatively new, introduced only just before the Visual Studio Beta 2 release. We both figure it was a rush job because here we see a major mangling of the object model. A pure object model is a blessing to programmers because it allows them to develop a "feeling" for the framework. When something new comes up, a programmer with a feel for the object model will know where to look and approximately what the object does. The creation of the Common namespace was designed to help organize the object model. And it does... sort of.

Here's what was meant to happen. The System.Data namespace was cluttered with many of the classes that were used in the creation of data providers, and the providers themselves weren't clearly distinguished from the other parts of ADO.NET. As you saw in Chapter 2, "Introduction to ADO.NET," the ADO.NET model divides neatly into two segments: the segment that deals with pure data manipulation, regardless of source, and the segment that deals directly with data sources.

In order to clean up the System.Data namespace, Microsoft moved several of the classes that dealt with the creation of data providers to the System.Data.Common namespace. This namespace, as mentioned previously, provides for the commonalities between the various data providers. Unfortunately, Microsoft moved only some of the classes. It moved the DbDataAdapter class but failed to move the IDbDataAdapter interface, which, when combined with the DbDataAdapter class, provides most of the common interface for accessing relational databases. It left the IDbCommand, and even the IDbConnection interfaces, in the System.Data namespace. Both are absolutely specific to the data provider layer and have nothing at all to do with the pure .NET data objects that are the majority of the System.Data namespace. Thus, a good idea gone awry. But, at least, you have a slight feel for the structure. Unfortunately, it won't get you all the way, but it'll get you closer.

RANT **I find this half-baked class hierarchy adjustment particularly galling. I was a VB programmer before Visual Basic .NET, and my pet peeve with VB was the lack of consistency. Some collections were zero based, others one based. Identical methods from different objects had different names, or even worse, were called with different signatures (one accepting a string, then integer—the other the same integer, then the string). This is what made VB nonrespectable. Yes, Microsoft was able to deploy new versions of VB more quickly, and, yes, they had to be compatible with previous releases. And, yes, VB was still a faster development tool than many other languages. But the lack of a well-thought-out structure made it always second rate to better structured languages.**

I watched new features grow on VB, useful features, but features that grew like distorted cancers, deforming the structure. Half the time programming was spent finding workarounds to problems caused by lack of consistency or foresight. Java got it right. Built from the ground up, it maintained its consistency, its beauty of design, and its elegance. C# also does it right, as does the new Visual Basic .NET. But, the object model that all of .NET shares, the .NET Framework, already shows signs of aging or hacks to maintain backward compatibility. And all of this in the first release. Read the guidelines written by Microsoft itself for naming objects in a custom data provider, then look at the SqlClient, where it has disregarded its own written advice and created a nonstandard naming scheme for the objects, prefixing some with Sql and some with SqlClient. Will it still work? Yes. Will programmers wonder why it doesn't make sense? Yes. Will Microsoft care? Maybe, but it will be too late. All the ugly warts of a poor design will remain with us forever to ensure backward compatibility. That's the end of my personal rant; thank you for listening.

System.Data.Common.DataAdapter

The DataAdapter class is the foundation class for all specific implementations of DataAdapter in each of the .NET data providers. It is a utility class that provides behaviors and functionality to assist in creating DataAdapters geared for all types of data sources. As such, it is an abstract (MustInherit) class, so you cannot create an instance of this class but must instead create instances of objects that inherit from this class (such as the SqlDataAdapter class).

The DataAdapter class contains many protected members that can be called only by classes that descend from it. These are implemented for the convenience of programmers creating their own data providers. Because the creation of data providers is beyond the scope of this book, these protected members will be not be listed.

Although the constructor is listed in the text that follows, it is a protected method, which means it can be called only by descendents of this class and cannot be used directly in data access code. It is listed only for informational purposes.

Multiple DataAdapters can be used with the same DataSet. In this way, several disparate data sources can be included in one DataSet. For instance, a customer list drawn from a small MS Access database could be combined with orders drawn from a SQL Server 2000 database into one DataSet. Data relationships between the two tables could be created internally to the DataSet, and the resulting in-memory database could be queried using SQL. Changes to the DataSet are then saved back to the multiple data sources by calling the Update() method of each DataAdapter.

For more information on working with a particular DataAdapter, see the sections dedicated to the various implementations of this class. The three covered in this book are the OleDataAdapter class, the SqlDataAdapter class, and the OdbcDataAdapter class.

Constructors

```
Dim myDataAdapter As New DataAdapter()
```

Parameters

None.

Members

AcceptChangesDuringFill

The AcceptChangesDuringFill property is a Boolean value that determines whether the AcceptChanges event is fired when the Fill() method is called. If the value is true, then the AcceptChanges event (see System.Data.DataRow class) is called for each DataRow object as it is added to the DataTable object, leaving the DataRowState = Unchanged (2). If false, the added DataRow objects are treated as added rows, leaving the DataRowState = Added (4). The default value is True.

Usage

```
myBoolean = myDataAdapter.AcceptChangesDuringFill
myDataAdapter.AcceptChangesDuringFill = myBoolean
```

Disposed

The Disposed event (inherited from Component) is fired when the component is to be disposed and its resources freed. The Disposed event can be caught just prior to the object being disposed, and clean up code can be executed. The FillError event passes a reference to the source of the event (the instantiated DataAdapter object) and a System. EventArgs object. The EventArgs object has very little meaningful information, and it is mainly there to conform to .NET Framework recommendations for raising events.

Usage

```
Private Sub myDataAdapter_Disposed(ByVal sender As Object, _
   ByVal e As System.EventArgs) Handles myDataAdapter.Disposed
```

Event Data

None.

Sample Code

```
Private Sub myDataAdapter_Disposed(ByVal sender As Object, _
    ByVal e As System.EventArgs) Handles myDataAdapter.Disposed
    MessageBox.Show("myDataAdapter is currently In Disposed. ;-)")
End Sub
```

Fill

The Fill() method for the DataAdapter is an abstract (MustOverride) method that provides a signature for all derived classes. There is only one implementation of the Fill() method for the DataAdapter. It accepts a DataSet to fill and returns an Integer specifying the number of rows that were added or updated. This is the most general of all Fill() methods in the various DataAdapter implementations, and it reflects the maximum flexibility. Not all data providers are built for relational databases, and these would inherit from this class.

Usage

```
myInteger = myDataAdapter.Fill(myDataSet)
```

Parameters

`myDataSet`	A System.Data.DataSet object to be filled.

Exceptions

As per Inherited class; see implemented DataAdapter class.

FillSchema

The FillSchema() method is an abstract (MustOverride) method that provides a signature for all derived classes. There is only one implementation of the FillSchema method for the DataAdapter object. It defines a signature to accept a new DataTable and fill it with the schema inherited from the data source. It then returns an array of DataTable objects containing the schema derived from the data source. The schema is configured based on the value of the SchemaType parameter. A SchemaType of "Source" applies the incoming schema to the DataSet with no transformation; "Mapped" applies the mappings of existing DataTable objects to the schema and then transforms the DataSet based on the transformed schema.

The FillSchema() method is particularly useful when creating data in a DataSet that must match the constraints imposed by the data source. Once a DataSet has inherited the schema from the data source, any additions to a DataTable or group of DataTable objects that violate one of the constraints will cause an error to be raised. This method does not add any data to the DataSet or DataTable, only the schema. To fill a DataSet or DataTable with data, use the Fill() method.

Usage

```
arrayDataTable() = myDbDataAdapter.FillSchema(myDataSet, mySchemaType)
```

Parameters

`myDataSet`	A System.Data.DataSet object to be updated.
`mySchemaType`	A System.Data.SchemaType enumeration specifying how existing schema mappings should be dealt with. This can be either Source or Mapped. (This should generally be set to Mapped. See SchemaType for more information.)

Exceptions

As per Inherited class; see implemented DataAdapter class.

GetFillParameters

The GetFillParameters() method is an abstract (MustOverride) method that provides a signature for all derived classes. It defines a method to return an array of IDataParameter objects specifying user-defined parameters to be passed in a SQL SELECT command.

NOTE Sometimes Microsoft's class definitions are a bit cluttered. Here is one example. The DataAdapter is the defining class for all (including non-SQL) data sources. Yet, here is a method specifically geared for SQL (read relational) data sources. This method should have more properly been assigned to the DbDataAdapter.

Usage

```
myIDataParameterArray() = myDataAdapter.GetFillParameters()
```

Parameters

None.

Exceptions

As per Inherited class; see implemented DataAdapter class.

MissingMappingAction

The MissingMappingAction property returns or sets a MissingMappingAction enumeration value that determines what to do when the incoming data does not have a matching table or column in the current DataSet. The default value is Passthrough.

Usage

```
myMissingMappingActionEnumeration = myDataAdapter.MissingMappingAction
myDataAdapter.MissingMappingAction = myMissingMappingActionEnumeration
```

Parameters

None.

MissingMappingAction Enumeration Values

Error (3)	A System.SystemException is thrown.
Ignore (2)	Any columns or tables without mappings are ignored, returning a null reference.
Passthrough (1)	(Default). The source column or table is added to the DataSet using its original name.

MissingSchemaAction

The MissingSchemaAction property returns or sets a MissingSchemaAction enumeration value that determines what to do when the incoming data does not have a matching schema in the current DataSet. The default value is Add.

Usage

```
myEnumeration = myDataAdapter.MissingSchemaAction
myDataAdapter.MissingSchemaAction = myEnumeration
```

Parameters

None.

MissingMappingAction Enumeration Values

Add (1)	(Default). Adds the columns required to complete the schema.
AddWithKey (4)	Adds the columns and primary key information required to complete the schema.
Error (3)	A System.SystemException is thrown.
Ignore (2)	Any columns without a matching schema are ignored.

ToString

The ToString method for DataAdapter simply returns "System.Data.Common.DataAdapter".

Usage

```
myString = myDataAdapter.ToString()
```

Parameters

None.

Exceptions

None.

Update

The Update() method is an abstract (MustOverride) method that provides a signature for all derived classes. It defines a method that calls the appropriate commands for each of the inserted, updated, or deleted rows and returns an Integer containing the number of rows successfully updated. In the case of a data source that supports SQL, these would be the INSERT, UPDATE, and DELETE commands.

Usage

```
myInteger = myDataAdapter.Update(myDataSet)
```

Parameters

`myDataSet`	A System.Data.DataSet object to be updated.

Exceptions

As per Inherited class; see the implemented DataAdapter class.

System.Data.Common.DataColumnMapping

The DataColumnMapping class coordinates the mapping between a DataTable column and a related column from a data source. A DataColumnMapping object allows you to use a column name in the DataSet that is different from that in the data source. This mapping is then referenced during an update of the DataSet or the data source.

Although it can exist as an independent object, a DataColumnMapping object is maintained in a DataColumnMappingCollection that is, in turn, generally stored in the ColumnMappings property of a DataTableMapping. Which, if truth be told, is generally included in a DataTableMappingCollection included as a property in a DataAdapter.

Constructors

```
Dim myDataColumnMapping As New DataColumnMapping()
Dim myDataColumnMapping As New DataColumnMapping(strSourceColumn, _
   strDataSetColumn)
```

Parameters

`strSourceColumn`	The case-sensitive name of the column from the data source, as a String. This sets the SourceColumn property.
`strDataSetColumn`	The noncase-sensitive name of the column from the DataSet, as a String. This sets the DataSet property.

Members

DataSetColumn

The DataSetColumn property gets or sets the name of the column in the DataSet (as a String). This property is not case sensitive. This column is matched with the Source-Column to establish a mapping between the data source and the DataSet.

Usage

```
myString = myDataColumnMapping.DataSetColumn
myDataColumnMapping.DataSetColumn= myString
```

Parameters

None.

SourceColumn

The SourceColumn property gets or sets the name of the column in the data source (as a String). This column is matched with the DataSetColumn to establish a mapping between the data source and the DataSet.

Usage

```
myString = myDataColumnMapping.SourceColumn
myDataColumnMapping.SourceColumn = myString
```

Parameters

None.

GetDataColumnBySchemaAction

The GetDataColumnBySchemaAction() method returns a DataColumn object from the passed DataTable object. The method accepts three parameters: the DataTable from which to pull the DataColumn object, the data type of the requested column, and a MissingSchemaAction enumeration value to determine what to do if the desired DataColumn does not exist in the passed DataTable. Be careful when using MissingSchemaAction.Add because,despite the name, it does not "Add" anything to the passed DataTable, but merely returns a value.

Usage

```
myDataColumn = myDataColumnMapping.GetDataColumnBySchemaAction( _
   dataTable, dataType, schemaAction)
```

Parameters

`dataTable`	The DataTable object from which to draw the requested DataColumn.
`dataType`	The Type of the data column.
`schemaAction`	A System.Data.MissingSchemaAction enumeration value to determine the action taken if the desired DataColumn doesn't exist in the passed DataTable.

MissingSchemaAction Enumeration Values

Error (3)	An exception is thrown.
Ignore (2)	DataColumn returned by method is null (`Nothing` in VB).
Add (1)	A DataColumn is generated with the passed type with the name of the DataSetColumn property, but nothing is added to the passed DataTable.

Exceptions

None.

ToString

The ToString method is overridden to return the current SourceColumn property.

Usage

```
myString = myDataColumnMapping.ToString()
```

Parameters
None.

Exceptions
None.

System.Data.Common.DataColumnMapping Collection

The DataColumnMappingCollection is a container class that maintains a collection of DataColumnMapping objects. An empty DataColumnMappingCollection is automatically created when a new DataTableMapping object is created. The constructor, though, can be used to create an empty standalone collection that can be manipulated.

Constructors

```
Dim myDataColumnMappingCollection As New DataColumnMappingCollection()
```

Parameters

None.

Members

Count

The read-only Count property returns an Integer specifying the number of DataColumnMapping objects contained in the collection. Because all arrays in .NET are zero based, Count returns a number one greater than the highest available index ordinal in any array.

Usage

```
myInteger = myDataColumnMappingCollection.Count
```

Parameters
None.

Exceptions
None.

Item

The Item property returns or sets a DataColumnMapping object contained in the DataColumnMappingCollection at a selected location. Because this is the default property of the object, placing the index directly after the DataColumnMapping is possible (see second usage example).

Usage

```
myDataColumnMapping = myDataColumnMappingCollection.Item(intIndex)
myDataColumnMapping = myDataColumnMappingCollection(intIndex)
```

Parameters

`intIndex`	The zero-based Integer valued index of the DataColumnMapping object to retrieve.

Exceptions

None.

Add

The Add() method adds a DataColumnMapping object to the collection and returns the index of the added object as an Integer. The object can be added either by adding an already created DataColumnMapping or by passing two strings representing the SourceColumn and DataSetColumn names.

Usage

```
myInteger = myDataColumnMappingCollection.Add(objectDataColumnMapping)
myInteger = myDataColumnMappingCollection.Add(strSourceColumn, _
    strDataSetColumn)
```

Parameters

`objectDataColumnMapping`	The Object to add to the collection, as a DataColumnMapping object.
`strSourceColumn`	The case-sensitive name of the column from the data source, as a String.
`strDataSetColumn`	The noncase-sensitive name of the column from the DataSet, as a String.

Exceptions

None.

AddRange

The AddRange() method copies the passed array of DataColumnMapping objects to the end of the DataColumnMappingCollection.

Usage

```
myDataColumnMappingCollection.AddRange(arrayDataColumnMapping)
```

Parameters

`arrayDataColumnMapping`	An array of DataColumnMapping objects to be added to the end of the DataColumnMapping-Collection.

Exceptions

None.

Clear

The Clear() method removes all DataColumnMapping objects from the DataColumn-MappingCollection.

Usage

```
myDataColumnMappingCollection.Clear()
```

Parameters

None.

Exceptions

None.

Contains

The Contains() method returns a Boolean indicating whether a DataColumnMapping object exists in the DataColumnMappingCollection. You can pass either a DataColumn-Mapping object or the source column name as a case-sensitive string.

Usage

```
myDataColumnMappingCollection.Contains(myDataColumnMapping)
myDataColumnMappingCollection.Contains(strSourceColumn)
```

Parameters

`myDataColumnMapping`	A DataColumnMapping object to compare for existence in the DataColumnMappingCollection.
`strSourceColumn`	The source column name to find in the DataColumn-MappingCollection as a case-sensitive String.

Exceptions

None.

CopyTo

The CopyTo() method copies the contained DataColumnMapping objects to a passed buffer array. You may also pass an index value to indicate where in the buffer array you wish to begin filling. Pass a value other than zero if your array already contains other objects that you don't want to overwrite.

Usage

```
myDataColumnMappingCollection.CopyTo(arrayBuffer, intIndex)
```

Parameters

`arrayBuffer`	The passed array to fill with DataColumnMapping objects.
`intIndex`	Location to begin filling array. For example: Passing a 3 will fill arrayBuffer (3) with the first DataColumnMapping object.

Exceptions

None.

GetByDataSetColumn

The GetByDataSetColumn() method returns a DataColumnMapping object with the passed DataSet column name.

Usage

```
myDataColumnMapping = _
   myDataColumnMappingCollection.GetByDataSetColumn(strDataSetColumn)
```

Parameters

`strDataSetColumn`	The DataSet column name as a noncase-sensitive String.

Exceptions

None.

GetColumnMappingBySchemaAction

The GetColumnMappingBySchemaAction() method is a static (shared) method that returns a DataColumnMapping object from a passed DataColumnMappingCollection. Because this is a shared method, an object does not have to be created to access it (see the example that follows). The method accepts three parameters: the DataColumn-MappingCollection from which to pull the DataColumnMapping object, the name of the source column, and a MissingMappingAction enumeration value to determine what to do if the desired DataColumnMapping does not exist in the passed Data-ColumnMappingCollection.

Usage

```
myDataColumnMapping = _
   myDataColumnMappingCollection.GetColumnMappingBySchemaAction( _
   columnMappings, strSourceColumn, mappingAction)
```

Parameters

`columnMappings`	The DataColumnMappingCollection object from which to draw the requested DataColumnMapping.
`strSourceColumn`	The source column name to find in the DataColumn-MappingCollection as a case-sensitive String.
`mappingAction`	A System.Data.MissingMappingAction enumeration value to determine the action taken if the desired DataColumnMapping doesn't exist in the passed DataColumnMappingCollection.

MissingMappingAction Enumeration Values

Error (3)	A System.SystemException is thrown.
Ignore (2)	Any columns or tables without mappings are ignored, returning a null reference.
Passthrough (1)	(Default). The source column or table is added to the DataSet using its original name.

Exceptions

None.

IndexOf

The IndexOf() method returns an Integer specifying the location of a specified DataColumnMapping within the DataColumnMappingCollection. Because this method is overloaded, you may pass either the DataColumnMapping object itself or a String representing the source column name.

Usage

```
myInteger = myDataColumnMappingCollection.IndexOf(objectDataColumn)
myInteger = myDataColumnMappingCollection.IndexOf(strSourceColumn)
```

Parameters

`objectDataColumn`	An Object that is the DataColumnMapping object for which to find the location. Although any Object may be passed, it must be a member of the DataColumnMapping class.
`strSourceColumn`	The source column name to find in the DataColumnMappingCollection as a case-sensitive String.

Exceptions

None.

IndexOfDataSetColumn

The IndexOfDataSetColumn() method returns an Integer specifying the location of the DataColumnMapping within the passed DataSet column name.

Usage

```
myInteger = myDataColumnMappingCollection.IndexOf(strDataSetColumn)
```

Parameters

`strDataSetColumn`	The DataSet column name to find in the DataColumnMappingCollection as a noncase-sensitive String.

Exceptions

None.

Insert

The Insert() method inserts a DataColumnMapping object into the DataColumnMappingCollection at the specified index. Passing an index of 3 will insert the DataColumnMapping at the Item(3) position.

Usage

```
myDataColumnMappingCollection.Insert(intIndex, objectDataColumn)
```

Parameters

`intIndex`	Location to begin filling array. For example: Passing a 3 will insert the DataColumnMapping object into the DataColumnMappingCollection.Item (3) position.
`objectDataColumn`	The Object to insert into the DataColumnMappingCollection. This Object must be a DataColumnMapping object.

Exceptions

None.

Remove

The Remove() method removes a specified DataColumnMapping object from the DataColumnMappingCollection.

Usage

```
myDataColumnMappingCollection.Remove(objectDataColumn)
```

Parameters

`objectDataColumn`	The Object to remove from the DataColumnMappingCollection. This Object must be a DataColumnMapping object.

Exceptions

SystemException	Either the objectDataColumn is not a DataColumnMapping object or the passed objectDataColumn object does not exist in the DataColumnMappingCollection.

RemoveAt

The RemoveAt() method removes a DataColumnMapping object from the DataColumnMappingCollection. The method is overloaded, so you can specify the DataColumnMapping object by passing either the location of the object or the name of the source column.

Usage

```
myDataColumnMappingCollection.RemoveAt(intIndex)
myDataColumnMappingCollection.RemoveAt(strSourceColumn)
```

Parameters

`intIndex`	Location of the DataMappingColumn to remove, as an Int32.
`strSourceColumn`	The source column name to remove from the DataColumnMappingCollection, as a case-sensitive String.

Exceptions

IndexOutOfRangeException	A DataMappingColumn object does not exist at the passed intIndex or with the passed strSourceColumn name.

System.Data.Common.DataTableMapping

The DataTableMapping class coordinates the mapping between a DataSet table and a related table from a data source. A DataTableMapping object allows you to use a table name in the DataSet that is different from that in the data source. This mapping is then referenced during an update of the DataSet or the data source.

Although it can exist as an independent object, a DataTableMapping object is maintained in a DataTableMappingCollection, which is, in turn, generally stored in the TableMappings property of a DataAdapter.

Constructors

```
Dim myDataTableMapping As New DataTableMapping()
Dim myDataTableMapping As New DataTableMapping(strSourceTable, _
   strDataSetTable)
```

Parameters

`strSourceTable`	The case-sensitive name of the table from the data source, as a String. This sets the SourceTable property.
`strDataSetTable`	The noncase-sensitive name of the table from the DataSet, as a String. This sets the DataSet property.

Members

DataSetTable

The DataSetTable property gets or sets the name of the table in the DataSet (as a String). This property is not case sensitive. This table is matched with the SourceTable to establish a mapping between the data source and the DataSet.

Usage

```
myString = myDataTableMapping.DataSetTable
myDataTableMapping.DataSetTable = myString
```

Parameters
None.

Exceptions
None.

SourceTable

The SourceTable property gets or sets the name of the table in the data source (as a String). This table is matched with the DataSetTable to establish a mapping between the data source and the DataSet.

Usage

```
myString = myDataTableMapping.SourceTable
myDataTableMapping.SourceTable = myString
```

Parameters
None.

Exceptions
None.

GetColumnMappingBySchemaAction

The GetColumnMappingBySchemaAction() method returns a DataColumnMapping object from the passed DataTable object. The method accepts two parameters: the name of the source column and a MissingSchemaAction enumeration value to determine what to do if no DataColumnMapping with the passed source column name exists in the current DataTableMapping.

Usage

```
myDataColumnMapping = _
   myDataTableMapping.GetColumnMappingBySchemaAction( _
   strSourceColumn, mappingAction)
```

Parameters

`strSourceColumn`	The source table name to find in the DataTableMapping-Collection as a case-sensitive String.
`mappingAction`	A System.Data.MissingMappingAction enumeration value to determine the action taken if the desired DataTableMapping doesn't exist in the passed DataTableMappingCollection.

MissingMappingAction Enumeration Values

Error (3)	A System.SystemException is thrown.
Ignore (2)	Any columns or tables without mappings are ignored, returning a null reference.
Passthrough (1)	(Default). The source column or table is added to the DataSet using its original name.

Exceptions

None.

ToString

The ToString method is overridden to return the current SourceTable property.

Usage

```
myString = myDataTableMapping.ToString()
```

Parameters

None.

Exceptions

None.

System.Data.Common. DataTableMappingCollection

The DataTableMappingCollection is a container class that maintains a collection of DataTableMapping objects. An empty DataTableMappingCollection is automatically created when a new DataAdapter object is created. The constructor, however, can be used to create an empty, standalone collection that can be manipulated.

Constructors

```
Dim myDataTableMappingCollection As New DataTableMappingCollection()
```

Parameters

None.

Members

Count

The read-only Count property returns an Integer specifying the number of DataTableMapping objects contained in the collection. Because all arrays in .NET are zero based, Count returns a number one greater than the highest available index ordinal in any array.

Usage

```
myInteger = myDataTableMappingCollection.Count
```

Parameters

None.

Exceptions

None.

Item

The Item property returns or sets a DataTableMapping object contained in the DataTableMappingCollection at a selected location. Because this is the default property of the object, placing the index directly after the DataTableMapping is possible (see second usage example).

Usage

```
myDataTableMapping = myDataTableMappingCollection.Item(intIndex)
myDataTableMapping = myDataTableMappingCollection(intIndex)
```

Parameters

`intIndex`	The zero-based Integer valued index of the DataTableMapping object to retrieve.

Exceptions

None.

Add

The Add() method adds a DataTableMapping object to the collection and returns the index of the added object as an Integer. The object can be added either by adding an already created DataTableMapping or by passing two strings representing the SourceTable and DataSetTable names.

Usage

```
myInteger = myDataTableMappingCollection.Add(objectDataTableMapping)
myInteger = myDataTableMappingCollection.Add(strSourceTable, _
   strDataSetTable)
```

Parameters

`objectDataTableMapping`	The Object to add to the collection, as a DataTableMapping object.
`strSourceTable`	The case-sensitive name of the table from the data source, as a String.
`strDataSetTable`	The noncase-sensitive name of the table from the DataSet, as a String.

Exceptions

SystemException	The objectDataTableMapping passed is not an instance of the DataTableMapping class.

AddRange

The AddRange() method copies the passed array of DataTableMapping objects to the end of the DataTableMappingCollection.

Usage

```
myDataTableMappingCollection.AddRange(arrayDataTableMapping)
```

Parameters

`arrayDataTableMapping`	An array of DataTableMapping objects to be added to the end of the DataTableMappingCollection.

Exceptions

None.

Clear

The Clear() method removes all DataTableMapping objects from the DataTableMappingCollection.

Usage

```
myDataTableMappingCollection.Clear()
```

Parameters

None.

Exceptions

None.

Contains

The Contains() method returns a Boolean indicating whether a DataTableMapping object exists in the DataTableMappingCollection. Because this method is overloaded, you can pass either a DataTableMapping object or the source table name as a case-sensitive String.

Usage

```
myDataTableMappingCollection.Contains(myDataTableMapping)
myDataTableMappingCollection.Contains(strSourceTable)
```

Parameters

`myDataTableMapping`	A DataTableMapping object to compare for existence in the DataTableMappingCollection.
`strSourceTable`	The source table name to find in the DataTableMappingCollection, as a case-sensitive String.

Exceptions

None.

CopyTo

The CopyTo() method copies the contained DataTableMapping objects to a passed buffer array. You may also pass an index value to indicate where in the buffer array you wish to begin filling. Pass a value other than zero if your array already contains other objects that you don't want to overwrite.

Usage

```
myDataTableMappingCollection.CopyTo(arrayBuffer, intIndex)
```

Parameters

`arrayBuffer`	The passed array to fill with DataTableMapping objects.
`intIndex`	Location to begin filling array. For example: Passing a 3 will fill arrayBuffer(3) with the first DataTableMapping object.

Exceptions

None.

GetByDataSetTable

The GetByDataSetTable() method returns a DataTableMapping object with the passed DataSet table name.

Usage

```
myDataTableMapping = _
   myDataTableMappingCollection.GetByDataSetTable(strDataSetTable)
```

Parameters

`strDataSetTable`	The DataSet table name as a non-case-sensitive String.

Exceptions

None.

GetTableMappingBySchemaAction

The GetTableMappingBySchemaAction() method is a static (shared) method that returns a DataTableMapping object from a passed DataTableMappingCollection. Because this is a shared method, an object does not have to be created to access it (see the example that follows). The method accepts four parameters: the DataTableMappingCollection from which to pull the DataTableMapping object, the name of the source table, the name of the DataSet table, and a MissingMappingAction enumeration value to determine what to do if the desired DataTableMapping does not exist in the passed DataTableMappingCollection.

Usage

```
myDataTableMapping = _
   myDataTableMappingCollection.GetTableMappingBySchemaAction( _
   tableMappings, strSourceTable, strDataSetTable, mappingAction)
```

Parameters

`tableMappings`	The DataTableMappingCollection object from which to draw the requested DataTableMapping.
`strSourceTable`	The source table name to find in the DataTableMapping-Collection as a case-sensitive String.
`strDataSetTable`	The DataSet table name to find in the DataTableMapping-Collection as a case-sensitive String.
`mappingAction`	A System.Data.MissingMappingAction enumeration value to determine the action taken if the desired Data-TableMapping doesn't exist in the passed DataTable-MappingCollection.

MissingMappingAction Enumeration Values

Error (3)	A System.SystemException is thrown.
Ignore (2)	Any columns or tables without mappings are ignored, returning a null reference.
Passthrough (1)	(Default). The source column or table is added to the DataSet using its original name.

Exceptions
None.

IndexOf

The IndexOf() method returns an Integer specifying the location of a specified DataTableMapping within the DataTableMappingCollection. Because this method is overloaded, you may pass either the DataTableMapping object itself or a String representing the source table name.

Usage

```
myInteger = myDataTableMappingCollection.IndexOf(objectDataTable)
myInteger = myDataTableMappingCollection.IndexOf(strSourceTable)
```

Parameters

`objectDataTable`	An Object that is the DataTableMapping object for which to find the location. The Object must be a member of the DataTableMapping class.
`strSourceTable`	The source table name to find in the DataTableMappingCollection as a case-sensitive String.

Exceptions
None.

IndexOfDataSetTable

The IndexOfDataSetTable() method returns an Integer specifying the location of the DataTableMapping within the passed DataSet table name.

Usage

```
myInteger = myDataTableMappingCollection.IndexOf(strDataSetTable)
```

Parameters

`strDataSetTable`	The DataSet table name to find in the DataTableMappingCollection as a noncase-sensitive String.

Exceptions
None.

Insert

The Insert() method inserts a DataTableMapping object into the DataTableMappingCollection at the specified index. Passing an index of 3 will insert the DataTableMapping at the Item (3) position.

Usage

```
myDataTableMappingCollection.Insert(intIndex, objectDataTable)
```

Parameters

`intIndex`	Location to begin filling array. For example: Passing a 3 will insert the DataTableMapping object into the DataTableMappingCollection.Item (3) position.

`objectDataTable`	The Object to insert into the DataTableMapping-Collection. This Object must be a DataTable-Mapping object.

Exceptions

None.

Remove

The Remove() method removes a specified DataTableMapping object from the Data-TableMappingCollection.

Usage

```
myDataTableMappingCollection.Remove(objectDataTable)
```

Parameters

`objectDataTable`	The Object to remove from the DataTableMapping-Collection. This Object must be a DataTable-Mapping object.

Exceptions

SystemException	Either the objectDataTable is not a DataTableMapping object or the passed objectDataTable object does not exist in the DataTableMappingCollection.

RemoveAt

The RemoveAt() method removes a DataTableMapping object from the DataTable-MappingCollection. The method is overloaded, so you can specify the DataTableMapping object by passing either the location of the object or the name of the source table.

Usage

```
myDataTableMappingCollection.RemoveAt(intIndex)
myDataTableMappingCollection.RemoveAt(strSourceTable)
```

Parameters

`intIndex`	Location of the DataMappingTable to remove, as an Int32.
`strSourceTable`	The source table name to remove from the Data-TableMappingCollection, as a case-sensitive String.

Exceptions

IndexOutOfRangeException	A DataMappingTable object does not exist at the passed intIndex, or with the passed strSourceTable name.

System.Data.Common.DbDataAdapter

The DbDataAdapter class inherits from the Data.Common.DataAdapter class. It is a utility class that provides behaviors and functionality to assist in creating DataAdapters geared for accessing relational databases. As such, it is an abstract (MustInherit) class, so you cannot create an instance of this class but must instead create instances of objects that inherit from this class (such as the OleDbDataAdapter class).

This class provides the foundational methods and properties for the interface between a data source and the .NET framework data objects. The DbDataAdapter class itself inherits from the Data.Common.DataAdapter class, specifically gearing the implementation toward relational databases. Classes that inherit from DbDataAdapter implement all of the inherited members and generally provide additional methods and properties that are specific for a particular data source.

The DbDataAdapter class contains many protected members that can be called only by classes that descend from it. These are implemented for the convenience of programmers creating their own data providers. Because the creation of data providers is beyond the scope of this book, these protected members will be not be listed.

Although the constructor is listed in the text that follows, it is a protected method, which means it can be called only by descendents of this class and cannot be used directly in data access code. It is listed for those who wish to create their own data providers.

For more information on working with a particular DataAdapter, see the sections dedicated to the various implementations of this class. The three covered in this book are the OleDbDataAdapter class, the SqlDataAdapter class, and the OdbcDataAdapter class.

Constructors

```
Dim myDbDataAdapter As New DbDataAdapter()
```

Parameters

None.

Members

AcceptChangesDuringFill

The AcceptChangesDuringFill property (inherited from the DataAdapter object) is a Boolean value that determines whether the AcceptChanges event is fired when the Fill() method is called. Please see DataAdapter.AcceptChangesDuringFill for more information.

Usage

```
myBoolean = myDbDataAdapter.AcceptChangesDuringFill
myDbDataAdapter.AcceptChangesDuringFill = myBoolean
```

Parameters

None.

Exceptions

None.

DefaultSourceTableName

The constant DefaultSourceTableName returns a String detailing the default name used by the DataAdapter object for table mappings. This property is used when an application uses Fill() to add data to a DataSet but does not specify a data table mapping name. Because this property is a constant it cannot be changed.

Usage

```
myString = myDbDataAdapter.DefaultSourceTableName
```

Parameters

None.

Exceptions

None.

Disposed

The Disposed event (inherited from Component) is fired when the component is to be disposed and its resources freed. The Disposed event can be caught just prior to the object being disposed, and cleanup code can be executed. The FillError event passes a reference to the source of the event (the instantiated DbDataAdapter object) and a System.EventArgs object. The EventArgs object has very little meaningful information, and it is mainly there to conform to .NET Framework recommendations for raising events.

Usage

```
Private Sub myDbDataAdapter_Disposed(ByVal sender As Object, _
   ByVal e As System.EventArgs) Handles myDbDataAdapter.Disposed
```

Event Data

None.

Exceptions

None.

Fill

The Fill() method adds or updates the rows in a DataSet, based on a SelectCommand, and returns an Integer specifying the number of records that were added or updated.

Fill() will automatically append rows to an existing DataTable if there is no primary key defined. If there is a primary key, the Fill() method will update the data in the DataTable from the data in the data source wherever matching primary keys are found.

When determining which of the possible Fill methods to use, there are a few things to keep in mind. When you use the DbDataAdapter.Fill(DataSet), the DataSet will add a DataTable with the default name "Table". When you call the DataAdapter.Update method, you may then use the Update(DataSet) because that operates only on the DataTable named "Table". Once you name the DataTable, you must then name the DataTable in any Update commands as well, or a System.ArgumentNullException will be raised.

If the Fill() method used does not return any rows, no rows are added to any DataTable, and no exception is raised. You can, however, use the integer returned by the Fill() method to determine if any rows have been added or changed.

Usage

```
myInteger = myDbDataAdapter.Fill(myDataSet)
myInteger = myDbDataAdapter.Fill(myDataTable)
myInteger = myDbDataAdapter.Fill(myDataTable, strSourceTable)
myInteger = myDbDataAdapter.Fill(myDataSet, intStartRecord, _
            intMaxRecords, strSourceTable)
```

Parameters

`myDataSet`	A System.Data.DataSet object to be filled.
`myDataTable`	A System.Data.DataTable object to be filled.
`strSourceTable`	A String designating the source table name.
`intStartRecord`	An Integer specifying the first record to retrieve.
`intMaxRecords`	An Integer specifying the maximum number of records to retrieve.

Exceptions

SystemException	Either the source table was invalid, or the DataSet was invalid.
InvalidOperationException	Either the source table was invalid, or the Fill method was called when Connection has not been specified.
InvalidCastException	A Connection object could not be found.
ArgumentException	intStartRecord or intMaxRecords less than zero.

FillError

The FillError event is fired whenever an error is encountered during a Fill() operation. The FillError event passes a reference to the source of the event (the class inheriting from DbDataAdapter) and a System.Data.FillErrorEventArgs object with data about the error. This event can be used by the application to determine whether to continue the Fill operation after an error has been encountered.

This event can be very useful when dealing with additions to the DataSet that violate previously established constraints or when dealing with the loss of precision when going from a SqlDataType to a .NET Framework data type.

Usage

```
Private Sub myDbDataAdapter_FillError(ByVal sender As Object, _
   ByVal e As System.Data.FillErrorEventArgs) Handles _
   myDbDataAdapter.FillError
```

Event Data

e.Continue	Gets or sets Boolean determining whether the fill operation should continue despite the error.

e.DataTable	Gets a reference to the DataTable that is currently being updated.
e.Errors	Gets an Exception object specifying the errors that occurred.
e.Values	Gets the values for the row being updated as an array of Object objects.

Exceptions

None.

FillSchema

The FillSchema() method creates a new DataTable and applies to it the schema inherited from the data source. It then returns the DataTable or array of DataTable objects containing the schema derived from the data source. The schema is configured based on the value of the SchemaType parameter. A SchemaType of "Source" (Value = 1) applies the incoming schema to the DataSet with no transformation; "Mapped" applies the mappings of existing DataTable objects to the schema and then transforms the DataSet based on the transformed schema.

The FillSchema() method is particularly useful when creating data in a DataSet that must match the constraints imposed by the data source. Once a DataSet has inherited the schema from the data source, any additions to a DataTable or group of DataTable objects that violates one of the constraints will cause an error to be raised. This method does not add any data to the DataSet or DataTable, only the schema. To fill a DataSet or DataTable with data, use the Fill() method.

Usage

```
arrayDataTable() = myDbDataAdapter.FillSchema(myDataSet, mySchemaType)
singleDataTable = myDbDataAdapter.FillSchema(myDataTable, mySchemaType)
arrayDataTable() = myDbDataAdapter.FillSchema(myDataSet, _
   mySchemaType, strSourceTable)
```

Parameters

`myDataSet`	A System.Data.DataSet object in which to insert the schema.
`mySchemaType`	A System.Data.SchemaType enumeration specifying how existing schema mappings should be dealt with. This can be either Source or Mapped. This should generally be set to Mapped. See SchemaType for more information.
`myDataTable`	A System.Data.DataTable object in which to insert the schema.
`strSourceTable`	A String designating the source table name.

Exceptions

SystemException	Either the source table was invalid, or the DataSet was invalid.
InvalidOperationException	Either the source table was invalid, or the Fill method was called when Connection has not been specified.

InvalidCastException	A Connection object could not be found.
ArgumentException	intStartRecord or intMaxRecords less than zero.

GetFillParameters

The GetFillParameters method returns an array of objects implementing the IDataParameter interface specifying user-defined parameters to be passed in a SQL SELECT command. This method can be used to verify the parameters when selecting data. The returned array of parameters will generally be in the form of the specific .NET data provider used. For example, if you are using a OleDbDataAdapter, the returned array will be typed OleDbParameter.

Usage

```
myIDataParameterArray() = myDbDataAdapter.GetFillParameters()
```

Parameters

None.

Exceptions

None.

MissingMappingAction

The MissingMappingAction property (inherited from System.Data.DataAdapter) returns or sets a MissingMappingAction enumeration value that determines what to do when the incoming data does not have a matching table or column in the current DataSet. The default value is Passthrough.

Usage

```
myMissingMappingActionEnumeration = myDbDataAdapter.MissingMappingAction
myDbDataAdapter.MissingMappingAction = myMissingMappingActionEnumeration
```

Parameters

None.

MissingMappingAction Enumeration Values

Error (3)	A System.SystemException is thrown.
Ignore (2)	Any columns or tables without mappings are ignored, returning a null reference.
Passthrough (1)	(Default). The source column or table is added to the DataSet using its original name.

Exceptions

None.

MissingSchemaAction

The MissingSchemaAction property (inherited from System.Data.DataAdapter) returns or sets a MissingSchemaAction enumeration value that determines what to do when the incoming data does not have a matching schema in the current DataSet. The default value is Add.

Usage

```
myEnumeration = myDbDataAdapter.MissingSchemaAction
myDbDataAdapter.MissingSchemaAction = myEnumeration
```

Parameters
None.

MissingMappingAction Enumeration Values

Add (1)	(Default). Adds the columns required to complete the schema.
AddWithKey (4)	Adds the columns and primary key information required to complete the schema.
Error (3)	A System.SystemException is thrown.
Ignore (2)	Any columns without a matching schema are ignored.

Exceptions
None.

TableMappings

The read-only TableMappings property (inherited from System.Data.DateAdapter) returns a DataTableMappingCollection object. This collection of DataTableMapping objects maps the table and column names used by the data source to the table and column names used by the DataSet. The default value is an empty collection. These mappings are used during an Update() to ensure the proper tables and columns are updated in the data source, despite possibly different names.

The DataTableMapping objects contained in the DataTableMappingCollection contain three public properties that permit access to the underlying mapping. They are the read-only ColumnMapping property, which returns the DataColumnMapping-Collection object describing the mappings of the columns between the data source and DataSet; the DataSetTable property, which is used to get or set the destination DataSet table name; and the SourceTable, which gets or sets the source table from which to retrieve the data.

For specific information on the DataTableMapping class, its members, or its usage, see the System.Data.Common.DataTableMapping namespace.

Usage

```
myDataTableMappingCollection = myDataAdapter.TableMapping
```

Parameters
None.

DataTableMappingCollection Members

ColumnMapping	Read-only property that returns the DataColumnMapping-Collection object describing the mappings of the columns between the data source and DataSet.
DataSetTable	Property that is used to get or set the destination DataSet table name.
SourceTable	Property that is used to get or set the destination DataSet table name.

Exceptions
None.

ToString

The ToString method for DbDataAdapter simply returns "System.Data.OleDb. DbDataAdapter".

Usage

```
myIDataParameterArray() = myDbDataAdapter.GetFillParameters()
```

Parameters

None.

Exceptions

None.

Update

The Update() method calls the INSERT, UPDATE, or DELETE commands for each of the inserted, updated, or deleted rows and returns an Integer containing the number of rows successfully updated. Several different parameters can be sent to the Update() method, depending on what set of rows you'd like to update. Basically, all of them boil down to some grouping of System.Data.DataRow objects. The difference is merely how they are collected and identified. One way is to send an array of DataRow objects for update. Another is to send a System.Data.DataTable, which is an object containing a collection of DataRows. Another is to pass a System.Data.DataSet object, which is a collection of DataTables and corresponding DataRows.

When calling Update() with the DataSet object, you must specify on which of the DataTables you wish to perform the update. You cannot send a DataSet to the Update() method and expect all contained DataTables to be updated. This can be a source of frustration for novice users. The Update(DataSet) method will send only a DataTable with the name of "Table" for update! This is the default name given to the first DataTable loaded into the DataSet. If no DataTable named "Table" exists, an exception is thrown. So, if you've given your DataTable objects meaningful names, you must also pass the given name of the table to be updated.

Be aware that the Update() method calls the Updates on a row-by-row basis according to the order in the DataSet. This means that deletions, updates, and additions can occur in mixed orders. This can cause occasional trouble if you have an application that requires that additions be processed before updates (a customer must exist in the database before you can change his or her phone number). To deal with these situations, use the DataSet.GetChanges method to return a DataTable with all of the changes filtered by DataRowState (see the DataSet.GetChanges method for more information).

Usage

```
myInteger = myDbDataAdapter.Update(arrayDataRow[])
myInteger = myDbDataAdapter.Update(myDataSet)
myInteger = myDbDataAdapter.Update(myDataTable)
myInteger = myDbDataAdapter.Update(myDataSet, strSourceTable)
```

Parameters

`arrayDataRow[])`	A System.Data.DataTable object to be updated.
`myDataSet`	A System.Data.DataSet object to be updated.

`myDataTable`	An array of System.Data.DataRow objects to be updated.
`strSourceTable`	A String designating the source table name.

Exceptions

ArgumentNullException	The source DataSet is invalid.
InvalidOperationException	The source DataTable is invalid.
SystemException	No DataRow exists to update, no DataSet exists to update, or no source DataSet exists.
DBConcurrencyException	An attempt to execute an INSERT, UPDATE, or DELETE command has resulted in no records affected.

System.Data.Common.RowUpdatedEventArgs

The RowUpdatedEventArgs class is an abstract (MustInherit) class that provides several general behaviors for its descending classes. Because it is an abstract class, you cannot create an instance of this class but must instead create instances of objects that inherit from this class (such as the OleDbRowUpdatedEventArgs class).

This class provides the foundation for the data that is provided during the RowUpdated event of a DataAdapter. This event is raised during the Update() method of the various implementations of the DataAdapter class. During the Update, every DataRow that has been inserted, updated, or deleted is sent to the data source for updating. Each change raises the RowUpdated event after changes have been made to the data source, but before they are accepted.

Once the event is intercepted, you have a great deal of control over what happens next. Although you cannot make changes to the row to be updated (we find this very unfortunate), you are able to examine the row, along with information about the data source, and what type of Update action will occur (Insert, Delete, etc.). You then have the ability to cancel the update for this particular row or for this row and all following rows. You can even stop processing rows and assign a custom exception (complete with errors) to be raised to the OleDbDataAdapter.

For more information on working with the RowUpdatedEventArgs, see the sections dedicated to the various implementations of this class. The three covered in this book are the OleDbRowUpdatedEventArgs class, the SqlRowUpdatedEventArgs class, and the OdbcRowUpdatedEventArgs class.

Although the constructor is listed in the text that follows, it is a protected method, which means it can be called only by descendents of this class and cannot be used directly in data access code. It is listed for those who wish to create their own data providers.

Constructors

```
Dim myRowUpdatedEventArgs As New myRowUpdatedEventArgs( _
   DataRow, IDbCommand, StatementType, DataTableMapping)
```

Parameters

Parameter	Description
`DataRow`	A System.Data.DataRow object that is to be deleted, inserted, or updated at the data source.
`IDbCommand`	An OleDbCommand object (implementing the System.Data.IDbCommand interface) representing the SQL statement to be executed.
`StatementType`	A System.Data.StatementType enumeration that specifies the type of SQL statement in the IDbCommand object. Valid values are: Delete (3), Insert (1), Select (0), Update (2).
`DataTableMapping`	A System.Data.Common.DataTableMapping object that describes the mapping between the DataTable object and the source data.

RowUpdatedEventArgs Sample Code

For sample code, please see the creatable class that inherits from this object. For instance, if you are using the OLE DB Data Provider, see System.Data.OleDb.OleDbRowUpdated-EventArgs for sample code.

Members

Command

The read-only Command property returns an object implementing the System.Data. IDbCommand interface that represents the SQL statement that was executed at the data source. In the case of the SQL Server Data Provider, the returned object is a Sql-Command object, and for the OLE DB Data Provider it is an OleDbCommand object. Thus, you can declare a variable with the type IDbCommand and then assign it to the object returned by the Command property. Its actual type will be one of the classes that implements the IDbCommand interface.

You can declare a variable with the type IDbCommand and then assign it to the object returned by the Command property; however, because IDbCommand is an interface and not a class, its actual type will be OleDbCommand.

Because this property is read only, changes to the Command cannot be made during the RowUpdated event—the Command has already been applied to the data source, so trying to change it now wouldn't make sense. If you wish to make changes to the Command, you can use the Command object of the RowUpdatingEventArgs (in the RowUpdating event) since that property is both read and write.

Usage

```
myIDbCommand = myRowUpdatedEventArgs.Command
```

Parameters

None.

Exceptions

None.

Errors

The Errors property returns a System.Exception object (or a descendant of the Exception class). It contains the errors generated by the .NET data provider when the command executes. The actual class type of the returned Errors property depends on the exception or error that was returned. For example, an exception originating from an OLE DB data source will return an OleDbException. Knowing the type of the exception raised allows you to assign the Errors property to a more specific exception object. (See the OleDbRowUpdatedEventArgs sample code for an example.)

Another major use of the Errors property is assigning your own Exception (or derived class) to the property and setting the Status property to ErrorsOccurred (1). This will cause the exception you've added to be thrown by the OleDbDataAdapter. In this way you can introduce custom exceptions into your data update code. Be aware, however, that this will cancel the update on the current and all future rows.

Usage

```
myException = myRowUpdatedEventArgs.Errors
myRowUpdatedEventArgs.Errors = myException
```

Parameters

None.

Exceptions

None.

RecordsAffected

The read-only RecordsAffected property returns an integer containing the number of records affected by the execution of the SQL statement specified in the Update. The number is the sum of all rows updated, added, and deleted. If no rows were affected or if there were errors, RecordsAffected is set to 0. If the SQL command executed was a SELECT command, it is set to -1. This is not the same as the Transact SQL @@Rowcount, which returns the number of selected rows returned from a SELECT command.

Usage

```
myInteger = myRowUpdatedEventArgs.RecordsAffected
```

Parameters

None.

Exceptions

None.

Row

The read-only Row property returns a System.Data.DataRow object, which contains the data that was updated at the data source. Because this property is read only, you cannot change the values of the data that will be committed at the completion of the RowUpdated event (when AcceptChanges is called).

Usage

```
myDataRow = myRowUpdatedEventArgs.Row
```

Parameters
None.

Exceptions
None.

StatementType

The read-only StatementType property returns a System.StatementType enumeration value specifying the type of SQL statement that was executed at the data source. This value should match the action specified by the Command object.

The value can be assigned to several different types of variables, including an Integer, String, or StatementType enumeration. The advantage to assigning the value to an enumeration is that the ToString method of the enumeration will return the enumeration member name, instead of merely its integer value—that is, "Delete" instead of "3".

Usage

```
myStatementType = myRowUpdatedEventArgs.StatementType
myInteger = myRowUpdatedEventArgs.StatementType
myString = myRowUpdatedEventArgs.StatementType ' returns the Integer _
   value as a String, i.e., "2"
myString = myRowUpdatedEventArgs.StatementType.ToString() ' returns _
  the Enumeration name, i.e., "Update"
```

Parameters
None.

StatementType Enumeration Values

Delete (3)	A SQL DELETE statement.
Insert (1)	A SQL INSERT statement.
Select (0)	A SQL SELECT statement.
Update (2)	A SQL UPDATE statement.

Exceptions
None.

Status

The Status property returns a System.Data.UpdateStatus enumeration value specifying the action that will be taken during the Update with regard to the current row and subsequent rows. The default value is *Continue*, which tells the DataAdapter to process this row and to continue processing rows. Other values are listed in the text that follows.

This allows you to cancel changes to the data source after the DataAdapter has executed the changes but before they are committed. By setting this value to SkipCurrentRow, the changes made to the data source are ignored and remaining rows continue to be processed normally.

Like other enumerations, the value can be assigned to several different types of variables, including an Integer, String, or UpdateStatus enumeration. The advantage to assigning the value to an enumeration is that the ToString method of the enumeration will return the enumeration member name, instead of merely its integer value—that is, "Continue" instead of "0".

Usage

```
myUpdateStatus = myRowUpdatedEventArgs.Status
myInteger = myRowUpdatedEventArgs.Status
myString = myRowUpdatedEventArgs.Status ' returns the Integer _
   value as a String, i.e., "2"
myString = myRowUpdatedEventArgs.Status.ToString() ' returns _
   the Enumeration name, i.e., "SkipCurrentRow"
```

Parameters

None.

UpdateStatus Enumeration Values

Continue (0)	(Default). Process this row, and continue processing rows.
ErrorsOccurred (1)	This update should be treated as an error. Setting this value will abort the update of this row and all remaining rows, as well as throw an Exception. To specify the Error to be thrown, add an Exception to the Errors property.
SkipAllRemainingRows (3)	Do not process this row or any remaining rows.
SkipCurrentRow (2)	Do not process this row, but continue processing rows.

Exceptions

None.

TableMapping

The read-only TableMapping property returns the System.Data.Common.DataTable-Mapping object that was sent by the Update() method. This object maps the table and columns used by the data source to the table and columns used by the DataSet, to facilitate updating the data at the data source. The DataTableMapping objects contained in the DataTableMappingCollection contain three public properties that permit access to the underlying mapping. They are the read-only ColumnMapping property, which returns the DataColumnMappingCollection object describing the mappings of the columns between the data source and DataSet; the DataSetTable property, which is used to get or set the destination DataSet table name; and the SourceTable, which gets or sets the source table from which to retrieve the data.

See System.Data.Common.DataTableMapping for more information.

Usage

```
myDataTableMapping = myRowUpdatedEventArgs.TableMapping
```

Parameters

None.

Exceptions

None.

ToString

The ToString method simply returns the object type—"System.Data.Common.RowUpdatedEventArgs".

Usage

```
myString = myDataAdapter.ToString()
```

Parameters

None.

Exceptions

None.

System.Data.Common.RowUpdatingEventArgs

The RowUpdatingEventArgs class is an abstract (MustInherit) class that provides several general behaviors for its descending classes. Because it is an abstract class, you cannot create an instance of this class, but must instead create instances of objects that inherit from this class (such as the OleDbRowUpdatingEventArgs class).

This class provides the foundation for the data that is provided during the RowUpdating event of a DataAdapter. This event is raised during the Update() method of the various implementations of the DataAdapter class. During the Update, every DataRow that has been inserted, updated, or deleted is sent to the data source for updating. Each change raises the RowUpdating event before any changes have been made to the data source.

Once the event is intercepted, you have a great deal of control over what happens next. Although you cannot make changes to the row to be updated (we find this very unfortunate), you are able to examine the row, along with information about the data source, and what type of Update action will occur (Insert, Delete, etc.). You then have the ability to cancel the update for this particular row or for this row and all following rows. You can even stop processing rows and assign a custom exception (complete with errors) to be raised to the DataAdapter.

For more information on working with the RowUpdatingEventArgs, see the sections dedicated to the various implementations of this class. The three covered in this book are the OleDbRowUpdatingEventArgs class, the SqlRowUpdatingEventArgs class, and the OdbcRowUpdatingEventArgs class.

Although the constructor is listed in the text that follows, it is a protected method, which means it can be called only by descendents of this class and cannot be used directly in data access code. It is listed for those who wish to create their own data providers.

Constructors

```
Dim myRowUpdatingEventArgs As New myRowUpdatingEventArgs ( _
   DataRow, IDbCommand, StatementType, DataTableMapping)
```

Parameters

`DataRow`	A System.Data.DataRow object that is to be deleted, inserted, or updated at the data source.
`IDbCommand`	An Object that implements the System.Data.IDb-Command interface, representing the SQL statement to be executed.
`StatementType`	A System.Data.StatementType enumeration that specifies the type of SQL statement in the IDbCommand object. Valid values are: Delete (3), Insert (1), Select (0), and Update (2).
`DataTableMapping`	A System.Data.Common.DataTableMapping object that describes the mapping between the DataTable object and the source data.

RowUpdatingEventArgs Sample Code

For sample code, please see the creatable class that inherits from this object. For instance, if you are using the OLE DB data provider, see System.Data.OleDb.OleDbRowUpdatingEventArgs for sample code.

Members

Command

The Command property returns an object implementing the System.Data.IDbCommand interface that represents the SQL statement to be executed at the data source. In the case of the SQL Server Data Provider, the returned object is a SqlCommand object, and for the OLE DB Data Provider it is an OleDbCommand object. Thus, you can declare a variable with the type IDbCommand and then assign it to the object returned by the Command property. Its actual type will be one of the classes that implements the IDbCommand interface.

Because this property can be modified, you can change the Command prior to the Command being executed against the data source. This, however, can be done only during the RowUpdating event because the property is read-only in the RowUpdated event. This makes sense because the Command property has already been fired by the time the RowUpdated event fires. Because an object of type IDbCommand cannot be created, you must instead assign an object that implements that interface.

Usage

```
myIDbCommand = myRowUpdatingEventArgs.Command
myRowUpdatingEventArgs.Command = myObjectImplementingIDbCommand
```

Parameters

None.

Exceptions

None.

Errors

The Errors property returns a System.Exception object (or a subclass that inherits from the Exception class). It contains the errors generated by the .NET data provider when the command executes. The actual class type of the returned Errors property depends on the exception or error that was returned. For example, an exception originating from an OLE DB data source will return an OleDbException. Knowing the type of the exception raised allows you to assign the Errors property to a more specific exception object.

Another major use of the Errors property is assigning your own Exception (or derived class) to the property and setting the Status property to ErrorsOccurred (value = 1). This will cause the exception you've added to be thrown by the DataAdapter. In this way you can introduce custom exceptions to your data update code. Be aware, however, that this will cancel the update on the current and all future rows.

See the OleDbRowUpdatingEventArgs sample code for an example.

Usage

```
myException = myRowUpdatingEventArgs.Errors
myRowUpdatingEventArgs.Errors = myException
```

Parameters

None.

Exceptions

None.

Row

The read-only Row property returns a System.Data.DataRow object, which contains the data that will be updated at the data source. Because this property is read only, you cannot change the values of the data to be updated during a RowUpdating event.

OPINION We find this very unfortunate because being able to correct data here would prevent having to cancel updates.

Usage

```
myDataRow = myRowUpdatingEventArgs.Row
```

Parameters

None.

Exceptions

None.

StatementType

The read-only StatementType property returns a System.StatementType enumeration value specifying the type of SQL statement to be executed at the data source. This value should match the action being specified by the Command object.

The value can be assigned to several different types of variables, including an Integer, String, or StatementType enumeration. The advantage to assigning the value to an enumeration is that the ToString method of the enumeration will return the enumeration member name, instead of merely its integer value—that is, "Delete" instead of "3".

Usage

```
myStatementType = myRowUpdatingEventArgs.StatementType
myInteger = myRowUpdatingEventArgs.StatementType
myString = myRowUpdatingEventArgs.StatementType ' returns the Integer _
   value as a String, i.e., "2"
myString = myRowUpdatingEventArgs.StatementType.ToString() ' returns _
   the Enumeration name, i.e., "Update")
```

Parameters

None.

StatementType Enumeration Values

Delete (3)	A SQL DELETE statement.
Insert (1)	A SQL INSERT statement.
Select (0)	A SQL SELECT statement.
Update (2)	A SQL UPDATE statement.

Exceptions

None.

Status

The Status property returns a System.Data.UpdateStatus enumeration value specifying the action that will be taken during the Update with regard to the current row and following rows. The default value is Continue, which tells the DataAdapter to process this row and to continue processing rows. Other values are listed in the text that follows.

This allows you to cancel changes to the data source. By setting this value to SkipCurrentRow, no changes will be made to the data source for this row; however, any remaining rows will continue to be processed normally.

Like other enumerations, the value can be assigned to several different types of variables, including an Integer, String, or UpdateStatus enumeration. The advantage to assigning the value to an enumeration is that the ToString method of the enumeration will return the enumeration member name, instead of merely its integer value—that is, "Continue" instead of "0".

Usage

```
myUpdateStatus = myRowUpdatingEventArgs.Status
myInteger = myRowUpdatingEventArgs.Status
myString = myRowUpdatingEventArgs.Status ' returns the Integer _
   value as a String, i.e., "2"
myString = myRowUpdatingEventArgs.Status.ToString() ' returns _
   the Enumeration name, i.e., "SkipCurrentRow"
```

Parameters

None.

UpdateStatus Enumeration Values

Continue (0)	(Default). Process this row, and continue processing rows.

ErrorsOccurred (1)	This update should be treated as an error. Setting this value will abort the update of this row and all remaining rows, as well as throw an Exception. To specify the Error to be thrown, add an Exception to the Errors property.
SkipAllRemainingRows (3)	Do not process this row or any remaining rows.
SkipCurrentRow (2)	Do not process this row, but continue processing rows.

Exceptions
None.

TableMapping

The read-only TableMapping property returns the System.Data.Common.DataTableMapping object that is being sent by the Update() method. This object maps the table and columns used by the data source to the table and columns used by the DataSet, to facilitate updating the data at the data source. The DataTableMapping objects contained in the DataTableMappingCollection contain three public properties that permit access to the underlying mapping. They are the read-only ColumnMapping property, which returns the DataColumnMappingCollection object describing the mappings of the columns between the data source and DataSet; the DataSetTable property, which is used to get or set the destination DataSet table name; and the SourceTable, which gets or sets the source table from which to retrieve the data.

See System.Data.Common.DataTableMapping for more information.

Usage

```
myDataTableMapping = myRowUpdatingEventArgs.TableMapping
```

Parameters
None.

Exceptions
None.

ToString

The ToString method simply returns the object type—"System.Data.Common.RowUpdatingEventArgs".

Usage

```
myString = myDataAdapter.ToString()
```

Parameters
None.

Exceptions
None.

CHAPTER

6

Microsoft.Data.Odbc

NOTE Microsoft renamed their ODBC .NET data provider namespace just prior to RTM, and although we tried to organize our reference section alphabetically, we feel that it fits here logically as well!

The ODBC .NET data provider is necessary to maintain wide support for scores of legacy data sources. During the last few years, not all software vendors were quick to develop OLE DB providers, but rather relied on their tried-and-true ODBC drivers to communicate to their data stores. Even though it came as a surprise to some, Microsoft recognized the need to support ODBC with its ODBC .NET data provider.

Because you cannot access the Microsoft OLE DB provider for ODBC Drivers (MSDASQL) from Microsoft.Data.OleDb, you must use the Odbc namespace to access your ODBC data sources. To use the ODBC .NET data provider you must have Microsoft Data Access Components 2.67 or later. You must also be using a supported driver. As of the Release Candidate Beta of this ODBC .NET data provider, Microsoft guarantees only that it will work with the following drivers:

- Microsoft SQL Server ODBC Driver
- Microsoft's ODBC Driver for Oracle
- Microsoft Jet ODBC driver

You should visit Microsoft's Web site periodically to check on the availability of other .NET-compatible ODBC drivers.

The ODBC .NET data provider is similar to the OLE DB .NET data provider in that both require expensive COM Interoperability in order to function. Thus, an extra layer of code, with the overhead of not being managed code, is required to access ODBC data sources from your .NET applications.

WE'RE CURIOUS **Why didn't Microsoft just enable the MSDASQL OLE DB provider from the OLEDB .NET data provider? That seemed to have been its original plan, as it was possible in Beta 1 of the .NET Framework.**

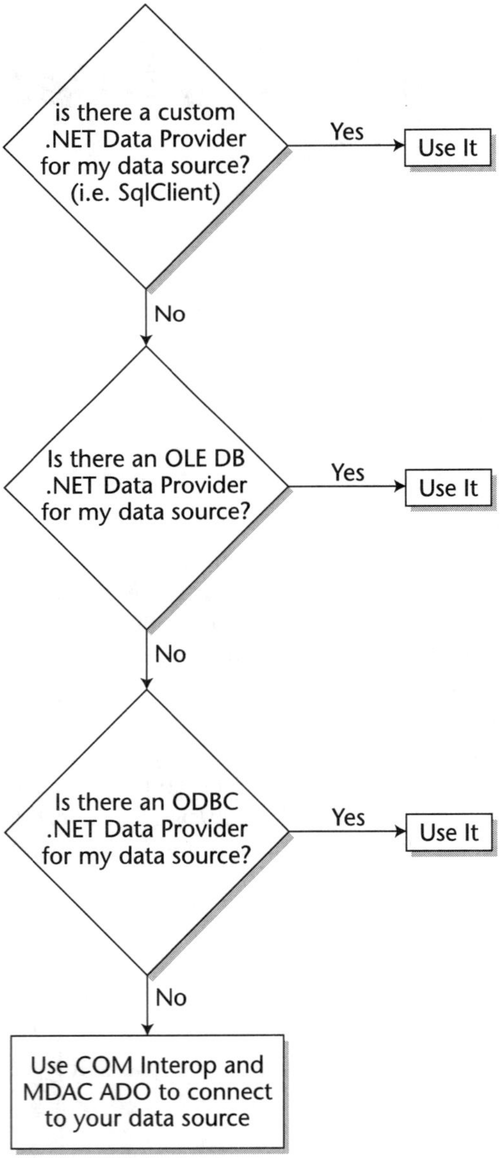

Figure 6.1 Which .NET data provider to use?

We see the ODBC .NET data provider as being a last resort. You should consider using any custom .NET data provider that targets your data source as your first choice, such as for SQL Server 7.0 or SQL Server 2000. If there is not a custom .NET data provider, then you should consider using the OLE DB .NET data provider, providing that you have a .NET-compatible OLE DB provider, such as for Access or Oracle. If there is not an OLE DB .NET data provider, then you will have to use the ODBC .NET data provider. We don't see a reason for using an ODBC .NET data provider when one of the other options is available.

See the Web Site

The ODBC .NET data provider is not shipping with the release of the .NET Framework, but it is included as a separate download from Microsoft. As of the publication of this book the ODBC .NET data provider is still going through multiple changes in its Beta release. Microsoft has even warned against using the RC Beta version for any production code—something that some shops might ignore. You will be able to research and download the ODBC .NET data provider from Microsoft's Web site: www.microsoft.com/data.

So, Where's the Chapter?

Due to the static nature of the printed page and the dynamic nature of the bits from Microsoft, please see the Wiley Web site supporting this book to download this chapter in PDF format. To download this chapter as well as all source code, visit this URL: www.wiley.com/cda/product/0,,0471201871,00.html.

CHAPTER

7

System.Data.OleDb

The OLE DB data provider for .NET is one of the key data access technologies for accessing relational databases of all types. By building a single provider to access OLE DB, Microsoft leveraged the huge amount of OLE DB interfaces already in existence. By creating this single interface, literally hundreds of databases have been opened up to .NET.

Using the OLE DB data provider has one very strong advantage: Code built using it will run with virtually any major (and most minor) relational databases in existence, with virtually no modifications. Also, it is reasonably fast, exposes a common set of functionality, and can be comfortable for programmers with extensive OLE DB experience.

There are drawbacks, however. The ability to interact with a database in OLE DB implies the interface layer between the exposed OLE DB standard and a database's native form. The OLE DB to .NET interface then adds an additional layer, on top of the OLE DB interface. Therefore, when possible, use a dedicated data provider for maximum performance. For instance, MS SQL Server uses TDS (Tabular Data Stream) as its native communication protocol. Accessing SQL Server with the OleDbDataAdapter implies any data retrieval to be morphed first into an OLE DB format, then morphed again to match the .NET data format. By using a SqlDataAdapter, the TDS protocol is changed only once, directly into a format accessible to .NET objects. Unfortunately, as of this writing, there is only one targeted, data provider—the SQL Server data provider—and it won't work for SQL Server 6.5 and below.

NOTE **Surprisingly, however, it works with Microsoft Data Engine files (MS Access 2000 and Access XP MSDE data), as well as SQL Server 7.0 and higher.**

Another drawback is that support for the OLE DB interface to ODBC (MSDASQL) has been disabled. You should instead use the ODBC data provider to .NET for ODBC data sources, which is found in the Microsoft.Data.Odbc namespace. This limits the flexibility of the OLE DB data provider, but it does ensure that three levels of interfaces aren't between you and your data source! Also, the OLE DB 2.5 interface is not yet supported. This means you cannot use the OLE DB providers for things such as MS Exchange and Internet publishing. Finally, the use of the OLE DB data provider requires the installation of MDAC 2.6 or later (available free from Microsoft).

Like the other data providers, the OLE DB data provider has the Connection, Command, DataAdapter, and DataReader classes as its heavy lifters. Other classes provide supporting functionality, such as the OleDbException and OleDbError classes, which provide detailed error information specific to OLE DB data sources. To use this data provider you must import the System.Data.OleDb namespace.

System.Data.OleDb.OleDbCommand

The OleDbCommand represents a SQL statement or a call to a stored procedure. If information is to be returned, the OleDbCommand can do so by returning an OleDbDataReader object, a scalar value, or output parameters and return values read via the Parameters collection.

You may instantiate an OleDbCommand object by itself or use the CreateCommand method on the OleDbConnection object.

Constructors

```
Dim myOleDbCommand As New OleDbCommand()
Dim myOleDbCommand As New OleDbCommand(CommandText)
Dim myOleDbCommand As New OleDbCommand(CommandText, OleDbConnection)
Dim myOleDbCommand As New OleDbCommand(CommandText, OleDbConnection, _
    OleDbTransaction)
```

Parameters

`CommandText`	The String to be used as the CommandText property.
`OleDbConnection`	The OleDbConnection object to assign to the Connection property.
`OleDbTransaction`	The OleDbTransaction object to assign to the Transaction property.

OleDbCommand Sample Code

```
Dim myOleDbConnection As New System.Data.OleDb.OleDbConnection()
Dim myOleDbCommand As New System.Data.OleDb.OleDbCommand()
Dim myOleDbDataReader As System.Data.OleDb.OleDbDataReader
```

```
Dim myConnectionString As String
myConnectionString = "Provider=Microsoft.Jet.OLEDB.4.0;" & _
   "Data Source=C:\Northwind.mdb"
myOleDbConnection.ConnectionString = myConnectionString
myOleDbConnection.Open()
myOleDbCommand.CommandType = CommandType.TableDirect
myOleDbCommand.CommandText = "Employees"
myOleDbCommand.Connection = myOleDbConnection
myOleDbDataReader = myOleDbCommand.ExecuteReader()
' Process OleDbDataReader here
myOleDbDataReader.Close
```

OleDbCommand Members

Cancel

The Cancel method cancels the execution of the OleDbCommand. If you had already assigned an OleDbDataReader object, it will not be disposed or reinitialized when you call the Cancel method.

The Cancel method is very forgiving, and it will not throw an exception even if there is no operation to cancel. Cancel also will not throw an exception if the OleDbCommand object has not been properly established or if the connection is closed.

NOTE Our guess is that Cancel is being implemented for future asynchronous support.

Usage

```
myOleDbCommand.Cancel()
```

Parameters

None.

Exceptions

None.

Sample Code

```
Dim myOleDbConnection As New System.Data.OleDb.OleDbConnection()
Dim myOleDbCommand As New System.Data.OleDb.OleDbCommand()
Dim myOleDbDataReader As System.Data.OleDb.OleDbDataReader
Dim myConnectionString As String
myConnectionString = "Provider=Microsoft.Jet.OLEDB.4.0;" & _
   "Data Source=C:\Northwind.mdb"
myOleDbConnection.ConnectionString = myConnectionString
myOleDbConnection.Open()
myOleDbCommand.CommandText = "SELECT * FROM Products"
myOleDbCommand.Connection = myOleDbConnection
myOleDbDataReader = myOleDbCommand.ExecuteReader()
myOleDbCommand.Connection = myOleDbConnection
myOleDbCommand.Cancel
```

```
' Process OleDbDataReader here
myOleDbDataReader.Close()
myOleDbConnection.Close()
```

CommandText

The CommandText property is a String value that gets or sets the SQL statement or name of a stored procedure to execute. The default value is an empty string. If the text references objects with spaces in their names, you'll need to put those names in delimiters (square brackets). The CommandText property works in conjunction with the CommandType property, specifying a StoredProcedure, TableDirect, or Text (the default), so ensure that the CommandText you specify in this property matches the expectations of the CommandType property.

As with the CommandType and Connection properties, the CommandText property cannot be set when the associated OleDbConnection object is performing a fetch or execute operation.

When the CommandType is set to Text, the OLE DB provider does not support named parameters, so any parameters must be designated with a "?" or built into the SQL statement directly by concatenating the SQL command and any parameters into a String. If you concatenate the SQL command programmatically, be careful to mind the delimiters—it can be very easy to get your quotation marks or apostrophes out of synch. If you want to use the question mark method, then you will need to create OleDbParameter objects and add them to the OleDbParameterCollection in the order in which they appear in the SQL statement.

```
SELECT * FROM [Order Details] WHERE ProductID = ? AND UnitPrice > ?
```

The benefit of using OleDbParameter objects is that your ADO.NET code can retrieve Return values and Output parameters from the stored procedures. The concatenation method cannot, as it supports only the passing of values to the stored procedure. The benefit of the concatenation method is in the reduction in overhead of having to use OleDbParameter objects. The deciding factor for you is whether you need to capture output variables from your stored procedures. Keep in mind that either method retrieves recordset data without concern.

Usage

```
myCommandText = myOleDbCommand.CommandText
myOleDbCommand.CommandText = "SELECT * FROM Products"
```

Parameters

None.

CommandTimeout

The CommandTimeout property gets or sets an Int32 value representing the amount of time (in seconds) to wait for a Command to execute before raising a timeout error. It is common to have a particular lengthy stored procedure or SQL statement that needs several minutes to finish processing. Ideally, longer batch processes are scheduled during the off hours and executed without the need of a user interface; however, there are times when you need to programmatically allow for a lengthy routine to run.

Setting CommandTimeout to a value of 0 indicates that there is no time limit. This should generally be avoided because it could result in hung applications.

The default CommandTimeout is 30 seconds.

Usage

```
myInt32 = myOleDbCommand.CommandTimeout
myOleDbCommand.CommandTimeout = 60
```

Parameters

None.

Exceptions

ArgumentException	The CommandTimeout value was less than 0.

Sample Code

```
Dim myOleDbConnection As New System.Data.OleDb.OleDbConnection()
Dim myOleDbCommand As New System.Data.OleDb.OleDbCommand()
Dim myConnectionString As String
myConnectionString = "Provider=SQLOLEDB;Initial Catalog=Northwind;" & _
   "Datasource=Neptune;Integrated Security=SSPI;"
myOleDbConnection.ConnectionString = myConnectionString
myOleDbConnection.Open()
myOleDbCommand.CommandText = "EXECUTE web_ArchiveAccounting"
myOleDbCommand.CommandTimeout = 7200 ' Two hours
myOleDbCommand.Connection = myOleDbConnection
myOleDbCommand.ExecuteNonQuery()
myOleDbConnection.Close()
```

CommandType

The CommandType property sets or returns a CommandType enumeration that determines how the CommandText property should be interpreted by the data source. Because of this, the CommandType property actually dictates the content of the CommandText property. For example, if you set the CommandType to TableDirect, you may not specify a SQL statement in the CommandText property.

As with the CommandText and Connection properties, the CommandType property cannot be set when the associated OleDbConnection object is performing a fetch or execute operation.

The default CommandType is Text.

Usage

```
myCommandType = myOleDbCommand.CommandType
myOleDbCommand.CommandType = CommandType.StoredProcedure
```

Parameters

None.

CommandType Enumeration

StoredProcedure (4)	CommandText should be set to the name of the stored procedure.
TableDirect (512)	CommandText should be the name of a table. All columns will be returned.
Text (1)	(Default). CommandText can be any valid SQL text command.

Exceptions

ArgumentException	The CommandType value does not correspond to a valid CommandType.

Sample Code

```
Dim myOleDbConnection As New System.Data.OleDb.OleDbConnection()
Dim myOleDbCommand As New System.Data.OleDb.OleDbCommand()
Dim myOleDbDataReader As System.Data.OleDb.OleDbDataReader
Dim myConnectionString As String
myConnectionString = "Provider=Microsoft.Jet.OLEDB.4.0;" & _
   "Data Source=C:\Northwind.mdb"
myOleDbConnection.ConnectionString = myConnectionString
myOleDbConnection.Open()
myOleDbCommand.CommandType = CommandType.TableDirect
myOleDbCommand.CommandText = "Employees"
myOleDbCommand.Connection = myOleDbConnection
myOleDbDataReader = myOleDbCommand.ExecuteReader()
' Process myOleDbDataReader here
myOleDbDataReader.Close()
myOleDbConnection.Close()
```

Connection

The Connection property sets or returns the OleDbConnection object associated with the OleDbCommand. The OleDbConnection object being associated with the OleDbCommand can be open or closed. As with the CommandText and CommandType properties, the Connection property cannot be set when the associated OleDbConnection object is performing a fetch or execute operation.

Setting the connection is not allowed if a transaction is active; however, if the transaction has already been committed or rolled back, then the transaction object will automatically be set to null when the connection object is set or changed.

The default Connection is a null reference, which is `Nothing` in Visual Basic.

Usage

```
myOleDbConnection = myOleDbCommand.Connection
myOleDbCommand.Connection = myOleDbConnection
```

Parameters

None.

Exceptions

InvalidOperationException	Attempt to change Connection value while a transaction was in progress.

CreateParameter

The CreateParameter method returns a new OleDbParameter object. You would want to call this method if you are constructing a parameter collection in preparation for a call to a stored procedure or query using replaceable parameters.

The CreateParameter method is available purely for convenience. The resulting OleDbParameter object is not initialized in any way, nor is it added automatically to the OleDbCommand.Parameters collection. You must manually initialize the object as well as add it to the Parameters collection.

Usage

```
myOleDbParameter = myOleDbCommand.CreateParameter()
```

Parameters

None.

Exceptions

None.

Sample Code

```
Dim myOleDbConnection As New System.Data.OleDb.OleDbConnection()
Dim myOleDbParameter As New System.Data.OleDb.OleDbParameter()
Dim myOleDbCommand As New System.Data.OleDb.OleDbCommand()
Dim myOleDbDataReader As System.Data.OleDb.OleDbDataReader
Dim myConnectionString As String
myConnectionString = "Provider=Microsoft.Jet.OLEDB.4.0;" & _
   "Data Source=C:\Northwind.mdb"
myOleDbConnection.ConnectionString = myConnectionString
myOleDbConnection.Open()
myOleDbCommand.CommandText = "SELECT * FROM Employees WHERE Region = ?"
myOleDbCommand.Connection = myOleDbConnection
myOleDbParameter = myOleDbCommand.CreateParameter()
myOleDbParameter.Value = "WA"
myOleDbCommand.Parameters.Add(myOleDbParameter)
myOleDbDataReader = myOleDbCommand.ExecuteReader()
' Process myOleDbDataReader here
myOleDbDataReader.Close()
myOleDbConnection.Close()
```

DesignTimeVisible

The DesignTimeVisible property gets or sets a Boolean determining whether the OleDbCommand object will be visible in a Windows Form Designer control.

Usage

```
myBoolean = myOleDbCommand.DesignTimeVisible
myOleDbCommand.DesignTimeVisible = False
```

Parameters

None.

ExecuteNonQuery

The ExecuteNonQuery method executes a SQL statement and returns an Int32 representing the number of rows affected. This is generally used for SQL statements that update or change the data source but return no data. If you require the ability to retrieve row data from an OleDbCommand, then you should consider using the ExecuteReader method. If you require the ability to retrieve a single value from an OleDbCommand, such as an average product price, then you should consider using the ExecuteScalar method.

The return value for Insert, Update, and Delete statements is the number of rows affected. For all other statements it is -1. Although no data is returned from an ExecuteNonQuery method call, any output parameters or return values that are mapped to parameters will be returned.

When executing a command against SQL Server, the number of rows affected will be the *sum* of all Insert, Update, and Delete statements executed in the batch or stored procedure, regardless of whether there are other output statements. This is not the case with the Access because the Jet OLE DB provider will not execute more than one SQL statement at a time.

Usage

```
myInt32 = myOleDbCommand.ExecuteNonQuery()
```

Parameters

None.

Exceptions

InvalidOperationException	The OleDbConnection does not exist or is not open.
OleDbException	The command syntax was invalid for the given OLE DB provider.

Sample Code

```
Dim myOleDbConnection As New System.Data.OleDb.OleDbConnection()
Dim myOleDbCommand As New System.Data.OleDb.OleDbCommand()
Dim myInt32 As Int32
Dim myConnectionString As String
myConnectionString = "Provider=SQLOLEDB;Initial Catalog=Northwind;" & _
   "Datasource=Neptune;Integrated Security=SSPI;"
myOleDbConnection.ConnectionString = myConnectionString
myOleDbConnection.Open()
myOleDbCommand.CommandText = _
   "UPDATE Products SET UnitPrice = UnitPrice * 1.1 WHERE " & _
   "UnitPrice < 10 " & _
   "UPDATE Products SET UnitPrice = UnitPrice * 1.2 WHERE " & _
   "UnitPrice > 20"
myOleDbCommand.Connection = myOleDbConnection
myInt32 = myOleDbCommand.ExecuteNonQuery
' myInt32 should equal 48 (11 from Update #1 + 37 from Update #2)
myOleDbConnection.Close()
```

ExecuteReader

The ExecuteReader method executes a SQL statement and returns an OleDb-DataReader object that returns rows of data. ExecuteReader is generally used to call a SQL statement, stored procedure, or table directly. If your intention is to Insert, Update, or Delete data, then you should consider using the ExecuteNonQuery method. If you require the ability to retrieve a single value from an OleDbCommand, such as an average product price, then you should consider using the ExecuteScalar method.

You may also specify a bitwise combination of System.Data.CommandBehavior enumeration values for additional control over how the OleDbCommand behaves. These behaviors are vaguely reminiscent of the CursorType property from MDAC ADO. Keep in mind that some behaviors are mutually exclusive of other ones and that there are no default behaviors.

The OleDbDataReader requires exclusive access to the OleDbConnection object. While you are manipulating the OleDbDataReader object, you may not perform any other operations on the OleDbConnection, other than closing it. Once you execute the OleDbDataReader.Close method, you may again use the OleDbConnection for other operations.

Usage

```
myOleDbDataReader = myOleDbCommand.ExecuteReader()
myOleDbDataReader = myOleDbCommand.ExecuteReader(CommandBehavior)
```

Parameters

`CommandBehavior`	A bit-wise combination of CommandBehavior enumeration values.

CommandBehavior Enumeration

CloseConnection (32)	After the command has executed and you have manually called the OleDbDataReader's Close method, ADO.NET will automatically close the connection.
KeyInfo (4)	KeyInfo appends hidden key and timestamp information to the results, in order to support later updates without having to keep the table locked. This behavior is fundamental to a client-side cursor design. If you query the OleDbDataReader's schema, you will see these additional descriptors. For KeyInfo to work, the Select statement may not contain a Union clause and the underlying table must have a timestamp field and a unique index. The Jet OLE DB provider does not support the KeyInfo behavior.
SchemaOnly (2)	The command returns only schema information and does not allow you to read any data rows. This behavior does not impact the database state. The schema information can be viewed by executing the OleDbDataReader's GetSchemaTable method.

SequentialAccess (16)	The command returns the results sequentially across all columns. You should select this behavior if your columns contain large binary values, such as embedded documents or images. The Sequential-Access behavior allows you to call the OleDb-DataReader's GetChars or GetBytes method.
SingleResult (1)	The query returns a single result. If your command returns multiple result sets, this behavior will allow only the first one to be returned; however, no error will be thrown if you call the OleDbDataReader's NextResult method.
SingleRow(8)	The query returns a single row. If your command returns multiple rows in one or more result sets, this behavior will allow only the first row to be returned. Selecting this behavior may result in an optimized execution of the command; however, not all OLE DB providers will optimize. If you are expecting back a single row of data, specifying this behavior can improve your application's performance.

Exceptions

InvalidOperationException	The OleDbConnection does not exist or is not open.
OleDbException	The command syntax was invalid for the given OLE DB provider.
InvalidCastException	The OLE DB provider does not support the CommandBehavior.

Sample Code

```
Dim myOleDbConnection As New System.Data.OleDb.OleDbConnection()
Dim myOleDbCommand As New System.Data.OleDb.OleDbCommand()
Dim myOleDbDataReader As System.Data.OleDb.OleDbDataReader
Dim myInt32 As Int32
Dim myConnectionString As String
myConnectionString = "Provider=Microsoft.Jet.OLEDB.4.0;" & _
  "Data Source=C:\Northwind.mdb"
myOleDbConnection.ConnectionString = myConnectionString
myOleDbConnection.Open()
myOleDbCommand.CommandType = CommandType.TableDirect
myOleDbCommand.CommandText = "Products"
myOleDbCommand.Connection = myOleDbConnection
myOleDbDataReader = _
   myOleDbCommand.ExecuteReader(CommandBehavior.SchemaOnly + _
   CommandBehavior.CloseConnection)
' Browse the SchemaTable in a DataGrid
DataGrid1.DataSource = myOleDbDataReader.GetSchemaTable
myOleDbDataReader.Close()
' myOleDbConnection is closed implicitly
Messagebox.Show(myOleDbConnection.State.ToString(),"Connection.State")
```

ExecuteScalar

The ExecuteScalar method executes a SQL statement and returns an Object referencing the first column of the first row of data. ExecuteScalar is generally used to call a SQL statement or stored procedure that will return a single value, such as an aggregate function, server version, or other system variable. If you require the ability to retrieve row data from an OleDbCommand, then you should consider using the ExecuteReader method. If your intention is to Insert, Update, or Delete data, then you should consider using the ExecuteNonQuery method.

If your SQL statement returns more than one column or more than one row, the extra information is ignored, and only the first column in the first row is returned. If your SQL statement doesn't return any information, the ExecuteScalar method will not throw an exception, but rather your numeric object will be set to zero and your string objects will be empty (""). Because of this, make sure that your SQL statement is valid before you execute it.

Usage

```
myObject = myOleDbCommand.ExecuteScalar()
```

Parameters

None.

Exceptions

InvalidOperationException	The OleDbConnection does not exist or is not open.
OleDbException	The command syntax was invalid for the given OLE DB provider.
InvalidCastException	The Object returned cannot be stored in your variable. For example, you may have returned a String value and tried to store it to an Int32 object.

Sample Code

```
Dim myOleDbConnection As New System.Data.OleDb.OleDbConnection()
Dim myOleDbCommand As New System.Data.OleDb.OleDbCommand()
Dim myMaxPrice As Double
Dim myConnectionString As String
myConnectionString = "Provider=Microsoft.Jet.OLEDB.4.0;" & _
   "Data Source=C:\Northwind.mdb"
myOleDbConnection.ConnectionString = myConnectionString
myOleDbConnection.Open()
myOleDbCommand.CommandText = "SELECT Max(UnitPrice) FROM Products"
myOleDbCommand.Connection = myOleDbConnection
myMaxPrice = myOleDbCommand.ExecuteScalar
Messagebox.Show(myMaxPrice.ToString("c")) ' Formatted as currency
myOleDbConnection.Close()
```

Parameters

The Parameters property returns an OleDbParameterCollection object that contains a collection of all parameters created for the OleDbCommand. The Parameters collection is meaningful only for an OleDbCommand with a CommandType of Text or StoredProcedure. If you are using a TableDirect command, the Parameters collection will be ignored. Parameters defaults to an empty collection.

If your SQL statement contains replaceable parameters or your stored procedure expects parameters, then you must create your parameters collection before executing the command. The order in which the parameters are expected in the statement must match exactly with the order in the Parameters collection. See the OleDbParameterCollection class for more information.

When calling stored procedures that do not return output parameters or return values, you do need to use the Parameters collection. Performance is improved if you concatenate literals and variables together to form a meaningful SQL statement or stored procedure call and then execute it directly:

```
myOleDbCommand.CommandType = CommandType.Text
myOleDbCommand.CommandText = "EXECUTE [Employee Sales by Country] '" & _
  myDate1.ToShortDateString & "','" & myDate2.ToShortDateString & "'"
```

Usage

```
myOleDbParameterCollection = myOleDbCommand.Parameters
```

Parameters

None.

Sample Code

```
Dim myOleDbConnection As New System.Data.OleDb.OleDbConnection()
Dim myOleDbParameter As New System.Data.OleDb.OleDbParameter()
Dim myOleDbCommand As New System.Data.OleDb.OleDbCommand()
Dim myOleDbDataReader As System.Data.OleDb.OleDbDataReader
Dim myConnectionString As String
myConnectionString = "Provider=Microsoft.Jet.OLEDB.4.0;" & _
   "Data Source=C:\Northwind.mdb"
myOleDbConnection.ConnectionString = myConnectionString
myOleDbConnection.Open()
myOleDbCommand.CommandType = CommandType.StoredProcedure
myOleDbCommand.CommandText = "[Employee Sales by Country]"
myOleDbParameter = myOleDbCommand.CreateParameter()
myOleDbParameter.Value = "07/01/1996"
myOleDbCommand.Parameters.Add(myOleDbParameter)
myOleDbParameter = myOleDbCommand.CreateParameter()
myOleDbParameter.Value = "07/15/1996"
myOleDbCommand.Parameters.Add(myOleDbParameter)
myOleDbCommand.Connection = myOleDbConnection
myOleDbDataReader = myOleDbCommand.ExecuteReader()
' Process myOleDbDataReader here
myOleDbDataReader.Close()
myOleDbConnection.Close()
```

Prepare

The Prepare method notifies the data source to prepare the SQL statement, which means to create a prepared or compiled version of the command at the data source and keep it handy for successive calls. If you plan on calling a SQL statement more than three or four times, then you should prepare it first. Statement preparation slows the first execution call. Because of the increased overhead, you shouldn't prepare statements that you call infrequently. Some OLE DB providers implement the prepared statements using temporary objects that use server resources.

Prepared execution dovetails nicely with the Parameters collection because, although the command syntax has to be the same for each successive call to a prepared command, you are allowed to vary the parameter values. You should consider calling Prepare only with an OleDbCommand that has a CommandType of Text. Invalid SQL command or commands that specify stored procedure execution should not be prepared.

Microsoft SQL Server 2000 is very efficient in its management of execution plans, even for those that are executed directly. Because everybody's ADO.NET application will be unique, it is up to you to test your implementation and determine if preparing the statement will gain you any increases in performance.

Usage

```
myOleDbCommand.Prepare()
```

Parameters

None.

Exceptions

InvalidOperationException	The OleDbConnection does not exist, is not open, or the command syntax has not yet been set.
OleDbException	The OLE DB provider could not prepare the command. Perhaps the command syntax was invalid.

Sample Code

```
Dim myOleDbConnection As New System.Data.OleDb.OleDbConnection()
Dim myOleDbParameter As New System.Data.OleDb.OleDbParameter()
Dim myOleDbCommand As New System.Data.OleDb.OleDbCommand()
Dim myOleDbDataReader As System.Data.OleDb.OleDbDataReader
Dim myInt32 As Int32
Dim myConnectionString As String
myConnectionString = "Provider=SQLOLEDB;Initial Catalog=Northwind;" & _
   "Datasource=Neptune;Integrated Security=SSPI;"
myOleDbConnection.ConnectionString = myConnectionString
myOleDbConnection.Open()
myOleDbCommand.CommandText = "UPDATE Products SET UnitsInStock = " & _
   "UnitsInStock - ? WHERE ProductName = ?"
myOleDbCommand.Connection = myOleDbConnection
myOleDbCommand.Prepare()
' First update
myOleDbParameter = myOleDbCommand.CreateParameter()
myOleDbParameter.Value = 20
myOleDbCommand.Parameters.Add(myOleDbParameter)
myOleDbParameter = myOleDbCommand.CreateParameter()
myOleDbParameter.Value = "Grandma's Boysenberry Spread"
myOleDbCommand.Parameters.Add(myOleDbParameter)
```

```
myInt32 = myOleDbCommand.ExecuteNonQuery
' Second update
myOleDbCommand.Parameters(0).Value = 10
myOleDbCommand.Parameters(1).Value = "Carnarvon Tigers"
myInt32 = myOleDbCommand.ExecuteNonQuery
' Third update
myOleDbCommand.Parameters(1).Value = "Sasquatch Ale"
myInt32 = myOleDbCommand.ExecuteNonQuery
myOleDbConnection.Close()
```

ResetCommandTimeout

The ResetCommandTimeout method resets the CommandTimeout property back to its default value of 30 seconds. Calling this method is functionally equivalent to executing this line of code:

```
myOleDbCommand.CommandTimeout = 30
```

Usage

```
myOleDbCommand.ResetCommandTimeout()
```

Parameters

None.

Exceptions

None.

Sample Code

```
Dim myOleDbConnection As New System.Data.OleDb.OleDbConnection()
Dim myOleDbCommand As New System.Data.OleDb.OleDbCommand()
Dim myConnectionString As String
myConnectionString = "Provider=SQLOLEDB;Initial Catalog=Northwind;" & _
   "Datasource=Neptune;Integrated Security=SSPI;"
myOleDbConnection.ConnectionString = myConnectionString
myOleDbConnection.Open()
' First execution (must finish in two hours)
myOleDbCommand.CommandText = "EXECUTE web_ArchiveAccounting"
myOleDbCommand.CommandTimeout = 7200 ' Two hours
myOleDbCommand.Connection = myOleDbConnection
myOleDbCommand.ExecuteNonQuery()
' Second execution (must finish in thirty seconds)
myOleDbCommand.CommandText = "EXECUTE web_Initialize"
myOleDbCommand.ResetCommandTimeout()
myOleDbCommand.ExecuteNonQuery()
myOleDbConnection.Close()
```

Transaction

The Transaction property returns an OleDbTransaction object that represents the transaction within which the OleDbCommand will execute. Although the transaction is typically created and managed at the OleDbConnection object, the OleDb-Command object can access its transaction object with the help of this reference.

You must create the OleDbTransaction first, using the associated OleDbConnection's BeginTransaction method, before you can reference and manipulate it. See the OleDbConnection class for more information on creating a transaction. See the OleDb-Transaction class for more information on manipulating a transaction.

Usage

```
myOleDbTransaction = myOleDbCommand.Transaction
myOleDbCommand.Transaction = myOleDbTransaction
```

Parameters

None.

Sample Code

```
Dim myOleDbConnection As New System.Data.OleDb.OleDbConnection()
Dim myOleDbCommand As New System.Data.OleDb.OleDbCommand()
Dim myConnectionString As String
myConnectionString = "Provider=Microsoft.Jet.OLEDB.4.0;" & _
   "Data Source=C:\Northwind.mdb"
myOleDbConnection.ConnectionString = myConnectionString
myOleDbConnection.Open()
myOleDbCommand.CommandText = "INSERT INTO Customers " & _
   "(CustomerID,CompanyName) VALUES ('WILEY','Wiley Publishing')"
myOleDbCommand.Connection = myOleDbConnection
myOleDbCommand.Transaction = myOleDbConnection.BeginTransaction()
myOleDbCommand.ExecuteNonQuery()     ' INSERT succeeds
Try
   myOleDbCommand.ExecuteNonQuery() ' INSERT fails on PK violation
   myOleDbCommand.Transaction.Commit()
   MessageBox.Show("Success!", "Both records written")
Catch ex As Exception
   myOleDbCommand.Transaction.Rollback()
   MessageBox.Show(ex.ToString(), "No records written")
Finally
   myOleDbConnection.Close()
End Try
```

UpdatedRowSource

The UpdatedRowSource property determines how command results are applied back to the DataRow when you call the Update method of an associated OleDb-DataAdapter. If you are setting this value, you must use a valid UpdateRowSource enumeration. See the table of enumeration values that follows.

Usage

```
myUpdateRowSource = myOleDbCommand.UpdatedRowSource
myOleDbCommand.UpdatedRowSource = UpdateRowSource.Both
```

Parameters

None.

UpdateRowSource Enumeration	
Both (3)	Both output parameters and first returned row are mapped to the changed row in the database. This is the default value if the OleDbCommand has *not* been automatically generated.
FirstReturnedRecord (2)	Data in the first returned row is mapped to the changed row in the DataSet.
None (0)	All returned parameters or rows are ignored. This is the default value if the OleDbCommand has been automatically generated.
OutputParameters (1)	Output parameters are mapped to the changed row in the DataSet.

Exceptions	
ArgumentException	The value entered was not one of the valid UpdateRowSource values.

System.Data.OleDb.OleDbCommandBuilder

The OleDbCommandBuilder is a helpful class in that it provides a mechanism to automatically generate commands used to facilitate the updates made in an OleDbDataSet to the underlying table. These changes may affect only a single table. If your DataSet object is composed of data from more than one table, then you will have to code a custom solution.

For the OleDbCommandBuilder to work, your tables must have a unique key established. This may be a primary key or a candidate key (implemented via a unique index or constraint). The OleDbCommandBuilder is smart enough to determine the original column names, even if your SQL statement or stored procedure renamed them from the base table. Also, any additional columns or literal columns are ignored when these statements get built. If your SQL statement or stored procedure returns more than one result set, the OleDbCommandBuilder will process only the first result.

THANK YOU **As database programmers who have manually created these same Insert, Update, and Delete statements to gain performance in our applications, we can appreciate the usefulness of this class.**

Constructors

```
Dim myOleDbCommandBuilder As New OleDbCommandBuilder()
Dim myOleDbCommandBuilder As New OleDbCommandBuilder(OleDbDataAdapter)
```

Parameters

`OleDbDataAdapter`	An OleDbDataAdapter object to associate with the OleDbCommandBuilder. If you don't specify one in the constructor, you'll need to assign it later to the DataAdapter property.

OleDbCommandBuilder Sample Code

```
Dim myOleDbConnection As New System.Data.OleDb.OleDbConnection()
Dim myOleDbDataAdapter As New System.Data.OleDb.OleDbDataAdapter()
Dim myOleDbCommandBuilder As System.Data.OleDb.OleDbCommandBuilder
Dim myConnectionString As String
myConnectionString = "Provider=Microsoft.Jet.OLEDB.4.0;" & _
   "Data Source=C:\Northwind.mdb"
myOleDbConnection.ConnectionString = myConnectionString
myOleDbConnection.Open()
myOleDbDataAdapter.SelectCommand = New OleDbCommand( _
   "SELECT * FROM Customers", myOleDbConnection)
myOleDbCommandBuilder = New OleDbCommandBuilder()
myOleDbCommandBuilder.DataAdapter = myOleDbDataAdapter
' Seems a little redundant here
myOleDbDataAdapter.DeleteCommand =
myOleDbCommandBuilder.GetDeleteCommand
myOleDbDataAdapter.InsertCommand =
myOleDbCommandBuilder.GetInsertCommand
myOleDbDataAdapter.UpdateCommand =
myOleDbCommandBuilder.GetUpdateCommand
' Read data from the DataAdapter and post any changes back
myOleDbConnection.Close()
```

Members

DataAdapter

The DataAdapter property sets or returns a reference to the OleDbDataAdapter required by the OleDbCommandBuilder. The DataAdapter is necessary for the OleDbCommand-Builder to properly construct the Insert, Update, and Delete SQL commands. This property can either be set during instantiation of the OleDbCommandBuilder object, by passing a valid OleDbDataAdapter object to the constructor, or by assigning it to this property at a later time.

By setting the DataAdapter property, you are essentially registering the OleDbCommandBuilder object as a listener for the OleDbDataAdapter's RowUpdating events.

Usage

```
myOleDbDataAdapter = myOleDbCommandBuilder.DataAdapter
myOleDbCommandBuilder.DataAdapter = myOleDbDataAdapter
```

Parameters

None.

Sample Code

```
Dim myOleDbConnection As New System.Data.OleDb.OleDbConnection()
Dim myOleDbDataAdapter As New System.Data.OleDb.OleDbDataAdapter()
Dim myOleDbCommandBuilder As System.Data.OleDb.OleDbCommandBuilder
Dim myConnectionString As String
myConnectionString = "Provider=Microsoft.Jet.OLEDB.4.0;" & _
   "Data Source=C:\Northwind.mdb"
myOleDbConnection.ConnectionString = myConnectionString
myOleDbConnection.Open()
myOleDbDataAdapter.SelectCommand = New OleDbCommand( _
   "SELECT * FROM Customers", myOleDbConnection)
myOleDbCommandBuilder = New OleDbCommandBuilder()
myOleDbCommandBuilder.DataAdapter = myOleDbDataAdapter
MessageBox.Show(myOleDbCommandBuilder.GetInsertCommand.CommandText)
MessageBox.Show(myOleDbCommandBuilder.GetUpdateCommand.CommandText)
MessageBox.Show(myOleDbCommandBuilder.GetDeleteCommand.CommandText)
myOleDbConnection.Close()
```

DeriveParameters

A very useful function, the DeriveParameters method enables you to automatically populate an OleDbCommand's Parameters collection with the parameter information for a data source stored procedure. These new parameters will overwrite any existing parameters in the OleDbCommand's collection. You do not need to run this method, but it saves time from having to define your Parameters collection by hand. This method is reminiscent of MDAC ADO's Parameters.Refresh method.

The ease-of-use of the DeriveParameters method comes at a price, as it requires an extra round trip to the data source before executing the command. If you have only a few parameters to define, you should consider doing it manually, in code.

Usage

```
myOleDbCommandBuilder.DeriveParameters(myOleDbCommand)
```

Parameters

`myOleDbCommand`	The System.Data.OleDb.OleDbCommand object for which you want to populate the parameters collection.

Exceptions

InvalidOperationException	The specified stored procedure doesn't exist.

Sample Code

```
Dim myOleDbCommandBuilder As New System.Data.OleDb.OleDbCommandBuilder()
Dim myOleDbConnection As New System.Data.OleDb.OleDbConnection()
Dim myOleDbParameter As System.Data.OleDb.OleDbParameter
Dim myOleDbCommand As System.Data.OleDb.OleDbCommand
' Establish Connection
myOleDbConnection.ConnectionString = _
   "Provider=SQLOLEDB;Initial Catalog=Northwind;" & _
```

```
    "Datasource=Neptune;Integrated Security=SSPI;"
myOleDbConnection.Open()
' Establish Command
myOleDbCommand = myOleDbConnection.CreateCommand()
myOleDbCommand.CommandText = "SalesByCategory"
myOleDbCommand.CommandType = CommandType.StoredProcedure
' Use CommandBuilder to Populate Parameters collection
myOleDbCommandBuilder.DeriveParameters(myOleDbCommand)
' Enumerate the Parameters collection (3 Items)
For Each myOleDbParameter In myOleDbCommand.Parameters
   MessageBox.Show(myOleDbParameter.ParameterName & " (" & _
      myOleDbParameter.OleDbType.ToString & ")", _
      myOleDbParameter.Direction.ToString & " Parameter")
Next
' Done
myOleDbConnection.Close()
```

GetDeleteCommand

Together with its colleagues, GetInsertCommand and GetUpdateCommand, this utility method returns a reference to the OleDbCommand object that is managing the deleting of any records. This reference should be treated as informational, meaning you should not try to manipulate the OleDbCommand directly. Some of the more interesting properties that you can query are the CommandText, CommandTimeout, CommandType, and Parameters collection. Although these properties are read only, no exception will be thrown if you try to write to them. See the OleDbCommand class for more information.

If you want to customize the SQL statement, you should capture the CommandText and make any changes to the OleDbDataAdapter DeleteCommand property. You could also create your own OleDbCommand and execute it manually. This workaround can solve the problem of trying to update multiple tables at once, which isn't currently supported with the OleDbCommandBuilder class.

Usage

```
myOleDbCommand = myOleDbCommandBuilder.GetDeleteCommand
```

Parameters

None.

Exceptions

None.

Sample Code

```
Dim myOleDbConnection As New System.Data.OleDb.OleDbConnection()
Dim myOleDbDataAdapter As New System.Data.OleDb.OleDbDataAdapter()
Dim myOleDbCommandBuilder As System.Data.OleDb.OleDbCommandBuilder
Dim myOleDbCommand As New System.Data.OleDb.OleDbCommand()
Dim myConnectionString As String
myConnectionString = "Provider=Microsoft.Jet.OLEDB.4.0;" & _
   "Data Source=C:\Northwind.mdb"
myOleDbConnection.ConnectionString = myConnectionString
myOleDbConnection.Open()
```

```
myOleDbDataAdapter.SelectCommand = New OleDbCommand( _
   "SELECT * FROM Customers", myOleDbConnection)
myOleDbCommandBuilder = New OleDbCommandBuilder()
myOleDbCommandBuilder.DataAdapter = myOleDbDataAdapter
' CommandBuilder approach (a SQL statement with many parameters)
myOleDbDataAdapter.DeleteCommand = _
   myOleDbCommandBuilder.GetDeleteCommand
' Custom approach (a lighter SQL statement)
' You'll need to manually create the parameter
myOleDbCommand.CommandText = _
   "DELETE FROM [Customers] WHERE CustomerID = ?"
myOleDbDataAdapter.DeleteCommand = myOleDbCommand
' Execute UPDATE and finish
```

GetInsertCommand

Together with its colleagues, GetDeleteCommand and GetUpdateCommand, this utility method returns a reference to the OleDbCommand object that is managing the insertion of any records. This reference should be treated as informational, meaning you should not try to manipulate the OleDbCommand directly. Some of the more interesting properties that you can query are the CommandText, CommandTimeout, CommandType, and Parameters collection. Although these properties are read only, no exception will be thrown if you try to write to them. See the OleDbCommand class for more information.

If you want to customize the SQL statement, you should capture the CommandText and make any changes to the OleDbDataAdapter InsertCommand property. You could also create your own OleDbCommand and execute it manually. This workaround can solve the problem of trying to update multiple tables at once, which isn't currently supported with the OleDbCommandBuilder class.

Usage

```
myOleDbCommand = myOleDbCommandBuilder.GetInsertCommand
```

Parameters

None.

Exceptions

None.

GetUpdateCommand

Together with its colleagues, GetDeleteCommand and GetInsertCommand, this utility method returns a reference to the OleDbCommand object that is managing the updating of any records. This reference should be treated as informational, meaning you should not try to manipulate the OleDbCommand directly. Some of the more interesting properties that you can query are the CommandText, CommandTimeout, CommandType, and Parameters collection. Although these properties are read only, no exception will be thrown if you try to write to them. See the OleDbCommand class for more information.

If you want to customize the SQL statement, you should capture the CommandText and make any changes to the OleDbDataAdapter UpdateCommand property. You could also create your own OleDbCommand and execute it manually. This workaround can solve the problem of trying to update multiple tables at once, which isn't currently supported with the OleDbCommandBuilder class.

Usage

```
myOleDbCommand = myOleDbCommandBuilder.GetUpdateCommand
```

Parameters

None.

Exceptions

None.

QuotePrefix

The QuotePrefix property allows you to set or return the beginning character to use when specifying database object names. Because some data sources allow their tables, views, stored procedures, and column names to contain spaces, ADO.NET must delimit those names accordingly. Here are some examples:

```
-- Bad SQL (especially since ORDER is a reserved keyword)
UPDATE Order Details SET UnitPrice = UnitPrice * 1.1
     -- Poor SQL (may work with SQL Server, won't work with Access)
UPDATE "Order Details" SET UnitPrice = UnitPrice * 1.1
-- Good SQL (works with SQL Server and Access)
UPDATE [Order Details] SET UnitPrice = UnitPrice * 1.1
```

By default, the QuotePrefix will be an empty string. Once you make your first call to GetDeleteCommand, GetInsertCommand, or GetUpdateCommand, ADO.NET will initialize the QuotePrefix with a quotation mark (") for SQL Server or an apostrophe (') for Access. Once this has happened, the QuotePrefix becomes read-only, and you may not change the character. For this reason, you should specify your custom delimiter before generating any of the SQL commands. A good alternative is a square left bracket ([).

Both SQL Server and Access support spaces in their object names. SQL Server can override the behavior of the quotation mark based on the QUOTED_IDENTIFIER setting. If it has been set to OFF, quotation marks will not work as delimiters, and you must use the square braces. For this reason, it is best to get into the habit of using square braces and manually setting them on QuotePrefix and QuoteSuffix.

Usage

```
myString = myOleDbCommandBuilder.QuotePrefix
myOleDbCommandBuilder.QuotePrefix = "["
```

Parameters

None.

Exceptions

InvalidOperationException	You are trying to assign the character after the OleDbCommandBuilder has generated the command. QuotePrefix becomes read only at that point.

Sample Code

```
Dim myOleDbConnection As New System.Data.OleDb.OleDbConnection()
Dim myOleDbDataAdapter As New System.Data.OleDb.OleDbDataAdapter()
Dim myOleDbCommandBuilder As System.Data.OleDb.OleDbCommandBuilder
Dim myConnectionString As String
myConnectionString = "Provider=Microsoft.Jet.OLEDB.4.0;" & _
   "Data Source=C:\Northwind.mdb"
myOleDbConnection.ConnectionString = myConnectionString
myOleDbConnection.Open()
myOleDbDataAdapter.SelectCommand = New OleDbCommand( _
   "SELECT * FROM [Order Details]", myOleDbConnection)
myOleDbCommandBuilder = New OleDbCommandBuilder(myOleDbDataAdapter)
myOleDbCommandBuilder.QuotePrefix = "["
myOleDbCommandBuilder.QuoteSuffix = "]"
MessageBox.Show(myOleDbCommandBuilder.GetInsertCommand.CommandText)
MessageBox.Show(myOleDbCommandBuilder.GetUpdateCommand.CommandText)
MessageBox.Show(myOleDbCommandBuilder.GetDeleteCommand.CommandText)
myOleDbConnection.Close()
```

QuoteSuffix

The QuoteSuffix property allows you to set or return the ending character to use when specifying database object names. Because some data sources allow their tables, views, stored procedures, and column names to contain spaces, ADO.NET must delimit those names accordingly. See the QuotePrefix method for more information.

By default, the QuoteSuffix will be an empty string. Once you make your first call to GetDeleteCommand, GetInsertCommand, or GetUpdateCommand, ADO.NET will initialize the QuoteSuffix with a quotation mark (") for SQL Server or an apostrophe (') for Access. Once this has happened, the QuoteSuffix becomes read only and you may not change the character. For this reason, you should specify your custom delimiter before generating any of the SQL commands. A good alternative is a square right bracket (]).

Both SQL Server and Access support spaces in their object names. SQL Server can override the behavior of the quotation mark based on the QUOTED_IDENTIFIER setting. If it has been set to OFF, quotation marks will not work as delimiters, and you must use the square braces. For this reason, it is best to get into the habit of using square braces and manually setting them on QuotePrefix and QuoteSuffix.

Usage

```
myString = myOleDbCommandBuilder.QuoteSuffix
myOleDbCommandBuilder.QuoteSuffix = "]"
```

Parameters

None.

Exceptions

Exception	Description
InvalidOperationException	You are trying to assign the character after the OleDbCommandBuilder has generated the command. QuoteSuffix becomes read only at that point.

RefreshSchema

The RefreshSchema method will force a reload of the schema information from the data source so that you can generate accurate Insert, Update, and Delete commands. If you change the SQL statement of the associated OleDbDataAdapter's SelectCommand property without calling RefreshSchema, you may generate commands based on the old command text.

Usage

```
myOleDbCommand.RefreshSchema()
```

Parameters

None.

Exceptions

None.

Sample Code

```
Dim myOleDbConnection As New System.Data.OleDb.OleDbConnection()
Dim myOleDbDataAdapter As New System.Data.OleDb.OleDbDataAdapter()
Dim myOleDbCommandBuilder As System.Data.OleDb.OleDbCommandBuilder
Dim myConnectionString As String
myConnectionString = "Provider=Microsoft.Jet.OLEDB.4.0;" & _
   "Data Source=C:\Northwind.mdb"
myOleDbConnection.ConnectionString = myConnectionString
myOleDbConnection.Open()
myOleDbDataAdapter.SelectCommand = New OleDbCommand( _
   "SELECT SupplierID, CompanyName FROM Suppliers", myOleDbConnection)
myOleDbCommandBuilder = New OleDbCommandBuilder(myOleDbDataAdapter)
MessageBox.Show(myOleDbCommandBuilder.GetUpdateCommand.CommandText)
' Change the underlying select command
myOleDbDataAdapter.SelectCommand.CommandText = _
   "SELECT SupplierID, ContactName FROM Suppliers"
MessageBox.Show(myOleDbCommandBuilder.GetUpdateCommand.CommandText)
' Refresh to show new update command
myOleDbCommandBuilder.RefreshSchema()
MessageBox.Show(myOleDbCommandBuilder.GetUpdateCommand.CommandText)
myOleDbConnection.Close()
```

System.Data.OleDb.OleDbConnection

An OleDbConnection represents a unique connection to an OLE DB data source. This connection mechanism uses the .NET OLE DB data provider that, in turn, uses COM Interop to enable data access to any existing OLE DB provider.

When an OleDbConnection object goes out of scope, it will not release the resources used by the OleDbConnection; therefore, it must be explicitly closed by calling the Close or Dispose method. We therefore recommend that a Close or Dispose method call be placed into the Finally block of a Try-Catch-Finally exception handler, to ensure that the connection is actually released, even in the event of an exception being raised.

Another reason to explicitly call Close rather than allowing your connection objects to simply go out of scope is garbage collection. Garbage collection in .NET does not happen immediately, and therefore your connection objects will still be alive and holding valuable server resources. It is actually possible to run out of connections on your data source with code written in this way. If you always explicitly call the Close method, you'll be fine.

Constructors

```
Dim myOleDbConnection As New OleDbConnection()
Dim myOleDbConnection As New OleDbConnection(String)
```

Parameters

`String` The connection string to be passed. See the ConnectionString property.

Members

BeginTransaction

The BeginTransaction method begins a database transaction and returns an OleDb-Transaction object. Any OleDbCommand objects that you execute as part of this transaction will be buffered. All changes will be flushed to the data source when you explicitly complete the transaction by using the Commit method. All changes will be rolled back when you explicitly call the Rollback method or if you happen to close the Connection with open transactions.

All ADO.NET transactions are handled within the database and are not supported by the Microsoft Distributed Transaction Coordinator (MTC) or any other transactional mechanism. Because .NET is brokering the transaction management, you shouldn't use the transaction support provided by the data source, or errors may result. In other words, don't embed a SQL *BEGIN TRANSACTION* in any command you execute. Most data sources implement transaction by way of locks. For this reason, you should keep the number and duration of your transactions to a minimum.

If you want to begin a transaction with a specific isolation level, you can call the BeginTransaction method by passing a valid IsolationLevel enumeration to the constructor. The IsolationLevel determines how one transaction is (or isn't) isolated from another. It describes how sensitive the data within your transaction is to changes by other transactions. The default IsolationLevel is ReadCommitted, which happens to be the safest.

See the OleDbTransaction class for more information.

Usage

```
myOleDbTransaction = myOleDbConnection.BeginTransaction()
myOleDbTransaction = myOleDbConnection.BeginTransaction(IsolationLevel)
```

Parameters

`IsolationLevel` A valid IsolationLevel enumeration.

IsolationLevel Enumeration

Chaos (16)	Any pending changes from transactions that are more highly isolated transactions cannot be overwritten. SQL Server 2000 and below does not support this isolation level.
ReadCommitted (4096)	(Default) Shared locks are held while the data is being read to avoid dirty reads, but the data can be changed before the end of the transaction, resulting in nonrepeatable reads or phantom data (a.k.a. CursorStability).
ReadUncommitted (256)	No shared locks or exclusive locks are honored, so dirty reads are possible (a.k.a. Browse).
RepeatableRead (65536)	All data used in a query is locked, preventing others from updating. This prevents nonrepeatable reads, but phantom rows are still possible.
Serializable (1048576)	A range lock is placed on the data preventing other users from updating or inserting rows into the dataset until the transaction is complete (a.k.a. Isolated).
Unspecified (-1)	A different isolation level than the one specified is being used, but the level cannot be determined. (This value cannot be passed when creating a Transaction.)

Exceptions

ArgumentException	An invalid IsolationLevel argument was passed.

Sample Code

```
Dim myOleDbConnection As New System.Data.OleDb.OleDbConnection()
Dim myOleDbTransaction As System.Data.OleDb.OleDbTransaction
Dim myOleDbCommand As New System.Data.OleDb.OleDbCommand()
Dim myConnectionString As String
myConnectionString = "Provider=Microsoft.Jet.OLEDB.4.0;" & _
   "Data Source=C:\Northwind.mdb"
myOleDbConnection.ConnectionString = myConnectionString
myOleDbConnection.Open()
myOleDbTransaction = myOleDbConnection.BeginTransaction()
myOleDbCommand.CommandText = "INSERT INTO Customers " & _
   "(CustomerID,CompanyName) VALUES ('WILEY','Wiley Publishing')"
myOleDbCommand.Connection = myOleDbConnection
myOleDbCommand.Transaction = myOleDbTransaction
myOleDbCommand.ExecuteNonQuery()    ' INSERT succeeds
Try
   myOleDbCommand.ExecuteNonQuery() ' INSERT fails on PK violation
   myOleDbTransaction.Commit()
   MessageBox.Show("Success!", "Both records written")
Catch ex As Exception
   myOleDbTransaction.Rollback()
   MessageBox.Show(ex.ToString(), "No records written")
Finally
   myOleDbConnection.Close()
End Try
```

ChangeDatabase

The ChangeDatabase method changes the current database for an open OleDbConnection. Some OLE DB providers, such as Microsoft's provider for Access, don't support this method.

NOTE We found it interesting that you can pass an invalid database name and it will *not* throw an exception. Only if the database name is empty or null will ADO.NET become upset.

Usage

```
myOleDbConnection.ChangeDatabase(String)
```

Parameters

`String`	A valid database name.

Exceptions

ArgumentException	An invalid database name was passed.
InvalidOperationException	The connection is not open.
OleDbException	The database cannot be changed.

Sample Code

```
Dim myOleDbConnection As New System.Data.OleDb.OleDbConnection()
Dim myConnectionString As String
myConnectionString = "Provider=SQLOLEDB;Initial Catalog=Northwind;" & _
   "Datasource=Neptune;Integrated Security=SSPI;"
myOleDbConnection.ConnectionString = myConnectionString
myOleDbConnection.Open()
MessageBox.Show(myOleDbConnection.Database, "Database")
Try
   myOleDbConnection.ChangeDatabase("Pubs")
   MessageBox.Show(myOleDbConnection.Database, "Database")
Catch ex As Exception
   MessageBox.Show(ex.ToString(), "Exception")
Finally
   myOleDbConnection.Close()
End Try
```

Close

The Close method is the preferred way of closing an open connection. In addition to releasing the connection to the connection pool (if applicable), the Close method also rolls back any pending transactions, just as though the OleDbTransaction.Rollback method was called.

Unlike prior versions of ADO, if you call the Close method on a connection that is closed, no exception is thrown. This makes it ideal to place in the Finally block of an exception handler. After a connection has been closed, it may be reopened with the Open method, without having to respecify the ConnectionString.

The difference between Close and Dispose is that Close releases the connection back to the connection pool to be possibly reused, whereas Dispose removes the connection from the connection pool. Close also maintains the ConnectionString property, whereas Dispose does not.

Usage

```
myOleDbConnection.Close()
```

Parameters

None.

Exceptions

None.

Sample Code

```
Dim myOleDbConnection As New System.Data.OleDb.OleDbConnection()
Dim myConnectionString As String
myConnectionString = "Provider=SQLOLEDB;Initial Catalog=Northwind;" & _
   "Datasource=Neptune;Integrated Security=SSPI;"
myOleDbConnection.ConnectionString = myConnectionString
myOleDbConnection.Open()
MessageBox.Show(myOleDbConnection.State.ToString(), "State")
myOleDbConnection.Close()
MessageBox.Show(myOleDbConnection.State.ToString(), "State")
```

ConnectionString

The ConnectionString property is probably the most important member of the OleDb-Connection class. The ConnectionString property specifies all of the parameters required to open a connection to the underlying data source. Many of these parameters have corresponding, read-only properties.

You can assign the ConnectionString in two possible ways: by passing the ConnectionString to the OleDbConnection constructor or by assigning the property directly. You may not, however, change the ConnectionString once the connection is open. If you want to change the connection information, such as the data source, you must first close the connection, reassign the ConnectionString, and then reopen the connection. Each parameter is separated with a semicolon, and the order in which they are listed does not matter.

At a minimum, a ConnectionString needs a Provider and a Data Source. This assumes that the data source is not secured or that it allows anonymous or guest login. If the Data Source is secure, then a User ID and Password parameter may be required. These four common parameters are supported by most OLE DB providers.

Not all ConnectionString parameters are supported by all providers. The listing that follows includes the common ones, typically supported by the more popular data sources.

Usage

```
myOleDbConnection.ConnectionString = myString
myString = myOleDbConnection.ConnectionString
```

Parameters

None.

Common ConnectionString Parameters

Connect Timeout	The number of seconds ADO.NET has to connect to the data source before "timing out" and returning an error. The default is 15 seconds. Passing a value of 0 will attempt to connect indefinitely!
Data Source	(Required). The database server (client/server DBMS) or the physical path to the database file (Access).
Initial Catalog	The database on the server (client/server DBMS). This parameter is not supported with Access.
Integrated Security	Used to specify Windows authentication rather than SQL Server authentication. If you want to pass the user and password transparently, then set this parameter to SSPI (Secured Support Provider Interface).
Password	When not using Integrated Security, or when connecting to Access, this is the password used for authentication.
Persist Security Info	When querying the ConnectionString and this parameter is true, the ConnectionString will return any password that was passed to the data source. If Persist Security Info is false, the ConnectionString will not include any password.
Prompt	When connecting, prompt the user to manually enter his or her connection information via a popup dialog box. (1) Always prompts the user for connection parameters. (2) Prompt the user only if ConnectionString didn't provide enough information. (3) Prompt the user only if ConnectionString didn't provide enough information and keep the user from selecting any optional settings. (Default) (4) Do not prompt the user.
Provider	(Required). This parameter specifies the OLE DB provider to use to access the data source. ADO.NET does not support all OLE DB providers. Refer to the Provider property for a list of supported providers.
User ID	When not using Integrated Security, or when connecting to Access, this is the user name used for authentication.

Exceptions

ArgumentException	A parameter value was invalid.
InvalidOperationException	You tried to assign the ConnectionString property while the connection was open.
SystemException	An invalid Provider is passed.

Sample Code

```
Dim myOleDbConnection As New System.Data.OleDb.OleDbConnection()
Dim myConnectionString As String
myConnectionString = "Provider=Microsoft.Jet.OLEDB.4.0;" & _
   "Data Source=C:\Northwind.mdb;User ID=Richard;Prompt=3"
myOleDbConnection.ConnectionString = myConnectionString
Try
   myOleDbConnection.Open()
Catch ex As Exception
   MessageBox.Show(ex.ToString(), "Exception")
Finally
   myOleDbConnection.Close()
End Try
```

ConnectionTimeout

The ConnectionTimeout property is read only and returns an Int32 specifying the number of seconds to wait while attempting to open a database connection before terminating the attempt and raising an error. By default, this value is 15 seconds, but it can be overridden by setting the Connect Timeout parameter in the ConnectionString. You can query the ConnectionTimeout property immediately after assigning the ConnectionString parameter. You do not need to wait until the OleDbConnection is open for the value to update.

Usage

```
myInt32 = myOleDbConnection.ConnectionTimeout
```

Parameters

None.

Sample Code

```
Dim myOleDbConnection As New System.Data.OleDb.OleDbConnection()
Dim myConnectionString As String
myConnectionString = "Provider=SQLOLEDB; Data Source=AsiaServer;" & _
   "Connect Timeout=30"
myOleDbConnection.ConnectionString = myConnectionString
Messagebox.Show(myOleDbConnection.ConnectionTimeout,"Timeout")
```

CreateCommand

The method provides a convenient way to create and return an OleDbCommand object associated with the current connection. OleDbCommand objects are the mechanisms by which you run queries, call stored procedures, or execute other SQL statements. See the OleDbCommand class reference for more information.

By using the CreateCommand method, it allows you to do two steps in one: Create the OleDbCommand object, and assign it to an OleDbConnection object.

The OleDbConnection does not need to be open for you to execute the CreateCommand method; however, the OleDbConnection must be open for you to execute the OleDbCommand.

If your connection is engaging in an OleDbTransaction, you must still assign the Transaction property of the OleDbCommand object manually:

```
myOleDbCommand.Transaction = myOleDbTransaction
```

Usage

```
myOleDbCommand = myOleDbConnection.CreateCommand()
```

Parameters

None.

Exceptions

None.

Sample Code

```
Dim myOleDbConnection As New System.Data.OleDb.OleDbConnection()
Dim myOleDbCommand As New System.Data.OleDb.OleDbCommand()
Dim myConnectionString As String
myConnectionString = "Provider=Microsoft.Jet.OLEDB.4.0;" & _
   "Data Source=C:\Northwind.mdb;"
myOleDbConnection.ConnectionString = myConnectionString
myOleDbConnection.Open()
myOleDbCommand = myOleDbConnection.CreateCommand
myOleDbCommand.CommandText = "INSERT INTO Customers " & _
   "(CustomerID,CompanyName) VALUES ('WILEY','Wiley Publishing')"
myOleDbCommand.ExecuteNonQuery()
myOleDbConnection.Close()
```

Database

The Database property returns the name of a connection's database as specified by the *Initial Catalog* parameter of the ConnectionString. The connection does not need to be open to query this read-only property. The database will default to an empty string, unless it has been assigned in one of four possible ways:

1. Pass a connection string with an Initial Catalog parameter to the OleDbConnection constructor during creation.
2. Assign a connection string, including the Initial Catalog parameter, directly to the OleDbConnection's ConnectionString property.
3. Call the ChangeDatabase method on an open connection. This is not supported by Microsoft Access.
4. Change the database programmatically, such as by executing a "USE Pubs" Transact-SQL command. A programmatic change such as this will be trapped by the connection's InfoMessage event.

Some OLE DB providers, such as Microsoft's provider for Access, won't support this property. One reason is because this property returns only the value passed over via the Initial Catalog parameter, so you cannot use it to query the name of a Microsoft Access database because its path and name are passed via the Data Source parameter in the ConnectionString. You should query the DataSource property instead.

Usage

```
myString = myOleDbConnection.Database
```

Parameters

None.

Sample Code

```
Dim myOleDbConnection As New System.Data.OleDb.OleDbConnection()
Dim myConnectionString As String
' Sample 1 - no open connection and database property is an empty string
MessageBox.Show(myOleDbConnection.Database)
' Sample 2 - no open connection, but database property = "Northwind"
myConnectionString = "Provider=SQLOLEDB;Initial Catalog=Northwind;" & _
   "Datasource=(local);Integrated Security=SSPI;"
myOleDbConnection = New System.Data.OleDb.OleDbConnection()
myOleDbConnection.ConnectionString = myConnectionString
MessageBox.Show(myOleDbConnection.Database)
' Sample 3 - connection is open and database property = "Northwind"
myConnectionString = "Provider=SQLOLEDB;Initial Catalog=Northwind;" & _
   "Datasource=(local);Integrated Security=SSPI;"
myOleDbConnection = New _
   System.Data.OleDb.OleDbConnection(myConnectionString)
myOleDbConnection.Open()
MessageBox.Show(myOleDbConnection.Database)
```

DataSource

The DataSource property returns the server or filename as specified by the *Data Source* parameter of the ConnectionString. The connection does not need to be open to query this read-only property. DataSource will default to an empty string, unless it has been assigned in one of two possible ways:

1. Pass a connection string with a Data Source parameter to the OleDbConnection constructor during creation.
2. Assign a connection string, including the Data Source parameter, directly to the OleDbConnection's ConnectionString property.

Usage

```
myString = myOleDbConnection.DataSource
```

Parameters

None.

Sample Code

```
Dim myOleDbConnection As System.Data.OleDb.OleDbConnection
```

```
Dim myConnectionString As String
' Sample 1 - no open connection and datasource property is an empty
' string
myOleDbConnection = New System.Data.OleDb.OleDbConnection()
MessageBox.Show(myOleDbConnection.DataSource, "DataSource")
' Sample 2 - no open connection, but datasource property is available
myConnectionString = "Provider=Microsoft.Jet.OLEDB.4.0;" & _
   "Data Source=C:\Northwind.mdb;"
myOleDbConnection = New System.Data.OleDb.OleDbConnection()
myOleDbConnection.ConnectionString = myConnectionString
MessageBox.Show(myOleDbConnection.DataSource, "DataSource")
' Sample 3 - connection is open and datasource property is available
myConnectionString = "Provider=Microsoft.Jet.OLEDB.4.0;" & _
   "Data Source=X:\Northwind.mdb;"
myOleDbConnection = New _
   System.Data.OleDb.OleDbConnection(myConnectionString)
myOleDbConnection.Open()
MessageBox.Show(myOleDbConnection.DataSource, "DataSource")
```

Dispose

Similar to Close, the Dispose method closes the current connection to the data source and then flushes the OleDbConnection from the connection pool. Before the connection is actually closed, all uncommitted transactions are rolled back and the connection is released. The Dispose method may be called even when the connection is not open and will not throw an exception or raise an error. Dispose not only frees all of the memory resources, but also clears the ConnectionString property. Thus, unlike using Close, once you have called Dispose, the connection cannot be simply reestablished by calling the Open method.

Usage

```
myOleDbConnection.Dispose()
```

Parameters

None.

Exceptions

None.

Sample Code

```
Dim myOleDbConnection As New System.Data.OleDb.OleDbConnection()
Dim myConnectionString As String
myConnectionString = "Provider=Microsoft.Jet.OLEDB.4.0;" & _
  "Data Source=C:\Northwind.mdb"
myOleDbConnection.ConnectionString = myConnectionString
myOleDbConnection.Open()
myOleDbConnection.Close()
MessageBox.Show(myOleDbConnection.ConnectionString, "ConnectionString")
myOleDbConnection.Open()
myOleDbConnection.Dispose()
MessageBox.Show(myOleDbConnection.ConnectionString, "ConnectionString")
```

GetOleDbSchemaTable

This method returns a DataTable object containing the schema and associated information. Essentially, this is a way to query a data source and receive a catalog of what tables, views, constraints, and more are available.

Usage

```
myDataTable = myOleDbConnection.GetOleDbSchemaTable _
   (OleDbSchemaGuid, Restrictions())
```

Parameters

`OleDbSchemaGuid`	A 128-bit integer representing which kind of schema table to return. Please refer to OleDbSchemaGuid for all possible values.
`Restrictions()`	An array of objects that serve as filter values. You'll need to have an understanding of what the DataTable to be returned will look like, so that you may put the appropriate column filters in place. For example, placing a SYSTEM TABLE in the fourth column position will force MS Access to return back a schema of only system tables.

Exceptions

InvalidOperationException	The connection is closed.
OleDbException	An incorrect parameter was passed.

Sample Code

```
Dim myOleDbConnection As New System.Data.OleDb.OleDbConnection()
Dim myDataTable As System.Data.DataTable
Dim myConnectionString As String
Dim myMessage As String
Dim iRow, iCol As Int32
myConnectionString = "Provider=Microsoft.Jet.OLEDB.4.0;" & _
   "Data Source=C:\Northwind.mdb"
myOleDbConnection.ConnectionString = myConnectionString
myOleDbConnection.Open()
myDataTable = myOleDbConnection.GetOleDbSchemaTable( _
   OleDbSchemaGuid.Tables,New Object()
{Nothing,Nothing,Nothing,"TABLE"})
For iRow = 0 To myDataTable.Rows.Count - 1
   myMessage = ""
   For iCol = 0 To myDataTable.Columns.Count - 1
      myMessage = myMessage + myDataTable.Columns(iCol).ColumnName + _
         ControlChars.Tab + myDataTable.Rows(iRow).Item(iCol) + _
         ControlChars.CrLf
   Next
   MessageBox.Show(myMessage, "Schema Record # " & iRow + 1 & _
     " of " & myDataTable.Rows.Count)
Next
myOleDbConnection.Close()
```

InfoMessage

The InfoMessage event can be used to catch informational, warning, or error messages passed back from the provider. This event handler is passed an argument of type OleDbInfoMessageEventArgs, which supplies all of the relevant data.

InfoMessages are delivered independently of any error messages or exceptions. In other words, just because you receive an ADO.NET exception does not mean that there will be any InfoMessage information; conversely, InfoMessages may be received that are not exceptions. An example of this would be a SQL PRINT statement—it is not row data, to be captured in a DataReader or DataSet, but yet it's not an error or exception to be captured by the exception handler. The InfoMessage event is where you would go to collect the information returned by those PRINT statements in stored procedures or queries.

NOTE SQL Server 2000 RAISERROR commands with a severity of 0 through 10 will raise an InfoMessage event without throwing an exception. RAISERROR with a severity of 11 or higher will throw an exception, without raising an InfoMessage event.

Usage

```
Private Sub myOleDbConnection_InfoMessage(ByVal sender As Object, & _
   ByVal e As System.Data.OleDb.OleDbInfoMessageEventArgs) & _
   Handles myOleDbConnection.InfoMessage
```

Parameters

`sender`	Contains a reference to the originator of the event.
`e`	Contains the OleDbInfoMessageEventArgs object. See the table below.

Event Argument Data

e.ErrorCode	Gets the HRESULT following the ANSI SQL standard for the database.
e.Errors	Gets the collection of information/warnings sent from the data source.
e.Message	Full text of the error sent from the data source.
e.Source	The name of the object that generated the message.

Sample Code

```
Private WithEvents myOleDbConnection As New OleDbConnection()
. . .
Dim myOleDbCommand As New OleDbCommand()
Dim myConnectionString As String
myConnectionString = "Provider=SQLOLEDB;Initial Catalog=Northwind;" & _
   "Datasource=(local);Integrated Security=SSPI;"
myOleDbConnection = New OleDbConnection(myConnectionString)
myOleDbConnection.Open()
myOleDbCommand.Connection = myOleDbConnection
myOleDbCommand.CommandText = "PRINT 'Hello World'"
```

```
myOleDbCommand.ExecuteNonQuery() ' Raises the InfoMessage event below
. . .

Private Sub myOleDbConnection_InfoMessage(ByVal sender As Object, _
   ByVal e As System.Data.OleDb.OleDbInfoMessageEventArgs) _
   Handles myOleDbConnection.InfoMessage
   MessageBox.Show(e.ToString(), e.Source)
End Sub
```

Open

This method establishes a connection to the data source as specified in the ConnectionString. Before calling Open, you must ensure that the ConnectionString specifies a valid Provider and Data Source and any optional security information. The OleDbConnection will use an open connection from the connection pool if there is one available. If not, a new connection will be established to the data source. If the OleDbConnection variable goes out of scope, the connection is not implicitly closed. You will have to manage the lifetime of your connection variables manually, using Close and Dispose.

Although some validation of the ConnectionString is performed at the time it is assigned, the final test is to call the Open method. Because so many variables can affect whether your data source can be opened, it is important to wrap your Open method in a Try-Catch-Finally block to catch and handle any exceptions.

Upon a successful call to Open, the StateChange event will fire and the OleDbConnection.State property will reflect the fact that the connection is now open. These indicators are handy to use in expressions.

Usage

```
myOleDbConnection.Open()
```

Parameters

None.

Exceptions

InvalidOperationException	The connection is already open.
OleDbException	The connection could not be opened. Several reasons can cause this: 1.) Could not find the data source (server or filename) 2.) Data source is locked or offline for maintenance 3.) An invalid user or password was passed 4.) Invalid ConnectionString parameter
SystemException	The provider is invalid.

Sample Code

```
Dim myOleDbConnection As New System.Data.OleDb.OleDbConnection()
Dim myConnectionString As String
```

```
Dim i As Integer
myConnectionString = "Provider=Microsoft.Jet.OLEDB.4.0;" & _
   "Data Source=C:\Zorthwind.mdb"
myOleDbConnection.ConnectionString = myConnectionString
Try
   myOleDbConnection.Open()
Catch exInvalidOpException As InvalidOperationException
   MessageBox.Show(exInvalidOpException.ToString(), _
      "Invalid Operation Exception")
Catch myOleDbException As OleDbException
   For i = 0 To myOleDbException.Errors.Count - 1
      MessageBox.Show("Error #" + ControlChars.Tab + i.ToString() + _
      ControlChars.Cr + "Message" + ControlChars.Tab + _
      myOleDbException.Errors(i).Message + ControlChars.Cr + _
      "Native" + ControlChars.Tab + _
      myOleDbException.Errors(i).NativeError.ToString() + _
      ControlChars.Cr + "Source" + ControlChars.Tab + _
      myOleDbException.Errors(i).Source + ControlChars.Cr + _
      "SQL" + ControlChars.Tab + _
      myOleDbException.Errors(i).SQLState + ControlChars.Cr, _
      "OleDb Exception")
   Next i
Catch ex As Exception
   MessageBox.Show(ex.ToString(), "Other Exception")
Finally
   myOleDbConnection.Close()
End Try
```

Provider

The Provider property returns the name of a connection's OLE DB provider. The connection does not need to be open. This read-only property will be empty, unless the provider has been assigned in one of two possible ways:

1. Pass a connection string, including the provider, to the OleDbConnection constructor during creation.
2. Assign the connection string, including the provider, directly to OleDbConnection.ConnectionString.

Usage

```
myString = myOleDbConnection.Provider
```

Parameters

None.

ReleaseObjectPool

The ReleaseObjectPool method signals to ADO.NET that the user is finished pooling the OleDbConnection objects and that the last underlying OLE DB provider may be released. To conserve resources, you should call this method when you are done using any OleDbConnection objects.

Calling this method by itself does not guarantee that the connection will be released from the pool. You must *Close* the connection, wait for it to time out, and then wait for or invoke garbage collection. See the sample code below for the exact order of events.

Usage

```
myOleDbConnection.ReleaseObjectPool()
```

Parameters

None.

Exceptions

None.

Sample Code

```
Dim myOleDbConnection As New System.Data.OleDb.OleDbConnection()
Dim myConnectionString As String
myConnectionString = "Provider=Microsoft.Jet.OLEDB.4.0;" & _
   "Data Source=C:\Northwind.mdb"
myOleDbConnection.ConnectionString = myConnectionString
myOleDbConnection.Open()
myOleDbConnection.Close()
' Allow enough time for the Connection to time out of the pool
myOleDbConnection.ReleaseObjectPool()
' Wait for or invoke garbage collection
```

ServerVersion

The ServerVersion property returns the major, minor, and release version of the connected database server. An open connection must be established in order to query the ServerVersion.

ServerVersion is returned in the format of XX.YY.ZZZZ:

XX	Major version
YY	Minor version
ZZZZ	Release version. A provider-specific description may also be appended to the release version.

Usage

```
myString = myOleDbConnection.ServerVersion
```

Parameters

None.

Microsoft ServerVersions

Microsoft SQL Server 2000	08.00.0194
Microsoft SQL Server 2000 SP1	08.00.0384
Microsoft SQL Server 2000 SP2	08.00.0534
Microsoft Access 2000	04.00.0000
Microsoft Access XP	04.00.0000

Exceptions

InvalidOperationException	The connection is closed.

Sample Code

```
Dim myOleDbConnection As New System.Data.OleDb.OleDbConnection()
Dim myConnectionString As String
myConnectionString = "Provider=Microsoft.Jet.OLEDB.4.0;" & _
   "Data Source=C:\Northwind.mdb"
myOleDbConnection.ConnectionString = myConnectionString
myOleDbConnection.Open()
MessageBox.Show(myOleDbConnection.ServerVersion,"Jet Version")
myOleDbConnection.Close()
myConnectionString = "Provider=SQLOLEDB;Initial Catalog=Northwind;" & _
   "Datasource=Neptune;Integrated Security=SSPI;"
myOleDbConnection.ConnectionString = myConnectionString
myOleDbConnection.Open()
MessageBox.Show(myOleDbConnection.ServerVersion,"SQL Version")
myOleDbConnection.Close()
```

State

The State property returns the current disposition of the connection, which could be one of several values: broken, closed, connecting, executing, fetching, or open. The values can be bitwise combinations of the various state properties, although some combinations are illogical and not supported.

You can also detect state changes by trapping the StateChange event on the OleDbConnection object. The StateChange event fires when the connection changes from closed to open or from open to closed. Because the OleDbConnection Open method executes synchronously, either approach will work similarly.

Usage

```
myConnectionState = myOleDbConnection.State
myString = myOleDbConnection.State.ToString()
```

Parameters

None.

ConnectionState Enumeration

Broken (16)	The connection has been broken. This state is not supported.
Closed (0)	(Default) The connection is closed.
Connecting (2)	The connection is connecting. This state is not supported.
Executing (4)	The connection is executing a command. This state is not supported.
Fetching (8)	Data is being retrieved. This state is not supported.
Open (1)	The connection is currently open.

Exceptions

InvalidOperationException	The connection is closed.

Sample Code

```
Dim myOleDbConnection As New System.Data.OleDb.OleDbConnection()
Dim myConnectionString As String
myConnectionString = "Provider=SQLOLEDB;Initial Catalog=Northwind;" & _
   "Datasource=Neptune;Integrated Security=SSPI;"
myOleDbConnection.ConnectionString = myConnectionString
myOleDbConnection.Open()
MessageBox.Show(myOleDbConnection.State.ToString(),"Connection State")
myOleDbConnection.Close()
MessageBox.Show(myOleDbConnection.State.ToString(),"Connection State")
```

StateChange

The StateChange event fires whenever the OleDbConnection's state changes, such as when it opens or closes. It is important to know that by the time the event is raised, the state has already changed. Any exceptions raised from within the event handler is propagated up to the caller of the Open or Close method.

Usage

```
Private Sub myOleDbConnection_StateChange(ByVal sender As Object, & _
   ByVal e As System.Data.StateChangeEventArgs) & _
   Handles myOleDbConnection.StateChange
```

Parameters

`sender`	Contains a reference to the originator of the event.
`e`	Contains the StateChangeEventArgs object. See the table that follows.

Event Argument Data

e.CurrentState	A ConnectionState enumeration representing the new, current state of the connection. The change has already occurred.
e.OriginalState	A ConnectionState enumeration representing the previous, original state of the connection.

ConnectionState Enumeration

Broken (16)	The connection has been broken. This state is not supported.
Closed (0)	(Default) The connection is closed.
Connecting (2)	The connection is connecting. This state is not supported.
Executing (4)	The connection is executing a command. This state is not supported.
Fetching (8)	Data is being retrieved. This state is not supported.
Open (1)	The connection is currently open.

Exceptions

InvalidOperationException	The connection is closed.

Sample Code

```
Private WithEvents myOleDbConnection As New OleDbConnection()
. . .
Dim myOleDbCommand As New OleDbCommand()
Dim myConnectionString As String
myConnectionString = "Provider=SQLOLEDB;Initial Catalog=Northwind;" & _
   "Datasource=(local);Integrated Security=SSPI;"
myOleDbConnection = New OleDbConnection(myConnectionString)
myOleDbConnection.Open()
myOleDbConnection.Close()
. . .
Private Sub myOleDbConnection_StateChange(ByVal sender As Object, _
   ByVal e As System.Data.StateChangeEventArgs) _
   Handles myOleDbConnection.StateChange
   MessageBox.Show("From " & e.OriginalState.ToString() & " to " & _
   e.CurrentState.ToString(), "State Changed")
End Sub
```

System.Data.OleDb.OleDbDataAdapter

The OleDbDataAdapter provides an interface between an OLE DB data source and the .NET Framework data-handling objects. The DataAdapter both retrieves data from a data source, populating a DataSet with data and constraints, and resolves updates, additions, and deletions back to the data source. The DataAdapter depends on the Connection object to provide the connection to the data source and the Command object to retrieve data from and resolve changes to the data source.

The DataAdapter uses the SelectCommand object to define which data to draw from the data source. This OleDbCommand object may reference a valid SQL statement, a stored procedure (with or without parameters), or, in the case of the OleDb-DataAdapter only, a single table name from which all columns are returned (equivalent to "SELECT * from myTable"). See OleDbCommand for more information on how to properly define Command objects. In order to process changes to the data source, the DataAdapter moves through the rows, one by one, calling the appropriate Insert, Update, Delete Command for every row in which changes have occurred. If an OleDbCommand object has not been specified for the DataAdapter, and if it is required during a Fill or Update operation, an exception will be raised. See Fill and Update in the text that follows for more information.

Multiple DataAdapters can be used with the same DataSet. In this way, several disparate data sources can be included in one DataSet. For instance, a customer list drawn from a small MS Access database could be combined with orders drawn from a SQL Server 2000 database into one DataSet. Data relationships between the two tables could be created internally to the DataSet, and the resulting in-memory database could be queried using SQL. Changes to the DataSet are then saved back to the multiple data sources by calling the Update method of each DataAdapter.

If a DataAdapter's SelectCommand returns more than one result set, each set is inserted into the DataSet as a new DataTable.

Constructors

```
Dim myOleDbDataAdapter As New OleDbDataAdapter()
Dim myOleDbDataAdapter As New OleDbDataAdapter(OleDbCommand)
Dim myOleDbDataAdapter As New OleDbDataAdapter(String, OleDbConnection)
Dim myOleDbDataAdapter As New OleDbDataAdapter(String, String2)
```

Parameters

`OleDbCommand`	An OleDbCommand object to assign to the Select-Command property.
`String`	A valid SQL SELECT statement to be used to select data from the data source. This string is assigned to the Select-Command.CommandText property.
`OleDbConnection`	The OleDbConnection object representing the connection to the data source.
`String2`	A valid connection string used to identify the data source.

OleDbDataAdapter Sample Code

```
Dim myOleDbConnection As New System.Data.OleDb.OleDbConnection()
Dim myOleDbDataAdapter As System.Data.OleDb.OleDbDataAdapter
Dim myOleDbCommand As System.Data.OleDb.OleDbCommand
Dim myDataSet As System.Data.DataSet
Dim myConnectionString As String
Dim intRowsUpdated As Int32
' Establish connection to the Northwind Database (Access 2000/XP)
myConnectionString = "Provider=Microsoft.Jet.OLEDB.4.0;" & _
   "Data Source=C:\Northwind.mdb;"
Try
   myOleDbConnection.ConnectionString = myConnectionString
   myOleDbConnection.Open()
Catch myOleDbException As OleDbException
   MessageBox.Show(myOleDbException.Message, "OleDbException Thrown")
Catch myException As Exception
   MessageBox.Show(myException.Message, "Other Exception")
End Try
' Create the OleDbCommand to use
myOleDbCommand = New OleDbCommand("SELECT * FROM Customers", _
   myOleDbConnection)
myOleDbCommand.CommandTimeout = 30
' Create the OleDbDataAdapter to use
myOleDbDataAdapter = New OleDbDataAdapter()
myOleDbDataAdapter.SelectCommand = myOleDbCommand
' Create an OleDbCommandBuilder to fill Insert, Update, Delete Commands
Dim myCmdBldr As OleDbCommandBuilder = _
   New OleDbCommandBuilder(myOleDbDataAdapter)
' We can see the Commands that the CommandBuilder has generated for us
```

```
' Warning: building myCmdBldr does not fill the Insert, Update
'  and DeleteCommand properties of the OleDbDataAdapter!  This
'  is done only during the raising of the updates!!!)
MessageBox.Show("Update Command is:" + _
   myCmdBldr.GetUpdateCommand.CommandText)
MessageBox.Show("Insert Command is: " + _
   myCmdBldr.GetInsertCommand.CommandText)
MessageBox.Show("Delete Command is: " + _
   myCmdBldr.GetDeleteCommand.CommandText)
' Running this line will throw an NullReferenceException
'
' MessageBox.Show("Update Command is: " + _
'      myOleDbDataAdapter.UpdateCommand.CommandText)
' Create the DataSet to be filled with data
myDataSet = New System.Data.DataSet()
' Specify the OleDbDataAdapter's behaviors when calling Fill()
' Here we're merely using the defaults
myOleDbDataAdapter.AcceptChangesDuringFill = True
myOleDbDataAdapter.MissingMappingAction =
MissingMappingAction.Passthrough
myOleDbDataAdapter.MissingSchemaAction = MissingSchemaAction.Add
' Fill the DataSet. Note that the "Customers" here is what I
'  chose to name the table INSIDE the DataSet, and is purely
'  coincidental that it is also the same name as from the data source
myOleDbDataAdapter.Fill(myDataSet, "Customers")
' **************************************************
' Without this line of code, the RowUpdating event will not pass a valid
' Command object in the OleDbRowUpdatingEventArgs object
' Comment this line out to see the error, leave it in and watch
' everything work nicely.
'
myOleDbDataAdapter = myOleDbDataAdapter
' Edit the first field of the first row (simply add an "R")
myDataSet.Tables(0).Rows(0).BeginEdit()
myDataSet.Tables(0).Rows(0).Item(1) += "R"
myDataSet.Tables(0).Rows(0).EndEdit()
Try
   ' Note that when we filled myDataSet we set the name of the table
   ' to "Customers". That means we cannot simply pass myDataSet
   ' to the Update method, since it is looking for DataTable
   ' with the default name of "Table"
   ' Instead we must pass a DataTable, or a DataSet and the table name
   ' WRONG
   '   intRowsUpdated = myOleDbDataAdapter.Update(myDataSet)
   ' RIGHT
   '   intRowsUpdated = myOleDbDataAdapter.Update(myDataSet.Tables(0))
   '   intRowsUpdated = myOleDbDataAdapter.Update(myDataSet, "Customers")
   ' *********************************
   intRowsUpdated = myOleDbDataAdapter.Update(myDataSet.Tables(0))
Catch myOleDbException As OleDbException
   MessageBox.Show(myOleDbException.Message)
Catch myException As Exception
```

```
    MessageBox.Show(myException.Message)
End Try
' Clean up
myDataSet.Dispose()
myOleDbCommand.Dispose()
myOleDbDataAdapter.Dispose()
myOleDbConnection.Close()
```

Members

AcceptChangesDuringFill

The AcceptChangesDuringFill property (inherited from the DataAdapter object) is a Boolean value that determines whether the AcceptChanges event is fired when the Fill method is called. If the value is true, then the AcceptChanges method is called for each DataRow object as it is added to the DataTable object, leaving the DataRowState = Unchanged (2). If false, the added DataRow objects are treated as added rows, leaving the DataRowState = Added (4). See System.Data.DataRow class for more information.

The default value is True.

Usage

```
myBoolean = myOleDbDataAdapter.AcceptChangesDuringFill
myOleDbDataAdapter.AcceptChangesDuringFill = myBoolean
```

Parameters

None.

DeleteCommand

The DeleteCommand property returns or sets the OleDbCommand object representing the SQL DELETE statement used to delete records from the data source when the Update method is called. In some instances, the DeleteCommand during an Update may be automatically generated by a CommandBuilder object. Even when the CommandBuilder is used, though, this property is not filled. Instead, the CommandBuilder listens for the RowUpdating and RowUpdated events, and it provides the proper commands at that time. See System.Data.OleDb.OleDbCommand and System.Data.OleDb.OleDbCommandBuilder for more information.

Before calling the Update method, the DeleteCommand, InsertCommand, or UpdateCommand properties of the DataAdapter must be initialized with valid SQL statements or OleDbCommand objects, or an OleDbCommandBuilder object must be associated with the OleDbDataAdapter. If not, an OleDbException will be thrown.

Usage

```
myOleDbCommand = myOleDbDataAdapter.DeleteCommand
myOleDbDataAdapter.DeleteCommand = myOleDbCommand
```

or, if the default OleDbCommand is acceptable, a shorter version is:

```
myOleDbDataAdapter.DeleteCommand.CommandText = mySqlDeleteString
```

Parameters

None.

Fill

The Fill method adds or updates the rows in a DataSet, based on the SelectCommand, and returns an Int32 specifying the number of records that were added or updated. The Fill method can accept an ADO Recordset or ADO Record as an input parameter; however, this is a one-way movement of data from the ADO Recordset/Record to the .NET DataSet. Once the DataSet is loaded, any changes to the DataSet must be handled programmatically because there is not sufficient meta data in an ADO Recordset (even a disconnected one) to support the .NET meta data requirements. (Warning: In order to consume ADO Records and Recordsets, you must import TlbImp.exe into your .NET application, either directly or through a reference to the .NET COM Interop Services.)

Before calling the Fill method, the SelectCommand of the DataAdapter must be initialized with a valid SQL SELECT statement or OleDbCommand object. If not, an OleDbException will be thrown.

Fill will automatically append rows to an existing DataTable if there is no primary key defined. If there is a primary key, the Fill method will update the data in the DataTable from the data in the data source wherever matching primary keys are found.

When determining which of the possible usages to use, there are a few things to keep in mind. When you use the OleDbDataAdapter.Fill(DataSet), the DataSet will add a DataTable with the default name *Table*. When you call the DataAdapter.Update method, you may then use the Update(DataSet) because that operates only on the DataTable named *Table*. If you once name the DataTable, you must then name the DataTable in any Update commands as well, or a System.ArgumentNullException will be raised.

Usage

```
myOleDbDataAdapter.Fill(DataTable, Object)
myOleDbDataAdapter.Fill(DataSet, Object, String)
myOleDbDataAdapter.Fill(DataTable)
myOleDbDataAdapter.Fill(DataSet)
myOleDbDataAdapter.Fill(DataSet, String)
myOleDbDataAdapter.Fill(DataSet, Int32a, Int32b, String)
```

Parameters

`DataTable`	A System.Data.DataTable object to be filled.
`Object`	The source ADO Recordset or Record object (only used to fill the DataSet).
`DataSet`	A System.Data.DataSet object to be filled.
`String`	A string designating the source table.
`Int32a`	An Int32 specifying the first record to be retrieve.
`Int32b`	An Int32 specifying the maximum number of records to retrieve.

Exceptions

InvalidOperationException	You called the Fill method when Connection has not been specified.

OleDbException	You called the Fill method when either an empty or invalid SelectCommand has been set, or you called the Update method when an empty or invalid DeleteCommand, InsertCommand, or UpdateCommand has been set.

FillError

The FillError event (inherited from System.Data.Common.DbDataAdapter) is fired whenever an error is encountered during a Fill operation. The FillError event passes a reference to the source of the event (the instantiated OleDbDataAdapter object), and a System.Data.FillErrorEventArgs object with data about the error.

For more information, please see the System.Data.Common.DbDataAdapter.FillError event.

Usage

```
Private Sub myOleDbDataAdapter_FillError(ByVal sender As Object, _
   ByVal e As System.Data.FillErrorEventArgs) Handles _
   myOleDbDataAdapter.FillError
```

Parameters

`sender`	Contains a reference to the originator of the event.
`e`	Contains the FillErrorEventArgs object.

Event Argument Data

e.Continue	Gets or sets Boolean determining whether the fill operation should continue despite the error.
e.DataTable	Gets a reference to the DataTable that is currently being updated.
e.Errors	Gets an Exception object specifying the errors that occurred.
e.Values	Gets the values for the row being updated as an array of Object objects.

FillSchema

The FillSchema method (inherited from System.Data.Common.DbDataAdapter class) creates a new DataTable and fills it with the schema inherited from the data source. It then returns a DataTable containing the schema derived from the data source. The schema is configured based on the value of the SchemaType parameter. A SchemaType of Source (value = 1) applies the incoming schema to the DataSet with no transformation; Mapped applies the mappings of existing DataTable objects to the schema and then transforms the DataSet based on the transformed schema.

Usage

```
myOleDbDataAdapter.FillSchema(DataTable, SchemaType)
myOleDbDataAdapter.FillSchema(DataSet, SchemaType)
myOleDbDataAdapter.FillSchema(DataSet, SchemaType, String)
```

Parameters

`DataTable`	A System.Data.DataTable object to receive the schema.
`SchemaType`	A System.Data.SchemaType enumeration value (Mapped (2) or Source (1)).
`DataSet`	A System.Data.DataSet object to receive the schema.
`String`	A string designating the source table to be used for the schema mapping.

Exceptions

ArgumentException	The source table from which to get the schema could not be found.

GetFillParameters

The GetFillParameters method (inherited from System.Data.Common.DbDataAdapter class) returns an array of IDataParameter objects specifying user-defined parameters to be passed in a SQL SELECT command. This method can be used to verify the parameters when selecting data. This is similar to the Parameters property of the OleDbCommand object, which returns an OleDbParameterCollection (a collection of OleDbParameter objects).

Usage

```
myIDataParameterArray() = myOleDbDataAdapter.GetFillParameters()
```

Parameters

None.

Exceptions

None.

InsertCommand

The InsertCommand property returns or sets an OleDbCommand object. The command represents the SQL INSERT statement to be used to insert new records into the data source when the Update method is called. In some instances, the InsertCommand may be automatically generated by a CommandBuilder object. Even when the CommandBuilder is used, though, this property is not filled. Instead, the CommandBuilder listens for the RowUpdating and RowUpdated events and provides the proper commands at that time. See System.Data.OleDb.OleDbCommand and System.Data.OleDb.OleDbCommandBuilder for more information.

Before calling the Update method, the DeleteCommand, InsertCommand, or UpdateCommand properties of the DataAdapter must be initialized with valid SQL statements or OleDbCommand objects, or an OleDbCommandBuilder object must be associated with the OleDbDataAdapter. If not, an OleDbException will be thrown.

Usage

```
myOleDbCommand = myOleDbDataAdapter.InsertCommand
myOleDbDataAdapter.InsertCommand = myOleDbCommand
```

or, if the default OleDbCommand is acceptable, a shorter version is:

```
myOleDbDataAdapter.InsertCommand.CommandText = mySqlInsertString
```

Parameters
None.

MissingMappingAction

The MissingMappingAction property (inherited from System.Data.DataAdapter) returns or sets a MissingMappingAction enumeration value that determines what to do when the incoming data does not have a matching table or column in the current DataSet. The default value is Passthrough.

Usage

```
myMissingMappingAction = myOleDbDataAdapter.MissingMappingAction
myOleDbDataAdapter.MissingMappingAction = myMissingMappingAction
```

Parameters
None.

MissingMappingAction Enumeration

Error (3)	A System.SystemException is thrown.
Ignore (2)	Any columns or tables without mappings are ignored, returning a null reference.
Passthrough (1)	(Default) The source column or table is added to the DataSet using its original name.

MissingSchemaAction

The MissingSchemaAction property (inherited from System.Data.DataAdapter) returns or sets a MissingSchemaAction enumeration value that determines what to do when the incoming data does not have a matching schema in the current DataSet. The default value is Add.

Usage

```
myMissingSchemaAction = myOleDbDataAdapter.MissingSchemaAction
myOleDbDataAdapter.MissingSchemaAction = myMissingSchemaAction
```

Parameters
None.

MissingSchemaAction Enumeration

Add (1)	(Default) Adds the columns required to complete the schema.
AddWithKey (4)	Adds the columns and primary key information required to complete the schema. Note: The OLE DB data source must support the DBPROP_UNIQUEROWS method for this parameter to be used.
Error (3)	A System.SystemException is thrown.
Ignore (2)	Any columns without a matching schema are ignored.

RowUpdated

The RowUpdated event is raised when the Update method is called. This event fires on every row that is being added, changed, or deleted from the data source. The event occurs after the changes have been made to the data source and before AcceptChanges is called. The event passes an OleDbRowUpdatedEventArgs object to the designated event handler.

NOTE Be aware that, in Visual Basic .NET, the OleDbDataAdapter object must be declared WithEvents in order for declared event handlers to be executed (unless the AddHandler statement is used). For a complete reference of the arguments passed to this event, see System.Data.OleDb.OleDbRowUpdatedEventArgs.

Usage

```
Private Sub myOleDbDataAdapter_RowUpdated(ByVal sender As Object, _
   ByVal e As System.Data.OleDb.OleDbRowUpdatedEventArgs) _
   Handles myOleDbDataAdapter.RowUpdated
```

Parameters

`sender`	Contains a reference to the originator of the event.
`e`	Contains the OleDbRowUpdatedEventArgs object. For more information, see the section on System.Data.OleDb.OleDbRow-UpdatedEventArgs.

RowUpdating

The RowUpdating event is raised when the Update method is called. This event fires on every row that is being added, changed, or deleted from the data source. The event occurs after the changes have been made to the data source and before AcceptChanges is called. The event passes an OleDbRowUpdatingEventArgs object to the designated event handler.

NOTE Be aware that, in Visual Basic .NET, the OleDbDataAdapter object must be declared WithEvents in order for declared event handlers to be executed (unless the AddHandler statement is used). For a complete reference of the arguments passed to this event, see System.Data.OleDb.OleDbRowUpdatingEventArgs.

Usage

```
Private Sub myOleDbDataAdapter_RowUpdating(ByVal sender As Object, _
   ByVal e As System.Data.OleDb.OleDbRowUpdatingEventArgs) _
   Handles myOleDbDataAdapter.RowUpdating
```

Parameters

`sender`	Contains a reference to the originator of the event.
`e`	Contains the OleDbRowUpdatingEventArgs object. For more information, see the section on System.Data.OleDb.OleDbRow-UpdatingEventArgs.

SelectCommand

The SelectCommand property returns or sets an OleDbCommand object. The command represents the SQL SELECT statement to be used to select records from the data source when the Fill method is called. Unlike the Delete, Insert, and Update Commands, the SelectCommand cannot be automatically generated by a CommandBuilder object.

Usage

```
myOleDbCommand = myOleDbDataAdapter.SelectCommand
myOleDbDataAdapter.SelectCommand = myOleDbCommand
```

or, if the default OleDbCommand is acceptable, a shorter version is:

```
myOleDbDataAdapter.SelectCommand.CommandText = mySqlSelectString
```

Parameters

None.

TableMappings

The read-only TableMappings property returns a DataTableMappingCollection object. This collection of DataTableMapping objects maps the table and column names used by the data source to the table and column names used by the DataSet. The default value is an empty collection. These mappings are used during an Update to ensure that the proper tables and columns are updated in the data source, despite possibly different names. The DataTableMapping objects contained in the DataTableMappingCollection contain three public properties that permit access to the underlying mapping. They are the read-only ColumnMapping property, which returns the DataColumnMappingCollection object describing the mappings of the columns between the data source and DataSet; the DataSetTable property, which is used to get or set the destination DataSet table name; and the SourceTable, which gets or sets the source table from which to retrieve the data.

Usage

```
myDataTableMappingCollection = myOleDbDataAdapter.TableMappings
```

Parameters

None.

ToString

The ToString method for OleDbDataAdapter simply returns "System.Data.OleDb.OleDbDataAdapter".

Usage

```
myString = myOleDbDataAdapter.ToString()
```

Parameters

None.

Exceptions

None.

Update

The Update method calls the INSERT, UPDATE, or DELETE commands for each of the inserted, updated, or deleted rows. Several different parameters can be sent to the Update method, depending on what set of rows you'd like to update. Basically, all of them boil down to a collection of System.Data.DataRow objects. The difference is merely how they are collected and identified. One way is to send an array of DataRow objects for update. Another is to send a System.Data.DataTable, which is an object containing a collection of DataRows. Another is to pass a System.Data.DataSet object, which is a collection of DataTables and corresponding DataRows.

When calling Update with the DataSet object, you must specify on which of the DataTables you wish to perform the update. You cannot send a DataSet to the Update method and expect all contained DataTables to be updated. This can be a source of frustration for first-time users. The Update(DataSet) method will send only a DataTable with the name of "Table" for update! This is the default name given to the first DataTable loaded into the DataSet. (If no DataTable named "Table" exists, an exception is thrown.) So, if you've given your DataTable objects meaningful names, you must also pass the given name of the table to be updated.

(Note: There are no Update methods that include an ADODB Recordset because a Fill operation with an ADODB Recordset object is one-way only.)

Usage

```
myOleDbDataAdapter.Update(DataRow[])
myOleDbDataAdapter.Update(DataSet)
myOleDbDataAdapter.Update(DataTable)
myOleDbDataAdapter.Update(DataRow[], DataTableMapping)
myOleDbDataAdapter.Update(DataSet, String)
```

Parameters

`DataRow[])`	An array of System.Data.DataRow objects to be updated.
`DataSet`	A System.Data.DataSet object to be updated.
`DataTable`	A System.Data.DataTable object to be updated.
`DataTableMapping`	A System.Data.DataTableMapping that contains a mapping between the DataTable and the data source.
`String`	A string designating the source table.

Exceptions

ArgumentNullException	The source DataSet is invalid.
DBConcurrencyException	Attempt to execute an INSERT, UPDATE, or DELETE command has resulted in no records affected.
InvalidOperationException	The source DataTable is invalid.
SystemException	Either no DataRow exists to update, or no DataSet exists to update or no source DataSet exists.

UpdateCommand

The UpdateCommand property returns or sets an OleDbCommand object. The command represents the SQL UPDATE statement to be used to update records into the data source when the Update method is called. In some instances, the UpdateCommand may be automatically generated by a CommandBuilder object. Even when the CommandBuilder is used, this property is not filled. Instead, the CommandBuilder listens for the RowUpdating and RowUpdated events, and it provides the proper commands at that time. See System.Data.OleDb.OleDbCommand and System.Data.OleDb. OleDbCommandBuilder for more information.

Before calling the Update method, the DeleteCommand, InsertCommand, or UpdateCommand properties of the DataAdapter must be initialized with valid SQL statements or OleDbCommand objects, or an OleDbCommandBuilder object must be associated with the OleDbDataAdapter. If not, an OleDbException will be thrown.

Usage

```
myOleDbCommand = myOleDbDataAdapter.UpdateCommand
myOleDbDataAdapter.UpdateCommand = myOleDbCommand
```

or, if the default OleDbCommand is acceptable, a shorter version is:

```
myOleDbDataAdapter.UpdateCommand.CommandText = mySqlUpdateString
```

Parameters

None.

System.Data.OleDb.OleDbDataReader

The OleDbDataReader provides read-only, forward-only access to an OLE DB data source. Because it maintains only one record in memory at a time, there is minimal resource impact. Unlike a DataTable object, the DataReader is specifically geared toward working with a particular type of data source. Because there is no need to create a DataSet object (or other data structures found in the System.Data namespace), and the DataReader is always fully connected to the database, it is much faster than other forms of data access. It can be an excellent choice for populating list boxes or providing data for Web pages. Be aware, though, that once a DataReader has been opened, the connection it is using cannot be used by any other object, and the connection to the data source is maintained until the DataReader's Close method is called. Once the DataReader is closed, the only two properties available are IsClosed and RecordsAffected. Any calls to other properties will result in a System.InvalidOperationException being thrown.

Unlike other data access objects, the DataReader can be instantiated only by using the ExecuteReader method of a Command object, and it cannot be maintained independently of an open Connection object. The primary method for retrieving data from a DataReader is the Read method. The Read method will return FALSE when there is no further data to read; thus, it can be used as the condition in a Do While Loop. See the code sample. There are several Get methods that return the data read as a particular data type. Because no type conversions are performed when the data is read, you must ensure that the data that is read is of the proper type!

Only one DataReader can use any given Connection object at a time; however, the Command that created the DataReader may return more than one set of data. In this case, the NextResult method can be used to begin processing the next set of data. When there are no further result sets, the NextResult method will return FALSE; otherwise, it will return TRUE and load the first row of data from the next result set.

Constructors

There is no public constructor. Instead, use the ExecuteReader method of an OleDb-Command object:

```
myOleDbDataReader = myOleDbCommand.ExecuteReader()
```

Parameters

None.

OleDbDataReader Sample Code

```
Dim myOleDbConnection As System.Data.OleDb.OleDbConnection
Dim myOleDbDataReader As System.Data.OleDb.OleDbDataReader
Dim myOleDbCommand As System.Data.OleDb.OleDbCommand
Dim myConnectionString As String
Dim myDisplayString As String
Dim mySingleValue As Object
Dim mySqlString As String
Dim myValues() As Object
Dim i As Integer
'SELECT the database to connect to by changing the commenting
'  one one of the next two databases. Note that Access will
'  not be able to demonstrate the NextRecordset method.
'myConnectionString = "Provider=Microsoft.Jet.OLEDB.4.0;" & _
'   "Data Source=C:\Northwind.mdb;"
myConnectionString = "Provider=SQLOLEDB;Initial Catalog=" & _
   "Northwind;Data Source=(local);Integrated Security=SSPI"
myOleDbConnection = New OleDbConnection(myConnectionString)
Try
   myOleDbConnection.Open()
Catch myOleDbException As OleDbException
   For i = 0 To myOleDbException.Errors.Count - 1
      MessageBox.Show("Error # " & i.ToString() & _
      ControlChars.Cr & myOleDbException.Errors(i).ToString())
   Next i
Catch myException As Exception
   MessageBox.Show(myException.ToString(), "Other Exception")
End Try
' Vary SELECT statements based on provider
If myOleDbConnection.Provider = "SQLOLEDB" Then
   mySqlString = "Select * from Employees order by LastName; " & _
      "Select * from Customers"
Else
```

```
    mySqlString = "Select * from Employees order by LastName"
End If
myOleDbCommand = New OleDbCommand(mySqlString, myOleDbConnection)
' Demonstrate use of the DataReader
Try
    myOleDbDataReader = myOleDbCommand.ExecuteReader
Catch myOleDbException As OleDbException
    MessageBox.Show(myOleDbException.ToString(), "OleDbException")
Catch myException As Exception
    MessageBox.Show(myException.ToString(), "Other Exception")
End Try
' Build an ugly string returning information from Employees table
Do While myOleDbDataReader.Read()
    For i = 0 To myOleDbDataReader.FieldCount - 1
        myDisplayString += myOleDbDataReader.GetName(i).ToString() + _
            ControlChars.Tab + _
            myOleDbDataReader.GetFieldType(i).ToString() + _
            ControlChars.Tab + _
            myOleDbDataReader.GetValue(i).ToString() + _
            ControlChars.Cr
    Next
    myDisplayString += ControlChars.Cr + ControlChars.Cr
Loop
MessageBox.Show(myDisplayString)
' Read the NextResult if using SQL Server
If myOleDbConnection.Provider = "SQLOLEDB" Then
    myOleDbDataReader.NextResult()
Else
    ' Create a new DataReader with a new Select Statement
    myOleDbDataReader.Close()
    myOleDbCommand.CommandText = "Select * from Customers"
    Try
        myOleDbDataReader = myOleDbCommand.ExecuteReader
    Catch myOleDbException As OleDbException
        MessageBox.Show(myOleDbException.ToString(), "OleDbException")
    Catch myException As Exception
        MessageBox.Show(myException.ToString(), "Other Exception")
    End Try
End If
' Build a string with all the fields available in the Customers table
' Dimension the array to the proper count
ReDim myValues(myOleDbDataReader.FieldCount - 1)
myDisplayString = ""
Do While myOleDbDataReader.Read()
    ' Retrieve all of the columns into an array of Objects
    myOleDbDataReader.GetValues(myValues)
    ' We can now use a For Each since the ReDim of myValues ensures
    ' we have the right number of fields
    For Each mySingleValue In myValues
        myDisplayString += mySingleValue.ToString()
        myDisplayString += ControlChars.Tab
```

```
        Next
        myDisplayString += ControlChars.Cr + ControlChars.Cr
    Loop
    MessageBox.Show(myDisplayString)
    ' Clean up
    myOleDbDataReader.Close()
    myOleDbCommand.Dispose()
    myOleDbConnection.Close()
```

Members

Close

The Close method closes the OleDbDataReader object and allows the associated OleDbConnection object to be used by other objects. The Close method must be EXPLICITLY closed to free the Connection object. Once Close has been called, only two properties remain set: IsClosed and RecordsAffected. Calls to any other properties after closing the DataReader will return a System.InvalidOperationException.

Usage

```
myOleDbDataReader.Close()
```

Parameters

None.

Exceptions

None.

Depth

The read-only Depth property returns an Int32 specifying the level of nesting of the current row. Any row in a single table will have a value of 0. This member is of primary use when using a multidimensional data provider, data shaping provider, or XML data. In these cases, the Depth property indicates the level of nesting.

Usage

```
myInt32 = myOleDbDataReader.Depth
```

Parameters

None.

Exceptions

InvalidOperationException	The OleDbDataReader is closed.

FieldCount

The read-only FieldCount property returns an Int32 specifying the number of fields in the current row. If the DataReader does not contain a valid row, FieldCount returns a 0. A value of -1 indicates that that the SQL statement filling the DataReader was a statement that does not return rows (i.e., update).

Usage

```
myInt32 = myOleDbDataReader.FieldCount
```

Parameters

None.

GetBoolean

The GetBoolean method retrieves the value of the specified column as a Boolean value. If the column does not contain a Boolean, a System.InvalidCastException will the raised.

Usage

```
myBoolean = myOleDbDataReader.GetBoolean(Index)
```

Parameters

`Index`	The zero-based column position (Int32).

Exceptions

IndexOutOfRangeException	Requested column does not exist.
InvalidCastException	Either the value in desired column is not a Boolean value, or the column name (as String) was passed instead of the ordinal position.
InvalidOperationException	Either the OleDbDataReader is closed, or the Read method has not yet been called (no data yet exists).

GetByte

The GetByte method retrieves the value of the specified column as a Byte value. If the column does not contain a Byte, a System.InvalidCastException will the raised.

Usage

```
myByte = myOleDbDataReader.GetByte(Index)
```

Parameters

`Index`	The zero-based column position (Int32).

Exceptions

IndexOutOfRangeException	Requested column does not exist.
InvalidCastException	Either the value in desired column is not a Byte value, or the column name (as String) was passed instead of the ordinal position.
InvalidOperationException	Either the OleDbDataReader is closed, or the Read method has not yet been called (no data yet exists).

GetBytes

The GetBytes method retrieves a stream of Bytes to be loaded into a passed Byte array (buffer) and returns an Int64 specifying the actual number of Bytes read. To receive the stream of Bytes, you must pass several parameters. The first is an Int32 specifying which column in the row contains data to read. The second is an Int64 value specifying the index in the column from which to begin reading data. Because this index is zero based, passing a value of 4 in a Byte array that contains "BROTHER" would cause "T" to be the first Byte read. The third is the destination Byte array. If a null reference (or an object set to `Nothing`, if using VB) is passed, the GetBytes method will return the length of the column in bytes.

The destination Byte array may already contain data because the fourth parameter is an Int32 identifying the array index to begin filling the Byte array. Passing a 5 will begin filling at myByteArray(4). The final value specifies the number of Bytes to read into the array. Passing a number larger than the number of bytes remaining will fill the buffer with the remaining bytes and leave the difference unfilled. No errors or exceptions will be raised.

If the column doesn't contain an array of Bytes, a System.InvalidCastException will be raised.

Usage

```
myInt64 = myOleDbDataReader.GetBytes(Index, FieldIndex, _
   ByteArray(), ByteArrayIndex, Length)
```

Parameters

`Index`	The zero-based column position (Int32).
`FieldIndex`	The zero-based index within the data field to begin taking data (Int64).
`ByteArray()`	The array of Bytes to fill with data. Passing a null reference (`Nothing` in VB) causes the GetBytes method to return an Int64 specifying the length of the column, in bytes.
`ByteArrayIndex`	The starting index of the passed array of Bytes to start filling with data (Int32).
`Length`	Int32 that specifies the number of bytes to read (length). If the number exceeds the number of Bytes left, all remaining Bytes are loaded into the array, and no error or exception is raised.

Exceptions

IndexOutOfRangeException	Requested column does not exist.
InvalidCastException	Either the value in desired column is not a Byte array, or the column name (as String) was passed instead of the ordinal position.
InvalidOperationException	Either the OleDbDataReader is closed or the Read method has not yet been called (no data yet exists).

GetChar

The GetChar method retrieves the value of the specified column as a Char value. If the column does not contain a Char, a System.InvalidCastException will be raised.

Usage

```
myChar = myOleDbDataReader.GetChar(Index)
```

Parameters

`Index`	The zero-based column position (Int32).

Exceptions

IndexOutOfRangeException	Requested column does not exist.
InvalidCastException	Either the value in desired column is not a Byte value, or the column name (as String) was passed instead of the ordinal position.
InvalidOperationException	Either the OleDbDataReader is closed, or the Read method has not yet been called (no data yet exists).

GetChars

The GetChars method retrieves a stream of characters to be loaded into a passed Char array (buffer), and it returns an Int64 specifying the actual number of characters read. To receive the stream of characters, you must pass several parameters. The first is an Int32 specifying which column in the row contains data to read. The second is an Int64 value specifying the index in the column from which to begin reading data. Because this index is zero based, passing a value of 4 in a Char array that contains "BROTHER" would cause "H" to be the first Char read. The third is the passed buffer in the form of a destination Char array. If a null reference (or an object set to `Nothing` in VB) is passed, the GetChars method will return the length of the column in chars. The destination Char array may already contain data because the fourth parameter is an Int32 identifying the array index to begin filling the Char array. Passing a 5 will begin filling at myCharArray(4). The final value specifies the number of characters to read into the array. Passing a number larger than the number of characters remaining will fill the buffer with the remaining characters and leave the difference unfilled. No errors or exceptions will be raised.

If the column doesn't contain an array of characters, a System.InvalidCastException will be raised.

Usage

```
myInt64 = myOleDbDataReader.GetChars(Index, FieldIndex, _
   CharArray(), CharArrayIndex, Length)
```

Parameters

`Index`	The zero-based column position (Int32).
`FieldIndex`	The zero-based index within the data field to begin taking data (Int64).
`CharArray()`	The array of characters to fill with data. Passing a null reference (`Nothing` in VB) causes the GetChars method to return an Int64 specifying the length of the column, in characters.

`CharArrayIndex`	The starting index of the passed array of characters to start filling with data (Int32).
`Length`	Int32 that specifies the number of bytes to read (length). If the number exceeds the number of characters left, all remaining characters are loaded into the array, and no error or exception is raised.

Exceptions

IndexOutOfRangeException	Requested column does not exist.
InvalidCastException	Either the value in desired column is not a Byte array, or the column name (as String) was passed instead of the ordinal position.
InvalidOperationException	Either the OleDbDataReader is closed, or the Read method has not yet been called (no data yet exists).

GetData

The GetData method is not currently supported by .NET (as of Visual Studio .NET Beta2 release). Currently, any attempt to call this method will raise a System.InvalidOperationException. In the future, it will likely return an OleDbDataReader object, based on the data that exists in a specified column.

Usage

```
myOleDbDataReader = myOleDbDataReader.GetData(Index)
```

Parameters

`Index`	The zero-based column position (Int32).

Exceptions

InvalidOperationException	Any call to this function will currently return this exception.

GetDataTypeName

The GetDataTypeName method returns a String specifying the name of the data type in the specified column. Note that the data type returned is the OLE DB data type (or provider-specific extension) from the data source and not necessarily one of the standardized .NET data types or one of the System.Data.DbType enumerations.

Usage

```
myString = myOleDbDataReader.GetDataType(Index)
```

Parameters

`Index`	The zero-based column position (Int32).

Exceptions

IndexOutOfRangeException	Requested column does not exist.

InvalidCastException	Column name (as String) passed instead of the ordinal position.
InvalidOperationException	Either the OleDbDataReader is closed, or the Read method has not yet been called (no data yet exists).

GetDateTime

The GetDateTime method retrieves the value of the specified column as a System.DateTime value. If the column does not contain a DateTime value, a System.InvalidCastException will be raised.

Usage

```
myDateTime = myOleDbDataReader.GetDateTime(Index)
```

Parameters

`Index`	The zero-based column position (Int32).

Exceptions

IndexOutOfRangeException	Requested column does not exist.
InvalidCastException	Either the value in the desired column is not a DateTime value, or the column name, as a string, was passed instead of the ordinal position.
InvalidOperationException	Either the OleDbDataReader is closed or the Read method has not yet been called (no data yet exists).

GetDecimal

The GetDecimal method retrieves the value of the specified column as a Decimal value. If the value is not a Decimal, a System.InvalidCastException will be raised.

Usage

```
myDecimal = myOleDbDataReader.GetDecimal(Index)
```

Parameters

`Index`	The zero-based column position (Int32).

Exceptions

IndexOutOfRangeException	Requested column does not exist.
InvalidCastException	Either the value in the desired column is not a Decimal value, or the column name, as a string, was passed instead of the ordinal position.
InvalidOperationException	Either the OleDbDataReader is closed, or the Read method has not yet been called (no data yet exists).

GetDouble

The GetDouble method retrieves the value of the specified column as a Double (double-precision floating point). If the value is not a Double, a System.InvalidCastException will be raised.

Usage

```
myDouble = myOleDbDataReader.GetDouble(Index)
```

Parameters

`Index`	The zero-based column position (Int32).

Exceptions

IndexOutOfRangeException	Requested column does not exist.
InvalidCastException	Either the value in the desired column is not a Double value, or the column name, as a string, was passed instead of the ordinal position.
InvalidOperationException	Either the OleDbDataReader is closed, or the Read method has not yet been called (no data yet exists).

GetFieldType

The GetFieldType method returns a System.Type object indicating the data type of the object contained in the specified column.

The returned Type object is primarily a way to access meta data about the underlying field. To do so, it acts as a gateway to the Reflection API. Use this method to get information about the specified column's type declaration, constructors, methods, fields, properties, and events (as well as staggering amounts of other information relating to the column's Type).

This is useful when reading the columns of a row as Object objects, and you need to determine whether the retrieved Object will support a particular method. For instance, some object types support a Parse method (Char, Boolean, Int32, etc.); others do not (GUID). Reflection can be used to find out this information, without needing to enumerate all possible .NET types in a huge IF-THEN structure.

This column differs from the GetDataTypeName method in that it returns the .NET data type as a Type object, whereas the GetDataTypeName method returns a String representing the data type supported by the data source (which may not be equivalent to a .NET data type).

Usage

```
myType = myOleDbDataReader.GetType(Index)
```

Parameters

`Index`	The zero-based column position (Int32).

Exceptions

IndexOutOfRangeException	Requested column does not exist.

InvalidCastException	The column name, as a string, was passed instead of the ordinal position.
InvalidOperationException	Either the OleDbDataReader is closed, or the Read method has not yet been called (no data yet exists).

GetFloat

The GetFloat method retrieves the value of the specified column as a Float (single-precision floating point). If the value is not a Float, a System.InvalidCastException will the raised.

Usage

```
myFloat = myOleDbDataReader.GetFloat(Index)
```

Parameters

`Index`	The zero-based column position (Int32).

Exceptions

IndexOutOfRangeException	Requested column does not exist.
InvalidCastException	Either the value in the desired column is not a Float value, or the column name, as a string, was passed instead of the ordinal position.
InvalidOperationException	Either the OleDbDataReader is closed, or the Read method has not yet been called (no data yet exists).

GetGuid

The GetGuid method retrieves the value of the specified column as a System.Guid (Globally Unique Identifier). If the value is not a Guid, a System.InvalidCastException will be raised.

Usage

```
myGuid = myOleDbDataReader.GetGuid(Index)
```

Parameters

`Index`	The zero-based column position (Int32).

Exceptions

IndexOutOfRangeException	Requested column does not exist.
InvalidCastException	Either the value in the desired column is not a Guid value, or the column name, as a string, was passed instead of the ordinal position.
InvalidOperationException	Either the OleDbDataReader is closed, or the Read method has not yet been called (no data yet exists).

GetInt16

The GetInt16 method retrieves the value of the specified column as a System.Int16 (16-bit signed integer). If the value is not an Int16, a System.InvalidCastException will be raised.

Usage

```
myInt16 = myOleDbDataReader.GetInt16(Index)
```

Parameters

`Index`	The zero-based column position (Int32).

Exceptions

IndexOutOfRangeException	Requested column does not exist.
InvalidCastException	Either the value in the desired column is not an Int16 value, or the column name, as a string, was passed instead of the ordinal position.
InvalidOperationException	Either the OleDbDataReader is closed, or the Read method has not yet been called (no data yet exists).

GetInt32

The GetInt32 method retrieves the value of the specified column as a System.Int32 (32-bit signed integer). If the value is not an Int32, a System.InvalidCastException will be raised.

Usage

```
myInt32 = myOleDbDataReader.GetInt32(Index)
```

Parameters

`Index`	The zero-based column position (Int32).

Exceptions

IndexOutOfRangeException	Requested column does not exist.
InvalidCastException	Either the value in the desired column is not an Int32 value, or the column name, as a string, was passed instead of the ordinal position.
InvalidOperationException	Either the OleDbDataReader is closed, or the Read method has not yet been called (no data yet exists).

GetInt64

The GetInt64 method retrieves the value of the specified column as a System.Int64 (64-bit signed integer). If the value is not an Int64, a System.InvalidCastException will be raised.

Usage

```
myInt64 = myOleDbDataReader.GetInt64(Index)
```

Parameters

`Index`	The zero-based column position (Int32).

Exceptions

IndexOutOfRangeException	Requested column does not exist.
InvalidCastException	Either the value in the desired column is not an Int64 value, or the column name, as a string, was passed instead of the ordinal position.
InvalidOperationException	Either the OleDbDataReader is closed, or the Read method has not yet been called (no data yet exists).

GetName

The GetName method returns a String indicating the name of the specified column.

Usage

```
myString = myOleDbDataReader.GetName(Index)
```

Parameters

`Index`	The zero-based column position (Int32).

Exceptions

IndexOutOfRangeException	Requested column does not exist.
InvalidCastException	The column name, as a string, was passed instead of the ordinal position.
InvalidOperationException	Either the OleDbDataReader is closed, or the Read method has not yet been called (no data yet exists).

GetOrdinal

The GetOrdinal method retrieves the ordinal value (Int32) when passed the column name as a String. If the passed column name does not exist in the current row, a System.IndexOutOfRangeException will be raised.

Usage

```
myInt32 = myOleDbDataReader.GetOrdinal(String)
```

Parameters

`String`	A String representing the column name.

Exceptions

IndexOutOfRangeException	Requested column does not exist.
InvalidOperationException	Either the OleDbDataReader is closed, or the Read method has not yet been called (no data yet exists).

GetSchemaTable

The GetSchemaTable method retrieves a System.DataTable representing the column meta data for all of the columns in the OleDbDataReader. Each column in the OleDbDataReader is described by a row in the returned DataTable. A listing of the column values in the DataTable is shown in the text that follows.

Be aware when using the GetSchemaTable that the meta data returned by an OleDbDataReader will be different from that returned by the SqlClientDataReader. The meta data from an OleDbDataReader returns the meta data required by an OLE DB provider (plus the .NET data type as an additional column), but it is not as robust as the meta data returned by SQL Server 2000.

Be very careful when using this with OLE DB. There are many differences between OLE DB providers, and many common ones support only a few of the meta data columns. For instance, the Jet .OLEDB.4.0 driver for MS Access 2000 and XP doesn't support (among other things) things as simple as IsUnique and IsKey, as well as incorrectly returning values for NumericalPrecision and NumericalScale ("255" instead of NULL for a System.String value). In addition, all of the BaseTable information fields return NULL, even when queried against a "SELECT * from myTableName".

WARNING The OleDbDataReader.GetSchemaTable that we tested seemed very buggy. Use it at your own risk. The SqlDataReader.GetSchemaTable works well, however.

Usage

```
myDataTable = myOleDbDataReader.GetSchemaTable()
```

Parameters

None.

Metadata

DATAREADER COLUMN	OLE DB COLUMN ID	DESCRIPTION
ColumnName	DBCOLUMN_NAME	The column name (not necessarily unique). A null value (`Nothing` in VB) is returned if the column name cannot be determined.
ColumnOrdinal	DBCOLUMN_NUMBER	The ordinal column number. Bookmark Columns, if any, have a value of 0. All others begin with 1. Somewhat counter-intuitively, this means that the ColumnOrdinal cannot be used as the ordinal in the DataReader Get methods. (ColumnOrdinal –1 can sometimes be used.)

DATAREADER COLUMN	OLE DB COLUMN ID	DESCRIPTION
ColumnSize	DBCOLUMN_ COLUMNSIZE	The maximum possible length for a value in this column. This is the size of the data type in the case of fixed-length data types (such as Integers).
NumericPrecision	DBCOLUMN_PRECISION	The maximum precision of the data type of this column, if it is a numeric type. Null, if it is not numeric.
NumericScale	DBCOLUMN_SCALE	The number of digits to right of the decimal point if DbType is DBTYPE_DECIMAL or DBTYPE_NUMERIC. Otherwise, this is a null value.
DataType	None	The .NET common language runtime type of DbType.
ProviderType (DbType in documentation and pre-Beta2 release)	DBCOLUMN_TYPE	Indicates the column's OLE DB data type. If data type varies, this is DBTYPE_VARIANT. (Beta2 MSDN still calls this column DbType, but the actual name has been changed.)
IsLong	DBCOLUMNFLAGS_ ISLONG	Provider-specific. Set to TRUE if the column contains a Binary Long Object (BLOB) that contains "very long" data. The definition of "very long" is provider specific.
AllowDBNull	DBCOLUMNFLAGS_ ISNULLABLE	TRUE if the column can be set to a null value, or if the OLE DB provider cannot determine whether it can be set to a null value. FALSE, otherwise. Note: In some cases, it may be impossible to set a null value, but the provider may still contain null values.

continues

DATAREADER COLUMN	OLE DB COLUMN ID	DESCRIPTION
IsReadOnly	DBCOLUMNFLAGS_ WRITE	TRUE if column is Read-Only. FALSE, otherwise. (Note: Visual Studio .NET Beta2 help reports this as "TRUE if column can be modified; otherwise FALSE"—this is an MSDN documentation bug and should be fixed as of final release.)
IsRowVersion	DBCOLUMNFLAGS_ ISROWID	Set if the column contains a persistent row identifier that cannot be written to and has no meaningful value except to identity the row.
IsUnique	DBCOLUMN_ISUNIQUE	Returns VARIANT_TRUE if no two rows in the DataReader can have the same value in this column. Returns VARIANT_FALSE if duplicates are allowed (default). Note: IsUnique may return VARIANT_FALSE if the column is PART of a primary key group; however, it will return VARIANT_TRUE if the column is, by itself, a key or if it has a UNIQUE constraint.
IsKeyColumn	DBCOLUMN_ KEYCOLUMN	VARIANT_TRUE if the column is the primary key, or one of several columns that together make up the primary key. VARIANT_FALSE if the column is not part of a primary key.
IsAutoIncrement	DBCOLUMN_ ISAUTOINCREMENT	VARIANT_TRUE if the column values are automatically assigned to new rows in increments. VARIANT_FALSE, otherwise.
BaseSchemaName	DBCOLUMN_ BASESCHEMANAME	Name of the schema used by the column's data store. Null if the schema name can't be determined (default).

DATAREADER COLUMN	OLE DB COLUMN ID	DESCRIPTION
BaseCatalogName	DBCOLUMN_ BASECATALOGNAME	Name of the catalog used by the column's data store. Null if the catalog name can't be determined (default).
BaseTableName	DBCOLUMN_ BASETABLENAME	Name of the table used by the column's data store. Null if the table name can't be determined (default).
BaseColumnName	DBCOLUMN_ BASECOLUMNNAME	Name of the column used by the column's data store. If an alias was used, this may be different from the ColumnName value. Null if the column name can't be determined or the column is derived (default).

Exceptions

InvalidOperationException	The OleDbDataReader is closed.

GetString

The GetString method retrieves the value of the specified column as a String. If the value is not a String, a System.InvalidCastException will be raised.

Usage

```
myString = myOleDbDataReader.GetString(Index)
```

Parameters

`Index`	The zero-based column position (Int32).

Exceptions

IndexOutOfRangeException	Requested column does not exist.
InvalidCastException	Either the value in the desired column is not a String value, or the column name, as a string, was passed instead of the ordinal position.
InvalidOperationException	Either the OleDbDataReader is closed, or the Read method has not yet been called (no data yet exists).

GetTimeSpan

The GetTimeSpan method retrieves the value of the specified column as a System. TimeSpan object. If the value is not a TimeSpan, a System.InvalidCastException will be raised. (A TimeSpan is a type that represents an interval of time, measured in

100-nanosecond increments. A TimeSpan does not maintain a Start and End time or date, simply the number of "ticks" (or 100-nanosecond increments) that has been passed to it. It does, however, have several methods allowing retrieval of Days, Hours, Milliseconds, etc.)

Usage

```
myTimeSpan = myOleDbDataReader.GetTimeSpan(Index)
```

Parameters

Index	The zero-based column position (Int32).

Exceptions

IndexOutOfRangeException	Requested column does not exist.
InvalidCastException	Either the value in the desired column is not a TimeSpan value, or the column name, as a string, was passed instead of the ordinal position.
InvalidOperationException	Either the OleDbDataReader is closed, or the Read method has not yet been called (no data yet exists).

GetValue

The GetValue method retrieves the value of the specified column in its native type (inherited from Object). Because every data type in the .NET Framework inherits from Object, any value retrieved from the GetValue method can be treated as an Object. Basically, this method is an easy way to retrieve a column of data, especially if you don't know beforehand what the column will return.

Usage

```
myObject = myOleDbDataReader.GetValue(Index)
```

Parameters

`Index`	The zero-based column position (Int32).

Exceptions

IndexOutOfRangeException	Requested column does not exist.
InvalidCastException	The column name, as a string, was passed instead of the ordinal position.
InvalidOperationException	Either the OleDbDataReader is closed, or the Read method has not yet been called (no data yet exists).

GetValues

The GetValues method retrieves an array of values in their native type (inherited from Object) and returns an Int32 specifying the number of values retrieved. The length of the array need not be the same as the number of fields to retrieve. If the length of the array is larger than the number of fields, all of the available fields will be filled in the lower indices of the array. If the array length is smaller than the number of fields, the array is filled to capacity with the first fields of the array.

NOTE When dealing with dynamic arrays, you can also use ReDim myArray(myOleDbDataReader.FieldCount - 1) to fit the number of fields exactly.

If you know the data types in the row are all a particular type, you can use an array of that type as the buffer array. Be aware that a System.ArrayTypeMismatchException will be raised if the types do not match. This includes any NULL values in the data source! Therefore, an exception can be thrown if the data source allows NULLs, even if the type of the field matches the type of the array.

Usage

```
myInt32= myOleDbDataReader.GetValues(myObjectArray)
```

Parameters

`myObjectArray`	An array of objects to fill with data from the row; also known as the buffer.

Exceptions

ArgumentNullException	The array of objects is a null reference; `Nothing` in VB.
ArrayTypeMismatchException	Buffer array received a value of a different type. This can occur when the buffer array is of a type descending from Object.
InvalidCastException	Parameter passed is not an array of Objects.
InvalidOperationException	Either the OleDbDataReader is closed, or the Read method has not yet been called (no data yet exists).

IsClosed

The read-only IsClosed property returns a Boolean specifying whether the DataReader is currently closed. IsClosed returns TRUE if the DataReader has been closed, FALSE if it is open. This property will not raise an Exception if the OleDbDataReader is closed.

Usage

```
myBoolean = myOleDbDataReader.IsClosed
```

Parameters

None.

IsDBNull

The IsDBNull method retrieves a Boolean specifying whether the specified column contains a nonexistent or missing value (DBNull). This is not equivalent to the data source having NULL assigned as a value. This method allows a program to differentiate between an assigned value of null and a field that has not yet been instantiated with any value (empty). Some data sources are unable to differentiate between empty and null; in that case, this value will return a TRUE or FALSE depending on the behavior of the data source.

Usage

```
myBoolean = myOleDbDataReader.IsDBNull(Index)
```

Parameters

`Index`	The zero-based column position (Int32).

Exceptions

IndexOutOfRangeException	Requested column does not exist.
InvalidCastException	The column name, as a string, was passed instead of the ordinal position.
InvalidOperationException	Either the OleDbDataReader is closed, or the Read method has not yet been called (no data yet exists).

NextResult

The NextResult method moves to the next set of data. (If a batch SQL statement returning more than one set of data was passed in the creation of the DataReader. It returns a Boolean TRUE if there is another set of data available, and a Boolean FALSE if the last set of data has been reached. Once the new data set is prepared, the position is set at just prior to the first record (requiring Read to be called to begin accessing data).

Usage

```
myBoolean = myOleDbDataReader.NextResult()
```

Parameters

None.

Exceptions

InvalidOperationException	The OleDbDataReader is closed.

Read

The Read method moves to the next record and returns a Boolean TRUE if one exists or a Boolean FALSE if the last record has been reached. After the DataReader has been created, the position is set just prior to the first record. Thus, a Read method must be called prior to accessing any of the data.

Usage

```
myBoolean = myOleDbDataReader.Read()
```

Parameters

None.

Exceptions

InvalidOperationException	The OleDbDataReader is closed.

RecordsAffected

The read-only RecordsAffected property returns an Int32 specifying the number of records that were affected during the use of the DataReader. Because an OleDb-DataReader is read only, the only time this will have a positive value is when the Ole-DbCommand.CommandText manipulates the data in some way.

Usage

```
myInt32 = myOleDbDataReader.RecordsAffected
```

Parameters

None.

Exceptions

InvalidOperationException	The OleDbDataReader is closed.

System.Data.OleDb.OleDbError

The OleDbError class communicates an individual warning or error generated by an OLE DB data source. In nearly all circumstances, an OleDbError is automatically created within an OleDbErrorCollection object, which is contained within an OleDbException object. This is true even if there is only one OleDbError class within the OleDbErrorCollection object. Because this class is automatically generated by the OleDbDataAdapter, it has no public constructors.

The OleDbException, OleDbErrorCollection, and OleDbError objects are all closely related. In the case of the OLE DB data provider, they are created only as sets of objects. Whenever a data access situation occurs that cannot be handled by the OLE DB data provider, an OleDbException is thrown, with an OleDbErrorCollection as its Errors property. The created OleDbErrorCollection will contain at least one OleDbError.

An OleDbError severity level that is too high may cause the OleDbConnection to be closed. If this is the case, you may reopen the database connection and continue working. Because of this behavior, be aware of trapping and dealing with an error, then later experiencing a closed OleDbConnection. This can be especially difficult to track down with other objects that depend on the connection. For instance, closing an OleDbConnection will cause an OleDbDataReader to call its Close method automatically. Reconnecting an OleDbConnection will still leave the OleDbDataReader closed.

There are literally thousands of different errors that can be raised from the data source. Due to the sheer number of OLE DB data sources and the multitude of errors and warnings each one can generate, it is beyond the scope of this book to enumerate all of them. For additional information, please see the documentation specific to your data source.

Constructors

There is no public constructor.

Parameters

None.

OleDbError Sample Code

```
Public Sub DisplayOleDbErrors(ByVal myOleDbException As OleDbException)
   Dim myError As OleDbError
   For Each myError In myOleDbException.Errors
      MessageBox.Show("Error Properties - " + ControlChars.Cr _
         + "Message: " + myError.Message + ControlChars.Cr _
         + "Native: " + myError.NativeError.ToString() + ControlChars.Cr _
         + "Source: " + myError.Source + ControlChars.Cr _
         + "SQL: " + myError.SQLState)
   Next
End Sub
```

Members

Message

The read-only Message property returns a short, human-readable description of the error as a String.

Usage

```
myString = myOleDbError.Message
```

Parameters

None.

NativeError

The read-only NativeError property returns the data source-specific error code as an Int32. To find further information on a specific error number, see the documentation included with the data source.

Usage

```
myInt32 = myOleDbError.NativeError
```

Parameters

None.

Source

The read-only Source property returns a String containing the name of the provider that generated the error.

Usage

```
myString = myOleDbError.Source
```

Parameters
None.

SQLState

The read-only SQLState property returns a String containing the five-character ANSI SQL error code for the data source. The SQLState originated as a set of common ODBC error messages. This enables errors to be shared across a large number of data providers and limits the number of provider-specific errors that must be considered. There are now standards defined in SQL-92, ISO SQL, and ODBC.

Usage

```
myString = myOleDbError.SQLState
```

Parameters
None.

ToString

The ToString method is overridden to return information relating to the OleDbError. The returned String contains the error message and stack trace. It is often simpler to use than constructing your own string with error information; the drawback is that it doesn't contain all of the information that you may need.

Usage

```
myString = myOleDbError.ToString()
```

Parameters
None.

Exceptions
None.

System.Data.OleDb.OleDbErrorCollection

The OleDbErrorCollection is created automatically by the OleDbException object to hold one or more OleDbError objects. It is a relatively simple collection object with only three native members. These are the Count and Item properties and the CopyTo method, which converts the OleDbErrorCollection to an array.

The OleDbException, OleDbErrorCollection, and OleDbError objects are all closely related. In the case of the OLE DB data provider, they are created only as sets of objects. Whenever a data access situation occurs that cannot be handled by the OLE DB data provider, an OleDbException is thrown, with an OleDbErrorCollection as its Errors property. The created OleDbErrorCollection will contain at least one OleDbError.

Constructors

There is no public constructor.

Parameters

None.

OleDbErrorCollection Sample Code

```
For example usage of the OleDbErrorCollection object,
see the example code for the OleDbError object.
```

Members

CopyTo

The CopyTo method copies the OleDbError objects into a passed Array, starting at the designated index within the Array. Because you can begin at any index within an array, you can create a single array with Error objects received from many different exceptions, each subsequent exception object copying the errors to a later part of the array.

Usage

`myOleDbErrorCollection.CopyTo(myArray, Index)`

Parameters

`myArray`	The passed array to fill with OleDbError objects.
`Index`	Location to begin filling array. (Example: Passing a 3 will fill arrayBuffer(3) with the first OleDbError object.)

Exceptions

ArgumentException	The sum of intIndex and the number of elements in the OleDbErrorCollection is greater than the length of arrayBuffer.
ArgumentNullException	arrayBuffer is null (`Nothing` in Visual Basic).
ArgumentOutOfRangeException	The intIndex is not valid for the passed buffer array.

Sample Code

```
Public Sub DemoCopyToMethod(ByVal myOleDbException As OleDbException)
    Dim myOleDbErrorCol As OleDbErrorCollection = _
        myOleDbException.Errors
    Dim myArray(myOleDbErrorCol.Count - 1) As Object
    myArray.Initialize()
    myOleDbErrorCol.CopyTo(myArray, 0)
    'myArray is now filled with the OleDbError objects
    '  any Array methods are available, such as Sort and Reverse
    myArray.Sort(myArray)
    myArray.Reverse(myArray)
```

```
        'now show them in reverse sorted order.
        Dim i As Int32
        For i = 0 To myArray.Length - 1
            MessageBox.Show(myArray(i).ToString())
        Next
    End Sub
```

Count

The read-only Count property returns an Int32 specifying the number of OleDbError objects contained in the collection. Because all arrays in .NET are zero based, Count returns a number that is one greater than the highest available index ordinal in any array. Because there is always at least one OleDbError object in this collection, this property will return at least 1.

Usage

```
myInt32 = myOleDbErrorCollection.Count
```

Parameters

None.

Item

The read-only Item property returns an OleDbError object from the collection as indicated by the Index parameter. This is the default property of the OleDbErrorCollection. Placing the index directly after the OleDbErrorCollection is possible, as a shortcut.

Usage

```
myOleDbError = myOleDbErrorCollection.Item(Index)
myOleDbError = myOleDbErrorCollection(Index)
```

Parameters

`Index`	Int32 valued index of the OleDbError object to retrieve.

System.Data.OleDb.OleDbException

The OleDbException is thrown whenever the OLE DB data source returns an error or a warning. The OleDbException.Errors collection will always contain at least one OleDbError object that provides detailed information on the error or warning thrown by the data source.

If the error returned is of high severity, the OleDbConnection may be closed. Please see OleDbError for more information on the possible consequences.

The OleDbException class has many members that can be of great use in tracking down errors. For instance, the InnerException member will return an Exception object or a subclass that contains the exception that raised this exception, if there has been a chain of errors. Similarly, the GetBaseException will return the Exception that first caused the chain of Exceptions to be initiated. The ToString method is overridden to provide the full name of this Exception, as well as possibly returning the error message, the name of the inner exception, and the stack trace.

Many of these properties are inherited from the System.Exception class; however, they will be covered next because of their usefulness.

Constructors

There is no public constructor.

Parameters

None.

OleDbException Sample Code

```
Dim myOleDbConnection As OleDbConnection
Dim myConnectionString As String
' Connect to a misspelled Northwind database
myConnectionString = "Provider=Microsoft.Jet.OLEDB.4.0;" & _
   "Data Source=C:\Zorthwind.mdb"
Try
   ' Since some validation is done during the assignment
   ' of the connection string, we'll include the creation
   ' of the new OleDbConnection within the Try-Catch.
   myOleDbConnection = New OleDbConnection(myConnectionString)
   myOleDbConnection.Open()
Catch myOleDbException As OleDbException
   ' Show the exception's major data
   MessageBox.Show(myOleDbException.ToString())
   ' Show a bit more detail
   MessageBox.Show("OleDbException Information" + ControlChars.Cr + _
      "Message:    " + myOleDbException.Message + ControlChars.Cr + _
      "Source:     " + myOleDbException.Source + ControlChars.Cr + _
      "ErrorCode:  " + myOleDbException.ErrorCode.ToString() + _
      ControlChars.Cr + _
      "HelpLink:   " + myOleDbException.HelpLink + ControlChars.Cr + _
      "StackTrace: " + myOleDbException.StackTrace)
   ' Display the InnerException if there is one
   If Not myOleDbException.InnerException Is Nothing Then
      MessageBox.Show("The InnerException info is " + _
         ControlChars.Cr + myOleDbException.InnerException.ToString())
   End If
   ' If the BaseException is not equal to the current exception,
   ' then display it as well.
   If Not myOleDbException.Equals(myOleDbException.GetBaseException) _
   Then
      MessageBox.Show("The base exception for this " + _
         "exception chain is : " + ControlChars.Cr + _
         myOleDbException.GetBaseException.ToString())
   End If
   ' Finally, show all of the individual errors that have been passed
```

```
    ' in the Errors collection. See example code for the OleDbError
    ' object for the DisplayOleDbErrors source code
    DisplayOleDbErrors(myOleDbException)
Catch myOtherException As Exception
    MessageBox.Show(myOtherException.ToString())
End Try
```

Members

ErrorCode

The read-only ErrorCode property (inherited from System.Runtime.InteropServices.ExternalException) returns an Int32 specifying the Win32 or HRESULT error identification number. This number is generated by the Windows operating system. For a list of possible errors, see the Windows help documentation.

Usage

```
myInt32 = myOleDbException.ErrorCode
```

Parameters

None.

Errors

The read-only Errors property returns an OleDbErrorCollection object containing all of the errors generated by the OLE DB provider or data source. The OleDbErrorCollection will contain at least one OleDbError. This property contains the majority of the information relating to the error raised by the OLE DB provider.

Usage

```
myOleDbErrorCollection = myOleDbException.Errors
```

Parameters

None.

GetBaseException

The GetBaseException method returns an Exception object containing the original exception. To return the original exception, it traverses the chain of InnerException objects. If the InnerException property of the current exception is null, GetBaseException will return a reference to the current Exception object.

To determine only the parent exception to the current exception, use the InnerException property.

Usage

```
myException = myOleDbException.GetBaseException()
```

Parameters

None.

Exceptions

None.

GetObjectData

The GetObjectData method (inherited from System.Exception) fills the passed SerializationInfo buffer object with information about the Exception object. There is no value returned by this method. Depending on the passed StreamingContext object, this method can be used to serialize the object to a stream or read serialization from a stream.

Because it deals mainly with serialization and not data access, further discussion of this property is beyond the scope of this book.

Usage

```
myOleDbException.GetObjectData(SerializationInfo, StreamingContext)
```

Parameters

`SerializationInfo`	A System.Runtime.Serialization.SerializationInfo buffer object to be filled with the exception's serialization data.
`StreamingContext`	A System.Runtime.Serialization.StreamingContext object specifying the stream to write the serialization info to or read the information from.

Exceptions

ArgumentNullException	The passed SerializationInfo buffer object is null (`Nothing` in VB).

HelpLink

The HelpLink property (inherited from Exception) returns or sets a String linking to a help file associated with the OleDbException. The HelpLink is formatted as a Uniform Resource Name (URN) or Uniform Resource Locator (URL). An example of this property that points to the MSDN help available with Visual Studio .NET would be: `ms-help://MS.VSCC/MS.MSDNVS/cpref/html/exceptionclasshelplinktopic.htm`.

The HelpLink is often not set, so it is wise to verify both that the HelpLink property itself is not an empty string and that the HelpLink points to a valid help file before exposing the HelpLink to a user of your program.

Usage

```
myString = myOleDbException.HelpLink
myOleDbException.HelpLink = myString
```

Parameters

None.

InnerException

The read-only InnerException property (inherited from Exception) returns the Exception object linking to a previous exception that caused the current exception to be thrown, if any, or a null value (`Nothing` in VB), if not. This permits a chain of InnerException objects to be generated, allowing a program to trace the exception chain all the way to the root exception. Be aware that many of the OleDbException exceptions do not have a parent exception, causing many InnerException values to be null.

For example, assume an OleDbException is thrown by the OleDbConnection.Open method when the database specified in the ConnectionString could not be found. Your code catches this exception and generates a myOwnDataBaseNotFoundException. Later code that catches the myOwnDataBaseNotFoundException can use the InnerException property to retrieve the OleDbException that triggered the new exception. This InnerException object can then be used to extract further information that may have been hidden by the myOwnDataBaseNotFoundException.

To find the base exception that originally was fired, use the GetBaseException method.

Usage

```
myException = myOleDbException.InnerException
```

Parameters

None.

Sample Code

```
' Accepts any Exception to subroutine, so recursion is possible
Public Sub ViewInnerExceptions(ByVal myException As Exception)
    'immediately leave subroutine if InnerException is null
    If myException.InnerException Is Nothing Then Exit Sub
    Dim myInnerException As Exception = myException.InnerException
    MessageBox.Show("InnerException Information" + ControlChars.Cr _
        + "Message:    " + myInnerException.Message + ControlChars.Cr _
        + "Source:     " + myInnerException.Source + ControlChars.Cr _
        + "HelpLink:   " + myInnerException.HelpLink + ControlChars.Cr _
        + "StackTrace: " + myInnerException.StackTrace)
    'recurse if necessary
    If Not myInnerException.InnerException Is Nothing Then
        ViewInnerExceptions(myInnerException)
    End If
End Sub
```

Message

The read-only Message property returns a String describing the first error that caused the exception. This property is merely a wrapper that allows simple access to the OleDbError.Message property of the first OleDbError contained in the Errors collection property.

Because it provides information only from the first error, use this property cautiously when building robust error handling.

Usage

```
myString = myOleDbException.Message
```

Parameters

None.

Source

The read-only Source property returns a String containing the name of the provider that generated the first error. This property is merely a wrapper that allows simple access to the OleDbError.Source property of the first OleDbError contained in the Errors collection property.

Because it provides information only from the first error, use this property cautiously when building robust error handling.

Usage

```
myString = myOleDbException.Source
```

Parameters

None.

StackTrace

The read-only StackTrace property returns a String containing a textual representation of the stack trace. The stack trace reports all of the methods that are in execution at the time just prior to the execution being thrown. It is read from top to bottom with the latest method in execution at the top.

The StackTrace can be invaluable in tracing difficult-to-find bugs because it provides a way to see all of the methods that could have led up to the error.

TIP To see the stack trace programmatically when no exception has been raised, use the Environment.StackTrace property.

Usage

```
myString = myOleDbException.StackTrace
```

Parameters

None.

TargetSite

The read-only TargetSite property returns an object inheriting from System.Reflection.MethodBase that contains a reference to the method that caused the error to be thrown.

This property is primarily used to programmatically find information about the method that raised the exception. The returned object will provide information, such as the methods parameters and return type, and whether the method is virtual, a constructor, public, private, etc. Because it deals mainly with reflection and not data access, further discussion of this property is beyond the scope of this book.

Usage

```
myMethodBase = myOleDbException.TargetSite
```

Parameters

None.

ToString

The ToString method is overridden to return information relating to the OleDbException. The returned String contains the full class name and also the error message, name of the inner exception, and stack trace, if they exist. If the error message is provided, it is the error message of the first OleDbError in the Errors collection.

Usage

```
myString = myOleDbException.ToString()
```

Parameters

None.

Exceptions

None.

System.Data.OleDb. OleDbInfoMessageEventArgs

The OleDbInfoMessageEventArgs class provides data for the OleDbConnection.InfoEvent event. This event is sent through an OleDbConnection object whenever the data source sends warnings or information to the .NET data provider. Because this class is automatically generated by the OleDbConnection, it has no public constructors.

Because many of the warnings and pieces of information sent from the data source will not throw an exception, the only way to receive notification of these events is by declaring a method that handles the OleDbConnection.InfoEvent event. In Visual Basic .NET, you must manually add a handler (using the AddHandler statement) or ensure that the OleDbConnection object is declared WithEvents. In C#, no special declaration is required, as it is implicit in object declaration.

Not all OLE DB data sources will behave the same when confronted with a statement that is not understood. Some will merely raise an InfoEvent with a given statement; others will throw an exception. The example that follows is one such case. The Microsoft.Jet.OLEDB.4.0 data provider will throw an exception, while the SQLOLEDB.1 data provider will raise the InfoMessage event.

Constructors

There is no public constructor.

Parameters

None.

OleDbInfoMessageEventArgs Sample Code

```
' To demonstrate the OleDbInfoMessageEventArgs class,
' we'll create a procedure to raise the OleDbConnection.InfoEvent event,
' and another to handle the event and demonstrate the passed
' OleDbInfoMessageEventArgs object. In this case, the data
' provider (SQL Server) will return a "General Warning" '
' (SQLState "01000"). (Use the SQLOLEDB data provider to raise
' the InfoMessage event. The Microsoft.Jet.OLEDB.4.0 will not
' raise the InfoMessage, but will throw an exception.)
```

```
' Declare as WithEvents just beneath the Class declaration
Public WithEvents myOleDbConnection As OleDbConnection
' Create an InfoMessage event handler
Private Sub myOleDbConnection_InfoMessage(ByVal sender As Object, _
   ByVal e As System.Data.OleDb.OleDbInfoMessageEventArgs) _
   Handles myOleDbConnection.InfoMessage
   MessageBox.Show(sender.GetType.ToString(),"Sender")
   MessageBox.Show(e.ErrorCode.ToString() & ControlChars.Cr & _
      "Errors: " & e.Errors.GetType.ToString() & ControlChars.Cr & _
      "Source: " & e.Source & ControlChars.Cr & _
      "Message: " & e.Message & ControlChars.Cr & _
      "ToString: " & e.ToString(),"ErrorCode")
End Sub
. . .
Dim myOleDbCommand As System.Data.OleDb.OleDbCommand
Dim myConnectionString As String
' Establish a connection to Northwind on SQL Server, which
' will raise the InfoMessage event
myConnectionString = "Provider=SQLOLEDB;Initial Catalog=Northwind;" & _
   "Data Source=(local);Integrated Security=SSPI;"
myOleDbConnection = New OleDbConnection(myConnectionString)
myOleDbConnection.Open()
myOleDbCommand = myOleDbConnection.CreateCommand
myOleDbCommand.CommandText = "PRINT 'Hello World'"
Try
   myOleDbCommand.ExecuteNonQuery() ' Raises the InfoMessage
Catch myOleDbException As OleDbException
   MessageBox.Show(myOleDbException.ToString())
Catch myException As Exception
   MessageBox.Show(myException.ToString())
End Try
```

Members

ErrorCode

The read-only ErrorCode property returns an Int32 specifying the HRESULT error identification number derived from the five-character ANSI SQL error code for the data source. This property is merely a wrapper that allows simple access to the OleDb-Error.SQLState property of the first OleDbError contained in the Errors collection property.

The SQLState originated as a set of common ODBC error messages. This enables errors to be shared across a large number of data providers and limits the number of provider-specific errors that must be considered. They are now standards defined in SQL-92, ISO SQL, and ODBC. The Int32 returned by ErrorCode is that error run through the Windows operating system.

To determine the actual SQLState (of the first error), use:

```
myString = myOleDbInfoMessageEventArgs.Errors(0).SQLState
```

Usage

```
myInt32 = myOleDbInfoMessageEventArgs.ErrorCode
```

Parameters

None.

Errors

The read-only Errors property returns an OleDbErrorCollection object containing all of the warnings generated by the OLE DB .NET data provider. The OleDbErrorCollection will contain at least one OleDbError object (representing the warning). This property contains the majority of the information relating to the warnings raised by the OLE DB provider.

Usage

```
myOleDbErrorCollection = myOleDbInfoMessageEventArgs.Errors
```

Parameters

None.

Message

The read-only Message property returns a String describing the first warning that caused the InfoMessage event to be raised. This property is merely a wrapper that allows simple access to the OleDbError.Message property of the first OleDbError contained in the Errors collection property.

Because it provides information from only the first warning, use this property cautiously when building robust error handling.

Usage

```
myString = myOleDbInfoMessageEventArgs.Message
```

Parameters

None.

Source

The read-only Source property returns a String containing the name of the provider that generated the first warning. This property is merely a wrapper that allows simple access to the OleDbError.Source property of the first OleDbError contained in the Errors collection property.

Because it provides information from only the first warning, use this property cautiously when building robust error handling.

Usage

```
myString = myOleDbInfoMessageEventArgs.Source
```

Parameters

None.

ToString

The ToString method is overridden to return information relating to the InfoMessage. The returned String contains the same information as provided by the Message property.

Usage

```
myString = myOleDbInfoMessageEventArgs.ToString()
```

Parameters

None.

Exceptions

None.

System.Data.OleDb.OleDbParameter

The OleDbParameter is a class that facilitates passing data to and from SQL commands and stored procedures.

Although an OleDbParameter is meaningful only when related to an OleDb-Command, its constructor is public; therefore, you can create standalone OleDbParameter objects. Later, you can add or insert them to an OleDbCommand's Parameters collection.

Parameter names are not case sensitive and are also not required. You may leave them null. Once you add the OleDbParameter to a collection, the names must be unique. If you fail to specify the ParameterName property, ADO.NET shall provide one for you at the time you add or insert the OleDbParameter to the collection. This ADO.NET-provided name will be a cryptic one like "@P1" or "Parameter1".

Constructors

```
Dim myOleDbParameter As New OleDbParameter()
Dim myOleDbParameter As New OleDbParameter(String,Object)
Dim myOleDbParameter As New OleDbParameter(String,OleDbType)
Dim myOleDbParameter As New OleDbParameter(String,OleDbType,Int32)
Dim myOleDbParameter As New OleDbParameter(String,OleDbType,Int32, _
    String2)
Dim myOleDbParameter As New OleDbParameter(String,OleDbType,Int32, _
    Direction,Boolean,Byte,Byte2,String2,DataRowVersion,Object)
```

Parameters

`String`	The name of the parameter. Must be unique in the collection.
`Object`	The value of the parameter.
`OleDbType`	The OleDbType of the parameter.
`Int32`	The size or width of the column.
`String2`	The name of the source column.
`Direction`	The ParameterDirection of the parameter. This can be Input, InputOutput, Output, or ReturnValue.
`Boolean`	The nullability of the column. If the column can contain null values, then this value will be True.

`Byte`	The precision of the column. This is the total number of digits to the left of the decimal point.
`Byte2`	The scale of the column. This is the total number of decimal places.
`DataRowVersion`	The DataRowVersion of the column. This will indicate if the DataRow contains Current, Default, Original, or Proposed values.

OleDbParameter Sample Code

```
Dim myOleDbConnection As New System.Data.OleDb.OleDbConnection()
Dim myOleDbParameter As New System.Data.OleDb.OleDbParameter()
Dim myOleDbCommand As New System.Data.OleDb.OleDbCommand()
Dim myOleDbDataReader As System.Data.OleDb.OleDbDataReader
Dim myConnectionString As String
' Establish connection
myConnectionString = "Provider=Microsoft.Jet.OLEDB.4.0;' & _
   "Data Source=C:\Northwind.mdb"
myOleDbConnection.ConnectionString = myConnectionString
myOleDbConnection.Open()
' OleDbCommand object
myOleDbCommand.CommandText = _
   "SELECT * FROM Customers WHERE CustomerID = ?"
myOleDbCommand.Connection = myOleDbConnection
' Create parameter and add to collection
myOleDbParameter.Value = 7
myOleDbParameter.DbType = DbType.Int32
myOleDbCommand.Parameters.Add(myOleDbParameter)
' Execute command
myOleDbDataReader = myOleDbCommand.ExecuteReader
' Done
myOleDbConnection.Close()
```

Members

DbType

The DbType property sets or returns the OleDbParameter's .NET data type. Because the DbType and the OleDbType are linked, when you change the DbType property, ADO.NET will change the OleDbType to the corresponding value. Be careful when setting the OleDbType because conversion errors, such as truncation, may result.

There are 24 DbTypes to select from. For a complete reference, see the System.Data.DbType enumeration. The default DbType is String.

Usage

```
myDbType = myOleDbParameter.DbType
myOleDbParameter.DbType = DbType.Guid
```

Parameters
None.

Exceptions

ArgumentOutOfRangeException	You attempted to assign an invalid DbType value.

Direction

The Direction property sets or returns the OleDbParameter's behavior as to whether it is an Input, Output, Input and Output, or a Return Value type of parameter. Based on the value of Direction property, ADO.NET shall allow or disallow certain behaviors of passing data to and receiving data from the data source via these parameters.

Usage

```
myParameterDirection = myOleDbParameter.Direction
myOleDbParameter.Direction = ParameterDirection.Output
```

Parameters
None.

ParameterDirection Enumeration

Input (1)	(Default) The parameter is an input parameter only. The purpose of this OleDbParameter is to provide a value to the SQL statement or stored procedure to enable it to run properly.
InputOutput (3)	The parameter serves as both an input and an output parameter. The idea here is that the stored procedure might change the value of the parameter, and you'll need to be able to receive the new value.
Output (2)	The parameter is an output parameter only. The purpose of this OleDbParameter is to receive a value back from a stored procedure. The corresponding parameter in the data source might need to be marked as OUTPUT.
ReturnValue (6)	The parameter will receive the return value.

Exceptions

ArgumentException	You attempted to assign an invalid ParameterDirection value.

IsNullable

The IsNullable property sets or returns the OleDbParameter's capability of storing a null value. If the IsNullable property is set to True, the parameter may be null. The default value is false.

Usage

```
myBoolean = myOleDbParameter.IsNullable
myOleDbParameter.IsNullable = False
```

Parameters
None.

Exceptions
None.

OleDbType

The OleDbType property sets or returns the OleDbParameter's underlying OLE DB provider data type. Because the DbType and the OleDbType are linked, when you change the OleDbType property, ADO.NET will change the DbType to the corresponding value. Be careful when setting the OleDbType because conversion errors, such as truncation, may result.

There are 37 OleDbTypes to select from. For a complete reference, see the System.Data.OleDb.OleDbType enumeration. The default OleDbType is VarWChar.

Usage

```
myOleDbType = myOleDbParameter.OleDbType
myOleDbParameter.OleDbType = OleDbType.Decimal
```

Parameters
None.

Exceptions

ArgumentOutOfRangeException	You attempted to assign an invalid OleDbType value.

ParameterName

The ParameterName property sets or returns the OleDbParameter's name that you may use to reference the OleDbParameter in the collection. For that matter, it is important to provide a short, unique, and meaningful name that represents the purpose of the parameter. Try to avoid using any spaces in the name. The default ParameterName is an empty string until such time when you add the OleDbParameter to a collection, and then it will be given a default name.

Because the OleDb .NET data provider doesn't support named parameters, you do not need to worry about how you name them or if they match the parameters in your stored procedures or queries. You should be more worried about their position in the collection.

Usage

```
myString = myOleDbParameter.ParameterName
myOleDbParameter.ParameterName = "SSN"
```

Parameters
None.

Precision

The Precision property sets or returns the maximum number of digits used to represent the OleDbParameter's Value property. Precision applies only to decimal and numeric Input parameters.

Usage

```
myByte = myOleDbParameter.Precision
myOleDbParameter.Precision = 8
```

Parameters

None.

Scale

The Scale property sets or returns the number of decimal places used to represent the OleDbParameter's Value property. Scale applies only to decimal and numeric Input parameters.

Usage

```
myByte = myOleDbParameter.Scale
myOleDbParameter.Scale = 4
```

Parameters

None.

Size

The Size property sets or returns the maximum number of bytes the OleDbParameter's Value property can hold. Size applies only to binary and string parameters. The Size property can be smaller than the size of the corresponding data type within the stored procedure. This will reduce the size of the data packet sent to the server. Be careful not to truncate any data, especially if the OleDbParameter is used for Output as well.

For variable-length data types, the Size property sets the maximum amount of data to transmit to the server. For nonstring data types and ANSI string data, the Size property sets the number of bytes. For fixed-width data types, the Size property is ignored, although it can be retrieved for informational purposes. The default size value is inferred from the value of the parameter.

Usage

```
myInt32 = myOleDbParameter.Size
myOleDbParameter.Size = myString.Length
```

Parameters

None.

Exceptions

SystemException	You attempted to assign an invalid Size value.

SourceColumn

The SourceColumn property sets or returns the name of the column in the corresponding DataSet. This information is used for loading or returning the OleDbParameter's Value. The default value for SourceColumn is an empty string.

Usage

```
myString = myOleDbParameter.SourceColumn
myOleDbParameter.SourceColumn = "Address1"
```

Parameters
None.

SourceVersion

The SourceVersion property sets or returns the DataRowVersion of the OleDb-Parameter value. The version is used by the UpdateCommand during an Update operation to determine whether the value is set to Current or Original. Based on the SourceVersion, ADO.NET can avoid work by not updating columns that haven't changed.

Usage

```
myDataRowVersion = myOleDbParameter.SourceVersion
myOleDbParameter.SourceVersion = DataRowVersion.Default
```

Parameters
None.

DataRowVersion Enumeration

Current (512)	(Default). The row contains current values.
Default (1536)	The row contains its default values.
Original (256)	The row contains its original values.
Proposed (1024)	The row contains proposed values.

Exceptions

ArgumentException	You attempted to assign an invalid SourceVersion value.

Value

The Value property sets or returns the value of the OleDbParameter. This is probably the most popular property of the OleDbParameter object.

If the OleDbParameter's direction is Input or InputOuput, then the Value property should be assigned before executing the command. If the OleDbParameter's direction is Output, InputOutput, or Return Value, then the Value property will not be set until after the command has executed and possibly not until the associated DataReader has finished processing the rows and/or is closed (depending on the provider). The Value property is overwritten by the Update method.

If you want to send a NULL value to the data source, then you'll need to specify DBNULL instead of the standard .NET null value.

```
myOleDbParameter.Value = DBNull.Value
```

Usage

```
myObject = myOleDbParameter.Value
myOleDbParameter.Value = "Bruce Campbell"
```

Parameters
None.

System.Data.OleDb. OleDbParameterCollection

The OleDbParameterCollection is created automatically by the OleDbCommand object to hold OleDbParameter objects. The OleDbParameterCollection and OleDbParameter class are closely related. The OleDbParameterCollection class has no public constructor, so you cannot create a standalone collection.

It is important that the number, type, direction, and position of each parameter in the collection match exactly with the expectations of the SQL statement or stored procedure. If the parameter information doesn't match, the OLE DB provider could raise an error.

The OleDbParameterCollection is essentially like any other .NET collection, with the same methods and properties that you've become accustomed to using.

Constructors

There is no public constructor.

Parameters

None.

OleDbParameterCollection Sample Code

```
Dim myOleDbParameterCollection As _
   System.Data.OleDb.OleDbParameterCollection
Dim myOleDbConnection As New System.Data.OleDb.OleDbConnection()
Dim myOleDbParameter As New System.Data.OleDb.OleDbParameter()
Dim myOleDbCommand As New System.Data.OleDb.OleDbCommand()
Dim myConnectionString As String
' Establish connection
myConnectionString = "Provider=Microsoft.Jet.OLEDB.4.0;" & _
   "Data Source=C:\Northwind.mdb"
myOleDbConnection.ConnectionString = myConnectionString
myOleDbConnection.Open()
' OleDbCommand object
myOleDbCommand.CommandText = _
   "SELECT * FROM Customers WHERE CustomerID = ?"
myOleDbCommand.Connection = myOleDbConnection
' Create parameter and add to collection
myOleDbParameter.Value = 7
myOleDbParameterCollection = myOleDbCommand.Parameters
myOleDbParameterCollection.Add(myOleDbParameter)
' Test
MessageBox.Show(myOleDbParameterCollection.Count,"Count")
```

```
MessageBox.Show(myOleDbParameterCollection(0).Value,"Item #1")
' Execute command and process data here
myOleDbConnection.Close()
```

Members

Add

The Add method adds a new OleDbParameter object to the collection. The Add method is overloaded in a number of ways, providing you with flexibility in how you add OleDbParameter objects to the collection. If you are trying to insert the new OleDbParameter object at a particular location in the collection, consider using the Insert method.

Usage

```
myOleDbParameterCollection.Add(Object)
myOleDbParameterCollection.Add(OleDbParameter)
myOleDbParameterCollection.Add(String, Object)
myOleDbParameterCollection.Add(String, OleDbType)
myOleDbParameterCollection.Add(String, OleDbType, Int32)
myOleDbParameterCollection.Add(String, OleDbType, Int32, String2)
```

Parameters

`Object`	Adds an OleDbParameter object to the collection with the specified value.
`OleDbParameter`	Adds the specified OleDbParameter object to the collection.
`String`	The name of the parameter to be added.
`OleDbType`	The OleDbType of the parameter to be added.
`Int32`	The size or width of the column.
`String2`	The name of the source column.

Exceptions

ArgumentException	The parameter name is not unique.
InvalidCastException	The parameter passed to the Add method was invalid.

Clear

The Clear method removes all OleDbParameter objects from the collection. You can call the Clear method on an empty collection without raising an error.

Usage

```
myOleDbParameterCollection.Clear()
```

Parameters

None.

Exceptions

None.

Contains

The Contains method provides a way to search for the existence of an OleDbParameter object within the collection. The Contains method is overloaded in two different ways, allowing you to use the same method to search by an OleDbParameter object or just the parameter name.

NOTE In testing, it seems that all properties of the OleDbParameter object you are looking for must match, not just the value.

Usage

```
myBoolean = myOleDbParameterCollection.Contains(OleDbParameter)
myBoolean = myOleDbParameterCollection.Contains(String)
```

Parameters

`OleDbParameter`	The OleDbParameter object you are attempting to locate.
`String`	The name of the parameter you are attempting to locate. This search is not case sensitive, but you may need to include the @ prefix.

Exceptions

None.

CopyTo

The CopyTo method copies the OleDbParameter objects into a passed array, starting at the designated index within the Array. You must specify both an Array and a starting index. There is no default index.

NOTE Remember that in .NET all arrays are zero based. When you Dim your array variable, make sure you dim it with a size one less than the number of parameters you are expecting.

Usage

```
myOleDbParameterCollection.CopyTo(Array,Index)
```

Parameters

`Array`	The passed array to fill with OleDbParameter objects.
`Index`	The starting index of the array. For example, if you pass a 3, ADO.NET will fill array (3) with the first OleDbParameter object.

Exceptions

ArgumentException	The sum of index and the number of elements in the OleDbParameterCollection is greater than the length of the array.

ArgumentNullException	The array is null (`Nothing` in Visual Basic).
ArgumentOutOfRangeException	The index is not valid for the passed array.

Count

The read-only Count property returns an Int32 representing the number of OleDbParameter objects contained in the collection. This count is base one. If you are going to use the Count to somehow size an array or enumerate through the collection by index, you'll need to subtract one. For example, a collection with a Count of 20 items will have items indexed 0 through 19.

Usage

```
myInt32 = myOleDbParameterCollection.Count
```

Parameters

None.

IndexOf

Similar to the Contains method, the IndexOf provides a way to search for the existence of an OleDbParameter object within the collection and return the location or Index of the object. If the IndexOf method cannot find the OleDbParameter object in the collection, then it will return a -1. The IndexOf method is overloaded in two different ways, allowing you to use the same method to search by an OleDbParameter object or just the parameter name.

NOTE **In testing, it seems that all properties of the OleDbParameter object you are looking for must match, not just the value.**

Usage

```
myIndex = myOleDbParameterCollection.IndexOf(OleDbParameter)
myIndex = myOleDbParameterCollection.IndexOf(String)
```

Parameters

`OleDbParameter`	The OleDbParameter object you are attempting to locate.
`String`	The name of the parameter you are attempting to locate. This search is not case sensitive, but you may need to include the @ prefix.

Insert

Similar to the Add method, the Insert method adds a new OleDbParameter object to the collection at the specified index. The Insert method is not overloaded and therefore always requires two parameters. If you are trying to simply add the new OleDbParameter object, consider using the Add method.

Usage

```
myOleDbParameterCollection.Insert(Index,OleDbParameter)
```

Parameters

`Index`	The index within the collection to insert the new OleDbParameter object. The collection is zero based, so an Index of 10 will insert the new object into position 11.
`OleDbParameter`	The OleDbParameter object to be added to the collection.

Exceptions

ArgumentException	The parameter name is not unique.
ArgumentOutOfRangeException	The index is not valid for the collection.

Item

The Item property sets or returns a particular OleDbParameter in the collection. When you want to reference a particular OleDbParameter for viewing or editing, you will need to use the Item property.

For safety, you should consider testing for the existence of the OleDbParameter object by using the Contains method.

```
If myOleDbParameterCollection.Contains("Comments") Then
   myOleDbParameter = myOleDbParameterCollection.Item("Comments")
End If
```

The Item property is also the default property for the class, so in many code examples you will not see it explicitly mentioned. This takes advantage of a shortcut in .NET and results in code that can sometimes be hard to understand and document:

```
' Fully qualified method
myValue = myOleDbParameterCollection.Item(5).Value
' Shortcut in .NET
myValue = myOleDbParameterCollection(5).Value
```

Usage

```
myOleDbParameter = myOleDbParameterCollection.Item(Int32)
myOleDbParameter = myOleDbParameterCollection.Item(String)
```

Parameters

`Int32`	The index of the OleDbParameter that you are attempting to reference. The collection is zero based, so an Index of 10 will reference the OleDbParameter at position 11.
`String`	The parameter name of the OleDbParameter that you are attempting to reference. The string is not case sensitive, but you may need to include the @ prefix.

Exceptions

IndexOutOfRangeException	The index or the parameter name was not found in the collection.

Remove

The Remove method is used to remove an OleDbParameter object from the OleDbParameterCollection. In contrast to the RemoveAt method, the Remove method requires you to have a reference to an OleDbParameter object in order to Remove it, where the RemoveAt method can remove by Index number or Parameter name.

Usage

```
myOleDbParameterCollection.Remove(OleDbParameter)
```

Parameters

`OleDbParameter`	The OleDbParameter object to remove from the collection.

Exceptions

InvalidCastException	The parameter is not of type OleDbParameter.
SystemException	You have attempted to remove an OleDb-Parameter that is not contained in the collection.

RemoveAt

Similar to the Remove method, the RemoveAt method is used to remove an OleDbParameter object from the OleDbParameterCollection by Index number or Parameter name. If you already have a reference to an OleDbParameter in the collection, then you should consider using the Remove method.

For safety, you should consider testing for the existence of the OleDbParameter object by using the Contains method:

```
If myOleDbParameterCollection.Contains("Comments") Then
   myOleDbParameterCollection.RemoveAt("Comments")
End If
```

Usage

```
myOleDbParameterCollection.RemoveAt(Int32)
myOleDbParameterCollection.RemoveAt(String)
```

Parameters

`Int32`	The index of the OleDbParameter that you are attempting to remove. The collection is zero based, so an Index of 10 will reference the OleDbParameter at position 11.
`String`	The parameter name of the OleDbParameter that you are attempting to remove. The string is not case sensitive, but you may need to include the @ prefix.

Exceptions

IndexOutOfRangeException	The index or the parameter name was not found in the collection.

System.Data.OleDb. OleDbRowUpdatedEventArgs

The OleDbRowUpdatedEventArgs class provides data for the OleDbDataAdapter. RowUpdated event. This event is raised during the Update method of the OleDb-DataAdapter class. During the Update, every DataRow that has been inserted, updated, or deleted is sent to the data source for updating. Each change raises the RowUpdated event after the changes have been made to the data source, but before they are committed.

Once the event is intercepted, you have a great deal of control over what happens next. Although you cannot make changes to the row to be updated, which we find to be very unfortunate, you are able to examine the row, along with information about the data source and what type of Update action will occur (Insert, Delete, etc.). You then have the ability to cancel the update for this particular row or for this row and all following rows. You can even stop processing rows and assign a custom exception, complete with errors, to be raised to the OleDbDataAdapter.

The majority of the OleDbRowUpdatedEventArgs class members are inherited from the System.Data.Common.RowUpdatedEventArgs class, which means that learning these will translate nicely to the other .NET data providers.

Defining a procedure to handle the OleDbDataAdapter.RowUpdated event is one way to catch errors or exceptions within a program. Another is to wrap the Fill and Update procedures in a Try-Catch-Finally block. Generally, if you're just catching exceptions, a Try-Catch-Finally block is preferable; however, if you have additional data validation to perform, handling the RowUpdating event is better. This is especially true because you may handle the RowUpdated events for more than one OleDb-DataAdapter with the same procedure. To do this, simply add any number of OleDbDataAdapter.RowUpdated event declarations after the Handles keyword in the procedure definition. Be sure to separate the declarations with commas.

Although the constructor is listed in the text that follows, it's unlikely you would actually use this constructor because the .NET Framework automatically generates this object when the RowUpdated event is raised.

Constructors

```
Dim myOleDbRowUpdatedEventArgs As New OleDbRowUpdatedEventArgs( _
   DataRow, IDbCommand, StatementType, DataTableMapping)
```

Parameters

`DataRow`	A System.Data.DataRow object that is to be deleted, inserted, or updated at the data source.
`IDbCommand`	An OleDbCommand object (implementing the System.Data.IDbCommand interface) representing the SQL statement to be executed.

`StatementType`	A System.Data.StatementType enumeration that specifies the type of SQL statement in the IDbCommand object. Valid values are Delete (3), Insert (1), Select (0), and Update (2).
`DataTableMapping`	A System.Data.Common.DataTableMapping object that describes the mapping between the DataTable object and the source data.

OleDbRowUpdatedEventArgs Sample Code

```
' The best way to approach sample code for this object is to
' trap the RowUpdated event of the OleDbDataAdapter object.
' Declare as WithEvents just beneath the Class declaration
Public WithEvents myOleDbDataAdapter As
System.Data.OleDb.OleDbDataAdapter
. . .
Private Sub myOleDbDataAdapter_RowUpdated(ByVal sender As Object, _
   ByVal e As System.Data.OleDb.OleDbRowUpdatedEventArgs) _
   Handles myOleDbDataAdapter.RowUpdated
   Dim myOleDbCommand As OleDbCommand
   Dim myIDbCmd As System.Data.IDbCommand
   Dim myException As System.Exception
   Dim i As Int32 'for loops
   Dim strDisplay As String
   ' Demonstrate some features of the OleDbRowUpdatingEventArgs object
   MessageBox.Show("Entering RowUpdated")
   myIDbCmd = e.Command
   ' Even though we have declared myIDbCmd as an IdbCommand object,
   ' the actual type is OleDbCommand
   MessageBox.Show("Command object type is: " + TypeName(myIDbCmd))
   ' If we choose we can assign myIDbCmd to myOleDbCommand, although
   ' this is not necessary since myIDbCmd already is an OleDbCommand
   ' NOTE: TypeOf-Is is MUCH faster than TypeName() = "stringValue"
   If TypeOf myIDbCmd Is OleDbCommand Then
      myOleDbCommand = myIDbCmd
   End If
   ' Occassionally the command may have a Null value (although
   ' it never SHOULD. It indicates a bug somewhere.
   If myIDbCmd Is Nothing Then
      MessageBox.Show("e.Command is null. Exiting")
      Exit Sub
   End If
   ' We can see the SQL command that was used to update the data source,
   ' as well as its type
   MessageBox.Show("SQL Command Type: " + e.StatementType.ToString())
   MessageBox.Show("SQL Command Text: " + e.Command.CommandText)
   ' And also any parameters sent along (see OleDbParameter for more)
   For i = 0 To e.Command.Parameters.Count - 1
```

```
        strDisplay += "Parameter #" + i.ToString() + ControlChars.Tab _
            + e.Command.Parameters.Item(i).Value + ControlChars.Cr
    Next
    MessageBox.Show(strDisplay)
    ' And also the DataRow sent for the update (this is the changed
    ' row and will reflect row at the source
    strDisplay = ""
    For i = 0 To e.Row.ItemArray.Length - 1
        strDisplay += "RowColumn #" + i.ToString() + ControlChars.Tab _
            + e.Row.Item(i) + ControlChars.Cr
    Next
    MessageBox.Show(strDisplay)
    ' We can also check to see how many rows have been impacted
    ' by our update statement.
    MessageBox.Show("Records affected: " + e.RecordsAffected.ToString())
    ' Next we can see if any errors have been raised
    If Not e.Errors Is Nothing Then
        'show the exception (recall e.Errors returns an Exception)
        MessageBox.Show("An exception has been raised. " _
            + ControlChars.Cr + e.Errors.ToString())
        MessageBox.Show(e.Errors.Source)
        Dim myOleEx As OleDbException = e.Errors
        MessageBox.Show(myOleEx.Errors.Item(0).ToString())
        ' Handle errors here...
    End If
    ' Once we've gathered the information we can determine what
    ' to do with the this row, and all remaining rows.
    ' To cancel updating of this row only we can use:
    e.Status = UpdateStatus.SkipCurrentRow
    ' If we have come across some business rule error in the
    ' data, we can also choose to raise our own exception.
    ' Comment out the lines below to avoid having exceptions raised
    e.Status = UpdateStatus.ErrorsOccurred
    e.Errors = New Exception("Personalized Exception from RowUpdated")
    MessageBox.Show("Exiting RowUpdated")
End Sub
```

Members

Command

The read-only Command property returns an object implementing the System.Data.IDbCommand interface that represents the SQL statement that was executed at the data source. In this case, the returned object can be assigned to an OleDbCommand object because it implements the IDbCommand interface.

You can declare a variable with the type IDbCommand, then assign it to the object returned by the Command property; however, because IDbCommand is an interface and not a class, its actual type will be OleDbCommand.

Because this property is read only, changes to the Command cannot be made during the RowUpdating or RowUpdated events.

Usage

```
myIDbCommand = myOleDbRowUpdatedEventArgs.Command
myOleDbCommand = myOleDbRowUpdatedEventArgs.Command
```

Parameters

None.

Errors

The Errors property (inherited from System.Data.Common.RowUpdatedEventArgs) returns a System.Exception object or a subclass that inherits from the Exception class. It contains the errors generated by the .NET data provider when the command executes. The actual class type of the returned Errors property depends on the exception or error that was returned. For example, an exception originating from the data source will return an OleDbException. Knowing the type of the exception raised allows you to assign the Errors property to a more specific exception object. See the OleDbRowUpdatedEventArgs code sample for an example.

Another major use of the Errors property is assigning your own Exception (or derived class) to the property and setting the Status property to ErrorsOccurred (1). This will cause the exception you've added to be thrown by the OleDbDataAdapter. In this way, you can introduce custom exceptions into your data update code. Be aware, however, that this will cancel the update on the current row and all future rows.

NOTE The naming of the Errors property is somewhat unfortunate. It is easy to confuse it with the OleDbException.Errors property, which is an OleDbErrorCollection object, yet this property returns an Exception object. Be aware of this difference, and you can avoid a frustrating coding session.

Usage

```
myException = myOleDbRowUpdatedEventArgs.Errors
myOleDbRowUpdatingEventArgs.Errors = myException
```

Parameters

None.

RecordsAffected

The read-only RecordsAffected property (inherited from System.Data.Common.RowUpdatedEventArgs) returns an Int32 containing the number of records affected by the execution of the SQL statement specified in the Update. The number is the sum of all rows updated, added, and deleted. If no rows were affected, or if there were errors, RecordsAffected will be set to 0. If the SQL command executed was a SELECT command, it is set to -1.

NOTE This is not the same as the Transact-SQL @@Rowcount, which returns the number of selected rows returned from the last SQL command.

Usage

```
myInt32 = myOleDbRowUpdatedEventArgs.RecordsAffected
```

Parameters

None.

Row

The read-only Row property (inherited from System.Data.Common.RowUpdated-EventArgs) returns a System.Data.DataRow object, which contains the data that was updated at the data source. Because this property is read only, you cannot change the values. The data that will be committed at the completion of the RowUpdated event, when AcceptChanges is called.

Usage

```
myDataRow = myOleDbRowUpdatedEventArgs.Row
```

Parameters

None.

StatementType

The read-only StatementType property (inherited from System.Data.Common.Row-UpdatedEventArgs) returns a System.StatementType enumeration value specifying the type of SQL statement that was executed at the data source. This value should match the action specified by the Command object.

The value can be assigned to several different types of variables, including an Int32, String, or StatementType enumeration. The advantage to assigning the value to an enumeration is that the ToString method of the enumeration will return the enumeration member name, instead of merely its integer value.

NOTE The StatementType method is a good example of when you might want to use the ToString method to return a more meaningful value. StatementType by itself returns a number, whereas StatementType.ToString returns a meaningful string such as Update.

Usage

```
myStatementType = myOleDbRowUpdatedEventArgs.StatementType
myInt32 = myOleDbRowUpdatedEventArgs.StatementType
```

Parameters

None.

StatementType Enumeration

Delete (3)	A SQL DELETE statement.
Insert (1)	A SQL INSERT statement.
Select (0)	(Default). A SQL SELECT statement.
Update (2)	A SQL UPDATE statement.

Status

The Status property (inherited from System.Data.Common.RowUpdatedEventArgs) returns a System.Data.UpdateStatus enumeration value specifying the action that will be taken during the Update with regard to the current row and following rows. The default value is Continue, which tells the DataAdapter to process this row and to continue processing rows. Other values are listed in the text that follows.

This allows you to cancel changes to the data source after the DataAdapter has executed the changes. By setting this value to SkipCurrentRow, the changes made to the data source are ignored, and remaining rows continue to be processed normally.

Like other enumerations, the value can be assigned to several different types of variables, including an Int32, String, or UpdateStatus enumeration. The advantage to assigning the value to an enumeration is that the ToString method of the enumeration will return the enumeration member name, instead of merely its integer value.

Usage

```
myStatus = myOleDbRowUpdatedEventArgs.Status
myInt32 = myOleDbRowUpdatedEventArgs.Status
```

Parameters

None.

UpdateStatus Enumeration

Continue (0)	(Default) Process this row, and continue processing rows.
ErrorsOccurred (1)	This update should be treated as an error. Setting this value will abort the update of this row and all remaining rows, as well as throw an Exception. To specify the Error to be thrown, add an Exception to the Errors property.
SkipAllRemainingRows (3)	Do not process this row or any remaining rows.
SkipCurrentRow (2)	Do not process this row, but continue processing rows.

TableMapping

The read-only TableMapping property (inherited from System.Data.Common.RowUpdatedEventArgs) returns the System.Data.Common.DataTableMapping object that was sent by the Update method. This object maps the table and columns used by the data source to the table and columns used by the DataSet, to facilitate updating the data at the data source. The DataTableMapping objects contained in the DataTableMappingCollection contain three public properties that permit access to the underlying mapping.

- The read-only ColumnMapping property, which returns the DataColumnMappingCollection object describing the mappings of the columns between the data source and DataSet.
- The DataSetTable property, which is used to get or set the destination DataSet table name.

- The SourceTable, which gets or sets the source table from which to retrieve the data.

See System.Data.Common.DataTableMapping for more information.

Usage

```
myDataTableMapping = myOleDbRowUpdatedEventArgs.TableMapping
```

Parameters

None.

System.Data.OleDb. OleDbRowUpdatingEventArgs

The OleDbRowUpdatingEventArgs class provides data for the OleDbDataAdapter. RowUpdating event. This event is raised during the Update method of the OleDb-DataAdapter class. During the Update, every DataRow that has been inserted, updated, or deleted is sent to the data source for updating. Each change raises the RowUpdating event before any changes have been made to the data source.

Once the event is intercepted, you have a great deal of control over what happens next. Although you cannot make changes to the row to be updated, which we find to be very unfortunate, you are able to examine the row, along with information about the data source, and what type of Update action will occur (Insert, Delete, etc.). You then have the ability to cancel the update for this particular row or for this row and all following rows. You can even stop processing rows and assign a custom exception, complete with errors, to be raised to the OleDbDataAdapter.

The majority of the OleDbRowUpdatingEventArgs class members are inherited from the System.Data.Common.RowUpdatingEventArgs class, which means that learning these will translate nicely to the other .NET data providers.

Defining a procedure to handle the OleDbDataAdapter.RowUpdating event is one way to catch errors or exceptions within a program. Another is to bracket the Fill and Update procedures in a Try-Catch-Finally block. Generally, if you're just catching exceptions, a Try-Catch-Finally block is preferable; however, if you have additional data validation to perform, handling the RowUpdating event is better. This is especially true because you may handle the RowUpdating events for more than one OleDb-DataAdapter with the same procedure. To do this, simply add any number of OleDbDataAdapter.RowUpdating event declarations after the Handles keyword in the procedure definition. Be sure to separate the declarations with commas.

Although the constructor is listed in the text that follows, it's unlikely you would actually use it because the OleDbDataAdapter automatically generates this object when the RowUpdating event is raised.

Constructors

```
Dim myOleDbRowUpdatingEventArgs As New OleDbRowUpdatingEventArgs ( _
   DataRow, IDbCommand, StatementType, DataTableMapping)
```

Parameters

`DataRow`	A System.Data.DataRow object that is to be deleted, inserted, or updated at the data source.
`IDbCommand`	An OleDbCommand object (implementing the System.Data.IDbCommand interface) representing the SQL statement to be executed.
`StatementType`	A System.Data.StatementType enumeration that specifies the type of SQL statement in the IDbCommand object. Valid values are Delete (3), Insert (1), Select (0), and Update (2).
`DataTableMapping`	A System.Data.Common.DataTableMapping object that describes the mapping between the DataTable object and the source data.

OleDbRowUpdatingEventArgs Sample Code

```
' The best way to approach sample code for this object is to
' trap the RowUpdating event of the OleDbDataAdapter cbject.
' Declare as WithEvents just beneath the Class declaration
Public WithEvents myOleDbDataAdapter As
System.Data.OleDb.OleDbDataAdapter
. . .
Private Sub myOleDbDataAdapter_RowUpdating(ByVal sender As Object, _
   ByVal e As System.Data.OleDb.OleDbRowUpdatingEventArgs) _
   Handles myOleDbDataAdapter.RowUpdating
   Dim myOleDbCommand As OleDbCommand
   Dim myIDbCmd As System.Data.IDbCommand
   Dim myException As System.Exception
   Dim i As Int32 'for loops
   Dim strDisplay As String
   ' Demonstrate some features of the OleDbRowUpdatingEventArgs object
   MessageBox.Show("Entering RowUpdating")
   myIDbCmd = e.Command
   ' Even though we have declared myIDbCmd as an IdbCommand object, the
   ' actual type is OleDbCommand
   MessageBox.Show("Command object type is: " + TypeName(myIDbCmd))
   ' If we choose we can assign myIDbCmd to myOleDbCommand, although
   ' this is not necessary since myIDbCmd already is an OleDbCommand
   ' NOTE: TypeOf-Is is MUCH faster than TypeName() = 'stringValue"
   If TypeOf myIDbCmd Is OleDbCommand Then
      myOleDbCommand = myIDbCmd
   End If
   ' We can see the SQL command  to be used to update the data source,
   ' as well as its type
   MessageBox.Show("SQL Command Type: " + e.StatementType.ToString())
   MessageBox.Show("SQL Command Text: " + e.Command.CommandText)
   ' And also any parameters sent along (see OleDbParameter for more)
```

```
    For i = 0 To e.Command.Parameters.Count - 1
        strDisplay += "Parameter #" + i.ToString() + ControlChars.Tab _
            + e.Command.Parameters.Item(i).Value + ControlChars.Cr
    Next
    MessageBox.Show(strDisplay)
    ' And also the DataRow sent for the update (this is the changed
    ' row NOT the row currently in the source.
    strDisplay = ""
    For i = 0 To e.Row.ItemArray.Length - 1
        strDisplay += "RowColumn #" + i.ToString() + ControlChars.Tab _
            + e.Row.Item(i) + ControlChars.Cr
    Next
    MessageBox.Show(strDisplay)
    ' Next we can see if any errors have been raised
    If Not e.Errors Is Nothing Then
        'show the exception (recall e.Errors returns an Exception)
        MessageBox.Show("An exception has been raised. " _
            + ControlChars.Cr + e.Errors.ToString())
        'deal with errors here...
    End If
    ' Once we've gathered the information we can determine what
    ' to do with the this row, and all remaining rows.
    ' To cancel updating of this row only we can use:
    ' (Be sure to comment out this line if you will have this
    ' code active, when checking out the RowUpdated, since
    ' it won't run, if it's cancelled here!!!)
    e.Status = UpdateStatus.SkipCurrentRow
    ' If we have come across some business rule error in the
    ' data, we can also choose to raise our own exception.
    ' Comment out the lines below to avoid having exceptions raised
    ' (Be sure to comment out these lines if you will have this
    ' code active, when checking out the RowUpdated, since
    ' it won't run, if an error is raised here!!!)
    e.Status = UpdateStatus.ErrorsOccurred
    e.Errors = New Exception("Personalized Exception from RowUpdating")
    MessageBox.Show("Exiting RowUpdating")
End Sub
```

Members

Command

The Command property returns an object implementing the System.Data.IDbCommand interface that represents the SQL statement that was executed at the data source. In this case, the returned object can be assigned to an OleDbCommand object because it implements the IDbCommand interface.

You can declare a variable with the type IDbCommand, then assign it to the object returned by the Command property; however, because IDbCommand is an interface and not a class, its actual type will be OleDbCommand.

Because this property is read only, changes to the Command cannot be made during the RowUpdating or RowUpdated events.

Usage

```
myIDbCommand = myOleDbRowUpdatingEventArgs.Command
myOleDbCommand = myOleDbRowUpdatingEventArgs.Command
```

Parameters

None.

Errors

The Errors property (inherited from System.Data.Common.RowUpdatingEventArgs) returns a System.Exception object or a subclass that inherits from the Exception class. It contains the errors generated by the .NET data provider when the command executes. The actual class type of the returned Errors property depends on the exception or error that was returned. For example, an exception originating from the data source will return an OleDbException. Knowing the type of the exception raised allows you to assign the Errors property to a more specific exception object. See the OleDbRowUpdatingEventArgs sample code for an example.

Another major use of the Errors property is assigning your own Exception (or derived class) to the property and setting the Status property to ErrorsOccurred (1). This will cause the exception you've added to be thrown by the OleDbDataAdapter. In this way, you can introduce custom exceptions into your data update code. Be aware, however, that this will cancel the update on the current and all future rows.

NOTE **The naming of the Errors property is somewhat unfortunate. It is easy to confuse it with the OleDbException.Errors property, which is an OleDbErrorCollection object, yet this property returns an Exception object. Be aware of this difference, and you can avoid a frustrating coding session.**

Usage

```
myException = myOleDbRowUpdatingEventArgs.Errors
myOleDbRowUpdatingEventArgs.Errors = myException
```

Parameters

None.

Row

The read-only Row property (inherited from System.Data.Common.RowUpdatingEventArgs) returns a System.Data.DataRow object, which contains the data that will be updated at the data source. Because this property is read only, you cannot change the values of the data to be updated during a RowUpdating event.

NOTE **We find this very unfortunate because being able to correct data here would prevent having to cancel updates.**

Usage

```
myDataRow = myOleDbRowUpdatingEventArgs.Row
```

Parameters

None.

StatementType

The read-only StatementType property (inherited from System.Data.Common.RowUpdatingEventArgs) returns a System.StatementType enumeration value specifying the type of SQL statement to be executed at the data source. This value should match the action being specified by the Command object.

The value can be assigned to several different types of variables, including an Int32, String, or StatementType enumeration. (The advantage to assigning the value to an enumeration is that the ToString method of the enumeration will return the enumeration member name, instead of merely its integer value—that is, "Delete" instead of "3".)

> **NOTE** **The StatementType method is a good example of when you might want to use the ToString method to return a more meaningful value. StatementType by itself returns a number, whereas StatementType.ToString returns a meaningful string such as Update.**

Usage

```
myStatementType = myOleDbRowUpdatingEventArgs.StatementType
myInt32 = myOleDbRowUpdatingEventArgs.StatementType
```

Parameters

None.

StatementType Enumeration

Delete (3)	A SQL DELETE statement.
Insert (1)	A SQL INSERT statement.
Select (0)	(Default). A SQL SELECT statement.
Update (2)	A SQL UPDATE statement.

Status

The Status property (inherited from System.Data.Common.RowUpdatingEventArgs) returns a System.Data.UpdateStatus enumeration value specifying the action that will be taken during the Update with regard to the current row and following rows. The default value is Continue, which tells the DataAdapter to process this row and to continue processing rows. Other values are listed in the text that follows.

This allows you to cancel changes to the data source. By setting this value to SkipCurrentRow, no changes will be made to the data source for this row; however, any remaining rows will continue to be processed normally.

Like other enumerations, the value can be assigned to several different types of variables, including an Int32, String, or UpdateStatus enumeration. The advantage to assigning the value to an enumeration is that the ToString method of the enumeration will return the enumeration member name, instead of merely its integer value—that is, "Continue" instead of "0".

Usage

```
myUpdateStatus = myOleDbRowUpdatingEventArgs.UpdateStatus
myInt32 = myOleDbRowUpdatingEventArgs.UpdateStatus
```

Parameters

None.

UpdateStatus Enumeration

Member	Description
Continue (0)	(Default) Process this row, and continue processing rows.
ErrorsOccurred (1)	This update should be treated as an error. Setting this value will abort the update of this row and all remaining rows, as well as throw an Exception. To specify the Error to be thrown, add an Exception to the Errors property.
SkipAllRemainingRows (3)	Do not process this row or any remaining rows.
SkipCurrentRow (2)	Do not process this row, but continue processing rows.

TableMapping

The read-only TableMapping property (inherited from System.Data.Common.RowUpdatingEventArgs) returns the System.Data.Common.DataTableMapping object that is being sent by the Update method. This object maps the table and columns used by the data source to the table and columns used by the DataSet, to facilitate updating the data at the data source. The DataTableMapping objects contained in the DataTableMapping-Collection contain three public properties that permit access to the underlying mapping.

- The read-only ColumnMapping property, which returns the DataColumnMappingCollection object describing the mappings of the columns between the data source and DataSet.
- The DataSetTable property, which is used to get or set the destination DataSet table name.
- The SourceTable, which gets or sets the source table from which to retrieve the data.

See System.Data.Common.DataTableMapping for more information.

Usage

```
myDataTableMapping = myOleDbRowUpdatingEventArgs.TableMapping
```

Parameters

None.

System.Data.OleDb.OleDbSchemaGuid

An OleDbSchemaGuid represents the type of schema table returned by the OleDbConnection's GetOleDbSchemaTable method. A schema is a catalog of information, or meta data, that describes the objects in a database. See the OleDbConnection object for more information about retrieving schema information from a data source.

When you call the OleDbConnection.GetOleDbSchemaTable method, you can pass it the type of schema you want back via a GUID (Globally Unique Identifier). Depending upon the GUID you pass to the GetOleDbSchemaTable method, you will receive back specific columns of data.

Thirty-five different GUIDs offer a wide range of meta data that you can query about a given data source. Not all GUIDs are valid for all OLE DB providers. Some are reserved for future versions of the databases. If you are ever curious as to the value of the GUID, you can use the ToString method:

```
MessageBox.Show(myOleDbSchemaGuid.Tables.ToString())
```

Returns:

```
c8b52229-5cf3-11ce-ade5-00aa0044773d
```

Some of the more popular schemas that you might request are the following:

- Catalogs
- Check_Constraints
- Columns
- Indexes
- Primary_Keys
- Procedures
- Tables
- Views

Remember that each schema returned is based on the user that is logged in. If there are objects that are not owned by the user ID and that user ID doesn't have administrative privileges in the database, then the schema may not show all possible information. Also, the schema may include hidden or system tables.

Also, please consider using a more robust API, such as SQL Server's Distributed Management Objects (SQL-DMO), or using system stored procedures to return information not available in these schemas.

Constructors

```
myOleDbSchemaGuid = New System.Data.OleDb.OleDbSchemaGuid
```

Parameters

None.

Members

Assertions

This GUID returns the assertions defined in the catalog. Assertions are similar to constraints and are not currently supported in Microsoft products.

As of this writing, the Assertions schema is not supported by either the SQL Server OLE DB provider or the Jet OLE DB provider.

Catalogs

This GUID returns the physical attributes associated with catalogs accessible from the data source. With SQL Server, the catalogs return a DataTable of all databases on the server.

As of this writing, the Catalogs schema is not supported by the Jet OLE DB provider.

Character_Sets

This GUID returns the character sets defined in the catalog. Character sets determine the types of characters stored in character and text fields.

As of this writing, the Character_Sets schema is not supported by either the SQL Server OLE DB provider or the Jet OLE DB provider.

Check_Constraints

This GUID returns any check constraints defined in the catalog. Check constraints are expressions that can be saved to a database that specify valid values to be entered into specific columns.

Check_Constraints_By_Table

Similar to the Check_Constraints schema, this GUID also returns additional information about the catalog and table.

As of this writing, the Check_Constraints_By_Table schema is not supported by the Jet OLE DB provider; however, the Check_Constraints schema is supported, and the same table information can be parsed out of the Constraint_Name field.

Collations

This GUID returns the character set collations defined in the catalog. Collations are sets of rules that determine how data is compared, sorted, and presented, including locale information, sorting order, and case sensitivity.

As of this writing, the Collations schema is not supported by either the SQL Server OLE DB provider or the Jet OLE DB provider.

Column_Domain_Usage

This GUID returns the columns defined in the catalog that are dependent on a domain. This table will show all of those columns in the current database that are based on user-defined data types.

As of this writing, the Column_Domain_Usage schema is not supported by either the SQL Server OLE DB provider or the Jet OLE DB provider.

Column_Privileges

This GUID returns the privileges on all table columns that have been granted to the current user. This can be a very large table of information, but also very useful in programmatically determining if the current user has Insert, Reference, Select, or Update permission for a given range of columns.

As of this writing, the Column_Privileges schema is not supported by the Jet OLE DB provider.

Columns

This GUID returns all columns of all tables and views in the database. This can be a very large table of information because it includes a lot of useful information about each column, including the data type, width, ordinal position, default information, nullable, flags, and many other descriptors.

Constraint_Column_Usage

This GUID returns those columns used in referential constraints, unique constraints, check constraints, and other constraints, such as assertions.

As of this writing, the Constraint_Column_Usage schema is not supported by the SQL Server OLE DB provider.

Constraint_Table_Usage

This GUID returns those tables used in referential constraints, unique constraints, check constraints, and other constraints, such as assertions. For Microsoft Access, this information can be retrieved by using the Constraint_Column_Usage GUID.

As of this writing, the Constraint_Table_Usage schema is not supported by either the SQL Server OLE DB provider or the Jet OLE DB provider.

DbInfoLiterals

This GUID returns a list of provider-specific literal keywords that can be used in text commands. In addition to returning the literal name and value, invalid characters, max length, and an ordinal number are also returned. It is good to review this schema before you start coding, to familiarize yourself with any escape sequences and delimiters for that particular provider.

Foreign_Keys

This GUID returns those columns that are used in foreign keys. Both primary key and foreign key information, such as database, table, and columns, are returned as well as any actions, such as cascading updates and deletes.

Indexes

This GUID returns all indexes defined in the database. In addition to the basic information, such as index name, table, and columns, technical information about the index is returned, such as whether it is clustered, unique, primary, initial size, automatic update, page counts, cardinal information, fill factor, and so on.

Keep in mind that several rows can constitute an index. For multikey indexes, you may have to read through the schema based on the Table_Name, Index_Name, and Ordinal fields to read the keys properly.

Key_Column_Usage

This GUID returns those database columns that are constrained as keys. This schema allows you to quickly find all of those columns that constitute primary key constraints, unique constraints, and foreign key constraints. Keep in mind that several rows can constitute a constraint. For multicolumned constraints, you may have to read through the schema based on the Table_Name, Constraint_Name, and Ordinal fields.

As of this writing, the Key_Column_Usage schema is not supported by the SQL Server OLE DB provider.

Primary_Keys

This GUID returns those columns that define primary keys. For multicolumned primary keys, you may have to read through the schema based on the Table_Name and Ordinal fields.

Procedure_Columns

This GUID returns a schema of rowset columns returned by stored procedures. In addition to column name information, descriptions, data types, lengths, scale, precision information, and other descriptors are returned.

As of this writing, the Procedure_Columns schema is not supported by either the SQL Server OLE DB provider or the Jet OLE DB provider.

Procedure_Parameters

This GUID returns all parameters to all stored procedures in the database. In addition to the procedure and parameter names, data types, lengths, scale, precision, and other descriptors are returned. To read all of the parameters for a given stored procedure in their natural order, pay attention to the Procedure_Name and Ordinal columns.

As of this writing, the Procedure_Parameters schema is not supported by the Jet OLE DB provider.

Procedures

This GUID returns a schema of all stored procedures in the database. The schema, however, does not include any information about triggers. With the Jet OLE DB provider, the schema returns a mix of information from query and report objects, as well as other embedded queries in the database.

Provider_Types

This GUID returns a schema listing the base data types supported by the ADO.NET data provider. In addition to the data type name, the schema also returns the size, prefix, suffix, nullability, case sensitivity, precision, and scale, as well as several other descriptors.

Referential_Constraints

This GUID returns a schema listing all of the Referential Integrity (RI) constraints defined in the database. With the Jet OLE DB provider, this schema will list any relationships you set up in the Relationships editor in Microsoft Access, including any action for updating and deleting.

As of this writing, the Referential_Constraints schema is not supported by the SQL Server OLE DB provider.

Schemata

This GUID returns a schema of all schema objects in the database. With SQL Server, this schema simply returns a table, where each row is a database that has permissions for the current user.

As of this writing, the Procedure_Parameters schema is not supported by the Jet OLE DB provider.

Sql_Languages

This GUID returns a schema listing the conformance levels, options, and dialects supported by the OLE DB provider's implementation of SQL.

As of this writing, the Procedure_Columns schema is not supported by either the SQL Server OLE DB provider or the Jet OLE DB provider.

Statistics

This GUID returns a schema of all tables in the database as well as the number of rows per table (which is also called the cardinality of the table). Keep in mind that the cardinality value may not be accurate due to ongoing transactions, locking, and other factors affecting the way the database maintains statistics. The only sure way to determine the accurate number of rows in a table is to execute a SELECT Count(*) query.

Table_Constraints

This GUID returns a schema of all table-level constraints defined in the database. These constraints may include check constraints, primary key constraints, foreign key constraints, and unique constraints.

Table_Privileges

This GUID returns the privileges on all tables that have been granted to the current user. This can be a very large table of information, but it can also be very useful in programmatically determining if the current user has Delete, Insert, Reference, Select, or Update permission for a given table.

As of this writing, the Table_Privileges schema is not supported by the Jet OLE DB provider.

Tables

This GUID returns a schema listing all system tables, user tables, and views defined in the database. This schema is an example of how you could use the restrictions() array on the GetOleDbSchemaTable method call to just return the user tables in the database.

Consider the OleDbSchemaGuid.Tables_Info schema for more detailed information.

Tables_Info

This GUID returns a schema listing all system tables, user tables, and views defined in the database. In addition to the object names, this schema lists bookmark, version, and cardinality (row count) information.

Table_Statistics

This GUID returns a schema listing the available sets of statistics for each table in the database. A rather technical schema, this one can assist in tuning your indexes and queries because it lists the cardinality for each row as well as each column. You can also view average column length, number of ranges, and sample percentage by statistic type.

As of this writing, the Table_Statistics schema is not supported by the Jet OLE DB provider.

Translations

This GUID returns a schema listing the code page character translations for the database. Knowing these translations is important when working with international databases that may use a mix of Unicode and non-Unicode character sets.

As of this writing, the Translations schema is not supported by either the SQL Server OLE DB provider or the Jet OLE DB provider.

Trustee

This GUID returns a schema listing all trustees defined in the database. Trustees are users or groups under whose security context an application or component runs.

As of this writing, the Trustee schema is not supported by either the SQL Server OLE DB provider or the Jet OLE DB provider.

Usage_Privileges

This GUID returns a schema listing all of the usage privileges on all objects that have been granted to the current user.

As of this writing, the Usage_Privileges schema is not supported by either the SQL Server OLE DB provider or the Jet OLE DB provider.

View_Column_Usage

This GUID returns a schema listing all dependent columns from all views in the database.

As of this writing, the View_Column_Usage schema is not supported by either the SQL Server OLE DB provider or the Jet OLE DB provider.

View_Table_Usage

This GUID returns a schema listing all dependent tables from all views in the database.

As of this writing, the View_Table_Usage schema is not supported by either the SQL Server OLE DB provider or the Jet OLE DB provider.

Views

This GUID returns a schema listing all views in the database. With the Jet OLE DB provider, the schema returns the names, descriptions, dates, SQL, and other descriptors for the query objects.

As of this writing, the Views schema is not supported by the SQL Server OLE DB provider.

System.Data.OleDb.OleDbTransaction

An OleDbTransaction represents a SQL transaction for a given OleDbConnection. A transaction is a logical group of database operations combined to form a single unit of work. An example of this would be an INSERT and a DELETE operation working together to facilitate "moving" data from one table to another. In this case, it is very important for both operations to happen together or not at all. Transactions see to that.

SQL programmers might be inclined to execute a SQL batch that contains BEGIN TRANSACTION and COMMIT TRANSACTION statements. You should not do this; rather, you should use ADO.NET's built-in transaction management features found in the OleDbTransaction and OleDbConnection classes.

ADO.NET creates an OleDbTransaction object when the BeginTransaction method is called on an OleDbConnection object. All ensuing operations associated with the transaction are performed on the OleDbTransaction object.

Although the OleDbTransaction class has a constructor method, it is private and cannot be called. You must use the BeginTransaction method of an existing OleDb-Connection object to create an instance of an OleDbTransaction.

Constructors

There is no public constructor.

Parameters

None.

Members

Begin

The Begin method commences a new, nested transaction within the context of an existing OleDbTransaction.

In order to simplify complicated data processing, you may want to create nested (inner) transactions, committing them as you go along, and then finally commit the parent (outer) transaction, always reserving the ability to roll back the entire unit of work. This allows you to take a modular approach to your database work.

If you want to begin a transaction with a specific isolation level, you can call the Begin method by passing a valid IsolationLevel enumeration to the constructor. The default IsolationLevel is ReadCommitted.

See the IsolationLevel property for a list of valid IsolationLevel enumeration values.

NOTE **Keep in mind that not all OLEDB providers support nested transactions. As of the RTM version, the JET (Access) Ole Db provider supports nested transactions, but the SQLOLEDB provider does not. We cannot explain the logic in this.**

Usage

```
myOleDbTrans2 = myOleDbTrans1.Begin()
myOleDbTrans2 = myOleDbTrans1.Begin(IsolationLevel)
```

Parameters

`IsolationLevel`	A valid IsolationLevel enumeration.

Exceptions

ArgumentException	An invalid IsolationLevel argument was passed.
NullReferenceException	The parent OleDbTransaction object has not yet been instantiated.
OleDbException	Parallel transactions are not supported. If you are trying to start a nested transaction, you must use an additional object variable.

Sample Code

```
Dim myOleDbConnection As New System.Data.OleDb.OleDbConnection()
Dim myOleDbTransaction1 As System.Data.OleDb.OleDbTransaction
Dim myOleDbTransaction2 As System.Data.OleDb.OleDbTransaction
Dim myOleDbCommand1 As New System.Data.OleDb.OleDbCommand()
Dim myOleDbCommand2 As New System.Data.OleDb.OleDbCommand()
Dim myConnectionString As String
' Open Connection
myConnectionString = "Provider=Microsoft.Jet.OLEDB.4.0;' & _
   "Data Source=C:\Northwind.mdb"
myOleDbConnection.ConnectionString = myConnectionString
myOleDbConnection.Open()
' Outer Transaction
myOleDbTransaction1 = myOleDbConnection.BeginTransaction()
myOleDbCommand1.CommandText = "INSERT INTO Customers " & _
   "(CustomerID,CompanyName) VALUES ('Cust1','Test Customer 1')"
myOleDbCommand1.Connection = myOleDbConnection
myOleDbCommand1.Transaction = myOleDbTransaction1
myOleDbCommand1.ExecuteNonQuery()
' Inner Transaction
myOleDbTransaction2 = myOleDbTransaction1.Begin()
```

```
myOleDbCommand2.CommandText = "INSERT INTO Customers " & _
   "(CustomerID,CompanyName) VALUES ('Cust2','Test Customer 2')"
myOleDbCommand2.Connection = myOleDbConnection
myOleDbCommand2.Transaction = myOleDbTransaction2
myOleDbCommand2.ExecuteNonQuery()
' Commit and Rollback
myOleDbTransaction2.Commit()   ' Commit Inner Transaction
myOleDbTransaction1.Rollback() ' Rollback Outer & Inner Transaction
myOleDbConnection.Close()
```

Commit

The Commit method saves all pending changes to the data source made since the start of the transaction. By definition, a Commit guarantees that all of the transaction's modifications are made successfully to the data source. The Commit method also frees locks and other resources at the data source.

You cannot Commit a transaction that has already been rolled back.

Usage

```
myOleDbTransaction.Commit()
```

Parameters

None.

Exceptions

Exception	An unspecified ADO.NET error occurred while trying to commit the transaction.
InvalidOperationException	There is no current transaction (perhaps it was already committed or rolled back), or the OleDbConnection is not open.

Sample Code

```
Dim myOleDbConnection As New System.Data.OleDb.OleDbConnection()
Dim myOleDbTransaction As System.Data.OleDb.OleDbTransaction
Dim myOleDbCommand As New System.Data.OleDb.OleDbCommand()
Dim myConnectionString As String
myConnectionString = "Provider=Microsoft.Jet.OLEDB.4.0;" & _
   "Data Source=C:\Northwind.mdb"
myOleDbConnection.ConnectionString = myConnectionString
myOleDbConnection.Open()
myOleDbTransaction = myOleDbConnection.BeginTransaction()
myOleDbCommand.Connection = myOleDbConnection
myOleDbCommand.Transaction = myOleDbTransaction
Try
   ' First Insert
   myOleDbCommand.CommandText = "INSERT INTO Customers " & _
      "(CustomerID,CompanyName) VALUES ('Wiley','Wiley Publishing')"
   myOleDbCommand.ExecuteNonQuery()
   ' Second Insert
```

```
    myOleDbCommand.CommandText = "INSERT INTO Customers " & _
        "(CustomerID,CompanyName) VALUES ('Wiley','Wiley Publishing')"
    myOleDbCommand.ExecuteNonQuery()
    myOleDbTransaction.Commit()
    MessageBox.Show("Both records were written", "Success!")
Catch ex As Exception
    myOleDbTransaction.Rollback()
    MessageBox.Show("Neither record was written" & _
        ControlChars.CrLf & ControlChars.CrLf & ex.ToString(), "Failure!")
Finally
    myOleDbConnection.Close()
End Try
```

IsolationLevel

The IsolationLevel property is the read-only value of the IsolationLevel for the OleDb-Transaction specified.

An IsolationLevel controls the degree by which your data is isolated from other processes. IsolationLevels guard against interference from other users running queries or changing data that you are currently working on in your transaction. The underlying data source may or may not support all of ADO.NET's IsolationLevels.

Usage

```
myIsolationLevel = myOleDbTransaction.IsolationLevel
myIsolationLevelString = myOleDbTransaction.IsolationLevel.ToString()
```

Parameters

None.

IsolationLevel Enumeration

Chaos (16)	Any pending changes from transactions that are more highly isolated transactions cannot be overwritten. SQL Server 2000 and below do not support this isolation level.
ReadCommitted (4096)	(Default) Shared locks are held while the data is being read to avoid dirty reads, but the data can be changed before the end of the transaction, resulting in nonrepeatable reads or phantom data (a.k.a. CursorStability).
ReadUncommitted (256)	No shared locks or exclusive locks are honored, so dirty reads are possible (a.k.a. Browse).
RepeatableRead (65536)	All data used in a query is locked, preventing others from updating. This prevents nonrepeatable reads, but phantom rows are still possible.
Serializable (1048576)	A range lock is placed on the data, preventing other users from updating or inserting rows into the dataset until the transaction is complete (a.k.a. Isolated).

Unspecified (-1)	A different isolation level than the one specified is being used, but the level cannot be determined. (This value cannot be passed when creating a Transaction.)

Sample Code

```
Dim myOleDbConnection As New System.Data.OleDb.OleDbConnection()
Dim myOleDbTransaction As System.Data.OleDb.OleDbTransaction
Dim myOleDbCommand As New System.Data.OleDb.OleDbCommand()
Dim myConnectionString As String
myConnectionString = "Provider=Microsoft.Jet.OLEDB.4.0;" & _
   "Data Source=C:\Northwind.mdb"
myOleDbConnection.ConnectionString = myConnectionString
myOleDbConnection.Open()
myOleDbTransaction = myOleDbConnection.BeginTransaction()
MessageBox.Show(myOleDbTransaction.IsolationLevel.ToString())
myOleDbConnection.Close()
```

Rollback

The opposite of the Commit method, Rollback removes any pending changes to the data source made since the start of the transaction. By definition, a Rollback maintains integrity because it puts the data source back to an original state in the event of an application or system failure. The Rollback method also frees locks and other resources at the data source. If you close an OleDbConnection with an activity transaction, ADO.NET will roll back any pending changes automatically.

You cannot roll back a transaction which has already been committed.

Usage

```
myOleDbTransaction.Rollback()
```

Parameters

None.

Exceptions

Exception	An unspecified system error occurred while trying to rollback the transaction.
InvalidOperationException	There is no current transaction (perhaps it was already committed or rolled back), or the OleDbConnection is not open.

CHAPTER

8

System.Data.SqlClient

The SQL Server .NET data provider is the provider of choice for accessing SQL Server 7.0, 2000, or MSDE (Microsoft Data Engine) databases. Although other .NET data providers would work and connect to these data sources, this provider is recommended, as it directly uses the application-level protocol to talk to SQL Server. This protocol is known as Tabular Data Stream (TDS) and came into being with SQL Server 7.0. TDS is used by SQL Server to transfer requests and responses between the client application and SQL Server.

Because the SQL Server .NET data provider speaks TDS as its mother tongue, there is no need for an OLE DB provider or ODBC driver to perform any translation. The fact that no extra layers are used means that you get a lightweight data access mechanism.

TIP If you need to access an earlier version of SQL Server, such as 6.0 or 6.5, then you must use the OLE DB .NET data provider. You may also want to download and use the ODBC .NET data provider.

Like the other data providers, the SQL Server .NET data provider has the Connection, Command, DataAdapter, and DataReader classes as its heavy lifters. Other classes provide supporting functionality, such as the SqlException and SqlError classes, which provide detailed error information specific to SQL Server. To use this data provider you must import the System.Data.SqlClient namespace.

You will find that the objects in the SqlClient namespace have subtle differences, such as the occasional addition method or property, to better support SQL Server.

System.Data.SqlClient.SqlCommand

The SqlCommand represents a SQL statement or call to a stored procedure. If information is to be returned, the SqlCommand can do so by returning a SqlDataReader object, an XMLReader object, a scalar value, or output parameters and return values read via the Parameters collection.

You may instantiate a SqlCommand object by itself or use the CreateCommand method on the SqlConnection object.

Constructors

```
Dim mySqlCommand As New SqlCommand()
Dim mySqlCommand As New SqlCommand(MyString)
Dim mySqlCommand As New SqlCommand(MyString, MySqlConnection)
Dim mySqlCommand As New SqlCommand(MyString, MySqlConnection, _
    MySqlTransaction)
```

Parameters

`MyString`	The String to be assigned to the CommandText property.
`MySqlConnection`	The SqlConnection object to assign to the Connection property.
`MySqlTransaction`	The SqlTransaction object to assign to the Transaction property.

SqlCommand Sample Code

```
Dim mySqlConnection As New System.Data.SqlClient.SqlConnection()
Dim mySqlTransaction As System.Data.SqlClient.SqlTransaction
Dim mySqlCommand As System.Data.SqlClient.SqlCommand
' Establish Connection
mySqlConnection.ConnectionString = _
   "Data Source=Omnibook;Integrated Security=SSPI;Database=Northwind"
mySqlConnection.Open()
' Establish Transaction
mySqlTransaction = mySqlConnection.BeginTransaction()
' Establish Command
mySqlCommand = New SqlCommand("INSERT Customers " & _
   "(CustomerID,CompanyName) VALUES ('WILEY','Wiley Publishing')", _
   mySqlConnection, mySqlTransaction)
' Attempt Execution(s)
mySqlCommand.ExecuteNonQuery()     ' INSERT succeeds
Try
   mySqlCommand.ExecuteNonQuery() ' INSERT fails on PK violation
   mySqlTransaction.Commit()
```

```
    MessageBox.Show("Success!", "Both records written")
Catch ex As Exception
    mySqlTransaction.Rollback()
    MessageBox.Show(ex.ToString(), "No records written")
Finally
    mySqlConnection.Close()
    mySqlConnection.Dispose()
End Try
```

Members

Cancel

The Cancel method cancels the execution of the SqlCommand. If you had already assigned a SqlDataReader object, it will not be disposed or reinitialized when you call the Cancel method.

The Cancel method is very forgiving, and it will not throw an exception even if there is no operation to cancel. Cancel also will not throw an exception if the SqlCommand object has not been properly established or if the connection is closed.

NOTE Because the Execute methods are synchronous by nature, the Cancel method will work only if you are implementing the SqlCommand in a multithreaded algorithm. Microsoft may also decide to add asynchronous behavior to the SqlCommand and SqlConnection at a later time. Both of these classes support a Cancel method.

Usage

```
mySqlCommand.Cancel()
```

Parameters

None.

Exceptions

None.

CommandText

The CommandText property is a String value that gets or sets the SQL statement or name of a stored procedure to execute. The default value is an empty String. If the text references objects with spaces in their names, you'll need to put those names in delimiters (square brackets). The CommandText property works in conjunction with the CommandType property, specifying either a StoredProcedure or Text (the default), so ensure that the CommandText you specify in this property matches the expectations of the CommandType property.

NOTE Incidentally, the TableDirect CommandType is not supported by SqlClient.

As with the CommandType and Connection properties, the CommandText property cannot be set when the associated SqlConnection object is performing a fetch or execute operation.

When calling a stored procedure, the CommandText requires named parameters, so any parameters must be prefixed with an "@" or built into the SQL statement directly by concatenating the SQL command and any parameters into a String. Unlike the OleDb .NET data provider, you cannot use the question mark (?) symbols to delimit your parameters.

If you decided to concatenate your SQL command programmatically, be careful to mind the delimiters—it can be very easy to get your quotation marks or apostrophes out of synch. If you want to use the named parameter method, then you will need to create SqlParameter objects and add them to the SqlParameterCollection in the order they appear in the SQL statement.

```
SELECT * FROM [Order Details] WHERE ProductID = @ProductID
   AND UnitPrice > @UnitPrice
```

The benefit of using SqlParameter objects is that your ADO.NET code can retrieve Return values and Output parameters from the stored procedures. The concatenation method cannot, as it supports only the passing of values to the stored procedure. The benefit of the concatenation method is in the reduction in overhead of having to use SqlParameter objects. The deciding factor for you is whether you need to capture output variables from your stored procedures. Keep in mind that either method retrieves recordset data without concern.

Usage

```
myCommandText = mySqlCommand.CommandText
mySqlCommand.CommandText = "SELECT * FROM Products"
```

Parameters

None.

Sample Code

```
Dim mySqlConnection As New System.Data.SqlClient.SqlConnection()
Dim mySqlCommand As System.Data.SqlClient.SqlCommand
' Establish Connection
mySqlConnection.ConnectionString = _
   "Data Source=Omnibook;Integrated Security=SSPI;Database=Northwind"
mySqlConnection.Open()
' Establish Command
mySqlCommand = mySqlConnection.CreateCommand
mySqlCommand.CommandText = "SELECT Count(*) FROM [Order Details] " & _
   "WHERE ProductID = @ProductID AND UnitPrice > @UnitPrice"
' Establish Parameters and Execute Command
mySqlCommand.Parameters.Add("@ProductID", 59)
mySqlCommand.Parameters.Add("@UnitPrice", 50)
MessageBox.Show(mySqlCommand.ExecuteScalar, "Product Count") ' 35
' Done
mySqlConnection.Close()
```

CommandTimeout

The CommandTimeout property gets or sets an Int32 value representing the amount of time (in seconds) to wait for a Command to execute before raising a timeout error. It is common to have a particular lengthy stored procedure or SQL statement that needs several minutes to finish processing. Ideally, longer batch processes are scheduled during the off hours and executed without the need of a user interface; however, there are times when you need to programmatically allow for a lengthy routine to run.

Setting CommandTimeout to a value of zero indicates that there is no time limit. This should generally be avoided because it could result in "hung" applications.

The default CommandTimeout is 30 seconds.

Usage

```
myInt32 = mySqlCommand.CommandTimeout
mySqlCommand.CommandTimeout = 60
```

Parameters

None.

Exceptions

ArgumentException	The CommandTimeout value was less than zero.

Sample Code

```
Dim mySqlConnection As New System.Data.SqlClient.SqlConnection()
Dim mySqlCommand As System.Data.SqlClient.SqlCommand
' Establish Connection
mySqlConnection.ConnectionString = _
   "Server=(local);Integrated Security=SSPI;Database=Accounting"
mySqlConnection.Open()
' Establish Command to perform lengthy archival routine
mySqlCommand = mySqlConnection.CreateCommand()
mySqlCommand.CommandText = "EXECUTE web_ArchiveAccounting"
mySqlCommand.CommandTimeout = 7200 ' Two hours
mySqlCommand.ExecuteNonQuery()
' Done
mySqlConnection.Close()
```

CommandType

The CommandType property sets or returns a CommandType enumeration that determines how the CommandText property should be interpreted by the data source. Because of this, the CommandType property actually dictates the content of the CommandText property. For example, if you set the CommandType to StoredProcedure, you may not specify a SQL statement in the CommandText property—you can specify only a stored procedure name.

As with the CommandText and Connection properties, the CommandType property cannot be set when the associated SqlConnection object is performing a fetch or execute operation.

The default CommandType is Text.

Usage

```
myCommandType = mySqlCommand.CommandType
mySqlCommand.CommandType = CommandType.StoredProcedure
```

Parameters

None.

CommandType Enumeration

StoredProcedure (4)	CommandText should be set to the name of the stored procedure.
TableDirect (512)	CommandText should be the name of a table. All columns will be returned. This CommandType is *not* supported with the SqlClient namespace.
Text (1)	(Default) CommandText can be any valid SQL text command.

Exceptions

ArgumentException	The CommandType value does not correspond to a valid CommandType.

Sample Code

```
Dim mySqlConnection As New System.Data.SqlClient.SqlConnection()
Dim mySqlDataReader As System.Data.SqlClient.SqlDataReader
Dim mySqlCommand As System.Data.SqlClient.SqlCommand
' Establish Connection
mySqlConnection.ConnectionString = _
  "Server=(local);Integrated Security=SSPI;"
mySqlConnection.Open()
mySqlConnection.ChangeDatabase("Northwind")
' Establish Command and Parameters
mySqlCommand = mySqlConnection.CreateCommand
mySqlCommand.CommandType = CommandType.StoredProcedure
mySqlCommand.CommandText = "[Sales By Year]"
mySqlCommand.Parameters.Add("@Beginning_Date", "10/01/1997")
mySqlCommand.Parameters.Add("@Ending_Date", "12/31/1997")
' Execute
mySqlDataReader = mySqlCommand.ExecuteReader()
' Process mySqlDataReader here
mySqlDataReader.Close()
mySqlConnection.Close()
```

Connection

The Connection property sets or returns the SqlConnection object associated with the SqlCommand. The SqlConnection object being associated with the SqlCommand can be open or closed. As with the CommandText and CommandType properties, the Connection property cannot be set when the associated SqlConnection object is performing a fetch or execute operation.

Setting the connection is not allowed if a transaction is active; however, if the transaction has already been committed or rolled back, then the transaction object will automatically be set to null when the connection object is set or changed.

The default Connection is a null reference, which is `Nothing` in Visual Basic.

TIP **You can take a shortcut and avoid having to assign the Connection property if you create your SqlCommand object by using the SqlConnection.CreateCommand method.**

Usage

```
mySqlConnection = mySqlCommand.Connection
mySqlCommand.Connection = mySqlConnection
```

Parameters

None.

Exceptions

InvalidOperationException	Attempt to change Connection value while a transaction was in progress.

Sample Code

```
Dim mySqlConnection As New System.Data.SqlClient.SqlConnection()
Dim mySqlCommand As New System.Data.SqlClient.SqlCommand()
Dim myInteger As Int32
' Establish Connection
mySqlConnection.ConnectionString = _
   "Server=(local);Integrated Security=SSPI;Database=Northwind"
mySqlConnection.Open()
' Determine Number of SysObjects
mySqlCommand.CommandText = "SELECT Count(*) FROM SysObjects"
mySqlCommand.Connection = mySqlConnection
myInteger = mySqlCommand.ExecuteScalar()
Messagebox.Show(myInteger,"Number of SysObjects")
mySqlConnection.Close()
```

CreateParameter

The CreateParameter method returns a new SqlParameter object. You would want to call this method if you are constructing a parameter collection in preparation for a call to a stored procedure or query using replaceable parameters.

The CreateParameter method is available purely for convenience. The resulting SqlParameter object is not initialized in any way, nor is it added automatically to the SqlCommand.Parameters collection. You must manually initialize the object as well as add it to the Parameters collection.

Usage

```
mySqlParameter = mySqlCommand.CreateParameter()
```

Parameters

None.

Exceptions

None.

Sample Code

```
Dim mySqlConnection As New System.Data.SqlClient.SqlConnection()
Dim mySqlDataReader As System.Data.SqlClient.SqlDataReader
Dim mySqlParameter As System.Data.SqlClient.SqlParameter
Dim mySqlCommand As System.Data.SqlClient.SqlCommand
' Establish Connection
mySqlConnection.ConnectionString = _
  "Server=(local);Integrated Security=SSPI;"
mySqlConnection.Open()
mySqlConnection.ChangeDatabase("Northwind")
' Establish Command
mySqlCommand = mySqlConnection.CreateCommand()
mySqlCommand.CommandType = CommandType.StoredProcedure
mySqlCommand.CommandText = "[Sales By Year]"
' Establish Parameter #1
mySqlParameter = mySqlCommand.CreateParameter()
mySqlParameter.ParameterName = "@Beginning_Date"
mySqlParameter.Value = "10/01/1997"
mySqlCommand.Parameters.Add(mySqlParameter)
' Establish Parameter #2
mySqlParameter = mySqlCommand.CreateParameter()
mySqlParameter.ParameterName = "@Ending_Date"
mySqlParameter.Value = "12/31/1997"
mySqlCommand.Parameters.Add(mySqlParameter)
' Execute
mySqlDataReader = mySqlCommand.ExecuteReader()
' Process mySqlDataReader here
mySqlDataReader.Close()
mySqlConnection.Close()
```

DesignTimeVisible

The DesignTimeVisible property gets or sets a Boolean determining whether the SqlCommand object will be visible in a Windows Form Designer control.

Usage

```
myBoolean = mySqlCommand.DesignTimeVisible
mySqlCommand.DesignTimeVisible = False
```

Parameters

None.

ExecuteNonQuery

The ExecuteNonQuery method executes a SQL statement and returns an Int32 representing the number of rows affected. This is generally used for SQL statements that update or change the data source but return no data. If you require the ability to retrieve row data from a SqlCommand, then you should consider using the ExecuteReader method. If you require the ability to retrieve a single value from a SqlCommand, such as an average product price, then you should consider using the ExecuteScalar method. If you are issuing a SQL command with the "FOR XML" clause, then you should call the ExecuteXmlReader method.

The return value for Insert, Update, and Delete statements is the number of rows affected. For all other statements it is -1. Although no data is returned from an ExecuteNonQuery method call, any output parameters or return values that are mapped to parameters will be returned.

When executing a command against SQL Server, the number of rows affected will be the *sum* of all Insert, Update, and Delete statements executed in the batch or stored procedure, regardless of whether there are other output statements.

Usage

```
myInt32 = mySqlCommand.ExecuteNonQuery()
```

Parameters

None.

Exceptions

InvalidOperationException	The SqlConnection does not exist or is not open.
SqlException	The command syntax is invalid.

Sample Code

```
Dim mySqlConnection As New System.Data.SqlClient.SqlConnection()
Dim mySqlCommand As System.Data.SqlClient.SqlCommand
Dim myInt32 As Int32
' Establish Connection
mySqlConnection.ConnectionString = _
   "Server=(local);Integrated Security=SSPI;"
mySqlConnection.Open()
mySqlConnection.ChangeDatabase("NorthWind")
' Establish Command to execute two UPDATES in a batch
mySqlCommand = mySqlConnection.CreateCommand()
mySqlCommand.CommandText = _
   "UPDATE Products SET UnitPrice = UnitPrice * 1.1 WHERE " & _
   "UnitPrice < 10 " & _
   "UPDATE Products SET UnitPrice = UnitPrice * 1.15 WHERE " & _
   "UnitPrice > 20"
myInt32 = mySqlCommand.ExecuteNonQuery()
MessageBox.Show(myInt32, "Total # of Rows Updated")
' myInt32 should equal 48 (11 from Update #1 + 37 from Update #2)
mySqlConnection.Close()
```

ExecuteReader

The ExecuteReader method executes a SQL statement and returns a SqlDataReader object. The ExecuteReader method is generally used to call a SQL statement or stored procedure that returns rows of data. If your intention is to Insert, Update, or Delete data, then you should consider using the ExecuteNonQuery method. If you require the ability to retrieve a single value from a SqlCommand, such as an average product price, then you should consider using the ExecuteScalar method. If you are issuing a SQL command with the "FOR XML" clause, then you should call the ExecuteXmlReader method.

You may also specify a bitwise combination of System.Data.CommandBehavior enumeration values for additional control over how the SqlCommand behaves. These behaviors are vaguely reminiscent of the CursorType property from MDAC ADO. Keep in mind that some behaviors are mutually exclusive of other ones and that there are no default behaviors.

The SqlDataReader requires exclusive access to the SqlConnection object. While you are manipulating the SqlDataReader object, you may not perform any other operations on the SqlConnection, other than closing it. Once you execute the SqlDataReader.Close method, you may again use the SqlConnection for other operations.

Usage

```
mySqlDataReader = mySqlCommand.ExecuteReader()
mySqlDataReader = mySqlCommand.ExecuteReader(MyCommandBehavior)
```

Parameters

`MyCommandBehavior`	A bit-wise combination of CommandBehavior enumeration values.

CommandBehavior Enumeration

CloseConnection (32)	After the command has executed and you have manually called the SqlDataReader's Close method, ADO.NET will automatically close the connection.
KeyInfo (4)	KeyInfo appends hidden key and timestamp information to the results, in order to support later updates without having to keep the table locked. This behavior is fundamental to a client-side cursor design. If you query the SqlDataReader's schema, you will see these additional descriptors. For KeyInfo to work, the Select statement may not contain a Union clause and the underlying table must have a timestamp field and a unique index.
SchemaOnly (2)	The command returns only schema information and does not allow you to read any data rows. This behavior does not impact the database state. The schema information can be viewed by executing the SqlDataReader's GetSchemaTable method.
SequentialAccess (16)	The command returns the results sequentially across all columns. You should select this behavior if your columns contain large binary values, such as embedded documents or images. The SequentialAccess behavior allows you to call the SqlDataReader's GetChars or GetBytes method.
SingleResult (1)	The query returns a single result. If your command returns multiple result sets, this behavior will allow only the first one to be returned; however, no error will be thrown if you call the SqlDataReader's NextResult method.

SingleRow(8)	The query returns a single row. If your command returns multiple rows in one or more result sets, this behavior will allow only the first row to be returned. If you are expecting back a single row of data, specifying this behavior can improve your application's performance. If you are querying only one column from one row, you might consider using the ExecuteScalar method instead. Also, if your query returns multiple results, they will all be returned—but only the first row of each.

Exceptions

InvalidCastException	The CommandBehavior or combination of CommandBehaviors is not valid.
InvalidOperationException	The SqlConnection does not exist or is not open.
SqlException	The command syntax is invalid.

Sample Code

```
Dim mySqlConnection As New System.Data.SqlClient.SqlConnection()
Dim mySqlCommand As System.Data.SqlClient.SqlCommand
Dim mySqlDataReader As System.Data.SqlClient.SqlDataReader
' Establish Connection
mySqlConnection.ConnectionString = _
   "Server=(local);Integrated Security=SSPI;Database=Northwind"
mySqlConnection.Open()
' Establish Command
mySqlCommand = mySqlConnection.CreateCommand()
mySqlCommand.CommandType = CommandType.Text
mySqlCommand.CommandText = "SELECT * FROM Products"
mySqlDataReader = mySqlCommand.ExecuteReader( _
   CommandBehavior.SchemaOnly + CommandBehavior.CloseConnection)
' Browse the SchemaTable in a DataGrid
DataGrid1.DataSource = mySqlDataReader.GetSchemaTable
mySqlDataReader.Close()
' mySqlConnection is closed implicitly
MessageBox.Show(mySqlConnection.State.ToString(), "Connection State")
```

ExecuteScalar

The ExecuteScalar method executes a SQL statement and returns an Object referencing the first column of the first row of data. ExecuteScalar is generally used to call a SQL statement or stored procedure that will return a single value, such as an aggregate function, server version, or other system variable. If you require the ability to retrieve row data from a SqlCommand, then you should consider using the ExecuteReader method. If your intention is to Insert, Update, or Delete data, then you should consider using the ExecuteNonQuery method. If you are issuing a SQL command with the "FOR XML" clause, then you should call the ExecuteXmlReader method.

If your SQL statement returns more than one column or more than one row, the extra information is ignored, and only the first column in the first row is returned. If your SQL statement doesn't return any information, the ExecuteScalar method will not throw an exception, but rather your numeric object will be set to zero and your string objects will be empty (""). Because of this, make sure that your SQL statement is valid before you execute it.

Usage

```
myObject = mySqlCommand.ExecuteScalar()
```

Parameters

None.

Exceptions

InvalidCastException	The Object returned cannot be stored in your variable. For example, you may have returned a String value and tried to store it to an Int32 object.
InvalidOperationException	The SqlConnection does not exist or is not open.
SqlException	The command syntax is invalid.

Sample Code

```
Dim mySqlConnection As New System.Data.SqlClient.SqlConnection()
Dim mySqlCommand As New System.Data.SqlClient.SqlCommand()
Dim myMaxPrice As Double
' Establish Connection
mySqlConnection.ConnectionString = _
   "Server=(local);Integrated Security=SSPI;Database=Northwind"
mySqlConnection.Open()
' Establish Command
mySqlCommand = mySqlConnection.CreateCommand()
mySqlCommand.CommandText = "SELECT Max(UnitPrice) FROM Products"
' ExecuteScalar
myMaxPrice = mySqlCommand.ExecuteScalar
MessageBox.Show(myMaxPrice.ToString("c")) ' Formatted as currency
' Done
mySqlConnection.Close()
```

ExecuteXmlReader

The ExecuteReader method executes a SQL statement and returns an XmlReader object. The ExecuteReader method is generally used to call a SQL statement or stored procedure that returns data with a valid *FOR XML* clause. You can also retrieve XML that you have programmatically stored in text columns. Remember, XML is Unicode.

If you require the ability to retrieve standard (non-XML) row data from a SqlCommand, then you should consider using the ExecuteReader method. If your intention is to Insert, Update, or Delete data, then you should consider using the ExecuteNonQuery method. If you require the ability to retrieve a single value from a SqlCommand, such as an average product price, then you should consider using the ExecuteScalar method.

Only SQL Server 2000 and later versions support this type of query. For more information on the syntax of the SELECT statement and the variations of the FOR XML clause, please consult SQL Server Books Online. An XmlReader object provides forward-only, read-only access to a stream of XML data.

The XmlReader requires exclusive access to the SqlConnection object. While you are manipulating the XMLReader object, you may not perform any other operations on the SqlConnection, other than closing it. Once you execute the XMLReader.Close method, you may again use the SqlConnection for other operations.

Usage

```
myXmlReader = mySqlCommand.ExecuteXmlReader()
```

Parameters

None.

Exceptions

InvalidCastException	The CommandBehavior or combination of CommandBehaviors is not valid.
InvalidOperationException	The SqlConnection does not exist or is not open.
SqlException	The command syntax is invalid.

Sample Code

```
Dim mySqlConnection As New System.Data.SqlClient.SqlConnection()
Dim mySqlCommand As System.Data.SqlClient.SqlCommand
Dim myXmlReader As System.Xml.XmlReader
Dim strAttributes As String
' Establish Connection
mySqlConnection.ConnectionString = _
   "Server=(local);Integrated Security=SSPI;Database=Northwind"
mySqlConnection.Open()
' Establish Command
mySqlCommand = mySqlConnection.CreateCommand()
mySqlCommand.CommandText = _
   "SELECT * FROM Products WHERE UnitPrice > 75 FOR XML AUTO"
' Assign results to XMLReader and Read
myXmlReader = mySqlCommand.ExecuteXmlReader()
While myXmlReader.Read()
   ' Display all attributes for current element
   strAttributes = ""
   While myXmlReader.MoveToNextAttribute()
      strAttributes = strAttributes & myXmlReader.Name & " : " & _
         myXmlReader.Value & ControlChars.CrLf
   End While
   MessageBox.Show(strAttributes, "Product Attributes")
End While
' Done
myXmlReader.Close()
mySqlConnection.Close()
```

Parameters

The Parameters property returns a SqlParameterCollection object that contains a collection of all parameters created for the SqlCommand. The SqlParameter objects are used to pass information to Transact-SQL statements or stored procedures, or they are used to receive information from stored procedures. Parameters default to an empty collection.

If your SQL statement contains replaceable parameters or your stored procedure expects parameters, then you must create your parameters collection before executing the command. The order in which the parameters are expected in the statement must match exactly with the order in the Parameters collection. See the SqlParameterCollection class for more information.

The SqlClient .NET data provider does not support the question mark (?) placeholder for parameters when parsing a SqlCommand. You should instead use named parameters, such as @CustomerID.

When calling stored procedures that do not return output parameters or return values, you do need to use the Parameters collection. Performance is improved if you concatenate literals and variables together to form a meaningful SQL statement or stored procedure call and then execute it directly:

```
mySqlCommand.CommandType = CommandType.Text
mySqlCommand.CommandText = "EXECUTE [Employee Sales by Country] '" & _
   myDate1.ToShortDateString & "','" & myDate2.ToShortDateString & "'"
```

Usage

```
mySqlParameterCollection = mySqlCommand.Parameters
```

Parameters

None.

Sample Code

```
Dim mySqlConnection As New System.Data.SqlClient.SqlConnection()
Dim mySqlCommand As System.Data.SqlClient.SqlCommand
' Establish Connection
mySqlConnection.ConnectionString = _
   "Data Source=Omnibook;Integrated Security=SSPI;Database=Northwind"
mySqlConnection.Open()
' Establish Command
mySqlCommand = mySqlConnection.CreateCommand
mySqlCommand.CommandText = "SELECT Count(*) FROM [Order Details] " & _
   "WHERE ProductID = @ProductID AND UnitPrice > @UnitPrice"
' Establish Parameters
mySqlCommand.Parameters.Add("@ProductID", 59)
mySqlCommand.Parameters.Add("@UnitPrice", 50)
MessageBox.Show(mySqlCommand.Parameters.Count, "Number of Parameters")
' Execute SqlCommand
MessageBox.Show(mySqlCommand.ExecuteScalar, "Product Count") ' 35
' Done
mySqlConnection.Close()
```

Prepare

The Prepare method notifies SQL Server to prepare the SQL statement, which means to create a prepared or compiled version of the command at the server and keep it handy for successive calls from this client. If you plan on calling a SQL statement more than three or four times, then you should prepare it first. Statement preparation slows the first execution call. Because of the increased overhead, you shouldn't prepare statements that you call infrequently. SQL Server implements prepared statements using temporary objects that use server resources.

Prepared execution dovetails nicely with the Parameters collection because, although the command syntax has to be the same for each successive call to a prepared command, you are allowed to vary the parameter values. You should consider calling Prepare only with a SqlCommand that has a CommandType of Text. Invalid SQL commands that specify stored procedure execution should not be prepared. All Parameters must have their types defined and their sizes defined, if they are variable length.

Microsoft SQL Server 2000 is very efficient in its management of execution plans, even for those that are not prepared but executed directly. Because everybody's ADO.NET application will be unique, it is up to you to test your implementation and determine if preparing the statement will gain you any increases in performance.

Usage

```
mySqlCommand.Prepare()
```

Parameters

None.

Exceptions

InvalidOperationException	The SqlConnection does not exist, or it is not open. The command syntax may not have been set yet or is invalid. All parameters must have an explicit type defined.
SqlException	SQL Server could not prepare the command. Perhaps the command syntax was invalid.

Sample Code

```
Dim mySqlConnection As New System.Data.SqlClient.SqlConnection()
Dim mySqlParameter As System.Data.SqlClient.SqlParameter
Dim mySqlCommand As System.Data.SqlClient.SqlCommand
Dim myInt32 As Int32
' Establish Connection
mySqlConnection.ConnectionString = _
   "Server=(local);Integrated Security=SSPI;"
mySqlConnection.Open()
mySqlConnection.ChangeDatabase("NorthWind")
' Create and Prepare Command
mySqlCommand = mySqlConnection.CreateCommand
mySqlCommand.CommandText = "UPDATE Products SET UnitsInStock = " & _
   "UnitsInStock - @UnitsSold WHERE ProductName = @ProductName"
```

```
' Create parameters
mySqlParameter = mySqlCommand.CreateParameter()
mySqlParameter.ParameterName = "@UnitsSold"
mySqlParameter.SqlDbType = SqlDbType.SmallInt
mySqlCommand.Parameters.Add(mySqlParameter)
mySqlParameter = mySqlCommand.CreateParameter()
mySqlParameter.ParameterName = "@ProductName"
mySqlParameter.SqlDbType = SqlDbType.NVarChar
mySqlParameter.Size = 80
mySqlCommand.Parameters.Add(mySqlParameter)
' Prepare Command
mySqlCommand.Prepare()
' First update
mySqlCommand.Parameters("@UnitsSold").Value = 5
mySqlCommand.Parameters("@ProductName").Value = "Ipoh Coffee"
myInt32 = mySqlCommand.ExecuteNonQuery
' Second update
mySqlCommand.Parameters("@UnitsSold").Value = 10
mySqlCommand.Parameters("@ProductName").Value = "Carnarvon Tigers"
myInt32 = mySqlCommand.ExecuteNonQuery
' Third update
mySqlCommand.Parameters("@ProductName").Value = "Sasquatch Ale"
myInt32 = mySqlCommand.ExecuteNonQuery
' Done
mySqlConnection.Close()
```

ResetCommandTimeout

The ResetCommandTimeout method resets the CommandTimeout property back to its default value of 30 seconds. Calling this method is functionally equivalent to executing this line of code:

```
mySqlCommand.CommandTimeout = 30
```

Usage

```
mySqlCommand.ResetCommandTimeout()
```

Parameters

None.

Exceptions

None.

Transaction

The Transaction property returns a SqlTransaction object that represents the transaction within which the SqlCommand will execute. Although the transaction is typically created and managed at the SqlConnection object, the SqlCommand object can access its transaction object through this property.

You must create the SqlTransaction first, using the associated SqlConnection's BeginTransaction method, before you can reference and manipulate it. See the SqlConnection class for more information on creating a transaction. See the SqlTransaction class for more information on manipulating a transaction.

You can place a Command inside a transaction in one of two ways:

1. Pass the SqlTransaction object to the SqlCommand constructor.
   ```
   mySqlCommand = _
       New SqlCommand(MyCommandText,MySqlConnection,MySqlTransaction)
   ```
2. Assign the SqlTransaction object to the SqlCommand Transaction property (see usage that follows).

Usage

```
mySqlTransaction = mySqlCommand.Transaction
mySqlCommand.Transaction = mySqlTransaction
```

Parameters

None.

Sample Code

```
Dim mySqlConnection As New System.Data.SqlClient.SqlConnection()
Dim mySqlTransaction As System.Data.SqlClient.SqlTransaction
Dim mySqlCommand As System.Data.SqlClient.SqlCommand
' Establish Connection
mySqlConnection.ConnectionString = _
   "Data Source=Omnibook;Integrated Security=SSPI;Database=Northwind"
mySqlConnection.Open()
' Establish Transaction
mySqlTransaction = mySqlConnection.BeginTransaction()
' Establish Command
mySqlCommand = mySqlConnection.CreateCommand
mySqlCommand.Connection = mySqlConnection
mySqlCommand.Transaction = mySqlTransaction
mySqlCommand.CommandText = _
   "INSERT Customers (CustomerID,CompanyName) " & _
   "VALUES ('WILEY','Wiley Publishing')"
' Attempt Execution(s)
mySqlCommand.ExecuteNonQuery()    ' INSERT succeeds
Try
   mySqlCommand.ExecuteNonQuery() ' INSERT fails on PK violation
   mySqlTransaction.Commit()
   MessageBox.Show("Success!", "Both records written")
Catch ex As Exception
   mySqlTransaction.Rollback()
   MessageBox.Show(ex.ToString(), "No records written")
Finally
   mySqlConnection.Close()
   mySqlConnection.Dispose()
End Try
```

UpdatedRowSource

The UpdatedRowSource property determines how command results are applied back to the DataRow when you call the Update method of an associated SqlDataAdapter. If you are setting this value, you must use a valid UpdateRowSource enumeration. See the table of enumeration values that follows.

Usage

```
myUpdateRowSource = mySqlCommand.UpdatedRowSource
mySqlCommand.UpdatedRowSource = UpdateRowSource.Both
```

Parameters

None.

UpdateRowSource Enumeration

Both (3)	Both output parameters and first returned row are mapped to the changed row in the database. This is the default value if the SqlCommand has not been automatically generated.
FirstReturnedRecord (2)	Data in the first returned row is mapped to the changed row in the DataSet.
None (0)	All returned parameters or rows are ignored. This is the default value if the SqlCommand has been automatically generated.
OutputParameters (1)	Output parameters are mapped to the changed row in the DataSet.

Exceptions

ArgumentException	The value entered was not one of the valid UpdateRowSource values.

System.Data.SqlClient.SqlCommandBuilder

The SqlCommandBuilder is a helpful class in that it provides a mechanism to automatically generate commands used to facilitate the updates made in a SqlDataSet to the underlying table. These changes may affect only a single table. If your DataSet object is composed of data from more than one table, then you will have to code a custom solution.

For the SqlCommandBuilder to work, your tables must have a unique key established. This may be a primary key or a candidate key (implemented via a unique index or constraint). The SqlCommandBuilder is smart enough to determine the original column names, even if your SQL statement or stored procedure renamed them from the base table. Also, any additional columns or literal columns are ignored when these statements get built. If your SQL statement or stored procedure returns more than one result set, the SqlCommandBuilder will process only the first result.

THANK YOU **As database programmers who have manually created these same Insert, Update, and Delete statements to gain performance in our applications, we can appreciate the usefulness of this class.**

Constructors

```
Dim mySqlCommandBuilder As New SqlCommandBuilder()
Dim mySqlCommandBuilder As New SqlCommandBuilder(MySqlDataAdapter)
```

Parameters

`MySqlDataAdapter`	A SqlDataAdapter object to associate with the SqlCommandBuilder. If you don't specify one in the constructor, you'll need to assign it later to the DataAdapter property. By associating a SqlDataAdapter with your CommandBuilder, you are registering the CommandBuilder as a *listener* for the RowUpdating events generated by the SqlDataAdapter.

SqlCommandBuilder Sample Code

```
Dim mySqlDataAdapter As New System.Data.SqlClient.SqlDataAdapter()
Dim mySqlCommandBuilder As System.Data.SqlClient.SqlCommandBuilder
Dim mySqlConnection As New System.Data.SqlClient.SqlConnection()
' Establish Connection
mySqlConnection.ConnectionString = _
  "Server=(local);Integrated Security=SSPI;"
mySqlConnection.Open()
mySqlConnection.ChangeDatabase("NorthWind")
' Establish DataAdapter and CommandBuilder
mySqlDataAdapter.SelectCommand = New SqlCommand( _
   "SELECT * FROM Customers", mySqlConnection)
mySqlCommandBuilder = New SqlCommandBuilder()
mySqlCommandBuilder.DataAdapter = mySqlDataAdapter
' Assign the generated commands, so we can query the DataAdapter's SQL
mySqlDataAdapter.InsertCommand = mySqlCommandBuilder.GetInsertCommand()
mySqlDataAdapter.UpdateCommand = mySqlCommandBuilder.GetUpdateCommand()
mySqlDataAdapter.DeleteCommand = mySqlCommandBuilder.GetDeleteCommand()
' Test
MessageBox.Show(mySqlDataAdapter.InsertCommand.CommandText, "Insert")
MessageBox.Show(mySqlDataAdapter.UpdateCommand.CommandText, "Update")
MessageBox.Show(mySqlDataAdapter.DeleteCommand.CommandText, "Delete")
' Process Data using the DataAdapter Here
mySqlConnection.Close()
```

Members

DataAdapter

The DataAdapter property sets or returns a reference to the SqlDataAdapter required by the SqlCommandBuilder. The DataAdapter is necessary for the SqlCommandBuilder to properly construct the Insert, Update, and Delete SQL commands. This property can be set during instantiation of the SqlCommandBuilder object, by passing a valid SqlDataAdapter object to the constructor, or by assigning it to this property at a later time.

By setting the DataAdapter property, you are essentially registering the SqlCommandBuilder object as a listener for the SqlDataAdapter RowUpdating events.

Usage

```
mySqlDataAdapter = mySqlCommandBuilder.DataAdapter
mySqlCommandBuilder.DataAdapter = mySqlDataAdapter
```

Parameters

None.

DeriveParameters

A very useful function, the DeriveParameters method enables you to automatically populate a SqlCommand's Parameters collection with the parameter information for a SQL Server stored procedure. These new parameters will overwrite any existing parameters in the SqlCommand's collection. You do not need to run this method, but it saves time from having to define your Parameters collection by hand. This method is reminiscent of MDAC ADO's Parameters.Refresh method.

The ease of use of the DeriveParameters method comes at a price, as it requires an extra round trip to the SQL Server before executing the command. If you have only a few parameters to define, you should consider doing it manually, in code.

Usage

```
mySqlCommandBuilder.DeriveParameters(mySqlCommand)
```

Parameters

`mySqlCommand`	The System.Data.SqlClient.SqlCommand object for which you want to populate the parameters collection.

Exceptions

InvalidOperationException	The specified stored procedure doesn't exist.

Sample Code

```
Dim mySqlCommandBuilder As New System.Data.SqlClient.SqlCommandBuilder()
Dim mySqlConnection As New System.Data.SqlClient.SqlConnection()
Dim mySqlParameter As System.Data.SqlClient.SqlParameter
Dim mySqlCommand As System.Data.SqlClient.SqlCommand
' Establish Connection
mySqlConnection.ConnectionString = _
   "Server=(local);Integrated Security=SSPI;Database=Northwind"
```

```
mySqlConnection.Open()
' Establish Command
mySqlCommand = mySqlConnection.CreateCommand()
mySqlCommand.CommandText = "SalesByCategory"
mySqlCommand.CommandType = CommandType.StoredProcedure
' Use CommandBuilder to Populate Parameters collection
mySqlCommandBuilder.DeriveParameters(mySqlCommand)
' Enumerate the Parameters collection (3 Items)
For Each mySqlParameter In mySqlCommand.Parameters
   MessageBox.Show(mySqlParameter.ParameterName & " (" & _
      mySqlParameter.SqlDbType.ToString & ")", _
      mySqlParameter.Direction.ToString & " Parameter")
Next
' Done
mySqlConnection.Close()
```

GetDeleteCommand

Together with its colleagues, GetInsertCommand and GetUpdateCommand, this utility method returns a reference to the SqlCommand object that is brokering the deleting of records from the SqlDataAdapter. This reference should be treated as informational, meaning you should not try to manipulate the SqlCommand directly. Some of the more interesting properties that you can query are the CommandText, CommandTimeout, CommandType, and Parameters collection. Although these properties are read only, no exception will be thrown if you try to write to them. See the SqlCommand class for more information.

If you want to customize the SQL statement, you should capture the CommandText and make any changes to the SqlDataAdapter DeleteCommand property. You could also create your own SqlCommand and execute it manually. This workaround can solve the problem of trying to update multiple tables at once, which isn't currently supported with the SqlCommandBuilder class.

Usage

```
mySqlCommand = mySqlCommandBuilder.GetDeleteCommand()
```

Parameters

None.

Exceptions

None.

GetInsertCommand

Together with its colleagues, GetDeleteCommand and GetUpdateCommand, this utility method returns a reference to the SqlCommand object that is brokering the insertion of any records from the SqlDataAdapter. This reference should be treated as informational, meaning you should not try to manipulate the SqlCommand directly. Some of the more interesting properties that you can query are the CommandText, CommandTimeout, CommandType, and Parameters collection. Although these properties are read only, no exception will be thrown if you try to write to them. See the SqlCommand class for more information.

If you want to customize the SQL statement, you should capture the CommandText and make any changes to the SqlDataAdapter InsertCommand property. You could also create your own SqlCommand and execute it manually. This workaround can solve the problem of trying to update multiple tables at once, which isn't currently supported with the SqlCommandBuilder class.

Usage

```
mySqlCommand = mySqlCommandBuilder.GetInsertCommand()
```

Parameters

None.

Exceptions

None.

GetUpdateCommand

Together with its colleagues, GetDeleteCommand and GetInsertCommand, this utility method returns a reference to the SqlCommand object that is brokering the updating of any records from the SqlDataAdapter. This reference should be treated as informational, meaning you should not try to manipulate the SqlCommand directly. Some of the more interesting properties that you can query are the CommandText, CommandTimeout, CommandType, and Parameters collection. Although these properties are read only, no exception will be thrown if you try to write to them. See the SqlCommand class for more information.

If you want to customize the SQL statement, you should capture the CommandText and make any changes to the SqlDataAdapter UpdateCommand property. You could also create your own SqlCommand and execute it manually. This workaround can solve the problem of trying to update multiple tables at once, which isn't currently supported with the SqlCommandBuilder class.

Usage

```
mySqlCommand = mySqlCommandBuilder.GetUpdateCommand()
```

Parameters

None.

Exceptions

None.

QuotePrefix

The QuotePrefix property allows you to set or return the beginning character to use when specifying database object names. Because SQL Server allows its tables, views, stored procedures, and column names to contain spaces, ADO.NET must delimit those names accordingly. Here are some examples:

```
-- Bad SQL (especially since ORDER is a reserved keyword)
UPDATE Order Details SET UnitPrice = UnitPrice * 1.1
-- Poor SQL (may work with SQL Server, but wouldn't work with Access)
UPDATE "Order Details" SET UnitPrice = UnitPrice * 1.1
-- Good SQL (works with SQL Server and Access)
```

```
UPDATE [Order Details] SET UnitPrice = UnitPrice * 1.1
```

By default, the QuotePrefix will be an empty string, which will cause problems when working with examples like the ones shown previously. For this reason, you should specify your custom delimiter before generating any of the SQL commands. A good choice is a square left bracket ([).

If you choose to use the quotation mark, keep in mind that SQL Server can override the behavior of the quotation mark based on the QUOTED_IDENTIFIER setting. If it has been set to OFF, quotation marks will not work as delimiters and you must use the square braces. For this reason, it is best to get into the habit of using square braces and manually setting them on QuotePrefix and QuoteSuffix.

Usage

```
myString = mySqlCommandBuilder.QuotePrefix
mySqlCommandBuilder.QuotePrefix = "["
```

Parameters

None.

Exceptions

InvalidOperationException	You are trying to assign the character after the SqlCommandBuilder has generated the command. QuotePrefix becomes read only at that point.

Sample Code

```
Dim mySqlDataAdapter As New System.Data.SqlClient.SqlDataAdapter()
Dim mySqlCommandBuilder As System.Data.SqlClient.SqlCommandBuilder
Dim mySqlConnection As New System.Data.SqlClient.SqlConnection()
' Establish Connection
mySqlConnection.ConnectionString = _
  "Server=(local);Integrated Security=SSPI;"
mySqlConnection.Open()
mySqlConnection.ChangeDatabase("NorthWind")
' Establish DataAdapter and CommandBuilder
mySqlDataAdapter.SelectCommand = New SqlCommand( _
   "SELECT * FROM [Order Details]", mySqlConnection)
mySqlCommandBuilder = New SqlCommandBuilder()
mySqlCommandBuilder.DataAdapter = mySqlDataAdapter
mySqlCommandBuilder.QuotePrefix = "["
mySqlCommandBuilder.QuoteSuffix = "]"
' Take a peek at the UpdateCommand to see the delimiters
MessageBox.Show(mySqlCommandBuilder.GetUpdateCommand().CommandText)
' Process Data using the DataAdapter Here
mySqlConnection.Close()
```

QuoteSuffix

The QuoteSuffix property allows you to set or return the ending character to use when specifying database object names. Because SQL Server allows its tables, views, stored procedures, and column names to contain spaces, ADO.NET must delimit those names accordingly. See the QuotePrefix method for more information.

By default, the QuoteSuffix will be an empty string, which will cause problems when working with SQL objects with spaces in their names. For this reason, you should specify your custom delimiter before generating any of the SQL commands. A good choice is a square right bracket (]).

If you choose to use the quotation mark, keep in mind that SQL Server can override the behavior of the quotation mark based on the QUOTED_IDENTIFIER setting. If it has been set to OFF, quotation marks will not work as delimiters and you must use the square braces. For this reason, it is best to get into the habit of using square braces and manually setting them on QuotePrefix and QuoteSuffix.

Usage

```
myString = mySqlCommandBuilder.QuoteSuffix
mySqlCommandBuilder.QuoteSuffix = "]"
```

Parameters

None.

Exceptions

InvalidOperationException	You are trying to assign the character after the SqlCommandBuilder has generated the command. QuoteSuffix becomes read only at that point.

RefreshSchema

The RefreshSchema method will force a reload of the schema information from the data source so that you can generate accurate Insert, Update, and Delete commands. If you change the SQL statement of the associated SqlDataAdapter's SelectCommand property without calling RefreshSchema, you may be generating commands based on the old, inaccurate CommandText.

Usage

```
mySqlCommand.RefreshSchema()
```

Parameters

None.

Exceptions

None.

Sample Code

```
Dim mySqlCommandBuilder As System.Data.SqlClient.SqlCommandBuilder
Dim mySqlDataAdapter As New System.Data.SqlClient.SqlDataAdapter()
Dim mySqlConnection As New System.Data.SqlClient.SqlConnection()
' Establish Connection
mySqlConnection.ConnectionString = _
   "Server=(local);Integrated Security=SSPI;Database=NorthWind"
mySqlConnection.Open()
' Establish DataAdapter and CommandBuilder
mySqlDataAdapter.SelectCommand = New SqlCommand( _
   "SELECT SupplierID, CompanyName FROM Suppliers", mySqlConnection)
```

```
mySqlCommandBuilder = New SqlCommandBuilder(mySqlDataAdapter)
' Show the UpdateCommand Text
MessageBox.Show(mySqlCommandBuilder.GetUpdateCommand.CommandText)
' Change the underlying select command
mySqlDataAdapter.SelectCommand.CommandText = _
    "SELECT SupplierID, ContactName FROM Suppliers"
' Show the UpdateCommand Text - it hasn't changed
MessageBox.Show(mySqlCommandBuilder.GetUpdateCommand.CommandText)
' Refresh the Schema and show the new UpdateCommand Text
mySqlCommandBuilder.RefreshSchema()
MessageBox.Show(mySqlCommandBuilder.GetUpdateCommand.CommandText)
' Done
mySqlConnection.Close()
```

System.Data.SqlClient.SqlConnection

A SqlConnection represents a unique connection to a SQL Server 7.0 or 2000 server. If you are connecting to those or newer versions of SQL Server, you should use this .NET data provider. If you are connecting to a SQL Server 6.5 or a non-SQL Server data source, you should consider using the .NET OLE DB or ODBC data providers. The SqlConnection is equivalent to a network connection to the SQL Server.

It's important to know that when a SqlConnection object goes out of scope, it will not release the resources used by the SqlConnection; therefore, it must be explicitly closed by calling the Close or Dispose method. We therefore recommend that a Close or Dispose method call be placed into the Finally block of a Try-Catch-Finally exception handler, to ensure that the connection is actually released, even in the event of an exception being raised.

If a SqlCommand causes a SQL Server error to be raised with a severity of 20 or greater, the SqlConnection will typically be closed as a result. In those situations, you should anticipate this, test for the state of SqlConnection, and proceed accordingly, reopening the SqlConnection if necessary.

Constructors

```
Dim mySqlConnection As New SqlConnection()
Dim mySqlConnection As New SqlConnection(myString)
```

Parameters

`myString`	The connection string to be passed. See the ConnectionString property.

Exceptions

ArgumentException	Your ConnectionString contains invalid parameters or values.

SqlConnection Sample Code

```
Dim mySqlConnection As New System.Data.SqlClient.SqlConnection()
mySqlConnection.ConnectionString = _
   "Data Source=Neptune;Integrated Security=SSPI"
mySqlConnection.Open()
```

Members

BeginTransaction

The BeginTransaction method begins a database transaction and returns a SqlTransaction object. Any SqlCommand objects that you execute as part of this transaction will be buffered. All changes will be flushed to the data source when you explicitly complete the transaction by using the Commit method. All changes will be rolled back when you explicitly call the Rollback method or if you happen to close the Connection with open transactions.

All ADO.NET transactions are handled within the database and are not supported by the Microsoft Distributed Transaction Coordinator (MTC) or any other transactional mechanism. Because .NET is brokering the transaction management, you shouldn't use the transaction support provided by the data source, or errors may result. In other words, don't embed a SQL BEGIN TRANSACTION in any command you execute. SQL Server implements transactions by way of locks. For this reason, you should keep the number and duration of your transactions to a minimum.

If you want to begin a transaction with a specific isolation level, you can call the BeginTransaction method by passing a valid IsolationLevel enumeration to the constructor. The IsolationLevel determines how one transaction is (or isn't) isolated from another. It describes how sensitive the data within your transaction is to changes by other transactions. The default IsolationLevel is ReadCommitted, which happens to be the safest.

You can also pass the transaction a String for its name. Named transactions give you better flexibility in how you roll back your transactions. You can also use the transaction's name if you call the transaction's Save method in order to name the savepoint the same as the transaction.

Usage

```
mySqlTransaction = mySqlConnection.BeginTransaction()
mySqlTransaction = mySqlConnection.BeginTransaction(IsolationLevel)
mySqlTransaction = mySqlConnection.BeginTransaction(MyString)
mySqlTransaction = _
   mySqlConnection.BeginTransaction(IsolationLevel,MyString)
```

Parameters

`IsolationLevel`	A valid IsolationLevel enumeration.
`MyString`	The name of the Transaction.

IsolationLevel Enumeration

Chaos (16)	Any pending changes from transactions that are more highly isolated transactions cannot be overwritten. SQL Server 2000 and below do not support this isolation level.
ReadCommitted (4096)	(Default) Shared locks are held while the data is being read to avoid dirty reads, but the data can be changed before the end of the transaction, resulting in nonrepeatable reads or phantom data (a.k.a. CursorStability).
ReadUncommitted (256)	No shared locks or exclusive locks are honored, so dirty reads are possible (a.k.a. Browse).
RepeatableRead (65536)	All data used in a query is locked, preventing others from updating. This prevents nonrepeatable reads, but phantom rows are still possible.
Serializable (1048576)	A range lock is placed on the data preventing other users from updating or inserting rows into the dataset until the transaction is complete (a.k.a. Isolated).
Unspecified (-1)	A different isolation level than the one specified is being used, but the level cannot be determined. (This value cannot be passed when creating a Transaction.)

Exceptions

ArgumentException	An invalid IsolationLevel argument was passed.
InvalidOperationException	You've tried to execute BeginTransaction a second time. Parallel transactions are not supported.

Sample Code

```
Dim mySqlConnection As New System.Data.SqlClient.SqlConnection()
Dim mySqlTransaction As System.Data.SqlClient.SqlTransaction
Dim mySqlCommand As System.Data.SqlClient.SqlCommand
' Establish Connection
mySqlConnection.ConnectionString = _
    "Data Source=Omnibook;Integrated Security=SSPI"
mySqlConnection.Open()
mySqlConnection.ChangeDatabase("Northwind")
' Establish Command
mySqlCommand = mySqlConnection.CreateCommand()
mySqlCommand.CommandText = "INSERT Customers " & _
    "(CustomerID,CompanyName) VALUES ('WILEY','Wiley Publishing')"
mySqlCommand.Connection = mySqlConnection
' Establish Transaction
mySqlTransaction = _
    mySqlConnection.BeginTransaction(IsolationLevel.ReadCommitted, _
    "NewCustomers")
```

```
mySqlCommand.Transaction = mySqlTransaction
' Attempt Execution(s)
mySqlCommand.ExecuteNonQuery()    ' INSERT succeeds
Try
   mySqlCommand.ExecuteNonQuery() ' INSERT fails on PK violation
   mySqlTransaction.Commit()
   MessageBox.Show("Success!", "Both records written")
Catch ex As Exception
   mySqlTransaction.Rollback("NewCustomers")
   MessageBox.Show(ex.ToString(), "No records written")
Finally
   mySqlConnection.Close()
   mySqlConnection.Dispose()
End Try
```

ChangeDatabase

The ChangeDatabase method changes the current database for an open SqlConnection.

Usage

```
mySqlConnection.ChangeDatabase(String)
```

Parameters

`String`	A valid database name.

Exceptions

ArgumentException	The database name is not valid.
InvalidOperationException	The connection is not open.
SqlException	The database may not be changed to the database specified.

Sample Code

```
Dim mySqlConnection As New System.Data.SqlClient.SqlConnection()
' Establish Connection
mySqlConnection.ConnectionString = _
   "Data Source=Omnibook;Integrated Security=SSPI"
mySqlConnection.Open()
mySqlConnection.ChangeDatabase("Northwind")
' Process Northwind Data Here
mySqlConnection.ChangeDatabase("Pubs")
' Process Pubs Data Here
mySqlConnection.Close()
mySqlConnection.Dispose()
```

Close

The Close method is the preferred way of closing an open connection. In addition to releasing the connection to the connection pool (if pooling is enabled), the Close method also rolls back any pending transactions, just as though the SqlTransaction.Rollback method was called.

Unlike prior versions of ADO, if you call the Close method on a connection that is closed, no exception is thrown. This makes it ideal to place in the Finally block of an exception handler. After a connection has been closed, it may be reopened with the Open method, without having to respecify the ConnectionString.

The difference between Close and Dispose is that Close releases the connection back to the connection pool to be possibly reused, whereas Dispose removes the connection from the connection pool. Close also maintains the ConnectionString property, whereas Dispose does not.

Another reason to explicitly call Close rather than allowing your connection objects to simply go out of scope is garbage collection. Garbage collection in .NET does not happen immediately, and therefore your connection objects will still be alive and holding valuable server resources. It is actually possible to run out of connections on your data source with code written in this way. If you always explicitly call the Close method, you'll be fine.

Usage

```
mySqlConnection.Close()
```

Parameters

None.

Exceptions

None.

Sample Code

```
Dim mySqlConnection As New System.Data.SqlClient.SqlConnection()
mySqlConnection.ConnectionString = _
   "Data Source=Omnibook;Integrated Security=SSPI"
mySqlConnection.Open()
MessageBox.Show(mySqlConnection.State.ToString(), "State")
mySqlConnection.Close()
MessageBox.Show(mySqlConnection.State.ToString(), "State")
```

ConnectionString

The ConnectionString property is probably the most important member of the SqlConnection class. The ConnectionString property specifies all of the parameters required to open a connection to the underlying data source. This ConnectionString is made up of name-value pairs. Each parameter is separated with a semicolon, and the order in which they are listed does not matter. You can delimit the values of the parameter in single or double quotes. If a semicolon is part of a parameter's value, then you must use delimiters. If you specify the same parameter twice in the ConnectionString, the last occurrence is used. Many of these parameters have corresponding, read-only properties in the Connection class.

You can assign the ConnectionString in two possible ways: by passing the ConnectionString to the SqlConnection constructor or by assigning the property directly. You may not, however, change the ConnectionString once the connection is open. If you want to change the connection information, such as the data source (the SQL Server), you must first close the connection, reassign the ConnectionString, and then reopen the connection. You can, however, change the Database by using the special ChangeDatabase method provided.

At a minimum, a ConnectionString needs a Data Source. This assumes that the data source is not secured or allows anonymous or guest login. If the Data Source is secure, then a User ID and Password parameter may be required. When setting the Boolean (True or False) properties, you can also use Yes or No for the values. You may not use DSNs (Data Source Names) with the SQL .NET data provider because DSNs are an ODBC construct.

The listing that follows includes some of the common ConnectionString parameters.

Usage

```
mySqlConnection.ConnectionString = myString
myString = mySqlConnection.ConnectionString
```

Parameters

None.

Common ConnectionString Parameters

Addr	Synonymous to Server.
Address	Synonymous to Server.
Application Name	An arbitrary name of your ADO.NET application. This value is useful if you are running SQL Profiler so that you can see which application is generating the traffic. The default value is *.Net SqlClient data provider*.
AttachDBFilename	Name of the primary .MDF database file, including the full path of an attachable database.
Connect Timeout	Synonymous to Connection Timeout.
Connection Timeout	The number of seconds ADO.NET has to connect to the data source before "timing out" and returning an error. The default is 15 seconds. Passing a value of 0 will attempt to connect indefinitely!
Connection Lifetime	The number of seconds a Connection will live in the Connection pool before it is destroyed.
Connection Reset	Indicates if the Connection is reset when being removed from the pool. If this is False, then a round trip to the SQL Server can be avoided when obtaining a connection. The default is True, which is a safer choice.
Current Language	SQL Server's language name. This setting drives how messages are selected and formatted. The language must be installed on the SQL Server, or else the Connection will fail when you attempt to open it.
Database	The database on the Sql Server to open. You may not need to specify this, if you have already associated a default database for the login account being used. This is also the only parameter that you can change once the connection is open—see the ChangeDatatabase method.
Data Source	Synonymous to Server.

Enlist	When this is set to true, which is the default value, the Connection Pooling manager automatically enlists the connection in the creating thread's current transaction context.
Extended Properties	Synonymous to AttachDBFilename.
Initial Catalog	Synonymous to Database.
Initial File Name	Synonymous to AttachDBFilename.
Integrated Security	Used to specify a secure authentication rather than SQL Server's standard authentication. Valid values are True, SSPI (Secured Support Provider Interface), or False. The values True and SSPI are synonymous. The default value is False. If you want to pass the user and password transparently, then set this parameter to SSPI.
Max Pool Size	The maximum number of Connections in the Connection pool. The default is 100.
Min Pool Size	The minimum number of Connections in the Connection pool. The default is 0.
Net	Synonymous to Network Library.
Network Address	Synonymous to Server.
Network Library	The network library used to connect to the SQL Server instance. The corresponding DLL must be installed before the network library can work. Supported values include the following: *dbnmpntw*—Named Pipes *dbmsrpcn*—Multiprotocol *dbmsadsn*—Apple Talk *dbmsgnet*—VIA (Virtual Interface Architecture) *dbmsipcn*—Shared Memory—default when connecting to (local) *dbmsspxn*—IPX/SPX *dbmssocn*—TCP/IP—default for a named server
Packet Size	The size in bytes of the network packets being sent to/from SQL Server. The size can range between 512 and 32,767. The default is 8192.
Password	When not using Integrated Security, this is the password used for authentication.
Persist Security Info	When querying the ConnectionString and this parameter is True, the ConnectionString will return any password that was passed to the data source. If Persist Security Info is False, the ConnectionString will not include any password. The default is False.
Pooling	The master switch to indicate whether the SqlConnection is drawn from the appropriate pool or created and added to the pool. The default is True.
Pwd	Synonymous to Password.

Server	(Required). The SQL Server name or network address. You can also specify *(local)* to connection to the SQL Server running on the local machine.
Trusted_Connection	Synonymous to Integrated Security.
User ID	When not using Integrated Security, this is the user name used for authentication.
Workstation ID	The name of your workstation. This value is useful if you are running SQL Profiler so that you can see which workstation is generating the traffic. The default value is your local computer's name.

Exceptions

ArgumentException	A parameter value is invalid.
InvalidOperationException	You tried to assign the ConnectionString property while the connection is open.

Sample Code

```
Dim mySqlConnection As New System.Data.SqlClient.SqlConnection()
Dim myConnectionString As String
' Build the ConnectionString
myConnectionString = "Server=Omnibook;" & _
   "Application Name='Programming ADO.NET';" & _
   "Connection Timeout=60;" & _
   "Database=Northwind;" & _
   "Integrated Security=False;" & _
   "Network Library=dbnmpntw;" & _
   "User ID=dotnet;" & _
   "Password=dotnet;"
' Assign and Test
mySqlConnection.ConnectionString = myConnectionString
MessageBox.Show(mySqlConnection.ConnectionString, "Connection String")
' Establish Connection
Try
   mySqlConnection.Open()
Catch ex As Exception
   MessageBox.Show(ex.ToString(), "Exception")
Finally
   mySqlConnection.Close()
   mySqlConnection.Dispose()
End Try
```

ConnectionTimeout

The ConnectionTimeout property is read only and returns an Int32 specifying the number of seconds to wait while attempting to open a database connection before terminating the attempt and raising an error. By default, this value is 15 seconds, but it can be overridden by setting the Connection Timeout parameter in the ConnectionString.

You can request this ConnectionTimeout property immediately after assigning the ConnectionString parameter. You do not need to wait until the SqlConnection is open for the property to become available.

Usage

```
myInt32 = mySqlConnection.ConnectionTimeout
```

Parameters

None.

CreateCommand

This method provides a convenient way to create and return a SqlCommand object associated with the current connection. SqlCommand objects are the mechanisms by which you run standard queries and XML queries, call stored procedures, or execute other SQL statements. See the SqlCommand class reference for more information.

By using the CreateCommand method, it allows you to do two steps in one: first, create the SqlCommand object and, second, assign it to a SqlConnection object. The SqlConnection does not need to be open for you to execute the CreateCommand method; however, the SqlConnection must be open prior to your executing the SqlCommand.

If your connection is engaging in a SqlTransaction, you must still assign the Transaction property of the SqlCommand object manually with this step:

```
mySqlCommand.Transaction = mySqlTransaction
```

Usage

```
mySqlCommand = mySqlConnection.CreateCommand()
```

Parameters

None.

Exceptions

None.

Sample Code

```
Dim mySqlConnection As New System.Data.SqlClient.SqlCcnnection()
Dim mySqlCommand As System.Data.SqlClient.SqlCommand
' Establish Connection
mySqlConnection.ConnectionString = _
   "Server=Omnibook;Integrated Security=True;"
mySqlConnection.Open()
mySqlConnection.ChangeDatabase("Northwind")
' Create and Execute Command
mySqlCommand = mySqlConnection.CreateCommand
mySqlCommand.CommandText = "SELECT @@Version"
MessageBox.Show(mySqlCommand.ExecuteScalar(), "@@Version")
' Done
mySqlConnection.Close()
mySqlConnection.Dispose()
```

Database

The Database property returns the name of the SqlConnection's database as specified by the *Database* or *Initial Catalog* parameter of the ConnectionString. The connection does not need to be open to query this read-only property. Database will default to an empty string unless it has been assigned in one of four possible ways:

1. Pass a connection string with a Database or Initial Catalog parameter to the SqlConnection constructor during creation.
2. Assign a connection string, including a Database or Initial Catalog parameter, directly to the SqlConnection's ConnectionString property.
3. Call the ChangeDatabase method on an open connection.
4. Change the database programmatically, such as by executing a "USE Pubs" Transact-SQL command. A programmatic change such as this may be trapped by the connection's InfoMessage event.

Usage

```
myString = mySqlConnection.Database
```

Parameters

None.

Sample Code

```
Dim mySqlConnection As New System.Data.SqlClient.SqlConnection()
Dim myConnectionString As String
' Sample 1 - no open connection and database property is an empty string
MessageBox.Show(mySqlConnection.Database)
' Sample 2 - no open connection, but database property is "Northwind"
myConnectionString = "Server=Omnibook;Database=Northwind;" & _
   "Integrated Security=SSPI;"
mySqlConnection.ConnectionString = myConnectionString
MessageBox.Show(mySqlConnection.Database)
' Sample 3 - connection is open and database property is "Northwind"
mySqlConnection.Open()
MessageBox.Show(mySqlConnection.Database)
' Sample 4 - database is then changed to "master"
mySqlConnection.ChangeDatabase("Master")
MessageBox.Show(mySqlConnection.Database)
' Sample 5 - database is then changed = "pubs"
Dim mySqlCommand As New System.Data.SqlClient.SqlCommand()
mySqlCommand = mySqlConnection.CreateCommand()
mySqlCommand.CommandText = "USE Pubs"
mySqlCommand.ExecuteNonQuery()
MessageBox.Show(mySqlConnection.Database)
```

DataSource

The DataSource property returns the name of the SQL Server instance. If you are connecting to a SQL Server 7.0 or SQL Server 2000 default instance, the DataSource property will simply list the name of the server. If you are connecting to a named instance, the DataSource property will list the <servername>\<instancename>. This property is the same as specified by the Server, Data Source, Addr, Address, or Network Address parameter of the ConnectionString. The connection does not need to be open to query this read-only property. DataSource will default to an empty string, unless it has been assigned in one of two possible ways:

1. Pass a connection string with a Server parameter (or one of the alternates) to the SqlConnection constructor during creation.
2. Assign a connection string, including a Server parameter (or one of the alternates), directly to the SqlConnection's ConnectionString property.

Usage

```
myString = mySqlConnection.DataSource
```

Parameters

None.

Sample Code

```
Dim mySqlConnection As New System.Data.SqlClient.SqlCcnnection()
Dim myConnectionString As String
' Sample 1 - no open connection and datasource property is an empty
string
MessageBox.Show(mySqlConnection.DataSource)
' Sample 2 - no open connection, but datasource property = "(local)"
myConnectionString = "Data Source=(local);Integrated Security=SSPI"
mySqlConnection.ConnectionString = myConnectionString
MessageBox.Show(mySqlConnection.DataSource)
' Sample 3 - connection is open and datasource property =
"Neptune\Fiscal"
myConnectionString = _
   "Data Source= Neptune\Fiscal;Integrated Security=SSPI"
mySqlConnection.ConnectionString = myConnectionString
mySqlConnection.Open()
MessageBox.Show(mySqlConnection.DataSource)
```

Dispose

Similar to Close, the Dispose method closes the current connection to the SQL Server and then flushes the SqlConnection from the connection pool. Before the connection is actually closed, all uncommitted transactions are rolled back and the connection is released. The Dispose method may be called even when the connection is not open and will not throw an exception or raise an error.

NOTE This Dispose method doesn't work like its counterparts in the OdbcConnection and OleDbConnection classes. Even after you call this Dispose method, you may still query the ConnectionString property and also reopen the connection by simply calling the Open method. As this may be a bug, I wouldn't plan on this functionality. It would be safer to reassign the ConnectionString property after calling Dispose.

Usage

```
mySqlConnection.Dispose()
```

Parameters

None.

Exceptions

None.

Sample Code

```
Dim mySqlConnection As New System.Data.SqlClient.SqlConnection()
Dim myConnectionString As String
myConnectionString = "Data Source=Neptune;Integrated Security=SSPI"
mySqlConnection.ConnectionString = myConnectionString
mySqlConnection.Open()
mySqlConnection.Close()
mySqlConnection.Dispose()
' Normally this next line is required to re-open after a Dispose
' mySqlConnection.ConnectionString = myConnectionString ' Assign again
mySqlConnection.Open()
mySqlConnection.Close()
```

InfoMessage

The InfoMessage event can be used to catch informational, warning, or error messages passed back from SQL Server. This event handler is passed an argument of type SqlInfoMessageEventArgs, which supplies all of the information.

InfoMessages are delivered independent of any error messages or exceptions. In other words, just because you receive an ADO.NET exception does not mean that there will be any InfoMessage information; conversely, InfoMessages may be received during operations that do not throw exceptions. An example of this would be a SQL PRINT statement. It is not row data, to be captured in a DataReader or DataSet, but yet it's not an error or exception to be captured by the exception handler. The InfoMessage event is where you would go to collect the information returned by those PRINT statements in stored procedures or queries.

NOTE SQL Server 2000 RAISERROR commands with a severity of 0 through 10 will raise an InfoMessage event without throwing an exception. A RAISERROR with a severity of 11 or higher will throw an exception without raising an InfoMessage event. Also, SqlClient doesn't raise InfoMessage events on opening or closing the connection, unlike OdbcConnection and OleDbConnection objects.

Usage

```
Private Sub mySqlConnection_InfoMessage(ByVal sender As Object, _
   ByVal e As System.Data.SqlClient.SqlInfoMessageEventArgs) _
   Handles mySqlConnection.InfoMessage
End Sub
```

Parameters

`sender`	Contains a reference to the originator of the event.
`e`	Contains the SqlInfoMessageEventArgs object. See the event arguments in the table below.

Event Argument Data

e.Errors	Gets the collection of information/warnings sent from the SQL Server.
e.Message	Full text of the error sent from the SQL Server.
e.Source	The name of the object that generated the message.

Sample Code

```
' A general procedure to handle the event
Private Sub myInfoMessageHandler(ByVal sender As Object, _
   ByVal e As System.Data.SqlClient.SqlInfoMessageEventArgs)
   MessageBox.Show(sender.GetType.ToString(), "Sender Type")
   MessageBox.Show(e.Errors(0).ToString(), "1st Error/Message")
End Sub
Private Sub MyTest
   Dim mySqlConnection As New System.Data.SqlClient.SqlConnection()
   Dim mySqlCommand As System.Data.SqlClient.SqlCommand
   Dim myConnectionString As String
   ' Specify the Event Handler
   AddHandler mySqlConnection.InfoMessage, AddressOf myInfoMessageHandler
   ' Establish the Connection
   mySqlConnection.ConnectionString = _
      "Server=(local);Integrated Security=SSPI"
   mySqlConnection.Open()
   ' Change database context, which will fire the InfoMessage event
   mySqlConnection.ChangeDatabase("Northwind")      ' InfoMessage fires
   ' Execute a SQL PRINT command, which will fire the InfoMessage event
   mySqlCommand = mySqlConnection.CreateCommand
   mySqlCommand.CommandText = "PRINT 'Hello World'"
   mySqlCommand.ExecuteNonQuery()                    ' InfoMessage fires
   ' Done
   mySqlConnection.Close()
End Sub
```

Open

This method establishes a connection to the SQL Server as specified in the ConnectionString. Before calling Open, you must ensure that the ConnectionString specifies a valid SQL Server. If you are going to specify any additional security, database, or connection behavior parameters in the ConnectionString, you must do that before calling Open.

The SqlConnection will use an open connection from the connection pool if there is one available. If not, a new connection will be established to the server. If the SqlConnection variables go out of scope, the connection is not implicitly closed. You will have to manage the lifetime of your connection variables manually, using the Close and Dispose methods.

Although some validation of the ConnectionString is performed at the time it is assigned, the final test is to call the Open method. Because so many variables can affect whether your data source can be opened, it is important to wrap your Open method in a Try-Catch-Finally block to catch and handle any exceptions.

Upon a successful call to Open, the StateChange event will fire and the SqlConnection.State property will reflect the fact that the connection is now open. These indicators are handy to use in expressions.

Usage

```
mySqlConnection.Open()
```

Parameters

None.

Exceptions

InvalidOperationException	The connection is already open.
SqlException	The connection could not be opened. Several reasons can cause this: ■ Could not find the SQL Server or Database. ■ SQL Server is offline for maintenance. ■ An invalid user or password was passed. ■ Invalid ConnectionString parameter.

Sample Code

```
Dim mySqlConnection As New System.Data.SqlClient.SqlConnection()
Dim iError As Integer
mySqlConnection.ConnectionString = _
   "Data Source=InvalidServer;Integrated Security=SSPI"
Try
   mySqlConnection.Open()
Catch exInvalidOpException As InvalidOperationException
   MessageBox.Show(exInvalidOpException.ToString(), _
      "Invalid Operation Exception")
Catch exSqlException As SqlException
   For iError = 0 To exSqlException.Errors.Count - 1
      MessageBox.Show("Error #" & ControlChars.Tab & iError.ToString() & _
      ControlChars.Cr & "Message" & ControlChars.Tab & _
      exSqlException.Errors(iError).Message & ControlChars.Cr & _
      "Native" & ControlChars.Tab & _
      exSqlException.Errors(iError).Number.ToString() & _
      ControlChars.Cr & "Source" & ControlChars.Tab & _
      exSqlException.Errors(iError).Source & ControlChars.Cr & _
      "SQL" & ControlChars.Tab & _
      exSqlException.Errors(iError).State & ControlChars.Cr, _
      "SqlClient Exception")
   Next
Catch ex As Exception
   MessageBox.Show(ex.ToString(), "Other Exception")
Finally
```

```
    mySqlConnection.Close()
    mySqlConnection.Dispose()
End Try
```

PacketSize

The PacketSize property returns the size of the network packets being sent to/from the SQL Server as an Int32. The PacketSize is expressed in bytes and will reflect the value specified in the Packet Size parameter established in the ConnectionString. If a Packet Size parameter was not specified, the default size will be 8192 bytes. The connection does not need to be open for you to request this property.

Larger PacketSizes can be advantageous in situations where bulk data is being transferred, such as large amounts of text or image data. This would result in fewer network read and write operations. Smaller amounts of data would benefit from a smaller PacketSize.

Usage

```
myInt32 = mySqlConnection.PacketSize
```

Parameters

None.

Sample Code

```
Dim mySqlConnection As New System.Data.SqlClient.SqlConnection()
' Establish Connection and Request PacketSize
mySqlConnection.ConnectionString = _
    "Data Source=Omnibook;Integrated Security=SSPI;Packet Size=4096;"
MessageBox.Show(mySqlConnection.PacketSize.ToString()) ' 4096
mySqlConnection.Open()
MessageBox.Show(mySqlConnection.PacketSize.ToString()) ' 4096
' Done
mySqlConnection.Close()
mySqlConnection.Dispose()
```

ServerVersion

The ServerVersion property returns the major, minor, and release version of the connected SQL Server. An open connection must be established in order to query the ServerVersion.

ServerVersion is returned in the format of XX.YY.ZZZZ:

XX Major version.

YY Minor version.

ZZZZ Release version. A provider-specific description may also be appended to the release version.

Usage

```
myString = mySqlConnection.ServerVersion
```

Parameters

None.

Microsoft SQL Server Versions	
Microsoft SQL Server 7.0	07.00.0623
Microsoft SQL Server 7.0 SP1	07.00.0699
Microsoft SQL Server 7.0 SP2	07.00.0842
Microsoft SQL Server 7.0 SP3	07.00.0961
Microsoft SQL Server 2000	08.00.0194
Microsoft SQL Server 2000 SP1	08.00.0384
Microsoft SQL Server 2000 SP2	08.00.0534

Exceptions

InvalidOperationException	The connection is closed.

Sample Code

```
Dim mySqlConnection As New System.Data.SqlClient.SqlConnection()
Dim mySqlCommand As System.Data.SqlClient.SqlCommand
' Establish Connection
mySqlConnection.ConnectionString = _
   "Server=Omnibook;Integrated Security=True;"
mySqlConnection.Open()
' Create and Execute @@Version Command
mySqlCommand = mySqlConnection.CreateCommand
mySqlCommand.CommandText = "SELECT @@Version"
MessageBox.Show(mySqlCommand.ExecuteScalar(), "@@Version")
' Compare with SqlConnection.ServerVersion
MessageBox.Show(mySqlConnection.ServerVersion, _
   "SqlConnection.ServerVersion")
' Done
mySqlConnection.Close()
mySqlConnection.Dispose()
```

State

The State property returns the current disposition of the connection, which could be one of several values: broken, closed, connecting, executing, fetching, or open. The values can be bitwise combinations of the various state properties, although some combinations are illogical and not supported at this time.

You can also detect state changes by trapping the StateChange event on the SqlConnection object. The StateChange event fires when the connection changes from closed to open or from open to closed. Because the SqlConnection Open method executes synchronously, either approach will work similarly.

Usage

```
myConnectionState = mySqlConnection.State
myString = mySqlConnection.State.ToString()
```

Parameters

None.

ConnectionState Enumeration

Broken (16)	The connection has been broken. This state is not supported.
Closed (0)	(Default) The connection is closed.
Connecting (2)	The connection is connecting. This state is not supported.
Executing (4)	The connection is executing a command. This state is not supported.
Fetching (8)	Data is being retrieved. This state is not supported.
Open (1)	The connection is currently open.

Exceptions

InvalidOperationException	The connection is closed.

Sample Code

```
Dim mySqlConnection As New System.Data.SqlClient.SqlConnection()
mySqlConnection.ConnectionString = _
   "Data Source=Omnibook;Integrated Security=SSPI"
mySqlConnection.Open()
MessageBox.Show(mySqlConnection.State.ToString(), "State")
mySqlConnection.Close()
MessageBox.Show(mySqlConnection.State.ToString(), "State")
```

StateChange

The StateChange event fires whenever the SqlConnection's state changes, such as when it opens or closes. Keep in mind that, by the time the event is raised, the state has already changed. You can, however, request the StateChangeEventArgs and compare the original with the current state. Any exception raised from within the event handler is propagated up to the caller of the Open or Close method.

Usage

```
Private Sub mySqlConnection_StateChange(ByVal sender As Object, _
   ByVal e As System.Data.StateChangeEventArgs) _
   Handles mySqlConnection.StateChange
End Sub
```

Parameters

`sender`	Contains a reference to the originator of the event.
`e`	Contains the StateChangeEventArgs object. See arguments in the table below.

Event Argument Data

e.CurrentState	A ConnectionState enumeration representing the new, current state of the connection. Remember, the change has already occurred.
e.OriginalState	A ConnectionState enumeration representing the previous, original state of the connection.

ConnectionState Enumeration

Broken (16)	The connection has been broken. This state is not supported.
Closed (0)	(Default) The connection is closed.
Connecting (2)	The connection is connecting. This state is not supported.
Executing (4)	The connection is executing a command. This state is not supported.
Fetching (8)	Data is being retrieved. This state is not supported.
Open (1)	The connection is currently open.

Exceptions

InvalidOperationException	The connection is closed.

Sample Code

```
' A general procedure to handle the event
Private Sub myStateChangeHandler(ByVal sender As Object, _
   ByVal e As System.Data.StateChangeEventArgs)
   MessageBox.Show(e.OriginalState.ToString() & " to " & _
      e.CurrentState.ToString(), "State Changed")
End Sub
Private Sub MyTest()
   Dim mySqlConnection As New System.Data.SqlClient.SqlConnection()
   ' Specify the Event Handler
   AddHandler mySqlConnection.StateChange, AddressOf
myStateChangeHandler
   ' Establish the Connection
   mySqlConnection.ConnectionString = _
      "Server=(local);Integrated Security=SSPI"
   mySqlConnection.Open()   ' StateChange fires
   mySqlConnection.Close() ' StateChange fires
End Sub
```

WorkstationId

The read-only WorkstationId property returns the Workstation ID specified in the ConnectionString. The WorkstationId, if not specified, will be the same as the name of the client computer. The connection does not need to be open for you to request this property.

Using a meaningful WorkstationId can aid in troubleshooting. When using SQL Server tools, such as the SQL Profiler, you are able to view and even filter out the traffic from a specific WorkstationId.

Larger PacketSizes can be advantageous in situations where bulk data is being transferred, such as large amounts of text or image data. This would result in fewer network read and write operations. Smaller amounts of data would benefit from a smaller PacketSize.

Usage

```
myInt32 = mySqlConnection.PacketSize
```

Parameters

None.

Sample Code

```
Dim mySqlConnection As New System.Data.SqlClient.SqlConnection()
' ConnectionString with no Workstation ID
mySqlConnection.ConnectionString = _
    "Server=(local);Integrated Security=SSPI"
MessageBox.Show(mySqlConnection.WorkstationId) ' Returns the
ComputerName
' ConnectionString with HAL9000 as the Workstation ID
mySqlConnection.ConnectionString = _
    "Server=(local);Integrated Security=SSPI;Workstation ID=HAL9000"
MessageBox.Show(mySqlConnection.WorkstationId) ' Returns HAL9000
mySqlConnection.Open()
MessageBox.Show(mySqlConnection.WorkstationId) ' Returns HAL9000
' Done
mySqlConnection.Close()
```

System.Data.SqlClient.SqlDataAdapter

The SqlDataAdapter provides an interface between the SQL Server data source and the .NET Framework data handling objects. The SqlDataAdapter both retrieves data from a data source, populating a DataSet with data and constraints, and resolves updates, additions, and deletions back to the data source. The SqlDataAdapter depends on the SqlConnection object to provide the connection to the data source and on the SqlCommand object to retrieve data from and resolve changes to the data source.

The SqlDataAdapter uses the SelectCommand object to define which data to draw from the data source. This SqlCommand object may reference a valid SQL statement or a stored procedure , with optional parameters. See SqlCommand for more information on how to properly define SqlCommand objects. In order to process changes to the data source, the SqlDataAdapter moves through the rows, one by one, calling the appropriate Insert, Update, Delete command for every row in which changes have occurred. If a SqlCommand object has not been specified for the SqlDataAdapter, and if it is required during a Fill or Update operation, an exception will be raised. See Fill and Update in the text that follows for more information.

Multiple SqlDataAdapters can be used with the same DataSet. In this way, several disparate data sources can be included in one DataSet. For instance, a customer list drawn from a small MS Access database could be combined with orders drawn from a SQL Server 2000 database into one DataSet. Data relationships between the two tables could be created internally to the DataSet, and the resulting in-memory database could be queried using SQL. Changes to the DataSet are then saved back to the multiple data sources by calling the Update method of each SqlDataAdapter.

If a SqlDataAdapter's SelectCommand returns more than one result set, each set is inserted into the DataSet as a new DataTable.

Constructors

```
Dim mySqlDataAdapter As New SqlDataAdapter()
Dim mySqlDataAdapter As New SqlDataAdapter(SqlCommand)
```

```
Dim mySqlDataAdapter As New SqlDataAdapter(String, SqlConnection)
Dim mySqlDataAdapter As New SqlDataAdapter(String, String2)
```

Parameters

`SqlCommand`	A SqlCommand object to assign to the SelectCommand property.
`String`	A valid SQL SELECT statement to be used to select data from the data source. This string is assigned to the SelectCommand.CommandText property.
`SqlConnection`	The SqlConnection object representing the connection to the data source.
`String2`	A valid connection string used to identify the data source.

SqlDataAdapter Sample Code

```
Dim mySqlCommandBuilder As New System.Data.SqlClient.SqlCommandBuilder()
Dim mySqlDataAdapter As New System.Data.SqlClient.SqlDataAdapter()
Dim mySqlConnection As New System.Data.SqlClient.SqlConnection()
Dim mySqlCommand As System.Data.SqlClient.SqlCommand
Dim myDataSet As New System.Data.DataSet()
Dim intRowsUpdated As Int32
' Establish connection
mySqlConnection.ConnectionString = _
   "Server=(local);Integrated Security=SSPI;Database=Northwind"
mySqlConnection.Open()
' Create a Command
mySqlCommand = mySqlConnection.CreateCommand
mySqlCommand.CommandText = "SELECT * FROM Customers"
' Assign the SelectCommand to the DataAdapter
mySqlDataAdapter.SelectCommand = mySqlCommand
' Use a SqlCommandBuilder to fill Insert, Update, Delete Commands
mySqlCommandBuilder.DataAdapter = mySqlDataAdapter
mySqlDataAdapter.InsertCommand = mySqlCommandBuilder.GetInsertCommand()
mySqlDataAdapter.UpdateCommand = mySqlCommandBuilder.GetUpdateCommand()
mySqlDataAdapter.DeleteCommand = mySqlCommandBuilder.GetDeleteCommand()
' View the generated Command text
MessageBox.Show(mySqlDataAdapter.InsertCommand.CommandText, "Insert
SQL")
MessageBox.Show(mySqlDataAdapter.UpdateCommand.CommandText, "Update
SQL")
MessageBox.Show(mySqlDataAdapter.DeleteCommand.CommandText, "Delete
SQL")
' Before filling a Dataset, you can specify SqlDataAdapter behaviors
mySqlDataAdapter.AcceptChangesDuringFill = True
mySqlDataAdapter.MissingMappingAction = MissingMappingAction.Passthrough
mySqlDataAdapter.MissingSchemaAction = MissingSchemaAction.Add
```

```
' Fill the DataSet - "Customers" is an arbitrary name within the table
mySqlDataAdapter.Fill(myDataSet, "Customers")
' Make a small change to one piece of data (append an asterisk)
myDataSet.Tables(0).Rows(0).BeginEdit()
myDataSet.Tables(0).Rows(0).Item(1) += "*"
myDataSet.Tables(0).Rows(0).EndEdit()
' Update the SQL Server
Try
   ' Note that when we filled myDataSet we set the name of the table
   ' to "Customers". That means we cannot simply pass myDataSet
   ' to the Update method, since it is looking for DataTable
   ' with the default name of "Table"
   ' Instead we must pass a DataTable, or a DataSet and the table name
   ' WRONG
   '   intRowsUpdated = mySqlDataAdapter.Update(myDataSet)
   ' RIGHT
   '   intRowsUpdated = mySqlDataAdapter.Update(myDataSet.Tables(0))
   '   intRowsUpdated = mySqlDataAdapter.Update(myDataSet, "Customers")
   ' **********************************
   intRowsUpdated = mySqlDataAdapter.Update(myDataSet.Tables(0))
Catch mySqlException As SqlException
   MessageBox.Show(mySqlException.Message, "SqlException")
Catch myException As Exception
   MessageBox.Show(myException.Message, "Exception")
End Try
' Clean up
myDataSet.Dispose()
mySqlCommand.Dispose()
mySqlDataAdapter.Dispose()
mySqlConnection.Close()
```

Members

AcceptChangesDuringFill

The AcceptChangesDuringFill property (inherited from the DataAdapter object) is a Boolean value that determines whether the AcceptChanges event is fired when the Fill method is called. If the value is True, then the AcceptChanges method is called for each DataRow object as it is added to the DataTable object, leaving the DataRowState = Unchanged (2). If False, the added DataRow objects are treated as added rows, leaving the DataRowState = Added (4). See System.Data.DataRow class for more information.

The default value is True.

Usage

```
myBoolean = mySqlDataAdapter.AcceptChangesDuringFill
mySqlDataAdapter.AcceptChangesDuringFill = myBoolean
```

Parameters

None.

ContinueUpdateOnError

The ContinueUpdateOnError property (inherited from the DataAdapter object) is a Boolean value that determines whether to generate an exception during the update of a row. If this property value is set to True, then no exception will be thrown, but rather the update of the row is skipped and the error information is placed in the RowError property of the row in error. If this property value is set to False, an exception is thrown when an error occurs during the update.

The default value is False.

Usage

```
myBoolean = mySqlDataAdapter.ContinueUpdateOnError
mySqlDataAdapter.ContinueUpdateOnError = myBoolean
```

Parameters

None.

DefaultSourceTableName

The DefaultSourceTableName is a constant, which the SqlDataAdapter uses for its default name for table mappings. Currently, this value is Table.

Usage

```
myString = mySqlDataAdapter.DefaultSourceTableName
```

Parameters

None.

DeleteCommand

The DeleteCommand property returns or sets the SqlCommand object representing the SQL DELETE statement used to delete records from the data source when the Update method is called. In some instances, the DeleteCommand during an Update may be automatically generated by a SqlCommandBuilder object. Even when the SqlCommandBuilder is used, this property is not filled. Instead, the SqlCommandBuilder listens for the RowUpdating and RowUpdated events and provides the proper commands at that time. See System.Data.SqlClient.SqlCommand and System.Data.SqlClient.SqlCommandBuilder for more information.

Before calling the Update method, the DeleteCommand, InsertCommand, or UpdateCommand properties of the SqlDataAdapter must be initialized with valid SQL statements or SqlCommand objects, or a SqlCommandBuilder object must be associated with the SqlDataAdapter. If not, a SqlException will be thrown.

Usage

```
mySqlCommand = mySqlDataAdapter.DeleteCommand
mySqlDataAdapter.DeleteCommand = mySqlCommand
```

or, if the default SqlCommand is acceptable, a shorter version is:

```
mySqlDataAdapter.DeleteCommand.CommandText = mySqlDeleteString
```

Parameters

None.

Fill

The Fill method adds or updates the rows in a DataSet, based on the SelectCommand and returns an Int32 specifying the number of records that were added or updated. Before calling the Fill method, the SelectCommand of the DataAdapter must be initialized with a valid SQL SELECT statement or SqlCommand object. If not, a SqlException will be thrown.

Fill will automatically append rows to an existing DataTable if there is no primary key defined. If there is a primary key, the Fill method will update the data in the DataTable from the data in the data source wherever matching primary keys are found.

When determining which of the possible usages below to use, there are a few things to keep in mind. When you use the SqlDataAdapter.Fill(DataSet), the DataSet will add a DataTable with the default name Table. When you call the DataAdapter.Update method, you may then use the Update(DataSet) because that operates only on the DataTable named Table. If you once name the DataTable, you must then name the DataTable in any Update commands as well, or a System.ArgumentNullException will be raised.

TIP Unlike the OleDbDataAdapter, the SqlDataAdapter cannot consume MDAC ADO Recordset or Record objects. If you desire that capability, you should consider using the OleDb .NET data provider.

Usage

```
mySqlDataAdapter.Fill(DataTable)
mySqlDataAdapter.Fill(DataSet)
mySqlDataAdapter.Fill(DataSet, String)
mySqlDataAdapter.Fill(DataSet, Int32a, Int32b, String)
```

Parameters

`DataTable`	A System.Data.DataTable object to be filled.
`DataSet`	A System.Data.DataSet object to be filled.
`String`	A string designating the source table.
`Int32a`	An Int32 specifying the first record to be retrieved.
`Int32b`	An Int32 specifying the maximum number of records to be retrieved.

Exceptions

InvalidOperationException	You called the Fill method when Connection has not been specified.
SqlException	You called the Fill method when either an empty or invalid SelectCommand has been set, or you called the Update method when an empty or invalid DeleteCommand, InsertCommand, or UpdateCommand has been set.

FillError

The FillError event (inherited from System.Data.Common.DbDataAdapter) is fired whenever an error is encountered during a Fill operation. The FillError event passes a reference to the source of the event (the instantiated SqlDataAdapter object) and a System.Data.FillErrorEventArgs object with data about the error.

For more information please see the System.Data.Common.DbDataAdapter.FillError event.

Usage

```
Private Sub mySqlDataAdapter_FillError(ByVal sender As Object, _
   ByVal e As System.Data.FillErrorEventArgs) Handles _
   mySqlDataAdapter.FillError
```

Parameters

`sender`	Contains a reference to the originator of the event.
`e`	Contains the FillErrorEventArgs object.

Event Argument Data

e.Continue	Gets or sets a Boolean determining whether the fill operation should continue despite the error.
e.DataTable	Gets a reference to the DataTable that is currently being updated.
e.Errors	Gets an Exception object specifying the errors that occurred.
e.Values	Gets the values for the row being updated as an array of Object objects.

FillSchema

The FillSchema method (inherited from System.Data.Common.DbDataAdapter class) creates a new DataTable and fills it with the schema inherited from the data source. It then returns a DataTable containing the schema derived from the data source. The schema is configured based on the value of the SchemaType parameter. A SchemaType of Source (value = 1) applies the incoming schema to the DataSet with no transformation; Mapped applies the mappings of existing DataTable objects to the schema and then transforms the DataSet based on the transformed schema.

Usage

```
mySqlDataAdapter.FillSchema(DataTable, SchemaType)
mySqlDataAdapter.FillSchema(DataSet, SchemaType)
mySqlDataAdapter.FillSchema(DataSet, SchemaType, String)
```

Parameters

`DataTable`	A System.Data.DataTable object to receive the schema.
`SchemaType`	A System.Data.SchemaType enumeration value (Mapped (2) or Source (1)).
`DataSet`	A System.Data.DataSet object to receive the schema.
`String`	A string designating the source table to be used for the schema mapping.

Exceptions

ArgumentException	The source table from which to get the schema could not be found.

GetFillParameters

The GetFillParameters method (inherited from System.Data.Common.DbDataAdapter class) returns an array of IDataParameter objects specifying user-defined parameters to be passed in a SQL SELECT command. This method can be used to verify the parameters when selecting data. This is similar to the Parameters property of the SqlCommand object, which returns a SqlParameterCollection (a collection of SqlParameter objects).

Usage

```
myIDataParaterArray() = mySqlDataAdapter.GetFillParameters()
```

Parameters

None.

Exceptions

None.

InsertCommand

The InsertCommand property returns or sets a SqlCommand object. The command represents the SQL INSERT statement to be used to insert new records into the data source when the Update method is called. In some instances, the InsertCommand may be automatically generated by a SqlCommandBuilder object. Even when the SqlCommandBuilder is used, this property is not filled. Instead, the SqlCommandBuilder listens for the RowUpdating and RowUpdated events and provides the proper commands at that time. See System.Data.SqlClient.SqlCommand and System.Data.SqlClient.SqlCommandBuilder for more information.

Before calling the Update method, the DeleteCommand, InsertCommand, or UpdateCommand properties of the SqlDataAdapter must be initialized with valid SQL statements or SqlCommand objects, or a SqlCommandBuilder object must be associated with the SqlDataAdapter. If not, a SqlException will be thrown.

Usage

```
mySqlCommand = mySqlDataAdapter.InsertCommand
mySqlDataAdapter.InsertCommand = mySqlCommand
```

or, if the default SqlCommand is acceptable, a shorter version is:

```
mySqlDataAdapter.InsertCommand.CommandText = mySqlInsertString
```

Parameters

None.

MissingMappingAction

The MissingMappingAction property (inherited from System.Data.DataAdapter) returns or sets a MissingMappingAction enumeration value that determines what to do when the incoming data does not have a matching table or column in the current DataSet. The default value is Passthrough.

Usage

```
myMissingMappingAction = mySqlDataAdapter.MissingMappingAction
mySqlDataAdapter.MissingMappingAction = myMissingMappingAction
```

Parameters

None.

MissingMappingAction Enumeration

Error (3)	A System.SystemException is thrown.
Ignore (2)	Any columns or tables without mappings are ignored, returning a null reference.
Passthrough (1)	(Default) The source column or table is added to the DataSet using its original name.

MissingSchemaAction

The MissingSchemaAction property (inherited from System.Data.DataAdapter) returns or sets a MissingSchemaAction enumeration value that determines what to do when the incoming data does not have a matching schema in the current DataSet. The default value is Add.

Usage

```
myMissingSchemaAction = mySqlDataAdapter.MissingSchemaAction
mySqlDataAdapter.MissingSchemaAction = myMissingSchemaAction
```

Parameters

None.

MissingSchemaAction Enumeration

Add (1)	(Default) Adds the columns required to complete the schema.
AddWithKey (4)	Adds the columns and primary key information required to complete the schema.
Error (3)	A System.SystemException is thrown.
Ignore (2)	Any columns without a matching schema are ignored.

RowUpdated

The RowUpdated event is raised when the Update method is called. This event fires on every row that is being added, changed, or deleted from the data source. The event occurs after the changes have been made to the data source and before AcceptChanges is called. The event passes a SqlRowUpdatedEventArgs object to the designated event handler.

NOTE **Be aware that, in Visual Basic .NET, the SqlDataAdapter object must be declared WithEvents in order for declared event handlers to be executed (unless the AddHandler statement is used). For a complete reference of the arguments passed to this event, see System.Data.SqlClient.SqlRowUpdatedEventArgs.**

Usage

```
Private Sub mySqlDataAdapter_RowUpdated(ByVal sender As Object, _
   ByVal e As System.Data.SqlClient.SqlRowUpdatedEventArgs) _
```

```
   Handles mySqlDataAdapter.RowUpdated
End Sub
```

Parameters

`sender`	Contains a reference to the originator of the event.
`e`	Contains the SqlRowUpdatedEventArgs object. For more information, see the section on System.Data.SqlClient.SqlRowUpdatedEventArgs.

RowUpdating

The RowUpdating event is raised when the Update method is called. This event fires on every row that is being added, changed, or deleted from the data source. The event occurs after the changes have been made to the data source and before AcceptChanges is called. The event passes a SqlRowUpdatingEventArgs object to the designated event handler.

NOTE Be aware that, in Visual Basic .NET, the SqlDataAdapter object must be declared WithEvents in order for declared event handlers to be executed (unless the AddHandler statement is used). For a complete reference of the arguments passed to this event, see System.Data.SqlClient.SqlRowUpdatingEventArgs.

Usage

```
Private Sub mySqlDataAdapter_RowUpdating(ByVal sender As Object, _
   ByVal e As System.Data.SqlClient.SqlRowUpdatingEventArgs) _
   Handles mySqlDataAdapter.RowUpdating
End Sub
```

Parameters

`sender`	Contains a reference to the originator of the event.
`e`	Contains the SqlRowUpdatingEventArgs object. For more information, see the section on System.Data.SqlClient.SqlRowUpdatingEventArgs.

SelectCommand

The SelectCommand property returns or sets a SqlCommand object. The command represents the SQL SELECT statement to be used to select records from the data source when the Fill method is called. Unlike the Delete, Insert, and Update Commands, the SelectCommand cannot be automatically generated by a CommandBuilder object.

Usage

```
mySqlCommand = mySqlDataAdapter.SelectCommand
mySqlDataAdapter.SelectCommand = mySqlCommand
```

or, if the default SqlCommand is acceptable, a shorter version is:

```
mySqlDataAdapter.SelectCommand.CommandText = mySqlSelectString
```

Parameters

None.

TableMappings

The read-only TableMappings property returns a DataTableMappingCollection object. This collection of DataTableMapping objects maps the table and column names used by the data source to the table and column names used by the DataSet. The default value is an empty collection. These mappings are used during an Update to ensure the proper tables and columns are updated in the data source, despite possibly different names. The DataTableMapping objects contained in the DataTableMappingCollection contain three public properties that permit access to the underlying mapping. They are the read-only ColumnMapping property, which returns the DataColumnMappingCollection object describing the mappings of the columns between the data source and DataSet; the DataSetTable property, which is used to get or set the destination DataSet table name; and the SourceTable, which gets or sets the source table from which to retrieve the data.

Usage

```
myDataTableMappingCollection = mySqlDataAdapter.TableMappings
```

Parameters

None.

DataTableMapping	Collection
ColumnMapping	Read-only property that returns the DataColumnMapping-Collection object describing the mappings of the columns between the data source and DataSet.
DataSetTable	Property that is used to get or set the destination DataSet table name.
SourceTable	Property that returns or sets the source table from which to retrieve the data.

ToString

The ToString method for SqlDataAdapter simply returns "System.Data.SqlClient.Sql-DataAdapter".

Usage

```
myString = mySqlDataAdapter.ToString()
```

Parameters

None.

Exceptions

None.

Update

The Update method calls the INSERT, UPDATE, or DELETE commands for each of the inserted, updated, or deleted rows. Several different parameters can be sent to the Update method, depending on what set of rows you'd like to update. Basically, all of them boil down to a collection of System.Data.DataRow objects. The difference is merely how they are collected and identified. One way is to send an array of DataRow objects for update. Another is to send a System.Data.DataTable, which is an object containing a collection of DataRows. Another is to pass a System.Data.DataSet object, which is a collection of DataTables and corresponding DataRows.

When calling Update with the DataSet object, you must specify on which of the DataTables you wish to perform the update. You cannot send a DataSet to the Update method and expect all contained DataTables to be updated. This can be a source of frustration for first-time users. The Update(DataSet) method will send only a DataTable with the name of "Table" for update! This is the default name given to the first DataTable loaded into the DataSet. (If no DataTable named "Table" exists, an exception is thrown.) If you've given your DataTable objects meaningful names, you must also pass the given name of the table to be updated.

Usage

```
mySqlDataAdapter.Update(DataSet)
mySqlDataAdapter.Update(DataRowArray)
mySqlDataAdapter.Update(DataTable)
mySqlDataAdapter.Update(DataSet, String)
```

Parameters

`DataSet`	A System.Data.DataSet object to be updated.
`DataRowArray`	An array of System.Data.DataRow objects to be updated.
`DataTable`	A System.Data.DataTable object to be updated.
`String`	A string designating the source table.

Exceptions

ArgumentNullException	The source DataSet is invalid.
DBConcurrencyException	Attempt to execute an INSERT, UPDATE, or DELETE command has resulted in no records affected.
InvalidOperationException	The source DataTable is invalid.
SystemException	Either no DataRow exists to update, or no DataSet exists to update or no source DataSet exists.

UpdateCommand

The UpdateCommand property returns or sets a SqlCommand object. The command represents the SQL UPDATE statement to be used to update records into the data source when the Update method is called. In some instances, the UpdateCommand may be automatically generated by a SqlCommandBuilder object. Even when the SqlCommandBuilder is used, this property is not filled. Instead, the SqlCommandBuilder listens for the RowUpdating and RowUpdated events and provides the proper commands at that time. See System.Data.SqlClient.SqlCommand and System.Data.SqlClient.SqlCommandBuilder for more information.

Before calling the Update method, the DeleteCommand, InsertCommand, or UpdateCommand properties of the SqlDataAdapter must be initialized with valid SQL statements or SqlCommand objects, or a SqlCommandBuilder object must be associated with the SqlDataAdapter. If not, a SqlException will be thrown.

Usage

```
mySqlCommand = mySqlDataAdapter.UpdateCommand
mySqlDataAdapter.UpdateCommand = mySqlCommand
```

or, if the default SqlCommand is acceptable, a shorter version is:

```
mySqlDataAdapter.UpdateCommand.CommandText = mySqlUpdateString
```

Parameters

None.

System.Data.SqlClient.SqlDataReader

The SqlDataReader provides read-only, forward-only access to SQL Server. Because it maintains only one record in memory at a time, there is minimal resource impact. Unlike a DataTable object, the DataReader is specifically geared toward working with a particular type of data source. Because there is no need to create a DataSet object (or other data structures found in the System.Data namespace), and because the DataReader is always fully connected to the database, it is much faster than other forms of data access. It can be an excellent choice for populating list boxes or providing data for Web pages. Be aware, though, that once a DataReader has been opened, the connection it is using cannot be used by any other object, and the connection to the data source is maintained until the DataReader's Close method is called. Once the DataReader is closed, the only two properties available are IsClosed and RecordsAffected. Any calls to other properties will result in a System.InvalidOperationException being thrown.

Unlike other data access objects, the DataReader can be instantiated only by using the ExecuteReader method of a Command object, and it cannot be maintained independently of an open Connection object. The primary method for retrieving data from a DataReader is the Read method. The Read method will return FALSE when there is no further data to read, thus it can be used as the condition in a Do While Loop. See the code sample. There are several Get methods that return the data read as a particular data type. Because no type conversions are performed when the data is read, you must ensure that the data that is read is of the proper type!

Only one DataReader can use any given Connection object at a time, however the Command that created the DataReader may return more than one set of data. In this case, the NextResult method can be used to begin processing the next set of data. When there are no further result sets, the NextResult method will return FALSE; otherwise, it will return TRUE and load the first row of data from the next result set.

Constructors

There is no public constructor. Instead, use the ExecuteReader method of a SqlCommand object:

```
mySqlDataReader = mySqlCommand.ExecuteReader()
```

Parameters

None.

SqlDataReader Sample Code

```
Dim mySqlConnection As New System.Data.SqlClient.SqlConnection()
Dim mySqlDataReader As System.Data.SqlClient.SqlDataReader
Dim mySqlCommand As System.Data.SqlClient.SqlCommand
Dim myDisplayString As String
Dim myValues() As Object
Dim myValue As Object
Dim i As Int32
' Establish Connection
mySqlConnection.ConnectionString = _
   "Server=(local);Integrated Security=SSPI;Database=Northwind"
mySqlConnection.Open()
' Create Command
mySqlCommand = mySqlConnection.CreateCommand
mySqlCommand.CommandText = _
   "SELECT * FROM Region;SELECT * FROM Territories WHERE RegionID = 4"
' ExecuteReader
mySqlDataReader = mySqlCommand.ExecuteReader()
' Construct a String from the Region table columns
Do While mySqlDataReader.Read()
   For i = 0 To mySqlDataReader.FieldCount - 1
      myDisplayString += "Field" + ControlChars.Tab + _
         mySqlDataReader.GetName(i).ToString() + ControlChars.CrLf + _
         "Type" + ControlChars.Tab + _
         mySqlDataReader.GetFieldType(i).ToString() + _
         ControlChars.CrLf + "Value" + ControlChars.Tab + _
         mySqlDataReader.GetValue(i).ToString() + _
         ControlChars.CrLf + ControlChars.CrLf
   Next
Loop
MessageBox.Show(myDisplayString, "Region Table")
' Read the NextResult
mySqlDataReader.NextResult()
' Use the GetValues() method to store data to an array
ReDim myValues(mySqlDataReader.FieldCount - 1)
myDisplayString = ""
Do While mySqlDataReader.Read()
   mySqlDataReader.GetValues(myValues)
   ' Use For Each statement to enumerate the array
   For Each myValue In myValues
      myDisplayString += myValue.ToString()
      myDisplayString += ControlChars.Tab
```

```
        Next
        myDisplayString += ControlChars.Cr + ControlChars.Cr
    Loop
    MessageBox.Show(myDisplayString, "Territories Table")
    ' Done
    mySqlDataReader.Close()
    mySqlConnection.Close()
    mySqlConnection.Dispose()
```

Members

Close

The Close method closes the SqlDataReader object and allows the associated SqlConnection object to be used by other objects. The Close method must be explicitly closed to free the Connection object. Once Close has been called, only two properties remain set: IsClosed and RecordsAffected. Calls to any other properties after closing the SqlDataReader will return a System.InvalidOperationException.

Usage

```
mySqlDataReader.Close()
```

Parameters

None.

Exceptions

None.

Depth

The read-only Depth property returns an Int32 specifying the level of nesting of the current row. Any row in a single table will have a value of 0. This member is of primary use when using a multidimensional data provider, data shaping provider, or XML data. In these cases, the Depth property indicates the level of nesting.

Usage

```
myInt32 = mySqlDataReader.Depth
```

Parameters

None.

Exceptions

InvalidOperationException	The SqlDataReader is closed.

FieldCount

The read-only FieldCount property returns an Int32 specifying the number of fields (columns) in the current row. If the SqlDataReader does not contain a valid row, FieldCount returns a 0. A value of -1 indicates that that the SQL statement filling the SqlDataReader was a statement that does not return rows (i.e., update).

Usage

```
myInt32 = mySqlDataReader.FieldCount
```

Parameters

None.

GetBoolean

The GetBoolean method retrieves the value of the specified column as a Boolean value. If the column does not contain a Boolean, a System.InvalidCastException will be raised.

Usage

```
myBoolean = mySqlDataReader.GetBoolean(Index)
```

Parameters

`Index`	The zero-based column position (Int32).

Exceptions

IndexOutOfRangeException	Requested column does not exist.
InvalidCastException	Either the value in desired column is not a Boolean value, or the column name (as String) was passed instead of the ordinal position.
InvalidOperationException	Either the SqlDataReader is closed, or the Read method has not yet been called (no data yet exists).

GetByte

The GetByte method retrieves the value of the specified column as a Byte value. If the column does not contain a Byte, a System.InvalidCastException will be raised.

Usage

```
myByte = mySqlDataReader.GetByte(Index)
```

Parameters

`Index`	The zero-based column position (Int32).

Exceptions

IndexOutOfRangeException	Requested column does not exist.
InvalidCastException	Either the value in the desired column is not a Byte value, or the column name (as String) was passed instead of the ordinal position.
InvalidOperationException	Either the SqlDataReader is closed, or the Read method has not yet been called (no data yet exists).

GetBytes

The GetBytes method retrieves a stream of Bytes to be loaded into a passed Byte array (buffer) and returns an Int64 specifying the actual number of Bytes read. To receive the stream of Bytes, you must pass several parameters. The first is an Int32 specifying which column in the row contains data to read. The second is an Int64 value specifying the index in the column from which to begin reading data. Because this index is zero based, passing a value of 4 in a Byte array that contains "BROTHER" would cause "T" to be the first Byte read. The third is the destination Byte array. If a null reference (or an object set to `Nothing`, if using VB) is passed, the GetBytes method will return the length of the column in bytes.

The destination Byte array may already contain data because the fourth parameter is an Int32 identifying the array index to begin filling the Byte array. Passing a 5 will begin filling at myByteArray(4). The final value specifies the number of Bytes to read into the array. Passing a number larger than the number of bytes remaining will fill the buffer with the remaining bytes and leave the difference unfilled. No errors or exceptions will be raised.

If the column doesn't contain an array of Bytes, a System.InvalidCastException will be raised.

Usage

```
myInt64 = mySqlDataReader.GetBytes(Index, FieldIndex, _
   ByteArray(), ByteArrayIndex, Length)
```

Parameters

`Index`	The zero-based column position (Int32).
`FieldIndex`	The zero-based index within the data field to begin taking data (Int64).
`ByteArray()`	The array of Bytes to fill with data. Passing a null reference (`Nothing`, in VB) causes the GetBytes method to return an Int64 specifying the length of the column, in bytes.
`ByteArrayIndex`	The starting index of the passed array of Bytes to start filling with data (Int32).
`Length`	Int32 that specifies the number of bytes to read (length). If the number exceeds the number of Bytes left, all remaining Bytes are loaded into the array, and no error or exception is raised.

Exceptions

IndexOutOfRangeException	Requested column does not exist.
InvalidCastException	Either the value in desired column is not a Byte array, or the column name (as String) was passed instead of the ordinal position.
InvalidOperationException	Either the SqlDataReader is closed, or the Read method has not yet been called (no data yet exists).

GetChar

The GetChar method retrieves the value of the specified column as a Char value. If the column does not contain a Char, a System.InvalidCastException will be raised.

Usage

```
myChar = mySqlDataReader.GetChar(Index)
```

Parameters

`Index`	The zero-based column position (Int32).

Exceptions

IndexOutOfRangeException	Requested column does not exist.

InvalidCastException	Either the value in desired column is not a Byte value, or the column name (as String) was passed instead of the ordinal position.
InvalidOperationException	Either the SqlDataReader is closed, or the Read method has not yet been called (no data yet exists).

GetChars

The GetChars method retrieves a stream of characters to be loaded into a passed Char array (buffer) and returns an Int64 specifying the actual number of characters read. To receive the stream of characters, you must pass several parameters. The first is an Int32 specifying which column in the row contains data to read. The second is an Int64 value specifying the index in the column from which to begin reading data. Because this index is zero based, passing a value of 4 in a Char array that contains "BROTHER" would cause "H" to be the first Char read. The third is the passed buffer in the form of a destination Char array. If a null reference (or an object set to `Nothing` in VB) is passed, the GetChars method will return the length of the column in chars. The destination Char array may already contain data because the fourth parameter is an Int32 identifying the array index to begin filling the Char array. Passing a 5 will begin filling at myCharArray(4). The final value specifies the number of characters to read into the array. Passing a number larger than the number of characters remaining will fill the buffer with the remaining characters and leave the difference unfilled. No errors or exceptions will be raised.

If the column doesn't contain an array of characters, a System.InvalidCastException will be raised.

Usage

```
myInt64 = mySqlDataReader.GetChars(Index, FieldIndex, _
   CharArray(), CharArrayIndex, Length)
```

Parameters

`Index`	The zero-based column position (Int32).
`FieldIndex`	The zero-based index within the data field to begin taking data (Int64).
`CharArray()`	The array of characters to fill with data. Passing a null reference (`Nothing`, in VB) causes the GetChars method to return an Int64 specifying the length of the column, in characters.
`CharArrayIndex`	The starting index of the passed array of characters to start filling with data (Int32).
`Length`	Int32 that specifies the number of bytes to read (length). If the number exceeds the number of characters left, all remaining characters are loaded into the array, and no error or exception is raised.

Exceptions

IndexOutOfRangeException	Requested column does not exist.
InvalidCastException	Either the value in desired column is not a Byte array, or the column name (as String) was passed instead of the ordinal position.

InvalidOperationException	Either the SqlDataReader is closed, or the Read method has not yet been called (no data yet exists).

GetData

The GetData method is not currently supported by .NET. Currently, any attempt to call this method will raise a System.InvalidOperationException. In the future, it will likely return a SqlDataReader object, based on the data that exists in a specified column.

Usage

```
mySqlDataReader = mySqlDataReader.GetData(Index)
```

Parameters

`Index`	The zero-based column position (Int32).

Exceptions

InvalidOperationException	Any call to this function will currently return this exception.

GetDataTypeName

The GetDataTypeName method returns a String specifying the name of the data type in the specified column. Note that the data type returned is the SQL Server data type and not necessarily one of the standardized .NET data types or one of the System. Data.DbType enumerations.

Usage

```
myString = mySqlDataReader.GetDataType(Index)
```

Parameters

`Index`	The zero-based column position (Int32).

Exceptions

IndexOutOfRangeException	Requested column does not exist.
InvalidCastException	Column name (as String) passed instead of the ordinal position.
InvalidOperationException	Either the SqlDataReader is closed, or the Read method has not yet been called (no data yet exists).

GetDateTime

The GetDateTime method retrieves the value of the specified column as a System. DateTime value. If the column does not contain a DateTime value, a System.Invalid-CastException will be raised.

Usage

```
myDateTime = mySqlDataReader.GetDateTime(Index)
```

Parameters

`Index`	The zero-based column position (Int32).

Exceptions

IndexOutOfRangeException	Requested column does not exist.
InvalidCastException	Either the value in the desired column is not a DateTime value, or the column name, as a string, was passed instead of the ordinal position.
InvalidOperationException	Either the SqlDataReader is closed, or the Read method has not yet been called (no data yet exists).

GetDecimal

The GetDecimal method retrieves the value of the specified column as a Decimal value. If the value is not a Decimal, a System.InvalidCastException will be raised.

Usage

```
myDecimal = mySqlDataReader.GetDecimal(Index)
```

Parameters

`Index`	The zero-based column position (Int32).

Exceptions

IndexOutOfRangeException	Requested column does not exist.
InvalidCastException	Either the value in the desired column is not a Decimal value, or the column name, as a string, was passed instead of the ordinal position.
InvalidOperationException	Either the SqlDataReader is closed, or the Read method has not yet been called (no data yet exists).

GetDouble

The GetDouble method retrieves the value of the specified column as a Double (double-precision floating point). If the value is not a Double, a System.InvalidCastException will be raised.

Usage

```
myDouble = mySqlDataReader.GetDouble(Index)
```

Parameters

`Index`	The zero-based column position (Int32).

Exceptions

IndexOutOfRangeException	Requested column does not exist.
InvalidCastException	Either the value in the desired column is not a Double value, or the column name, as a string, was passed instead of the ordinal position.
InvalidOperationException	Either the SqlDataReader is closed, or the Read method has not yet been called (no data yet exists).

GetFieldType

The GetFieldType method returns a System.Type object indicating the data type of the object contained in the specified column.

The returned Type object is primarily a way to access meta data about the underlying field. To do so, it acts as a gateway to the Reflection API. Use this method to get information about the specified column's type declaration, constructors, methods, fields, properties, and events (as well as staggering amounts of other information relating to the column's Type).

This is useful when reading the columns of a row as Object objects, and you need to determine whether the retrieved Object will support a particular method. For instance, some object types support a Parse method (Char, Boolean, Int32, etc.) where others do not (GUID). Reflection can be used to find out this information, without needing to enumerate all possible .NET types in a huge IF-THEN structure.

This column differs from the GetDataTypeName method, in that it returns the .NET data type as a Type object, whereas the GetDataTypeName method returns a String representing the SQL Server data type (which may not be equivalent to a .NET data type).

Usage

```
myType = mySqlDataReader.GetType(Index)
```

Parameters

`Index`	The zero-based column position (Int32).

Exceptions

IndexOutOfRangeException	Requested column does not exist.
InvalidCastException	The column name, as a string, was passed instead of the ordinal position.
InvalidOperationException	Either the SqlDataReader is closed, or the Read method has not yet been called (no data yet exists).

GetFloat

The GetFloat method retrieves the value of the specified column as a Float (single-precision floating point). If the value is not a Float, a System.InvalidCastException will be raised.

Usage

```
myFloat = mySqlDataReader.GetFloat(Index)
```

Parameters

`Index`	The zero-based column position (Int32).

Exceptions

IndexOutOfRangeException	Requested column does not exist.
InvalidCastException	Either the value in the desired column is not a Float value, or the column name, as a string, was passed instead of the ordinal position.
InvalidOperationException	Either the SqlDataReader is closed, or the Read method has not yet been called (no data yet exists).

GetGuid

The GetGuid method retrieves the value of the specified column as a System.Guid (Globally Unique Identifier). If the value is not a Guid, a System.InvalidCastException will the raised.

Usage

```
myGuid = mySqlDataReader.GetGuid(Index)
```

Parameters

`Index`	The zero-based column position (Int32).

Exceptions

IndexOutOfRangeException	Requested column does not exist.
InvalidCastException	Either the value in the desired column is not a Guid value or the column name, as a string, was passed instead of the ordinal position.
InvalidOperationException	Either the SqlDataReader is closed, or the Read method has not yet been called (no data yet exists).

GetInt16

The GetInt16 method retrieves the value of the specified column as a System.Int16 (16-bit signed integer). If the value is not an Int16, a System.InvalidCastException will be raised.

Usage

```
myInt16 = mySqlDataReader.GetInt16(Index)
```

Parameters

`Index`	The zero-based column position (Int32).

Exceptions

IndexOutOfRangeException	Requested column does not exist.
InvalidCastException	Either the value in the desired column is not an Int16 value, or the column name, as a string, was passed instead of the ordinal position.
InvalidOperationException	Either the SqlDataReader is closed, or the Read method has not yet been called (no data yet exists).

GetInt32

The GetInt32 method retrieves the value of the specified column as a System.Int32 (32-bit signed integer). If the value is not an Int32, a System.InvalidCastException will be raised.

Usage

```
myInt32 = mySqlDataReader.GetInt32(Index)
```

Parameters

`Index`	The zero-based column position (Int32).

Exceptions

IndexOutOfRangeException	Requested column does not exist.
InvalidCastException	Either the value in the desired column is not an Int32 value, or the column name, as a string, was passed instead of the ordinal position.
InvalidOperationException	Either the SqlDataReader is closed, or the Read method has not yet been called (no data yet exists).

GetInt64

The GetInt64 method retrieves the value of the specified column as a System.Int64 (64-bit signed integer). If the value is not an Int64, a System.InvalidCastException will be raised.

Usage

```
myInt64 = mySqlDataReader.GetInt64(Index)
```

Parameters

`Index`	The zero-based column position (Int32).

Exceptions

IndexOutOfRangeException	Requested column does not exist.
InvalidCastException	Either the value in the desired column is not an Int64 value, or the column name, as a string, was passed instead of the ordinal position.
InvalidOperationException	Either the SqlDataReader is closed, or the Read method has not yet been called (no data yet exists).

GetName

The GetName method returns a String indicating the name of the specified column.

Usage

```
myString = mySqlDataReader.GetName(Index)
```

Parameters

`Index`	The zero-based column position (Int32).

Exceptions

IndexOutOfRangeException	Requested column does not exist.
InvalidCastException	The column name, as a string, was passed instead of the ordinal position.
InvalidOperationException	Either the SqlDataReader is closed, or the Read method has not yet been called (no data yet exists).

GetOrdinal

The GetOrdinal method retrieves the ordinal value (Int32) when passed the column name as a String. If the passed column name does not exist in the current row, a System.IndexOutOfRangeException will be raised.

Usage

```
myInt32 = mySqlDataReader.GetOrdinal(String)
```

Parameters

`String`	A String representing the column name.

Exceptions

IndexOutOfRangeException	Requested column does not exist.
InvalidOperationException	Either the SqlDataReader is closed, or the Read method has not yet been called (no data yet exists).

GetSchemaTable

The GetSchemaTable method retrieves a System.DataTable representing the column meta data for all of the columns in the SqlDataReader. Each column in the SqlDataReader is described by a row in the returned DataTable. The column values in the DataTable are listed in the text that follows.

Usage

```
myDataTable = mySqlDataReader.GetSchemaTable()
```

Parameters

None.

Meta data

ColumnName	The column name (not necessarily unique). A null value (`Nothing` in VB) is returned if the column name cannot be determined.
ColumnOrdinal	The ordinal column number. Bookmark Columns, if any, have a value of zero. All others begin with one. Somewhat counter-intuitively, this means that the ColumnOrdinal cannot be used as the ordinal in the DataReader Get methods. (However, Column-Ordinal –1 can sometimes be used.)
ColumnSize	The maximum possible length for a value in this column. This is the size of the data type in the case of fixed-length data types (such as Integers).
NumericPrecision	The maximum precision of the data type of this column, if it is a numeric type. Null, if it is not numeric.
NumericScale	The number of digits to the right of the decimal point if SqlDbType is Decimal. If the DbType is not a Decimal, then this is a null value.
IsUnique	Returns True if no two rows in the SqlDataReader can have the same value in this column. Returns False if duplicates are allowed (default). IsUnique may be False if the column is *part* of a primary key group; however, it will return True if the column is, by itself, a key or if it has a UNIQUE constraint.

IsKey	True if the column is the primary key or one of several columns that together make up the primary key. False if the column is not part of a primary key.
BaseCatalogName	Name of the catalog used by the column's data store. This will be null if the catalog name can't be determined. The default value is null.
BaseColumnName	Name of the column used by the column's data store. If an alias was used, this may be different from the ColumnName value. This will be null if the column name can't be determined or if the column is derived. The default value is null.
BaseSchemaName	Name of the schema used by the column's data store. This will be null if the schema name can't be determined. The default value is null.
BaseTableName	Name of the table used by the column's data store. This will be null if the table name can't be determined. The default value is null.
DataType	The .NET common language runtime type of DbType.
AllowDBNull	True if the column can be set to a null value or if the provider cannot determine whether it can be set to a null value. This will be False otherwise. In some cases, it may be impossible to set a null value, but the provider may still contain null values.
ProviderType	Indicates the column's data type. If data type varies, this is Variant.
IsAliased	True if the column name is an alias, and False if otherwise.
IsExpression	True if the column name is an expression, and False if otherwise.
IsIdentity	True if the column name is an identity column, and False if otherwise.
IsAutoIncrement	True if the column assigned values to new rows in some fixed increment, False if otherwise. The default value is False.
IsRowVersion	True if the column contains a read-only row identifier, and False if otherwise.
IsHidden	True if the column name is hidden, and False if otherwise.
IsLong	True if the column contains a Binary Long Object (BLOB) that contains "very long" data, and False if otherwise.
IsReadOnly	True if the column is read-only, and False if otherwise.

Exceptions

InvalidOperationException	The SqlDataReader is closed.

GetSqlBinary

The GetSqlBinary method retrieves the value of the specified column as a SqlBinary. By retrieving this value as one of the System.Data.SqlTypes, no conversions are required, so you gain a performance increase. SqlTypes may also contain null values. See System. Data.SqlTypes for more information.

Usage

```
mySqlBinary = mySqlDataReader.GetSqlBinary(Index)
```

Parameters

`Index`	The zero-based column position (Int32).

Exceptions

IndexOutOfRangeException	Requested column does not exist.
InvalidCastException	Either the value in the desired column could not be coerced to a SqlBinary value, or the column name, as a string, was passed instead of the ordinal position.
InvalidOperationException	Either the SqlDataReader is closed, or the Read method has not yet been called (no data yet exists).

GetSqlBoolean

The GetSqlBoolean method retrieves the value of the specified column as a SqlBoolean. By retrieving this value as one of the System.Data.SqlTypes, no conversions are required, so you gain a performance increase. SqlTypes may also contain null values. See System.Data.SqlTypes for more information.

Usage

```
mySqlBoolean = mySqlDataReader.GetSqlBoolean(Index)
```

Parameters

`Index`	The zero-based column position (Int32).

Exceptions

IndexOutOfRangeException	Requested column does not exist.
InvalidCastException	Either the value in the desired column could not be coerced to a SqlBinary value, or the column name, as a string, was passed instead of the ordinal position.
InvalidOperationException	Either the SqlDataReader is closed, or the Read method has not yet been called (no data yet exists).

GetSqlByte

The GetSqlByte method retrieves the value of the specified column as a SqlByte. By retrieving this value as one of the System.Data.SqlTypes, no conversions are required, so you gain a performance increase. SqlTypes may also contain null values. See System. Data.SqlTypes for more information.

Usage

```
mySqlByte = mySqlDataReader.GetSqlByte(Index)
```

Parameters

`Index`	The zero-based column position (Int32).

Exceptions

IndexOutOfRangeException	Requested column does not exist.
InvalidCastException	Either the value in the desired column could not be coerced to a SqlByte value, or the column name, as a string, was passed instead of the ordinal position.
InvalidOperationException	Either the SqlDataReader is closed, or the Read method has not yet been called (no data yet exists).

GetSqlDateTime

The GetSqlDateTime method retrieves the value of the specified column as a SqlDateTime. By retrieving this value as one of the System.Data.SqlTypes, no conversions are required, so you gain a performance increase. SqlTypes may also contain null values. See System.Data.SqlTypes for more information.

Usage

```
mySqlDateTime = mySqlDataReader.GetSqlDateTime(Index)
```

Parameters

`Index`	The zero-based column position (Int32).

Exceptions

IndexOutOfRangeException	Requested column does not exist.
InvalidCastException	Either the value in the desired column could not be coerced to a SqlDateTime value, or the column name, as a string, was passed instead of the ordinal position.
InvalidOperationException	Either the SqlDataReader is closed, or the Read method has not yet been called (no data yet exists).

GetSqlDecimal

The GetSqlDecimal method retrieves the value of the specified column as a SqlDecimal. By retrieving this value as one of the System.Data.SqlTypes, no conversions are required, so you gain a performance increase. SqlTypes may also contain null values. See System.Data.SqlTypes for more information.

Usage

```
mySqlDecimal = mySqlDataReader.GetSqlDecimal(Index)
```

Parameters

`Index`	The zero-based column position (Int32).

Exceptions

IndexOutOfRangeException	Requested column does not exist.
InvalidCastException	Either the value in the desired column could not be coerced to a SqlDecimal value, or the column name, as a string, was passed instead of the ordinal position.
InvalidOperationException	Either the SqlDataReader is closed, or the Read method has not yet been called (no data yet exists).

GetSqlDouble

The GetSqlDouble method retrieves the value of the specified column as a SqlDouble. By retrieving this value as one of the System.Data.SqlTypes, no conversions are required, so you gain a performance increase. SqlTypes may also contain null values. See System.Data.SqlTypes for more information.

Usage

```
mySqlDouble = mySqlDataReader.GetSqlDouble(Index)
```

Parameters

`Index`	The zero-based column position (Int32).

Exceptions

IndexOutOfRangeException	Requested column does not exist.
InvalidCastException	Either the value in the desired column could not be coerced to a SqlDouble value, or the column name, as a string, was passed instead of the ordinal position.
InvalidOperationException	Either the SqlDataReader is closed, or the Read method has not yet been called (no data yet exists).

GetSqlGuid

The GetSqlGuid method retrieves the value of the specified column as a SqlGuid. By retrieving this value as one of the System.Data.SqlTypes, no conversions are required, so you gain a performance increase. SqlTypes may also contain null values. See System.Data.SqlTypes for more information.

Usage

```
mySqlGuid = mySqlDataReader.GetSqlGuid(Index)
```

Parameters

`Index`	The zero-based column position (Int32).

Exceptions

IndexOutOfRangeException	Requested column does not exist.
InvalidCastException	Either the value in the desired column could not be coerced to a SqlGuid value, or the column name, as a string, was passed instead of the ordinal position.

InvalidOperationException	Either the SqlDataReader is closed, or the Read method has not yet been called (no data yet exists).

GetSqlInt16

The GetSqlInt16 method retrieves the value of the specified column as a SqlInt16. By retrieving this value as one of the System.Data.SqlTypes, no conversions are required, so you gain a performance increase. SqlTypes may also contain null values. See System. Data.SqlTypes for more information.

Usage

```
mySqlInt16 = mySqlDataReader.GetSqlInt16(Index)
```

Parameters

`Index`	The zero-based column position (Int32).

Exceptions

IndexOutOfRangeException	Requested column does not exist.
InvalidCastException	Either the value in the desired column could not be coerced to a SqlInt16 value, or the column name, as a string, was passed instead of the ordinal position.
InvalidOperationException	Either the SqlDataReader is closed, or the Read method has not yet been called (no data yet exists).

GetSqlInt32

The GetSqlInt32 method retrieves the value of the specified column as a SqlInt32. By retrieving this value as one of the System.Data.SqlTypes, no conversions are required, so you gain a performance increase. SqlTypes may also contain null values. See System. Data.SqlTypes for more information.

Usage

```
mySqlInt32 = mySqlDataReader.GetSqlInt32(Index)
```

Parameters

`Index`	The zero-based column position (Int32).

Exceptions

IndexOutOfRangeException	Requested column does not exist.
InvalidCastException	Either the value in the desired column could not be coerced to a SqlInt32 value, or the column name, as a string, was passed instead of the ordinal position.
InvalidOperationException	Either the SqlDataReader is closed, or the Read method has not yet been called (no data yet exists).

GetSqlInt64

The GetSqlInt64 method retrieves the value of the specified column as a SqlInt64. By retrieving this value as one of the System.Data.SqlTypes, no conversions are required, so you gain a performance increase. SqlTypes may also contain null values. See System.Data.SqlTypes for more information.

Usage

```
mySqlInt64 = mySqlDataReader.GetSqlInt64(Index)
```

Parameters

`Index`	The zero-based column position (Int32).

Exceptions

IndexOutOfRangeException	Requested column does not exist.
InvalidCastException	Either the value in the desired column could not be coerced to a SqlInt64 value, or the column name, as a string, was passed instead of the ordinal position.
InvalidOperationException	Either the SqlDataReader is closed, or the Read method has not yet been called (no data yet exists).

GetSqlMoney

The GetSqlMoney method retrieves the value of the specified column as a SqlMoney. By retrieving this value as one of the System.Data.SqlTypes, no conversions are required, so you gain a performance increase. SqlTypes may also contain null values. See System.Data.SqlTypes for more information.

Usage

```
mySqlMoney = mySqlDataReader.GetSqlMoney(Index)
```

Parameters

`Index`	The zero-based column position (Int32).

Exceptions

IndexOutOfRangeException	Requested column does not exist.
InvalidCastException	Either the value in the desired column could not be coerced to a SqlMoney value, or the column name, as a string, was passed instead of the ordinal position.
InvalidOperationException	Either the SqlDataReader is closed, or the Read method has not yet been called (no data yet exists).

GetSqlSingle

The GetSqlSingle method retrieves the value of the specified column as a SqlSingle. By retrieving this value as one of the System.Data.SqlTypes, no conversions are required, so you gain a performance increase. SqlTypes may also contain null values. See System.Data.SqlTypes for more information.

Usage

```
mySqlSingle = mySqlDataReader.GetSqlSingle(Index)
```

Parameters

`Index`	The zero-based column position (Int32).

Exceptions

IndexOutOfRangeException	Requested column does not exist.
InvalidCastException	Either the value in the desired column could not be coerced to a SqlSingle value, or the column name, as a string, was passed instead of the ordinal position.
InvalidOperationException	Either the SqlDataReader is closed, or the Read method has not yet been called (no data yet exists).

GetSqlString

The GetSqlString method retrieves the value of the specified column as a SqlString. By retrieving this value as one of the System.Data.SqlTypes, no conversions are required, so you gain a performance increase. SqlTypes may also contain null values. See System. Data.SqlTypes for more information.

Usage

```
mySqlString = mySqlDataReader.GetSqlString(Index)
```

Parameters

`Index`	The zero-based column position (Int32).

Exceptions

IndexOutOfRangeException	Requested column does not exist.
InvalidCastException	Either the value in the desired column could not be coerced to a SqlString value, or the column name, as a string, was passed instead of the ordinal position.
InvalidOperationException	Either the SqlDataReader is closed, or the Read method has not yet been called (no data yet exists).

GetSqlValue

The GetSqlValue method retrieves the value of the specified column as an Object. You would use this method to retrieve SQL Server Variant column data. If you want the column Value as a standard .NET type, use the GetValue method.

Usage

```
myObject = mySqlDataReader.GetSqlValue(Index)
```

Parameters

`Index`	The zero-based column position (Int32).

Exceptions

IndexOutOfRangeException	Requested column does not exist.
InvalidOperationException	Either the SqlDataReader is closed, or the Read method has not yet been called (no data yet exists).

GetSqlValues

The GetSqlValues method retrieves all of the values of the current row and stores them into an object array. This proves to be a very efficient way to retrieve and store all columns, rather than retrieving them individually with the various GetXXX methods. The array does not have to be the exact size as the number of columns. The returned Integer is the number of elements stored in the array.

Usage

```
myInt32 = mySqlDataReader.GetSqlValues(ObjectArray)
```

Parameters

`ObjectArray`	An array of Objects. The array does not have to be the exact size as the number of columns.

Exceptions

ArgumentNullException	The array of objects is a null reference or a dynamic array that hasn't been redimensioned.
InvalidOperationException	Either the SqlDataReader is closed, or the Read method has not yet been called (no data yet exists).

GetString

The GetString method retrieves the value of the specified column as a String. If the value is not a String, a System.InvalidCastException will be raised.

Usage

```
myString = mySqlDataReader.GetString(Index)
```

Parameters

`Index`	The zero-based column position (Int32).

Exceptions

IndexOutOfRangeException	Requested column does not exist.
InvalidCastException	Either the value in the desired column is not a String value, or the column name, as a string, was passed instead of the ordinal position.
InvalidOperationException	Either the SqlDataReader is closed, or the Read method has not yet been called (no data yet exists).

GetValue

The GetValue method retrieves the value of the specified column in its native type (inherited from Object). Because every data type in the .NET Framework inherits from Object, any value retrieved from the GetValue method can be treated as an Object. Basically, this method is an easy way to retrieve a column of data, especially if you don't know beforehand what the column will return.

Usage

```
myObject = mySqlDataReader.GetValue(Index)
```

Parameters

`Index`	The zero-based column position (Int32).

Exceptions

IndexOutOfRangeException	Requested column does not exist.
InvalidCastException	The column name, as a string, was passed instead of the ordinal position.
InvalidOperationException	Either the SqlDataReader is closed, or the Read method has not yet been called (no data yet exists).

GetValues

The GetValues method retrieves an array of values in their native type (inherited from Object) and returns an Int32 specifying the number of values retrieved. The length of the array need not be the same as the number of fields to retrieve. If the length of the array is larger than the number of fields, all of the available fields will be filled in the lower indices of the array. If the array length is smaller than the number of fields, the array is filled to capacity with the first fields of the array. The returned Integer is the number of elements stored in the array.

TIP When dealing with dynamic arrays, you can also use ReDim myArray(mySqlDataReader.FieldCount - 1) to fit the number of fields exactly.

NOTE If you know the data types in the row are all a particular type, you can use an array of that type as the buffer array. Be aware that an ArrayTypeMismatchException will be raised if the types do not match. This includes any NULL values in the data source! Therefore, an exception can be thrown if the data source allows NULLs, even if the type of the field matches the type of the array.

Usage

```
myInt32 = mySqlDataReader.GetValues(myObjectArray)
```

Parameters

`myObjectArray`	An array of objects to fill with data from the row; also known as the buffer.

Exceptions

ArgumentNullException	The array of objects is a null reference or a dynamic array that hasn't been redimensioned.
ArrayTypeMismatchException	Buffer array received a value of a different type. This can occur when the buffer array is of a type descending from Object.
InvalidCastException	Parameter passed is not an array of Objects.
InvalidOperationException	Either the SqlDataReader is closed, or the Read method has not yet been called (no data yet exists).

IsClosed

The read-only IsClosed property returns a Boolean specifying whether the DataReader is currently closed. IsClosed returns True if the DataReader has been closed, False if it is open. This property will not raise an Exception if the SqlDataReader is closed.

Usage

```
myBoolean = mySqlDataReader.IsClosed
```

Parameters

None.

IsDBNull

The IsDBNull method retrieves a Boolean specifying whether the specified column contains a nonexistent or missing value (DBNull). This is not equivalent to the data source having NULL assigned as a value. This method allows a program to differentiate between an assigned value of NULL and a field that has not yet been instantiated with any value (empty).

Usage

```
myBoolean = mySqlDataReader.IsDBNull(Index)
```

Parameters

`Index`	The zero-based column position (Int32).

Exceptions

IndexOutOfRangeException	Requested column does not exist.
InvalidCastException	The column name, as a string, was passed instead of the ordinal position.
InvalidOperationException	Either the SqlDataReader is closed, or the Read method has not yet been called (no data yet exists).

Item

The read-only Item property is similar to the GetValue method, in that it allows you to retrieve the value of the specified column in its native type (inherited from Object). Because every data type in the .NET Framework inherits from Object, any value retrieved from the Item property can be treated as an Object. This method is an easy way to retrieve a column of data, especially if you don't know beforehand what the column will return.

```
' These two lines of code are functionally identical
myObject = mySqlDataReader.Item(Index)
myObject = mySqlDataReader.GetValue(Index)
```

The advantage the Item property has over the GetValue method is that it is overloaded so you can pass it the column name, instead of the ordinal position.

```
' These two lines of code are functionally identical
myObject = mySqlDataReader.Item("ProductName")
myObject = mySqlDataReader.GetValue(mySqlDataReader.GetOrdinal( _
    "ProductName"))
```

Usage

```
myObject = mySqlDataReader.GetValue(Index)
myObject = mySqlDataReader.GetValue(ColumnName)
```

Parameters

Index	The zero-based column position (Int32).
ColumnName	A String containing the column name.

Exceptions

IndexOutOfRangeException	Requested column does not exist.
InvalidOperationException	Either the SqlDataReader is closed, or the Read method has not yet been called (no data yet exists).

NextResult

The NextResult method moves to the next set of data (if a batch SQL statement returning more than one set of data was passed in the creation of the DataReader). It returns a Boolean True if there is another set of data available and a Boolean False if the last set of data has been reached. Once the new data set is prepared, the position is set at just prior to the first record (requiring Read to be called to begin accessing data).

Usage

```
myBoolean = mySqlDataReader.NextResult()
```

Parameters

None.

Exceptions

InvalidOperationException	The SqlDataReader is closed.

Read

The Read method moves to the next record and returns a Boolean True if one exists or a Boolean False if the last record has been reached. After the DataReader has been created, the position is set just prior to the first record. Thus, a Read method must be called prior to accessing any of the data.

Usage

```
myBoolean = mySqlDataReader.Read()
```

Parameters

None.

Exceptions

InvalidOperationException	The SqlDataReader is closed.

RecordsAffected

The read-only RecordsAffected property returns an Int32 specifying the number of records that were affected during the use of the DataReader. Because a SqlDataReader is read only, the only time this will have a positive value is when the SqlCommand.CommandText manipulates the data in some way. SELECT statements will return a -1.

Usage

```
myInt32 = mySqlDataReader.RecordsAffected
```

Parameters

None.

Exceptions

InvalidOperationException	The SqlDataReader is closed.

System.Data.SqlClient.SqlDebugging

The SqlDebugging class merely supports the .NET Framework and is not intended to be called from your code.

Constructors

```
Dim mySqlDebugging As New System.Data.SqlClient.SqlDebugging()
```

Parameters

None.

Members

None.

System.Data.SqlClient.SqlError

The SqlError class communicates an individual warning or error generated by SQL Server. In nearly all circumstances, a SqlError is automatically created within a SqlErrorCollection object, which is contained within a SqlException object. This is true even if there is only one SqlError class within the SqlErrorCollection object. This class is automatically generated and therefore has no public constructor.

The SqlException, SqlErrorCollection, and SqlError objects are all closely related. In the case of the SqlClient .NET data provider, they are created only as sets of objects. Whenever a data access situation occurs that cannot be handled by the SQLClient data provider, a SqlException is thrown, with a SqlErrorCollection as its Errors property. The created SqlErrorCollection will contain at least one SqlError.

A SqlError severity level that is too high may cause the SqlConnection to be closed. If this is the case, you may reopen the database connection and continue working. Because of this behavior, be aware of trapping and dealing with an error, then later experiencing a closed SqlConnection. This can be especially difficult to track down with other objects that depend on the connection. For instance, closing a SqlConnection will cause a SqlDataReader to call its Close method automatically. Reconnecting a SqlConnection will still leave the SqlDataReader closed.

Here is a breakdown of the various error severity levels, as defined by SQL Server:

Severity < 10—Informational messages or minor problems with data entered.

Severity 11–16—User-generated messages; can be corrected by the user.

Severity 17–19—Software or hardware errors; you may keep working with some minor interruption.

Severity 20–25—Software or hardware errors; connection will be closed.

To view the master list of error messages and their severities, issue the following SQL command:

```
SELECT * FROM Master.dbo.SysMessages
```

Literally thousands of different errors can be raised from SQL Server. Discussing even a small number of them is beyond the scope of this book. For additional information, please refer to SQL Server Books Online.

Constructors

There is no public constructor.

Parameters

None.

SqlError Sample Code

```
Dim mySqlConnection As New System.Data.SqlClient.SqlConnection()
Dim mySqlCommand As System.Data.SqlClient.SqlCommand
Dim myError As System.Data.SqlClient.SqlError
' Establish Connection
mySqlConnection.ConnectionString = _
   "Server=(local);Integrated Security=SSPI;Database=NorthWind"
mySqlConnection.Open()
' Create a SqlCommand to simply ask SQL Server to Raise an Error
' This error will be raised with a Severity of 13 and a State of 1
mySqlCommand = mySqlConnection.CreateCommand()
mySqlCommand.CommandText = _
   "RAISERROR (21283,13,1,'AccountID','AccountsReceivable')"
Try
   mySqlCommand.ExecuteNonQuery()
Catch MySqlException As SqlException
   For Each myError In MySqlException.Errors
      MessageBox.Show("Message: " & myError.Message & ControlChars.Cr _
         & "Class: " & myError.Class & ControlChars.Cr _
         & "LineNumber: " & myError.LineNumber & ControlChars.Cr _
         & "Number: " & myError.Number & ControlChars.Cr _
         & "Procedure: " & myError.Procedure & ControlChars.Cr _
```

```
            & "Server: " & myError.Server.ToString() & ControlChars.Cr _
            & "Source: " & myError.Source & ControlChars.Cr _
            & "State: " & myError.State, "Error Properties")
    Next
Finally
    mySqlConnection.Close()
    mySqlConnection.Dispose()
End Try
```

Members

Class

The read-only Class property returns the SQL Server severity level of the error. A SQL Server severity can be from 1 to 25. The default severity is 0. For more information on the different severity levels, see the notes for SqlError or refer to SQL Server Books Online.

Usage

```
myByte = mySqlError.Class
```

Parameters

None.

LineNumber

The read-only LineNumber property returns the line number within the SQL command batch or stored procedure that raised the error. In SQL Server, valid line numbers begin at 1. A value of 0 would indicate that a LineNumber was not applicable to the raising of the error.

Usage

```
myInt32 = mySqlError.LineNumber
```

Parameters

None.

Message

The read-only Message property returns a short, human-readable description of the error as a String.

Usage

```
myString = mySqlError.Message
```

Parameters

None.

Number

The read-only Number property returns the number that identifies the type of SQL Server error. This number corresponds to the Error column from the SysMessages table in the Master database.

TIP **You can take this number and search on Microsoft.com, TechNet, or MSDN to find articles relating to the error's cause and possible solutions. For example, if you were to search on 1205 at www.Microsoft.com, you'd find several articles discussing Deadlock errors and workarounds. You may need to get creative and search for other combinations as well.**

Usage

```
myInt32 = mySqlError.Number
```

Parameters

None.

Procedure

The read-only Procedure property returns the name of the stored procedure or remote procedure call (RPC) that generated the error.

Usage

```
MyString = mySqlError.Procedure
```

Parameters

None.

Server

The read-only Server property returns the name of the SQL Server instance that generated the error.

Usage

```
MyString = mySqlError.Server
```

Parameters

None.

Source

The read-only Source property returns a String containing the name of the provider that generated the error. This will default to the .Net SqlClient data provider.

Usage

```
myString = mySqlError.Source
```

Parameters

None.

State

The read-only State property returns a byte indicating the state of the error code. This State value is an arbitrary integer, ranging from 1 through 127, that your DBA can use to further convey information back to the client application.

Usage

```
myByte = mySqlError.State
```

Parameters
None.

System.Data.SqlClient.SqlErrorCollection

The SqlErrorCollection is created automatically by the SqlException object to hold one or more SqlError objects. It is a simple collection object with only three native members. These are the Count and Item properties and the CopyTo method, which converts the SqlErrorCollection to an array.

The SqlException, SqlErrorCollection, and SqlError objects are all closely related. In the case of the SqlClient .NET data provider, they are created as sets of objects. Whenever a situation occurs that cannot be handled by the SqlClient .NET data provider, a SqlException is thrown, with a SqlErrorCollection as its Errors property. The created SqlErrorCollection will contain at least one SqlError.

Constructors

There is no public constructor.

Parameters

None.

SqlErrorCollection Sample Code

See the SqlError sample code.

Members

CopyTo

The CopyTo method copies the SqlError objects into a passed Array, starting at the designated index within the Array. Because you can begin at any index within an array, you can create a single array with Error objects received from many different exceptions, each subsequent exception object copying the errors to a later part of the array.

Usage

```
MySqlErrorCollection.CopyTo(myArray, myIndex)
```

Parameters

`myArray`	The passed array to fill with SqlError objects.
`myIndex`	Location to begin filling array. (Example: Passing a 3 will fill arrayBuffer(3) with the first SqlError object.)

Exceptions

ArgumentException	The sum of intIndex and the number of elements in the SqlErrorCollection is greater than the length of arrayBuffer.
ArgumentNullException	arrayBuffer is null (`Nothing` in Visual Basic).
ArgumentOutOfRangeException	The intIndex is not valid for the passed buffer array.

Sample Code

```
Public Sub DemoCopyToMethod(ByVal mySqlException As SqlException)
   Dim mySqlErrorCol As SqlErrorCollection = mySqlException.Errors
   Dim myArray(mySqlErrorCol.Count - 1) As Object
   Dim i As Int32
   ' Initialize Array
   myArray.Initialize()
   mySqlErrorCol.CopyTo(myArray, 0)
   ' myArray is now filled with the SqlError objects
   myArray.Sort(myArray)
   myArray.Reverse(myArray)
   ' Show them in reverse sorted order.
   For i = 0 To myArray.Length - 1
      MessageBox.Show(myArray(i).ToString())
   Next
End Sub
```

Count

The read-only Count property returns an Int32 specifying the number of SqlError objects contained in the collection. Because all arrays in .NET are zero based, Count returns a number that is one greater than the highest available index ordinal in any array. Because there is always at least one SqlError object in this collection, this property will return at least 1.

Usage

```
myInt32 = mySqlErrorCollection.Count
```

Parameters

None.

Item

The read-only Item property returns a SqlError object from the collection, as indicated by the Index parameter. This is the default property of the SqlErrorCollection. Placing the index directly after the SqlErrorCollection is possible, as a shortcut.

Usage

```
mySqlError = mySqlErrorCollection.Item(Index)
mySqlError = mySqlErrorCollection(Index)
```

Parameters

`Index`	Int32 valued index of the SqlError object to retrieve.

System.Data.SqlClient.SqlException

The SqlException is thrown whenever SQL Server returns an error or a warning. The Errors collection will always contain at least one SqlError object that provides detailed information on the error or warning. Most of the properties of the SqlException are actually wrappers of the same-named properties of the first error in the Errors collection.

If the error returned is of high severity, the SqlConnection may be closed. See SqlError for more information on the various severity levels.

The SqlException class has many members that can be of great use in tracking down errors. For instance, the InnerException member will return an Exception object or a subclass that contains the exception that raised this exception, if there has been a chain of errors. Similarly, the GetBaseException will return the Exception that first caused the chain of Exceptions to be initiated. The ToString method is overridden to provide the full name of this Exception, as well as possibly returning the error message, the name of the inner exception, and the stack trace.

Many of these properties are inherited from the System.Exception class; however, they will be covered in the text that follows because of their usefulness.

Constructors

There is no public constructor.

Parameters

None.

SqlException Sample Code

```
Dim mySqlConnection As New System.Data.SqlClient.SqlConnection()
Dim mySqlError As System.Data.SqlClient.SqlError
' Attempt to establish a connection to an invalid SQL Server
mySqlConnection.ConnectionString = _
   "Server=BadServer;Integrated Security=SSPI;Database=Northwind"
Try
   mySqlConnection.Open()
Catch mySqlException As SqlException
   ' Show Exception thumbnail by using the handy ToString() method
   MessageBox.Show(mySqlException.ToString())
   ' Show all Exception details
   MessageBox.Show("Message: " & mySqlException.Message & _
      ControlChars.Cr _
      & "Class: " & mySqlException.Source & ControlChars.Cr _
      & "HelpLink: " & mySqlException.HelpLink & ControlChars.Cr _
      & "LineNumber: " & mySqlException.LineNumber & ControlChars.Cr _
      & "Message: " & mySqlException.Message & ControlChars.Cr _
      & "Number: " & mySqlException.Number & ControlChars.Cr _
      & "Procedure: " & mySqlException.Procedure & ControlChars.Cr _
```

```
         & "Server: " & mySqlException.Server & ControlChars.Cr _
         & "Source: " & mySqlException.Source & ControlChars.Cr _
         & "State: " & mySqlException.State & ControlChars.Cr _
         & "StackTrace: " & mySqlException.StackTrace & ControlChars.Cr _
         & "TargetSite: " & mySqlException.TargetSite.ToString(), _
         "Exception Properties")
      ' Display the Inner Exception if available
      If Not mySqlException.InnerException Is Nothing Then
         MessageBox.Show(mySqlException.InnerException.ToString(), _
            "Inner Exception")
      End If
      ' Display the Base Exception if it is not equal to current exception
      If Not mySqlException.Equals(mySqlException.GetBaseException) Then
         MessageBox.Show(mySqlException.GetBaseException.ToString(), _
            "Base Exception")
      End If
      ' Display all individual errors in the Errors collection
      For Each mySqlError In mySqlException.Errors
         MessageBox.Show("Message: " & mySqlError.Message & _
            ControlChars.Cr _
            & "Class: " & mySqlError.Class & ControlChars.Cr _
            & "LineNumber: " & mySqlError.LineNumber & ControlChars.Cr _
            & "Number: " & mySqlError.Number & ControlChars.Cr _
            & "Procedure: " & mySqlError.Procedure & ControlChars.Cr _
            & "Server: " & mySqlError.Server.ToString() & ControlChars.Cr _
            & "Source: " & mySqlError.Source & ControlChars.Cr _
            & "State: " & mySqlError.State, "Error Properties")
      Next
   Catch myOtherException As Exception
      MessageBox.Show(myOtherException.ToString())
   Finally
      mySqlConnection.Close()
      mySqlConnection.Dispose()
   End Try
```

Members

Class

The read-only Class property returns the SQL Server severity level of the error. A SQL Server severity can be from 1 to 25. The default severity is 0. For more information on the different severity levels, see the notes for SqlError or refer to SQL Server Books Online.

Usage

```
myByte = mySqlException.Class
```

Parameters

None.

Errors

The read-only Errors property returns a SqlErrorCollection object containing all of the errors generated by the SqlClient .NET data provider or the SQL Server. The SqlErrorCollection will contain at least one SqlError. This property contains the majority of the information relating to the error raised by the SqlClient .NET data provider.

Usage

```
mySqlErrorCollection = mySqlException.Errors
```

Parameters

None.

GetBaseException

The GetBaseException method returns an Exception object containing the original exception. To return the original exception, it traverses the chain of InnerException objects. If the InnerException property of the current exception is null, GetBaseException will return a reference to the current Exception object.

To determine only the parent exception to the current exception, use the InnerException property.

Usage

```
myException = mySqlException.GetBaseException()
```

Parameters

None.

Exceptions

None.

GetObjectData

The GetObjectData method (inherited from System.Exception) fills the passed SerializationInfo buffer object with information about the Exception object. There is no value returned by this method. Depending on the passed StreamingContext object, this method can be used to serialize the object to a stream or read serialization from a stream.

Because it deals mainly with Serialization and not data access, further discussion of this property is beyond the scope of this book.

Usage

```
mySqlException.GetObjectData(SerializationInfo, StreamingContext)
```

Parameters

`SerializationInfo`	A System.Runtime.Serialization.SerializationInfo buffer object to be filled with the exception's serialization data.
`StreamingContext`	A System.Runtime.Serialization.StreamingContext object specifying the stream to write the serialization info to or read the information from.

Exceptions

ArgumentNullException	The passed SerializationInfo buffer object is null (`Nothing` in VB)

HelpLink

The HelpLink property (inherited from Exception) returns or sets a String linking to a help file associated with the SqlException. The HelpLink is formatted as a Uniform Resource Name (URN) or Uniform Resource Locator (URL). An example of this property that points to the MSDN help available with Visual Studio .NET would be: `ms-help://MS.VSCC/MS.MSDNVS/cpref/html/exceptiontopic.htm.`

The HelpLink is often not set, so it is wise to verify both that the HelpLink property itself is not an empty string and that the HelpLink points to a valid help file before exposing the HelpLink to a user of your program.

Usage

```
myString = mySqlException.HelpLink
mySqlException.HelpLink = myString
```

Parameters

None.

InnerException

The read-only InnerException property (inherited from Exception) returns the Exception object linking to a previous exception that caused the current exception to be thrown, if any, or a null value (`Nothing` in VB), if not. This permits a chain of InnerException objects to be generated, allowing a program to trace the exception chain all the way to the root exception. Be aware that many of the SqlException exceptions do not have a parent exception, causing many InnerException values to be null.

For example, assume a SqlException is thrown by the SqlConnection.Open method when the database specified in the ConnectionString could not be found. Your code catches this exception and generates a myOwnDataBaseNotFoundException. Later code that catches the myOwnDataBaseNotFoundException can use the InnerException property to retrieve the SqlException that triggered the new exception. This InnerException object can then be used to extract further information that may have been hidden by the myOwnDataBaseNotFoundException.

To find the base exception that originally was fired, use the GetBaseException method.

Usage

```
myException = mySqlException.InnerException
```

Parameters

None.

Sample Code

```
' Accepts any Exception to subroutine, so recursion is possible
Public Sub ViewInnerExceptions(ByVal myException As Exception)
    ' Bail out if InnerException is null
    If myException.InnerException Is Nothing Then Exit Sub
    Dim myInnerException As Exception = myException.InnerException
```

```
        MessageBox.Show("Message: " & myInnerException.Message & _
           ControlChars.Cr & "Source: " & myInnerException.Source & _
           ControlChars.Cr & "HelpLink: " & myInnerException.HelpLink & _
           ControlChars.Cr & "StackTrace: " & myInnerException.StackTrace, _
           "InnerException Information")
        ' Recurse if necessary
        If Not myInnerException.InnerException Is Nothing Then
           ViewInnerExceptions(myInnerException)
        End If
    End Sub
```

LineNumber

The read-only LineNumber property returns the line number within the SQL command batch or stored procedure that raised the error. In SQL Server, valid line numbers begin at 1. A value of 0 would indicate that a LineNumber was not applicable to the raising of the error.

Usage

```
myInt32 = mySqlException.LineNumber
```

Parameters

None.

Message

The read-only Message property returns a short, human-readable description of the error as a String.

Usage

```
myString = mySqlException.Message
```

Parameters

None.

Number

The read-only Number property returns the number that identifies the type of SQL Server error. This number corresponds to the Error column from the SysMessages table in the Master database.

> **TIP You can take this number and search on Microsoft.com, TechNet, or MSDN to find articles relating to the error's cause and possible solutions. For example, if you were to search on 1205 at www.Microsoft.com, you'd find several articles discussing Deadlock errors and workarounds. You may need to get creative and search for other combinations as well.**

Usage

```
myInt32 = mySqlException.Number
```

Parameters

None.

Procedure

The read-only Procedure property returns the name of the stored procedure or remote procedure call (RPC) that generated the error.

Usage

```
MyString = mySqlException.Procedure
```

Parameters

None.

Server

The read-only Server property returns the name of the SQL Server instance that generated the error.

Usage

```
MyString = mySqlException.Server
```

Parameters

None.

Source

The read-only Source property returns a String containing the name of the provider that generated the error. This will default to the .Net SqlClient data provider.

Usage

```
myString = mySqlException.Source
```

Parameters

None.

StackTrace

The read-only StackTrace property returns a String containing a textual representation of the stack trace. The stack trace reports all of the methods that are in execution at the time just prior to the execution being thrown. It is read from top to bottom with the latest method in execution at the top.

The StackTrace can be invaluable in tracing difficult-to-find bugs because it provides a way to see all of the methods that could have led up to the error.

TIP To see the stack trace programmatically when no exception has been raised, use the Environment.StackTrace property.

Usage

```
myString = mySqlException.StackTrace
```

Parameters

None.

State

The read-only State property returns a byte indicating the state of the error code. This State value is an arbitrary integer, ranging from 1 through 127, that your DBA can use to further convey information back to the client application.

Usage

```
myByte = mySqlException.State
```

Parameters

None.

TargetSite

The read-only TargetSite property returns an object inheriting from System.Reflection. MethodBase that contains a reference to the method that caused the error to be thrown.

This property is primarily used to programmatically find information about the method that raised the exception. The returned object will provide information such as the methods parameters and return type and whether the method is virtual, a constructor, public, private, etc. Because it deals mainly with Reflection and not data access, further discussion of this property is beyond the scope of this book.

Usage

```
myMethodBase = mySqlException.TargetSite
```

Parameters

None.

ToString

The ToString method is overridden to return information relating to the SqlException. The returned String contains the full class name, the error message, and the stack trace, if they exist. If the error message is provided, it is the error message of the first SqlError in the Errors collection.

Usage

```
myString = mySqlException.ToString()
```

Parameters

None.

Exceptions

None.

System.Data.SqlClient. SqlInfoMessageEventArgs

The SqlInfoMessageEventArgs class provides data for the SqlConnection.InfoEvent event. This event is sent through a SqlConnection object whenever the SQL Server sends warnings or information to the SqlClient .NET data provider. Because this class is automatically generated by the SqlConnection, it has no public constructors.

Many of the warnings and pieces of information sent from the SQL Server will not throw an exception. In fact, InfoMessage events will generate whenever a SQL Server message with a severity of 10 or less occurs. The only way to receive notification of these events is by declaring a method that handles the SqlConnection.InfoEvent event. In Visual Basic .NET, you must manually add a handler (using the AddHandler statement) or ensure that the SqlConnection object is declared WithEvents. In C#, no special declaration is required, as it is implicit in object declaration.

Constructors

There is no public constructor.

Parameters

None.

SqlInfoMessageEventArgs Sample Code

```
' A general procedure to handle the InfoMessage event
Private Sub myInfoMessageHandler(ByVal sender As Object, _
   ByVal e As System.Data.SqlClient.SqlInfoMessageEventArgs)
   MessageBox.Show(sender.GetType.ToString(), "Sender Type")
   MessageBox.Show(e.Message,"InfoMessage")
   MessageBox.Show(e.Source,"InfoMessage Source")
   MessageBox.Show(e.Errors(0).ToString(), "1st Error/Message")
End Sub
Private Sub MyTest
   Dim mySqlConnection As New System.Data.SqlClient.SqlConnection()
   Dim mySqlCommand As System.Data.SqlClient.SqlCommand
   Dim myConnectionString As String
   ' Specify the Event Handler
   AddHandler mySqlConnection.InfoMessage, AddressOf
myInfoMessageHandler
   ' Establish the Connection
   mySqlConnection.ConnectionString = _
      "Server=(local);Integrated Security=SSPI"
   mySqlConnection.Open()
   ' Change database context, which will fire the InfoMessage event
   mySqlConnection.ChangeDatabase("Northwind")      ' InfoMessage fires
   ' Execute a SQL PRINT command, which will fire the InfoMessage event
   mySqlCommand = mySqlConnection.CreateCommand
   mySqlCommand.CommandText = "PRINT 'Hello World'"
   mySqlCommand.ExecuteNonQuery()                   ' InfoMessage fires
   ' Done
   mySqlConnection.Close()
End Sub
```

Members

Errors

The read-only Errors property returns a SqlErrorCollection object containing all of the errors generated by the SqlClient .NET data provider or the SQL Server. The

SqlErrorCollection will contain at least one SqlError. This property contains the majority of the information relating to the warning, error, or information passed back from SQL Server.

Usage

```
mySqlErrorCollection = mySqlInfoMessageEventArgs.Errors
```

Parameters

None.

Message

The read-only Message property returns a String describing the first warning that caused the InfoMessage event to be raised. This property is merely a wrapper that allows simple access to the SqlError.Message property of the first SqlError contained in the Errors collection property.

Because it provides information only from the first warning, use this property cautiously when building robust error handling.

Usage

```
myString = mySqlInfoMessageEventArgs.Message
```

Parameters

None.

Source

The read-only Source property returns a String containing the name of the provider that generated the first warning. This property is merely a wrapper that allows simple access to the SqlError.Source property of the first SqlError contained in the Errors collection property.

Because it provides information only from the first warning, use this property cautiously when building robust error handling.

Usage

```
myString = mySqlInfoMessageEventArgs.Source
```

Parameters

None.

ToString

The ToString method is overridden to return information relating to the InfoMessage. The returned String contains the same information as provided by the Message property.

Usage

```
myString = mySqlInfoMessageEventArgs.ToString()
```

Parameters

None.

Exceptions

None.

System.Data.SqlClient.SqlParameter

The SqlParameter is a class that facilitates passing data to and from SQL commands and stored procedures. A SqlParameter is meaningful only when related to a SqlCommand. Its constructor, however, is public so you can create standalone SqlParameter objects. The intention is for you to add or insert these SqlParameter objects to a SqlCommand's Parameters collection at a later time.

Parameter names are not case sensitive, but they are required. Unlike the other .NET data providers, SqlClient requires you to specify a name, both in the CommandText as well as on the Parameter objects themselves. Once you add the SqlParameter to a collection, the names must be unique.

Constructors

```
Dim mySqlParameter As New SqlParameter()
Dim mySqlParameter As New SqlParameter(String,Object)
Dim mySqlParameter As New SqlParameter(String,SqlDbType)
Dim mySqlParameter As New SqlParameter(String,SqlDbType,Int32)
Dim mySqlParameter As New SqlParameter(String,SqlDbType,Int32, _
   String2)
Dim mySqlParameter As New SqlParameter(String,SqlDbType,Int32, _
   Direction,Boolean,Byte,Byte2,String2,DataRowVersion,Object)
```

Parameters

`String`	The name of the parameter. Must be unique in the collection.
`Object`	The value of the parameter.
`SqlDbType`	The SqlDbType of the parameter.
`Int32`	The size or width of the column.
`String2`	The name of the source column.
`Direction`	The ParameterDirection of the parameter. This can be Input, InputOutput, Output, or ReturnValue.
`Boolean`	The nullability of the column. If the column can contain null values, then this value will be True.
`Byte`	The precision of the column. This is the total number of digits to the left of the decimal point.
`Byte2`	The scale of the column. This is the total number of decimal places.
`DataRowVersion`	The DataRowVersion of the column. This will indicate if the DataRow contains Current, Default, Original, or Proposed values.

SqlParameter Sample Code

```
Dim mySqlConnection As New System.Data.SqlClient.SqlConnection()
Dim mySqlParameter As System.Data.SqlClient.SqlParameter
Dim mySqlCommand As System.Data.SqlClient.SqlCommand
Dim myInt32 As Int32
' Establish Connection
mySqlConnection.ConnectionString = _
   "Server=(local);Integrated Security=SSPI;"
mySqlConnection.Open()
mySqlConnection.ChangeDatabase("NorthWind")
' Create Command
mySqlCommand = mySqlConnection.CreateCommand
mySqlCommand.CommandText = "UPDATE Products SET UnitsInStock = " & _
   "UnitsInStock - @UnitsSold WHERE ProductName = @ProductName"
' Create Parameters
mySqlParameter = mySqlCommand.CreateParameter()
mySqlParameter.ParameterName = "@UnitsSold"
mySqlParameter.SqlDbType = SqlDbType.SmallInt
mySqlCommand.Parameters.Add(mySqlParameter)
mySqlParameter = mySqlCommand.CreateParameter()
mySqlParameter.ParameterName = "@ProductName"
mySqlParameter.SqlDbType = SqlDbType.NVarChar
mySqlParameter.Size = 80
mySqlCommand.Parameters.Add(mySqlParameter)
' Perform Update
mySqlCommand.Parameters("@UnitsSold").Value = 5
mySqlCommand.Parameters("@ProductName").Value = "Ipoh Coffee"
myInt32 = mySqlCommand.ExecuteNonQuery
' Done
mySqlConnection.Close()
```

Members

DbType

The DbType property sets or returns the SqlParameter's .NET data type. Because the DbType and the SqlDbType are linked, when you change the DbType property, ADO.NET will change the SqlDbType to the corresponding value. Be careful when setting the SqlDbType because conversion errors, such as truncation, may result.

There are 24 DbTypes to select from. For a complete reference, see the System.Data.DbType enumeration. The default DbType is String.

Usage

```
myDbType = mySqlParameter.DbType
mySqlParameter.DbType = DbType.Guid
```

Parameters
None.

Exceptions

ArgumentOutOfRangeException	You attempted to assign an invalid DbType value.

Direction

The Direction property sets or returns the SqlParameter's behavior as to whether it is an Input, Output, Input and Output, or a Return Value type of parameter. Based on the value of Direction property, ADO.NET shall allow or disallow certain behaviors of passing data to and receiving data from the data source via these parameters.

Usage

```
myParameterDirection = mySqlParameter.Direction
mySqlParameter.Direction = ParameterDirection.Output
```

Parameters
None.

ParameterDirection Enumeration

Input (1)	(Default) The parameter is an input parameter only. The purpose of this SqlParameter is to provide a value to the SQL statement or stored procedure to enable it to run properly.
InputOutput (3)	The parameter serves as both an input and an output parameter. The idea here is that the stored procedure might change the value of the parameter, and you'll need to be able to receive the new value.
Output (2)	The parameter is an output parameter only. The purpose of this SqlParameter is to receive a value back from a stored procedure. The corresponding parameter in the data source might need to be marked as OUTPUT.
ReturnValue (6)	The parameter will receive the return value.

Exceptions

ArgumentException	You attempted to assign an invalid ParameterDirection value.

IsNullable

The IsNullable property sets or returns the SqlParameter's capability of storing a null value. If the IsNullable property is set to True, the parameter may be null. The default value is false.

Usage

```
myBoolean = mySqlParameter.IsNullable
mySqlParameter.IsNullable = False
```

Parameters
None.

Exceptions
None.

Offset

The Offset property gets or sets the Offset value for binary or string types. The Offset is the number of bytes for binary types and the number of characters for strings. The default Offset is 0.

Usage
```
myInt32 = mySqlParameter.Offset
mySqlParameter.Offset = 3
```

Parameters
None.

Exceptions
None.

ParameterName

The ParameterName property gets or sets the name of the SqlParameter. ParameterNames must be prefixed with a Klammeraffe (the @ symbol). You must specify a valid ParameterName before executing the SqlCommand that uses those parameters. Once you add the SqlParameter to a collection, the names must be unique. The default ParameterName is an empty string.

Usage
```
myString = mySqlParameter.ParameterName
mySqlParameter.ParameterName = "@ArmorClass"
```

Parameters
None.

Exceptions
None.

Precision

The Precision property gets or sets the maximum number of digits used to represent the Value property of the SqlParameter. This setting is used by SqlParameters that have a SqlDbType of Decimal. The default Precision is 0.

Usage
```
myByte = mySqlParameter.Precision
mySqlParameter.Precision = 8
```

Parameters
None.

Exceptions
None.

Scale

The Scale property gets or sets the number of decimal places for which to resolve the Value property of the SqlParameter. This setting is used by SqlParameters that have a SqlDbType of Decimal. The default Scale is 0.

Usage

```
myByte = mySqlParameter.Scale
mySqlParameter.Scale = 8
```

Parameters

None.

Exceptions

None.

Size

The Size property sets or returns the maximum number of bytes the SqlParameter's Value property can hold. Size applies only to binary and string parameters. The Size property can be smaller than the size of the corresponding data type within the stored procedure. This will reduce the size of the data packet sent to the server. Be careful not to truncate any data, especially if the SqlParameter is used for Output as well.

For variable-length data types, the Size property sets the maximum amount of data to transmit to the server. For nonstring data types and ANSI string data, the Size property sets the number of bytes. For fixed-width data types, the Size property is ignored, although it can be retrieved for informational purposes. The default size value is inferred from the value of the parameter.

Usage

```
myInt32 = mySqlParameter.Size
mySqlParameter.Size = 80
```

Parameters

None.

Exceptions

None.

SourceColumn

The SourceColumn property sets or returns the name of the column in the corresponding DataSet. This information is used for loading or returning the SqlParameter's Value. The default value for SourceColumn is an empty string.

Usage

```
myString = mySqlParameter.SourceColumn
mySqlParameter.SourceColumn = "Address1"
```

Parameters

None.

SourceVersion

The SourceVersion property sets or returns the DataRowVersion of the SqlParameter value. The version is used by the UpdateCommand during an Update operation to determine whether the value is set to Current or Original. Based on the SourceVersion, ADO.NET can avoid work by not updating columns that haven't changed.

Usage

```
myDataRowVersion = mySqlParameter.SourceVersion
mySqlParameter.SourceVersion = DataRowVersion.Default
```

Parameters

None.

DataRowVersion Enumeration

Current (512)	(Default) The row contains current values.
Default (1536)	The row contains its default values.
Original (256)	The row contains its original values.
Proposed (1024)	The row contains proposed values.

Exceptions

ArgumentException	You attempted to assign an invalid SourceVersion value.

SqlDbType

The SqlDbType property sets or returns the SqlParameter's underlying SQL Server data type. Because the DbType and the SqlDbType are linked, when you change the SqlDbType property, ADO.NET will change the DbType to the corresponding value. Be careful when setting the SqlDbType because conversion errors, such as truncation, may result.

There are 24 SqlDbTypes to select from. For a complete reference, see the chapter on the System.Data.SqlTypes namespace. The default SqlDbType is NVarChar.

Usage

```
mySqlDbType = mySqlParameter.SqlDbType
mySqlParameter.SqlDbType = SqlDbType.Decimal
```

Parameters

None.

Exceptions

ArgumentOutOfRangeException	You attempted to assign an invalid SqlDbType value.

Value

The Value property sets or returns the value of the SqlParameter. This is probably the most popular property of the SqlParameter object.

If the SqlParameter's direction is Input or InputOuput, then the Value property should be assigned before executing the command. If the SqlParameter's direction is Output, InputOutput, or Return Value, then the Value property will not be set until after the command has executed and possibly not until the associated DataReader has finished processing the rows and/or is closed (depending on the provider). The Value property is overwritten by the Update method.

If you want to send a NULL value to the data source, then you'll need to specify DBNULL instead of the standard .NET null value.

```
mySqlParameter.Value = DBNull.Value
```

Usage

```
myObject = mySqlParameter.Value
mySqlParameter.Value = "Bruce Campbell"
```

Parameters

None.

System.Data.SqlClient.SqlParameterCollection

The SqlParameterCollection is created automatically by the SqlCommand object to hold SqlParameter objects. The SqlParameterCollection and SqlParameter class are closely related. The SqlParameterCollection class has no public constructor, so you cannot create a standalone collection.

It is important that the name, type, and direction of each parameter in the collection match exactly with the expectations of the SQL statement or stored procedure. If the parameter information doesn't match, the SqlClient .NET data provider could raise an error.

The SqlParameterCollection is essentially like any other .NET collection, with the same methods and properties that you've become accustomed to using.

Constructors

There is no public constructor.

Parameters

None.

SqlParameterCollection Sample Code

```
Dim mySqlConnection As New System.Data.SqlClient.SqlConnection()
Dim mySqlParameter As System.Data.SqlClient.SqlParameter
Dim mySqlCommand As System.Data.SqlClient.SqlCommand
Dim mySqlParameterCollection As _
   System.Data.SqlClient.SqlParameterCollection
```

```
Dim myInt32 As Int32
' Establish Connection
mySqlConnection.ConnectionString = _
   "Server=(local);Integrated Security=SSPI;"
mySqlConnection.Open()
mySqlConnection.ChangeDatabase("NorthWind")
' Create Command
mySqlCommand = mySqlConnection.CreateCommand
mySqlCommand.CommandText = "UPDATE Products SET UnitsInStock = " & _
   "UnitsInStock - @UnitsSold WHERE ProductName = @ProductName"
' Assign an object reference to SqlCommand.Parameters collection
mySqlParameterCollection = mySqlCommand.Parameters
' Create Parameters
mySqlParameter = mySqlCommand.CreateParameter()
mySqlParameter.ParameterName = "@UnitsSold"
mySqlParameter.SqlDbType = SqlDbType.SmallInt
mySqlParameterCollection.Add(mySqlParameter)
mySqlParameter = mySqlCommand.CreateParameter()
mySqlParameter.ParameterName = "@ProductName"
mySqlParameter.SqlDbType = SqlDbType.NVarChar
mySqlParameter.Size = 80
mySqlParameterCollection.Add(mySqlParameter)
' Perform Update
mySqlParameterCollection("@UnitsSold").Value = 5
mySqlParameterCollection("@ProductName").Value = "Ipoh Coffee"
myInt32 = mySqlCommand.ExecuteNonQuery
' Done
mySqlConnection.Close()
```

Members

Add

The Add method adds a new SqlParameter object to the collection. The Add method is overloaded in a number of ways, providing you with flexibility in how you add Sql-Parameter objects to the collection. If you are trying to insert the new SqlParameter object at a particular location in the collection, consider using the Insert method.

Usage

```
mySqlParameterCollection.Add(Object)
mySqlParameterCollection.Add(SqlParameter)
mySqlParameterCollection.Add(String, Object)
mySqlParameterCollection.Add(String, SqlDbType)
mySqlParameterCollection.Add(String, SqlDbType, Int32)
mySqlParameterCollection.Add(String, SqlDbType, Int32, String2)
```

Parameters

`Object`	Adds a SqlParameter object to the collection with the specified value.
`SqlParameter`	Adds the specified SqlParameter object to the collection.

`String`	The name of the parameter to be added.
`SqlDbType`	The SqlDbType of the parameter to be added.
`Int32`	The size or width of the column.
`String2`	The name of the source column.

Exceptions

ArgumentException	The parameter name is not unique.
InvalidCastException	The parameter passed to the Add method was invalid.

Clear

The Clear method removes all SqlParameter objects from the collection. You can call the Clear method on an empty collection without raising an error.

Usage

```
mySqlParameterCollection.Clear()
```

Parameters

None.

Exceptions

None.

Contains

The Contains method provides a way to search for the existence of a SqlParameter object within the collection. The Contains method is overloaded in two different ways, allowing you to use the same method to search by a SqlParameter object or just the parameter name.

NOTE In testing, it seems that all properties of the SqlParameter object you are looking for must match, not just the value.

Usage

```
myBoolean = mySqlParameterCollection.Contains(SqlParameter)
myBoolean = mySqlParameterCollection.Contains(String)
```

Parameters

`SqlParameter`	The SqlParameter object you are attempting to locate.
`String`	The name of the parameter you are attempting to locate. This search is not case sensitive, but you must include the @ prefix.

Exceptions

None.

CopyTo

The CopyTo method copies the SqlParameter objects into a passed array, starting at the designated index within the Array. You must specify both an Array and a starting index. There is no default index.

NOTE **Remember that in .NET all arrays are zero based. When you Dim your array variable, make sure you dim it with a size one less than the number of parameters you are expecting.**

Usage

```
mySqlParameterCollection.CopyTo(Array,Index)
```

Parameters

`Array`	The passed array to fill with SqlParameter objects.
`Index`	The starting index of the array. For example, if you pass a 3, ADO.NET will fill array (3) with the first SqlParameter object.

Exceptions

ArgumentException	The sum of index and the number of elements in the SqlParameterCollection is greater than the length of the array.
ArgumentNullException	The array is null (`Nothing` in Visual Basic).
ArgumentOutOfRangeException	The index is not valid for the passed array.

Count

The read-only Count property returns an Int32 representing the number of SqlParameter objects contained in the collection. This count is base one. If you are going to use the Count to somehow size an array or enumerate through the collection by index, you'll need to subtract one. For example, a collection with a Count of 20 items will have items indexed 0 through 19.

Usage

```
myInt32 = mySqlParameterCollection.Count
```

Parameters

None.

GetEnumerator

The SqlParameterCollection supports the basic IEnumerator interface. By calling the GetEnumerator method, you are returned an IEnumerator interface object. You may use this interface to read the data in the collection in an easy, enumerated fashion.

When the IEnumerator is instantiated, it essentially takes a snapshot of the collection. Therefore, the IEnumerator will not have exclusive access to the collection and may not be used to make changes. Be careful when updating the collection while you have an IEnumerator instantiated, as it might throw an exception. Your best bet would be to re-create the IEnumerator.

You should refer to Microsoft's IEnumerator documentation for more information.

Usage

```
myEnumerator = mySqlParameterCollection.GetEnumerator()
```

Parameters

None.

IndexOf

Similar to the Contains method, the IndexOf provides a way to search for the existence of a SqlParameter object within the collection and return the location or Index of the object. If the IndexOf method cannot find the SqlParameter object in the collection, then it will return a -1.

The IndexOf method is overloaded in two different ways, allowing you to use the same method to search by a SqlParameter object or just the parameter name.

NOTE In testing, it seems that all properties of the SqlParameter object you are looking for must match, not just the value.

Usage

```
myIndex = mySqlParameterCollection.IndexOf(SqlParameter)
myIndex = mySqlParameterCollection.IndexOf(String)
```

Parameters

`SqlParameter`	The SqlParameter object you are attempting to locate.
`String`	The name of the parameter you are attempting to locate. This search is not case sensitive, but you must include the @ prefix.

Insert

Similar to the Add method, the Insert method adds a new SqlParameter object to the collection at the specified index. The Insert method is not overloaded and therefore always requires two parameters. If you are trying to simply add the new SqlParameter object, consider using the Add method.

Usage

```
mySqlParameterCollection.Insert(Index,SqlParameter)
```

Parameters

`Index`	The index within the collection to insert the new SqlParameter object. The collection is zero based, so an Index of 10 will insert the new object into position 11.
`SqlParameter`	The SqlParameter object to be added to the collection.

Exceptions

ArgumentException	The parameter name is not unique.
ArgumentOutOfRangeException	The index is not valid for the collection.

Item

The Item property sets or returns a particular SqlParameter in the collection. When you want to reference a particular SqlParameter for viewing or editing, you will need to use the Item property. For safety, you should consider testing for the existence of the SqlParameter object by using the Contains method.

```
If mySqlParameterCollection.Contains("Comments") Then
   mySqlParameter = mySqlParameterCollection.Item("Comments")
End If
```

The Item property is also the default property for the class, so in many code examples you will not see it explicitly mentioned. This takes advantage of a shortcut in .NET and results in code that can sometimes be hard to understand and document:

```
' Fully qualified method
myValue = mySqlParameterCollection.Item(5).Value
' Shortcut in Visual Basic .NET
myValue = mySqlParameterCollection(5).Value
```

Usage

```
mySqlParameter = mySqlParameterCollection.Item(Int32)
mySqlParameter = mySqlParameterCollection.Item(String)
```

Parameters

`Int32`	The index of the SqlParameter that you are attempting to reference. The collection is zero based, so an Index of 10 will reference the SqlParameter at position 11.
`String`	The name of the parameter you are attempting to reference. This search is not case sensitive, but you must include the @ prefix.

Exceptions

IndexOutOfRangeException	The index or the parameter name was not found in the collection.

Remove

The Remove method is used to remove a SqlParameter object from the SqlParameter-Collection. In contrast to the RemoveAt method, the Remove method requires you to have a reference to a SqlParameter object in order to Remove it, where the RemoveAt method can remove by Index number or Parameter name.

Usage

```
mySqlParameterCollection.Remove(SqlParameter)
```

Parameters

`SqlParameter`	The SqlParameter object to remove from the collection

Exceptions

InvalidCastException	The parameter is not of type SqlParameter.
SystemException	You have attempted to remove a SqlParameter that is not contained in the collection.

RemoveAt

Similar to the Remove method, the RemoveAt method is used to remove a SqlParameter object from the SqlParameterCollection by Index number or Parameter name. If you already have a reference to a SqlParameter in the collection, then you should consider using the Remove method. For safety, you should consider testing for the existence of the SqlParameter object by using the Contains method:

```
If mySqlParameterCollection.Contains("Comments") Then
   mySqlParameterCollection.RemoveAt("Comments")
End If
```

Usage

```
mySqlParameterCollection.RemoveAt(Int32)
mySqlParameterCollection.RemoveAt(String)
```

Parameters

`Int32`	The index of the SqlParameter that you are attempting to remove. The collection is zero based, so an Index of 10 will reference the SqlParameter at position 11.
`String`	The parameter name of the SqlParameter that you are attempting to remove. This search is not case sensitive, but you must include the @ prefix.

Exceptions

IndexOutOfRangeException	The index or the parameter name was not found in the collection.

System.Data.SqlClient.SqlRowUpdatedEventArgs

The SqlRowUpdatedEventArgs class provides data for the SqlDataAdapter.RowUpdated event. This event is raised during the Update method of the SqlDataAdapter class. During the Update, every DataRow that has been inserted, updated, or deleted is sent to the data source for updating. Each change raises the RowUpdated event after the changes have been made to the data source, but before they are committed.

Once the event is intercepted, you have a great deal of control over what happens next. Although you cannot make changes to the row to be updated, which we find to be very unfortunate, you are able to examine the row, along with information about the data source, and what type of Update action will occur (Insert, Delete, etc.). You then have the ability to cancel the update for this particular row or for this row and all following rows. You can even stop processing rows and assign a custom exception, complete with errors, to be raised to the SqlDataAdapter.

The majority of the SqlRowUpdatedEventArgs class members are inherited from the System.Data.Common.RowUpdatedEventArgs class, which means that learning these will translate nicely to the other .NET data providers.

Defining a procedure to handle the SqlDataAdapter.RowUpdated event is one way to catch errors or exceptions within a program. Another is to wrap the Fill and Update procedures in a Try-Catch-Finally block. Generally, if you're just catching exceptions, a

Try-Catch-Finally block is preferable; however, if you have additional data validation to perform, handling the RowUpdating event is better. This is especially true because you may handle the RowUpdated events for more than one SqlDataAdapter with the same procedure. To do this, simply add any number of SqlDataAdapter.RowUpdated event declarations after the Handles keyword in the procedure definition. Be sure to separate the declarations with commas.

Although the constructor is listed in the text that follows, it's unlikely you would actually use this constructor because the .NET Framework automatically generates this object when the RowUpdated event is raised.

Constructors

```
Dim mySqlRowUpdatedEventArgs As New SqlRowUpdatedEventArgs( _
   DataRow, IDbCommand, StatementType, DataTableMapping)
```

Parameters

`DataRow`	A System.Data.DataRow object that is to be deleted, inserted, or updated at the data source.
`IdbCommand`	A SqlCommand object (implementing the System.Data.IDbCommand interface) representing the SQL statement to be executed.
`StatementType`	A System.Data.StatementType enumeration that specifies the type of SQL statement in the IDbCommand object. Valid values are Delete (3), Insert (1), Select (0), and Update (2).
`DataTableMapping`	A System.Data.Common.DataTableMapping object that describes the mapping between the DataTable object and the source data.

SqlRowUpdatedEventArgs Sample Code

```
' The best way to approach sample code for this object is to
' trap the RowUpdated event of the SqlDataAdapter object.
' Declare as WithEvents just beneath the Class declaration
Public WithEvents mySqlDataAdapter As
System.Data.SqlClient.SqlDataAdapter
. . .
Private Sub mySqlDataAdapter_RowUpdated(ByVal sender As Object, ByVal e
As System.Data.SqlClient.SqlRowUpdatedEventArgs) Handles
mySqlDataAdapter.RowUpdated
   Dim mySqlCommand As System.Data.SqlClient.SqlCommand
   Dim myIDbCommand As System.Data.IDbCommand
   Dim myException As System.Exception
   Dim strDisplay As String
   Dim i As Int32
   ' Demonstrate some features of the SqlRowUpdatingEventArgs object
   MessageBox.Show("Entering RowUpdated")
```

```
myIDbCommand = e.Command
' Even though we have declared myIDbCommand as an IdbCommand
' object, the actual type is SqlCommand
MessageBox.Show(TypeName(myIDbCommand), "Object Type")
' If we choose, we can assign myIDbCommand to mySqlCommand, although
' this is not necessary since myIDbCommand already is a SqlCommand
' NOTE: TypeOf-Is is MUCH faster than TypeName() = "stringValue"
If TypeOf myIDbCommand Is SqlCommand Then
   mySqlCommand = myIDbCommand
End If
' Occasionally the command may have a Null value (although
' it never SHOULD. It indicates a bug somewhere.
If myIDbCommand Is Nothing Then
   MessageBox.Show("e.Command is null.", "Exiting")
   Exit Sub
End If
' We can see the SQL command that was used to update
' the data source, as well as its type
MessageBox.Show(e.StatementType.ToString(), "SQL Command Type")
MessageBox.Show(e.Command.CommandText, "SQL Command Text")
' And also any parameters sent along (see SqlParameter for more)
For i = 0 To e.Command.Parameters.Count - 1
   strDisplay += "Parameter #" + i.ToString() + ControlChars.Tab _
      + e.Command.Parameters.Item(i).Value + ControlChars.Cr
Next
MessageBox.Show(strDisplay)
' And also the DataRow sent for the update (this is the changed
' row and will reflect row at the source
strDisplay = ""
For i = 0 To e.Row.ItemArray.Length - 1
   strDisplay += "RowColumn #" + i.ToString() + ControlChars.Tab _
      + e.Row.Item(i) + ControlChars.Cr
Next
MessageBox.Show(strDisplay)
' We can also check to see how many rows have been impacted
' by our update statement.
MessageBox.Show(e.RecordsAffected.ToString(), "Records affected")
' Next we can see if any errors have been raised
If Not e.Errors Is Nothing Then
   'show the exception (recall e.Errors returns an Exception)
   MessageBox.Show("An exception has been raised. " _
      & ControlChars.Cr & e.Errors.ToString())
   MessageBox.Show(e.Errors.Source)
   Dim myEx As SqlException = e.Errors
   MessageBox.Show(myEx.Errors.Item(0).ToString())
   ' Handle errors here ...
End If
' Once we've gathered the information we can determine what
' to do with the this row, and all remaining rows.
' To cancel updating of this row only we can use:
e.Status = UpdateStatus.SkipCurrentRow
```

```
        ' If we have come across some business rule error in the
        ' data, we can also choose to raise our own exception.
        ' Comment out the lines below to avoid having exceptions raised
        e.Status = UpdateStatus.ErrorsOccurred
        e.Errors = New Exception("Personalized Exception from RowUpdated")
        MessageBox.Show("Exiting RowUpdated")
    End Sub
```

Members

Command

The read-only Command property returns an object implementing the System.Data.IDbCommand interface that represents the SQL statement that was executed at the data source. In this case, the returned object can be assigned to a SqlCommand object because it implements the IDbCommand interface.

You can declare a variable with the type IDbCommand and then assign it to the object returned by the Command property; however, because IDbCommand is an interface and not a class, its actual type will be SqlCommand.

Because this property is read only, changes to the Command cannot be made during the RowUpdating or RowUpdated events.

Usage

```
myIDbCommand = mySqlRowUpdatedEventArgs.Command
mySqlCommand = mySqlRowUpdatedEventArgs.Command
```

Parameters

None.

Errors

The Errors property (inherited from System.Data.Common.RowUpdatedEventArgs) returns a System.Exception object or a subclass that inherits from the Exception class. It contains the errors generated by the SqlClient .NET data provider when the command executes. The actual class type of the returned Errors property depends on the exception or error that was returned. For example, an exception originating from the SqlClient .NET data provider will return a SqlException. Knowing the type of the exception raised allows you to assign the Errors property to a more specific exception object.

Another major use of the Errors property is assigning your own Exception (or derived class) to the property and setting the Status property to ErrorsOccurred (1). This will cause the exception you've added to be thrown by the SqlDataAdapter. In this way, you can introduce custom exceptions into your data update code. Be aware, however, that this will cancel the update on the current and all future rows.

OPINION **The naming of the Errors property is somewhat unfortunate. It is easy to confuse with the SqlException.Errors property, which is a SqlErrorCollection object, yet this property returns an Exception object. Be aware of this difference, and you can avoid a frustrating coding session.**

Usage

```
myException = mySqlRowUpdatedEventArgs.Errors
mySqlRowUpdatingEventArgs.Errors = myException
```

Parameters

None.

RecordsAffected

The read-only RecordsAffected property (inherited from System.Data.Common. RowUpdatedEventArgs) returns an Int32 containing the number of records affected by the execution of the SQL statement specified in the Update. The number is the sum of all rows updated, added, and deleted. If no rows were affected, or if there were errors, RecordsAffected will be set to 0. If the SQL command executed was a SELECT command, it is set to -1.

NOTE This is not the same as the Transact-SQL @@Rowcount, which returns the number of selected rows returned from the last SQL command.

Usage

```
myInt32 = mySqlRowUpdatedEventArgs.RecordsAffected
```

Parameters

None.

Row

The read-only Row property (inherited from System.Data.Common.RowUpdated-EventArgs) returns a System.Data.DataRow object, which contains the data that was updated at the data source. Because this property is read only, you cannot change the values. The data will be committed at the completion of the RowUpdated event, when AcceptChanges is called.

Usage

```
myDataRow = mySqlRowUpdatedEventArgs.Row
```

Parameters

None.

StatementType

The read-only StatementType property (inherited from System.Data.Common. RowUpdatedEventArgs) returns a System.StatementType enumeration value specifying the type of SQL statement that was executed at the data source. This value should match the action specified by the Command object.

The value can be assigned to several different types of variables, including an Int32, String, or StatementType enumeration. The advantage to assigning the value to an enumeration is that the ToString method of the enumeration will return the enumeration member name, instead of merely its integer value.

NOTE **The StatementType method is a good example of when you might want to use the ToString method to return a more meaningful value. StatementType by itself returns a number, whereas StatementType.ToString() returns a meaningful string such as "Update."**

Usage

```
myStatementType = mySqlRowUpdatedEventArgs.StatementType
myInt32 = mySqlRowUpdatedEventArgs.StatementType
```

Parameters

None.

StatementType Enumeration

Delete (3)	A SQL DELETE statement.
Insert (1)	A SQL INSERT statement.
Select (0)	(Default) A SQL SELECT statement.
Update (2)	A SQL UPDATE statement.

Status

The Status property (inherited from System.Data.Common.RowUpdatedEventArgs) returns a System.Data.UpdateStatus enumeration value specifying the action that will be taken during the Update with regard to the current row and following rows. The default value is Continue, which tells the DataAdapter to process this row and to continue processing rows. Other values are listed in the text that follows.

This allows you to cancel changes to the data source after the DataAdapter has executed the changes. By setting this value to SkipCurrentRow, the changes made to the data source are ignored and remaining rows continue being processed normally.

Like other enumerations, the value can be assigned to several different types of variables, including an Int32, String, or UpdateStatus enumeration. The advantage to assigning the value to an enumeration is that the ToString method of the enumeration will return the enumeration member name, instead of merely its integer value.

Usage

```
myStatus = mySqlRowUpdatedEventArgs.Status
myInt32 = mySqlRowUpdatedEventArgs.Status
```

Parameters

None.

UpdateStatus Enumeration

Continue (0)	(Default) Process this row, and continue processing rows.
ErrorsOccurred (1)	This update should be treated as an error. Setting this value will abort the update of this row and all remaining rows, as well as throw an Exception. To specify the Error to be thrown add an Exception to the Errors property.

SkipAllRemainingRows (3)	Do not process this row or any remaining rows.
SkipCurrentRow (2)	Do not process this row, but continue processing rows.

TableMapping

The read-only TableMapping property (inherited from System.Data.Common. RowUpdatedEventArgs) returns the System.Data.Common.DataTableMapping object that was sent by the Update method. This object maps the table and columns used by the data source to the table and columns used by the DataSet, to facilitate updating the data at the data source. The DataTableMapping objects contained in the DataTable-MappingCollection contain three public properties that permit access to the underlying mapping.

- The read-only ColumnMapping property, which returns the DataColumnMappingCollection object describing the mappings of the columns between the data source and DataSet
- The DataSetTable property, which is used to get or set the destination DataSet table name
- The SourceTable, which gets or sets the source table from which to retrieve the data

See System.Data.Common.DataTableMapping for more information.

Usage

```
myDataTableMapping = mySqlRowUpdatedEventArgs.TableMapping
```

Parameters

None.

System.Data.SqlClient. SqlRowUpdatingEventArgs

The SqlRowUpdatingEventArgs class provides data for the SqlDataAdapter.RowUpdating event. This event is raised during the Update method of the SqlDataAdapter class. During the Update, every DataRow that has been inserted, updated, or deleted is sent to the data source for updating. Each change raises the RowUpdating event before any changes have been made to the data source.

Once the event is intercepted, you have a great deal of control over what happens next. Although you cannot make changes to the row to be updated, which we find to be very unfortunate, you are able to examine the row, along with information about the data source and what type of Update action will occur (Insert, Delete, etc.). You then have the ability to cancel the update for this particular row or for this row and all following rows. You can even stop processing rows and assign a custom exception, complete with errors, to be raised to the SqlDataAdapter.

The majority of the SqlRowUpdatingEventArgs class members are inherited from the System.Data.Common.RowUpdatingEventArgs class, which means that learning these will translate nicely to the other .NET data providers.

Defining a procedure to handle the SqlDataAdapter.RowUpdating event is one way to catch errors or exceptions within a program. Another is to bracket the Fill and Update procedures in a Try-Catch-Finally block. Generally, if you're just catching exceptions, a Try-Catch-Finally block is preferable; however, if you have additional data validation to perform, handling the RowUpdating event is better. This is especially true because you may handle the RowUpdating events for more than one SqlDataAdapter with the same procedure. To do this simply add any number of SqlDataAdapter.RowUpdating event declarations after the Handles keyword in the procedure definition. Be sure to separate the declarations with commas.

Although the constructor is listed in the text that follows, it's unlikely you would actually use it because the SqlDataAdapter automatically generates this object when the RowUpdating event is raised.

Constructors

```
Dim mySqlRowUpdatingEventArgs As New SqlRowUpdatingEventArgs ( _
   DataRow, IDbCommand, StatementType, DataTableMapping)
```

Parameters

`DataRow`	A System.Data.DataRow object that is to be deleted, inserted, or updated at the data source.
`IDbCommand`	A SqlCommand object (implementing the System.Data.IDbCommand interface) representing the SQL statement to be executed.
`StatementType`	A System.Data.StatementType enumeration that specifies the type of SQL statement in the IDbCommand object. Valid values are Delete (3), Insert (1), Select (0), and Update (2).
`DataTableMapping`	A System.Data.Common.DataTableMapping object that describes the mapping between the DataTable object and the source data.

SqlRowUpdatingEventArgs Sample Code

```
' The best way to approach sample code for this object is to
' trap the RowUpdating event of the SqlDataAdapter object.
' Declare as WithEvents just beneath the Class declaration
Public WithEvents mySqlDataAdapter As
System.Data.SqlClient.SqlDataAdapter
. . .
```

```
Private Sub mySqlDataAdapter_RowUpdating(ByVal sender As Object, _
   ByVal e As System.Data.SqlClient.SqlRowUpdatingEventArgs) _
   Handles mySqlDataAdapter.RowUpdating
   Dim mySqlCommand As System.Data.SqlClient.SqlCommand
   Dim myIDbCommand As System.Data.IDbCommand
   Dim myException As System.Exception
   Dim strDisplay As String
   Dim i As Int32
   ' Demonstrate some features of the SqlRowUpdatingEventArgs object
   MessageBox.Show("Entering RowUpdating")
   myIDbCommand = e.Command
   ' Even though we have declared myIDbCommand as an IdbCommand
   ' object, the actual type is SqlCommand
   MessageBox.Show(TypeName(myIDbCommand), "Object Type")
   ' If we choose, we can assign myIDbCommand to mySqlCommand, although
   ' this is not necessary since myIDbCommand already is a SqlCommand
   ' NOTE: TypeOf-Is is MUCH faster than TypeName() = "stringValue"
   If TypeOf myIDbCommand Is SqlCommand Then
      mySqlCommand = myIDbCommand
   End If
   ' Occasionally the command may have a Null value (although
   ' it never SHOULD. It indicates a bug somewhere.
   If myIDbCommand Is Nothing Then
      MessageBox.Show("e.Command is null.", "Exiting")
      Exit Sub
   End If
   ' We can see the SQL command that was used to update
   ' the data source, as well as its type
   MessageBox.Show(e.StatementType.ToString(), "SQL Command Type")
   MessageBox.Show(e.Command.CommandText, "SQL Command Text")
   ' And also any parameters sent along (see SqlParameter for more)
   For i = 0 To e.Command.Parameters.Count - 1
      strDisplay += "Parameter #" + i.ToString() + ControlChars.Tab _
         + e.Command.Parameters.Item(i).Value + ControlChars.Cr
   Next
   MessageBox.Show(strDisplay)
   ' And also the DataRow sent for the update (this is the changed
   ' row NOT the row currently in the source).
   strDisplay = ""
   For i = 0 To e.Row.ItemArray.Length - 1
      strDisplay += "RowColumn #" + i.ToString() + ControlChars.Tab _
         + e.Row.Item(i) + ControlChars.Cr
   Next
   MessageBox.Show(strDisplay)
   ' Next we can see if any errors have been raised
   If Not e.Errors Is Nothing Then
      'show the exception (recall e.Errors returns an Exception)
      MessageBox.Show("An exception has been raised. " _
         & ControlChars.Cr & e.Errors.ToString())
      'deal with errors here...
   End If
```

```
    ' Once we've gathered the information we can determine what
    ' to do with the this row, and all remaining rows.
    ' To cancel updating of this row only we can use:
    ' (Be sure to comment out this line if you will have this
    ' code active, when checking out the RowUpdated, since
    ' it won't run, if it's cancelled here!!!)
    e.Status = UpdateStatus.SkipCurrentRow
    ' If we have come across some business rule error in the
    ' data, we can also choose to raise our own exception.
    ' Comment out the lines below to avoid having exceptions raised
    ' (Be sure to comment out these lines if you will have this
    ' code active, when checking out the RowUpdated, since
    ' it won't run, if an error is raised here!!!)
    e.Status = UpdateStatus.ErrorsOccurred
    e.Errors = New Exception("Personalized Exception from RowUpdating")
    MessageBox.Show("Exiting RowUpdating")
End Sub
```

Members

Command

The Command property returns an object implementing the System.Data.IDbCommand interface that represents the SQL statement that was executed at the data source. In this case, the returned object can be assigned to a SqlCommand object because it implements the IDbCommand interface.

You can declare a variable with the type IDbCommand, then assign it to the object returned by the Command property; however, because IDbCommand is an interface and not a class, its actual type will be SqlCommand.

Because this property is read only, changes to the Command cannot be made during the RowUpdating or RowUpdated events.

Usage

```
myIDbCommand = mySqlRowUpdatingEventArgs.Command
mySqlCommand = mySqlRowUpdatingEventArgs.Command
```

Parameters

None.

Errors

The Errors property (inherited from System.Data.Common.RowUpdatingEventArgs) returns a System.Exception object or a subclass that inherits from the Exception class. It contains the errors generated by the SqlClient .NET data provider when the command executes. The actual class type of the returned Errors property depends on the exception or error that was returned. For example, an exception originating from the SqlClient .NET data provider will return a SqlException. Knowing the type of the exception raised allows you to assign the Errors property to a more specific exception object. See the SqlRowUpdatingEventArgs sample code for an example.

Another major use of the Errors property is assigning your own Exception (or derived class) to the property and setting the Status property to ErrorsOccurred (1). This will cause the exception you've added to be thrown by the SqlDataAdapter. In this way, you can introduce custom exceptions into your data update code. Be aware, however, that this will cancel the update on the current and all future rows.

OPINION **The naming of the Errors property is somewhat unfortunate. It is easy to confuse with the SqlException.Errors property, which is a SqlErrorCollection object, yet this property returns an Exception object. Be aware of this difference, and you can avoid a frustrating coding session.**

Usage

```
myException = mySqlRowUpdatingEventArgs.Errors
mySqlRowUpdatingEventArgs.Errors = myException
```

Parameters

None.

Row

The read-only Row property (inherited from System.Data.Common.RowUpdatingEventArgs) returns a System.Data.DataRow object, which contains the data that will be updated at the data source. Because this property is read only, you cannot change the values of the data to be updated during a RowUpdating event.

OPINION **We find this very unfortunate because being able to correct data here would prevent having to cancel updates.**

Usage

```
myDataRow = mySqlRowUpdatingEventArgs.Row
```

Parameters

None.

StatementType

The read-only StatementType property (inherited from System.Data.Common.RowUpdatingEventArgs) returns a System.StatementType enumeration value specifying the type of SQL statement to be executed at the data source. This value should match the action being specified by the Command object.

The value can be assigned to several different types of variables, including an Int32, String, or StatementType enumeration. (The advantage to assigning the value to an enumeration is that the ToString method of the enumeration will return the enumeration member name, instead of merely its integer value—that is, "Delete" instead of "3".)

NOTE **The StatementType method is a good example of when you might want to use the ToString method to return a more meaningful value. StatementType by itself returns a number, whereas StatementType.ToString returns a meaningful string such as Update.**

Usage

```
myStatementType = mySqlRowUpdatingEventArgs.StatementType
myInt32 = mySqlRowUpdatingEventArgs.StatementType
```

Parameters

None.

StatementType Enumeration

Delete (3)	A SQL DELETE statement.
Insert (1)	A SQL INSERT statement.
Select (0)	(Default) A SQL SELECT statement.
Update (2)	A SQL UPDATE statement.

Status

The Status property (inherited from System.Data.Common.RowUpdatingEventArgs) returns a System.Data.UpdateStatus enumeration value specifying the action that will be taken during the Update with regard to the current row and following rows. The default value is Continue, which tells the DataAdapter to process this row and to continue processing rows. Other values are listed in the text that follows.

This allows you to cancel changes to the data source. By setting this value to SkipCurrentRow, no changes will be made to the data source for this row; however, any remaining rows will continue to be processed normally.

Like other enumerations, the value can be assigned to several different types of variables, including an Int32, String, or UpdateStatus enumeration. The advantage to assigning the value to an enumeration is that the ToString method of the enumeration will return the enumeration member name, instead of merely its integer value—that is, Continue instead of 0.

Usage

```
myUpdateStatus = mySqlRowUpdatingEventArgs.UpdateStatus
myInt32 = mySqlRowUpdatingEventArgs.UpdateStatus
```

Parameters

None.

UpdateStatus Enumeration

Continue (0)	(Default) Process this row, and continue processing rows.
ErrorsOccurred (1)	This update should be treated as an error. Setting this value will abort the update of this row and all remaining rows, as well as throw an Exception. To specify the Error to be thrown, add an Exception to the Errors property.
SkipAllRemainingRows (3)	Do not process this row or any remaining rows.
SkipCurrentRow (2)	Do not process this row, but continue processing rows.

TableMapping

The read-only TableMapping property (inherited from System.Data.Common.RowUpdatingEventArgs) returns the System.Data.Common.DataTableMapping object that is being sent by the Update method. This object maps the table and columns used by the data source to the table and columns used by the DataSet, to facilitate updating the data at the data source. The DataTableMapping objects contained in the DataTableMappingCollection contain three public properties that permit access to the underlying mapping.

- The read-only ColumnMapping property, which returns the DataColumnMappingCollection object describing the mappings of the columns between the data source and DataSet
- The DataSetTable property, which is used to get or set the destination DataSet table name
- The SourceTable, which gets or sets the source table from which to retrieve the data.

See System.Data.Common.DataTableMapping for more information.

Usage

```
myDataTableMapping = mySqlRowUpdatingEventArgs.TableMapping
```

Parameters

None.

System.Data.SqlClient.SqlTransaction

A SqlTransaction represents an Transact-SQL transaction for a given SqlConnection. A transaction is a logical group of database operations combined to form a single unit of work. An example of this would be an INSERT and a DELETE operation working together to facilitate "moving" data from one table to another. In this case, it is very important for both operations to happen together or neither at all. Transactions see to that.

SQL programmers might be inclined to execute a SQL batch that contains *BEGIN TRANSACTION* and *COMMIT TRANSACTION* statements. You should not do this, but rather you should use ADO.NET's built-in transaction management features found in the SqlTransaction and SqlConnection classes.

ADO.NET creates a SqlTransaction object when the BeginTransaction method is called on a SqlConnection object. All ensuing operations associated with the transaction are performed on the SqlTransaction object.

Although the SqlTransaction class has a constructor method, it is private and cannot be called. You must use the BeginTransaction method of an existing SqlConnection object to create an instance of a SqlTransaction.

NOTE **Unlike the Transaction object in the OleDb .NET data provider, the SqlTransaction class does not implement a Begin method. This means that**

the SqlClient .NET data provider will not allow you to implement nested transactions. You can work around this limitation by executing your own BEGIN, COMMIT, and ROLLBACK statements as SQL commands. In general, doing this is not recommended; you should always opt for ADO.NET to broker the transaction for you, but this is a situation where that support is not provided.

Constructors

There is no public constructor.

Parameters

None.

SqlTransaction Sample Code

```
Dim mySqlConnection As New System.Data.SqlClient.SqlConnection()
Dim mySqlTransaction As System.Data.SqlClient.SqlTransaction
Dim mySqlCommand As System.Data.SqlClient.SqlCommand
' Establish Connection
mySqlConnection.ConnectionString = _
   "Data Source=Omnibook;Integrated Security=SSPI;Database=Northwind"
mySqlConnection.Open()
' Create Transaction and Command
mySqlTransaction = mySqlConnection.BeginTransaction("AddNewCustomers")
mySqlCommand = mySqlConnection.CreateCommand()
mySqlCommand.Transaction = mySqlTransaction
' Insert a customer
mySqlCommand.CommandText = "INSERT Customers " & _
   "(CustomerID,CompanyName) VALUES ('CUST1','Wiley Publishing')"
mySqlCommand.ExecuteNonQuery()
' Request a Transaction Savepoint
mySqlTransaction.Save("AddNewCustomer1")
' Try to insert two more customers, but with the duplicate IDs
mySqlCommand.CommandText = "INSERT Customers " & _
   "(CustomerID,CompanyName) VALUES ('CUST2','Wiley Publishing')"
mySqlCommand.ExecuteNonQuery()     ' This Insert succeeds
Try
   mySqlCommand.ExecuteNonQuery() ' This Insert fails on PK violation
Catch ex As Exception
   mySqlTransaction.Rollback("AddNewCustomer1") ' Rollback to Savepoint
Finally
   mySqlTransaction.Commit()
   mySqlConnection.Close()
   mySqlConnection.Dispose()
   MessageBox.Show("Only the first Customer was added", "Commit")
End Try
```

Members

Commit

The Commit method saves all pending changes to the SQL Server made since the start of the transaction. By definition, a Commit guarantees that all of the transaction's modifications are made successfully to the data source. The Commit method also frees locks and other resources at the data source.

You cannot commit a transaction that has already been rolled back.

Usage

```
mySqlTransaction.Commit()
```

Parameters

None.

Exceptions

Exception	An unspecified ADO.NET error occurred while trying to commit the transaction.
InvalidOperationException	There is no current transaction (perhaps it was already committed or rolled back), or the SqlConnection is not open.

Connection

The Connection property is the read-only value of the SqlConnection object that is associated with the SqlTransaction. This property may also return a null reference (`Nothing` in Visual Basic .NET) if the transaction is no longer valid.

Usage

```
mySqlConnection = mySqlTransaction.Connection
```

Parameters

None.

IsolationLevel

The IsolationLevel property is the read-only value of the IsolationLevel for the SqlTransaction specified. An IsolationLevel controls the degree by which your data is isolated from other processes. IsolationLevels guard against interference from other users running queries or changing data that you are currently working on in your transaction. The SQL Server version you are connected to may not support all of ADO.NET's IsolationLevels.

Usage

```
myIsolationLevel = mySqlTransaction.IsolationLevel
myIsolationLevelString = mySqlTransaction.IsolationLevel.ToString()
```

Parameters

None.

IsolationLevel Enumeration

Chaos (16)	Any pending changes from transactions that are more highly isolated transactions cannot be overwritten. SQL Server 2000 and below do not support this isolation level.
ReadCommitted (4096)	(Default) Shared locks are held while the data is being read to avoid dirty reads, but the data can be changed before the end of the transaction, resulting in non-repeatable reads or phantom data (a.k.a. CursorStability).
ReadUncommitted (256)	No shared locks or exclusive locks are honored, so dirty reads are possible (a.k.a. Browse).
RepeatableRead (65536)	All data used in a query is locked, preventing others from updating. This prevents nonrepeatable reads, but phantom rows are still possible.
Serializable (1048576)	A range lock is placed on the data, preventing other users from updating or inserting rows into the dataset until the transaction is complete (a.k.a. Isolated).
Unspecified (-1)	A different isolation level than the one specified is being used, but the level cannot be determined. (This value cannot be passed when creating a Transaction.)

Sample Code

```
Dim mySqlConnection As New System.Data.SqlClient.SqlConnection()
Dim mySqlTransaction As System.Data.SqlClient.SqlTransaction
Dim mySqlCommand As System.Data.SqlClient.SqlCommand
' Establish Connection
mySqlConnection.ConnectionString = _
   "Server=(local);Integrated Security=SSPI;Database=Northwind"
mySqlConnection.Open()
' Establish Transaction
mySqlTransaction = mySqlConnection.BeginTransaction
MessageBox.Show(mySqlTransaction.IsolationLevel.ToString(), _
    "Isolation Level")
' Done
mySqlConnection.Close()
```

Rollback

The opposite of the Commit method, Rollback removes any pending changes to the SQL Server made since the start of the transaction. By definition, a Rollback maintains integrity because it puts SQL Server back to an original state in the event of an application or system failure. The Rollback method also frees locks and other resources at the server. If you close a SqlConnection with an activity transaction, ADO.NET will roll back any pending changes automatically.

If you know the name of the transaction, you can specify when calling the Rollback method. If you want to roll back the transaction to a specific savepoint, you can do that also—just specify the savepoint name when calling the Rollback method. You cannot roll back a transaction that has already been committed.

Usage

```
mySqlTransaction.Rollback()
mySqlTransaction.Rollback(MyString)
```

Parameters

`MyString`	The name of the transaction to roll back or the savepoint for which to roll back. You can specify the name of the transaction when you create it—see SqlConnection.BeginTransaction. You can also specify periodic savepoints, to which you can roll back; see SqlTransaction.Save.

Exceptions

Exception	An unspecified system error occurred while trying to roll back the transaction.
InvalidOperationException	There is no current transaction (perhaps it was already committed or rolled back) or the SqlConnection is not open.
SqlException	You have attempted to roll back a transaction to a savepoint that doesn't exist.

Save

The Save method allows you to create a *savepoint* in the transaction. A savepoint is a marker that allows an application to roll back part of a transaction, in the event a minor error is encountered. If you roll back a transaction to a savepoint, the transaction is still active and you'll need to follow up with another rollback or commit to complete the transaction.

This method call is functionally equivalent to the Transact-SQL SAVE TRANSACTION statement.

Usage

```
mySqlTransaction.Save(MyString)
```

Parameters

`MyString`	The name of the savepoint.

Exceptions

Exception	An unspecified system error occurred while trying to define the savepoint.
InvalidOperationException	There is no current transaction (perhaps it was already committed or rolled back), or the SqlConnection is not open.

CHAPTER

9

System.Data.SqlTypes

The System.Data.SqlTypes namespace serves an important utility role in ADO.NET. This namespace provides classes and structures to better support the native data types in SQL Server 7.0 and 2000 and, thus, is intended to complement the System.Data.SqlClient namespace. These SqlTypes are alternative data types that are safer and faster to use when working with SQL Server.

Remember that one of the key functions of the .NET Framework is to serve as a giant type converter, serving many languages while simultaneously serving many platforms. The width of the Framework's support is impressive; however, the depth could be improved for specific applications. Because SQL Server is such a key data source for .NET developers, Microsoft created the SqlTypes namespace to give extra depth when working with this particular data source.

Tables built within SQL Server 7.0 and SQL Server 2000 can consist of up to 25 different data types. This number jumps to nearly 40 if you consider all the various ANSI synonyms that SQL Server supports. Without the use of SqlTypes to better map the SQL Server data types to be used in ADO.NET, you could lose precision or functionality.

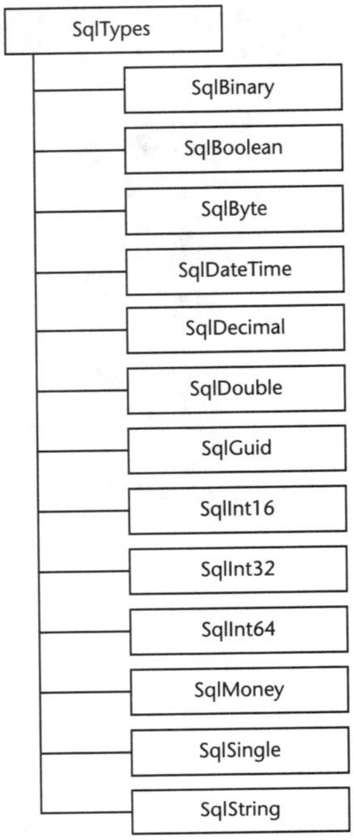

Figure 9.1 System.Data.SqlTypes structures.

Can you manipulate data from SQL Server without explicitly using the SqlTypes? Yes; internally, however, ADO.NET manipulates the data types being returned from System.Data.SqlClient calls anyway. One benefit of using the SqlTypes over the standard .NET types is that these structures implement the INullable interface, which allows each of the SqlTypes to contain *null* values. Each of the numeric SqlTypes knows what its minimum and maximum values are, which is important because the precision and scale supported by Sql Server is different from what the .NET Framework supports.

Although you can instantiate each of the SqlTypes manually and then populate, transform, and convert, the more likely scenario will find you working with these types as a result of calling one of the SqlDataReader methods. These methods are listed in Figure 9.2 and will return the corresponding SqlType.

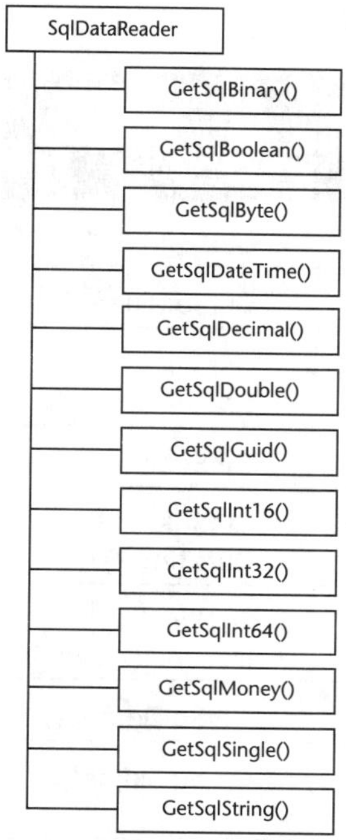

Figure 9.2 SqlDataReader SqlTypes methods.

Table 9.1 shows the SQL Server data types and how they are handled in ADO.NET.

Operators

Because the various SqlTypes are complex objects, you cannot simply add, subtract, compare, or assign their values without using overloaded operators. Visual Basic .NETdoes not support overloaded operators. Other languages, such as C#, support overloaded operators, so these operations behave just as though the SqlTypes were standard, primitive .NET objects.

Table 9.1 SQL Server Data Types

SQL SERVER DATA TYPE	.NET FRAMEWORK DATA TYPE	TYPENAME() FUNCTION	CORRESPONDING SQLTYPE	CORRESPONDING SQLDATAREADER METHOD
bigint *	System.Int64	Long	SqlInt64	GetSqlInt64()
binary	System.Byte[]	Byte[]	SqlBinary	GetSqlBinary()
bit	System.Boolean	Boolean	SqlBoolean	GetSql-Boolean()
char	System.String	String	SqlString	GetSqlString()
datetime	System.Datetime	Date	SqlDateTime	GetSql-DateTime()
decimal	System.Decimal	Decimal	SqlDecimal	GetSql-Decimal()
float	System.Double	Double	SqlDouble	GetSqlDouble()
float (n < 25) **	System.Single	Single	SqlSingle	GetSqlSingle()
float (n > 24) **	System.Double	Double	SqlDouble	GetSqlDouble()
image	System.Byte[]	Byte[]	SqlBinary	GetSqlBinary()
int	System.Int32	Integer	SqlInt32	GetSqlInt32()
money	System.Decimal	Decimal	SqlMoney	GetSqlMoney()
nchar	System.String	String	SqlString	GetSqlString()
ntext	System.String	String	SqlString	GetSqlString()
numeric	System.Decimal	Decimal	SqlDecimal	GetSql-Decimal()
nvarchar	System.String	String	SqlString	GetSqlString()
real	System.Single	Single	SqlSingle	GetSqlSingle()
smalldatetime	System.Datetime	Date	SqlDateTime	GetSql-DateTime()
smallint	System.Int16	Short	SqlInt16	GetSqlInt16()
smallmoney	System.Decimal	Decimal	SqlMoney	GetSqlMoney()
sql_variant *	System.Object	*Will Vary*	*Will Vary*	*Will Vary*

SQL SERVER DATA TYPE	.NET FRAMEWORK DATA TYPE	TYPENAME() FUNCTION	CORRESPONDING SQLTYPE	CORRESPONDING SQLDATAREADER METHOD
sysname	System.String	String	SqlString	GetSqlString()
text	System.String	String	SqlString	GetSqlString()
timestamp	System.Byte[]	Byte[]	SqlBinary	GetSqlBinary()
tinyint	System.Byte	Byte	SqlByte	GetSqlByte()
unique-identifier	System.Guid	Guid	SqlGuid	GetSqlGuid()
varbinary	System.Byte[]	Byte[]	SqlBinary	GetSqlBinary()
varchar	System.String	String	SqlString	GetSqlString()

* Not available in SQL Server 7.0.

** n = number of mantissa bits—essentially the precision; float ($n<25$) is implemented in SQL Server as a *real.*

Table 9.2 is the SqlTypes operators and the Visual Basic .NET and C# calling conventions.

Table 9.2 SqlTypes Operators

VISUAL BASIC .NET	C#
`op_Addition(mySqlType1,mySqlType2)`	`mySqlType1 + mySqlType2`
`op_Subtraction(mySqlType1,mySqlType2)`	`mySqlType1 - mySqlType2`
`op_Division(mySqlType1,mySqlType2)`	`mySqlType1 / mySqlType2`
`op_Multiply(mySqlType1,mySqlType2)`	`mySqlType1 * mySqlType2`
`op_Modulus(mySqlType1,mySqlType2)`	`mySqlType1 % mySqlType2`
`op_Equality(mySqlType1,mySqlType2)`	`mySqlType1 == mySqlType2`
`op_GreaterThan(mySqlType1,mySqlType2)`	`mySqlType1 > mySqlType2`
`op_GreaterThanOrEqual (mySqlType1,mySqlType2)`	`mySqlType1 >= mySqlType2`

continues

Table 9.2 (Continued)

VISUAL BASIC .NET	C#
`op_Inequality(mySqlType1,mySqlType2)`	`mySqlType1 != mySqlType2`
`op_LessThan(mySqlType1,mySqlType2)`	`mySqlType1 < mySqlType2`
`op_LessThanOrEqual (mySqlType1,mySqlType2)`	`mySqlType1 <= mySqlType2`
`op_BitwiseAnd(mySqlType1,mySqlType2)`	`mySqlType1 & mySqlType2`
`op_BitwiseOr(mySqlType1,mySqlType2)`	`mySqlType1 | mySqlType2`
`op_ExclusiveOr(mySqlType1,mySqlType2)`	`mySqlType1 ^ mySqlType2`
`op_LogicalNot(mySqlType)`	`! mySqlType`
`op_OnesCompliment(mySqlType)`	`~ mySqlType`
`op_UnaryNegation(mySqlType)`	`- mySqlType`

Accessing Class Members

Visual Basic .NET and C# differ in how you call the static members of the SqlTypes structures. Visual Basic .NET allows you to call every method, property, and field that the structure offers via the instantiated object. C#, however, does not let you access static members from an instantiated object, but it requires you to reference the member from the class, structure, or type directly.

For example, in Visual Basic .NET you can access the True field of a SqlBoolean using either approach:

```
mySqlBoolean = mySqlBoolean.True   ' Accesses the object
mySqlBoolean = SqlBoolean.True     ' Accesses the structure
```

In C# you can access only the True field of the structure:

```
mySqlBoolean = mySqlBoolean.True; ' Gives you a build error
mySqlBoolean = SqlBoolean.True;   ' Accesses the structure
```

In C#, the rule of thumb with the SqlTypes namespace is that all fields and some methods must be referenced by the structure. You will know as soon as you try to compile your C# code that you cannot reference the member by the instantiated object because you will receive a build error:

```
Static member 'System.Data.SqlTypes.SqlBoolean.True' cannot be accessed
with an instance reference; qualify it with a type name instead.
```

System.Data.SqlTypes.INullable

All of the structures in System.Data.SqlTypes implement the INullable interface. By implementing this interface, the SqlTypes may contain a null value—something that *most* of the standard .NET data types cannot do. By default all SqlTypes are null. This changes once a nonnull value is assigned, either from the DataReader or DataSet classes, or by some other means. The SqlType can always be returned to a null value by assigning it the value of null.

Assigning a null value is done differently with the SqlTypes than with other .NET data types (that may support null values) in the . NET Framework. For those .NET data types that may be set to null, you must use the singleton class, System.DbNull, and assign its Value property to the data type. This is a little different from previous language versions, where you may have used vbNull or Nothing. Each of the System. Data.SqlTypes implements a field that is used to set itself to null.

Here is a quick comparison of the ways you can assign a null value in Visual Basic .NET:

```
' Use this approach for those .NET objects that support null values
myObject = System.DbNull.Value
MessageBox.Show(IsDBNull(myObject))    ' True
' Use this approach, however, for the various SqlTypes
mySqlMoney = mySqlMoney.Null
MessageBox.Show(mySqlMoney.IsNull())    ' True
' Beware of these approaches as they are hard to test for
myObject = VbNull
MessageBox.Show(IsDBNull(myObject))    ' False
myObject = VariantType.Null
MessageBox.Show(IsDBNull(myObject))    ' False
```

NOTE The "Db" prefix in the System.DbNull class might throw you at first, especially because its usage extends beyond database applications, such as with COM Interop to distinguish between object values. We guess Microsoft simply believed that the majority of the programmers would be using it for database applications.

Constructors

None.

Parameters

None.

INullable Interface Sample Code

See the sample code for the IsNull member.

Members

IsNull

The read-only IsNull property returns a Boolean indicating whether the SqlType is null. The value will be true if the value of the SqlType is null and false if it contains a value.

Usage

```
myBoolean = mySqlDataType.IsNull
```

Event Data

None.

Sample Code

```
Dim myGuid As System.Guid
Dim myObject As System.Object
Dim mySqlGuid As System.Data.SqlTypes.SqlGuid
' Attempt to set to NULL values
' Compile fails because a System.Guid cannot be assigned null
myGuid = System.DBNull.Value
' Works fine because a System.Object can be null
myObject = System.DBNull.Value
' Compile fails because SqlTypes are not set to null in this way
mySqlGuid = System.DBNull.Value
' Instead, all SqlTypes have a null field for just such a task
mySqlGuid = mySqlGuid.Null
' Test
MessageBox.Show(mySqlGuid.IsNull, "IsNull") ' True
' Assign a Guid using an overloaded constructor
mySqlGuid = New System.Data.SqlTypes.SqlGuid(System.Guid.NewGuid)
' Test
MessageBox.Show(mySqlGuid.ToString, "Value")
MessageBox.Show(mySqlGuid.IsNull, "IsNull") ' False
```

System.Data.SqlTypes.SqlBinary

The SqlBinary structure represents a variable-length stream of binary data. Use the SqlBinary structure to manipulate the following SQL Server data types:

- binary
- image
- timestamp
- varbinary
- sql_variant (if the data is one the above types)

Constructors

```
Dim mySqlBinary As New SqlBinary(myByteArray)
```

Parameters

`myByteArray` An array of bytes.

SqlBinary Sample Code

```
Private Sub ReadSqlType(ByVal myConnectionString As String, _
                        ByVal myCommandText As String)
   Dim mySqlConnection As System.Data.SqlClient.SqlConnection
   Dim mySqlDataReader As System.Data.SqlClient.SqlDataReader
   Dim mySqlCommand As System.Data.SqlClient.SqlCommand
   Dim mySqlBinary As System.Data.SqlTypes.SqlBinary
   ' Establish connection
   mySqlConnection = New SqlConnection(myConnectionString)
   mySqlConnection.Open()
   ' Build and execute command
   mySqlCommand = New SqlCommand(myCommandText)
   mySqlCommand.Connection = mySqlConnection
   mySqlDataReader = mySqlCommand.ExecuteReader
   ' Read first row
   If mySqlDataReader.Read Then
      ' Save column as appropriate SqlTypes structure
      mySqlBinary = mySqlDataReader.GetSqlBinary(1)
      MessageBox.Show(mySqlBinary.Length)
   End If
   ' Done
   mySqlConnection.Close()
End Sub
```

Members

CompareTo

The CompareTo method allows you to compare the SqlBinary value with another supplied object to return an indication of their relative values. The returned Int32 object will indicate the comparison:

Less than Zero. The SqlBinary value was less than the supplied object, or the SqlBinary was null.

Zero. The SqlBinary value was the same as the supplied object.

Greater than zero. The SqlBinary value was greater than the supplied object, or the object was null.

Usage

```
myInt32 = mySqlBinary.CompareTo(myObject)
```

Parameters

`myObject`	Any object that implements the IComparable interface.

Exceptions

ArgumentException	The supplied object isn't valid for comparison.

Concat

The Concat method allows you to concatenate two SqlBinary values together. The method returns a SqlBinary object. If either of the two SqlBinary values being concatenated is null, the resulting concatenation will be null.

In addition to the Concat method, you may also use the op_Addition operator method, or, if your language supports overloaded operators, you may use that construct instead.

Usage

```
mySqlBinary = mySqlBinary.Concat(mySqlBinary1,mySqlBinary2)
mySqlBinary = mySqlBinary.op_Addition(mySqlBinary1,mySqlBinary2) ' VB
mySqlBinary = mySqlBinary1 + mySqlBinary2; // C#
```

Parameters

`mySqlBinary1`	A SqlBinary object.
`mySqlBinary2`	A SqlBinary object.

Equals

The Equals method allows you to compare the SqlBinary value with a supplied object or compare the values of two supplied objects or SqlBinary values. The result will be either a Boolean or a SqlBoolean, depending on which overloaded method is called. The SqlBoolean result can be True, False, or Null (if either of the SqlBinary values being compared is null).

In addition to the Equals method, you may also use the op_Equality operator method, or, if your language supports overloaded operators, you may use that construct instead.

Usage

```
mySqlBoolean = mySqlBinary.Equals(mySqlBinary1,mySqlBinary2)
myBoolean = mySqlBinary.Equals(myObject)
myBoolean = mySqlBinary.Equals(myObject,myObject2)
mySqlBoolean = mySqlBinary.op_Equality(mySqlBinary1,mySqlBinary2) ' VB
mySqlBoolean = (mySqlBinary1 == mySqlBinary2); // C#
```

Parameters

`mySqlBinary1`	A SqlBinary object.
`mySqlBinary2`	A SqlBinary object.
`myObject`	Any System.Object or descendant.
`myObject2`	Any System.Object or descendant.

GetHashCode

The GetHashCode method returns a hash code for the SqlBinary value. The hash code represents a unique value corresponding to the particular set of bytes in the SqlBinary value. Keep in mind that even the smallest change to the SqlBinary value will result in a different hash code. Requesting the hash code for a null SqlBinary will return 0.

Usage

```
myInt32 = mySqlBinary.GetHashCode()
```

Parameters

None.

GreaterThan

The GreaterThan method compares two SqlBinary values and returns a SqlBoolean value indicating whether the first SqlBinary value is greater than the second SqlBinary value. A null value would indicate that one of the SqlBinary values is null.

In addition to the GreaterThan method, you may also use the op_GreaterThan operator method, or, if your language supports overloaded operators, you may use that construct instead.

Usage

```
mySqlBoolean = mySqlBinary.GreaterThan(mySqlBinary1,mySqlBinary2)
mySqlBoolean = mySqlBinary.op_GreaterThan(mySqlBinary1,mySqlBinary2) ' VB
mySqlBoolean = (mySqlBinary1 > mySqlBinary2); // C#
```

Parameters

`mySqlBinary1`	A SqlBinary object.
`mySqlBinary2`	A SqlBinary object.

GreaterThanOrEqual

The GreaterThanOrEqual method compares two SqlBinary values and returns a SqlBoolean value indicating whether the first SqlBinary value is greater than or equal to the second SqlBinary value. A null value would indicate that one of the SqlBinary values is null.

In addition to the GreaterThanOrEqual method, you may also use the op_GreaterThanOrEqual operator method, or, if your language supports overloaded operators, you may use that construct instead.

Usage

```
mySqlBoolean = mySqlBinary.GreaterThanOrEqual(mySqlBinary1,mySqlBinary2)
mySqlBoolean = _
   mySqlBinary.op_GreaterThanOrEqual(mySqlBinary1,mySqlBinary2) ' VB
mySqlBoolean = (mySqlBinary1 >= mySqlBinary2); // C#
```

Parameters

`mySqlBinary1`	A SqlBinary object.
`mySqlBinary2`	A SqlBinary object.

IsNull

The read-only IsNull property returns a Boolean indicating whether the SqlBinary is null. The value will be true if the value of the SqlBinary is null and false if it contains a value.

Usage

```
myBoolean = mySqlBinary.IsNull
```

Parameters

None.

Item

The read-only Item property allows you to retrieve a specific byte from the SqlBinary. You will need to pass the Item property the index (zero based) of the byte you are requesting. The value returned is an ASCII value, so you may want to use the Convert class (see second usage example).

Usage

```
myByte = mySqlBinary.Item(Index)
myChar = Convert.ToChar(mySqlBinary.Item(Index))
```

Parameters

`Index`	An Int32 indicating which byte position to return.

Exceptions

IndexOutOfRangeException	The index was negative or higher than the maximum number of bytes in the structure's value. Remember this is zero based.

Length

The read-only Length property returns the number of bytes contained in the SqlBinary. The SqlBinary object may not be null to reference the Length property.

Usage

```
myInt32 = mySqlBinary.Length
```

Parameters

None.

Exceptions

SqlNullValueException	You cannot check the length of a null value. Be sure to check the IsNull property, or use another exception handling technique.

LessThan

The LessThan method compares two SqlBinary values and returns a SqlBoolean value indicating whether the first SqlBinary value is less than the second SqlBinary value. A null value would indicate that one of the SqlBinary values is null.

In addition to the LessThan method, you may also use the op_LessThan operator method, or, if your language supports overloaded operators, you may use that construct instead.

Usage

```
mySqlBoolean = mySqlBinary.LessThan(mySqlBinary1,mySqlBinary2)
mySqlBoolean = mySqlBinary.op_LessThan(mySqlBinary1,mySqlBinary2) ' VB
mySqlBoolean = mySqlBinary1 < mySqlBinary2; // C#
```

Parameters

`mySqlBinary1`	A SqlBinary object.
`mySqlBinary2`	A SqlBinary object.

LessThanOrEqual

The LessThanOrEqual method compares two SqlBinary values and returns a SqlBoolean value indicating whether the first SqlBinary value is less than or equal to the second SqlBinary value. A null value would indicate that one of the SqlBinary values is null.

In addition to the LessThanOrEqual method, you may also use the op_LessThanOrEqual operator method, or, if your language supports overloaded operators, you may use that construct instead.

Usage

```
mySqlBoolean = mySqlBinary.LessThanOrEqual(mySqlBinary1,mySqlBinary2)
mySqlBoolean = _
   mySqlBinary.op_LessThanOrEqual(mySqlBinary1,mySqlBinary2) ' VB
mySqlBoolean = mySqlBinary1 <= mySqlBinary2; // C#
```

Parameters

`mySqlBinary1`	A SqlBinary object.
`mySqlBinary2`	A SqlBinary object.

NotEquals

The NotEquals method compares two SqlBinary values and returns a SqlBoolean value indicating whether the two SqlBinary values are not equal. A null value would indicate that one of the SqlBinary values is null.

In addition to the NotEquals method, you may also use the op_Inequality operator method, or, if your language supports overloaded operators, you may use that construct instead.

Usage

```
mySqlBoolean = mySqlBinary.NotEquals(mySqlBinary1,mySqlBinary2)
mySqlBoolean = mySqlBinary.op_Inequality(mySqlBinary1,mySqlBinary2) ' VB
mySqlBoolean = (mySqlBinary1 != mySqlBinary2); // C#
```

Parameters

`mySqlBinary1`	A SqlBinary object.
`mySqlBinary2`	A SqlBinary object.

Null

The Null field represents a read-only null value that can be assigned to a SqlBinary object. You cannot use the standard .NET way of assigning a null value with the System.DBNull.Value, but rather you must use this approach.

Usage

```
mySqlBinary = mySqlBinary.Null
```

Parameters

None.

op_Explicit

The op_Explicit method represents a special SqlBinary converter that allows SqlBinary values to be explicitly assigned to and from other SqlTypes. This method is overloaded in two ways. The first usage allows for the value of a SqlBinary to be returned as a byte array. The second usage allows for the value of a SqlGuid to be returned as a SqlBinary.

If you are using ADO.NET with C#, then you will not call the op_Explicit method directly, but rather you are allowed to cast from one SqlType to the other.

Usage

```
myByteArray = mySqlBinary.op_Explicit(mySqlBinary) ' Visual Basic .NET
myByteArray = (Byte[])mySqlBinary;                 // C#
mySqlBinary = mySqlBinary.op_Explicit(mySqlGuid)   ' Visual Basic .NET
mySqlBinary = (SqlBinary)mySqlGuid;                // C#
```

Parameters

`mySqlBinary`	A SqlBinary object.
`mySqlGuid`	A SqlGuid object.

op_Implicit

The op_Implicit method represents a special SqlBinary converter that allows for a byte array to be assigned to the SqlBinary. The SqlBinary will be set to a null value if an empty byte array was passed.

If you are using ADO.NET with C#, then you will not call the op_Implicit method directly, but rather you are allowed to cast from one SqlType to the other. See the example that follows:

Usage

```
mySqlBinary = mySqlBinary.op_Implicit(myByteArray) ' Visual Basic .NET
mySqlBinary = (SqlBinary)myByteArray;              // C#
```

Parameters

`myByteArray`	An array of bytes.

ToSqlGuid

The ToSqlGuid method returns the SqlBinary value as a SqlGuid. A null value would indicate that the SqlBinary value is null.

Usage

```
mySqlGuid = mySqlBinary.ToSqlGuid()
```

Parameters

None.

Exceptions

ArgumentException	The SqlBinary value is not a valid array of bytes to return a SqlGuid. The SqlBinary must contain exactly 16 bytes.

ToString

The ToString method returns the SqlBinary value as a String. A null value would indicate that the SqlBinary value is null.

NOTE **The .NET Framework RTM version simply returns the type of the SqlTypes structure and its length in parentheses, such as "SqlBinary(10)".**

Usage

```
myString = mySqlBinary.ToString()
```

Parameters

None.

Value

The read-only Value property allows you to retrieve the value of the SqlBinary. Remember that this property is read-only—you may not assign a SqlBinary its value using its Value property.

In addition to using the Value property, you may also use the op_Explicit conversion method, or, if your language supports overloaded operators, you may use that construct instead.

Usage

```
myByteArray = mySqlBinary.Value                      ' Visual Basic .NET
myByteArray = mySqlBinary.op_Explicit(mySqlBinary)  ' Visual Basic .NET
myByteArray = (Byte[])mySqlBinary;                   // C#
```

Parameters

None.

Exceptions

SqlNullValueException	You cannot retrieve a null value. Be sure to check the IsNull property or use another exception-handling technique.

System.Data.SqlTypes.SqlBoolean

The SqlBoolean structure represents a bit or Boolean field. The SqlBoolean value can be True, False, or Null. Use the SqlBoolean structure to manipulate the following SQL Server data types:

- bit
- sql_variant (if the data is of type bit)

Constructors

```
Dim mySqlBoolean As New SqlBoolean(myBoolean)
Dim mySqlBoolean As New SqlBoolean(myInt32)
```

Parameters

`myBoolean`	A Boolean object.
`myInt32`	A 32-bit Integer object.

SqlBoolean Sample Code

```
Private Sub ReadSqlType(ByVal myConnectionString As String, _
                        ByVal myCommandText As String)
   Dim mySqlConnection As System.Data.SqlClient.SqlConnection
   Dim mySqlDataReader As System.Data.SqlClient.SqlDataReader
   Dim mySqlCommand As System.Data.SqlClient.SqlCommand
   Dim mySqlBoolean As System.Data.SqlTypes.SqlBoolean
   ' Establish connection
   mySqlConnection = New SqlConnection(myConnectionString)
   mySqlConnection.Open()
   ' Build and execute command
   mySqlCommand = New SqlCommand(myCommandText)
   mySqlCommand.Connection = mySqlConnection
   mySqlDataReader = mySqlCommand.ExecuteReader
   ' Read first row
   If mySqlDataReader.Read Then
      ' Save column as appropriate SqlTypes structure
      mySqlBoolean = mySqlDataReader.GetSqlBoolean(1)
      MessageBox.Show(mySqlBoolean.ToString)
   End If
   ' Done
   mySqlConnection.Close()
End Sub
```

Members

And

The And method performs a Boolean *and* operation on two SqlBoolean values. The method returns a SqlBoolean object. If both SqlBoolean values are True, the resulting value will be True; otherwise, it will be False. If either of the two values being compared is null, the resulting SqlBoolean will be null.

In addition to the And method, you may also use the op_BitwiseAnd operator method, or, if your language supports overloaded operators, you may use that construct instead.

Usage

```
mySqlBoolean = mySqlBoolean.And(mySqlBoolean1,mySqlBoolean2)
mySqlBoolean = _
   mySqlBoolean.op_BitwiseAnd(mySqlBoolean1,mySqlBoolean2) ' VB
mySqlBoolean = mySqlBoolean1 & mySqlBoolean2; // C#
```

Parameters

mySqlBoolean1	A SqlBoolean object.
mySqlBoolean2	A SqlBoolean object.

ByteValue

The read-only ByteValue property returns a Byte representing the SqlBoolean value. The ByteValue will return the following values, based on the SqlBoolean value:

0 The SqlBoolean is False.

1 The SqlBoolean is True.

Usage

```
myByte = mySqlBoolean.ByteValue
```

Parameters

None.

Exceptions

SqlNullValueException	The SqlBoolean value was null.

CompareTo

The CompareTo method allows you to compare the SqlBoolean value with another supplied object to return an indication of their relative values. The returned Int32 object will indicate the comparison:

Less than Zero. The SqlBoolean value was less than the supplied object, or the SqlBoolean was null.

Zero. The SqlBoolean value was the same as the supplied object.

Greater than zero. The SqlBoolean value was greater than the supplied object, or the object was null.

Usage

```
myInt32 = mySqlBoolean.CompareTo(myObject)
```

Parameters

`myObject`	Any object that implements the IComparable interface.

Exceptions

ArgumentException	The supplied object isn't valid for comparison.

Equals

The Equals method allows you to compare the SqlBoolean value with a supplied object or compare the values of two supplied objects or SqlBoolean values. The result will be either a Boolean or a SqlBoolean, depending on which overloaded method is called. The SqlBoolean result can be True, False, or Null (if either of the SqlBoolean values being compared is null).

In addition to the Equals method, you may also use the op_Equality operator method, or, if your language supports overloaded operators, you may use that construct instead.

Usage

```
mySqlBoolean = mySqlBoolean.Equals(mySqlBoolean1,mySqlBoolean2)
myBoolean = mySqlBoolean.Equals(myObject)
myBoolean = mySqlBoolean.Equals(myObject,myObject2)
mySqlBoolean = mySqlBoolean.op_Equality(mySqlBoolean1,mySqlBoolean2) ' VB
mySqlBoolean = (mySqlBoolean1 == mySqlBoolean2); // C#
```

Parameters

`mySqlBoolean1`	A SqlBoolean object.
`mySqlBoolean2`	A SqlBoolean object.
`myObject`	Any System.Object or descendant.
`myObject2`	Any System.Object or descendant.

False

The False field represents a read-only False value that can be assigned to a SqlBoolean object.

Usage

```
mySqlBoolean = mySqlBoolean.False
```

Parameters

None.

GetHashCode

The GetHashCode method returns a hash code for the SqlBoolean value. The hash code represents a unique value corresponding to the particular value of the SqlBoolean object. Requesting the hash code for a null SqlBoolean will return 0.

BE CAREFUL **The hash code returned for a False SqlBoolean is 0, which is the same for a SqlBoolean with a null value.**

Usage

```
myInt32 = mySqlBoolean.GetHashCode()
```

Parameters

None.

IsFalse

The read-only IsFalse property returns a Boolean indicating whether the SqlBoolean is False. The value will be True if the value of the SqlBoolean is False and False if it is True.

In addition to the IsFalse property, you may also use the op_False operator method, or, if your language supports overloaded operators, you may use that construct instead.

NOTE **Now you can really keep your code confusing!**

Usage

```
myBoolean = mySqlBoolean.IsFalse
myBoolean = mySqlBoolean.op_False(mySqlBoolean) ' VB
myBoolean = (MySqlBoolean ? false : true); // C#
```

Parameters

`mySqlBoolean`	A SqlBoolean object.

IsNull

The read-only IsNull property returns a Boolean indicating whether the SqlBoolean is null. The value will be True if the value of the SqlBoolean is null and False otherwise.

Usage

```
myBoolean = mySqlBoolean.IsNull
```

Parameters

None.

IsTrue

The read-only IsTrue property returns a Boolean indicating whether the SqlBoolean is True. The value will be True if the value of the SqlBoolean is True and False if it is False.

In addition to the IsTrue property, you may also use the op_True operator method, or, if your language supports overloaded operators, you may use that construct instead.

Usage

```
myBoolean = mySqlBoolean.IsTrue
myBoolean = mySqlBoolean.op_True(mySqlBoolean) ' VB
myBoolean = (MySqlBoolean ? true : false); // C#
```

Parameters

None.

NotEquals

The NotEquals method compares two SqlBoolean values and returns a SqlBoolean value indicating whether the two SqlBoolean values are not equal. A null value would indicate that one of the SqlBoolean values is null.

In addition to the NotEquals method, you may also use the op_Inequality operator method, or, if your language supports overloaded operators, you may use that construct instead.

Usage

```
mySqlBoolean = mySqlBoolean.NotEquals(mySqlBoolean1,mySqlBoolean2)
mySqlBoolean = _
   mySqlBoolean.op_Inequality(mySqlBoolean1,mySqlBoolean2) ' VB
mySqlBoolean = (mySqlBoolean1 != mySqlBoolean2); // C#
```

Parameters

`mySqlBoolean1`	A SqlBoolean object.
`mySqlBoolean2`	A SqlBoolean object.

Null

The Null field represents a read-only null value that can be assigned to a SqlBoolean object. You cannot use the standard .NET way of assigning a null value with the System.DBNull.Value, but rather you must use this approach.

Usage

```
mySqlBoolean = mySqlBoolean.Null
```

Parameters

None.

One

The One field represents a read-only value of (1) that can be assigned to a SqlBoolean object. This is functionally equivalent to assigning a value of True.

Usage

```
mySqlBoolean = mySqlBoolean.One
```

Parameters

None.

OnesComplement

The OnesComplement method will return the bitwise one's complement of the specified SqlBoolean. This will effectively toggle the SqlBoolean value. If the SqlBoolean value that you are complementing is null, then the method will return a null value.

In addition to the OnesComplement method, you may also use the op_OnesComplement operator method, or, if your language supports overloaded operators, you may use that construct instead.

NOTE The one's complement operator is sometimes referred to as the *bitwise complement* or *bitwise not* operator.

Usage

```
mySqlBoolean = mySqlBoolean.OnesComplement(mySqlBoolean2)
mySqlBoolean = mySqlBoolean.op_OnesComplement(mySqlBoolean2) ' VB
mySqlBoolean = ~ mySqlBoolean2; // C#
```

Parameters

mySqlBoolean2	A SqlBoolean object.

op_Explicit

The op_Explicit method represents a special SqlBoolean converter that allows SqlBoolean values to be assigned from other SqlTypes. This method is overloaded in several ways. The example that follows shows how to retrieve the SqlBoolean value as a simple Boolean. The other examples show how to assign the SqlBoolean value.

When assigning the SqlBoolean value from one of the numeric SqlTypes, any nonzero numeric value becomes a True. A zero value becomes a False. A null value becomes a null.

When assigning the SqlBoolean value from a SqlString object, a numeric value that parses to a nonzero value or the string "True" becomes a True. A value that parses to "0" or "False" becomes a False. Converting from a SqlString object can throw a FormatException if ADO.NET can't parse the string.

If you are using ADO.NET with C#, then you will not call the op_Explicit method directly, but rather you are allowed to cast from one SqlType to the other.

Usage

```
myBoolean = mySqlBoolean.op_Explicit(mySqlBoolean)     ' Visual Basic .NET
myBoolean = (Boolean)mySqlBoolean;                     // C#
mySqlBoolean = mySqlBoolean.op_Explicit(mySqlByte)     ' Visual Basic .NET
mySqlBoolean = (SqlBoolean)mySqlByte;                  // C#
mySqlBoolean = mySqlBoolean.op_Explicit(mySqlDecimal)  ' Visual Basic .NET
mySqlBoolean = (SqlBoolean)mySqlDecimal;               // C#
mySqlBoolean = mySqlBoolean.op_Explicit(mySqlDouble)   ' Visual Basic .NET
mySqlBoolean = (SqlBoolean)mySqlDouble;                // C#
mySqlBoolean = mySqlBoolean.op_Explicit(mySqlInt16)    ' Visual Basic .NET
mySqlBoolean = (SqlBoolean)mySqlInt16;                 // C#
mySqlBoolean = mySqlBoolean.op_Explicit(mySqlInt32)    ' Visual Basic .NET
mySqlBoolean = (SqlBoolean)mySqlInt32;                 // C#
mySqlBoolean = mySqlBoolean.op_Explicit(mySqlInt64)    ' Visual Basic .NET
mySqlBoolean = (SqlBoolean)mySqlInt64;                 // C#
mySqlBoolean = mySqlBoolean.op_Explicit(mySqlMoney)    ' Visual Basic .NET
mySqlBoolean = (SqlBoolean)mySqlMoney;                 // C#
mySqlBoolean = mySqlBoolean.op_Explicit(mySqlSingle)   ' Visual Basic .NET
mySqlBoolean = (SqlBoolean)mySqlSingle;                // C#
mySqlBoolean = mySqlBoolean.op_Explicit(mySqlString)   ' Visual Basic .NET
mySqlBoolean = (SqlBoolean)mySqlString;                // C#
```

Parameters

mySqlByte	A SqlByte object.
mySqlDecimal	A SqlDecimal object.
mySqlDouble	A SqlDouble object.

`mySqlInt16`	A SqlInt16 object.
`mySqlInt32`	A SqlInt32 object.
`mySqlInt64`	A SqlInt64 object.
`mySqlMoney`	A SqlMoney object.
`mySqlSingle`	A SqlSingle object.
`mySqlString`	A SqlString object.

Exceptions

FormatException	ADO.NET couldn't parse the string.
SqlNullValueException	You cannot assign a null value to a Boolean class. Be sure to check the IsNull property, or use another exception-handling technique.

op_Implicit

The op_Implicit method represents a special SqlBoolean converter that allows for a Boolean value to be assigned to the SqlBoolean.

If you are using ADO.NET with C#, then you will not call the op_Implicit method directly, but rather you are allowed to cast from one SqlType to the other.

Usage

```
mySqlBoolean = mySqlBoolean.op_Implicit(myBoolean) ' VB
mySqlBoolean = (SqlBoolean)myBoolean; // C#
```

Parameters

`myBoolean`	A Boolean object.

op_LogicalNot

The op_LogicalNot operator method performs a Boolean not operation on a SqlBoolean, essentially toggling its value. The method returns a SqlBoolean object. If the value being toggled is null, the resulting SqlBoolean will be null. If your language supports overloaded operators, you may use that construct instead.

NOTE Given how thorough System.Data.SqlTypes is, it's funny that there is not a corresponding SqlBoolean.Not() method.

Usage

```
mySqlBoolean = mySqlBoolean.op_LogicalNot(mySqlBoolean) ' VB
mySqlBoolean = ! mySqlBoolean; // C#
```

Parameters

`mySqlBoolean`	A SqlBoolean object.

Or

The Or method performs a Boolean or operation on two SqlBoolean values. The method returns a SqlBoolean object. If either SqlBoolean values are True, the resulting value will be True; otherwise, it will be False. If either of the two values being compared is null, the resulting SqlBoolean will be null.

In addition to the Or method, you may also use the op_BitwiseOr operator method, or, if your language supports overloaded operators, you may use that construct instead.

Usage

```
mySqlBoolean = mySqlBoolean.Or(mySqlBoolean1,mySqlBoolean2)
mySqlBoolean = mySqlBoolean.op_BitwiseOr(mySqlBoolean1,mySqlBoolean2) ' VB
mySqlBoolean = (mySqlBoolean1 | mySqlBoolean2); // C#
```

Parameters

`mySqlBoolean1`	A SqlBoolean object.
`mySqlBoolean2`	A SqlBoolean object.

Parse

The Parse method will evaluate a string and return a SqlBoolean. If the string contains a nonzero number, the SqlBoolean will be True. If the string contains a zero, the SqlBoolean will be False. If the string contains the words "True" or "False" (case insensitive), then the SqlBoolean will be returned accordingly. Keep in mind that converting from a String can throw a FormatException if ADO.NET can't parse the string.

Usage

```
mySqlBoolean = mySqlBoolean.Parse(myString)
```

Parameters

`myString`	A case-insensitive String object containing a valid Boolean value, such as "0", "1", "true", "false".

Exceptions

FormatException	ADO.NET couldn't parse the string.

ToSqlByte

The ToSqlByte method returns the SqlBoolean value as a SqlByte (8-bit integer). A null value would indicate that the SqlBoolean value is null.

Usage

```
mySqlByte = mySqlBoolean.ToSqlByte()
```

Parameters

None.

ToSqlDecimal

The ToSqlDecimal method returns the SqlBoolean value as a SqlDecimal. A null value would indicate that the SqlBoolean value is null.

Usage

```
mySqlDecimal = mySqlBoolean.ToSqlDecimal()
```

Parameters

None.

ToSqlDouble

The ToSqlDouble method returns the SqlBoolean value as a SqlDouble. A null value would indicate that the SqlBoolean value is null.

Usage

```
mySqlDouble = mySqlBoolean.ToSqlDouble()
```

Parameters

None.

ToSqlInt16

The ToSqlInt16 method returns the SqlBoolean value as a SqlInt16 (16-bit integer). A null value would indicate that the SqlBoolean value is null.

Usage

```
mySqlInt16 = mySqlBoolean.ToSqlInt16()
```

Parameters

None.

ToSqlInt32

The ToSqlInt32 method returns the SqlBoolean value as a SqlInt32 (32-bit integer). A null value would indicate that the SqlBoolean value is null.

Usage

```
mySqlInt32 = mySqlBoolean.ToSqlInt32()
```

Parameters

None.

ToSqlInt64

The ToSqlInt64 method returns the SqlBoolean value as a SqlInt64 (64-bit integer). A null value would indicate that the SqlBoolean value is null.

Usage

```
mySqlInt64 = mySqlBoolean.ToSqlInt64()
```

Parameters

None.

ToSqlMoney

The ToSqlMoney method returns the SqlBoolean value as a SqlMoney. A null value would indicate that the SqlBoolean value is null.

Usage

```
mySqlMoney = mySqlBoolean.ToSqlMoney()
```

Parameters

None.

ToSqlSingle

The ToSqlSingle method returns the SqlBoolean value as a SqlSingle. A null value would indicate that the SqlBoolean value is null.

Usage

```
mySqlSingle = mySqlBoolean.ToSqlSingle()
```

Parameters

None.

ToSqlString

The ToSqlString method returns the SqlBoolean value as a SqlString. A null value would indicate that the SqlBoolean value is null.

Usage

```
mySqlString = mySqlBoolean.ToSqlString()
```

Parameters

None.

ToString

The ToString method returns the SqlBoolean value as a readable value, "True", "False", or "Null".

Usage

```
myString = mySqlBoolean.ToString()
```

Parameters

None.

True

The True field represents a read-only True value that can be assigned to a SqlBoolean object.

Usage

```
mySqlBoolean = mySqlBoolean.True
```

Parameters

None.

Value

The read-only Value property allows you to retrieve the value of the SqlBoolean. Remember that this property is read-only—you may not assign a SqlBoolean its value using its Value property.

In addition to using the Value property, you may also use the op_Explicit conversion method, or, if your language supports overloaded operators, you may use that construct instead.

Usage

```
myBoolean = mySqlBoolean.Value                          ' Visual Basic .NET
myBoolean = mySqlBoolean.op_Explicit(mySqlBoolean) ' Visual Basic .NET
myBoolean = (Boolean)mySqlBoolean;                      // C#
```

Parameters

None.

Exceptions

SqlNullValueException	You cannot retrieve a null value. Be sure to check the IsNull property, or use another exception-handling technique.

Xor

The Xor method performs a Boolean xor operation—a bitwise exclusive OR operation on two SqlBoolean values. The method returns a SqlBoolean object. If exactly one of the two SqlBoolean values is true, the resulting value will be True. If both operands have the same value, the resulting value will be False. If either of the two values being compared is null, the resulting SqlBoolean will be null.

In addition to the Xor method, you may also use the op_ExclusiveOr operator method, or, if your language supports overloaded operators, you may use that construct instead.

Usage

```
mySqlBoolean = mySqlBoolean.Xor(mySqlBoolean1,mySqlBoolean2)
mySqlBoolean = _
   mySqlBoolean.op_ExclusiveOr(mySqlBoolean1,mySqlBoolean2) ' VB
mySqlBoolean = mySqlBoolean1 ^ mySqlBoolean2; // C#
```

Parameters

`mySqlBoolean1`	A SqlBoolean object.
`mySqlBoolean2`	A SqlBoolean object.

Zero

The Zero field represents a read-only value of (0) that can be assigned to a SqlBoolean object. This is functionally equivalent to assigning a value of False.

Usage

```
mySqlBoolean = mySqlBoolean.Zero
```

Parameters

None.

System.Data.SqlTypes.SqlByte

The SqlByte structure represents a single byte value that is an 8-bit unsigned integer in the range of 0 through 255 inclusive. SqlByte is the structure you would use to manipulate the following SQL Server data types:

- tinyint
- sql_variant (if the data is of type tinyint)

Constructors

```
Dim mySqlByte As New SqlByte(myByte)
```

Parameters

`myByte` A Byte object.

SqlByte Sample Code

```
Private Sub ReadSqlType(ByVal myConnectionString As String, _
                        ByVal myCommandText As String)
   Dim mySqlConnection As System.Data.SqlClient.SqlConnection
   Dim mySqlDataReader As System.Data.SqlClient.SqlDataReader
   Dim mySqlCommand As System.Data.SqlClient.SqlCommand
   Dim mySqlByte As System.Data.SqlTypes.SqlByte
   ' Establish connection
   mySqlConnection = New SqlConnection(myConnectionString)
   mySqlConnection.Open()
   ' Build and execute command
   mySqlCommand = New SqlCommand(myCommandText)
   mySqlCommand.Connection = mySqlConnection
   mySqlDataReader = mySqlCommand.ExecuteReader
   ' Read first row
   If mySqlDataReader.Read Then
      ' Save column as appropriate SqlTypes structure
      mySqlByte = mySqlDataReader.GetSqlByte(1)
      MessageBox.Show(mySqlByte.ToString)
   End If
   ' Done
   mySqlConnection.Close()
End Sub
```

Members

Add

The Add method will add two SqlByte values together and return a SqlByte object whose Value property contains the results of the addition. Keep in mind the MinValue and MaxValue that a SqlByte can hold. If either SqlByte value is null, the resulting SqlByte will be null.

In addition to the Add method, you may also use the op_Addition operator method, or, if your language supports overloaded operators, you may use that construct instead.

Usage

```
mySqlByte = mySqlByte.Add(mySqlByte1,mySqlByte2)
mySqlByte = mySqlByte.op_Addition(mySqlByte1,mySqlByte2) ' VB
mySqlByte = mySqlByte1 + mySqlByte2; // C#
```

Parameters

`mySqlByte1`	A SqlByte object.
`mySqlByte2`	A SqlByte object.

Exceptions

OverflowException	The operation returned a value outside of the range of a SqlByte value.

BitwiseAnd

The BitwiseAnd method performs a Boolean and operation on two SqlByte objects. The method returns a SqlByte object. If either of the two values being compared is null, the resulting SqlByte will be null.

In addition to the BitwiseAnd method, you may also use the op_BitwiseAnd operator method, or, if your language supports overloaded operators, you may use that construct instead.

Usage

```
mySqlByte = mySqlByte.BitwiseAnd(mySqlByte1,mySqlByte2)
mySqlByte = mySqlByte.op_BitwiseAnd(mySqlByte1,mySqlByte2) ' VB
mySqlByte = mySqlByte1 & mySqlByte2; // C#
```

Parameters

`mySqlByte1`	A SqlByte object.
`mySqlByte2`	A SqlByte object.

BitwiseOr

The BitwiseOr method performs a Boolean or operation on two SqlByte objects. The method returns a SqlByte object. If either of the two values being compared is null, the resulting SqlByte will be null.

In addition to the BitwiseOr method, you may also use the op_BitwiseOr operator method, or, if your language supports overloaded operators, you may use that construct instead.

Usage

```
mySqlByte = mySqlByte.BitwiseOr(mySqlByte1,mySqlByte2)
mySqlByte = mySqlByte.op_BitwiseOr(mySqlByte1,mySqlByte2) ' VB
mySqlByte = mySqlByte1 | mySqlByte2; // C#
```

Parameters

`mySqlByte1`	A SqlByte object.
`mySqlByte2`	A SqlByte object.

CompareTo

The CompareTo method allows you to compare the SqlByte value with another supplied object to return an indication of their relative values. The returned Int32 object will indicate the comparison:

Less than Zero. The SqlByte value was less than the supplied object, or the SqlByte was null.

Zero. The SqlByte value was the same as the supplied object.

Greater than zero. The SqlByte value was greater than the supplied object, or the object was null.

Usage

```
myInt32 = mySqlByte.CompareTo(myObject)
```

Parameters

`myObject`	Any object that implements the IComparable interface.

Exceptions

ArgumentException	The supplied object isn't valid for comparison.

Divide

The Divide method will divide the first SqlByte by the second SqlByte. This method will return a SqlByte object whose Value property contains the results of the division. Because a SqlByte object can store only whole numbers, any remainders after the division will be discarded. If either SqlByte value is null, the resulting SqlByte will be null.

In addition to the Divide method, you may also use the op_Division operator method or, if your language supports overloaded operators, you may use that construct instead.

Usage

```
mySqlByte = mySqlByte.Divide(mySqlByte1,mySqlByte2)
mySqlByte = mySqlByte.op_Division(mySqlByte1,mySqlByte2) ' VB
mySqlByte = mySqlByte1 / mySqlByte2; // C#
```

Parameters

`mySqlByte1`	A SqlByte object.
`mySqlByte2`	A SqlByte object.

Exceptions

DivideByZeroException	You tried to divide by zero.

Equals

The Equals method allows you to compare the SqlByte value with a supplied object or compare the values of two supplied objects or SqlByte values. The result will be either a Boolean or a SqlBoolean, depending on which overloaded method is called. The result may be null if either of the SqlByte values being compared is null.

In addition to the Equals method, you may also use the op_Equality operator method, or, if your language supports overloaded operators, you may use that construct instead.

Usage

```
mySqlBoolean = mySqlByte.Equals(mySqlByte1,mySqlByte2)
myBoolean = mySqlByte.Equals(myObject)
myBoolean = mySqlByte.Equals(myObject,myObject2)
mySqlBoolean = mySqlByte.op_Equality(mySqlByte1,mySqlByte2) ' VB
mySqlBoolean = (mySqlByte1 == mySqlByte2); // C#
```

Parameters

`mySqlByte1`	A SqlByte object.
`mySqlByte2`	A SqlByte object.
`myObject`	Any System.Object or descendant.
`myObject2`	Any System.Object or descendant.

GetHashCode

The GetHashCode method returns a hash code for the SqlByte value. The hash code represents a unique value corresponding to the particular value of the SqlByte object. Keep in mind that even the smallest change to the SqlByte value will result in a different hash code. Requesting the hash code for a SqlInt16 object with a null value will return 0.

NOTE **Be careful because the hash code returned for a SqlByte with a value of 0 is 0, which is the same for a SqlByte with a null value.**

Usage

```
myInt32 = mySqlByte.GetHashCode()
```

Parameters

None.

GreaterThan

The GreaterThan method compares two SqlByte values and returns a SqlBoolean value indicating whether the first SqlByte value is greater than the second SqlByte value. A null value would indicate that one of the SqlByte values is null.

In addition to the GreaterThan method, you may also use the op_GreaterThan operator method, or, if your language supports overloaded operators, you may use that construct instead.

Usage

```
mySqlBoolean = mySqlByte.GreaterThan(mySqlByte1,mySqlByte2)
mySqlBoolean = mySqlByte.op_GreaterThan(mySqlByte1,mySqlByte2) ' VB
mySqlBoolean = (mySqlByte1 > mySqlByte2); // C#
```

Parameters

`mySqlByte1`	A SqlByte object.
`mySqlByte2`	A SqlByte object.

GreaterThanOrEqual

The GreaterThanOrEqual method compares two SqlByte values and returns a SqlBoolean value indicating whether the first SqlByte value is greater than or equal to the second SqlByte value. A null value would indicate that one of the SqlByte values is null.

In addition to the GreaterThanOrEqual method, you may also use the op_GreaterThanOrEqual operator method, or, if your language supports overloaded operators, you may use that construct instead.

Usage

```
mySqlBoolean = mySqlByte.GreaterThanOrEqual(mySqlByte1,mySqlByte2)
mySqlBoolean = mySqlByte.op_GreaterThanOrEqual(mySqlByte1,mySqlByte2) ' VB
mySqlBoolean = (mySqlByte1 >= mySqlByte2); // C#
```

Parameters

`mySqlByte1`	A SqlByte object.
`mySqlByte2`	A SqlByte object.

IsNull

The read-only IsNull property returns a Boolean indicating whether the SqlByte is null. The value will be True if the value of the SqlByte is null and False if it is otherwise.

Usage

```
myBoolean = mySqlByte.IsNull
```

Parameters

None.

LessThan

The LessThan method compares two SqlByte values and returns a SqlBoolean value indicating whether the first SqlByte value is less than the second SqlByte value. A null value would indicate that one of the SqlByte values is null.

In addition to the LessThan method, you may also use the op_LessThan operator method, or, if your language supports overloaded operators, you may use that construct instead.

Usage

```
mySqlBoolean = mySqlByte.LessThan(mySqlByte1,mySqlByte2)
mySqlBoolean = mySqlByte.op_LessThan(mySqlByte1,mySqlByte2) ' VB
mySqlBoolean = (mySqlByte1 < mySqlByte2); // C#
```

Parameters

`mySqlByte1`	A SqlByte object.
`mySqlByte2`	A SqlByte object.

LessThanOrEqual

The LessThanOrEqual method compares two SqlByte values and returns a SqlBoolean value indicating whether the first SqlByte value is less than or equal to the second SqlByte value. A null value would indicate that one of the SqlByte values is null.

In addition to the LessThanOrEqual method, you may also use the op_LessThanOrEqual operator method, or, if your language supports overloaded operators, you may use that construct instead.

Usage

```
mySqlBoolean = mySqlByte.LessThanOrEqual(mySqlByte1,mySqlByte2)
mySqlBoolean = mySqlByte.op_LessThanOrEqual(mySqlByte1,mySqlByte2) ' VB
mySqlBoolean = (mySqlByte1 <= mySqlByte2); // C#
```

Parameters

`mySqlByte1`	A SqlByte object.
`mySqlByte2`	A SqlByte object.

MaxValue

The read-only MaxValue field represents the largest number that a SqlByte can hold, which is 255. By using the MaxValue field, you can build flexible, readable exception-handling code.

Usage

```
mySqlByte = mySqlByte.MaxValue
```

Parameters

None.

MinValue

The read-only MinValue field represents the smallest number that a SqlByte can hold, which is 0. By using the MinValue field, you can build flexible, readable exception-handling code.

Usage

```
mySqlByte = mySqlByte.MinValue
```

Parameters

None.

Mod

The Mod method will divide the first SqlByte by the second SqlByte and return only the modulus (remainder portion) as a SqlByte object. If either SqlByte value is null, the resulting SqlByte will be null.

In addition to the Mod method, you may also use the op_Modulus operator method, or, if your language supports overloaded operators, you may use that construct instead.

Usage

```
mySqlByte = mySqlByte.Mod(mySqlByte1,mySqlByte2)
mySqlByte = mySqlByte.op_Modulus(mySqlByte1,mySqlByte2) ' VB
mySqlByte = mySqlByte1 % mySqlByte2; // C#
```

Parameters

mySqlByte1	A SqlByte object.
mySqlByte2	A SqlByte object.

Exceptions

DivideByZeroException	You tried to divide by zero.

Multiply

The Multiply method will multiply the first SqlByte by the second SqlByte and return a SqlByte object whose Value property contains the results of the multiplication. Keep in mind the MaxValue that a SqlByte can hold. If either SqlByte value is null, the resulting SqlByte will be null.

In addition to the Multiply method, you may also use the op_Multiply operator method, or, if your language supports overloaded operators, you may use that construct instead.

Usage

```
mySqlByte = mySqlByte.Multiply(mySqlByte1,mySqlByte2)
mySqlByte = mySqlByte.op_Multiply(mySqlByte1,mySqlByte2) ' VB
mySqlByte = mySqlByte1 * mySqlByte2; // C#
```

Parameters

mySqlByte1	A SqlByte object.
mySqlByte2	A SqlByte object.

Exceptions

OverflowException	The operation returned a value outside of the range of a SqlByte value.

NotEquals

The NotEquals method compares two SqlByte values and returns a SqlBoolean value indicating whether the two SqlByte values are not equal. A null value would indicate that one of the SqlByte values is null.

In addition to the NotEquals method, you may also use the op_Inequality operator method, or, if your language supports overloaded operators, you may use that construct instead.

Usage

```
mySqlBoolean = mySqlByte.NotEquals(mySqlByte1,mySqlByte2)
mySqlBoolean = mySqlByte.op_Inequality(mySqlByte1,mySqlByte2) ' VB
mySqlBoolean = (mySqlByte1 != mySqlByte2); // C#
```

Parameters

mySqlByte1	A SqlByte object.
mySqlByte2	A SqlByte object.

Null

The Null field represents a read-only null value that can be assigned to a SqlByte object. You cannot use the standard .NET way of assigning a null value with the System. DBNull.Value, but rather you must use this approach.

Usage

```
mySqlByte = mySqlByte.Null
```

Parameters

None.

OnesComplement

The OnesComplement method will return the bitwise one's complement of the specified SqlByte. If the SqlByte value that you are complementing is null, then the method will return a null value.

In addition to the OnesComplement method, you may also use the op_OnesComplement operator method, or, if your language supports overloaded operators, you may use that construct instead.

NOTE **The one's complement operator is sometimes referred to as the *bitwise complement* or *bitwise not* operator.**

Usage

```
mySqlByte = mySqlByte.OnesComplement(mySqlByte2)
mySqlByte = mySqlByte.op_OnesComplement(mySqlByte2) ' VB
mySqlByte = ~ mySqlByte2; // C#
```

Parameters

`mySqlByte2`	A SqlByte object.

op_Explicit

The op_Explicit method represents a special SqlByte converter that allows SqlByte values to be assigned from other SqlTypes. This method is overloaded in several ways. The first two examples that follow show how to retrieve the SqlByte value as a simple Byte. The other examples show how to assign the SqlByte value.

When assigning the SqlByte value from one of the other SqlTypes, keep in mind the MinValue and MaxValue. Any value that exceeds those limits will throw an OverflowException. Any null values will convert to a SqlByte null value.

When assigning the SqlByte value from a SqlString object, be sure that the string parses to a valid SqlByte value. Converting from a SqlString object can throw a FormatException if ADO.NET can't parse the string.

If you are using ADO.NET with C#, then you will not call the op_Explicit method directly, but rather you are allowed to cast from one SqlType to the other.

Usage

```
myByte = mySqlByte.op_Explicit(mySqlByte)         ' Visual Basic .NET
myByte = (Byte)mySqlByte;                         // C#
mySqlByte = mySqlByte.op_Explicit(mySqlBoolean)   ' Visual Basic .NET
mySqlByte = (SqlByte)mySqlBoolean;                // C#
```

```
mySqlByte = mySqlByte.op_Explicit(mySqlDecimal) ' Visual Basic .NET
mySqlByte = (SqlByte)mySqlDecimal;              // C#
mySqlByte = mySqlByte.op_Explicit(mySqlDouble)  ' Visual Basic .NET
mySqlByte = (SqlByte)mySqlDouble;               // C#
mySqlByte = mySqlByte.op_Explicit(mySqlInt16)   ' Visual Basic .NET
mySqlByte = (SqlByte)mySqlInt16;                // C#
mySqlByte = mySqlByte.op_Explicit(mySqlInt32)   ' Visual Basic .NET
mySqlByte = (SqlByte)mySqlInt32;                // C#
mySqlByte = mySqlByte.op_Explicit(mySqlInt64)   ' Visual Basic .NET
mySqlByte = (SqlByte)mySqlInt64;                // C#
mySqlByte = mySqlByte.op_Explicit(mySqlMoney)   ' Visual Basic .NET
mySqlByte = (SqlByte)mySqlMoney;                // C#
mySqlByte = mySqlByte.op_Explicit(mySqlSingle)  ' Visual Basic .NET
mySqlByte = (SqlByte)mySqlSingle;               // C#
mySqlByte = mySqlByte.op_Explicit(mySqlString)  ' Visual Basic .NET
mySqlByte = (SqlByte)mySqlString;               // C#
```

Parameters

`mySqlBoolean`	A SqlBoolean object.
`mySqlDecimal`	A SqlDecimal object.
`mySqlDouble`	A SqlDouble object.
`mySqlInt16`	A SqlInt16 object.
`mySqlInt32`	A SqlInt32 object.
`mySqlInt64`	A SqlInt64 object.
`mySqlMoney`	A SqlMoney object.
`mySqlSingle`	A SqlSingle object.
`mySqlString`	A SqlString object.

Exceptions

FormatException	ADO.NET couldn't parse the string.
OverflowException	The operation returned a value outside of the range of a SqlByte value.
SqlNullValueException	You cannot assign a null value to a Byte class. Be sure to check the IsNull property, or use another exception-handling technique.

op_Implicit

The op_Implicit method represents a special SqlByte converter that allows for a Byte value to be assigned to the SqlByte. If you are using ADO.NET with C#, then you will not call the op_Implicit method directly, but rather you are allowed to cast from one SqlType to the other.

Usage

```
mySqlByte = mySqlByte.op_Implicit(myByte) ' Visual Basic .NET
mySqlByte = (SqlByte)myByte;              // C#
```

Parameters

`myByte`	A Byte object.

Parse

The Parse method will evaluate a string and return a SqlByte. Keep in mind that converting from a String can throw a FormatException if ADO.NET can't parse the string.

Usage

```
mySqlByte = mySqlByte.Parse(myString)
```

Parameters

`myString`	A case-insensitive String object containing a valid Byte value, such as "0", "100", or "255".

Exceptions

OverflowException	The operation returned a value outside of the range of a SqlByte value.
FormatException	ADO.NET couldn't parse the string.

Subtract

The Subtract method will subtract the second SqlByte from the first SqlByte and return a SqlByte object whose Value property contains the results of the subtraction. Keep in mind the MinValue and MaxValue that a SqlByte can hold. If either SqlByte value is null, the resulting SqlByte will be null.

In addition to the Subtract method, you may also use the op_Subtraction operator method, or, if your language supports overloaded operators, you may use that construct instead.

Usage

```
mySqlByte = mySqlByte.Subtract(mySqlByte1,mySqlByte2)
mySqlByte = mySqlByte.op_Subtraction(mySqlByte1,mySqlByte2) ' VB
mySqlByte = mySqlByte1 - mySqlByte2; // C#
```

Parameters

`mySqlByte1`	A SqlByte object.
`mySqlByte2`	A SqlByte object.

Exceptions

OverflowException	The operation returned a value outside of the range of a SqlByte value.

ToSqlBoolean

The ToSqlBoolean method returns the SqlByte value as a SqlBoolean object. Any nonzero SqlByte value will return in a True SqlBoolean. A zero SqlByte value will return a False SqlBoolean. A null SqlByte value will return a null SqlBoolean.

Usage

```
mySqlBoolean = mySqlByte.ToSqlBoolean()
```

Parameters

None.

ToSqlDecimal

The ToSqlDecimal method returns the SqlByte value as a SqlDecimal. A null value would indicate that the SqlByte value is null.

Usage

```
mySqlDecimal = mySqlByte.ToSqlDecimal()
```

Parameters

None.

ToSqlDouble

The ToSqlDouble method returns the SqlByte value as a SqlDouble. A null value would indicate that the SqlByte value is null.

Usage

```
mySqlDouble = mySqlByte.ToSqlDouble()
```

Parameters

None.

ToSqlInt16

The ToSqlInt16 method returns the SqlByte value as a SqlInt16 (16-bit integer). A null value would indicate that the SqlByte value is null.

Usage

```
mySqlInt16 = mySqlByte.ToSqlInt16()
```

Parameters

None.

ToSqlInt32

The ToSqlInt32 method returns the SqlByte value as a SqlInt32 (32-bit integer). A null value would indicate that the SqlByte value is null.

Usage

```
mySqlInt32 = mySqlByte.ToSqlInt32()
```

Parameters

None.

ToSqlInt64

The ToSqlInt64 method returns the SqlByte value as a SqlInt64 (64-bit integer). A null value would indicate that the SqlByte value is null.

Usage

```
mySqlInt64 = mySqlByte.ToSqlInt64()
```

Parameters

None.

ToSqlMoney

The ToSqlMoney method returns the SqlByte value as a SqlMoney. A null value would indicate that the SqlByte value is null.

Usage

```
mySqlMoney = mySqlByte.ToSqlMoney()
```

Parameters

None.

ToSqlSingle

The ToSqlSingle method returns the SqlByte value as a SqlSingle. A null value would indicate that the SqlByte value is null.

Usage

```
mySqlSingle = mySqlByte.ToSqlSingle()
```

Parameters

None.

ToSqlString

The ToSqlString method returns the SqlByte value as a SqlString. A null value would indicate that the SqlByte value is null.

Usage

```
mySqlString = mySqlByte.ToSqlString()
```

Parameters

None.

ToString

The ToString method returns the SqlByte value as a readable value.

Usage

```
myString = mySqlByte.ToString()
```

Parameters

None.

Value

The read-only Value property allows you to retrieve the value of the SqlByte. Remember that this property is read-only—you may not assign a SqlByte its value using its Value property.

In addition to using the Value property, you may also use the op_Explicit conversion method, or, if your language supports overloaded operators, you may use that construct instead.

Usage

```
myByte = mySqlByte.Value                      ' Visual Basic .NET
myByte = mySqlByte.op_Explicit(mySqlByte)  ' Visual Basic .NET
myByte = (Byte)mySqlByte;                     // C#
```

Parameters

None.

Exceptions

SqlNullValueException	You cannot retrieve a null value. Be sure to check the IsNull property, or use another exception-handling technique.

Xor

The Xor method performs a Boolean xor operation—a bitwise exclusive OR operation on two SqlByte values. The method returns a SqlByte object. If either of the two values being compared is null, the resulting SqlByte will be null.

In addition to the Xor method, you may also use the op_ExclusiveOr operator method, or, if your language supports overloaded operators, you may use that construct instead.

Usage

```
mySqlByte = mySqlByte.Xor(mySqlByte1,mySqlByte2)
mySqlByte = mySqlByte.op_ExclusiveOr(mySqlByte1,mySqlByte2) ' VB
mySqlByte = mySqlByte1 ^ mySqlByte2; // C#
```

Parameters

`mySqlByte1`	A SqlByte object.
`mySqlByte2`	A SqlByte object.

Zero

The Zero field represents a read-only value of (0) that can be assigned to a SqlByte object. This is functionally equivalent to assigning a value of MinValue.

Usage

```
mySqlByte = mySqlByte.Zero
```

Parameters

None.

System.Data.SqlTypes.SqlCompareOptions

The SqlCompareOptions enumeration gives you named constants to use when instantiating a SqlString object or verifying later the SqlCompareOptions of a SqlString. The combination of these enumeration values you pass to the constructor will dictate the sorting and comparing behavior of the SqlString object.

These enumeration values correspond to those supported by Sql Server. When you install SQL Server, you are prompted to select a sorting order, such as the Binary sorting order. You may also select one or more sorting styles to use with the Collation Designator (the Windows collation name). With the ability to specify your own SqlCompareOption on the SqlString values you are using in ADO.NET, you may perform comparisons that might not be possible, or very hard to achieve, with stored procedures given the way the server was installed.

By default, when you create a SqlString, the IgnoreCase, IgnoreKanaType, and IgnoreWidth comparison options are automatically selected. This makes it very easy to sort and compare strings.

SqlCompareOptions Enumeration

BinarySort (32768)	ADO.NET will sort and compare based on the bit patterns defined for each character. This means BinarySort forces case sensitivity.
IgnoreCase (1)	ADO.NET will not distinguish between uppercase and lowercase letters. ADO.NET will consider both cases to be equal.
IgnoreKanaType (8)	ADO.NET will not distinguish between the two types of Japanese kana characters: Hiragana and Katakana. ADO.NET will consider Hiragana and Katakana characters to be equal.
IgnoreNonSpace (2)	ADO.NET will not distinguish between accented and unaccented characters. ADO.NET will consider all diacritics of the same letter to be equal.
IgnoreWidth (16)	ADO.NET will not distinguish between single-byte (half-width) and the same character when represented as a double-byte (full-width) character.

None.(0)

Sample Code

```
Dim mySqlString1 As System.Data.SqlTypes.SqlString
Dim mySqlString2 As System.Data.SqlTypes.SqlString
' Remove comment characters and test each comparison
' BinarySort (Uppercase less than lowercase)
mySqlString1 = New _
   SqlString("ADO.NET",1033,SqlCompareOptions.BinarySort)
mySqlString2 = New _
   SqlString("ado.net",1033,SqlCompareOptions.BinarySort)
' IgnoreCase (will be equal)
'mySqlString1 = New _
'   SqlString("ADO.NET",1033,SqlCompareOptions.IgnoreCase)
'mySqlString2 = New _
'   SqlString("ado.net",1033,SqlCompareOptions.IgnoreCase)
' IgnoreNonSpace (will be equal - note the use of the diacritic)
'mySqlString1 = New _
'   SqlString("ADO.NET",1033,SqlCompareOptions.IgnoreNonSpace)
'mySqlString2 = New _
'   SqlString("ÄDO.NET",1033,SqlCompareOptions.IgnoreWidth)
' Compare
If mySqlString1.LessThan(mySqlString1,mySqlString2).IsTrue Then
   MessageBox.Show(mySqlString1.ToString & " < " & _
     mySqlString2.ToString)
ElseIf mySqlString1.GreaterThan(mySqlString1,mySqlString2).IsTrue Then
   MessageBox.Show(mySqlString1.ToString & " > " & _
     mySqlString2.ToString)
```

```
Else
   MessageBox.Show(mySqlString1.ToString & " = " & _
     mySqlString2.ToString)
End If
```

System.Data.SqlTypes.SqlDateTime

The SqlDateTime structure represents a date and time value, which is physically stored in two four-byte integers. The first integer stores the number of days before or after the base date of January 1, 1900, which is the system reference date. The second integer stores the time of the day represented as the number of milliseconds after midnight.

A SqlDateTime object can store dates from January 1, 1753, through December 31, 9999 (which is the end of time as database programmers know it). Time, down to an accuracy of 3.33 milliseconds, can be stored in a SqlDateTime object. SqlDateTime is the structure you would use to manipulate the following SQL Server data types:

- datetime
- smalldatetime
- sql_variant (if the data is one the above types)

Constructors

```
Dim mySqlDateTime As New SqlDateTime(myDateTime)
Dim mySqlDateTime As New SqlDateTime(myDayTicks,myTimeTicks)
Dim mySqlDateTime As New SqlDateTime(myYear,myMonth,myDay)
Dim mySqlDateTime As New SqlDateTime(myYear,myMonth,myDay, _
   myHour,myMinute,mySecond)
Dim mySqlDateTime As New SqlDateTime(myYear,myMonth,myDay, _
   myHour,myMinute,mySecond,myMilliSecond)
Dim mySqlDateTime As New SqlDateTime(myYear,myMonth,myDay, _
   myHour,myMinute,mySecond,myMilliSecond)
Dim mySqlDateTime As New SqlDateTime(myYear,myMonth,myDay, _
   myHour,myMinute,mySecond,myBiliSecond)
```

Parameters

`myDateTime`	A System.DateTime object.
`myDayTicks`	An Int32 object representing the number of days +/- from January 1, 1900.
`myTimeTicks`	An Int32 object representing the number of 3.33 millisecond units from midnight. This value must be positive. A TimeTick of 300 = 1 second.
`myYear`	An Int32 object representing the year. Valid values can be between 1753 and 9999, inclusively.

`myMonth`	An Int32 object representing the month. Valid values can be between 1 and 12, inclusively.
`myDay`	An Int32 object representing the day of the month. Valid values can be between 1 and 31, inclusively. An exception will be thrown if the number of days is higher than the month allows.
`myHour`	An Int32 object representing the hour of the day. Valid values can be between 0 and 23, inclusively.
`myMinute`	An Int32 object representing the minute of the hour. Valid values can be between 0 and 59, inclusively.
`mySecond`	An Int32 object representing the second of the minute. Valid values can be between 0 and 59, inclusively.
`myMilliSecond`	A Double object representing the number of milliseconds (millionths of a second).
`myBiliSecond`	An Int32 object representing the number of biliseconds (billionths of a second).

Exceptions

OverflowException	Invalid parameters were passed to the constructor, and ADO.NET was not able to instantiate a DateTime object with a valid Value.
SqlTypeException	Invalid parameters were passed to the constructor, and ADO.NET was not able to instantiate a DateTime object with a valid Value.

SqlDateTime Sample Code

```
Private Sub ReadSqlType(ByVal myConnectionString As String, _
                        ByVal myCommandText As String)
   Dim mySqlConnection As System.Data.SqlClient.SqlConnection
   Dim mySqlDataReader As System.Data.SqlClient.SqlDataReader
   Dim mySqlCommand As System.Data.SqlClient.SqlCommand
   Dim mySqlDateTime As System.Data.SqlTypes.SqlDateTime
   ' Establish connection
   mySqlConnection = New SqlConnection(myConnectionString)
   mySqlConnection.Open()
   ' Build and execute command
   mySqlCommand = New SqlCommand(myCommandText)
   mySqlCommand.Connection = mySqlConnection
   mySqlDataReader = mySqlCommand.ExecuteReader
   ' Read first row
   If mySqlDataReader.Read Then
      ' Save column as appropriate SqlTypes structure
      mySqlDateTime = mySqlDataReader.GetSqlDateTime(1)
```

```
        MessageBox.Show(mySqlDateTime.ToString)
    End If
    ' Done
    mySqlConnection.Close()
End Sub
```

Members

NOTE It seems that Microsoft forgot to include the Add and Subtract methods to the SqlDateTime structure. They did, however, leave the hidden op_Addition and op_Subtraction methods and, if your language supports overloaded operators, then you can use the (+) and (-) constructs as well. Each of these approaches uses a TimeSpan structure to specify the number of days, hours, minutes, etc. to adjust the SqlDateTime value.

CompareTo

The CompareTo method allows you to compare the SqlDateTime value with another supplied object to return an indication of their relative values. The returned Int32 object will indicate the comparison:

Less than Zero. The SqlDateTime value was less than the supplied object, or the SqlDateTime was null.

Zero. The SqlDateTime value was the same as the supplied object.

Greater than zero. The SqlDateTime value was greater than the supplied object, or the object was null.

Usage

```
myInt32 = mySqlDateTime.CompareTo(myObject)
```

Parameters

`myObject`	Any object that implements the IComparable interface.

Exceptions

ArgumentException	The supplied object doesn't implement the IComparable interface.

DayTicks

The read-only DayTicks property allows you to retrieve the difference in days between the value of SqlDateTime object and January 1, 1900. This value can be positive or negative. Remember that this property is read-only—you may not assign a SqlDateTime its DayTicks value using this property.

If you try to reference the DayTicks value when the SqlDateTime is null, an exception will be thrown.

Usage

```
myInt32 = mySqlDateTime.DayTicks
```

Parameters

None.

Exceptions

SqlNullValueException	You cannot retrieve a null value. Be sure to check the IsNull property, or use another exception-handling technique.

Equals

The Equals method allows you to compare the SqlDateTime value with a supplied object or compare the values of two supplied objects or SqlDateTime values. The result will be either a Boolean or a SqlBoolean, depending on which overloaded method is called. The result may be null if either of the SqlDateTime values being compared were null.

In addition to the Equals method, you may also use the op_Equality operator method, or, if your language supports overloaded operators, you may use that construct instead.

Usage

```
mySqlBoolean = mySqlDateTime.Equals(mySqlDateTime1,mySqlDateTime2)
myBoolean = mySqlDateTime.Equals(myObject)
myBoolean = mySqlDateTime.Equals(myObject,myObject2)
mySqlBoolean = _
   mySqlDateTime.op_Equality(mySqlDateTime1,mySqlDateTime2) ' VB
mySqlBoolean = (mySqlDateTime1 == mySqlDateTime2); // C#
```

Parameters

`mySqlDateTime1`	A SqlDateTime object.
`mySqlDateTime2`	A SqlDateTime object.
`myObject`	Any System.Object or descendant.
`myObject2`	Any System.Object or descendant.

GetHashCode

The GetHashCode method returns a hash code for the SqlDateTime value. The hash code represents a unique value corresponding to the particular value of the SqlDateTime object. Keep in mind that even the smallest change to the SqlDateTime value will result in a different hash code. Requesting the hash code for a SqlDateTime object with a null value will return 0.

NOTE **Be careful because the hash code returned for a SqlDateTime with a value of 0 is 0, which is the same for a SqlDateTime with a null value.**

Usage

```
myInt32 = mySqlDateTime.GetHashCode()
```

Parameters

None.

GreaterThan

The GreaterThan method compares two SqlDateTime values and returns a SqlBoolean value indicating whether the first SqlDateTime value is greater than the second SqlDateTime value. A null value would indicate that one of the SqlDateTime values is null.

In addition to the GreaterThan method, you may also use the op_GreaterThan operator method, or, if your language supports overloaded operators, you may use that construct instead.

Usage

```
mySqlBoolean = mySqlDateTime.GreaterThan(mySqlDateTime1,mySqlDateTime2)
mySqlBoolean = _
   mySqlDateTime.op_GreaterThan(mySqlDateTime1,mySqlDateTime2) ' VB
mySqlBoolean = (mySqlDateTime1 > mySqlDateTime2); // C#
```

Parameters

`mySqlDateTime1`	A SqlDateTime object.
`mySqlDateTime2`	A SqlDateTime object.

GreaterThanOrEqual

The GreaterThanOrEqual method compares two SqlDateTime values and returns a SqlBoolean value indicating whether the first SqlDateTime value is greater than or equal to the second SqlDateTime value. A null value would indicate that one of the SqlDateTime values is null.

In addition to the GreaterThanOrEqual method, you may also use the op_GreaterThanOrEqual operator method, or, if your language supports overloaded operators, you may use that construct instead.

Usage

```
mySqlBoolean = _
   mySqlDateTime.GreaterThanOrEqual(mySqlDateTime1,mySqlDateTime2)
mySqlBoolean = _
   mySqlDateTime.op_GreaterThanOrEqual(mySqlDateTime1,mySqlDateTime2) ' VB
mySqlBoolean = (mySqlDateTime1 >= mySqlDateTime2); // C#
```

Parameters

`mySqlDateTime1`	A SqlDateTime object.
`mySqlDateTime2`	A SqlDateTime object.

IsNull

The read-only IsNull property returns a Boolean indicating whether the SqlDateTime is null. The value will be True if the value of the SqlDateTime is null and False if it is otherwise.

Usage

```
myBoolean = mySqlDateTime.IsNull
```

Parameters

None.

LessThan

The LessThan method compares two SqlDateTime values and returns a SqlBoolean value indicating whether the first SqlDateTime value is less than the second SqlDateTime value. A null value would indicate that one of the SqlDateTime values is null.

In addition to the LessThan method, you may also use the op_LessThan operator method, or, if your language supports overloaded operators, you may use that construct instead.

Usage

```
mySqlBoolean = mySqlDateTime.LessThan(mySqlDateTime1,mySqlDateTime2)
mySqlBoolean = _
   mySqlDateTime.op_LessThan(mySqlDateTime1,mySqlDateTime2) ' VB
mySqlBoolean = (mySqlDateTime1 < mySqlDateTime2); // C#
```

Parameters

`mySqlDateTime1`	A SqlDateTime object.
`mySqlDateTime2`	A SqlDateTime object.

LessThanOrEqual

The LessThanOrEqual method compares two SqlDateTime values and returns a SqlBoolean value indicating whether the first SqlDateTime value is less than or equal to the second SqlDateTime value. A null value would indicate that one of the SqlDateTime values is null.

In addition to the LessThanOrEqual method, you may also use the op_LessThanOrEqual operator method, or, if your language supports overloaded operators, you may use that construct instead.

Usage

```
mySqlBoolean = _
   mySqlDateTime.LessThanOrEqual(mySqlDateTime1,mySqlDateTime2)
mySqlBoolean = _
   mySqlDateTime.op_LessThanOrEqual(mySqlDateTime1,mySqlDateTime2) ' VB
mySqlBoolean = (mySqlDateTime1 <= mySqlDateTime2); // C#
```

Parameters

`mySqlDateTime1`	A SqlDateTime object.
`mySqlDateTime2`	A SqlDateTime object.

MaxValue

The read-only MaxValue field represents the largest number that a SqlDateTime can hold, which is 12/31/1999 11:59:59 PM. By using the MaxValue field, you can build flexible, readable exception-handling code.

Usage

```
mySqlDateTime = mySqlDateTime.MaxValue
```

Parameters

None.

MinValue

The read-only MinValue field represents the smallest number that a SqlDateTime can hold, which is 1/1/1753 12:00:00 AM. By using the MinValue field, you can build flexible, readable exception-handling code.

Usage

```
mySqlDateTime = mySqlDateTime.MinValue
```

Parameters

None.

NotEquals

The NotEquals method compares two SqlDateTime values and returns a SqlBoolean value indicating whether the two SqlDateTime values are not equal. A null value would indicate that one of the SqlDateTime values is null.

In addition to the NotEquals method, you may also use the op_Inequality operator method, or, if your language supports overloaded operators, you may use that construct instead.

Usage

```
mySqlBoolean = mySqlDateTime.NotEquals(mySqlDateTime1,mySqlDateTime2)
mySqlBoolean = _
   mySqlDateTime.op_Inequality(mySqlDateTime1,mySqlDateTime2) ' VB
mySqlBoolean = (mySqlDateTime1 != mySqlDateTime2); // C#
```

Parameters

`mySqlDateTime1`	A SqlDateTime object.
`mySqlDateTime2`	A SqlDateTime object.

Null

The Null field represents a read-only null value that can be assigned to a SqlDateTime object. You cannot use the standard .NET way of assigning a null value with the System.DBNull.Value, but rather you must use this approach.

Usage

```
mySqlDateTime = mySqlDateTime.Null
```

Parameters

None.

op_Explicit

The op_Explicit method represents a special SqlDateTime converter that allows SqlDateTime values to be explicitly assigned to and from other SqlTypes. This method is overloaded in two ways. The first two examples that follow show how to retrieve the SqlDateTime value as a DateTime object. The other examples show how to assign the SqlDateTime value.

When assigning the SqlDateTime value from a SqlString object, be sure that the string parses to a valid SqlDateTime value. Converting from a SqlString object can throw a FormatException if ADO.NET can't parse the string.

If you are using ADO.NET with C#, then you will not call the op_Explicit method directly, but rather you are allowed to cast from one SqlType to the other.

Usage

```
myDateTime = mySqlDateTime.op_Explicit(mySqlDateTime)   ' Visual Basic .NET
myDateTime = (DateTime)mySqlDateTime;                   // C#
mySqlDateTime = mySqlDateTime.op_Explicit(mySqlString) ' Visual Basic .NET
mySqlDateTime = (SqlDateTime)mySqlString;               // C#
```

Parameters

`mySqlDateTime`	A SqlDateTime object.
`mySqlString`	A SqlString object.

Exceptions

FormatException	ADO.NET couldn't parse the string.
SqlNullValueException	You cannot assign a null value to a DateTime class. Be sure to check the IsNull property, or use another exception-handling technique.
SqlTypeException	The operation returned a value outside of the range of a SqlDateTime value.

op_Implicit

The op_Implicit method represents a special SqlDateTime converter that allows SqlDateTime values to be implicitly assigned from a DateTime object.

If you are using ADO.NET with C#, then you will not call the op_Implicit method directly, but rather you are allowed to cast from a DateTime object to a SqlDateTime structure.

Usage

```
mySqlDateTime = mySqlDateTime.op_Implicit(myDateTime) ' Visual Basic .NET
mySqlDateTime = (SqlDateTime)myDateTime;              // C#
```

Parameters

`myDateTime`	A System.DateTime object.

Exceptions

None.

Parse

The Parse method will evaluate a string and return a SqlDateTime. Keep in mind that converting from a String can throw a FormatException if ADO.NET can't parse the string. That having been said, this method is very liberal and accepts most every DateTime format you can imagine.

Usage

```
mySqlDateTime = mySqlDateTime.Parse(myString)
```

Parameters

`myString`	A case-insensitive String object containing a valid DateTime value, such as "12/25/1812", "15 Jul 1968 10:55 AM", "April 19, 1999 16:42:15".

Exceptions

OverflowException	The operation returned a value outside of the range of a SqlDateTime value.
FormatException	ADO.NET couldn't parse the string.

SQLTicksPerHour

The SQLTicksPerHour field represents the number of ticks equivalent to one hour, which is 1,080,000. By using the SQLTicksPerHour field, you can build flexible, readable exception-handling code.

Usage

```
myInt32 = mySqlDateTime.SQLTicksPerHour
```

Parameters

None.

SQLTicksPerMinute

The SQLTicksPerMinute field represents the number of ticks equivalent to one minute, which is 18,000. By using the SQLTicksPerMinute field, you can build flexible, readable exception-handling code.

Usage

```
myInt32 = mySqlDateTime.SQLTicksPerMinute
```

Parameters

None.

SQLTicksPerSecond

The SQLTicksPerSecond field represents the number of ticks equivalent to one second, which is 300. By using the SQLTicksPerSecond field, you can build flexible, readable exception-handling code.

Usage

```
myInt32 = mySqlDateTime.SQLTicksPerSecond
```

Parameters

None.

TimeTicks

The read-only TimeTicks property allows you to retrieve the difference between the time value of SqlDateTime object and midnight, in TimeTicks. You may not assign a SqlDateTime its DayTicks value using this property.

If you try to reference the TimeTicks value when the SqlDateTime is null, an exception will be thrown.

NOTE Remember that 300 TimeTicks equal 1 second.

Usage

```
myInt32 = mySqlDateTime.DayTicks
```

Parameters

None.

Exceptions

SqlNullValueException	You cannot retrieve a null value. Be sure to check the IsNull property, or use another exception-handling technique.

ToSqlString

The ToSqlString method returns the SqlDateTime value as a SqlString. A null value would indicate that the SqlDateTime value is null.

Usage

```
mySqlString = mySqlDateTime.ToSqlString()
```

Parameters

None.

ToString

The ToString method returns the SqlDateTime value as a readable value.

Usage

```
myString = mySqlDateTime.ToString()
```

Parameters

None.

Value

The read-only Value property allows you to retrieve the value of the SqlDateTime. Remember that this property is read-only—you may not assign a SqlDateTime its value using its Value property.

In addition to using the Value property, you may also use the op_Explicit conversion method, or, if your language supports overloaded operators, you may use that construct instead.

NOTE C# handles requests for null SqlDateTime values a bit differently. In Visual Basic .NET, a request of a null SqlDateTime value will throw a SqlNullValueException. C#, however, simply returns a DateTime value of Jan 1, 1900 12:00:00 AM.

Usage

```
myDateTime = mySqlDateTime.Value                          ' Visual Basic .NET
myDateTime = mySqlDateTime.op_Explicit(mySqlDateTime)  ' Visual Basic .NET
myDateTime = (DateTime)mySqlDateTime;                  // C#
```

Parameters

None.

Exceptions

SqlNullValueException	You cannot retrieve a null value. Be sure to check the IsNull property, or use another exception-handling technique.

System.Data.SqlTypes.SqlDecimal

The SqlDecimal structure represents a numeric value with fixed precision and scale. The decimal value may be between -10^{38} and 10^{38}. Use the SqlDecimal to manipulate the following SQL Server data types:

- decimal
- numeric
- sql_variant (if the data is one the above types)

Constructors

```
Dim mySqlDecimal As New SqlDecimal(myDecimal)
Dim mySqlDecimal As New SqlDecimal(myDouble)
Dim mySqlDecimal As New SqlDecimal(myInt32)
Dim mySqlDecimal As New SqlDecimal(myInt64)
Dim mySqlDecimal As New
SqlDecimal(myPrecision,myScale,myPositive,myBits)
Dim mySqlDecimal As New SqlDecimal(myPrecision,myScale,myPositive, _
   myData1,myData2,myData3,myData4)
```

Parameters

`myDecimal`	A Decimal object.
`myDouble`	A Double object.
`myInt32`	An Int32 object (Integer in Visual Basic .NET).
`myInt64`	An Int64 object (Long in Visual Basic .NET).
`myPrecision`	A Byte object indicating the maximum number of digits that can be used to represent the Decimal value.
`myScale`	A Byte object indicating the number of decimal places.

`myPositive`	A Boolean object indicating if the decimal is to be positive (True) or negative (False).
`myBits`	An array of Int32 objects.
`myData1`	An Int32 object.
`myData2`	An Int32 object.
`myData3`	An Int32 object.
`myData4`	An Int32 object.

Exceptions

OverflowException	The operation returned a value outside of the range of a SqlDecimal value. If you are using one of the overloaded constructors that allows you to specify the Precision and Scale, ensure that they are adequate to hold the Value.

SqlDecimal Sample Code

```
Private Sub ReadSqlType(ByVal myConnectionString As String, _
                        ByVal myCommandText As String)
   Dim mySqlConnection As System.Data.SqlClient.SqlConnection
   Dim mySqlDataReader As System.Data.SqlClient.SqlDataReader
   Dim mySqlCommand As System.Data.SqlClient.SqlCommand
   Dim mySqlDecimal As System.Data.SqlTypes.SqlDecimal
   ' Establish connection
   mySqlConnection = New SqlConnection(myConnectionString)
   mySqlConnection.Open()
   ' Build and execute command
   mySqlCommand = New SqlCommand(myCommandText)
   mySqlCommand.Connection = mySqlConnection
   mySqlDataReader = mySqlCommand.ExecuteReader
   ' Read first row
   If mySqlDataReader.Read Then
      ' Save column as appropriate SqlTypes structure
      mySqlDecimal = mySqlDataReader.GetSqlDecimal(1)
      MessageBox.Show(mySqlDecimal.ToString)
   End If
   ' Done
   mySqlConnection.Close()
End Sub
```

Members

Abs

The Abs method will return the absolute value of a given SqlDecimal value. The absolute value of a number is its unsigned magnitude. The absolute value will be returned as SqlDecimal object. If the SqlDecimal value is null, the resulting SqlDecimal will be null.

Usage

```
mySqlDecimal = mySqlDecimal.Abs(mySqlDecimal)
```

Parameters

`mySqlDecimal`	A SqlDecimal object.

Add

The Add method will add two SqlDecimal values together and return a SqlDecimal object whose Value property contains the results of the addition. Keep in mind the MinValue and MaxValue that a SqlDecimal can hold. If either SqlDecimal value is null, the resulting SqlDecimal will be null.

In addition to the Add method, you may also use the op_Addition operator method, or, if your language supports overloaded operators, you may use that construct instead.

Usage

```
mySqlDecimal = mySqlDecimal.Add(mySqlDecimal1, mySqlDecimal2)
mySqlDecimal = mySqlDecimal.op_Addition(mySqlDecimal1, mySqlDecimal2) ' VB
mySqlDecimal = mySqlDecimal1 + mySqlDecimal2; // C#
```

Parameters

`mySqlDecimal1`	A SqlDecimal object.
`mySqlDecimal2`	A SqlDecimal object.

Exceptions

OverflowException	The operation returned a value outside of the range of a SqlDecimal value.

AdjustScale

The AdjustScale method is used to change the scale (number of decimal places) for a given SqlDecimal. Remember, if you decrease the scale, there is a chance that you will lose data. To somewhat alleviate this, you can ask the AdjustScale method to round, rather than truncate, the new value. If the SqlDecimal value is null, the resulting SqlDecimal will be null.

WARNING This method doesn't seem to work as advertised in the Microsoft documentation. The second parameter is actually a *change* in the scale, rather than a new scale value, as you'd be inclined to believe. So, If you wanted to change from a scale of 7 down to 3, you would pass a -4, rather than a 3.

Usage

```
mySqlDecimal =
mySqlDecimal.AdjustScale(mySqlDecimal,myAdjustment,myRound)
```

Parameters

`mySqlDecimal`	A SqlDecimal object.
`myAdjustment`	An Int16 object indicating the change in the number of decimal places in the adjusted structure.

myRound	A Boolean object indicating whether to round (True) or truncate (False).

Exceptions

SqlTruncateException	You have specified an invalid scale adjustment.

BinData

The BinData property returns the value of the SqlDecimal as an array of Byte values, representing the 16 bytes that physically compose the SqlDecimal value in memory. The array returned will always have 16 elements.

Whether the SqlDecimal has a value of 0 or is Null, each array element will contain a Byte value of 0.

NOTE **Here is another example of inconsistency within the SqlTypes namespace. A SqlDecimal structure has a BinData property that performs exactly like the SqlGuid ToByteArray method.**

Usage

```
myByteArray = mySqlDecimal.BinData
```

Parameters

None.

Ceiling

The Ceiling method returns the smallest integer greater than or equal to the specified SqlDecimal. This method returns a SqlDecimal. If the SqlDecimal value is null, the resulting SqlDecimal will be null.

Requesting the ceiling of a SqlDecimal of 125.35 would return 126. Requesting the ceiling of a SqlDecimal of -45 would return -45.

Usage

```
mySqlDecimal = mySqlDecimal.Ceiling()
```

Parameters

None.

Exceptions

None.

CompareTo

The CompareTo method allows you to compare the SqlDecimal value with another supplied object to return an indication of their relative values. The returned Int32 object will indicate the comparison:

Less than Zero. The SqlDecimal value was less than the supplied object, or the SqlDecimal was null.

Zero. The SqlDecimal value was the same as the supplied object.

Greater than zero. The SqlDecimal value was greater than the supplied object, or the object was null.

Usage

```
myInt32 = mySqlDecimal.CompareTo(myObject)
```

Parameters

`myObject`	Any object that implements the IComparable interface.

Exceptions

ArgumentException	The supplied object isn't valid for comparison.

ConvertToPrecScale

Where the AdjustScale method simply altered with scale, the ConvertToPrecScale method allows you to convert a SqlDecimal to a new decimal with a different precision and/or scale.

If the new SqlDecimal has a smaller precision or scale such that data will be lost, ADO.NET will *round* the Value to the new scale, rather than truncate. If the SqlDecimal value is null, the resulting SqlDecimal will be null.

Usage

```
mySqlDecimal = _
   mySqlDecimal.ConvertToPrecScale(mySqlDecimal,myPrecision,myScale)
```

Parameters

`mySqlDecimal`	A SqlDecimal object.
`myPrecision`	An Int32 representing the precision of the new SqlDecimal object.
`myScale`	An Int32 representing the scale of the new SqlDecimal object.

Exceptions

SqlTruncateException	You have specified an invalid precision or scale value. Make sure that your precision is > 0 and < MaxPrecision and that your Scale is >= 0 and <= Precision.
SqlTypeException	You have specified an invalid precision or scale value. Make sure that your precision is > 0 and < MaxPrecision and that your Scale is >= 0 and <= Precision.

Data

The Data property returns the value of the SqlDecimal as an array of Int32 values, representing the 16 bytes that physically compose the SqlDecimal value in memory. The array returned will always have four elements.

Whether the SqlDecimal has a value of 0 or is Null, each array element will contain an Int32 value of 0.

Usage

```
myInt32Array = mySqlDecimal.Data
```

Parameters

None.

Divide

The Divide method will divide the first SqlDecimal by the second SqlDecimal. This method will return a SqlDecimal object whose Value property contains the results of the division. If either SqlDecimal value is null, the resulting SqlDecimal will be null.

In addition to the Divide method, you may also use the op_Division operator method, or, if your language supports overloaded operators, you may use that construct instead.

Usage

```
mySqlDecimal = mySqlDecimal.Divide(mySqlDecimal1,mySqlDecimal2)
mySqlDecimal = mySqlDecimal.op_Division(mySqlDecimal1,mySqlDecimal2) ' VB
mySqlDecimal = mySqlDecimal1 / mySqlDecimal2; // C#
```

Parameters

`mySqlDecimal1`	A SqlDecimal object.
`mySqlDecimal2`	A SqlDecimal object.

Exceptions

DivideByZeroException	You tried to divide by zero.

Equals

The Equals method allows you to compare the SqlDecimal value with a supplied object or compare the values of two supplied objects or SqlDecimal values. The result will be either a Boolean or a SqlBoolean, depending on which overloaded method is called. The result may be null if either of the SqlDecimal values being compared were null.

In addition to the Equals method, you may also use the op_Equality operator method, or, if your language supports overloaded operators, you may use that construct instead.

Usage

```
mySqlBoolean = mySqlDecimal.Equals(mySqlDecimal1,mySqlDecimal2)
myBoolean = mySqlDecimal.Equals(myObject)
myBoolean = mySqlDecimal.Equals(myObject,myObject2)
mySqlBoolean = mySqlDecimal.op_Equality(mySqlDecimal1,mySqlDecimal2) ' VB
mySqlBoolean = (mySqlDecimal1 == mySqlDecimal2); // C#
```

Parameters

`mySqlDecimal1`	A SqlDecimal object.
`mySqlDecimal2`	A SqlDecimal object.
`myObject`	Any System.Object or descendant.
`myObject2`	Any System.Object or descendant.

Floor

The Floor method returns the larger integer less than or equal to the specified SqlDecimal. This method returns a SqlDecimal. If the SqlDecimal value is null, the resulting SqlDecimal will be null.

Requesting the Floor of a SqlDecimal of 125.35 would return 125. Requesting the Floor of a SqlDecimal of -45 would return -45.

Usage
```
mySqlDecimal = mySqlDecimal.Floor()
```

Parameters
None.

Exceptions
None.

GetHashCode

The GetHashCode method returns a hash code for the SqlDecimal value. The hash code represents a unique value corresponding to the particular value of the SqlDecimal object. Keep in mind that even the smallest change to the SqlDecimal value will result in a different hash code. Requesting the hash code for a SqlDecimal object with a null value will return 0.

BE CAREFUL **The hash code returned for a SqlDecimal with a value of 0 is 0, which is the same for a SqlDecimal with a null value.**

Usage
```
myInt32 = mySqlDecimal.GetHashCode()
```

Parameters
None.

GreaterThan

The GreaterThan method compares two SqlDecimal values and returns a SqlBoolean value indicating whether the first SqlDecimal value is greater than the second SqlDecimal value. A null value would indicate that one of the SqlDecimal values is null.

In addition to the GreaterThan method, you may also use the op_GreaterThan operator method, or, if your language supports overloaded operators, you may use that construct instead.

Usage
```
mySqlBoolean = mySqlDecimal.GreaterThan(mySqlDecimal1,mySqlDecimal2)
mySqlBoolean = _
   mySqlDecimal.op_GreaterThan(mySqlDecimal1,mySqlDecimal2) ' VB
mySqlBoolean = mySqlDecimal1 > mySqlDecimal2; // C#
```

Parameters

`mySqlDecimal1`	A SqlDecimal object.
`mySqlDecimal2`	A SqlDecimal object.

GreaterThanOrEqual

The GreaterThanOrEqual method compares two SqlDecimal values and returns a SqlBoolean value indicating whether the first SqlDecimal value is greater than or equal to the second SqlDecimal value. A null value would indicate that one of the SqlDecimal values is null.

In addition to the GreaterThanOrEqual method, you may also use the op_GreaterThanOrEqual operator method, or, if your language supports overloaded operators, you may use that construct instead.

Usage

```
mySqlBoolean = _
   mySqlDecimal.GreaterThanOrEqual(mySqlDecimal1,mySqlDecimal2)
mySqlBoolean = _
  mySqlDecimal.op_GreaterThanOrEqual(mySqlDecimal1,mySqlDecimal2) ' VB
mySqlBoolean = mySqlDecimal1 >= mySqlDecimal2; // C#
```

Parameters

`mySqlDecimal1`	A SqlDecimal object.
`mySqlDecimal2`	A SqlDecimal object.

IsNull

The read-only IsNull property returns a Boolean indicating whether the SqlDecimal is null. The value will be True if the value of the SqlDecimal is null and False if it is otherwise.

Usage

```
myBoolean = mySqlDecimal.IsNull
```

Parameters

None.

IsPositive

The read-only IsPositive property returns a Boolean indicating whether the SqlDecimal is positive. The value will be True if the value of the SqlDecimal is positive, zero, or null and False if it is negative.

NOTE **It's interesting that there is no corresponding IsNegative property. With the SqlBoolean structure, Microsoft gave us both an IsTrue and IsFalse property. They must trust us to use the Not operator with a SqlDecimal!**

Usage

```
myBoolean = mySqlDecimal.IsPositive
```

Parameters

None.

LessThan

The LessThan method compares two SqlDecimal values and returns a SqlBoolean value indicating whether the first SqlDecimal value is less than the second SqlDecimal value. A null value would indicate that one of the SqlDecimal values is null.

In addition to the LessThan method, you may also use the op_LessThan operator method, or, if your language supports overloaded operators, you may use that construct instead.

Usage

```
mySqlBoolean = mySqlDecimal.LessThan(mySqlDecimal1,mySqlDecimal2)
mySqlBoolean = mySqlDecimal.op_LessThan(mySqlDecimal1,mySqlDecimal2) ' VB
mySqlBoolean = mySqlDecimal1 < mySqlDecimal2; // C#
```

Parameters

`mySqlDecimal1`	A SqlDecimal object.
`mySqlDecimal2`	A SqlDecimal object.

LessThanOrEqual

The LessThanOrEqual method compares two SqlDecimal values and returns a SqlBoolean value indicating whether the first SqlDecimal value is less than or equal to the second SqlDecimal value. A null value would indicate that one of the SqlDecimal values is null.

In addition to the LessThanOrEqual method, you may also use the op_LessThanOrEqual operator method, or, if your language supports overloaded operators, you may use that construct instead.

Usage

```
mySqlBoolean = _
   mySqlDecimal.LessThanOrEqual(mySqlDecimal1,mySqlDecimal2)
mySqlBoolean = _
   mySqlDecimal.op_LessThanOrEqual(mySqlDecimal1,mySqlDecimal2) ' VB
mySqlBoolean = mySqlDecimal1 <= mySqlDecimal2; // C#
```

Parameters

`mySqlDecimal1`	A SqlDecimal object.
`mySqlDecimal2`	A SqlDecimal object.

MaxPrecision

The read-only MaxPrecision field represents the highest precision (number of digits) that a SqlDecimal can hold, which is 38. By using the MaxPrecision field, you can build flexible, readable exception-handling code.

Usage

```
mySqlDecimal = mySqlDecimal.MaxPrecision
```

Parameters

None.

MaxScale

The read-only MaxScale field represents the highest scale (number of decimal places) that a SqlDecimal can hold, which is 38 (same as MaxPrecision). By using the MaxScale field, you can build flexible, readable exception-handling code.

Usage

```
mySqlDecimal = mySqlDecimal.MaxScale
```

Parameters

None.

MaxValue

The read-only MaxValue field represents the largest number that a SqlDecimal can hold, which is 38 digits (99,999,999,999,999,999,999,999,999,999,999,999,999). By using the MaxValue field, you can build flexible, readable exception-handling code.

Usage

```
mySqlDecimal = mySqlDecimal.MaxValue
```

Parameters

None.

MinValue

The read-only MinValue field represents the smallest number that a SqlDecimal can hold, which is negative 38 digits (-99,999,999,999,999,999,999,999,999,999,999,999,999). By using the MinValue field, you can build flexible, readable exception-handling code.

Usage

```
mySqlDecimal = mySqlDecimal.MinValue
```

Parameters

None.

Multiply

The Multiply method will multiply the first SqlDecimal by the second SqlDecimal and return a SqlDecimal object whose Value property contains the results of the multiplication. Keep in mind the MaxValue that a SqlDecimal can hold. If either SqlDecimal value is null, the resulting SqlDecimal will be null.

In addition to the Multiply method, you may also use the op_Multiply operator method, or, if your language supports overloaded operators, you may use that construct instead.

Usage

```
mySqlDecimal = mySqlDecimal.Multiply(mySqlDecimal1,mySqlDecimal2)
mySqlDecimal = mySqlDecimal.op_Multiply(mySqlDecimal1,mySqlDecimal2) ' VB
mySqlDecimal = mySqlDecimal1 * mySqlDecimal2; // C#
```

Parameters

`mySqlDecimal1`	A SqlDecimal object.
`mySqlDecimal2`	A SqlDecimal object.

Exceptions

OverflowException	The operation returned a value outside of the range of a SqlDecimal value.

NotEquals

The NotEquals method compares two SqlDecimal values and returns a SqlBoolean value indicating whether the two SqlDecimal values are not equal. A null value would indicate that one of the SqlDecimal values is null.

In addition to the NotEquals method, you may also use the op_Inequality operator method, or, if your language supports overloaded operators, you may use that construct instead.

Usage

```
mySqlBoolean = mySqlDecimal.NotEquals(mySqlDecimal1,mySqlDecimal2)
mySqlBoolean = _
   mySqlDecimal.op_Inequality(mySqlDecimal1,mySqlDecimal2) ' VB
mySqlBoolean = (mySqlDecimal1 != mySqlDecimal2); // C#
```

Parameters

mySqlDecimal1	A SqlDecimal object.
mySqlDecimal2	A SqlDecimal object.

Null

The Null field represents a read-only null value that can be assigned to a SqlDecimal object. You cannot use the standard .NET way of assigning a null value with the System.DBNull.Value, but rather you must use this approach.

Usage

```
mySqlDecimal = mySqlDecimal.Null
```

Parameters

None.

op_Explicit

The op_Explicit method represents a special SqlDecimal converter that allows SqlDecimal values to be explicitly assigned to and from other SqlTypes. This method is overloaded in several ways. The first two examples show how to retrieve the SqlDecimal value as a Decimal object. The other examples show how to assign the SqlDecimal value.

When assigning the SqlDecimal value from one of the other SqlTypes, keep in mind the MinValue and MaxValue. Any value that exceeds those limits will throw an OverflowException. Any null values will convert to a SqlDecimal null value.

When assigning the SqlDecimal value from a SqlString object, be sure that the string parses to a valid SqlDecimal value. Converting from a SqlString object can throw a FormatException if ADO.NET can't parse the string.

If you are using ADO.NET with C#, then you will not call the op_Explicit method directly, but rather you are allowed to cast from one SqlType to the other.

Usage

```
myDecimal = mySqlDecimal.op_Explicit(mySqlDecimal)     ' Visual Basic .NET
myDecimal = (Decimal)mySqlDecimal;                     // C#
mySqlDecimal = mySqlDecimal.op_Explicit(mySqlBoolean) ' Visual Basic .NET
mySqlDecimal = (SqlDecimal)mySqlBoolean;               // C#
```

```
mySqlDecimal = mySqlDecimal.op_Explicit(mySqlDouble)   ' Visual Basic .NET
mySqlDecimal = (SqlDecimal)mySqlDouble;                // C#
mySqlDecimal = mySqlDecimal.op_Explicit(mySqlSingle)   ' Visual Basic .NET
mySqlDecimal = (SqlDecimal)mySqlSingle;                // C#
mySqlDecimal = mySqlDecimal.op_Explicit(mySqlString)   ' Visual Basic .NET
mySqlDecimal = (SqlDecimal)mySqlString;                // C#
```

Parameters

`mySqlDecimal`	A SqlDecimal object.
`mySqlBoolean`	A SqlBoolean object.
`mySqlDouble`	A SqlDouble object.
`mySqlSingle`	A SqlSingle object.
`mySqlString`	A SqlString object.

Exceptions

FormatException	ADO.NET couldn't parse the string.
OverflowException	The operation returned a value outside of the range of a SqlDecimal value.
SqlNullValueException	You cannot assign a null value to a Decimal class. Be sure to check the IsNull property, or use another exception-handling technique.

op_Implicit

The op_Implicit method represents a special SqlDecimal converter that allows SqlDecimal values to be implicitly assigned from other SqlTypes. This method is overloaded in several ways.

NOTE **It appears that you can pass any numeric object to the op_Implicit method. When assigning the SqlDecimal value from numeric types with a larger precision, keep in mind the MinValue and MaxValue. Any value that exceeds those limits will throw an OverflowException.**

If you are using ADO.NET with C#, then you will not call the op_Implicit method directly, but rather you are allowed to cast from one SqlType to the other.

Usage

```
mySqlDecimal = mySqlDecimal.op_Implicit(myDecimal)     ' Visual Basic .NET
mySqlDecimal = (SqlDecimal)myDecimal;                  // C#
mySqlDecimal = mySqlDecimal.op_Implicit(mySqlByte)     ' Visual Basic .NET
mySqlDecimal = (SqlDecimal)mySqlByte;                  // C#
mySqlDecimal = mySqlDecimal.op_Implicit(mySqlInt16)    ' Visual Basic .NET
mySqlDecimal = (SqlDecimal)mySqlInt16;                 // C#
mySqlDecimal = mySqlDecimal.op_Implicit(mySqlInt32)    ' Visual Basic .NET
mySqlDecimal = (SqlDecimal)mySqlInt32;                 // C#
mySqlDecimal = mySqlDecimal.op_Implicit(mySqlInt64)    ' Visual Basic .NET
mySqlDecimal = (SqlDecimal)mySqlInt64;                 // C#
mySqlDecimal = mySqlDecimal.op_Implicit(mySqlMoney)    ' Visual Basic .NET
mySqlDecimal = (SqlDecimal)mySqlMoney;                 // C#
```

Parameters

`myDecimal`	A Decimal object.
`mySqlByte`	A SqlByte object.
`mySqlInt16`	A SqlInt16 object.
`mySqlInt32`	A SqlInt32 object.
`mySqlInt64`	A SqlInt64 object.
`mySqlMoney`	A SqlMoney object.

Exceptions

OverflowException	The operation returned a value outside of the range of a SqlDecimal value.

Parse

The Parse method will evaluate a string and return a SqlDecimal. Keep in mind that converting from a String can throw a FormatException if ADO.NET can't parse the string.

Usage

```
mySqlDecimal = mySqlDecimal.Parse(myString)
```

Parameters

`myString`	A case-insensitive String object containing a valid Decimal value, such as "-123.45, "0", "100.5" or "1250.23550".

Exceptions

OverflowException	The operation returned a value outside of the range of a SqlDecimal value.
FormatException	ADO.NET couldn't parse the string.

Power

The Power method will raise the SqlDecimal value (the base) to the power passed in the second argument (the exponent). This method is essentially X^Y, where X is a SqlDecimal object.

NOTE If you are planning on using the Power method to return a square root, cube root, etc. by passing a 0.5 or 0.33 value as the exponent, you will be disappointed. For some reason, the Power method rounds the results to the nearest integer. For example, both the square root and the cube root of a SqlDecimal with the value of 5 will return a SqlDecimal with the value of 2.

Usage

```
mySqlDecimal = mySqlDecimal.Power(mySqlDecimal, myDouble)
```

Parameters

`mySqlDecimal`	A SqlDecimal object, representing the base.
`myDouble`	A Double object, representing the exponent.

Exceptions

OverflowException	The operation returned a value outside the range of a SqlDecimal value.
SqlNullValueException	You may not use the Power method with a SqlDecimal that is null.

Precision

The read-only Precision property allows you to see the precision of the SqlDecimal. Valid precision values range from 0 to MaxPrecision (which is 38). Remember that this property is read-only—you may not assign a SqlDecimal its precision directly.

If you need to change the precision of a SqlDecimal, consider using the ConvertTo-PrecScale method, which creates a new SqlDecimal object.

Usage

```
myByte = mySqlDecimal.Precision
```

Parameters

None.

Round

The Round method will return a SqlDecimal rounded to the specified number of decimal places. If the SqlDecimal is null, the Round method will return a null value.

> **NOTE** **An interesting side effect can be witnessed if you round to a negative number of decimal places. You can actually set a certain number of digits to the left of the decimal point to zero and round one as well!**

Usage

```
mySqlDecimal = mySqlDecimal.Round(mySqlDecimal, myInt32)
```

Parameters

`mySqlDecimal`	A SqlDecimal object.
`myInt32`	The number of decimal places to round.

Exceptions

None.

Scale

The read-only Scale property allows you to see the precision of the SqlDecimal. Valid precision values range from 0 to MaxScale (which is 38). Remember that this property is read-only—you may not assign a SqlDecimal its scale directly.

If you need to change the scale of a SqlDecimal, consider using the AdjustScale or ConvertToPrecScale method, which creates a new SqlDecimal object.

Usage

```
myByte = mySqlDecimal.Scale
```

Parameters

None.

Sign

The Sign method will return a SqlInt32 indicating the sign of the SqlDecimal value. The SqlInt32 will be one of these values:

-1	The SqlDecimal has a negative value.
0	The SqlDecimal has a value of zero (0).
1	The SqlDecimal has a positive value.
null	The SqlDecimal has a null value.

Usage

```
mySqlInt32 = mySqlDecimal.Sign(mySqlDecimal)
```

Parameters

`mySqlDecimal`	A SqlDecimal object.

Exceptions

None.

Subtract

The Subtract method will subtract the second SqlDecimal from the first SqlDecimal and return a SqlDecimal object whose Value property contains the results of the subtraction. Keep in mind the MinValue and MaxValue that a SqlDecimal can hold. If either SqlDecimal value is null, the resulting SqlDecimal will be null.

In addition to the Subtract method, you may also use the op_Subtraction operator method, or, if your language supports overloaded operators, you may use that construct instead.

Usage

```
mySqlDecimal = mySqlDecimal.Subtract(mySqlDecimal1,mySqlDecimal2)
mySqlDecimal = _
   mySqlDecimal.op_Subtraction(mySqlDecimal1,mySqlDecimal2) ' VB
mySqlDecimal = mySqlDecimal1 - mySqlDecimal2; // C#
```

Parameters

`mySqlDecimal1`	A SqlDecimal object.
`mySqlDecimal2`	A SqlDecimal object.

Exceptions

OverflowException	The operation returned a value outside of the range of a SqlDecimal value.

ToDouble

The ToDouble method returns the SqlDecimal value as a Double object. Be mindful that the Double may not hold the precision or scale of your SqlDecimal object and that data may be lost. A null SqlDecimal value will throw an exception.

Usage

```
myDouble = mySqlDecimal.ToDouble()
```

Parameters

None.

Exceptions

SqlNullValueException	You cannot retrieve a null value. Be sure to check the IsNull property, or use another exception-handling technique.

ToSqlBoolean

The ToSqlBoolean method returns the SqlDecimal value as a SqlBoolean object. Any nonzero SqlDecimal value will return in a True SqlBoolean. A zero SqlDecimal value will return a False SqlBoolean. A null SqlDecimal value will return a null SqlBoolean.

Usage

```
mySqlBoolean = mySqlDecimal.ToSqlBoolean()
```

Parameters

None.

ToSqlByte

The ToSqlByte method returns the SqlDecimal value as a SqlByte object. Be mindful of the range of values that the SqlByte class supports and that it holds only positive integer values. A null SqlDecimal value will return a null SqlByte.

Usage

```
mySqlByte = mySqlDecimal.ToSqlByte()
```

Parameters

None.

Exceptions

OverflowException	The operation returned a value outside of the range of a SqlByte value.

ToSqlDouble

The ToSqlDouble method returns the SqlDecimal value as a SqlDouble. Be mindful that the SqlDouble may not hold the precision or scale of your SqlDecimal object and that data may be lost. A null value would indicate that the SqlDecimal value is null.

Usage

```
mySqlDouble = mySqlDecimal.ToSqlDouble()
```

Parameters

None.

ToSqlInt16

The ToSqlInt16 method returns the SqlDecimal value as a SqlInt16 (16 bit integer). Be mindful of the range of values that the SqlInt16 class supports and that it holds only integer values. A null value would indicate that the SqlDecimal value is null.

Usage

```
mySqlInt16 = mySqlDecimal.ToSqlInt16()
```

Parameters

None.

Exceptions

OverflowException	The operation returned a value outside of the range of a SqlInt16 value.

ToSqlInt32

The ToSqlInt32 method returns the SqlDecimal value as a SqlInt32 (32 bit integer). Be mindful of the range of values that the SqlInt32 class supports and that it holds only integer values. A null value would indicate that the SqlDecimal value is null.

Usage

```
mySqlInt32 = mySqlDecimal.ToSqlInt32()
```

Parameters

None.

Exceptions

OverflowException	The operation returned a value outside of the range of a SqlInt32 value.

ToSqlInt64

The ToSqlInt64 method returns the SqlDecimal value as a SqlInt64 (64 bit integer). Be mindful of the range of values that the SqlInt64 class supports and that it holds only integer values. A null value would indicate that the SqlDecimal value is null.

Usage

```
mySqlInt64 = mySqlDecimal.ToSqlInt64()
```

Parameters

None.

Exceptions

OverflowException	The operation returned a value outside of the range of a SqlInt64 value.

ToSqlMoney

The ToSqlMoney method returns the SqlDecimal value as a SqlMoney. Be mindful of the range of values that the SqlMoney class supports. A null value would indicate that the SqlDecimal value is null.

Usage

```
mySqlMoney = mySqlDecimal.ToSqlMoney()
```

Parameters

None.

Exceptions

OverflowException	The operation returned a value outside of the range of a SqlMoney value.

ToSqlSingle

The ToSqlSingle method returns the SqlDecimal value as a SqlSingle. Be mindful that the SqlSingle may not hold the precision or scale of your SqlDecimal object and that data may be lost. A null value would indicate that the SqlDecimal value is null.

Usage

```
mySqlSingle = mySqlDecimal.ToSqlSingle()
```

Parameters

None.

ToSqlString

The ToSqlString method returns the SqlDecimal value as a SqlString. A null value would indicate that the SqlDecimal value is null.

Usage

```
mySqlString = mySqlDecimal.ToSqlString()
```

Parameters

None.

ToString

The ToString method returns the SqlDecimal value as a readable value.

Usage

```
myString = mySqlDecimal.ToString()
```

Parameters

None.

Truncate

The Truncate method will return a SqlDecimal truncated to the specified number of decimal places. If the SqlDecimal is null, the Truncate method will return a null value.

NOTE An interesting side effect can be witnessed if you truncate to a negative number of decimal places. You can actually set a specified number of digits to the left of the decimal point to zero.

Usage

```
mySqlDecimal = mySqlDecimal.Truncate(mySqlDecimal, myInt32)
```

Parameters

mySqlDecimal	A SqlDecimal object.
myInt32	The number of decimal places to truncate.

Exceptions

None.

Value

The read-only Value property allows you to retrieve the value of the SqlDecimal. Remember that this property is read-only—you may not assign a SqlDecimal its value using its Value property.

In addition to using the Value property, you may also use the op_Explicit conversion method, or, if your language supports overloaded operators, you may use that construct instead.

Usage

```
myDecimal = mySqlDecimal.Value                            ' Visual Basic .NET
myDecimal = mySqlDecimal.op_Explicit(mySqlDecimal)        ' Visual Basic .NET
myDecimal = (decimal)mySqlDecimal;                        // C#
```

Parameters

None.

Exceptions

SqlNullValueException	You cannot retrieve a null value. Be sure to check the IsNull property, or use another exception-handling technique.

System.Data.SqlTypes.SqlDouble

The SqlDouble structure represents a floating-point number. The value may be between -1.79E+308 and 1.79E + 308. Use the SqlDouble structure to manipulate the following SQL Server data types:

- float (n) - where n > 24
- float - where no mantissa is mentioned
- sql_variant (if the data is one the above types)

Constructors

```
Dim mySqlDouble As New SqlDouble(myDouble)
```

Parameters

`myDouble`	A Double object.

SqlDouble Sample Code

```
Private Sub ReadSqlType(ByVal myConnectionString As String, _
                        ByVal myCommandText As String)
   Dim mySqlConnection As System.Data.SqlClient.SqlConnection
   Dim mySqlDataReader As System.Data.SqlClient.SqlDataReader
```

```
        Dim mySqlCommand As System.Data.SqlClient.SqlCommand
        Dim mySqlDouble As System.Data.SqlTypes.SqlDouble
        ' Establish connection
        mySqlConnection = New SqlConnection(myConnectionString)
        mySqlConnection.Open()
        ' Build and execute command
        mySqlCommand = New SqlCommand(myCommandText)
        mySqlCommand.Connection = mySqlConnection
        mySqlDataReader = mySqlCommand.ExecuteReader
        ' Read first row
        If mySqlDataReader.Read Then
            ' Save column as appropriate SqlTypes structure
            mySqlDouble = mySqlDataReader.GetSqlDouble(1)
            MessageBox.Show(mySqlDouble.ToString)
        End If
        ' Done
        mySqlConnection.Close()
    End Sub
```

Members

Add

The Add method will add two SqlDouble values together and return a SqlDouble object whose Value property contains the results of the addition. Keep in mind the MinValue and MaxValue that a SqlDouble can hold. If either SqlDouble value is null, the resulting SqlDouble will be null.

In addition to the Add method, you may also use the op_Addition operator method or, if your language supports overloaded operators, you may use that construct instead.

Usage

```
mySqlDouble = mySqlDouble.Add(mySqlDouble1,mySqlDouble2)
mySqlDouble = mySqlDouble.op_Addition(mySqlDouble1,mySqlDouble2) ' VB
mySqlDouble = mySqlDouble1 + mySqlDouble2; // C#
```

Parameters

`mySqlDouble1`	A SqlDouble object.
`mySqlDouble2`	A SqlDouble object.

Exceptions

OverflowException	The operation returned a value outside of the range of a SqlDouble value.

CompareTo

The CompareTo method allows you to compare the SqlDouble value with another supplied object to return an indication of their relative values. The returned Int32 object will indicate the comparison:

Less Than Zero. The SqlDouble value was less than the supplied object, or the SqlDouble was null.

Zero. The SqlDouble value was the same as the supplied object.

Greater than zero. The SqlDouble value was greater than the supplied object, or the object was null.

Usage

```
myInt32 = mySqlDouble.CompareTo(myObject)
```

Parameters

`myObject`	Any object that implements the IComparable interface.

Exceptions

ArgumentException	The supplied object isn't valid for comparison.

Divide

The Divide method will divide the first SqlDouble by the second SqlDouble. This method will return a SqlDouble object whose Value property contains the results of the division. If either SqlDouble value is null, the resulting SqlDouble will be null.

In addition to the Divide method, you may also use the op_Division operator method, or, if your language supports overloaded operators, you may use that construct instead.

Usage

```
mySqlDouble = mySqlDouble.Divide(mySqlDouble1,mySqlDouble2)
mySqlDouble = mySqlDouble.op_Division(mySqlDouble1,mySqlDouble2) ' VB
mySqlDouble = mySqlDouble1 / mySqlDouble2; // C#
```

Parameters

`mySqlDouble1`	A SqlDouble object.
`mySqlDouble2`	A SqlDouble object.

Exceptions

DivideByZeroException	You tried to divide by zero.

Equals

The Equals method allows you to compare the SqlDouble value with a supplied object or compare the values of two supplied objects or SqlDouble values. The result will be either a Boolean or a SqlBoolean, depending on which overloaded method is called. The result may be null if either of the SqlDouble values being compared were null.

In addition to the Equals method, you may also use the op_Equality operator method, or, if your language supports overloaded operators, you may use that construct instead.

Usage

```
mySqlBoolean = mySqlDouble.Equals(mySqlDouble1,mySqlDouble2)
myBoolean = mySqlDouble.Equals(myObject)
myBoolean = mySqlDouble.Equals(myObject,myObject2)
```

```
mySqlBoolean = mySqlDouble.op_Equality(mySqlDouble1,mySqlDouble2) ' VB
mySqlBoolean = (mySqlDouble1 == mySqlDouble2); // C#
```

Parameters

`mySqlDouble1`	A SqlDouble object.
`mySqlDouble2`	A SqlDouble object.
`myObject`	Any System.Object or descendant.
`myObject2`	Any System.Object or descendant.

GetHashCode

The GetHashCode method returns a hash code for the SqlDouble value. The hash code represents a unique value corresponding to the particular value of the SqlDouble object. Keep in mind that even the smallest change to the SqlDouble value will result in a different hash code. Requesting the hash code for a SqlDouble object with a null value will return 0.

BE CAREFUL **The hash code returned for a SqlDouble with a value of 0 is 0, which is the same for a SqlDouble with a null value.**

Usage

```
myInt32 = mySqlDouble.GetHashCode()
```

Parameters

None.

GreaterThan

The GreaterThan method compares two SqlDouble values and returns a SqlBoolean value indicating whether the first SqlDouble value is greater than the second SqlDouble value. A null value would indicate that one of the SqlDouble values is null.

In addition to the GreaterThan method, you may also use the op_GreaterThan operator method, or, if your language supports overloaded operators, you may use that construct instead.

Usage

```
mySqlBoolean = mySqlDouble.GreaterThan(mySqlDouble1,mySqlDouble2)
mySqlBoolean = mySqlDouble.op_GreaterThan(mySqlDouble1,mySqlDouble2) ' VB
mySqlBoolean = (mySqlDouble1 > mySqlDouble2); // C#
```

Parameters

`mySqlDouble1`	A SqlDouble object.
`mySqlDouble2`	A SqlDouble object.

GreaterThanOrEqual

The GreaterThanOrEqual method compares two SqlDouble values and returns a SqlBoolean value indicating whether the first SqlDouble value is greater than or equal to the second SqlDouble value. A null value would indicate that one of the SqlDouble values is null.

In addition to the GreaterThanOrEqual method, you may also use the op_GreaterThanOrEqual operator method, or, if your language supports overloaded operators, you may use that construct instead.

Usage

```
mySqlBoolean = _
   mySqlDouble.GreaterThanOrEqual(mySqlDouble1,mySqlDouble2)
mySqlBoolean = _
   mySqlDouble.op_GreaterThanOrEqual(mySqlDouble1,mySqlDouble2) ' VB
mySqlBoolean = (mySqlDouble1 >= mySqlDouble2); // C#
```

Parameters

`mySqlDouble1`	A SqlDouble object.
`mySqlDouble2`	A SqlDouble object.

IsNull

The read-only IsNull property returns a Boolean indicating whether the SqlDouble is null. The value will be True if the value of the SqlDouble is null and False if it is otherwise.

Usage

```
myBoolean = mySqlDouble.IsNull
```

Parameters

None.

LessThan

The LessThan method compares two SqlDouble values and returns a SqlBoolean value indicating whether the first SqlDouble value is less than the second SqlDouble value. A null value would indicate that one of the SqlDouble values is null.

In addition to the LessThan method, you may also use the op_LessThan operator method, or, if your language supports overloaded operators, you may use that construct instead.

Usage

```
mySqlBoolean = mySqlDouble.LessThan(mySqlDouble1,mySqlDouble2)
mySqlBoolean = mySqlDouble.op_LessThan(mySqlDouble1,mySqlDouble2) ' VB
mySqlBoolean = (mySqlDouble1 < mySqlDouble2); // C#
```

Parameters

`mySqlDouble1`	A SqlDouble object.
`mySqlDouble2`	A SqlDouble object.

LessThanOrEqual

The LessThanOrEqual method compares two SqlDouble values and returns a SqlBoolean value indicating whether the first SqlDouble value is less than or equal to the second SqlDouble value. A null value would indicate that one of the SqlDouble values is null.

In addition to the LessThanOrEqual method, you may also use the op_LessThanOrEqual operator method, or, if your language supports overloaded operators, you may use that construct instead.

Usage

```
mySqlBoolean = mySqlDouble.LessThanOrEqual(mySqlDouble1,mySqlDouble2)
mySqlBoolean = _
   mySqlDouble.op_LessThanOrEqual(mySqlDouble1,mySqlDouble2) ' VB
mySqlBoolean = (mySqlDouble1 <= mySqlDouble2); // C#
```

Parameters

`mySqlDouble1`	A SqlDouble object.
`mySqlDouble2`	A SqlDouble object.

MaxValue

The read-only MaxValue field represents the largest number that a SqlDouble can hold, which is 1.79E + 308 (1.79769313486232E+308). By using the MaxValue field, you can build flexible, readable exception-handling code.

Usage

```
mySqlDouble = mySqlDouble.MaxValue
```

Parameters

None.

MinValue

The read-only MinValue field represents the smallest number that a SqlDouble can hold, which is -1.79E+308 (-1.79769313486232E+308). By using the MinValue field, you can build flexible, readable exception-handling code.

Usage

```
mySqlDouble = mySqlDouble.MinValue
```

Parameters

None.

Multiply

The Multiply method will multiply the first SqlDouble by the second SqlDouble and return a SqlDouble object whose Value property contains the results of the multiplication. Keep in mind the MaxValue that a SqlDouble can hold. If either SqlDouble value is null, the resulting SqlDouble will be null.

In addition to the Multiply method, you may also use the op_Multiply operator method, or, if your language supports overloaded operators, you may use that construct instead.

Usage

```
mySqlDouble = mySqlDouble.Multiply(mySqlDouble1,mySqlDouble2)
mySqlDouble = mySqlDouble.op_Multiply(mySqlDouble1,mySqlDouble2) ' VB
mySqlDouble = mySqlDouble1 * mySqlDouble2; // C#
```

Parameters

`mySqlDouble1`	A SqlDouble object.
`mySqlDouble2`	A SqlDouble object.

Exceptions

OverflowException	The operation returned a value outside of the range of a SqlDouble value.

NotEquals

The NotEquals method compares two SqlDouble values and returns a SqlBoolean value indicating whether the two SqlDouble values are not equal. A null value would indicate that one of the SqlDouble values is null.

In addition to the NotEquals method, you may also use the op_Inequality operator method, or, if your language supports overloaded operators, you may use that construct instead.

Usage

```
mySqlBoolean = mySqlDouble.NotEquals(mySqlDouble1,mySqlDouble2)
mySqlBoolean = mySqlDouble.op_Inequality(mySqlDouble1,mySqlDouble2) ' VB
mySqlBoolean = (mySqlDouble1 != mySqlDouble2); // C#
```

Parameters

`mySqlDouble1`	A SqlDouble object.
`mySqlDouble2`	A SqlDouble object.

Null

The Null field represents a read-only null value that can be assigned to a SqlDouble object. You cannot use the standard .NET way of assigning a null value with the System.DBNull.Value, but rather you must use this approach.

Usage

```
mySqlDouble = mySqlDouble.Null
```

Parameters

None.

op_Explicit

The op_Explicit method represents a special SqlDouble converter the allows SqlDouble values to be explicitly assigned to and from other SqlTypes. This method is overloaded in several ways. The first two examples that follow show how to retrieve the SqlDouble value as a Decimal object. The other examples show how to assign the SqlDouble value.

When assigning the SqlDouble value from one of the other SqlTypes, keep in mind the MinValue and MaxValue. Any value that exceeds those limits will throw an OverflowException. Any null values will convert to a SqlDouble null value.

When assigning the SqlDouble value from a SqlString object, be sure that the string parses to a valid SqlDouble value. Converting from a SqlString object can throw a FormatException if ADO.NET can't parse the string.

If you are using ADO.NET with C#, then you will not call the op_Explicit method directly, but rather you are allowed to cast from one SqlType to the other.

Usage

```
myDouble = mySqlDouble.op_Explicit(mySqlDouble)      ' Visual Basic .NET
myDouble = (Double)mySqlDouble;                      // C#
mySqlDouble = mySqlDouble.op_Explicit(mySqlBoolean)  ' Visual Basic .NET
mySqlDouble = (SqlDouble)mySqlBoolean;               // C#
mySqlDouble = mySqlDouble.op_Explicit(mySqlString)   ' Visual Basic .NET
mySqlDouble = (SqlDouble)mySqlString;                // C#
```

Parameters

`mySqlDouble`	A SqlDouble object.
`mySqlBoolean`	A SqlBoolean object.
`mySqlString`	A SqlString object.

Exceptions

FormatException	ADO.NET couldn't parse the string.
OverflowException	The operation returned a value outside of the range of a SqlDouble value.
SqlNullValueException	You cannot assign a null value to a Double class. Be sure to check the IsNull property, or use another exception-handling technique.

op_Implicit

The op_Implicit method represents a special SqlDouble converter that allows SqlDouble values to be implicitly assigned from other SqlTypes. This method is overloaded in several ways.

NOTE It appears that you can pass any numeric object to the op_Implicit method. When assigning the SqlDouble value from numeric types with a larger precision, keep in mind the MinValue and MaxValue. Any value that exceeds those limits will throw an OverflowException.

If you are using ADO.NET with C#, then you will not call the op_Implicit method directly, but rather you are allowed to cast from one SqlType to the other.

Usage

```
mySqlDouble = mySqlDouble.op_Implicit(myDouble)      ' Visual Basic .NET
mySqlDouble = (SqlDouble)myDouble;                   // C#
mySqlDouble = mySqlDouble.op_Implicit(mySqlByte)     ' Visual Basic .NET
mySqlDouble = (SqlDouble)mySqlByte;                  // C#
mySqlDouble = mySqlDouble.op_Implicit(mySqlDecimal)  ' Visual Basic .NET
mySqlDouble = (SqlDouble)mySqlDecimal;               // C#
mySqlDouble = mySqlDouble.op_Implicit(mySqlInt16)    ' Visual Basic .NET
mySqlDouble = (SqlDouble)mySqlInt16;                 // C#
mySqlDouble = mySqlDouble.op_Implicit(mySqlInt32)    ' Visual Basic .NET
mySqlDouble = (SqlDouble)mySqlInt32;                 // C#
```

```
mySqlDouble = mySqlDouble.op_Implicit(mySqlInt64)    ' Visual Basic .NET
mySqlDouble = (SqlDouble)mySqlInt64;                 // C#
mySqlDouble = mySqlDouble.op_Implicit(mySqlSingle)   ' Visual Basic .NET
mySqlDouble = (SqlDouble)mySqlSingle;                // C#
mySqlDouble = mySqlDouble.op_Implicit(mySqlMoney)    ' Visual Basic .NET
mySqlDouble = (SqlDouble)mySqlMoney;                 // C#
```

Parameters

`myDouble`	A Decimal object.
`mySqlByte`	A SqlByte object.
`mySqlDecimal`	A SqlDecimal object.
`mySqlInt16`	A SqlInt16 object.
`mySqlInt32`	A SqlInt32 object.
`mySqlInt64`	A SqlInt64 object.
`mySqlSingle`	A SqlSingle object.
`mySqlMoney`	A SqlMoney object.

Exceptions

OverflowException	The operation returned a value outside of the range of a SqlDouble value.

Parse

The Parse method will evaluate a string and return a SqlDouble. Keep in mind that converting from a String can throw a FormatException if ADO.NET can't parse the string.

Usage

```
mySqlDouble = mySqlDouble.Parse(myString)
```

Parameters

`myString`	A case-insensitive String object containing a valid Double value, such as "-17305.25", "0", "100", or "1.79E + 308".

Exceptions

OverflowException	The operation returned a value outside of the range of a SqlDouble value.
FormatException	ADO.NET couldn't parse the string.

Subtract

The Subtract method will subtract the second SqlDouble from the first SqlDouble and return a SqlDouble object whose Value property contains the results of the subtraction. Keep in mind the MinValue and MaxValue that a SqlDouble can hold. If either Sql-Double value is null, the resulting SqlDouble will be null.

In addition to the Subtract method, you may also use the op_Subtraction operator method, or, if your language supports overloaded operators, you may use that construct instead.

Usage

```
mySqlDouble = mySqlDouble.Subtract(mySqlDouble1,mySqlDouble2)
mySqlDouble = mySqlDouble.op_Subtraction(mySqlDouble1,mySqlDouble2) ' VB
mySqlDouble = mySqlDouble1 - mySqlDouble2; // C#
```

Parameters

mySqlDouble1	A SqlDouble object.
mySqlDouble2	A SqlDouble object.

Exceptions

OverflowException	The operation returned a value outside of the range of a SqlDouble value.

ToSqlBoolean

The ToSqlBoolean method returns the SqlDouble value as a SqlBoolean object. Any nonzero SqlDouble value will return in a True SqlBoolean. A zero SqlDouble value will return a False SqlBoolean. A null SqlDouble value will return a null SqlBoolean.

Usage

```
mySqlBoolean = mySqlDouble.ToSqlBoolean()
```

Parameters

None.

ToSqlByte

The ToSqlByte method returns the SqlDouble value as a SqlByte object. Be mindful of the range of values that the SqlByte class supports and that it holds only positive integer values. A null SqlDouble value will return a null SqlByte.

Usage

```
mySqlByte = mySqlDouble.ToSqlByte()
```

Parameters

None.

Exceptions

OverflowException	The operation returned a value outside of the range of a SqlByte value.

ToSqlDecimal

The ToSqlDecimal method returns the SqlDouble value as a SqlDecimal. A null value would indicate that the SqlDouble value is null.

Usage

```
mySqlDecimal = mySqlDouble.ToSqlDecimal()
```

Parameters

None.

Exceptions

OverflowException	The operation returned a value outside of the range of a SqlDecimal value.

ToSqlInt16

The ToSqlInt16 method returns the SqlDouble value as a SqlInt16 (16-bit integer). Be mindful of the range of values that the SqlInt16 class supports and that it holds only integer values. A null value would indicate that the SqlDouble value is null.

Usage

```
mySqlInt16 = mySqlDouble.ToSqlInt16()
```

Parameters

None.

Exceptions

OverflowException	The operation returned a value outside of the range of a SqlInt16 value.

ToSqlInt32

The ToSqlInt32 method returns the SqlDouble value as a SqlInt32 (32-bit integer). Be mindful of the range of values that the SqlInt32 class supports and that it holds only integer values. A null value would indicate that the SqlDouble value is null.

Usage

```
mySqlInt32 = mySqlDouble.ToSqlInt32()
```

Parameters

None.

Exceptions

OverflowException	The operation returned a value outside of the range of a SqlInt32 value.

ToSqlInt64

The ToSqlInt64 method returns the SqlDouble value as a SqlInt64 (64 bit integer). Be mindful of the range of values that the SqlInt64 class supports and that it holds only integer values. A null value would indicate that the SqlDouble value is null.

Usage

```
mySqlInt64 = mySqlDouble.ToSqlInt64()
```

Parameters

None.

Exceptions

OverflowException	The operation returned a value outside of the range of a SqlInt64 value.

ToSqlMoney

The ToSqlMoney method returns the SqlDouble value as a SqlMoney. A null value would indicate that the SqlDouble value is null.

Usage

```
mySqlMoney = mySqlDouble.ToSqlMoney()
```

Parameters

None.

Exceptions

OverflowException	The operation returned a value outside of the range of a SqlMoney value.

ToSqlSingle

The ToSqlSingle method returns the SqlDouble value as a SqlSingle. A null value would indicate that the SqlDouble value is null.

Usage

```
mySqlSingle = mySqlDouble.ToSqlSingle()
```

Parameters

None.

ToSqlString

The ToSqlString method returns the SqlDouble value as a SqlString. A null value would indicate that the SqlDouble value is null.

Usage

```
mySqlString = mySqlDouble.ToSqlString()
```

Parameters

None.

ToString

The ToString method returns the SqlDouble value as a readable value.

Usage

```
myString = mySqlDouble.ToString()
```

Parameters

None.

Value

The read-only Value property allows you to retrieve the value of the SqlDouble. Remember that this property is read-only—you may not assign a SqlDouble its value using its Value property.

In addition to using the Value property, you may also use the op_Explicit conversion method, or, if your language supports overloaded operators, you may use that construct instead.

Usage

```
myDouble = mySqlDouble.Value                      ' Visual Basic .NET
myDouble = mySqlDouble.op_Explicit(mySqlDouble)   ' Visual Basic .NET
myDouble = (Double)mySqlDouble;                   // C#
```

Parameters

None.

Exceptions

SqlNullValueException	You cannot retrieve a null value. Be sure to check the IsNull property, or use another exception-handling technique.

Zero

The Zero field represents a read-only value of (0) that can be assigned to a SqlDouble object.

Usage

```
mySqlDouble = mySqlDouble.Zero
```

Parameters

None.

System.Data.SqlTypes.SqlGuid

The SqlGuid structure represents a Globally Unique IDentifier (GUID). Internally, the value is stored as a 16-byte (128-bit) value, but outwardly is represented as a 36-byte string (32 characters + 6 hyphens). Each hexadecimal character can be 0-9 or a-f.

A GUID is formatted like this:

```
########-####-####-####-############
```

Here is an example:

```
4a985849-fc57-4c70-8c50-09636c771c5a
```

SqlGuid is the structure you would use to manipulate the following SQL Server data types:

- uniqueidentifier
- sql_variant (if the data is of type uniqueidentifier)

Constructors

```
Dim mySqlGuid As New SqlGuid(myByteArray)
Dim mySqlGuid As New SqlGuid(myGuid)
Dim mySqlGuid As New SqlGuid(myString)
```

```
Dim mySqlGuid As New SqlGuid(myInt32,myInt16a,myInt16b,myByte1,myByte2,_
   myByte3,myByte4,myByte5,myByte6,myByte7,myByte8)
```

Parameters

`myByteArray`	A 16-element array of bytes.
`myGuid`	A System.Guid object.
`myString`	A String object, in the format.
`myInt32`	An Int32 object representing the first four bytes (position 0-3) of the SqlGuid.
`myInt16a`	An Int16 object representing the next two bytes (position 4-5) of the SqlGuid.
`myInt16b`	An Int16 object representing the next two bytes (position 6-7) of the SqlGuid.
`myByte1`	A Byte object representing the next byte (position 8) of the SqlGuid.
`myByte2`	A Byte object representing the next byte (position 9) of the SqlGuid.
`myByte3`	A Byte object representing the next byte (position 10) of the SqlGuid.
`myByte4`	A Byte object representing the next byte (position 11) of the SqlGuid.
`myByte5`	A Byte object representing the next byte (position 12) of the SqlGuid.
`myByte6`	A Byte object representing the next byte (position 13) of the SqlGuid.
`myByte7`	A Byte object representing the next byte (position 14) of the SqlGuid.
`myByte8`	A Byte object representing the next byte (position 15) of the SqlGuid.

Exceptions

FormatException	The values passed to the constructor were invalid. If you are using the overload that accepts a string, make sure you are passing the correct format.

SqlGuid Sample Code

```
Private Sub ReadSqlType(ByVal myConnectionString As String, _
                        ByVal myCommandText As String)
   Dim mySqlConnection As System.Data.SqlClient.SqlConnection
   Dim mySqlDataReader As System.Data.SqlClient.SqlDataReader
```

```
    Dim mySqlCommand As System.Data.SqlClient.SqlCommand
    Dim mySqlGuid As System.Data.SqlTypes.SqlGuid
    ' Establish connection
    mySqlConnection = New SqlConnection(myConnectionString)
    mySqlConnection.Open()
    ' Build and execute command
    mySqlCommand = New SqlCommand(myCommandText)
    mySqlCommand.Connection = mySqlConnection
    mySqlDataReader = mySqlCommand.ExecuteReader
    ' Read first row
    If mySqlDataReader.Read Then
        ' Save column as appropriate SqlTypes structure
        mySqlGuid = mySqlDataReader.GetSqlGuid(1)
        MessageBox.Show(mySqlGuid.ToString)
    End If
    ' Done
    mySqlConnection.Close()
End Sub
```

Members

CompareTo

The CompareTo method allows you to compare the SqlGuid value with another supplied object to return an indication of their relative values. The returned Int32 object will indicate the comparison:

Less Than Zero. The SqlGuid value was less than the supplied object, or the SqlGuid was null.

Zero. The SqlGuid value was the same as the supplied object.

Greater than zero. The SqlGuid value was greater than the supplied object, or the object was null.

Usage

```
myInt32 = mySqlGuid.CompareTo(myObject)
```

Parameters

`myObject`	Any object that implements the IComparable interface.

Exceptions

ArgumentException	The supplied object isn't valid for comparison.

Equals

The Equals method allows you to compare the SqlGuid value with a supplied object or compare the values of two supplied objects or SqlGuid values. The result will be either a Boolean or a SqlBoolean, depending on which overloaded method is called. The result will be null if either of the SqlGuid values being compared is null.

In addition to the Equals method, you may also use the op_Equality operator method, or, if your language supports overloaded operators, you may use that construct instead.

Usage

```
mySqlBoolean = mySqlGuid.Equals(mySqlGuid1,mySqlGuid2)
myBoolean = mySqlGuid.Equals(myObject)
myBoolean = mySqlGuid.Equals(myObject,myObject2)
mySqlBoolean = mySqlGuid.op_Equality(mySqlGuid1,mySqlGuid2) ' VB
mySqlBoolean = (mySqlGuid1 == mySqlGuid2); // C#
```

Parameters

`mySqlGuid1`	A SqlGuid object.
`mySqlGuid2`	A SqlGuid object.
`myObject`	Any System.Object or descendant.
`myObject2`	Any System.Object or descendant.

GetHashCode

The GetHashCode method returns a hash code for the SqlGuid value. The hash code represents a unique value corresponding to the particular value of the SqlGuid object. Keep in mind that even the smallest change to the SqlGuid value will result in a different hash code. Requesting the hash code for a SqlGuid object with a null value will return 0.

BE CAREFUL The hash code returned for a SqlGuid with all 0s is 0, which is the same for a SqlGuid with a null value.

Usage

```
myInt32 = mySqlGuid.GetHashCode()
```

Parameters

None.

GreaterThan

The GreaterThan method compares two SqlGuid values and returns a SqlBoolean value indicating whether the first SqlGuid value is greater than the second SqlGuid value. A null value would indicate that one of the SqlGuid values is null.

In addition to the GreaterThan method, you may also use the op_GreaterThan operator method, or, if your language supports overloaded operators, you may use that construct instead.

Usage

```
mySqlBoolean = mySqlGuid.GreaterThan(mySqlGuid1,mySqlGuid2)
mySqlBoolean = mySqlGuid.op_GreaterThan(mySqlGuid1,mySqlGuid2) ' VB
mySqlBoolean = (mySqlGuid1 > mySqlGuid2); // C#
```

Parameters

`mySqlGuid1`	A SqlGuid object.
`mySqlGuid2`	A SqlGuid object.

GreaterThanOrEqual

The GreaterThanOrEqual method compares two SqlGuid values and returns a SqlBoolean value indicating whether the first SqlGuid value is greater than or equal to the second SqlGuid value. A null value would indicate that one of the SqlGuid values is null.

In addition to the GreaterThanOrEqual method, you may also use the op_GreaterThanOrEqual operator method, or, if your language supports overloaded operators, you may use that construct instead.

Usage

```
mySqlBoolean = mySqlGuid.GreaterThanOrEqual(mySqlGuid1,mySqlGuid2)
mySqlBoolean = mySqlGuid.op_GreaterThanOrEqual(mySqlGuid1,mySqlGuid2) ' VB
mySqlBoolean = (mySqlGuid1 >= mySqlGuid2); // C#
```

Parameters

`mySqlGuid1`	A SqlGuid object.
`mySqlGuid2`	A SqlGuid object.

IsNull

The read-only IsNull property returns a Boolean indicating whether the SqlGuid is null. The value will be True if the value of the SqlGuid is null and False if it is otherwise.

Usage

```
myBoolean = mySqlGuid.IsNull
```

Parameters

None.

LessThan

The LessThan method compares two SqlGuid values and returns a SqlBoolean value indicating whether the first SqlGuid value is less than the second SqlGuid value. A null value would indicate that one of the SqlGuid values is null.

In addition to the LessThan method, you may also use the op_LessThan operator method, or, if your language supports overloaded operators, you may use that construct instead.

Usage

```
mySqlBoolean = mySqlGuid.LessThan(mySqlGuid1,mySqlGuid2)
mySqlBoolean = mySqlGuid.op_LessThan(mySqlGuid1,mySqlGuid2) ' VB
mySqlBoolean = (mySqlGuid1 < mySqlGuid2); // C#
```

Parameters

`mySqlGuid1`	A SqlGuid object.
`mySqlGuid2`	A SqlGuid object.

LessThanOrEqual

The LessThanOrEqual method compares two SqlGuid values and returns a SqlBoolean value indicating whether the first SqlGuid value is less than or equal to the second SqlGuid value. A null value would indicate that one of the SqlGuid values is null.

In addition to the LessThanOrEqual method, you may also use the op_LessThanOrEqual operator method, or, if your language supports overloaded operators, you may use that construct instead.

Usage

```
mySqlBoolean = mySqlGuid.LessThanOrEqual(mySqlGuid1,mySqlGuid2)
mySqlBoolean = mySqlGuid.op_LessThanOrEqual(mySqlGuid1,mySqlGuid2) ' VB
mySqlBoolean = (mySqlGuid1 <= mySqlGuid2); // C#
```

Parameters

`mySqlGuid1`	A SqlGuid object.
`mySqlGuid2`	A SqlGuid object.

NotEquals

The NotEquals method compares two SqlGuid values and returns a SqlBoolean value indicating whether the two SqlGuid values are not equal. A null value would indicate that one of the SqlGuid values is null.

In addition to the NotEquals method, you may also use the op_Inequality operator method, or, if your language supports overloaded operators, you may use that construct instead.

Usage

```
mySqlBoolean = mySqlGuid.NotEquals(mySqlGuid1,mySqlGuid2)
mySqlBoolean = mySqlGuid.op_Inequality(mySqlGuid1,mySqlGuid2) ' VB
mySqlBoolean = (mySqlGuid1 != mySqlGuid2); // C#
```

Parameters

`mySqlGuid1`	A SqlGuid object.
`mySqlGuid2`	A SqlGuid object.

Null

The Null field represents a read-only null value that can be assigned to a SqlGuid object. You cannot use the standard .NET way of assigning a null value with the System.DBNull.Value, but rather you must use this approach.

Usage

```
mySqlGuid = mySqlGuid.Null
```

Parameters

None.

op_Explicit

The op_Explicit method represents a special SqlGuid converter that allows SqlGuid values to be explicitly assigned to and from other SqlTypes. This method is overloaded in a couple of ways. The first two examples that follow show how to retrieve the SqlGuid value as a GUID object. The other examples show how to assign the SqlGuid value.

When assigning the SqlGuid value from a SqlString object, be sure that the string parses to a valid SqlGuid value. Converting from a SqlString object can throw a FormatException if ADO.NET can't parse the string.

If you are using ADO.NET with C#, then you will not call the op_Explicit method directly, but rather you are allowed to cast from one SqlType to the other.

Usage

```
myGuid = mySqlGuid.op_Explicit(mySqlGuid)      ' Visual Basic .NET
myGuid = (Guid)mySqlGuid;                      // C#
mySqlGuid = mySqlGuid.op_Explicit(mySqlBinary) ' Visual Basic .NET
mySqlGuid = (SqlGuid)mySqlBinary;              // C#
mySqlGuid = mySqlGuid.op_Explicit(mySqlString) ' Visual Basic .NET
mySqlGuid = (SqlGuid)mySqlString;              // C#
```

Parameters

`mySqlGuid`	A SqlGuid object.
`mySqlBinary`	A SqlBinary object.
`mySqlString`	A SqlString object.

Exceptions

FormatException	ADO.NET couldn't parse the string.
SqlNullValueException	You cannot assign a null value to a GUID class. Be sure to check the IsNull property, or use another exception-handling technique.

op_Implicit

The op_Implicit method represents a special SqlGuid converter that allows SqlGuid values to be implicitly assigned from a GUID object.

If you are using ADO.NET with C#, then you will not call the op_Implicit method directly, but rather you are allowed to cast from a GUID object to a SqlGuid structure.

Usage

```
mySqlGuid = mySqlGuid.op_Implicit(myGuid) ' Visual Basic .NET
mySqlGuid = (SqlGuid)myGuid;              // C#
```

Parameters

`myGuid`	A System.Guid object.

Exceptions

None.

Parse

The Parse method will evaluate a string and return a SqlGuid. Keep in mind that converting from a String can throw a FormatException if ADO.NET can't parse the string.

Usage

```
mySqlGuid = mySqlGuid.Parse(myString)
```

Parameters

`myString`	A case-insensitive String object containing a valid GUID value, such as "4a985849-fc57-4c70-8c50-09636c771c5a".

Exceptions

FormatException	ADO.NET couldn't parse the string.

ToByteArray

The ToByteArray method returns the value of the SqlGuid as an array of Byte values, representing the 16 bytes that physically compose the SqlGuid value in memory. The array returned will always have 16 elements.

Whether the SqlGuid has a value of all 0s or is Null, each array element will contain a Byte value of 0.

NOTE Here is another example of inconsistency within the SqlTypes namespace. A SqlDecimal structure has a BinData property that performs exactly like the SqlGuid ToByteArray method.

Usage

```
myByteArray = mySqlGuid.ToByteArray()
```

Parameters

None.

ToSqlBinary

The ToSqlBinary method returns the SqlGuid value as a SqlBinary. A null value would indicate that the SqlGuid value is null.

Usage

```
mySqlBinary = mySqlGuid.ToSqlBinary()
```

Parameters

None.

ToSqlString

The ToSqlString method returns the SqlGuid value as a SqlString. A null value would indicate that the SqlGuid value is null.

Usage

```
mySqlString = mySqlGuid.ToSqlString()
```

Parameters

None.

ToString

The ToString method returns the SqlGuid value as a readable value.

Usage

```
myString = mySqlGuid.ToString()
```

Parameters

None.

Value

The read-only Value property allows you to retrieve the value of the SqlGuid. Remember that this property is read-only—you may not assign a SqlGuid its value using its Value property.

In addition to using the Value property, you may also use the op_Explicit conversion method, or, if your language supports overloaded operators, you may use that construct instead.

Usage

```
myGuid = mySqlGuid.Value                     ' Visual Basic .NET
myGuid = mySqlGuid.op_Explicit(mySqlGuid)    ' Visual Basic .NET
myGuid = (Guid)mySqlGuid;                    // C#
```

Parameters

None.

Exceptions

SqlNullValueException	You cannot retrieve a null value. Be sure to check the IsNull property, or use another exception-handling technique.

System.Data.SqlTypes.SqlInt16

The SqlInt16 structure represents a 16-bit signed integer stored in 2 bytes. The integer's data value can range from 2^15 (-32,768) through 2^15 - 1 (32,767). Use the SqlInt16 structure to manipulate the following SQL Server data types:

- smallint
- ssql_variant (if the data is of type smallint)

Constructors

```
Dim mySqlInt16 As New SqlInt16(myInt16)
Dim mySqlInt16 As New SqlInt16(myShort)
```

Parameters

myInt16	An Int16 object.
myShort	A Short object (Visual Basic .NET).

SqlInt16 Sample Code

```
Private Sub ReadSqlType(ByVal myConnectionString As String, _
                        ByVal myCommandText As String)
   Dim mySqlConnection As System.Data.SqlClient.SqlConnection
```

```
    Dim mySqlDataReader As System.Data.SqlClient.SqlDataReader
    Dim mySqlCommand As System.Data.SqlClient.SqlCommand
    Dim mySqlInt16 As System.Data.SqlTypes.SqlInt16
    ' Establish connection
    mySqlConnection = New SqlConnection(myConnectionString)
    mySqlConnection.Open()
    ' Build and execute command
    mySqlCommand = New SqlCommand(myCommandText)
    mySqlCommand.Connection = mySqlConnection
    mySqlDataReader = mySqlCommand.ExecuteReader
    ' Read first row
    If mySqlDataReader.Read Then
        ' Save column as appropriate SqlTypes structure
        mySqlInt16 = mySqlDataReader.GetSqlInt16(1)
        MessageBox.Show(mySqlInt16.ToString)
    End If
    ' Done
    mySqlConnection.Close()
End Sub
```

Members

Add

The Add method will add two SqlInt16 values together and return a SqlInt16 object whose Value property contains the results of the addition. Keep in mind the MinValue and MaxValue that a SqlInt16 can hold. If either SqlInt16 value is null, the resulting SqlInt16 will be null.

In addition to the Add method, you may also use the op_Addition operator method, or, if your language supports overloaded operators, you may use that construct instead.

Usage

```
mySqlInt16 = mySqlInt16.Add(mySqlInt16a,mySqlInt16b)
mySqlInt16 = mySqlInt16.op_Addition(mySqlInt16a,mySqlInt16b) ' VB
mySqlInt16 = mySqlInt16a + mySqlInt16b; // C#
```

Parameters

`mySqlInt16a`	A SqlInt16 object.
`mySqlInt16b`	A SqlInt16 object.

Exceptions

OverflowException	The operation returned a value outside of the range of a SqlInt16 value.

BitwiseAnd

The BitwiseAnd method performs a Boolean and operation on two SqlInt16 objects. The method returns a SqlInt16 object. If either of the two values being compared is null, the resulting SqlInt16 will be null.

In addition to the BitwiseAnd method, you may also use the op_BitwiseAnd operator method, or, if your language supports overloaded operators, you may use that construct instead.

Usage

```
mySqlInt16 = mySqlInt16.BitwiseAnd(mySqlInt16a,mySqlInt16b)
mySqlInt16 = mySqlInt16.op_BitwiseAnd(mySqlInt16a,mySqlInt16b) ' VB
mySqlInt16 = mySqlInt16a & mySqlInt16b; // C#
```

Parameters

`mySqlInt16a`	A SqlInt16 object.
`mySqlInt16b`	A SqlInt16 object.

BitwiseOr

The BitwiseOr method performs a Boolean or operation on two SqlInt16 objects. The method returns a SqlInt16 object. If either of the two values being compared is null, the resulting SqlInt16 will be null.

In addition to the BitwiseOr method, you may also use the op_BitwiseOr operator method, or, if your language supports overloaded operators, you may use that construct instead.

Usage

```
mySqlInt16 = mySqlInt16.BitwiseOr(mySqlInt16a,mySqlInt16b)
mySqlInt16 = mySqlInt16.op_BitwiseOr(mySqlInt16a,mySqlInt16b) ' VB
mySqlInt16 = mySqlInt16a | mySqlInt16b; // C#
```

Parameters

`mySqlInt16a`	A SqlInt16 object.
`mySqlInt16b`	A SqlInt16 object.

CompareTo

The CompareTo method allows you to compare the SqlInt16 value with another supplied object to return an indication of their relative values. The returned Int32 object will indicate the comparison:

Less Than Zero. The SqlInt16 value was less than the supplied object, or the SqlInt16 was null.

Zero. The SqlInt16 value was the same as the supplied object.

Greater than zero. The SqlInt16 value was greater than the supplied object, or the object was null.

Usage

```
myInt32 = mySqlInt16.CompareTo(myObject)
```

Parameters

`myObject`	Any object that implements the IComparable interface.

Exceptions

ArgumentException	The supplied object isn't valid for comparison.

Divide

The Divide method will divide the first SqlInt16 by the second SqlInt16. This method will return a SqlInt16 object whose Value property contains the results of the division. Because a SqlInt16 object can store only whole numbers, any remainders after the division will be discarded. If either SqlInt16 value is null, the resulting SqlInt16 will be null.

In addition to the Divide method, you may also use the op_Division operator method, or, if your language supports overloaded operators, you may use that construct instead.

Usage

```
mySqlInt16 = mySqlInt16.Divide(mySqlInt16a,mySqlInt16b)
mySqlInt16 = mySqlInt16.op_Division(mySqlInt16a,mySqlInt16b) ' VB
mySqlInt16 = mySqlInt16a / mySqlInt16b; // C#
```

Parameters

`mySqlInt16a`	A SqlInt16 object.
`mySqlInt16b`	A SqlInt16 object.

Exceptions

DivideByZeroException	You tried to divide by zero.

Equals

The Equals method allows you to compare the SqlInt16 value with a supplied object or compare the values of two supplied objects or SqlInt16 values. The result will be either a Boolean or a SqlBoolean, depending on which overloaded method is called. The result may be null if either of the SqlInt16 values being compared is null.

In addition to the Equals method, you may also use the op_Equality operator method, or, if your language supports overloaded operators, you may use that construct instead.

Usage

```
mySqlBoolean = mySqlInt16.Equals(mySqlInt16a,mySqlInt16b)
myBoolean = mySqlInt16.Equals(myObject)
myBoolean = mySqlInt16.Equals(myObject,myObject2)
mySqlBoolean = mySqlInt16.op_Equality(mySqlInt16a,mySqlInt16b) ' VB
mySqlBoolean = (mySqlInt16a == mySqlInt16b); // C#
```

Parameters

`mySqlInt16a`	A SqlInt16 object.
`mySqlInt16b`	A SqlInt16 object.
`myObject`	Any System.Object or descendant.
`myObject2`	Any System.Object or descendant.

GetHashCode

The GetHashCode method returns a hash code for the SqlInt16 value. The hash code represents a unique value corresponding to the particular value of the SqlInt16 object. Keep in mind that even the smallest change to the SqlInt16 value will result in a different hash code. Requesting the hash code for a SqlInt16 object with a null value will return 0.

BE CAREFUL The hash code returned for a SqlInt16 with a value of 0 is 0, which is the same for a SqlInt16 with a null value.

Usage

```
myInt32 = mySqlInt16.GetHashCode()
```

Parameters

None.

GreaterThan

The GreaterThan method compares two SqlInt16 values and returns a SqlBoolean value indicating whether the first SqlInt16 value is greater than the second SqlInt16 value. A null value would indicate that one of the SqlInt16 values is null.

In addition to the GreaterThan method, you may also use the op_GreaterThan operator method, or, if your language supports overloaded operators, you may use that construct instead.

Usage

```
mySqlBoolean = mySqlInt16.GreaterThan(mySqlInt16a,mySqlInt16b)
mySqlBoolean = mySqlInt16.op_GreaterThan(mySqlInt16a,mySqlInt16b) ' VB
mySqlBoolean = (mySqlInt16a > mySqlInt16b); // C#
```

Parameters

mySqlInt16a	A SqlInt16 object.
mySqlInt16b	A SqlInt16 object.

GreaterThanOrEqual

The GreaterThanOrEqual method compares two SqlInt16 values and returns a SqlBoolean value indicating whether the first SqlInt16 value is greater than or equal to the second SqlInt16 value. A null value would indicate that one of the SqlInt16 values is null.

In addition to the GreaterThanOrEqual method, you may also use the op_GreaterThanOrEqual operator method, or, if your language supports overloaded operators, you may use that construct instead.

Usage

```
mySqlBoolean = mySqlInt16.GreaterThanOrEqual(mySqlInt16a,mySqlInt16b)
mySqlBoolean = _
   mySqlInt16.op_GreaterThanOrEqual(mySqlInt16a,mySqlInt16b) ' VB
mySqlBoolean = (mySqlInt16a >= mySqlInt16b); // C#
```

Parameters

`mySqlInt16a`	A SqlInt16 object.
`mySqlInt16b`	A SqlInt16 object.

IsNull

The read-only IsNull property returns a Boolean indicating whether the SqlInt16 is null. The value will be True if the value of the SqlInt16 is null and False if it is otherwise.

Usage

```
myBoolean = mySqlInt16.IsNull
```

Parameters

None.

LessThan

The LessThan method compares two SqlInt16 values and returns a SqlBoolean value indicating whether the first SqlInt16 value is less than the second SqlInt16 value. A null value would indicate that one of the SqlInt16 values is null.

In addition to the LessThan method, you may also use the op_LessThan operator method, or, if your language supports overloaded operators, you may use that construct instead.

Usage

```
mySqlBoolean = mySqlInt16.LessThan(mySqlInt16a,mySqlInt16b)
mySqlBoolean = mySqlInt16.op_LessThan(mySqlInt16a,mySqlInt16b) ' VB
mySqlBoolean = (mySqlInt16a < mySqlInt16b); // C#
```

Parameters

`mySqlInt16a`	A SqlInt16 object.
`mySqlInt16b`	A SqlInt16 object.

LessThanOrEqual

The LessThanOrEqual method compares two SqlInt16 values and returns a SqlBoolean value indicating whether the first SqlInt16 value is less than or equal to the second SqlInt16 value. A null value would indicate that one of the SqlInt16 values is null.

In addition to the LessThanOrEqual method, you may also use the op_LessThanOrEqual operator method, or, if your language supports overloaded operators, you may use that construct instead.

Usage

```
mySqlBoolean = mySqlInt16.LessThanOrEqual(mySqlInt16a,mySqlInt16b)
mySqlBoolean = mySqlInt16.op_LessThanOrEqual(mySqlInt16a,mySqlInt16b) ' VB
mySqlBoolean = (mySqlInt16a <= mySqlInt16b); // C#
```

Parameters

`mySqlInt16a`	A SqlInt16 object.
`mySqlInt16b`	A SqlInt16 object.

MaxValue

The read-only MaxValue field represents the largest number that a SqlInt16 can hold, which is 32767. By using the MaxValue field, you can build flexible, readable exception-handling code.

Usage

```
mySqlInt16 = mySqlInt16.MaxValue
```

Parameters

None.

MinValue

The read-only MinValue field represents the smallest number that a SqlInt16 can hold, which is -32768. By using the MinValue field, you can build flexible, readable exception-handling code.

Usage

```
mySqlInt16 = mySqlInt16.MinValue
```

Parameters

None.

Mod

The Mod method will divide the first SqlInt16 by the second SqlInt16 and return only the modulus (remainder portion) as a SqlInt16 object. If either SqlInt16 value is null, the resulting SqlInt16 will be null.

In addition to the Mod method, you may also use the op_Modulus operator method, or, if your language supports overloaded operators, you may use that construct instead.

Usage

```
mySqlInt16 = mySqlInt16.Mod(mySqlInt16a,mySqlInt16b)
mySqlInt16 = mySqlInt16.op_Modulus(mySqlInt16a,mySqlInt15b) ' VB
mySqlInt16 = mySqlInt16a % mySqlInt16b; // C#
```

Parameters

`mySqlInt16a`	A SqlInt16 object.
`mySqlInt16b`	A SqlInt16 object.

Exceptions

DivideByZeroException	You tried to divide by zero.

Multiply

The Multiply method will multiply the first SqlInt16 by the second SqlInt16 and return a SqlInt16 object whose Value property contains the results of the multiplication. Keep in mind the MaxValue that a SqlInt16 can hold. If either SqlInt16 value is null, the resulting SqlInt16 will be null.

In addition to the Multiply method, you may also use the op_Multiply operator method, or, if your language supports overloaded operators, you may use that construct instead.

Usage

```
mySqlInt16 = mySqlInt16.Multiply(mySqlInt16a,mySqlInt16b)
mySqlInt16 = mySqlInt16.op_Multiply(mySqlInt16a,mySqlInt16b) ' VB
mySqlInt16 = mySqlInt16a * mySqlInt16b; // C#
```

Parameters

`mySqlInt16a`	A SqlInt16 object.
`mySqlInt16b`	A SqlInt16 object.

Exceptions

OverflowException	The operation returned a value outside of the range of a SqlInt16 value.

NotEquals

The NotEquals method compares two SqlInt16 values and returns a SqlBoolean value indicating whether the two SqlInt16 values are not equal. A null value would indicate that one of the SqlInt16 values is null.

In addition to the NotEquals method, you may also use the op_Inequality operator method, or, if your language supports overloaded operators, you may use that construct instead.

Usage

```
mySqlBoolean = mySqlInt16.NotEquals(mySqlInt16a,mySqlInt16b)
mySqlBoolean = mySqlInt16.op_Inequality(mySqlInt16a,mySqlInt16b) ' VB
mySqlBoolean = (mySqlInt16a != mySqlInt16b); // C#
```

Parameters

`mySqlInt16a`	A SqlInt16 object.
`mySqlInt16b`	A SqlInt16 object.

Null

The Null field represents a read-only null value that can be assigned to a SqlInt16 object. You cannot use the standard .NET way of assigning a null value with the System.DBNull.Value, but rather you must use this approach.

Usage

```
mySqlInt16 = mySqlInt16.Null
```

Parameters

None.

OnesComplement

The OnesComplement method will return the bitwise one's complement of the specified SqlInt16. If the SqlInt16 value that you are complementing is null, then the method will return a null value.

In addition to the OnesComplement method, you may also use the op_OnesComplement operator method, or, if your language supports overloaded operators, you may use that construct instead.

NOTE **The one's complement operator is sometimes referred to as the *bitwise complement* or *bitwise not* operator.**

Usage

```
mySqlInt16 = mySqlInt16.OnesComplement(mySqlInt16a)
mySqlInt16 = mySqlInt16.op_OnesComplement(mySqlInt16a) ' VB
mySqlInt16 = ~ mySqlInt16a; // C#
```

Parameters

`mySqlInt16a`	A SqlInt16 object.

op_Explicit

The op_Explicit method represents a special SqlInt16 converter that allows SqlInt16 values to be assigned from other SqlTypes. This method is overloaded in several ways. The first three examples that follow show how to retrieve the SqlInt16 value as simple Int16 or Short (Visual Basic .NET) objects. The other examples show how to assign the SqlInt16 value.

When assigning the SqlInt16 value from one of the other SqlTypes, keep in mind the MinValue and MaxValue. Any value that exceeds those limits will throw an OverflowException. Any null values will convert to a SqlInt16 null value.

When assigning the SqlInt16 value from a SqlString object, be sure that the string parses to a valid SqlInt16 value. Converting from a SqlString object can throw a FormatException if ADO.NET can't parse the string.

If you are using ADO.NET with C#, then you will not call the op_Explicit method directly, but rather you are allowed to cast from one SqlType to the other.

Usage

```
myShort = mySqlInt16.op_Explicit(mySqlInt16)          ' Visual Basic .NET
myInt16 = mySqlInt16.op_Explicit(mySqlInt16)          ' Visual Basic .NET
myInt16 = (Int16)mySqlInt16;                          // C#
mySqlInt16 = mySqlInt16.op_Explicit(mySqlBoolean)     ' Visual Basic .NET
mySqlInt16 = (SqlInt16)mySqlBoolean;                  // C#
mySqlInt16 = mySqlInt16.op_Explicit(mySqlDecimal)     ' Visual Basic .NET
mySqlInt16 = (SqlInt16)mySqlDecimal;                  // C#
mySqlInt16 = mySqlInt16.op_Explicit(mySqlDouble)      ' Visual Basic .NET
mySqlInt16 = (SqlInt16)mySqlDouble;                   // C#
mySqlInt16 = mySqlInt16.op_Explicit(mySqlInt32)       ' Visual Basic .NET
mySqlInt16 = (SqlInt16)mySqlInt32;                    // C#
mySqlInt16 = mySqlInt16.op_Explicit(mySqlInt64)       ' Visual Basic .NET
mySqlInt16 = (SqlInt16)mySqlInt64;                    // C#
mySqlInt16 = mySqlInt16.op_Explicit(mySqlMoney)       ' Visual Basic .NET
mySqlInt16 = (SqlInt16)mySqlMoney;                    // C#
mySqlInt16 = mySqlInt16.op_Explicit(mySqlSingle)      ' Visual Basic .NET
mySqlInt16 = (SqlInt16)mySqlSingle;                   // C#
mySqlInt16 = mySqlInt16.op_Explicit(mySqlString)      ' Visual Basic .NET
mySqlInt16 = (SqlInt16)mySqlString;                   // C#
```

Parameters

`mySqlBoolean`	A SqlBoolean object.
`mySqlDecimal`	A SqlDecimal object.
`mySqlDouble`	A SqlDouble object.
`mySqlInt32`	A SqlInt32 object.
`mySqlInt64`	A SqlInt64 object.
`mySqlMoney`	A SqlMoney object.
`mySqlSingle`	A SqlSingle object.
`mySqlString`	A SqlString object.

Exceptions

FormatException	ADO.NET couldn't parse the string.
OverflowException	The operation returned a value outside of the range of a SqlInt16 value.
SqlNullValueException	You cannot assign a null value to an Int16 or Short class. Be sure to check the IsNull property, or use another exception-handling technique.

op_Implicit

The op_Implicit method represents a special SqlInt16 converter that allows for an Int16 (Short integer in Visual Basic .NET) or a SqlByte value to be assigned to the SqlInt16.

NOTE It appears that you can pass any numeric object to the op_Implicit method. When assigning the SqlInt16 value from numeric types with a larger precision, keep in mind the MinValue and MaxValue. Any value that exceeds those limits will throw an OverflowException.

If you are using ADO.NET with C#, then you will not call the op_Implicit method directly, but rather you are allowed to cast from one SqlType to the other.

Usage

```
mySqlInt16 = mySqlInt16.op_Implicit(myInt16)    ' Visual Basic .NET
mySqlInt16 = (SqlInt16)myInt16;                 // C#
mySqlInt16 = mySqlInt16.op_Implicit(mySqlByte) ' Visual Basic .NET
mySqlInt16 = (SqlInt16)mySqlByte;               // C#
```

Parameters

`myInt16`	An Int16 object (Short in Visual Basic .NET).
`mySqlByte`	A SqlByte object.

Exceptions

OverflowException	The operation returned a value outside of the range of a SqlInt16 value.

Parse

The Parse method will evaluate a string and return a SqlInt16. Keep in mind that converting from a String can throw a FormatException if ADO.NET can't parse the string.

Usage

```
mySqlInt16 = mySqlInt16.Parse(myString)
```

Parameters

`myString`	A case-insensitive String object containing a valid Int16 value, such as "-32768", "100" or "32767".

Exceptions

OverflowException	The operation returned a value outside of the range of a SqlInt16 value.
FormatException	ADO.NET couldn't parse the string.

Subtract

The Subtract method will subtract the second SqlInt16 from the first SqlInt16 and return a SqlInt16 object whose Value property contains the results of the subtraction. Keep in mind the MinValue and MaxValue that a SqlInt16 can hold. If either SqlInt16 value is null, the resulting SqlInt16 will be null.

In addition to the Subtract method, you may also use the op_Subtraction operator method, or, if your language supports overloaded operators, you may use that construct instead.

Usage

```
mySqlInt16 = mySqlInt16.Subtract(mySqlInt16a,mySqlInt16b)
mySqlInt16 = mySqlInt16.op_Subtraction(mySqlInt16a,mySqlInt16b) ' VB
mySqlInt16 = mySqlInt16a - mySqlInt16b; // C#
```

Parameters

`mySqlInt16a`	A SqlInt16 object.
`mySqlInt16b`	A SqlInt16 object.

Exceptions

OverflowException	The operation returned a value outside of the range of a SqlInt16 value.

ToSqlBoolean

The ToSqlBoolean method returns the SqlInt16 value as a SqlBoolean object. Any nonzero SqlInt16 value will return in a True SqlBoolean. A zero SqlInt16 value will return a False SqlBoolean. A null SqlInt16 value will return a null SqlBoolean.

Usage

```
mySqlBoolean = mySqlInt16.ToSqlBoolean()
```

Parameters

None.

ToSqlByte

The ToSqlByte method returns the SqlInt16 value as a SqlByte object. Be mindful of the range of values that the SqlByte class supports. A null SqlInt16 value will return a null SqlByte.

Usage

```
mySqlByte = mySqlInt16.ToSqlByte()
```

Parameters

None.

Exceptions

OverflowException	The operation returned a value outside of the range of a SqlByte value.

ToSqlDecimal

The ToSqlDecimal method returns the SqlInt16 value as a SqlDecimal. A null value would indicate that the SqlInt16 value is null.

Usage

```
mySqlDecimal = mySqlInt16.ToSqlDecimal()
```

Parameters

None.

ToSqlDouble

The ToSqlDouble method returns the SqlInt16 value as a SqlDouble. A null value would indicate that the SqlInt16 value is null.

Usage

```
mySqlDouble = mySqlInt16.ToSqlDouble()
```

Parameters

None.

ToSqlInt32

The ToSqlInt32 method returns the SqlInt16 value as a SqlInt32 (32 bit integer). A null value would indicate that the SqlInt16 value is null.

Usage

```
mySqlInt32 = mySqlInt16.ToSqlInt32()
```

Parameters

None.

ToSqlInt64

The ToSqlInt64 method returns the SqlInt16 value as a SqlInt64 (64 bit integer). A null value would indicate that the SqlInt16 value is null.

Usage

```
mySqlInt64 = mySqlInt16.ToSqlInt64()
```

Parameters
None.

ToSqlMoney

The ToSqlMoney method returns the SqlInt16 value as a SqlMoney. A null value would indicate that the SqlInt16 value is null.

Usage
```
mySqlMoney = mySqlInt16.ToSqlMoney()
```

Parameters
None.

ToSqlSingle

The ToSqlSingle method returns the SqlInt16 value as a SqlSingle. A null value would indicate that the SqlInt16 value is null.

Usage
```
mySqlSingle = mySqlInt16.ToSqlSingle()
```

Parameters
None.

ToSqlString

The ToSqlString method returns the SqlInt16 value as a SqlString. A null value would indicate that the SqlInt16 value is null.

Usage
```
mySqlString = mySqlInt16.ToSqlString()
```

Parameters
None.

ToString

The ToString method returns the SqlInt16 value as a readable value.

Usage
```
myString = mySqlInt16.ToString()
```

Parameters
None.

Value

The read-only Value property allows you to retrieve the value of the SqlInt16. Remember that this property is read-only—you may not assign a SqlInt16 its value using its Value property.

In addition to using the Value property, you may also use the op_Explicit conversion method, or, if your language supports overloaded operators, you may use that construct instead.

Usage

```
myInt16 = mySqlInt16.Value                      ' Visual Basic .NET
myInt16 = mySqlInt16.op_Explicit(mySqlInt16)    ' Visual Basic .NET
myInt16 = (Int16)mySqlInt16;                    // C#
```

Parameters

None.

Exceptions

SqlNullValueException	You cannot retrieve a null value. Be sure to check the IsNull property, or use another exception-handling technique.

Xor

The Xor method performs a Boolean xor operation—a bitwise exclusive OR operation on two SqlInt16 values. The method returns a SqlInt16 object. If either of the two values being compared is null, the resulting SqlInt16 will be null.

In addition to the Xor method, you may also use the op_ExclusiveOr operator method, or, if your language supports overloaded operators, you may use that construct instead.

Usage

```
mySqlInt16 = mySqlInt16.Xor(mySqlInt16a,mySqlInt16b)
mySqlInt16 = mySqlInt16.op_ExclusiveOr(mySqlInt16a,mySqlInt16b)  ' VB
mySqlInt16 = mySqlInt16a ^ mySqlInt16b; // C#
```

Parameters

`mySqlInt16a`	A SqlInt16 object.
`mySqlInt16b`	A SqlInt16 object.

Zero

The Zero field represents a read-only value of (0) that can be assigned to a SqlInt16 object.

Usage

```
mySqlInt16 = mySqlInt16.Zero
```

Parameters

None.

System.Data.SqlTypes.SqlInt32

The SqlInt32 structure represents a 32-bit signed integer stored in 4 bytes. The integer's data value can range from -2^31 (-2,147,483,648) through 2^31 – 1 (2,147,483,647). Use the SqlInt32 structure to manipulate the following SQL Server data types:

- int
- sql_variant (if the data is of type int)

Constructors

```
Dim mySqlInt32 As New SqlInt32(myInt32)
Dim mySqlInt32 As New SqlInt32(myInteger)
```

Parameters

`myInt32`	An Int32 object.
`myInteger`	An Integer object (Visual Basic .NET).

SqlInt32 Sample Code

```
Private Sub ReadSqlType(ByVal myConnectionString As String, _
                        ByVal myCommandText As String)
   Dim mySqlConnection As System.Data.SqlClient.SqlConnection
   Dim mySqlDataReader As System.Data.SqlClient.SqlDataReader
   Dim mySqlCommand As System.Data.SqlClient.SqlCommand
   Dim mySqlInt32 As System.Data.SqlTypes.SqlInt32
   ' Establish connection
   mySqlConnection = New SqlConnection(myConnectionString)
   mySqlConnection.Open()
   ' Build and execute command
   mySqlCommand = New SqlCommand(myCommandText)
   mySqlCommand.Connection = mySqlConnection
   mySqlDataReader = mySqlCommand.ExecuteReader
   ' Read first row
   If mySqlDataReader.Read Then
      ' Save column as appropriate SqlTypes structure
      mySqlInt32 = mySqlDataReader.GetSqlInt32(1)
      MessageBox.Show(mySqlInt32.ToString)
   End If
   ' Done
   mySqlConnection.Close()
End Sub
```

Members

Add

The Add method will add two SqlInt32 values together and return a SqlInt32 object whose Value property contains the results of the addition. Keep in mind the MinValue and MaxValue that a SqlInt32 can hold. If either SqlInt32 value is null, the resulting SqlInt32 will be null.

In addition to the Add method, you may also use the op_Addition operator method, or, if your language supports overloaded operators, you may use that construct instead.

Usage

```
mySqlInt32 = mySqlInt32.Add(mySqlInt32a,mySqlInt32b)
mySqlInt32 = mySqlInt32.op_Addition(mySqlInt32a,mySqlInt32b) ' VB
mySqlInt32 = mySqlInt32a + mySqlInt32b; // C#
```

Parameters

`mySqlInt32a`	A SqlInt32 object.
`mySqlInt32b`	A SqlInt32 object.

Exceptions

OverflowException	The operation returned a value outside of the range of a SqlInt32 value.

BitwiseAnd

The BitwiseAnd method performs a Boolean and operation on two SqlInt32 objects. The method returns a SqlInt32 object. If either of the two values being compared is null, the resulting SqlInt32 will be null.

In addition to the BitwiseAnd method, you may also use the op_BitwiseAnd operator method, or, if your language supports overloaded operators, you may use that construct instead.

Usage

```
mySqlInt32 = mySqlInt32.BitwiseAnd(mySqlInt32a,mySqlInt32b)
mySqlInt32 = mySqlInt32.op_BitwiseAnd(mySqlInt32a,mySqlInt32b) ' VB
mySqlInt32 = mySqlInt32a & mySqlInt32b; // C#
```

Parameters

`mySqlInt32a`	A SqlInt32 object.
`mySqlInt32b`	A SqlInt32 object.

BitwiseOr

The BitwiseOr method performs a Boolean or operation on two SqlInt32 objects. The method returns a SqlInt32 object. If either of the two values being compared is null, the resulting SqlInt32 will be null.

In addition to the BitwiseOr method, you may also use the op_BitwiseOr operator method, or, if your language supports overloaded operators, you may use that construct instead.

Usage

```
mySqlInt32 = mySqlInt32.BitwiseOr(mySqlInt32a,mySqlInt32b)
mySqlInt32 = mySqlInt32.op_BitwiseOr(mySqlInt32a,mySqlInt32b) ' VB
mySqlInt32 = mySqlInt32a | mySqlInt32b; // C#
```

Parameters

`mySqlInt32a`	A SqlInt32 object.
`mySqlInt32b`	A SqlInt32 object.

CompareTo

The CompareTo method allows you to compare the SqlInt32 value with another supplied object to return an indication of their relative values. The returned Int32 object will indicate the comparison:

Less Than Zero. The SqlInt32 value was less than the supplied object, or the SqlInt32 was null.

Zero. The SqlInt32 value was the same as the supplied object.

Greater than zero. The SqlInt32 value was greater than the supplied object, or the object was null.

Usage

```
myInt32 = mySqlInt32.CompareTo(myObject)
```

Parameters

`myObject`	Any object that implements the IComparable interface.

Exceptions

ArgumentException	The supplied object isn't valid for comparison.

Divide

The Divide method will divide the first SqlInt32 by the second SqlInt32. This method will return a SqlInt32 object whose Value property contains the results of the division. Because a SqlInt32 object can store only whole numbers, any remainders after the division will be discarded. If either SqlInt32 value is null, the resulting SqlInt32 will be null.

In addition to the Divide method, you may also use the op_Division operator method, or, if your language supports overloaded operators, you may use that construct instead.

Usage

```
mySqlInt32 = mySqlInt32.Divide(mySqlInt32a,mySqlInt32b)
mySqlInt32 = mySqlInt32.op_Division(mySqlInt32a,mySqlInt32b) ' VB
mySqlInt32 = mySqlInt32a / mySqlInt32b; // C#
```

Parameters

`mySqlInt32a`	A SqlInt32 object.
`mySqlInt32b`	A SqlInt32 object.

Exceptions

DivideByZeroException	You tried to divide by zero.

Equals

The Equals method allows you to compare the SqlInt32 value with a supplied object or compare the values of two supplied objects or SqlInt32 values. The result will be either a Boolean or a SqlBoolean, depending on which overloaded method is called. The result may be null if either of the SqlInt32 values being compared is null.

In addition to the Equals method, you may also use the op_Equality operator method, or, if your language supports overloaded operators, you may use that construct instead.

Usage

```
mySqlBoolean = mySqlInt32.Equals(mySqlInt32a,mySqlInt32b)
myBoolean = mySqlInt32.Equals(myObject)
myBoolean = mySqlInt32.Equals(myObject,myObject2)
mySqlBoolean = mySqlInt32.op_Equality(mySqlInt32a,mySqlInt32b) ' VB
mySqlBoolean = (mySqlInt32a == mySqlInt32b); // C#
```

Parameters

mySqlInt32a	A SqlInt32 object.
mySqlInt32b	A SqlInt32 object.
myObject	Any System.Object or descendant.
myObject2	Any System.Object or descendant.

GetHashCode

The GetHashCode method returns a hash code for the SqlInt32 value. The hash code represents a unique value corresponding to the particular value of the SqlInt32 object. Keep in mind that even the smallest change to the SqlInt32 value will result in a different hash code. Requesting the hash code for a SqlInt32 object with a null value will return 0.

BE CAREFUL **The hash code returned for a SqlInt32 with a value of 0 is 0, which is the same for a SqlInt32 with a null value.**

Usage

```
myInt32 = mySqlInt32.GetHashCode()
```

Parameters

None.

GreaterThan

The GreaterThan method compares two SqlInt32 values and returns a SqlBoolean value indicating whether the first SqlInt32 value is greater than the second SqlInt32 value. A null value would indicate that one of the SqlInt32 values is null.

In addition to the GreaterThan method, you may also use the op_GreaterThan operator method, or, if your language supports overloaded operators, you may use that construct instead.

Usage

```
mySqlBoolean = mySqlInt32.GreaterThan(mySqlInt32a,mySqlInt32b)
mySqlBoolean = mySqlInt32.op_GreaterThan(mySqlInt32a,mySqlInt32b) ' VB
mySqlBoolean = (mySqlInt32a > mySqlInt32b); // C#
```

Parameters

mySqlInt32a	A SqlInt32 object.
mySqlInt32b	A SqlInt32 object.

GreaterThanOrEqual

The GreaterThanOrEqual method compares two SqlInt32 values and returns a SqlBoolean value indicating whether the first SqlInt32 value is greater than or equal to the second SqlInt32 value. A null value would indicate that one of the SqlInt32 values is null.

In addition to the GreaterThanOrEqual method, you may also use the op_GreaterThanOrEqual operator method, or, if your language supports overloaded operators, you may use that construct instead.

Usage

```
mySqlBoolean = mySqlInt32.GreaterThanOrEqual(mySqlInt32a,mySqlInt32b)
mySqlBoolean = _
   mySqlInt32.op_GreaterThanOrEqual(mySqlInt32a,mySqlInt32b) ' VB
mySqlBoolean = (mySqlInt32a >= mySqlInt32b); // C#
```

Parameters

`mySqlInt32a`	A SqlInt32 object.
`mySqlInt32b`	A SqlInt32 object.

IsNull

The read-only IsNull property returns a Boolean indicating whether the SqlInt32 is null. The value will be True if the value of the SqlInt32 is null and False if it is otherwise.

Usage

```
myBoolean = mySqlInt32.IsNull
```

Parameters

None.

LessThan

The LessThan method compares two SqlInt32 values and returns a SqlBoolean value indicating whether the first SqlInt32 value is less than the second SqlInt32 value. A null value would indicate that one of the SqlInt32 values is null.

In addition to the LessThan method, you may also use the op_LessThan operator method, or, if your language supports overloaded operators, you may use that construct instead.

Usage

```
mySqlBoolean = mySqlInt32.LessThan(mySqlInt32a,mySqlInt32b)
mySqlBoolean = mySqlInt32.op_LessThan(mySqlInt32a,mySqlInt32b) ' VB
mySqlBoolean = (mySqlInt32a < mySqlInt32b); // C#
```

Parameters

`mySqlInt32a`	A SqlInt32 object.
`mySqlInt32b`	A SqlInt32 object.

LessThanOrEqual

The LessThanOrEqual method compares two SqlInt32 values and returns a SqlBoolean value indicating whether the first SqlInt32 value is less than or equal to the second SqlInt32 value. A null value would indicate that one of the SqlInt32 values is null.

In addition to the LessThanOrEqual method, you may also use the op_LessThanOrEqual operator method, or, if your language supports overloaded operators, you may use that construct instead.

Usage

```
mySqlBoolean = mySqlInt32.LessThanOrEqual(mySqlInt32a,mySqlInt32b)
mySqlBoolean = mySqlInt32.op_LessThanOrEqual(mySqlInt32a,mySqlInt32b) ' VB
mySqlBoolean = (mySqlInt32a <= mySqlInt32b); // C#
```

Parameters

`mySqlInt32a`	A SqlInt32 object.
`mySqlInt32b`	A SqlInt32 object.

MaxValue

The read-only MaxValue field represents the largest number that a SqlInt32 can hold, which is 2^31 - 1 (2,147,483,647). By using the MaxValue field, you can build flexible, readable exception-handling code.

Usage

```
mySqlInt32 = mySqlInt32.MaxValue
```

Parameters

None.

MinValue

The read-only MinValue field represents the smallest number that a SqlInt32 can hold, which is -2^31 (-2,147,483,648). By using the MinValue field, you can build flexible, readable exception-handling code.

Usage

```
mySqlInt32 = mySqlInt32.MinValue
```

Parameters

None.

Mod

The Mod method will divide the first SqlInt32 by the second SqlInt32 and return only the modulus (remainder portion) as a SqlInt32 object. If either SqlInt32 value is null, the resulting SqlInt32 will be null.

In addition to the Mod method, you may also use the op_Modulus operator method, or, if your language supports overloaded operators, you may use that construct instead.

Usage

```
mySqlInt32 = mySqlInt32.Mod(mySqlInt32a,mySqlInt32b)
mySqlInt32 = mySqlInt32.op_Modulus(mySqlInt32a,mySqlInt32b) ' VB
mySqlInt32 = mySqlInt32a % mySqlInt32b; // C#
```

Parameters

`mySqlInt32a`	A SqlInt32 object.
`mySqlInt32b`	A SqlInt32 object.

Exceptions

DivideByZeroException	You tried to divide by zero.

Multiply

The Multiply method will multiply the first SqlInt32 by the second SqlInt32 and return a SqlInt32 object whose Value property contains the results of the multiplication. Keep in mind the MaxValue that a SqlInt32 can hold. If either SqlInt32 value is null, the resulting SqlInt32 will be null.

In addition to the Multiply method, you may also use the op_Multiply operator method, or, if your language supports overloaded operators, you may use that construct instead.

Usage

```
mySqlInt32 = mySqlInt32.Multiply(mySqlInt32a,mySqlInt32b)
mySqlInt32 = mySqlInt32.op_Multiply(mySqlInt32a,mySqlInt32b) ' VB
mySqlInt32 = mySqlInt32a * mySqlInt32b; // C#
```

Parameters

`mySqlInt32a`	A SqlInt32 object.
`mySqlInt32b`	A SqlInt32 object.

Exceptions

OverflowException	The operation returned a value outside of the range of a SqlInt32 value.

NotEquals

The NotEquals method compares two SqlInt32 values and returns a SqlBoolean value indicating whether the two SqlInt32 values are not equal. A null value would indicate that one of the SqlInt32 values is null.

In addition to the NotEquals method, you may also use the op_Inequality operator method, or, if your language supports overloaded operators, you may use that construct instead.

Usage

```
mySqlBoolean = mySqlInt32.NotEquals(mySqlInt32a,mySqlInt32b)
mySqlBoolean = mySqlInt32.op_Inequality(mySqlInt32a,mySqlInt32b) ' VB
mySqlBoolean = (mySqlInt32a != mySqlInt32b); // C#
```

Parameters

`mySqlInt32a`	A SqlInt32 object.
`mySqlInt32b`	A SqlInt32 object.

Null

The Null field represents a read-only null value that can be assigned to a SqlInt32 object. You cannot use the standard .NET way of assigning a null value with the System.DBNull.Value, but rather you must use this approach.

Usage

```
mySqlInt32 = mySqlInt32.Null
```

Parameters

None.

OnesComplement

The OnesComplement method will return the bitwise one's complement of the specified SqlInt32. If the SqlInt32 value that you are complementing is null, then the method will return a null value.

In addition to the OnesComplement method, you may also use the op_OnesComplement operator method, or, if your language supports overloaded operators, you may use that construct instead.

> **NOTE** **The one's complement operator is sometimes referred to as the *bitwise complement* or *bitwise not* operator.**

Usage

```
mySqlInt32 = mySqlInt32.OnesComplement(mySqlInt32a)
mySqlInt32 = mySqlInt32.op_OnesComplement(mySqlInt32a)  ' VB
mySqlInt32 = ~ mySqlInt32a; // C#
```

Parameters

`mySqlInt32a`	A SqlInt32 object.

op_Explicit

The op_Explicit method represents a special SqlInt32 converter that allows SqlInt32 values to be assigned from other SqlTypes. This method is overloaded in several ways. The first three examples that follow show how to retrieve the SqlInt32 value as simple Int32 or Integer (Visual Basic .NET) objects. The other examples show how to assign the SqlInt32 value.

When assigning the SqlInt16 value from one of the other SqlTypes, keep in mind the MinValue and MaxValue. Any value that exceeds those limits will throw an OverflowException. Any null values will convert to a SqlInt32 null value.

When assigning the SqlInt32 value from a SqlString object, be sure that the string parses to a valid SqlInt32 value. Converting from a SqlString object can throw a FormatException if ADO.NET can't parse the string.

If you are using ADO.NET with C#, then you will not call the op_Explicit method directly, but rather you are allowed to cast from one SqlType to the other.

Usage

```
myInteger = mySqlInt32.op_Explicit(mySqlInt32)          ' Visual Basic .NET
myInt32 = mySqlInt32.op_Explicit(mySqlInt32)            ' Visual Basic .NET
myInt32 = (Int32)mySqlInt32;                            // C#
mySqlInt32 = mySqlInt32.op_Explicit(mySqlBoolean)       ' Visual Basic .NET
mySqlInt32 = (SqlInt32)mySqlBoolean;                    // C#
mySqlInt32 = mySqlInt32.op_Explicit(mySqlDecimal)       ' Visual Basic .NET
mySqlInt32 = (SqlInt32)mySqlDecimal;                    // C#
```

```
mySqlInt32 = mySqlInt32.op_Explicit(mySqlDouble)  ' Visual Basic .NET
mySqlInt32 = (SqlInt32)mySqlDouble;               // C#
mySqlInt32 = mySqlInt32.op_Explicit(mySqlInt64)   ' Visual Basic .NET
mySqlInt32 = (SqlInt32)mySqlInt64;                // C#
mySqlInt32 = mySqlInt32.op_Explicit(mySqlMoney)   ' Visual Basic .NET
mySqlInt32 = (SqlInt32)mySqlMoney;                // C#
mySqlInt32 = mySqlInt32.op_Explicit(mySqlSingle)  ' Visual Basic .NET
mySqlInt32 = (SqlInt32)mySqlSingle;               // C#
mySqlInt32 = mySqlInt32.op_Explicit(mySqlString)  ' Visual Basic .NET
mySqlInt32 = (SqlInt32)mySqlString;               // C#
```

Parameters

`mySqlBoolean`	A SqlBoolean object.
`mySqlDecimal`	A SqlDecimal object.
`mySqlDouble`	A SqlDouble object.
`mySqlInt64`	A SqlInt64 object.
`mySqlMoney`	A SqlMoney object.
`mySqlSingle`	A SqlSingle object.
`mySqlString`	A SqlString object.

Exceptions

FormatException	ADO.NET couldn't parse the string.
OverflowException	The operation returned a value outside of the range of a SqlInt32 value.
SqlNullValueException	You cannot assign a null value to an Int32 or Integer class. Be sure to check the IsNull property, or use another exception-handling technique.

op_Implicit

The op_Implicit method represents a special SqlInt32 converter that is overloaded a couple of different ways. It allows for an Integer, SqlByte, or SqlInt16 to be assigned to the SqlInt32.

NOTE It appears that you can pass any numeric object to the op_Implicit method. When assigning the SqlInt32 value from numeric types with a larger precision, keep in mind the MinValue and MaxValue. Any value that exceeds those limits will throw an OverflowException.

If you are using ADO.NET with C#, then you will not call the op_Implicit method directly, but rather you are allowed to cast from one SqlType to the other.

Usage

```
mySqlInt32 = mySqlInt32.op_Implicit(myInt32)      ' Visual Basic .NET
mySqlInt32 = (SqlInt32)myInt32;                   // C#
mySqlInt32 = mySqlInt32.op_Implicit(mySqlByte)    ' Visual Basic .NET
mySqlInt32 = (SqlInt32)mySqlByte;                 // C#
mySqlInt32 = mySqlInt32.op_Implicit(mySqlInt16)   ' Visual Basic .NET
mySqlInt32 = (SqlInt32)mySqlInt16;                // C#
```

Parameters

`myInt32`	An Int32 (Integer in Visual Basic .NET) object.
`mySqlByte`	A SqlByte object.
`mySqlInt16`	A SqlInt16 object.

Exceptions

OverflowException	The operation returned a value outside of the range of a SqlInt32 value.

Parse

The Parse method will evaluate a string and return a SqlInt32. Keep in mind that converting from a String can throw a FormatException if ADO.NET can't parse the string.

Usage

```
mySqlInt32 = mySqlInt32.Parse(myString)
```

Parameters

`myString`	A case-insensitive String object containing a valid Int32 value, such as "-2147483648", "0", "100", or "2147483647".

Exceptions

OverflowException	The operation returned a value outside of the range of a SqlInt32 value.
FormatException	ADO.NET couldn't parse the string.

Subtract

The Subtract method will subtract the second SqlInt32 from the first SqlInt32 and return a SqlInt32 object whose Value property contains the results of the subtraction. Keep in mind the MinValue and MaxValue that a SqlInt32 can hold. If either SqlInt32 value is null, the resulting SqlInt32 will be null.

In addition to the Subtract method, you may also use the op_Subtraction operator method, or, if your language supports overloaded operators, you may use that construct instead.

Usage

```
mySqlInt32 = mySqlInt32.Subtract(mySqlInt32a,mySqlInt32b)
mySqlInt32 = mySqlInt32.op_Subtraction(mySqlInt32a,mySqlInt32b) ' VB
mySqlInt32 = mySqlInt32a - mySqlInt32b; // C#
```

Parameters

`mySqlInt32a`	A SqlInt32 object.
`mySqlInt32b`	A SqlInt32 object.

Exceptions

OverflowException	The operation returned a value outside of the range of a SqlInt32 value.

ToSqlBoolean

The ToSqlBoolean method returns the SqlInt32 value as a SqlBoolean object. Any nonzero SqlInt32 value will return in a True SqlBoolean. A zero SqlInt32 value will return a False SqlBoolean. A null SqlInt32 value will return a null SqlBoolean.

Usage

```
mySqlBoolean = mySqlInt32.ToSqlBoolean()
```

Parameters

None.

ToSqlByte

The ToSqlByte method returns the SqlInt32 value as a SqlByte object. Be mindful of the range of values that the SqlByte class supports. A null SqlInt32 value will return a null SqlByte.

Usage

```
mySqlByte = mySqlInt32.ToSqlByte()
```

Parameters

None.

Exceptions

OverflowException	The operation returned a value outside of the range of a SqlByte value.

ToSqlDecimal

The ToSqlDecimal method returns the SqlInt32 value as a SqlDecimal. A null value would indicate that the SqlInt32 value is null.

Usage

```
mySqlDecimal = mySqlInt32.ToSqlDecimal()
```

Parameters

None.

ToSqlDouble

The ToSqlDouble method returns the SqlInt32 value as a SqlDouble. A null value would indicate that the SqlInt32 value is null.

Usage

```
mySqlDouble = mySqlInt32.ToSqlDouble()
```

Parameters

None.

ToSqlInt16

The ToSqlInt16 method returns the SqlInt32 value as a SqlInt16 (16-bit integer). Be mindful of the range of values that the SqlInt16 class supports. A null value would indicate that the SqlInt32 value is null.

Usage

```
mySqlInt16 = mySqlInt32.ToSqlInt16()
```

Parameters

None.

Exceptions

OverflowException	The operation returned a value outside of the range of a SqlInt16 value.

ToSqlInt64

The ToSqlInt64 method returns the SqlInt32 value as a SqlInt64 (64-bit integer). A null value would indicate that the SqlInt32 value is null.

Usage

```
mySqlInt64 = mySqlInt32.ToSqlInt64()
```

Parameters

None.

ToSqlMoney

The ToSqlMoney method returns the SqlInt32 value as a SqlMoney. A null value would indicate that the SqlInt32 value is null.

Usage

```
mySqlMoney = mySqlInt32.ToSqlMoney()
```

Parameters

None.

ToSqlSingle

The ToSqlSingle method returns the SqlInt32 value as a SqlSingle. A null value would indicate that the SqlInt32 value is null.

Usage

```
mySqlSingle = mySqlInt32.ToSqlSingle()
```

Parameters

None.

ToSqlString

The ToSqlString method returns the SqlInt32 value as a SqlString. A null value would indicate that the SqlInt32 value is null.

Usage

```
mySqlString = mySqlInt32.ToSqlString()
```

Parameters

None.

ToString

The ToString method returns the SqlInt32 value as a readable value.

Usage

```
myString = mySqlInt32.ToString()
```

Parameters

None.

Value

The read-only Value property allows you to retrieve the value of the SqlInt32. Remember that this property is read only—you may not assign a SqlInt32 its value using its Value property.

In addition to using the Value property, you may also use the op_Explicit conversion method, or, if your language supports overloaded operators, you may use that construct instead.

Usage

```
myInt32 = mySqlInt32.Value                      ' Visual Basic .NET
myInt32 = mySqlInt32.op_Explicit(mySqlInt32)   ' Visual Basic .NET
myInt32 = (Int32)mySqlInt32;                    // C#
```

Parameters

None.

Exceptions

SqlNullValueException	You cannot retrieve a null value. Be sure to check the IsNull property, or use another exception-handling technique.

Xor

The Xor method performs a Boolean xor operation—a bitwise exclusive OR operation on two SqlInt32 values. The method returns a SqlInt32 object. If either of the two values being compared is null, the resulting SqlInt32 will be null.

In addition to the Xor method, you may also use the op_ExclusiveOr operator method, or, if your language supports overloaded operators, you may use that construct instead.

Usage

```
mySqlInt32 = mySqlInt32.Xor(mySqlInt32a,mySqlInt32b)
mySqlInt32 = mySqlInt32.op_ExclusiveOr(mySqlInt32a,mySqlInt32b) ' VB
mySqlInt32 = (mySqlInt32a ^ mySqlInt32b); // C#
```

Parameters

mySqlInt32a	A SqlInt32 object.
mySqlInt32b	A SqlInt32 object.

Zero

The Zero field represents a read-only value of (0) that can be assigned to a SqlInt32 object.

Usage

```
mySqlInt32 = mySqlInt32.Zero
```

Parameters

None.

System.Data.SqlTypes.SqlInt64

The SqlInt64 structure represents a 64-bit signed integer stored in 8 bytes. The integer's data value can range from -2^63 (-9,223,372,036,854,775,808) through 2^63 – 1 (9,223,372,036,854,775,807). This SqlTypes structure will not be used with SQL Server 7.0 applications, as the *bigint* data type is not supported. Use the SqlInt64 structure to manipulate the following SQL Server data types:

- bigint
- sql_variant (if the data is of type bigint)

Constructors

```
Dim mySqlInt64 As New SqlInt64(myInt64)
Dim mySqlInt64 As New SqlInt64(myLong)
```

Parameters

`myInt64`	An Int64 object.
`myLong`	A Long object (Visual Basic .NET).

SqlInt64 Sample Code

```
Private Sub ReadSqlType(ByVal myConnectionString As String, _
                        ByVal myCommandText As String)
   Dim mySqlConnection As System.Data.SqlClient.SqlConnection
   Dim mySqlDataReader As System.Data.SqlClient.SqlDataReader
   Dim mySqlCommand As System.Data.SqlClient.SqlCommand
   Dim mySqlInt64 As System.Data.SqlTypes.SqlInt64
   ' Establish connection
   mySqlConnection = New SqlConnection(myConnectionString)
   mySqlConnection.Open()
   ' Build and execute command
   mySqlCommand = New SqlCommand(myCommandText)
```

```
    mySqlCommand.Connection = mySqlConnection
    mySqlDataReader = mySqlCommand.ExecuteReader
    ' Read first row
    If mySqlDataReader.Read Then
        ' Save column as appropriate SqlTypes structure
        mySqlInt64 = mySqlDataReader.GetSqlInt64(1)
        MessageBox.Show(mySqlInt64.ToString)
    End If
    ' Done
    mySqlConnection.Close()
End Sub
```

Members

Add

The Add method will add two SqlInt64 values together and return a SqlInt64 object whose Value property contains the results of the addition. Keep in mind the MinValue and MaxValue that a SqlInt64 can hold. If either SqlInt64 value is null, the resulting SqlInt64 will be null.

In addition to the Add method, you may also use the op_Addition operator method, or, if your language supports overloaded operators, you may use that construct instead.

Usage

```
mySqlInt64 = mySqlInt64.Add(mySqlInt64a,mySqlInt64b)
mySqlInt64 = mySqlInt64.op_Addition(mySqlInt64a,mySqlInt64b) ' VB
mySqlInt64 = mySqlInt64a + mySqlInt64b; // C#
```

Parameters

`mySqlInt64a`	A SqlInt64 object.
`mySqlInt64b`	A SqlInt64 object.

Exceptions

OverflowException	The operation returned a value outside of the range of a SqlInt64 value.

BitwiseAnd

The BitwiseAnd method performs a Boolean and operation on two SqlInt64 objects. The method returns a SqlInt64 object. If either of the two values being compared is null, the resulting SqlInt64 will be null.

In addition to the BitwiseAnd method, you may also use the op_BitwiseAnd operator method, or, if your language supports overloaded operators, you may use that construct instead.

Usage

```
mySqlInt64 = mySqlInt64.BitwiseAnd(mySqlInt64a,mySqlInt64b)
mySqlInt64 = mySqlInt64.op_BitwiseAnd(mySqlInt64a,mySqlInt64b) ' VB
mySqlInt64 = mySqlInt64a & mySqlInt64b; // C#
```

Parameters

`mySqlInt64a`	A SqlInt64 object.
`mySqlInt64b`	A SqlInt64 object.

BitwiseOr

The BitwiseOr method performs a Boolean or operation on two SqlInt64 objects. The method returns a SqlInt64 object. If either of the two values being compared is null, the resulting SqlInt64 will be null.

In addition to the BitwiseOr method, you may also use the op_BitwiseOr operator method, or, if your language supports overloaded operators, you may use that construct instead.

Usage

```
mySqlInt64 = mySqlInt64.BitwiseOr(mySqlInt64a,mySqlInt64b)
mySqlInt64 = mySqlInt64.op_BitwiseOr(mySqlInt64a,mySqlInt64b) ' VB
mySqlInt64 = mySqlInt64a | mySqlInt64b; // C#
```

Parameters

`mySqlInt64a`	A SqlInt64 object.
`mySqlInt64b`	A SqlInt64 object.

CompareTo

The CompareTo method allows you to compare the SqlInt64 value with another supplied object to return an indication of their relative values. The returned Int32 object will indicate the comparison:

Less Than Zero. The SqlInt64 value was less than the supplied object, or the SqlInt64 was null.

Zero. The SqlInt64 value was the same as the supplied object.

Greater than zero. The SqlInt64 value was greater than the supplied object, or the object was null.

Usage

```
myInt32 = mySqlInt64.CompareTo(myObject)
```

Parameters

`myObject`	Any object that implements the IComparable interface.

Exceptions

ArgumentException	The supplied object isn't valid for comparison.

Divide

The Divide method will divide the first SqlInt64 by the second SqlInt64. This method will return a SqlInt64 object whose Value property contains the results of the division. Because a SqlInt64 object can store only whole numbers, any remainders after the division will be discarded. If either SqlInt64 value is null, the resulting SqlInt64 will be null.

In addition to the Divide method, you may also use the op_Division operator method, or, if your language supports overloaded operators, you may use that construct instead.

Usage

```
mySqlInt64 = mySqlInt64.Divide(mySqlInt64a,mySqlInt64b)
mySqlInt64 = mySqlInt64.op_Division(mySqlInt64a,mySqlInt54b) ' VB
mySqlInt64 = mySqlInt64a / mySqlInt64b; // C#
```

Parameters

`mySqlInt64a`	A SqlInt64 object.
`mySqlInt64b`	A SqlInt64 object.

Exceptions

DivideByZeroException	You tried to divide by zero.

Equals

The Equals method allows you to compare the SqlInt64 value with a supplied object or compare the values of two supplied objects or SqlInt64 values. The result will be either a Boolean or a SqlBoolean, depending on which overloaded method is called. The result may be null if either of the SqlInt64 values being compared is null.

In addition to the Equals method, you may also use the op_Equality operator method, or, if your language supports overloaded operators, you may use that construct instead.

Usage

```
mySqlBoolean = mySqlInt64.Equals(mySqlInt64a,mySqlInt64b)
myBoolean = mySqlInt64.Equals(myObject)
myBoolean = mySqlInt64.Equals(myObject,myObject2)
mySqlBoolean = mySqlInt64.op_Equality(mySqlInt64a,mySqlInt64b) ' VB
mySqlBoolean = (mySqlInt64a == mySqlInt64b); // C#
```

Parameters

`mySqlInt64a`	A SqlInt64 object.
`mySqlInt64b`	A SqlInt64 object.
`myObject`	Any System.Object or descendant.
`myObject2`	Any System.Object or descendant.

GetHashCode

The GetHashCode method returns a hash code for the SqlInt64 value. The hash code represents a unique value corresponding to the particular value of the SqlInt64 object. Keep in mind that even the smallest change to the SqlInt64 value will result in a different hash code. Requesting the hash code for a SqlInt64 object with a null value will return 0.

BE CAREFUL **The hash code returned for a SqlInt64 with a value of 0 is 0, which is the same for a SqlInt64 with a null value.**

Usage

```
myInt32 = mySqlInt64.GetHashCode()
```

Parameters

None.

GreaterThan

The GreaterThan method compares two SqlInt64 values and returns a SqlBoolean value indicating whether the first SqlInt64 value is greater than the second SqlInt64 value. A null value would indicate that one of the SqlInt64 values is null.

In addition to the GreaterThan method, you may also use the op_GreaterThan operator method, or, if your language supports overloaded operators, you may use that construct instead.

Usage

```
mySqlBoolean = mySqlInt64.GreaterThan(mySqlInt64a,mySqlInt64b)
mySqlBoolean = mySqlInt64.op_GreaterThan(mySqlInt64a,mySqlInt64b) ' VB
mySqlBoolean = (mySqlInt64a > mySqlInt64b); // C#
```

Parameters

`mySqlInt64a`	A SqlInt64 object.
`mySqlInt64b`	A SqlInt64 object.

GreaterThanOrEqual

The GreaterThanOrEqual method compares two SqlInt64 values and returns a SqlBoolean value indicating whether the first SqlInt64 value is greater than or equal to the second SqlInt64 value. A null value would indicate that one of the SqlInt64 values is null.

In addition to the GreaterThanOrEqual method, you may also use the op_GreaterThanOrEqual operator method, or, if your language supports overloaded operators, you may use that construct instead.

Usage

```
mySqlBoolean = mySqlInt64.GreaterThanOrEqual(mySqlInt64a,mySqlInt64b)
mySqlBoolean = _
   mySqlInt64.op_GreaterThanOrEqual(mySqlInt64a,mySqlInt64b) ' VB
mySqlBoolean = (mySqlInt64a >= mySqlInt64b); // C#
```

Parameters

`mySqlInt64a`	A SqlInt64 object.
`mySqlInt64b`	A SqlInt64 object.

IsNull

The read-only IsNull property returns a Boolean indicating whether the SqlInt64 is null. The value will be True if the value of the SqlInt64 is null and False if it is otherwise.

Usage

```
myBoolean = mySqlInt64.IsNull
```

Parameters

None.

LessThan

The LessThan method compares two SqlInt64 values and returns a SqlBoolean value indicating whether the first SqlInt64 value is less than the second SqlInt64 value. A null value would indicate that one of the SqlInt64 values is null.

In addition to the LessThan method, you may also use the op_LessThan operator method, or, if your language supports overloaded operators, you may use that construct instead.

Usage

```
mySqlBoolean = mySqlInt64.LessThan(mySqlInt64a,mySqlInt64b)
mySqlBoolean = mySqlInt64.op_LessThan(mySqlInt64a,mySqlInt64b) ' VB
mySqlBoolean = (mySqlInt64a < mySqlInt64b); // C#
```

Parameters

`mySqlInt64a`	A SqlInt64 object.
`mySqlInt64b`	A SqlInt64 object.

LessThanOrEqual

The LessThanOrEqual method compares two SqlInt64 values and returns a SqlBoolean value indicating whether the first SqlInt64 value is less than or equal to the second SqlInt64 value. A null value would indicate that one of the SqlInt64 values is null.

In addition to the LessThanOrEqual method, you may also use the op_LessThanOrEqual operator method, or, if your language supports overloaded operators, you may use that construct instead.

Usage

```
mySqlBoolean = mySqlInt64.LessThanOrEqual(mySqlInt64a,mySqlInt64b)
mySqlBoolean = mySqlInt64.op_LessThanOrEqual(mySqlInt64a,mySqlInt64b) ' VB
mySqlBoolean = (mySqlInt64a <= mySqlInt64b); // C#
```

Parameters

`mySqlInt64a`	A SqlInt64 object.
`mySqlInt64b`	A SqlInt64 object.

MaxValue

The read-only MaxValue field represents the largest number that a SqlInt64 can hold, which is 2^63 – 1 (9,223,372,036,854,775,807). By using the MaxValue field, you can build flexible, readable exception-handling code.

Usage

```
mySqlInt64 = mySqlInt64.MaxValue
```

Parameters

None.

MinValue

The read-only MinValue field represents the smallest number that a SqlInt64 can hold, which is -2^63 (-9,223,372,036,854,775,808). By using the MinValue field, you can build flexible, readable exception-handling code.

Usage

```
mySqlInt64 = mySqlInt64.MinValue
```

Parameters

None.

Mod

The Mod method will divide the first SqlInt64 by the second SqlInt64 and return only the modulus (remainder portion) as a SqlInt64 object. If either SqlInt64 value is null, the resulting SqlInt64 will be null.

In addition to the Mod method, you may also use the op_Modulus operator method, or, if your language supports overloaded operators, you may use that construct instead.

Usage

```
mySqlInt64 = mySqlInt64.Mod(mySqlInt64a,mySqlInt64b)
mySqlInt64 = mySqlInt64.op_Modulus(mySqlInt64a,mySqlInt64b) ' VB
mySqlInt64 = mySqlInt64a % mySqlInt64b; // C#
```

Parameters

mySqlInt64a	A SqlInt64 object.
mySqlInt64b	A SqlInt64 object.

Exceptions

DivideByZeroException	You tried to divide by zero.

Multiply

The Multiply method will multiply the first SqlInt64 by the second SqlInt64 and return a SqlInt64 object whose Value property contains the results of the multiplication. Keep in mind the MaxValue that a SqlInt64 can hold. If either SqlInt64 value is null, the resulting SqlInt64 will be null.

In addition to the Multiply method, you may also use the op_Multiply operator method, or, if your language supports overloaded operators, you may use that construct instead.

Usage

```
mySqlInt64 = mySqlInt64.Multiply(mySqlInt64a,mySqlInt64b)
mySqlInt64 = mySqlInt64.op_Multiply(mySqlInt64a,mySqlInt64b) ' VB
mySqlInt64 = mySqlInt64a * mySqlInt64b; // C#
```

Parameters

mySqlInt64a	A SqlInt64 object.
mySqlInt64b	A SqlInt64 object.

Exceptions

OverflowException	The operation returned a value outside of the range of a SqlInt64 value.

NotEquals

The NotEquals method compares two SqlInt64 values and returns a SqlBoolean value indicating whether the two SqlInt64 values are not equal. A null value would indicate that one of the SqlInt64 values is null.

In addition to the NotEquals method, you may also use the op_Inequality operator method, or, if your language supports overloaded operators, you may use that construct instead.

Usage

```
mySqlBoolean = mySqlInt64.NotEquals(mySqlInt64a,mySqlInt64b)
mySqlBoolean = mySqlInt64.op_Inequality(mySqlInt64a,mySqlInt64b) ' VB
mySqlBoolean = (mySqlInt64a != mySqlInt64b); // C#
```

Parameters

`mySqlInt64a`	A SqlInt64 object.
`mySqlInt64b`	A SqlInt64 object.

Null

The Null field represents a read-only null value that can be assigned to a SqlInt64 object. You cannot use the standard .NET way of assigning a null value with the System.DBNull.Value, but rather you must use this approach.

Usage

```
mySqlInt64 = mySqlInt64.Null
```

Parameters

None.

OnesComplement

The OnesComplement method will return the bitwise one's complement of the specified SqlInt64. If the SqlInt64 value that you are complementing is null, then the method will return a null value.

In addition to the OnesComplement method, you may also use the op_OnesComplement operator method, or, if your language supports overloaded operators, you may use that construct instead.

NOTE The one's complement operator is sometimes referred to as the bitwise complement or bitwise not operator.

Usage

```
mySqlInt64 = mySqlInt64.OnesComplement(mySqlInt64a)
mySqlInt64 = mySqlInt64.op_OnesComplement(mySqlInt64a) ' VB
mySqlInt64 = ~ mySqlInt64a; // C#
```

Parameters

`mySqlInt64a`	A SqlInt64 object.

op_Explicit

The op_Explicit method represents a special SqlInt64 converter that allows SqlInt64 values to be assigned from other SqlTypes. This method is overloaded in several ways. The first three examples that follow show how to retrieve the SqlInt64 value as simple Int64 or Long (Visual Basic .NET) objects. The other examples show how to assign the SqlInt64 value.

When assigning the SqlInt64 value from one of the other SqlTypes, keep in mind the MinValue and MaxValue. Any value that exceeds those limits will throw an OverflowException. Any null values will convert to a SqlInt64 null value.

When assigning the SqlInt64 value from a SqlString object, be sure that the string parses to a valid SqlInt64 value. Converting from a SqlString object can throw a FormatException if ADO.NET can't parse the string.

If you are using ADO.NET with C#, then you will not call the op_Explicit method directly, but rather you are allowed to cast from one SqlType to the other.

Usage

```
myLong = mySqlInt64.op_Explicit(mySqlInt64)         ' Visual Basic .NET
myInt64 = mySqlInt64.op_Explicit(mySqlInt64)        ' Visual Basic .NET
myInt64 = (Int64)mySqlInt64;                        // C#
mySqlInt64 = mySqlInt64.op_Explicit(mySqlBoolean)   ' Visual Basic .NET
mySqlInt64 = (SqlInt64)mySqlBoolean;                // C#
mySqlInt64 = mySqlInt64.op_Explicit(mySqlDecimal)   ' Visual Basic .NET
mySqlInt64 = (SqlInt64)mySqlDecimal;                // C#
mySqlInt64 = mySqlInt64.op_Explicit(mySqlDouble)    ' Visual Basic .NET
mySqlInt64 = (SqlInt64)mySqlDouble;                 // C#
mySqlInt64 = mySqlInt64.op_Explicit(mySqlMoney)     ' Visual Basic .NET
mySqlInt64 = (SqlInt64)mySqlMoney;                  // C#
mySqlInt64 = mySqlInt64.op_Explicit(mySqlSingle)    ' Visual Basic .NET
mySqlInt64 = (SqlInt64)mySqlSingle;                 // C#
mySqlInt64 = mySqlInt64.op_Explicit(mySqlString)    ' Visual Basic .NET
mySqlInt64 = (SqlInt64)mySqlString;                 // C#
```

Parameters

`mySqlBoolean`	A SqlBoolean object.
`mySqlDecimal`	A SqlDecimal object.
`mySqlDouble`	A SqlDouble object.
`mySqlMoney`	A SqlMoney object.
`mySqlSingle`	A SqlSingle object.
`mySqlString`	A SqlString object.

Exceptions

FormatException	ADO.NET couldn't parse the string.
OverflowException	The operation returned a value outside of the range of a SqlInt64 value.
SqlNullValueException	You cannot assign a null value to an Int64 or Long class. Be sure to check the IsNull property, or use another exception-handling technique.

op_Implicit

The op_Implicit method represents a special SqlInt64 converter that is overloaded a couple of different ways. It allows for an Int64 (Long), SqlByte, SqlInt16, or SqlInt32 to be assigned to the SqlInt64.

NOTE It appears that you can pass any numeric object to the op_Implicit method. When assigning the SqlInt64 value from numeric types with a larger precision, keep in mind the MinValue and MaxValue. Any value that exceeds those limits will throw an OverflowException.

If you are using ADO.NET with C#, then you will not call the op_Implicit method directly, but rather you are allowed to cast from one SqlType to the other.

Usage

```
mySqlInt64 = mySqlInt64.op_Implicit(myInt64)      ' Visual Basic .NET
mySqlInt64 = (SqlInt64)myInt64;                   // C#
mySqlInt64 = mySqlInt64.op_Implicit(mySqlByte)    ' Visual Basic .NET
mySqlInt64 = (SqlInt64)mySqlByte;                 // C#
mySqlInt64 = mySqlInt64.op_Implicit(mySqlInt16)   ' Visual Basic .NET
mySqlInt64 = (SqlInt64)mySqlInt16;                // C#
mySqlInt64 = mySqlInt64.op_Implicit(mySqlInt32)   ' Visual Basic .NET
mySqlInt64 = (SqlInt64)mySqlInt32;                // C#
```

Parameters

`myInt64`	An Int64 (Long in Visual Basic .NET) object.
`mySqlByte`	A SqlByte object.
`mySqlInt16`	A SqlInt16 object.
`mySqlInt32`	A SqlInt32 object.

Exceptions

OverflowException	The operation returned a value outside of the range of a SqlInt64 value.

Parse

The Parse method will evaluate a string and return a SqlInt64. Keep in mind that converting from a String can throw a FormatException if ADO.NET can't parse the string.

Usage

```
mySqlInt64 = mySqlInt64.Parse(myString)
```

Parameters

`myString`	A case-insensitive String object containing a valid Int64 value, such as "-9223372036854775808", "0", "100", or "9223372036854775807".

Exceptions

OverflowException	The operation returned a value outside of the range of a SqlInt64 value.
FormatException	ADO.NET couldn't parse the string.

Subtract

The Subtract method will subtract the second SqlInt64 from the first SqlInt64 and return a SqlInt64 object whose Value property contains the results of the subtraction. Keep in mind the MinValue and MaxValue that a SqlInt64 can hold. If either SqlInt64 value is null, the resulting SqlInt64 will be null.

In addition to the Subtract method, you may also use the op_Subtraction operator method, or, if your language supports overloaded operators, you may use that construct instead.

Usage

```
mySqlInt64 = mySqlInt64.Subtract(mySqlInt64a,mySqlInt64b)
mySqlInt64 = mySqlInt64.op_Subtraction(mySqlInt64a,mySqlInt64b) ' VB
mySqlInt64 = mySqlInt64a + mySqlInt64b; // C#
```

Parameters

`mySqlInt64a`	A SqlInt64 object.
`mySqlInt64b`	A SqlInt64 object.

Exceptions

OverflowException	The operation returned a value outside of the range of a SqlInt64 value.

ToSqlBoolean

The ToSqlBoolean method returns the SqlInt64 value as a SqlBoolean object. Any nonzero SqlInt64 value will return in a True SqlBoolean. A zero SqlInt64 value will return a False SqlBoolean. A null SqlInt64 value will return a null SqlBoolean.

Usage

```
mySqlBoolean = mySqlInt64.ToSqlBoolean()
```

Parameters

None.

ToSqlByte

The ToSqlByte method returns the SqlInt64 value as a SqlByte object. Be mindful of the range of values that the SqlByte class supports. A null SqlInt64 value will return a null SqlByte.

Usage

```
mySqlByte = mySqlInt64.ToSqlByte()
```

Parameters

None.

Exceptions

OverflowException	The operation returned a value outside of the range of a SqlByte value.

ToSqlDecimal

The ToSqlDecimal method returns the SqlInt64 value as a SqlDecimal. A null value would indicate that the SqlInt64 value is null.

Usage

```
mySqlDecimal = mySqlInt64.ToSqlDecimal()
```

Parameters

None.

ToSqlDouble

The ToSqlDouble method returns the SqlInt64 value as a SqlDouble. A null value would indicate that the SqlInt64 value is null.

Usage

```
mySqlDouble = mySqlInt64.ToSqlDouble()
```

Parameters

None.

ToSqlInt16

The ToSqlInt16 method returns the SqlInt64 value as a SqlInt16 (16 bit integer). Be mindful of the range of values that the SqlInt16 class supports. A null value would indicate that the SqlInt64 value is null.

Usage

```
mySqlInt16 = mySqlInt64.ToSqlInt16()
```

Parameters

None.

Exceptions

OverflowException	The operation returned a value outside of the range of a SqlInt16 value.

ToSqlInt32

The ToSqlInt32 method returns the SqlInt64 value as a SqlInt32 (32 bit integer). Be mindful of the range of values that the SqlInt32 class supports. A null value would indicate that the SqlInt64 value is null.

Usage

```
mySqlInt32 = mySqlInt64.ToSqlInt32()
```

Parameters

None.

Exceptions

OverflowException	The operation returned a value outside of the range of a SqlInt32 value.

ToSqlMoney

The ToSqlMoney method returns the SqlInt64 value as a SqlMoney. A null value would indicate that the SqlInt64 value is null.

Usage

```
mySqlMoney = mySqlInt64.ToSqlMoney()
```

Parameters

None.

Exceptions

OverflowException	The operation returned a value outside of the range of a SqlMoney value.

ToSqlSingle

The ToSqlSingle method returns the SqlInt64 value as a SqlSingle. A null value would indicate that the SqlInt64 value is null.

Usage

```
mySqlSingle = mySqlInt64.ToSqlSingle()
```

Parameters

None.

ToSqlString

The ToSqlString method returns the SqlInt64 value as a SqlString. A null value would indicate that the SqlInt64 value is null.

Usage

```
mySqlString = mySqlInt64.ToSqlString()
```

Parameters

None.

ToString

The ToString method returns the SqlInt64 value as a readable value.

Usage

```
myString = mySqlInt64.ToString()
```

Parameters

None.

Value

The read-only Value property allows you to retrieve the value of the SqlInt64. Remember that this property is read only—you may not assign a SqlInt64 its value using its Value property.

In addition to using the Value property, you may also use the op_Explicit conversion method, or, if your language supports overloaded operators, you may use that construct instead.

Usage

```
myInt64 = mySqlInt64.Value                        ' Visual Basic .NET
myInt64 = mySqlInt64.op_Explicit(mySqlInt64)      ' Visual Basic .NET
myInt64 = (Int64)mySqlInt64;                      // C#
```

Parameters

None.

Exceptions

SqlNullValueException	You cannot retrieve a null value. Be sure to check the IsNull property, or use another exception-handling technique.

Xor

The Xor method performs a Boolean xor operation—a bitwise exclusive OR operation on two SqlInt64 values. The method returns a SqlInt64 object. If either of the two values being compared is null, the resulting SqlInt64 will be null.

In addition to the Xor method, you may also use the op_ExclusiveOr operator method, or, if your language supports overloaded operators, you may use that construct instead.

Usage

```
mySqlInt64 = mySqlInt64.Xor(mySqlInt64a,mySqlInt64b)
mySqlInt64 = mySqlInt64.op_ExclusiveOr(mySqlInt64a,mySqlInt64b) ' VB
mySqlInt64 = mySqlInt64a ^ mySqlInt64b; // C#
```

Parameters

`mySqlInt64a`	A SqlInt64 object.
`mySqlInt64b`	A SqlInt64 object.

Zero

The Zero field represents a read-only value of (0) that can be assigned to a SqlInt64 object.

Usage

```
mySqlInt64 = mySqlInt64.Zero
```

Parameters

None.

System.Data.SqlTypes.SqlMoney

The SqlMoney structure represents a 64-bit currency value stored in 8 bytes. The data value can range from -2^63 (-922,337,203,685,477.5808) through 2^63 – 1 (922,337,203,685,477.5807). Use the SqlMoney structure to manipulate the following SQL Server data types:

- money
- smallmoney
- sql_variant (if the data is one of the above types)

Constructors

```
Dim mySqlMoney As New SqlMoney(myDecimal)
Dim mySqlMoney As New SqlMoney(myDouble)
Dim mySqlMoney As New SqlMoney(myInt32)
Dim mySqlMoney As New SqlMoney(myInt64)
```

Parameters

`myDecimal`	A Decimal object.
`myDouble`	A Double object.
`myInt32`	An Int32 object.
`myInt64`	An Int64 object.

SqlMoney Sample Code

```
Private Sub ReadSqlType(ByVal myConnectionString As String, _
                        ByVal myCommandText As String)
   Dim mySqlConnection As System.Data.SqlClient.SqlConnection
   Dim mySqlDataReader As System.Data.SqlClient.SqlDataReader
   Dim mySqlCommand As System.Data.SqlClient.SqlCommand
   Dim mySqlMoney As System.Data.SqlTypes.SqlMoney
   ' Establish connection
   mySqlConnection = New SqlConnection(myConnectionString)
   mySqlConnection.Open()
   ' Build and execute command
   mySqlCommand = New SqlCommand(myCommandText)
   mySqlCommand.Connection = mySqlConnection
   mySqlDataReader = mySqlCommand.ExecuteReader
   ' Read first row
   If mySqlDataReader.Read Then
      ' Save column as appropriate SqlTypes structure
      mySqlMoney = mySqlDataReader.GetSqlMoney(1)
      MessageBox.Show(mySqlMoney.ToString)
   End If
   ' Done
   mySqlConnection.Close()
End Sub
```

Members

Add

The Add method will add two SqlMoney values together and return a SqlMoney object whose Value property contains the results of the addition. Keep in mind the MinValue and MaxValue that a SqlMoney can hold. If either SqlMoney value is null, the resulting SqlMoney will be null.

In addition to the Add method, you may also use the op_Addition operator method, or, if your language supports overloaded operators, you may use that construct instead.

Usage

```
mySqlMoney = mySqlMoney.Add(mySqlMoney1,mySqlMoney2)
mySqlMoney = mySqlMoney.op_Addition(mySqlMoney1,mySqlMoney2) ' VB
mySqlMoney = mySqlMoney1 + mySqlMoney2; // C#
```

Parameters

`mySqlMoney1`	A SqlMoney object.
`mySqlMoney2`	A SqlMoney object.

Exceptions

OverflowException	The operation returned a value outside of the range of a SqlMoney value.

CompareTo

The CompareTo method allows you to compare the SqlMoney value with another supplied object to return an indication of their relative values. The returned Int32 object will indicate the comparison:

Less Than Zero. The SqlMoney value was less than the supplied object, or the SqlMoney was null.

Zero. The SqlMoney value was the same as the supplied object.

Greater than zero. The SqlMoney value was greater than the supplied object, or the object was null.

Usage

```
myInt32 = mySqlMoney.CompareTo(myObject)
```

Parameters

`myObject`	Any object that implements the IComparable interface.

Exceptions

ArgumentException	The supplied object isn't valid for comparison.

Divide

The Divide method will divide the first SqlMoney by the second SqlMoney. This method will return a SqlMoney object whose Value property contains the results of the division. If either SqlMoney value is null, the resulting SqlMoney will be null.

In addition to the Divide method, you may also use the op_Division operator method, or, if your language supports overloaded operators, you may use that construct instead.

Usage

```
mySqlMoney = mySqlMoney.Divide(mySqlMoney1,mySqlMoney2)
mySqlMoney = mySqlMoney.op_Division(mySqlMoney1,mySqlMoney2) ' VB
mySqlMoney = mySqlMoney1 / mySqlMoney2; // C#
```

Parameters

`mySqlMoney1`	A SqlMoney object.
`mySqlMoney2`	A SqlMoney object.

Exceptions

DivideByZeroException	You tried to divide by zero.

Equals

The Equals method allows you to compare the SqlMoney value with a supplied object or compare the values of two supplied objects or SqlMoney values. The result will be either a Boolean or a SqlBoolean, depending on which overloaded method is called. The result may be null if either of the SqlMoney values being compared were null.

In addition to the Equals method, you may also use the op_Equality operator method, or, if your language supports overloaded operators, you may use that construct instead.

Usage

```
mySqlBoolean = mySqlMoney.Equals(mySqlMoney1,mySqlMoney2)
myBoolean = mySqlMoney.Equals(myObject)
myBoolean = mySqlMoney.Equals(myObject,myObject2)
mySqlBoolean = mySqlMoney.op_Equality(mySqlMoney1,mySqlMoney2) ' VB
mySqlBoolean = (mySqlMoney1 == mySqlMoney2); // C#
```

Parameters

`mySqlMoney1`	A SqlMoney object.
`mySqlMoney2`	A SqlMoney object.
`myObject`	Any System.Object or descendant.
`myObject2`	Any System.Object or descendant.

GetHashCode

The GetHashCode method returns a hash code for the SqlMoney value. The hash code represents a unique value corresponding to the particular value of the SqlMoney object. Keep in mind that even the smallest change to the SqlMoney value will result in a different hash code. Requesting the hash code for a SqlMoney object with a null value will return 0.

BE CAREFUL **The hash code returned for a SqlMoney with a value of 0 is 0, which is the same for a SqlMoney with a null value.**

Usage

```
myInt32 = mySqlMoney.GetHashCode()
```

Parameters

None.

GreaterThan

The GreaterThan method compares two SqlMoney values and returns a SqlBoolean value indicating whether the first SqlMoney value is greater than the second SqlMoney value. A null value would indicate that one of the SqlMoney values is null.

In addition to the GreaterThan method, you may also use the op_GreaterThan operator method, or, if your language supports overloaded operators, you may use that construct instead.

Usage

```
mySqlBoolean = mySqlMoney.GreaterThan(mySqlMoney1,mySqlMcney2)
mySqlBoolean = mySqlMoney.op_GreaterThan(mySqlMoney1,mySqlMoney2) ' VB
mySqlBoolean = (mySqlMoney1 > mySqlMoney2); // C#
```

Parameters

mySqlMoney1	A SqlMoney object.
mySqlMoney2	A SqlMoney object.

GreaterThanOrEqual

The GreaterThanOrEqual method compares two SqlMoney values and returns a SqlBoolean value indicating whether the first SqlMoney value is greater than or equal to the second SqlMoney value. A null value would indicate that one of the SqlMoney values is null.

In addition to the GreaterThanOrEqual method, you may also use the op_GreaterThanOrEqual operator method, or, if your language supports overloaded operators, you may use that construct instead.

Usage

```
mySqlBoolean = mySqlMoney.GreaterThanOrEqual(mySqlMoney1,mySqlMoney2)
mySqlBoolean = _
   mySqlMoney.op_GreaterThanOrEqual(mySqlMoney1,mySqlMoney2) ' VB
mySqlBoolean = (mySqlMoney1 >= mySqlMoney2); // C#
```

Parameters

mySqlMoney1	A SqlMoney object.
mySqlMoney2	A SqlMoney object.

IsNull

The read-only IsNull property returns a Boolean indicating whether the SqlMoney is null. The value will be True if the value of the SqlMoney is null and False if it is otherwise.

Usage

```
myBoolean = mySqlMoney.IsNull
```

Parameters

None.

LessThan

The LessThan method compares two SqlMoney values and returns a SqlBoolean value indicating whether the first SqlMoney value is less than the second SqlMoney value. A null value would indicate that one of the SqlMoney values is null.

In addition to the LessThan method, you may also use the op_LessThan operator method, or, if your language supports overloaded operators, you may use that construct instead.

Usage

```
mySqlBoolean = mySqlMoney.LessThan(mySqlMoney1,mySqlMoney2)
mySqlBoolean = mySqlMoney.op_LessThan(mySqlMoney1,mySqlMoney2) ' VB
mySqlBoolean = (mySqlMoney1 < mySqlMoney2); // C#
```

Parameters

`mySqlMoney1`	A SqlMoney object.
`mySqlMoney2`	A SqlMoney object.

LessThanOrEqual

The LessThanOrEqual method compares two SqlMoney values and returns a Sql-Boolean value indicating whether the first SqlMoney value is less than or equal to the second SqlMoney value. A null value would indicate that one of the SqlMoney values is null.

In addition to the LessThanOrEqual method, you may also use the op_LessThanOr-Equal operator method, or, if your language supports overloaded operators, you may use that construct instead.

Usage

```
mySqlBoolean = mySqlMoney.LessThanOrEqual(mySqlMoney1,mySqlMoney2)
mySqlBoolean = mySqlMoney.op_LessThanOrEqual(mySqlMoney1,mySqlMoney2) ' VB
mySqlBoolean = (mySqlMoney1 <= mySqlMoney2); // C#
```

Parameters

`mySqlMoney1`	A SqlMoney object.
`mySqlMoney2`	A SqlMoney object.

MaxValue

The read-only MaxValue field represents the largest number that a SqlMoney can hold, which is 2^63 – 1 (922,337,203,685,477.5807). By using the MaxValue field, you can build flexible, readable exception-handling code.

Usage

```
mySqlMoney = mySqlMoney.MaxValue
```

Parameters

None.

MinValue

The read-only MinValue field represents the smallest number that a SqlMoney can hold, which is -2^63 (-922,337,203,685,477.5808). By using the MinValue field, you can build flexible, readable exception-handling code.

Usage

```
mySqlMoney = mySqlMoney.MinValue
```

Parameters

None.

Multiply

The Multiply method will multiply the first SqlMoney by the second SqlMoney and return a SqlMoney object whose Value property contains the results of the multiplication. Keep in mind the MaxValue that a SqlMoney can hold. If either SqlMoney value is null, the resulting SqlMoney will be null.

In addition to the Multiply method, you may also use the op_Multiply operator method, or, if your language supports overloaded operators, you may use that construct instead.

Usage

```
mySqlMoney = mySqlMoney.Multiply(mySqlMoney1,mySqlMoney2)
mySqlMoney = mySqlMoney.op_Multiply(mySqlMoney1,mySqlMoney2) ' VB
mySqlMoney = mySqlMoney1 * mySqlMoney2; // C#
```

Parameters

mySqlMoney1	A SqlMoney object.
mySqlMoney2	A SqlMoney object.

Exceptions

OverflowException	The operation returned a value outside of the range of a SqlMoney value.

NotEquals

The NotEquals method compares two SqlMoney values and returns a SqlBoolean value indicating whether the two SqlMoney values are not equal. A null value would indicate that one of the SqlMoney values is null.

In addition to the NotEquals method, you may also use the op_Inequality operator method, or, if your language supports overloaded operators, you may use that construct instead.

Usage

```
mySqlBoolean = mySqlMoney.NotEquals(mySqlMoney1,mySqlMoney2)
mySqlBoolean = mySqlMoney.op_Inequality(mySqlMoney1,mySqlMoney2) ' VB
mySqlBoolean = (mySqlMoney1 != mySqlMoney2); // C#
```

Parameters

`mySqlMoney1`	A SqlMoney object.
`mySqlMoney2`	A SqlMoney object.

Null

The Null field represents a read-only null value that can be assigned to a SqlMoney object. You cannot use the standard .NET way of assigning a null value with the System.DBNull.Value, but rather you must use this approach.

Usage

```
mySqlMoney = mySqlMoney.Null
```

Parameters

None.

op_Explicit

The op_Explicit method represents a special SqlMoney converter that allows SqlMoney values to be explicitly assigned to and from other SqlTypes. This method is overloaded in several ways. The first two examples that follow show how to retrieve the SqlMoney value as a Decimal object. The other examples show how to assign the SqlMoney value.

When assigning the SqlMoney value from one of the other SqlTypes, keep in mind the MinValue and MaxValue. Any value that exceeds those limits will throw an OverflowException. Any null values will convert to a SqlMoney null value.

When assigning the SqlMoney value from a SqlString object, be sure that the string parses to a valid SqlMoney value. Converting from a SqlString object can throw a FormatException if ADO.NET can't parse the string.

If you are using ADO.NET with C#, then you will not call the op_Explicit method directly, but rather you are allowed to cast from one SqlType to the other.

Usage

```
myDecimal = mySqlMoney.op_Explicit(mySqlMoney)      ' Visual Basic .NET
myDecimal = (Decimal)mySqlMoney;                    // C#
mySqlMoney = mySqlMoney.op_Explicit(mySqlBoolean)   ' Visual Basic .NET
mySqlMoney = (SqlMoney)mySqlBoolean;                // C#
mySqlMoney = mySqlMoney.op_Explicit(mySqlDecimal)   ' Visual Basic .NET
mySqlMoney = (SqlMoney)mySqlDecimal;                // C#
mySqlMoney = mySqlMoney.op_Explicit(mySqlDouble)    ' Visual Basic .NET
mySqlMoney = (SqlMoney)mySqlDouble;                 // C#
mySqlMoney = mySqlMoney.op_Explicit(mySqlSingle)    ' Visual Basic .NET
mySqlMoney = (SqlMoney)mySqlSingle;                 // C#
mySqlMoney = mySqlMoney.op_Explicit(mySqlString)    ' Visual Basic .NET
mySqlMoney = (SqlMoney)mySqlString;                 // C#
```

Parameters

`mySqlMoney`	A SqlMoney object.
`mySqlBoolean`	A SqlBoolean object.
`mySqlDecimal`	A SqlDecimal object.

`mySqlDouble`	A SqlDouble object.
`mySqlSingle`	A SqlSingle object.
`mySqlString`	A SqlString object.

Exceptions

FormatException	ADO.NET couldn't parse the string.
OverflowException	The operation returned a value outside of the range of a SqlMoney value.
SqlNullValueException	You cannot assign a null value to a Decimal class. Be sure to check the IsNull property, or use another exception-handling technique.

op_Implicit

The op_Implicit method represents a special SqlMoney converter that allows SqlMoney values to be implicitly assigned from other SqlTypes. This method is overloaded in several ways.

NOTE **It appears that you can pass any numeric object to the op_Implicit method. When assigning the SqlMoney value from numeric types with a larger precision, keep in mind the MinValue and MaxValue. Any value that exceeds those limits will throw an OverflowException.**

If you are using ADO.NET with C#, then you will not call the op_Implicit method directly, but rather you are allowed to cast from one SqlType to the other.

Usage

```
mySqlMoney = mySqlMoney.op_Implicit(mySqlByte)     ' Visual Basic .NET
mySqlMoney = (SqlMoney)mySqlByte;                  // C#
mySqlMoney = mySqlMoney.op_Implicit(mySqlDecimal)  ' Visual Basic .NET
mySqlMoney = (SqlMoney)mySqlDecimal;               // C#
mySqlMoney = mySqlMoney.op_Implicit(mySqlInt16)    ' Visual Basic .NET
mySqlMoney = (SqlMoney)mySqlInt16;                 // C#
mySqlMoney = mySqlMoney.op_Implicit(mySqlInt32)    ' Visual Basic .NET
mySqlMoney = (SqlMoney)mySqlInt32;                 // C#
mySqlMoney = mySqlMoney.op_Implicit(mySqlInt64)    ' Visual Basic .NET
mySqlMoney = (SqlMoney)mySqlInt64;                 // C#
```

Parameters

`mySqlByte`	A SqlByte object.
`mySqlDecimal`	A SqlDecimal object.
`mySqlInt16`	A SqlInt16 object.
`mySqlInt32`	A SqlInt32 object.
`mySqlInt64`	A SqlInt64 object.

Exceptions

OverflowException	The operation returned a value outside of the range of a SqlMoney value.

Parse

The Parse method will evaluate a string and return a SqlMoney value. Keep in mind that converting from a String can throw a FormatException if ADO.NET can't parse the string.

Usage

```
mySqlMoney = mySqlMoney.Parse(myString)
```

Parameters

`myString`	A case-insensitive String object containing a valid Money value, such as "-17305.25", "0", "100", "$11,725.32", or "922,337,203,685,477.5807".

Exceptions

OverflowException	The operation returned a value outside of the range of a SqlMoney value.
FormatException	ADO.NET couldn't parse the string.

Subtract

The Subtract method will subtract the second SqlMoney from the first SqlMoney and return a SqlMoney object whose Value property contains the results of the subtraction. Keep in mind the MinValue and MaxValue that a SqlMoney can hold. If either SqlMoney value is null, the resulting SqlMoney will be null.

In addition to the Subtract method, you may also use the op_Subtraction operator method, or, if your language supports overloaded operators, you may use that construct instead.

Usage

```
mySqlMoney = mySqlMoney.Subtract(mySqlMoney1,mySqlMoney2)
mySqlMoney = mySqlMoney.op_Subtraction(mySqlMoney1,mySqlMoney2) ' VB
mySqlMoney = mySqlMoney1 - mySqlMoney2; // C#
```

Parameters

`mySqlMoney1`	A SqlMoney object.
`mySqlMoney2`	A SqlMoney object.

Exceptions

OverflowException	The operation returned a value outside of the range of a SqlMoney value.

ToDecimal

The ToDecimal method returns the SqlMoney value as a Decimal object. A null SqlMoney value will throw an exception.

Usage

```
myDecimal = mySqlMoney.ToDecimal()
```

Parameters

None.

Exceptions

SqlNullValueException	You cannot retrieve a null value. Be sure to check the IsNull property, or use another exception-handling technique.

ToDouble

The ToDouble method returns the SqlMoney value as a Double object. Be mindful that the Double may not hold the precision or scale of your SqlMoney object and that data may be lost. A null SqlMoney value will throw an exception.

Usage

```
myDouble = mySqlMoney.ToDouble()
```

Parameters

None.

Exceptions

SqlNullValueException	You cannot retrieve a null value. Be sure to check the IsNull property, or use another exception-handling technique.

ToInt32

The ToInt32 method returns the SqlMoney value as an Int32 object. Be mindful of the range of values that the Int32 class supports and that it holds only integer values. A null SqlMoney value will throw an exception.

Usage

```
myInt32 = mySqlMoney.ToInt32()
```

Parameters

None.

Exceptions

OverflowException	The operation returned a value outside of the range of an Int32 value.
SqlNullValueException	You cannot retrieve a null value. Be sure to check the IsNull property, or use another exception-handling technique.

ToInt64

The ToInt64 method returns the SqlMoney value as an Int64 object. Be mindful that the Int64 class holds only integer values. A null SqlMoney value will throw an exception.

Usage

```
myInt64 = mySqlMoney.ToInt64()
```

Parameters

None.

Exceptions

SqlNullValueException	You cannot retrieve a null value. Be sure to check the IsNull property, or use another exception-handling technique.

ToSqlBoolean

The ToSqlBoolean method returns the SqlMoney value as a SqlBoolean object. Any nonzero SqlMoney value will return in a True SqlBoolean. A zero SqlMoney value will return a False SqlBoolean. A null SqlMoney value will return a null SqlBoolean.

Usage

```
mySqlBoolean = mySqlMoney.ToSqlBoolean()
```

Parameters

None.

ToSqlByte

The ToSqlByte method returns the SqlMoney value as a SqlByte object. Be mindful of the range of values that the SqlByte class supports and that it holds only positive integer values. A null SqlMoney value will return a null SqlByte.

Usage

```
mySqlByte = mySqlMoney.ToSqlByte()
```

Parameters

None.

Exceptions

OverflowException	The operation returned a value outside of the range of a SqlByte value.

ToSqlDecimal

The ToSqlDecimal method returns the SqlMoney value as a SqlDecimal. A null value would indicate that the SqlMoney value is null.

Usage

```
mySqlDecimal = mySqlMoney.ToSqlDecimal()
```

Parameters

None.

ToSqlDouble

The ToSqlDouble method returns the SqlMoney value as a SqlDouble. Be mindful that the SqlDouble may not hold the precision or scale of your SqlMoney object and that data may be lost. A null value would indicate that the SqlMoney value is null.

Usage

```
mySqlDouble = mySqlMoney.ToSqlDouble()
```

Parameters

None.

ToSqlInt16

The ToSqlInt16 method returns the SqlMoney value as a SqlInt16 (16-bit integer). Be mindful of the range of values that the SqlInt16 class supports and that it holds only integer values. A null value would indicate that the SqlMoney value is null.

Usage

```
mySqlInt16 = mySqlMoney.ToSqlInt16()
```

Parameters

None.

Exceptions

OverflowException	The operation returned a value outside of the range of a SqlInt16 value.

ToSqlInt32

The ToSqlInt32 method returns the SqlMoney value as a SqlInt32 (32 bit integer). Be mindful of the range of values that the SqlInt32 class supports and that it holds only integer values. A null value would indicate that the SqlMoney value is null.

Usage

```
mySqlInt32 = mySqlMoney.ToSqlInt32()
```

Parameters

None.

Exceptions

OverflowException	The operation returned a value outside of the range of a SqlInt32 value.

ToSqlInt64

The ToSqlInt64 method returns the SqlMoney value as a SqlInt64 (64 bit integer). Be mindful of the range of values that the SqlInt64 class supports and that it holds only integer values. A null value would indicate that the SqlMoney value is null.

Usage

```
mySqlInt64 = mySqlMoney.ToSqlInt64()
```

Parameters

None.

Exceptions

OverflowException	The operation returned a value outside of the range of a SqlInt64 value.

ToSqlSingle

The ToSqlSingle method returns the SqlMoney value as a SqlSingle. Be mindful that the SqlSingle may not hold the precision or scale of your SqlMoney object and that data may be lost. A null value would indicate that the SqlMoney value is null.

Usage

```
mySqlMoney = mySqlMoney.ToSqlMoney()
```

Parameters

None.

ToSqlString

The ToSqlString method returns the SqlMoney value as a SqlString. A null value would indicate that the SqlMoney value is null.

Usage

```
mySqlString = mySqlMoney.ToSqlString()
```

Parameters

None.

ToString

The ToString method returns the SqlMoney value as a readable value.

Usage

```
myString = mySqlMoney.ToString()
```

Parameters

None.

Value

The read-only Value property allows you to retrieve the value of the SqlMoney. Remember that this property is read-only—you may not assign a SqlMoney its value using its Value property.

In addition to using the Value property, you may also use the op_Explicit conversion method, or, if your language supports overloaded operators, you may use that construct instead.

Usage

```
myDecimal = mySqlMoney.Value                       ' Visual Basic .NET
myDecimal = mySqlMoney.op_Explicit(mySqlMoney)     ' Visual Basic .NET
myDecimal = (Decimal)mySqlMoney;                   // C#
```

Parameters

None.

Exceptions

SqlNullValueException	You cannot retrieve a null value. Be sure to check the IsNull property, or use another exception-handling technique.

Zero

The Zero field represents a read-only value of (0) that can be assigned to a SqlMoney object.

Usage

```
mySqlMoney = mySqlMoney.Zero
```

Parameters

None.

System.Data.SqlTypes.SqlNullValueException

The SqlNullValueException is thrown whenever the value of a SqlTypes object that contains a null value is requested. Most of the standard .NET data types cannot hold null values, so an exception is raised when you attempt to do so. The SqlNullValue-Exception class inherits from the SqlTypeException class.

Microsoft has provided a public constructor for this exception class, allowing you to instantiate and throw your own SqlNullValueException.

Constructors

```
Dim mySqlNullValueException As New SqlNullValueException()
Dim mySqlNullValueException As New SqlNullValueException(myString)
```

Parameters

`myString` A String object that will initialize the Message property.

SqlNullValueException Sample Code

```
Dim mySqlNullValueException As SqlNullValueException
mySqlNullValueException = New mySqlNullValueException("Data is Missing!")
Throw mySqlNullValueException
```

Members

GetBaseException

The GetBaseException method returns an Exception object containing the original exception. To return the original exception, it traverses the chain of InnerException objects. If the InnerException property of the current exception is null, GetBaseException will return a reference to the current Exception object.

To determine only the parent exception to the current exception, use the Inner-Exception property.

Usage

```
myException = mySqlNullValueException.GetBaseException()
```

Parameters
None.

Exceptions
None.

GetObjectData

The GetObjectData method fills the passed System.Runtime.Serialization.SerializationInfo buffer object with information about the Exception object. There is no value returned by this method. Depending on the passed System.Runtime.Serialization.StreamingContext object, this method can be used to serialize the object to a stream or read serialization from a stream.

Because it deals mainly with serialization and not data access, further discussion of this property is beyond the scope of this book.

Usage
```
mySqlNullValueException.GetObjectData(mySerializationInfo, _
   myStreamingContext)
```

Parameters

`mySerializationInfo`	A System.Runtime.Serialization.SerializationInfo buffer object to be filled with the exception's serialization data.
`myStreamingContext`	A System.Runtime.Serialization.StreamingContext object specifying the stream to write the serialization info to or read the information from.

Exceptions

ArgumentNullException	The passed SerializationInfo buffer object is null (`Nothing` in Visual Basic .NET).

HelpLink

The HelpLink property returns or sets a String linking to a help file associated with the SqlNullValueException. The HelpLink is formatted as a Uniform Resource Name (URN) or Uniform Resource Locator (URL). An example of this property that points to the MSDN help available with Visual Studio .NET would be: `ms-help://MS.VSCC/MS.MSDNVS/cpref/html/frlrfsystemexceptionclasshelplinktopic.htm`.

The HelpLink is often not set, so it is wise to verify both that the HelpLink property itself is not an empty string and that the HelpLink points to a valid help file before exposing the HelpLink to a user of your program.

Usage
```
myString = mySqlNullValueException.HelpLink
mySqlNullValueException.HelpLink = myString
```

Parameters
None.

InnerException

The read-only InnerException property returns the Exception object linking to a previous exception that caused the current exception to be thrown, if any, or a null value (`Nothing` in Visual Basic .NET), if not. This permits a chain of InnerException objects to be generated, allowing a program to trace the exception chain all the way to the root exception. Be aware that InnerException may be null.

To find the base exception that originally was fired, use the GetBaseException method.

Usage

```
myException = mySqlNullValueException.InnerException
```

Parameters

None.

Sample Code

```
' Accepts any Exception to subroutine, so recursion is possible
Public Sub ViewInnerExceptions(ByVal myException As Exception)
    'immediately leave subroutine if InnerException is null
    If myException.InnerException Is Nothing Then Exit Sub
    Dim myInnerException As Exception = myException.InnerException
    MessageBox.Show("InnerException Information" & ControlChars.Cr _
        & "Message:    " & myInnerException.Message & ControlChars.Cr _
        & "Source:     " & myInnerException.Source & ControlChars.Cr _
        & "HelpLink:   " & myInnerException.HelpLink & ControlChars.Cr _
        & "StackTrace: " & myInnerException.StackTrace)
    'recurse if necessary
    If Not myInnerException.InnerException Is Nothing Then
        ViewInnerExceptions(myInnerException)
    End If
End Sub
```

Message

The read-only Message property returns a String describing the first error that caused the exception. Because it provides information from only the first error, use this property cautiously when building robust error handling.

Usage

```
myString = mySqlNullValueException.Message
```

Parameters

None.

Source

The Source property sets or returns a String containing the name of the provider that generated the first error. Because it provides information from only the first error, use this property cautiously when building robust error handling.

Usage

```
myString = mySqlNullValueException.Source
mySqlNullValueException.Source = myString
```

Parameters

None.

StackTrace

The read-only StackTrace property returns a String containing a textual representation of the stack trace. The stack trace reports all of the methods that are in execution at the time just prior to the execution being thrown. It is read from top to bottom with the latest method in execution at the top.

The StackTrace can be invaluable in tracing difficult-to-find bugs because it provides a way to see all of the methods that could have led up to the error.

NOTE To see the stack trace programmatically when no exception has been raised, use the Environment.StackTrace property.

Usage

```
myString = mySqlNullValueException.StackTrace
```

Parameters

None.

TargetSite

The read-only TargetSite property returns an object inheriting from System.Reflection. MethodBase that contains a reference to the method that caused the error to be thrown.

This property is primarily used to programmatically find information about the method that raised the exception. The returned object will provide information such as the methods parameters and return type and whether the method is virtual, a constructor, public, private, etc. Because it deals mainly with reflection and not data access, further discussion of this property is beyond the scope of this book.

Usage

```
myMethodBase = mySqlNullValueException.TargetSite
```

Parameters

None.

ToString

The ToString method is overridden to return information relating to the SqlNullValueException. The returned String contains the full class name and also the error message, name of the inner exception, and stack trace, if they exist.

Usage

```
myString = mySqlNullValueException.ToString()
```

Parameters

None.

Exceptions
None.

System.Data.SqlTypes.SqlSingle

The SqlSingle structure represents a floating-point number. The value may be between -3.40E + 38 and 3.40E + 38. Use the SqlSingle structure to manipulate the following SQL Server data types:

- float (n) - where n < 25
- real
- sql_variant (if the data is one the above types)

Constructors

```
Dim mySqlSingle As New SqlSingle(mySingle)
Dim mySqlSingle As New SqlSingle(myDouble)
```

Parameters

`mySingle`	A Single object.
`myDouble`	A Double object.

SqlSingle Sample Code

```
Private Sub ReadSqlType(ByVal myConnectionString As String, _
                        ByVal myCommandText As String)
   Dim mySqlConnection As System.Data.SqlClient.SqlConnection
   Dim mySqlDataReader As System.Data.SqlClient.SqlDataReader
   Dim mySqlCommand As System.Data.SqlClient.SqlCommand
   Dim mySqlSingle As System.Data.SqlTypes.SqlSingle
   ' Establish connection
   mySqlConnection = New SqlConnection(myConnectionString)
   mySqlConnection.Open()
   ' Build and execute command
   mySqlCommand = New SqlCommand(myCommandText)
   mySqlCommand.Connection = mySqlConnection
   mySqlDataReader = mySqlCommand.ExecuteReader
   ' Read first row
   If mySqlDataReader.Read Then
      ' Save column as appropriate SqlTypes structure
      mySqlSingle = mySqlDataReader.GetSqlSingle(1)
      MessageBox.Show(mySqlSingle.ToString)
   End If
   ' Done
   mySqlConnection.Close()
End Sub
```

Members

Add

The Add method will add two SqlSingle values together and return a SqlSingle object whose Value property contains the results of the addition. Keep in mind the MinValue and MaxValue that a SqlSingle can hold. If either SqlSingle value is null, the resulting SqlSingle will be null.

In addition to the Add method, you may also use the op_Addition operator method, or, if your language supports overloaded operators, you may use that construct instead.

Usage

```
mySqlSingle = mySqlSingle.Add(mySqlSingle1,mySqlSingle2)
mySqlSingle = mySqlSingle.op_Addition(mySqlSingle1,mySqlSingle2) ' VB
mySqlSingle = mySqlSingle1 + mySqlSingle2; // C#
```

Parameters

`mySqlSingle1`	A SqlSingle object.
`mySqlSingle2`	A SqlSingle object.

Exceptions

OverflowException	The operation returned a value outside of the range of a SqlSingle value.

CompareTo

The CompareTo method allows you to compare the SqlSingle value with another supplied object to return an indication of their relative values. The returned Int32 object will indicate the comparison:

Less Than Zero. The SqlSingle value was less than the supplied object, or the SqlSingle was null.

Zero. The SqlSingle value was the same as the supplied object.

Greater than zero. The SqlSingle value was greater than the supplied object, or the object was null.

Usage

```
myInt32 = mySqlSingle.CompareTo(myObject)
```

Parameters

`myObject`	Any object that implements the IComparable interface.

Exceptions

ArgumentException	The supplied object isn't valid for comparison.

Divide

The Divide method will divide the first SqlSingle by the second SqlSingle. This method will return a SqlSingle object whose Value property contains the results of the division. If either SqlSingle value is null, the resulting SqlSingle will be null.

In addition to the Divide method, you may also use the op_Division operator method, or, if your language supports overloaded operators, you may use that construct instead.

Usage

```
mySqlSingle = mySqlSingle.Divide(mySqlSingle1,mySqlSingle2)
mySqlSingle = mySqlSingle.op_Division(mySqlSingle1,mySqlSingle2) ' VB
mySqlSingle = mySqlSingle1 / mySqlSingle2; // C#
```

Parameters

`mySqlSingle1`	A SqlSingle object.
`mySqlSingle2`	A SqlSingle object.

Exceptions

DivideByZeroException	You tried to divide by zero.

Equals

The Equals method allows you to compare the SqlSingle value with a supplied object or compare the values of two supplied objects or SqlSingle values. The result will be either a Boolean or a SqlBoolean, depending on which overloaded method is called. The result may be null if either of the SqlSingle values being compared were null.

In addition to the Equals method, you may also use the op_Equality operator method, or, if your language supports overloaded operators, you may use that construct instead.

Usage

```
mySqlBoolean = mySqlSingle.Equals(mySqlSingle1,mySqlSingle2)
myBoolean = mySqlSingle.Equals(myObject)
myBoolean = mySqlSingle.Equals(myObject,myObject2)
mySqlBoolean = mySqlSingle.op_Equality(mySqlSingle1,mySqlSingle2) ' VB
mySqlBoolean = (mySqlSingle1 == mySqlSingle2); // C#
```

Parameters

`mySqlSingle1`	A SqlSingle object.
`mySqlSingle2`	A SqlSingle object.
`myObject`	Any System.Object or descendant.
`myObject2`	Any System.Object or descendant.

GetHashCode

The GetHashCode method returns a hash code for the SqlSingle value. The hash code represents a unique value corresponding to the particular value of the SqlSingle object. Keep in mind that even the smallest change to the SqlSingle value will result in a different hash code. Requesting the hash code for a SqlSingle object with a null value will return 0.

BE CAREFUL The hash code returned for a SqlSingle with a value of 0 is 0, which is the same for a SqlSingle with a null value.

Usage

```
myInt32 = mySqlSingle.GetHashCode()
```

Parameters

None.

GreaterThan

The GreaterThan method compares two SqlSingle values and returns a SqlBoolean value indicating whether the first SqlSingle value is greater than the second SqlSingle value. A null value would indicate that one of the SqlSingle values is null.

In addition to the GreaterThan method, you may also use the op_GreaterThan operator method, or, if your language supports overloaded operators, you may use that construct instead.

Usage

```
mySqlBoolean = mySqlSingle.GreaterThan(mySqlSingle1,mySqlSingle2)
mySqlBoolean = mySqlSingle.op_GreaterThan(mySqlSingle1,mySqlSingle2) ' VB
mySqlBoolean = (mySqlSingle1 > mySqlSingle2); // C#
```

Parameters

`mySqlSingle1`	A SqlSingle object.
`mySqlSingle2`	A SqlSingle object.

GreaterThanOrEqual

The GreaterThanOrEqual method compares two SqlSingle values and returns a SqlBoolean value indicating whether the first SqlSingle value is greater than or equal to the second SqlSingle value. A null value would indicate that one of the SqlSingle values is null.

In addition to the GreaterThanOrEqual method, you may also use the op_GreaterThanOrEqual operator method, or, if your language supports overloaded operators, you may use that construct instead.

Usage

```
mySqlBoolean = _
   mySqlSingle.GreaterThanOrEqual(mySqlSingle1,mySqlSingle2)
mySqlBoolean = _
   mySqlSingle.op_GreaterThanOrEqual(mySqlSingle1,mySqlSingle2) ' VB
mySqlBoolean = (mySqlSingle1 >= mySqlSingle2); // C#
```

Parameters

`mySqlSingle1`	A SqlSingle object.
`mySqlSingle2`	A SqlSingle object.

IsNull

The read-only IsNull property returns a Boolean indicating whether the SqlSingle is null. The value will be True if the value of the SqlSingle is null and False if it is otherwise.

Usage

```
myBoolean = mySqlSingle.IsNull
```

Parameters
None.

LessThan

The LessThan method compares two SqlSingle values and returns a SqlBoolean value indicating whether the first SqlSingle value is less than the second SqlSingle value. A null value would indicate that one of the SqlSingle values is null.

In addition to the LessThan method, you may also use the op_LessThan operator method, or, if your language supports overloaded operators, you may use that construct instead.

Usage

```
mySqlBoolean = mySqlSingle.LessThan(mySqlSingle1,mySqlSingle2)
mySqlBoolean = mySqlSingle.op_LessThan(mySqlSingle1,mySqlSingle2) ' VB
mySqlBoolean = (mySqlSingle1 < mySqlSingle2); // C#
```

Parameters

`mySqlSingle1`	A SqlSingle object.
`mySqlSingle2`	A SqlSingle object.

LessThanOrEqual

The LessThanOrEqual method compares two SqlSingle values and returns a SqlBoolean value indicating whether the first SqlSingle value is less than or equal to the second SqlSingle value. A null value would indicate that one of the SqlSingle values is null.

In addition to the LessThanOrEqual method, you may also use the op_LessThanOrEqual operator method, or, if your language supports overloaded operators, you may use that construct instead.

Usage

```
mySqlBoolean = mySqlSingle.LessThanOrEqual(mySqlSingle1,mySqlSingle2)
mySqlBoolean = _
   mySqlSingle.op_LessThanOrEqual(mySqlSingle1,mySqlSingle2) ' VB
mySqlBoolean = (mySqlSingle1 <= mySqlSingle2); // C#
```

Parameters

`mySqlSingle1`	A SqlSingle object.
`mySqlSingle2`	A SqlSingle object.

MaxValue

The read-only MaxValue field represents the largest number that a SqlSingle can hold, which is 3.40E + 38 (3.402823E+38). By using the MaxValue field, you can build flexible, readable exception-handling code.

Usage

```
mySqlSingle = mySqlSingle.MaxValue
```

Parameters
None.

MinValue

The read-only MinValue field represents the smallest number that a SqlSingle can hold, which is -3.40E + 38 (-3.402823E+38). By using the MinValue field, you can build flexible, readable exception-handling code.

Usage

```
mySqlSingle = mySqlSingle.MinValue
```

Parameters

None.

Multiply

The Multiply method will multiply the first SqlSingle by the second SqlSingle and return a SqlSingle object whose Value property contains the results of the multiplication. Keep in mind the MaxValue that a SqlSingle can hold. If either SqlSingle value is null, the resulting SqlSingle will be null.

In addition to the Multiply method, you may also use the op_Multiply operator method, or, if your language supports overloaded operators, you may use that construct instead.

Usage

```
mySqlSingle = mySqlSingle.Multiply(mySqlSingle1,mySqlSingle2)
mySqlSingle = mySqlSingle.op_Multiply(mySqlSingle1,mySqlSingle2) ' VB
mySqlSingle = mySqlSingle1 * mySqlSingle2; // C#
```

Parameters

`mySqlSingle1`	A SqlSingle object.
`mySqlSingle2`	A SqlSingle object.

Exceptions

OverflowException	The operation returned a value outside of the range of a SqlSingle value.

NotEquals

The NotEquals method compares two SqlSingle values and returns a SqlBoolean value indicating whether the two SqlSingle values are not equal. A null value would indicate that one of the SqlSingle values is null.

In addition to the NotEquals method, you may also use the op_Inequality operator method, or, if your language supports overloaded operators, you may use that construct instead.

Usage

```
mySqlBoolean = mySqlSingle.NotEquals(mySqlSingle1,mySqlSingle2)
mySqlBoolean = mySqlSingle.op_Inequality(mySqlSingle1,mySqlSingle2) ' VB
mySqlBoolean = (mySqlSingle1 != mySqlSingle2); // C#
```

Parameters

`mySqlSingle1`	A SqlSingle object.
`mySqlSingle2`	A SqlSingle object.

Null

The Null field represents a read-only null value that can be assigned to a SqlSingle object. You cannot use the standard .NET way of assigning a null value with the System.DBNull.Value, but rather you must use this approach.

Usage

```
mySqlSingle = mySqlSingle.Null
```

Parameters

None.

op_Explicit

The op_Explicit method represents a special SqlSingle converter that allows SqlSingle values to be explicitly assigned to and from other SqlTypes. This method is overloaded in several ways. The first two examples that follow show how to retrieve the SqlSingle value as a Decimal object. The other examples show how to assign the SqlSingle value.

When assigning the SqlSingle value from one of the other SqlTypes, keep in mind the MinValue and MaxValue. Any value that exceeds those limits will throw an OverflowException. Any null values will convert to a SqlSingle null value.

When assigning the SqlSingle value from a SqlString object, be sure that the string parses to a valid SqlSingle value. Converting from a SqlString object can throw a FormatException if ADO.NET can't parse the string.

If you are using ADO.NET with C#, then you will not call the op_Explicit method directly, but rather you are allowed to cast from one SqlType to the other.

Usage

```
mySingle = mySqlSingle.op_Explicit(mySqlSingle)      ' Visual Basic .NET
mySingle = (Single)mySqlSingle;                      // C#
mySqlSingle = mySqlSingle.op_Explicit(mySqlBoolean)  ' Visual Basic .NET
mySqlSingle = (SqlSingle)mySqlBoolean;               // C#
mySqlSingle = mySqlSingle.op_Explicit(mySqlDouble)   ' Visual Basic .NET
mySqlSingle = (SqlSingle)mySqlDouble;                // C#
mySqlSingle = mySqlSingle.op_Explicit(mySqlString)   ' Visual Basic .NET
mySqlSingle = (SqlSingle)mySqlString;                // C#
```

Parameters

`mySqlSingle`	A SqlSingle object.
`mySqlBoolean`	A SqlBoolean object.
`mySqlDouble`	A SqlDouble object.
`mySqlString`	A SqlString object.

Exceptions

FormatException	ADO.NET couldn't parse the string.
OverflowException	The operation returned a value outside of the range of a SqlSingle value.
SqlNullValueException	You cannot assign a null value to a Single class. Be sure to check the IsNull property, or use another exception-handling technique.

op_Implicit

The op_Implicit method represents a special SqlSingle converter that allows SqlSingle values to be implicitly assigned from other SqlTypes. This method is overloaded in several ways.

NOTE It appears that you can pass any numeric object to the op_Implicit method. When assigning the SqlSingle value from numeric types with a larger precision, keep in mind the MinValue and MaxValue. Any value that exceeds those limits will throw an OverflowException.

If you are using ADO.NET with C#, then you will not call the op_Implicit method directly, but rather you are allowed to cast from one SqlType to the other.

Usage

```
mySqlSingle = mySqlSingle.op_Implicit(mySingle)      ' Visual Basic .NET
mySqlSingle = (SqlSingle)mySingle;                   // C#
mySqlSingle = mySqlSingle.op_Implicit(mySqlByte)     ' Visual Basic .NET
mySqlSingle = (SqlSingle)mySqlByte;                  // C#
mySqlSingle = mySqlSingle.op_Implicit(mySqlDecimal)  ' Visual Basic .NET
mySqlSingle = (SqlSingle)mySqlDecimal;               // C#
mySqlSingle = mySqlSingle.op_Implicit(mySqlInt16)    ' Visual Basic .NET
mySqlSingle = (SqlSingle)mySqlInt16;                 // C#
mySqlSingle = mySqlSingle.op_Implicit(mySqlInt32)    ' Visual Basic .NET
mySqlSingle = (SqlSingle)mySqlInt32;                 // C#
mySqlSingle = mySqlSingle.op_Implicit(mySqlInt64)    ' Visual Basic .NET
mySqlSingle = (SqlSingle)mySqlInt64;                 // C#
mySqlSingle = mySqlSingle.op_Implicit(mySqlMoney)    ' Visual Basic .NET
mySqlSingle = (SqlSingle)mySqlMoney;                 // C#
```

Parameters

`mySingle`	A Decimal object.
`mySqlByte`	A SqlByte object.
`mySqlDecimal`	A SqlDecimal object.
`mySqlInt16`	A SqlInt16 object.
`mySqlInt32`	A SqlInt32 object.
`mySqlInt64`	A SqlInt64 object.
`mySqlMoney`	A SqlMoney object.

Exceptions

OverflowException	The operation returned a value outside of the range of a SqlSingle value.

Parse

The Parse method will evaluate a string and return a SqlSingle. Keep in mind that converting from a String can throw a FormatException if ADO.NET can't parse the string.

Usage

```
mySqlSingle = mySqlSingle.Parse(myString)
```

Parameters

`myString`	A case-insensitive String object containing a valid Single value, such as "-17305.25", "0", "100", or "3.40E+38".

Exceptions

OverflowException	The operation returned a value outside of the range of a SqlSingle value.
FormatException	ADO.NET couldn't parse the string.

Subtract

The Subtract method will subtract the second SqlSingle from the first SqlSingle and return a SqlSingle object whose Value property contains the results of the subtraction. Keep in mind the MinValue and MaxValue that a SqlSingle can hold. If either SqlSingle value is null, the resulting SqlSingle will be null.

In addition to the Subtract method, you may also use the op_Subtraction operator method, or, if your language supports overloaded operators, you may use that construct instead.

Usage

```
mySqlSingle = mySqlSingle.Subtract(mySqlSingle1,mySqlSingle2)
mySqlSingle = mySqlSingle.op_Subtraction(mySqlSingle1,mySqlSingle2) ' VB
mySqlSingle = mySqlSingle1 - mySqlSingle2; // C#
```

Parameters

`mySqlSingle1`	A SqlSingle object.
`mySqlSingle2`	A SqlSingle object.

Exceptions

OverflowException	The operation returned a value outside of the range of a SqlSingle value.

ToSqlBoolean

The ToSqlBoolean method returns the SqlSingle value as a SqlBoolean object. Any nonzero SqlSingle value will return in a True SqlBoolean. A zero SqlSingle value will return a False SqlBoolean. A null SqlSingle value will return a null SqlBoolean.

Usage

```
mySqlBoolean = mySqlSingle.ToSqlBoolean()
```

Parameters

None.

ToSqlByte

The ToSqlByte method returns the SqlSingle value as a SqlByte object. Be mindful of the range of values that the SqlByte class supports and that it holds only positive integer values. A null SqlSingle value will return a null SqlByte.

Usage

```
mySqlByte = mySqlSingle.ToSqlByte()
```

Parameters

None.

Exceptions

OverflowException	The operation returned a value outside of the range of a SqlByte value.

ToSqlDecimal

The ToSqlDecimal method returns the SqlSingle value as a SqlDecimal. A null value would indicate that the SqlSingle value is null.

Usage

```
mySqlDecimal = mySqlSingle.ToSqlDecimal()
```

Parameters

None.

Exceptions

OverflowException	The operation returned a value outside of the range of a SqlDecimal value.

ToSqlDouble

The ToSqlDouble method returns the SqlSingle value as a SqlDouble. A null value would indicate that the SqlSingle value is null.

Usage

```
mySqlDouble = mySqlSingle.ToSqlDouble()
```

Parameters

None.

ToSqlInt16

The ToSqlInt16 method returns the SqlSingle value as a SqlInt16 (16 bit integer). Be mindful of the range of values that the SqlInt16 class supports and that it holds only integer values. A null value would indicate that the SqlSingle value is null.

Usage

```
mySqlInt16 = mySqlSingle.ToSqlInt16()
```

Parameters

None.

Exceptions

OverflowException	The operation returned a value outside of the range of a SqlInt16 value.

ToSqlInt32

The ToSqlInt32 method returns the SqlSingle value as a SqlInt32 (32 bit integer). Be mindful of the range of values that the SqlInt32 class supports and that it holds only integer values. A null value would indicate that the SqlSingle value is null.

Usage

```
mySqlInt32 = mySqlSingle.ToSqlInt32()
```

Parameters

None.

Exceptions

OverflowException	The operation returned a value outside of the range of a SqlInt32 value.

ToSqlInt64

The ToSqlInt64 method returns the SqlSingle value as a SqlInt64 (64 bit integer). Be mindful of the range of values that the SqlInt64 class supports and that it holds only integer values. A null value would indicate that the SqlSingle value is null.

Usage

```
mySqlInt64 = mySqlSingle.ToSqlInt64()
```

Parameters

None.

Exceptions

OverflowException	The operation returned a value outside of the range of a SqlInt64 value.

ToSqlMoney

The ToSqlMoney method returns the SqlSingle value as a SqlMoney. A null value would indicate that the SqlSingle value is null.

Usage

```
mySqlMoney = mySqlSingle.ToSqlMoney()
```

Parameters

None.

Exceptions

OverflowException	The operation returned a value outside of the range of a SqlMoney value.

ToSqlString

The ToSqlString method returns the SqlSingle value as a SqlString. A null value would indicate that the SqlSingle value is null.

Usage

```
mySqlString = mySqlSingle.ToSqlString()
```

Parameters

None.

ToString

The ToString method returns the SqlSingle value as a readable value.

Usage

```
myString = mySqlSingle.ToString()
```

Parameters

None.

Value

The read-only Value property allows you to retrieve the value of the SqlSingle. Remember that this property is read-only—you may not assign a SqlSingle its value using its Value property.

In addition to using the Value property, you may also use the op_Explicit conversion method, or, if your language supports overloaded operators, you may use that construct instead.

Usage

```
mySingle = mySqlSingle.Value                        ' Visual Basic .NET
mySingle = mySqlSingle.op_Explicit(mySqlSingle)  ' Visual Basic .NET
mySingle = (Single)mySqlSingle;                     // C#
```

Parameters

None.

Exceptions

SqlNullValueException	You cannot retrieve a null value. Be sure to check the IsNull property, or use another exception-handling technique.

Zero

The Zero field represents a read-only value of (0) that can be assigned to a SqlSingle object.

Usage

```
mySqlSingle = mySqlSingle.Zero
```

Parameters

None.

System.Data.SqlTypes.SqlString

The SqlString structure represents a variable-length stream of characters. Use the SqlString structure to manipulate the following SQL Server data types:

- char
- nchar (Unicode)
- ntext (Unicode)
- nvarchar (Unicode)
- sysname (equivalent to nvarchar(128))
- text
- varchar
- sql_variant (if the data is one of the above types)

Constructors

```
Dim mySqlString As New SqlString(myString)
Dim mySqlString As New SqlString(myString,myInt32)
Dim mySqlString As New SqlString(myInt32,mySqlCompareOptions,myByteArray)
Dim mySqlString As New SqlString(myString,myInt32,mySqlCompareOptions)
Dim mySqlString As New SqlString(myInt32,mySqlCompareOptions, _
   myByteArray, myBoolean)
Dim mySqlString As New SqlString(myInt32,mySqlCompareOptions, _
   myByteArray, myInt32a, myInt32b)
Dim mySqlString As New SqlString(myInt32,mySqlCompareOptions, _
   myByteArray, myInt32a, myInt32b, myBoolean)
```

Parameters

`myString`	The String object to be stored.
`myInt32`	An Int32 object representing the language ID (LCID). This defaults to your locale setting in Control Panel.
`mySqlCompareOptions`	A valid SqlCompareOptions enumeration value. See that section for more information.
`myByteArray`	A Byte array containing the data elements to be stored as a SqlString.
`myBoolean`	A Boolean object indicating if data is Unicode encoded (True) or not (False).
`myInt32a`	An Int32 object representing the starting index within the array to be stored.
`myInt32b`	An Int32 object representing the number of elements from the array to be stored.

Exceptions

ArgumentOutOfRangeException	You have passed an invalid LCID, SqlCompareOption value, or invalid index within the byte array.

SqlString Sample Code

```
Private Sub ReadSqlType(ByVal myConnectionString As String, _
                        ByVal myCommandText As String)
   Dim mySqlConnection As System.Data.SqlClient.SqlConnection
   Dim mySqlDataReader As System.Data.SqlClient.SqlDataReader
   Dim mySqlCommand As System.Data.SqlClient.SqlCommand
   Dim mySqlString As System.Data.SqlTypes.SqlString
   ' Establish connection
   mySqlConnection = New SqlConnection(myConnectionString)
   mySqlConnection.Open()
   ' Build and execute command
   mySqlCommand = New SqlCommand(myCommandText)
   mySqlCommand.Connection = mySqlConnection
   mySqlDataReader = mySqlCommand.ExecuteReader
   ' Read first row
   If mySqlDataReader.Read Then
      ' Save column as appropriate SqlTypes structure
      mySqlString = mySqlDataReader.GetSqlString(1)
      MessageBox.Show(mySqlString.ToString)
   End If
   ' Done
   mySqlConnection.Close()
End Sub
```

Members

BinarySort

The BinarySort field is a read-only value, synonymous with the SqlCompareOptions. BinarySort enumeration value. ADO.NET, in providing you with a very friendly object model, has duplicated all of the SqlCompareOptions enumeration values as SqlString fields. The value of this field is 32768.

Normally, ADO.NET will sort and compare data based on the sorting and comparison rules as defined by the associated language or alphabet. By specifying the BinarySort option, ADO.NET will sort and compare based on the bit patterns defined for each character. This means BinarySort forces case sensitivity.

Usage

```
myInt32 = mySqlString.BinarySort
```

Parameters

None.

Clone

The Clone method allows you to create a full copy of the SqlString object. Use this method to assign the SqlString to a second variable.

NOTE We think it's interesting that SqlString is the only structure in SqlTypes that supports the Clone method, and, as far as we can tell, it's not even necessary. Simply setting a second object variable equal to the first will cause the .NET Framework to automatically use the Clone method (behind the scenes) to create a new copy.

Usage

```
myNewSqlString = mySqlString.Clone()
```

Parameters

None.

CompareInfo

The CompareInfo method returns cultural (locale) information about the SqlString. This property will return the LCID value (for example, 1033). It is important to have this cultural information set correctly when sorting or comparing. This information is similar to that returned by the LCID property; however, requesting a CompareInfo value for a string with an invalid LCID will throw an exception.

Usage

```
myCompareInfo = mySqlString.CompareInfo
```

Parameters

None.

Exceptions

ArgumentException	The Language ID (LCID) is not a supported culture. Make sure the LCID is valid when you create the SqlString object.
SqlNullValueException	You cannot request the CompareInfo property of a null SqlString.

CompareOptionsFromSqlCompareOptions

The CompareOptionsFromSqlCompareOptions method returns a CompareOptions value containing the requested culture information.

NOTE ADO.NET is very redundant. The CompareOptionsFromSqlCompareOptions method simply wraps a request to the SqlCompareOptions enumeration.

Usage

```
myCompareOptions = _
   mySqlString.CompareOptionsFromSqlCompareOptions(SqlCompareOptions)
```

Parameters

None.

Exceptions

ArgumentOutOfRangeException	You have passed an invalid SqlCompareOption value. Be careful using the BinarySort option, as it is not a valid enumeration value in this context.

CompareTo

The CompareTo method allows you to compare the SqlString value with another supplied object to return an indication of their relative values. The returned Int32 object will indicate the comparison:

Less Than Zero. The SqlString value was less than the supplied object, or the SqlString was null.

Zero. The SqlString value was the same as the supplied object.

Greater than zero. The SqlString value was greater than the supplied object, or the object was null.

Usage

```
myInt32 = mySqlString.CompareTo(myObject)
```

Parameters

`myObject`	Any object that implements the IComparable interface.

Exceptions

ArgumentException	The supplied object isn't valid for comparison.

Concat

The Concat method allows you to concatenate two SqlString values together. The method returns a SqlString object. If either of the two SqlString values being concatenated is null, the resulting concatenation will be null.

In addition to the Concat method, you may also use the op_Addition operator method, or, if your language supports overloaded operators, you may use that construct instead.

Usage

```
mySqlString = mySqlString.Concat(mySqlString1, mySqlString2)
mySqlString = mySqlString.op_Addition(mySqlString1, mySqlString2) ' VB
mySqlString = mySqlString1 + mySqlString2; // C#
```

Parameters

`mySqlString1`	A SqlString object.
`mySqlString2`	A SqlString object.

CultureInfo

The CultureInfo method returns cultural (locale) information about the SqlString. This property will return the culture value (for example, en-US). It is important to have this cultural information set correctly when sorting or comparing. Requesting a CultureInfo value for a string with an invalid LCID will throw an exception.

Usage

```
myCultureInfo = mySqlString.CultureInfo
```

Parameters

None.

Exceptions

ArgumentException	The Language ID (LCID) is not a supported culture. Make sure the LCID is valid when you create the SqlString object.
SqlNullValueException	You cannot request the CultureInfo property of a null SqlString.

Equals

The Equals method allows you to compare the SqlString value with a supplied object or compare the values of two supplied objects or SqlString values. The result will be either a Boolean or a SqlBoolean, depending on which overloaded method is called. The result may be null if either of the SqlString values being compared was null.

In addition to the Equals method, you may also use the op_Equality operator method, or, if your language supports overloaded operators, you may use that construct instead.

Usage

```
mySqlBoolean = mySqlString.Equals(mySqlString1,mySqlString2)
myBoolean = mySqlString.Equals(myObject)
myBoolean = mySqlString.Equals(myObject,myObject2)
mySqlBoolean = mySqlString.op_Equality(mySqlString1,mySqlString2) ' VB
mySqlBoolean = (mySqlString1 == mySqlString2); // C#
```

Parameters

`mySqlString1`	A SqlString object.
`mySqlString2`	A SqlString object.
`myObject`	Any System.Object or descendant.
`myObject2`	Any System.Object or descendant.

GetHashCode

The GetHashCode method returns a hash code for the SqlString value. The hash code represents a unique value corresponding to the particular value of the SqlString object. Keep in mind that even the smallest change to the SqlString value will result in a different hash code. Requesting the hash code for a SqlString object with a null value will return 0.

NOTE SqlStrings with the same value, but with different LCIDs or CompareOptions, will return the same hash code; however, SqlStrings with different Unicode settings will return different hash codes.

Usage

```
myInt32 = mySqlString.GetHashCode()
```

Parameters

None.

GetNonUnicodeBytes

The GetNonUnicodeBytes method returns an array of bytes containing the value of the SqlString in ANSI format. The length of the array will be equal to the number of bytes in the SqlString.

Usage

```
myAnsiByteArray = mySqlString.GetNonUnicodeBytes()
```

Parameters

None.

GetUnicodeBytes

The GetUnicodeBytes method returns an array of bytes containing the value of the SqlString in Unicode (double-byte) format. The length of the array will be equal to twice the number of bytes in the SqlString.

Usage

```
myUnicodeByteArray = mySqlString.GetUnicodeBytes()
```

Parameters

None.

GreaterThan

The GreaterThan method compares two SqlString values and returns a SqlBoolean value indicating whether the first SqlString value is greater than the second SqlString value. A null value would indicate that one of the SqlString values is null.

In addition to the GreaterThan method, you may also use the op_GreaterThan operator method, or, if your language supports overloaded operators, you may use that construct instead.

Usage

```
mySqlBoolean = mySqlString.GreaterThan(mySqlString1,mySqlString2)
mySqlBoolean = mySqlString.op_GreaterThan(mySqlString1,mySqlString2) ' VB
mySqlBoolean = (mySqlString1 > mySqlString2); // C#
```

Parameters

`mySqlString1`	A SqlString object.
`mySqlString2`	A SqlString object.

GreaterThanOrEqual

The GreaterThanOrEqual method compares two SqlString values and returns a SqlBoolean value indicating whether the first SqlString value is greater than or equal to the second SqlString value. A null value would indicate that one of the SqlString values is null.

In addition to the GreaterThanOrEqual method, you may also use the op_GreaterThanOrEqual operator method, or, if your language supports overloaded operators, you may use that construct instead.

Usage

```
mySqlBoolean = mySqlString.GreaterThanOrEqual(mySqlString1,mySqlString2)
mySqlBoolean = _
   mySqlString.op_GreaterThanOrEqual(mySqlString1,mySqlString2) ' VB
mySqlBoolean = (mySqlString1 >= mySqlString2); // C#
```

Parameters

`mySqlString1`	A SqlString object.
`mySqlString2`	A SqlString object.

IgnoreCase

The IgnoreCase field is a read-only value, synonymous with the SqlCompareOptions.IgnoreCase enumeration value. ADO.NET, in providing you with a very friendly object model, has duplicated all of the SqlCompareOptions enumeration values as SqlString fields. The value of this field is 1.

By specifying the IgnoreCase option, ADO.NET will not distinguish between uppercase and lowercase letters. ADO.NET will consider both cases to be equal.

Usage

```
myInt32 = mySqlString.IgnoreCase
```

Parameters

None.

IgnoreKanaType

The IgnoreKanaType field is a read-only value, synonymous with the SqlCompareOptions.IgnoreKanaType enumeration value. ADO.NET, in providing you with a very friendly object model, has duplicated all of the SqlCompareOptions enumeration values as SqlString fields. The value of this field is 8.

By specifying the IgnoreKanaType option, ADO.NET will not distinguish between the two types of Japanese kana characters: Hiragana and Katakana. ADO.NET will consider Hiragana and Katakana characters to be equal.

Usage

```
myInt32 = mySqlString.IgnoreKanaType
```

Parameters

None.

IgnoreNonSpace

The IgnoreNonSpace field is a read-only value, synonymous with the SqlCompareOptions.IgnoreNonSpace enumeration value. ADO.NET, in providing you with a very friendly object model, has duplicated all of the SqlCompareOptions enumeration values as SqlString fields. The value of this field is 2.

By specifying the IgnoreNonSpace option, ADO.NET will not distinguish between accented and unaccented characters. ADO.NET will consider all diacritics of the same letter to be equal. For example, all versions of the capital letter A, whether accented or not, will be considered equal: A = À = Á = Ä.

Usage

```
myInt32 = mySqlString.IgnoreNonSpace
```

Parameters

None.

IgnoreWidth

The IgnoreWidth field is a read-only value, synonymous with the SqlCompareOptions.IgnoreWidth enumeration value. ADO.NET, in providing you with a very friendly object model, has duplicated all of the SqlCompareOptions enumeration values as SqlString fields. The value of this field is 16.

By specifying the IgnoreWidth option, ADO.NET will not distinguish between a single-byte (half-width) character and the same character when represented as a double-byte (full-width) character.

Usage

```
myInt32 = mySqlString.IgnoreWidth
```

Parameters

None.

IsNull

The read-only IsNull property returns a Boolean indicating whether the SqlString is null. The value will be True if the value of the SqlString is null and False if it is otherwise.

Usage

```
myBoolean = mySqlString.IsNull
```

Parameters

None.

LCID

The read-only LCID property returns the locale identifier for the SqlString. This attribute defines certain behaviors related to the language of the locale, such as the code page and the order in which characters are sorted. Unless a different LCID was specified when the SqlString was instantiated, the LCID will be equal to that set in your Regional Settings in Control Panel.

The U.S. English locale is 1033 (equivalent to the CultureInfo value of "en-us").

Usage

```
myInt32 = mySqlString.LCID
```

Parameters

None.

Exceptions

SqlNullValueException	You cannot request the LCID property of a null SqlString.

LessThan

The LessThan method compares two SqlString values and returns a SqlBoolean value indicating whether the first SqlString value is less than the second SqlString value. A null value would indicate that one of the SqlString values is null.

In addition to the LessThan method, you may also use the op_LessThan operator method, or, if your language supports overloaded operators, you may use that construct instead.

Usage

```
mySqlBoolean = mySqlString.LessThan(mySqlString1,mySqlString2)
mySqlBoolean = mySqlString.op_LessThan(mySqlString1,mySqlString2) ' VB
mySqlBoolean = (mySqlString1 < mySqlString2); // C#
```

Parameters

mySqlString1	A SqlString object.
mySqlString2	A SqlString object.

LessThanOrEqual

The LessThanOrEqual method compares two SqlString values and returns a SqlBoolean value indicating whether the first SqlString value is less than or equal to the second SqlString value. A null value would indicate that one of the SqlString values is null.

In addition to the LessThanOrEqual method, you may also use the op_LessThanOrEqual operator method, or, if your language supports overloaded operators, you may use that construct instead.

Usage

```
mySqlBoolean = mySqlString.LessThanOrEqual(mySqlString1,mySqlString2)
mySqlBoolean = _
   mySqlString.op_LessThanOrEqual(mySqlString1,mySqlString2) ' VB
mySqlBoolean = (mySqlString1 <= mySqlString2); // C#
```

Parameters

mySqlString1	A SqlString object.
mySqlString2	A SqlString object.

NotEquals

The NotEquals method compares two SqlString values and returns a SqlBoolean value indicating whether the two SqlString values are not equal. A null value would indicate that one of the SqlString values is null.

In addition to the NotEquals method, you may also use the op_Inequality operator method, or, if your language supports overloaded operators, you may use that construct instead.

Usage

```
mySqlBoolean = mySqlString.NotEquals(mySqlString1,mySqlString2)
mySqlBoolean = mySqlString.op_Inequality(mySqlString1,mySqlString2) ' VB
mySqlBoolean = (mySqlString1 != mySqlString2); // C#
```

Parameters

`mySqlString1`	A SqlString object.
`mySqlString2`	A SqlString object.

Null

The Null field represents a read-only null value that can be assigned to a SqlString object. You cannot use the standard .NET way of assigning a null value with the System.DBNull.Value, but rather you must use this approach.

Usage

```
mySqlString = mySqlString.Null
```

Parameters

None.

op_Explicit

The op_Explicit method represents a special SqlString converter that allows SqlString values to be explicitly assigned to and from other SqlTypes. This method is overloaded in a couple of ways. The first two examples that follow show how to retrieve the SqlString value as a String object. The other examples show how to assign the SqlString value.

If you are using ADO.NET with C#, then you will not call the op_Explicit method directly, but rather you are allowed to cast from one SqlType to the other.

Usage

```
myString = mySqlString.op_Explicit(mySqlString)        ' Visual Basic .NET
myString = (String)mySqlString;                        // C#
mySqlString = mySqlString.op_Explicit(mySqlBoolean)    ' Visual Basic .NET
mySqlString = (SqlString)mySqlBoolean;                 // C#
mySqlString = mySqlString.op_Explicit(mySqlByte)       ' Visual Basic .NET
mySqlString = (SqlString)mySqlByte;                    // C#
mySqlString = mySqlString.op_Explicit(mySqlDateTime)   ' Visual Basic .NET
mySqlString = (SqlString)mySqlDateTime;                // C#
mySqlString = mySqlString.op_Explicit(mySqlDecimal)    ' Visual Basic .NET
mySqlString = (SqlString)mySqlDecimal;                 // C#
mySqlString = mySqlString.op_Explicit(mySqlDouble)     ' Visual Basic .NET
mySqlString = (SqlString)mySqlDouble;                  // C#
```

```
mySqlString = mySqlString.op_Explicit(mySqlGuid)      ' Visual Basic .NET
mySqlString = (SqlString)mySqlGuid;                   // C#
mySqlString = mySqlString.op_Explicit(mySqlInt16)     ' Visual Basic .NET
mySqlString = (SqlString)mySqlInt16;                  // C#
mySqlString = mySqlString.op_Explicit(mySqlInt32)     ' Visual Basic .NET
mySqlString = (SqlString)mySqlInt32;                  // C#
mySqlString = mySqlString.op_Explicit(mySqlInt64)     ' Visual Basic .NET
mySqlString = (SqlString)mySqlInt64;                  // C#
mySqlString = mySqlString.op_Explicit(mySqlMoney)     ' Visual Basic .NET
mySqlString = (SqlString)mySqlMoney;                  // C#
mySqlString = mySqlString.op_Explicit(mySqlSingle)    ' Visual Basic .NET
mySqlString = (SqlString)mySqlSingle;                 // C#
```

Parameters

`mySqlString`	A SqlString object.
`mySqlBoolean`	A SqlBoolean object.
`mySqlByte`	A SqlByte object.
`mySqlDateTime`	A SqlDateTime object.
`mySqlDecimal`	A SqlDecimal object.
`mySqlDouble`	A SqlDouble object.
`mySqlGuid`	A SqlGuid object.
`mySqlInt16`	A SqlInt16 object.
`mySqlInt32`	A SqlInt32 object.
`mySqlInt64`	A SqlInt64 object.
`mySqlMoney`	A SqlMoney object.
`mySqlSingle`	A SqlSingle object.

Exceptions

SqlNullValueException	You cannot assign a null value to a String class. Be sure to check the IsNull property, or use another exception-handling technique.

op_Implicit

The op_Implicit method represents a special SqlString converter that allows SqlString values to be implicitly assigned from a String object.

If you are using ADO.NET with C#, then you will not call the op_Implicit method directly, but rather you are allowed to cast from a String object to a SqlString structure.

Usage

```
mySqlString = mySqlString.op_Implicit(myString) ' Visual Basic .NET
mySqlString = (SqlString)myString;              // C#
```

Parameters

`myString`	A String object.

Exceptions

None.

SqlCompareOptions

The read-only SqlCompareOptions property returns those comparison options specified when the SqlString was instantiated. If you want to change the SqlCompareOptions, you'll need to create a new SqlString with the desired options and assign the value from the old SqlString.

By default, the following SqlCompareOptions are selected:

- IgnoreCase
- IgnoreKanaType
- IgnoreWidth

Usage

```
myCompareOptions = mySqlString.SqlCompareOptions
```

Parameters

None.

Exceptions

SqlNullValueException	You cannot request the SqlCompareOptions property of a null SqlString.

ToSqlBoolean

The ToSqlBoolean method returns the SqlString value as a SqlBoolean object. The SqlString must evaluate to an integer (where 0 = false and anything else = true) or the word "True" or "False". A null SqlString value will return a null SqlBoolean.

Usage

```
mySqlBoolean = mySqlString.ToSqlBoolean()
```

Parameters

None.

Exceptions

FormatException	The SqlString was not recognized as a valid SqlBoolean value. Valid values might be "0", "1", "-1", "True", "False".

ToSqlByte

The ToSqlByte method returns the SqlString value as a SqlByte object. Be mindful of the range of values that the SqlByte class supports and that it holds only positive integer values. A null SqlString value will return a null SqlByte.

Usage

```
mySqlByte = mySqlString.ToSqlByte()
```

Parameters

None.

Exceptions

FormatException	The SqlString was not recognized as a valid SqlByte value. Valid values might be "0", "1", "255".

OverflowException	The operation returned a value outside of the range of a SqlByte value.

ToSqlDateTime

The ToSqlDateTime method returns the SqlString value as a SqlDateTime object. Keep in mind that converting from a SqlString to a SqlDateTime object can throw a FormatException if ADO.NET can't parse the string. That having been said, this method is very liberal and accepts most every DateTime format you can imagine. A null SqlString value will return a null SqlDateTime.

Usage

```
mySqlByte = mySqlString.ToSqlDateTime()
```

Parameters

None.

Exceptions

FormatException	The SqlString was not recognized as a valid SqlDateTime value. Valid values might be "12/25/1812", "15 Jul 1968 10:55 AM", "April 19, 1999 16:42:15".
SqlTypeException	The date must be between 1/1/1753 and 12/31/9999.

ToSqlDecimal

The ToSqlDecimal method returns the SqlString value as a SqlDecimal object. Be mindful of the range of values that the SqlDecimal class supports. A null SqlString value will return a null SqlDecimal.

Usage

```
mySqlDecimal = mySqlString.ToSqlDecimal()
```

Parameters

None.

Exceptions

FormatException	The SqlString was not recognized as a valid SqlDecimal value. Valid values might be "-123.45, "0", "100.5", or "1250.23550".
OverflowException	The operation returned a value outside of the range of a SqlDecimal value.

ToSqlDouble

The ToSqlDouble method returns the SqlString value as a SqlDouble object. Be mindful of the range of values that the SqlDouble class supports. A null SqlString value will return a null SqlDouble.

Usage

```
mySqlDouble = mySqlString.ToSqlDouble()
```

Parameters

None.

Exceptions

FormatException	The SqlString was not recognized as a valid SqlDouble value. Valid values might be "-17305.25", "0", "100", or "1.79E + 308".
OverflowException	The operation returned a value outside of the range of a SqlDouble value.

ToSqlGuid

The ToSqlGuid method returns the SqlString value as a SqlGuid. Keep in mind that converting from a SqlString to a SqlGuid object can throw a FormatException if the SqlString is not formatted properly. A null value would indicate that the SqlBinary value is null.

Usage

```
mySqlGuid = mySqlString.ToSqlGuid()
```

Parameters

None.

Exceptions

ArgumentException	The SqlString value is not formatted properly. It must contain 32 digits with 4 dashes. A valid value might be "4a985849-fc57-4c70-8c50-09636c771c5a".

ToSqlInt16

The ToSqlInt16 method returns the SqlString value as a SqlInt16 object. Be mindful of the range of values that the SqlInt16 class supports. A null SqlString value will return a null SqlInt16.

Usage

```
mySqlInt16 = mySqlString.ToSqlInt16()
```

Parameters

None.

Exceptions

FormatException	The SqlString was not recognized as a valid SqlInt16 value. Valid values might be "-32768", "100", or "32767".
OverflowException	The operation returned a value outside of the range of a SqlInt16 value.

ToSqlInt32

The ToSqlInt32 method returns the SqlString value as a SqlInt32 object. Be mindful of the range of values that the SqlInt32 class supports. A null SqlString value will return a null SqlInt32.

Usage

```
mySqlInt32 = mySqlString.ToSqlInt32()
```

Parameters

None.

Exceptions

FormatException	The SqlString was not recognized as a valid SqlInt32 value. Valid values might be "-2147483648", "0", "100", or "2147483647".
OverflowException	The operation returned a value outside of the range of a SqlInt32 value.

ToSqlInt64

The ToSqlInt64 method returns the SqlString value as a SqlInt64 object. Be mindful of the range of values that the SqlInt64 class supports. A null SqlString value will return a null SqlInt64.

Usage

```
mySqlInt64 = mySqlString.ToSqlInt64()
```

Parameters

None.

Exceptions

FormatException	The SqlString was not recognized as a valid SqlInt64 value. Valid values might be "-9223372036854775808", "0", "100", or "9223372036854775807".
OverflowException	The operation returned a value outside of the range of a SqlInt64 value.

ToSqlMoney

The ToSqlMoney method returns the SqlString value as a SqlMoney object. A null value would indicate that the SqlString value is null.

Usage

```
mySqlMoney = mySqlString.ToSqlMoney()
```

Parameters

None.

Exceptions

FormatException	The SqlString was not recognized as a valid SqlMoney value. Valid values might be "-17305.25", "0", "100", "$11,725.32", or "922,337,203,685,477.5807".
OverflowException	The operation returned a value outside of the range of a SqlMoney value.

ToSqlSingle

The ToSqlSingle method returns the SqlString value as a SqlSingle object. Be mindful of the range of values that the SqlSingle class supports. A null SqlString value will return a null SqlSingle.

Usage

```
mySqlSingle = mySqlString.ToSqlSingle()
```

Parameters

None.

Exceptions

FormatException	The SqlString was not recognized as a valid SqlSingle value. Valid values might be "-17305.25", "0", "100", or "3.40E+38".
OverflowException	The operation returned a value outside of the range of a SqlSingle value.

ToString

The ToString method returns the SqlString value as a String object.

Usage

```
myString = mySqlString.ToString()
```

Parameters

None.

Value

The read-only Value property allows you to retrieve the value of the SqlString. Remember that this property is read-only—you may not assign a SqlString its value using its Value property.

In addition to using the Value property, you may also use the op_Explicit conversion method, or, if your language supports overloaded operators, you may use that construct instead.

Usage

```
myString = mySqlString.Value                     ' Visual Basic .NET
myString = mySqlString.op_Explicit(mySqlString)  ' Visual Basic .NET
myString = (String)mySqlString;                  // C#
```

Parameters

None.

Exceptions

SqlNullValueException	You cannot retrieve a null value. Be sure to check the IsNull property, or use another exception-handling technique.

System.Data.SqlTypes.SqlTruncateException

The SqlTruncateException is thrown whenever a SqlDecimal has its scale adjusted to an illegal value. This will occur when you attempt to change the scale to less than 0 or greater than the precision of the SqlDecimal. The SqlTruncateException class inherits from the SqlTypeException class.

Microsoft has provided a public constructor for this exception class, allowing you to instantiate and throw your own SqlTruncateException.

Constructors

```
Dim mySqlTruncateException As New SqlTruncateException()
Dim mySqlTruncateException As New SqlTruncateException(myString)
```

Parameters

`myString` A String object that will initialize the Message property.

SqlTruncateException Sample Code

```
Dim mySqlTruncateException As SqlTruncateException
mySqlTruncateException = New SqlTruncateException("Data Truncated!")
Throw mySqlTruncateException
```

Members

GetBaseException

The GetBaseException method returns an Exception object containing the original exception. To return the original exception, it traverses the chain of InnerException objects. If the InnerException property of the current exception is null, GetBaseException will return a reference to the current Exception object.

To determine only the parent exception to the current exception, use the InnerException property.

Usage

```
myException = mySqlTruncateException.GetBaseException()
```

Parameters

None.

Exceptions

None.

GetObjectData

The GetObjectData method fills the passed System.Runtime.Serialization.SerializationInfo buffer object with information about the Exception object. There is no value returned by this method. Depending on the passed System.Runtime.Serialization.StreamingContext object, this method can be used to serialize the object to a stream or read serialization from a stream.

Because it deals mainly with serialization and not data access, further discussion of this property is beyond the scope of this book.

Usage

```
mySqlTruncateException.GetObjectData(mySerializationInfo, _
   myStreamingContext)
```

Parameters

`mySerializationInfo`	A System.Runtime.Serialization.SerializationInfo buffer object to be filled with the exception's serialization data.
`myStreamingContext`	A System.Runtime.Serialization.StreamingContext object specifying the stream to write the serialization info to or read the information from.

Exceptions

ArgumentNullException	The passed SerializationInfo buffer object is null (`Nothing` in Visual Basic .NET).

HelpLink

The HelpLink property returns or sets a String linking to a help file associated with the SqlTruncateException. The HelpLink is formatted as a Uniform Resource Name (URN) or Uniform Resource Locator (URL). An example of this property that points to the MSDN help available with Visual Studio .NET would be: `ms-help://MS.VSCC/MS.MSDNVS/cpref/html/frlrfsystemexceptionclasshelplinktopic.htm.`

The HelpLink is often not set, so it is wise to verify both that the HelpLink property itself is not an empty string and that the HelpLink points to a valid help file before exposing the HelpLink to a user of your program.

Usage

```
myString = mySqlTruncateException.HelpLink
mySqlTruncateException.HelpLink = myString
```

Parameters

None.

InnerException

The read-only InnerException property returns the Exception object linking to a previous exception that caused the current exception to be thrown, if any, or a null value (`Nothing` in Visual Basic .NET), if not. This permits a chain of InnerException objects to be generated, allowing a program to trace the exception chain all the way to the root exception. Be aware that InnerException may be null.

To find the base exception that originally was fired, use the GetBaseException method.

Usage

```
myException = mySqlTruncateException.InnerException
```

Parameters

None.

Sample Code

```
' Accepts any Exception to subroutine, so recursion is possible
Public Sub ViewInnerExceptions(ByVal myException As Exception)
    'immediately leave subroutine if InnerException is null
    If myException.InnerException Is Nothing Then Exit Sub
    Dim myInnerException As Exception = myException.InnerException
    MessageBox.Show("InnerException Information" & ControlChars.Cr _
        & "Message:    " & myInnerException.Message & ControlChars.Cr _
        & "Source:     " & myInnerException.Source & ControlChars.Cr _
        & "HelpLink:   " & myInnerException.HelpLink & ControlChars.Cr _
        & "StackTrace: " & myInnerException.StackTrace)
    'recurse if necessary
    If Not myInnerException.InnerException Is Nothing Then
        ViewInnerExceptions(myInnerException)
    End If
End Sub
```

Message

The read-only Message property returns a String describing the first error that caused the exception. Because it provides information from only the first error, use this property cautiously when building robust error handling.

Usage

```
myString = mySqlTruncateException.Message
```

Parameters

None.

Source

The Source property sets or returns a String containing the name of the provider that generated the first error. Because it provides information from only the first error, use this property cautiously when building robust error handling.

Usage

```
myString = mySqlTruncateException.Source
mySqlTruncateException.Source = myString
```

Parameters

None.

StackTrace

The read-only StackTrace property returns a String containing a textual representation of the stack trace. The stack trace reports all of the methods that are in execution at the time just prior to the execution being thrown. It is read from top to bottom with the latest method in execution at the top.

The StackTrace can be invaluable in tracing difficult-to-find bugs because it provides a method to see all of the methods that could have led up to the error.

TIP **To see the stack trace programmatically when no exception has been raised, use the Environment.StackTrace property.**

Usage

```
myString = mySqlTruncateException.StackTrace
```

Parameters

None.

TargetSite

The read-only TargetSite property returns an object inheriting from System.Reflection. MethodBase that contains a reference to the method that caused the error to be thrown.

This property is primarily used to programmatically find information about the method that raised the exception. The returned object will provide information such as the methods parameters and return type and whether the method is virtual, a constructor, public, private, etc. Because it deals mainly with reflection and not data access, further discussion of this property is beyond the scope of this book.

Usage

```
myMethodBase = mySqlTruncateException.TargetSite
```

Parameters

None.

ToString

The ToString method is overridden to return information relating to the SqlTruncateException. The returned String contains the full class name and also the error message, name of the inner exception, and stack trace, if they exist.

Usage

```
myString = mySqlTruncateException.ToString()
```

Parameters

None.

Exceptions

None.

System.Data.SqlTypes.SqlTypeException

The SqlTypeException is thrown when ADO.NET cannot construct a valid SqlType object. In the case of a SqlDateTime object, ADO.NET might not recognize the format passed to the constructor or the date might fall outside of the range of a SqlDateTime. In the case of a SqlDecimal object, you might have specified an invalid precision or scale. The SqlTypeException class is the parent class for the other two exception classes in the SqlTypes namespace: SqlNullValueException and SqlTruncateException.

Microsoft has provided a public constructor for this exception class, allowing you to instantiate and throw your own SqlTypeException.

Constructors

```
Dim mySqlTypeException As New SqlTypeException(myString)
```

Parameters

`myString`	A String object that will initialize the Message property.

SqlTypeException Sample Code

```
Dim mySqlTypeException As SqlTypeException
mySqlTypeException = New SqlTypeException("Type Exception!")
Throw mySqlTypeException
```

Members

GetBaseException

The GetBaseException method returns an Exception object containing the original exception. To return the original exception, it traverses the chain of InnerException objects. If the InnerException property of the current exception is null, GetBaseException will return a reference to the current Exception object.

To determine only the parent exception to the current exception, use the InnerException property.

Usage

```
myException = mySqlTypeException.GetBaseException()
```

Parameters

None.

Exceptions

None.

GetObjectData

The GetObjectData method fills the passed System.Runtime.Serialization.SerializationInfo buffer object with information about the Exception object. There is no value returned by this method. Depending on the passed System.Runtime.Serialization.StreamingContext object, this method can be used to serialize the object to a stream or read serialization from a stream.

Because it deals mainly with serialization and not data access, further discussion of this property is beyond the scope of this book.

Usage

```
mySqlTypeException.GetObjectData(mySerializationInfo,
myStreamingContext)
```

Parameters

`mySerializationInfo`	A System.Runtime.Serialization.SerializationInfo buffer object to be filled with the exception's serialization data.
`myStreamingContext`	A System.Runtime.Serialization.StreamingContext object specifying the stream to write the serialization info to or read the information from.

Exceptions

ArgumentNullException	The passed SerializationInfo buffer object is null (`Nothing` in Visual Basic .NET).

HelpLink

The HelpLink property returns or sets a String linking to a help file associated with the SqlTypeException. The HelpLink is formatted as a Uniform Resource Name (URN) or Uniform Resource Locator (URL). An example of this property that points to the MSDN help available with Visual Studio .NET would be: `ms-help://MS.VSCC/MS.MSDNVS/cpref/html/frlrfsystemexceptionclasshelplinktopic.htm`

The HelpLink is often not set, so it is wise to verify both that the HelpLink property itself is not an empty string and that the HelpLink points to a valid help file before exposing the HelpLink to a user of your program.

Usage

```
myString = mySqlTypeException.HelpLink
mySqlTypeException.HelpLink = myString
```

Parameters

None.

InnerException

The read-only InnerException property returns the Exception object linking to a previous exception that caused the current exception to be thrown, if any, or a null value (`Nothing` in Visual Basic .NET), if not. This permits a chain of InnerException objects to be generated, allowing a program to trace the exception chain all the way to the root exception. Be aware that InnerException may be null.

To find the base exception that originally was fired, use the GetBaseException method.

Usage

```
myException = mySqlTypeException.InnerException
```

Parameters

None.

Sample Code

```
' Accepts any Exception to subroutine, so recursion is possible
Public Sub ViewInnerExceptions(ByVal myException As Exception)
    'immediately leave subroutine if InnerException is null
    If myException.InnerException Is Nothing Then Exit Sub
    Dim myInnerException As Exception = myException.InnerException
    MessageBox.Show("InnerException Information" & ControlChars.Cr _
        & "Message:    " & myInnerException.Message & ControlChars.Cr _
        & "Source:     " & myInnerException.Source & ControlChars.Cr _
        & "HelpLink:   " & myInnerException.HelpLink & ControlChars.Cr _
        & "StackTrace: " & myInnerException.StackTrace)
    'recurse if necessary
    If Not myInnerException.InnerException Is Nothing Then
        ViewInnerExceptions(myInnerException)
    End If
End Sub
```

Message

The read-only Message property returns a String describing the first error that caused the exception. Because it provides information from only the first error, use this property cautiously when building robust error handling.

Usage

```
myString = mySqlTypeException.Message
```

Parameters

None.

Source

The Source property sets or returns a String containing the name of the provider that generated the first error. Because it provides information from only the first error, use this property cautiously when building robust error handling.

Usage

```
myString = mySqlTypeException.Source
mySqlTypeException.Source = myString
```

Parameters

None.

StackTrace

The read-only StackTrace property returns a String containing a textual representation of the stack trace. The stack trace reports all of the methods that are in execution at the time just prior to the execution being thrown. It is read from top to bottom with the latest method in execution at the top.

The StackTrace can be invaluable in tracing difficult-to-find bugs because it provides a method to see all of the methods that could have led up to the error.

TIP **To see the stack trace programmatically when no exception has been raised, use the Environment.StackTrace property.**

Usage

```
myString = mySqlTypeException.StackTrace
```

Parameters

None.

TargetSite

The read-only TargetSite property returns an object inheriting from System.Reflection. MethodBase that contains a reference to the method that caused the error to be thrown.

This property is primarily used to programmatically find information about the method that raised the exception. The returned object will provide information such as the methods parameters and return type and whether the method is virtual, a constructor, public, private, etc. Because it deals mainly with reflection and not data access, further discussion of this property is beyond the scope of this book.

Usage

```
myMethodBase = mySqlTypeException.TargetSite
```

Parameters

None.

ToString

The ToString method is overridden to return information relating to the SqlType-Exception. The returned String contains the full class name and also the error message, name of the inner exception, and stack trace, if they exist.

Usage

```
myString = mySqlTypeException.ToString()
```

Parameters

None.

Exceptions

None.

PART Three

Tutorial

We designed this primarily as a reference book, however, we wanted to devote a few chapters to teaching you how to create and manipulate ADO.NET objects. Rather than introduce a business problem and solve it over the next few chapters, we will introduce smaller, more manageable code segments to tutor you on using the key ADO.NET classes. Although the reference section of our book contains hundreds of useful code examples, this section will arrange the crucial ones together, grouped by specific task and with more detailed syntax.

Everyone who uses ADO.NET to interact with a database will need to begin at the connected layer. We spend a chapter teaching you how to use those classes in ADO.NET that pertain to connecting to a data source, managing errors and exceptions, querying data, updating data, and managing transactions.

Next, we will teach you how to use the classes in the disconnected layer of ADO.NET. This will be a natural progression from the connected layer tutorial, and we will walk you through the creation, filling, manipulation, merging, and updating of a DataSet. It is important for you to become comfortable using the DataSet class, as it is the most important class in ADO.NET. The DataSet class does not require a connection to a data source to be populated or to update, so we will teach you how to populate a DataSet from scratch, allowing you to specify all schema information manually, including table relations and even data. We'll also show how to create and update a DataSet using data stored in database.

Finally, we leave you with a tutorial on ADO.NET's flexible integration with XML. ADO.NET works with traditional relational data just as its MDAC ADO counterpart does, by referencing rows and columns. When faced with data that is better expressed hierarchically, you ought to consider manipulating your data in XML. Read this chapter to learn how to retrieve data as XML strings to be rendered by whatever client you choose. Once your ADO.NET data is in XML format, it can be parsed, searched (XPath), or transformed (XSLT) by any of the current technologies in .NET or otherwise. We will also demonstrate how to serialize and deserialize your ADO.NET DataSet — to maintain not only your data, but the state of the data as well. This technique will serve you when you need to serialize and later deserialize other .NET objects, as well.

CHAPTER

10

Accessing Data Sources Using ADO.NET

This chapter, the first in our tutorial section, will illustrate through sample code how to use the objects in the connected layer of ADO.NET. Remember, the connected layer is responsible for the connection to the data source, including the retrieval and updating of data. Nearly all of the classes in each .NET data provider are members of the connected layer. Only a few classes, primarily to support errors and exceptions, fall into the gray area of a supporting role.

While we could demonstrate ample ODBC and OLE DB .NET data provider samples in this section, we will focus primarily on the SQL Server .NET data provider, with the occasional OLE DB sample. Keep in mind, however, that about 90 percent of the sample code in this chapter will work in *all* of the .NET data providers.

ADO.NET, like most of the .NET Framework, is all about separation of duties. Each namespace has its purpose in life, and there is very little redundancy overall. Take System.Data, for example. System.Data is the primary namespace for ADO.NET, but what does that mean? In addition to containing the classes, enumerations, exceptions, and members for the ADO.NET architecture, it also provides the IDbConnection, IDbCommand, IDbParameter, IDbDataReader, IDbDataAdapter, and IDbTransaction interfaces, but these by themselves do little for the ADO.NET developer. System.Data contains these foundation classes and interfaces that get inherited, overridden, and implemented in the specific .NET data providers or in .NET data providers that you build yourself. System.Data also contains other supporting classes, enumerations, and exceptions. We have categorized these as Supporting.

System.Data, as you will see in the next chapter, also defines the core classes for the disconnected layer. Disconnected classes are not defined in the specific .NET data providers, as they are not specific and do not need to be overridden for a particular data source or access mechanism.

System.Data.Common contains those classes that are common to each of the .NET data providers. This sounds very familiar to System.Data's purpose. If you remember our rant from Chapter 5, "System.Data.Common," then you'll know how we feel about Microsoft's decision to place .NET data provider interfaces in System.Data instead of System.Data.Common.

In order to clean up the System.Data namespace, Microsoft moved several of the classes that dealt with the creation of data providers to the System.Data.Common namespace. System.Data.Common provides for the commonalities between the various data providers. Unfortunately, Microsoft moved only some of the classes. For example, it moved the DbDataAdapter class but failed to move the IDbDataAdapter interface, which, when combined with the DbDataAdapter class, provides most of the common interface for accessing relational databases. Microsoft left the IDbCommand, and even the IDbConnection interfaces, in the System.Data namespace. Both are absolutely specific to the data provider layer and have nothing at all to do with the pure .NET data objects that are the majority of the System.Data namespace.

If you compare System.Data and System.Data.Common, you'll see that, for the most part, the connected layer interfaces are defined in System.Data and partially implemented in System.Data.Common. If you then look to any of the .NET data providers, you'll see additional or overridden functionality over and above what is defined in System.Data.Common. System.Data.Common specifies a lowest common denominator of functionality and support that a .NET data provider must support. If you are building your own .NET data provider, you can implement and inherit from these classes. Look in MSDN for an article titled "Implementing a .NET Data Provider" for more information (see Figure 10.1).

TASKS PERFORMED IN THE CONNECTED LAYER

- **Establish, monitor and close a connection to a database**
- **Listen for database server errors, warnings, and alerts**
- **Return row data from a database in a quick, read-only, forward-only mode**
- **Execute a SQL command or stored procedure to perform an insert, update, delete, or other action**
- **Execute a SQL command or stored procedure to return row data**
- **Execute a SQL command or stored procedure to return a single value**
- **Execute a SQL command or stored procedure to return XML, if supported by the data source**
- **Define the name, number, and types of parameters for a stored procedure**
- **Establish, commit, or roll back a transaction**
- **Retrieve schema information from a database**
- **Initialize a DataAdapter using a CommandBuilder in order to broker DataSet updates**
- **Post changes from a DataSet to the database using a DataAdapter**

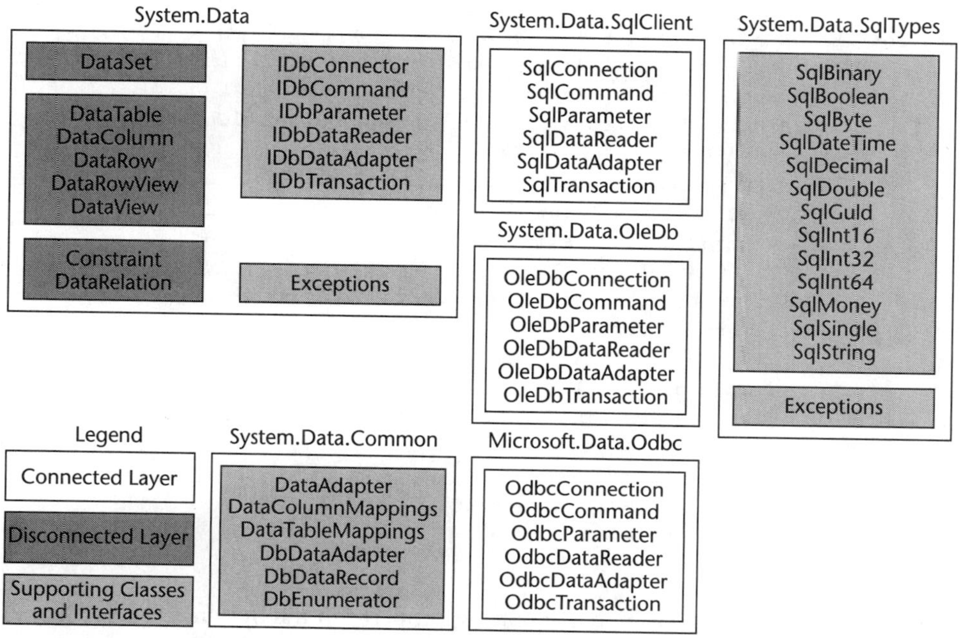

Figure 10.1 ADO.NET namespaces and layers.

Connecting to SQL Server 7.0/2000

The trick to connecting to SQL Server is knowing your connection string. Connection strings, without a doubt, are the most common technical support question with Microsoft database programmers. Even seasoned veterans forget the name of a driver, provider, server, or database. Not only do you have to know the syntax of the string, you have to know the names of all the resources—and you have to spell everything correctly.

Sample Code

```
Dim mySqlConnection As New System.Data.SqlClient.SqlConnection()
Dim iError As Integer
' Specify a ConnectionString to the Neptune server, using Windows
' authentication and defaulting to the Northwind database
mySqlConnection.ConnectionString = _
   "Server=Neptune;Integrated Security=SSPI;Database=Northwind"
Try
   mySqlConnection.Open()
Catch exSqlException As SqlException
```

```
      ' Loop through all errors in the errors collection
      For iError = 0 To exSqlException.Errors.Count - 1
         MessageBox.Show("Error #" & ControlChars.Tab & iError.ToString() & _
            ControlChars.Cr & "Message" & ControlChars.Tab & _
            exSqlException.Errors(iError).Message & ControlChars.Cr & _
            "Native" & ControlChars.Tab & _
            exSqlException.Errors(iError).Number.ToString() & _
            ControlChars.Cr & "Source" & ControlChars.Tab & _
            exSqlException.Errors(iError).Source & ControlChars.Cr & _
            "SQL" & ControlChars.Tab & _
            exSqlException.Errors(iError).State & ControlChars.Cr, _
            "SqlClient Exception")
      Next
   Catch ex As Exception
      MessageBox.Show(ex.ToString(), "Other Exception")
   Finally
      mySqlConnection.Close()
      mySqlConnection.Dispose()
      mySqlConnection = Nothing
   End Try
```

You should refer back to ConnectionString property in the System.Data.SqlClient. SqlConnection class in Chapter 8, "System.Data.SqlClient," for all of the possible parameters that you can specify in a ConnectionString. Remember that some of the parameters are synonyms for other parameters. In other words, the preceding ConnectionString could have been written like this:

```
mySqlConnection.ConnectionString = _
   "Data Source=Neptune;Integrated Security=SSPI;" & _
   "Initial Catalog=Northwind"
```

Remember that the default timeout is 15 seconds. If you are connecting via a long-distance network connection to your SQL Server, you may need to bump this value up. Use the Connection Timeout parameter to do so.

Best Practices

- Use the SQL Server .NET data provider, even though other providers might allow connection to SQL Server.
- Connection pooling on SqlConnection objects is enabled implicitly. Do not alter this default behavior, by setting ConnectionString properties, unless you have good reason to do so.
- Use the Windows *Performance Monitor* utility to watch connection pool information. This information will help you fine-tune your settings.
- Open the connection as late as possible, meaning don't open the connection until you're ready to use it.

- Close the connection as soon as possible. This means that your code shouldn't linger with an open connection.
- Close the connection explicitly. If you do not close or dispose the connection yourself, but rather rely on the object dropping out of scope, keep in mind that you'll have to wait for the garbage collector to run before the connection is physically closed.
- .NET has wonderful garbage collection, but this does not mitigate your responsibility to release any resources that you no longer need.

Connecting to SQL Server 6.5

To connect to a version of SQL Server prior to 7.0, you'll need to use either the OLE DB .NET data provider or the ODBC .NET data provider. Again, the bulk of the work is in establishing the connection string. Here's an example of connecting to SQL Server 6.5 using OLE DB. This example does not implement as robust an example of error handling as the prior example.

Sample Code

```
Dim myOleDbConnection As New System.Data.OleDb.OleDbConnection()
myOleDbConnection.ConnectionString = _
    "Provider=SQLOLEDB;Datasource=Neptune;" & _
    "Initial Catalog=Northwind;Integrated Security=SSPI;"
myOleDbConnection.Open()
myOleDbConnection.Close()
myOleDbConnection = Nothing
```

Connecting to Microsoft Access

Microsoft has not yet made a dedicated Jet .NET data provider, and until it does so, you'll need to use either the OLE DB .NET data provider or the ODBC .NET data provider to connect to an MDB database. With ODBC data sources, you can use DSNs (Data Source Names), which are file or registry settings made through Windows. With OLE DB, you can use UDLs (Universal Data Links), which are files with a .UDL extension that specify all of the OLE DB connection string information needed to connect to an OLE DB data source.

UDL Files are nice because you can modify them very easily and they are external to your compiled application, so an administrator or implementer can easily point the application toward a different data source. This dynamic capability comes at a price, as the UDL file must be loaded and parsed on each call to Open. For more information on creating UDL files, search MSDN for an article titled "Data Link API Overview."

Sample Code

```
''''''''''''''''''''''''''''''''''''''''''''''''''''''''''''''''
' Example using ODBC ConnectionString
Dim myOdbcConnection As New Microsoft.Data.Odbc.OdbcConnection()
Dim iError As Integer
' Open Connection
myOdbcConnection.ConnectionString = _
   "Driver={Microsoft Access Driver (*.mdb)};DBQ=c:\northwind.mdb"
Try
   myOdbcConnection.Open()
Catch exOdbcException As OdbcException
   ' Loop through all errors in the errors collection
   For iError = 0 To exOdbcException.Errors.Count - 1
      MessageBox.Show("Error #" & ControlChars.Tab & iError.ToString() & _
        ControlChars.Cr & "Message" & ControlChars.Tab & _
        exOdbcException.Errors(iError).Message & ControlChars.Cr & _
        "Native" & ControlChars.Tab & _
        exOdbcException.Errors(iError).NativeError.ToString() & _
        ControlChars.Cr & "Source" & ControlChars.Tab & _
        exOdbcException.Errors(iError).Source & ControlChars.Cr & _
        "SQL" & ControlChars.Tab & _
        exOdbcException.Errors(iError).SQLState & ControlChars.Cr)
   Next
Catch ex As Exception
   MessageBox.Show(ex.ToString(), "Other Exception")
Finally
   myOdbcConnection.Close()
   myOdbcConnection = Nothing
End Try
''''''''''''''''''''''''''''''''''''''''''''''''''''''''''''''''
' Example using ODBC DSN
Dim myOdbcConnection As New Microsoft.Data.Odbc.OdbcConnection()
myOdbcConnection.ConnectionString = "DSN=Northwind" ' MS Access XP
myOdbcConnection.Open()
''''''''''''''''''''''''''''''''''''''''''''''''''''''''''''''''
' Example using OLE DB
Dim myOleDbConnection As New System.Data.OleDb.OleDbConnection()
myOleDbConnection.ConnectionString = _
   "Provider=Microsoft.Jet.OLEDB.4.0;" & _
   "Data Source=C:\Northwind.mdb"
myOleDbConnection.Open()
''''''''''''''''''''''''''''''''''''''''''''''''''''''''''''''''
' Example using a UDL File
'
' The contents of the UDL File:
'
' [oledb]
' ; Everything after this line is an OLE DB initstring
```

```
' Provider=Microsoft.Jet.OLEDB.4.0;Data Source=X:\Northwind.mdb;
' Persist Security Info=False
Dim myOleDbConnection As New System.Data.OleDb.OleDbConnection()
myOleDbConnection.ConnectionString = "File Name=c:\northwind.udl"
myOleDbConnection.Open()
```

Best Practices

- Hard-coding ConnectionStrings into your application will result in the fastest code.
- Using a DSN or UDL file will result in code that can be ported to other servers or databases easily, but you'll take a small hit on performance as your application must read the registry or open the UDL file.

Determining the Server Version

It's always a good idea to have your code make smart decisions—decisions based on facts that it can gather itself. For example, if you know that your application will be connecting to two different versions of a database and that some of the features of your application won't function correctly on an earlier version, it would be nice if your code could make that distinction for itself. The ServerVersion property enables this.

Sample Code

```
Dim mySqlConnection As New System.Data.SqlClient.SqlConnection()
mySqlConnection.ConnectionString = _
   "Server=(local);Integrated Security=True;"
mySqlConnection.Open()
MessageBox.Show(mySqlConnection.ServerVersion, "ServerVersion")
mySqlConnection.Close()
mySqlConnection.Dispose()
mySqlConnection = Nothing
```

If you are connecting to SQL Server, then you can also query the Server and request its @@Server scalar function value. In addition to the major, minor, and release version information, @@Server will return the build date and time, copyright, edition, and operating system version. See the section titled *Returning Scalar Data Using a Command Object* in this chapter.

Best Practices

- Use the SqlConnection ServerVersion property over the @@Server approach, if the information will suffice. This will save a round trip to the SQL Server.

Determining a State Change on Your Connection

You can always query a Connection object's State property to see if it is open (1) or closed (0). Microsoft has included a couple of other ConnectionState values, but they are not supported as of the RTM version of the .NET Framework. In addition to exception handling, the detecting of these changes in the connection state will subsidize your error handling code nicely.

Sample Code

```
Dim mySqlConnection As New System.Data.SqlClient.SqlConnection()
mySqlConnection.ConnectionString = _
   "Server=(local);Integrated Security=SSPI;Database=Northwind"
mySqlConnection.Open()
If mySqlConnection.State = 1 Then
   ' Connection Is open, do something important here
End If
mySqlConnection.Close()
mySqlConnection.Dispose()
mySqlConnection = Nothing
```

What is more useful than just querying the State property value is being informed of a State change automatically. ADO.NET Connection objects implement the StateChange event for just such a purpose. You can include code in this event to prompt the user to reconnect if a disconnect has occurred prematurely.

In the following example, we demonstrate how you could put logic in the StateChange event to detect a closure and prompt the user if he or she should reopen the connection. You could improve this code to avoid asking the question if the connection was closed for a valid reason.

Sample Code

```
' Declare a form-level variable withEvents
Private WithEvents mySqlConnection As _
   New System.Data.SqlClient.SqlConnection()
' Event handler will prompt the user to reopen the connection
Private Sub mySqlConnection_StateChange(ByVal sender As Object, _
   ByVal e As System.Data.StateChangeEventArgs) _
   Handles mySqlConnection.StateChange
   If e.CurrentState = ConnectionState.Open Then
      MessageBox.Show("Welcome to Northwind", "Connection Opened")
   ElseIf e.CurrentState = ConnectionState.Closed Then
      If MessageBox.Show("Shall I attempt to reopen the Connection?", _
            "Connection Closed!", MessageBoxButtons.YesNo, _
            MessageBoxIcon.Question) = DialogResult.Yes Then
         Try
            mySqlConnection.Open()
```

```
            Catch ex As Exception
                MessageBox.Show(ex.ToString, "Couldn't Reopen Connection")
            End Try
        End If
    End If
End Sub
' Test
Private Sub myTest()
    mySqlConnection.ConnectionString = _
        "Server=(local);Integrated Security=SSPI;Database=Northwind"
    mySqlConnection.Open()
    mySqlConnection.Close()
    mySqlConnection = Nothing
End Sub
```

Best Practices

- Establish a StateChange event handler to listen for connection drops. Remember that this event will fire when critical exceptions occur *as well as* when you close your connection normally.

Listening for SQL Server Information

The other important event on a Connection object is the InfoMessage event. This event has been around since the RDO (Remote Data Objects) days and proves to be a useful mechanism to listen for information, warnings, and critical errors from SQL Server. When using the Ole Db or Odbc .NET data providers, keep in mind that not all data sources will utilize the InfoMessage event.

With SQL Server, the InfoMessage event will inform you when an error with a state of 10 or less has been raised or when a PRINT statement has been encountered.

Sample Code

```
' Declare a form level variable withEvents
Private WithEvents mySqlConnection As _
    New System.Data.SqlClient.SqlConnection()
' Event handler will prompt the user to reopen the connection
Private Sub mySqlConnection_InfoMessage(ByVal sender As Object, _
    ByVal e As System.Data.SqlClient.SqlInfoMessageEventArgs) _
    Handles mySqlConnection.InfoMessage
    MessageBox.Show(e.ToString(), "Informational Message, Level " & _
        e.Errors(0).State.ToString(), MessageBoxButtons.OK, _
        MessageBoxIcon.Information)
End Sub
' Test
Private Sub myTest()
    Dim mySqlCommand As System.Data.SqlClient.SqlCommand
```

```
        ' Establish Connection
        mySqlConnection.ConnectionString = _
           "Server=(local);Integrated Security=SSPI;Database=Northwind"
        mySqlConnection.Open()
        ' Manually raise a SQL Server error
        mySqlCommand = mySqlConnection.CreateCommand
        mySqlCommand.CommandText = _
           "RAISERROR('This is a sample error message',5,1)"
        mySqlCommand.ExecuteNonQuery()
        ' Execute a SQL PRINT Statement
        mySqlCommand.CommandText = "PRINT 'Hello World'"
        mySqlCommand.ExecuteNonQuery()
        ' Done
        mySqlConnection.Close()
        mySqlConnection.Dispose()
        mySqlConnection = Nothing
    End Sub
```

Best Practices

- Don't bother establishing an InfoMessage event handler unless you know that your connection will be monitoring code that raises informational errors (those with a severity of 10 or less) or executing PRINT commands. Most other events that the InfoMessage event responds to will be caught by the StateChange event, or were caused by your code anyway.

Changing a Database with an Open Connection

In SQL Server, you must specify a default database for a given User ID and password. This means that when that user connects to SQL Server, a predetermined database is associated with that connection. By default, this is the *master* database, which is a bad choice for a default database. The master database is where the bulk of SQL Server's settings are maintained. You could think of it as SQL Server's registry—a place that the average user should avoid.

In ADO.NET when you establish a connection, you've got the ability to set the database with the *Initial Catalog* or *Database* parameters in the ConnectionString. This is the preferred way of establishing a connection to a specific database, but it is not the only way. You can always leave the database parameter out of the ConnectionString and then change the database from the default database (as established by your SQL Server DBA), which is typically the master database. In the past, ADO programmers have had to execute a USE command on the connection, which changes the current database. This is still an option, but ADO.NET has a separate method, one that is better suited.

Sample Code

```
Dim mySqlConnection As New System.Data.SqlClient.SqlConnection()
Dim mySqlCommand As System.Data.SqlClient.SqlCommand
' Open Connection with Default Database
mySqlConnection.ConnectionString = _
   "Server=(local);Integrated Security=SSPI"
mySqlConnection.Open()
' Switch Database using SQL
mySqlCommand = mySqlConnection.CreateCommand
mySqlCommand.CommandText = "USE Pubs"
mySqlCommand.ExecuteNonQuery()
MessageBox.Show(mySqlConnection.Database, "Current Database")
' Switch Database using ADO.NET
mySqlConnection.ChangeDatabase("Northwind")
MessageBox.Show(mySqlConnection.Database, "Current Database")
' Done
mySqlConnection.Close()
mySqlConnection.Dispose()
mySqlConnection = Nothing
```

Best Practices

- It's always best to target the database you want to open in your ConnectionString. This will save you from having to execute another method or command to change it later.
- If you must change your database context, you should use the SqlConnection.ChangeDatabase method over the SQL USE Database command.
- Always be careful when changing database context, as any commands executed on that connection may not work correctly or produce unexpected results.

Returning Row Data Quickly Using a DataReader

The DataReader returns data to your application quickly, as a read-only, forward-only mechanism. It is meant to be used in a situation where performance counts and there will be no managed interaction with the data. If you would like to return data to be casually browsed and possibly edited, consider using a DataSet object.

Microsoft designed this object because it determined that a great number of applications were requesting a single record, a single value, or a set of data for the purpose of reporting or displaying on a Web page. Clever developers were then constructing client-side or middle-tier components to broker any updates back to the database via stored procedures or SQL statements. This alleviated the need for server-side cursors or having the MDAC ADO Recordsets manage any updates for us at all.

When dealing with SQL Server data, the SqlDataReader can directly expose the returned columns as SqlTypes, by referring to the accessor method with the same name as the SqlType. By calling these accessor methods, there is no need to convert the data to .NET Framework types. Consult Chapter 9, "System.Data.SqlTypes," for more information on SqlTypes.

Sample Code

```
Dim mySqlConnection As New System.Data.SqlClient.SqlConnection()
Dim mySqlDataReader As System.Data.SqlClient.SqlDataReader
Dim mySqlCommand As System.Data.SqlClient.SqlCommand
Dim myDisplay As String
Dim myValues() As Object
Dim myValue As Object
Dim i As Int32
' Establish Connection
mySqlConnection.ConnectionString = _
   "Server=(local);Integrated Security=SSPI;Database=Northwind"
mySqlConnection.Open()
' Create Command to return two sets of results:
' #1 - Customer, country, count of orders and date of first order
' #2 - All employees
mySqlCommand = mySqlConnection.CreateCommand
mySqlCommand.CommandText = _
   "SELECT C.CompanyName, C.Country, Count(O.OrderID) as Orders," & _
   "Min(O.OrderDate) as [FirstOrder] " & _
   "FROM Customers C INNER JOIN Orders O " & _
   "ON C.CustomerID = O.CustomerID " & _
   "GROUP BY C.CompanyName, C.Country " & _
   "HAVING(Count(O.OrderID) > 20); SELECT * FROM Employees"
' ExecuteReader
mySqlDataReader = mySqlCommand.ExecuteReader()
' Must execute a Read to prime the DataReader
Do While mySqlDataReader.Read()
   ' Construct a String from the Region table columns
   myDisplay += mySqlDataReader.GetString(0) + ControlChars.Tab + _
   mySqlDataReader.GetSqlDateTime(3).ToString + ControlChars.CrLf
Loop
MessageBox.Show(myDisplay, "Customer First Orders")
' Read the NextResult
mySqlDataReader.NextResult()
' Display Information about the DataReader
MessageBox.Show(mySqlDataReader.FieldCount, "FieldCount")
' Determine the column ordinal position when passing a column name
MessageBox.Show(mySqlDataReader.GetOrdinal("Title"), _
   "Which column number is Title")
' Determine the column name when passing a column ordinal position
```

```
MessageBox.Show(mySqlDataReader.GetName(5), _
    "What column name is in position 5")
' Position DataReader on first row to begin reading data
mySqlDataReader.Read()
' Compare and contrast the various ways to request a column
' Request by ordinal position
MessageBox.Show(mySqlDataReader.GetString(1), "Employee #1 LastName")
' Request by ordinal position as a SqlType (notice the need for
ToString)
MessageBox.Show(mySqlDataReader.GetSqlString(1).ToString, _
    "Employee #1 LastName")
' Request by ordinal position as an Object, using GetValue
MessageBox.Show(mySqlDataReader.GetValue(1), "Employee #1 LastName")
' Request by ordinal position by using the Item shortcut
MessageBox.Show(mySqlDataReader.Item(1), "Employee #1 LastName")
' Request by name by using the Item shortcut (a very clean approach)
MessageBox.Show(mySqlDataReader.Item("LastName"), "Employee #1
LastName")
' Done
mySqlDataReader.Close()   ' Always close the DataReader when you're done
mySqlConnection.Close()
mySqlConnection.Dispose()
mySqlConnection = Nothing
```

Best Practices

- Use the DataReader over a DataSet whenever possible, especially when you don't need to cache the data offline or update your data.
- Only one DataReader per Connection can be open at a given time. You'll have to create a second connection if you want to execute additional queries based on the values of the current DataReader.
- Return the minimum number of rows as necessary (use a WHERE clause).
- Return the minimum number of columns as necessary (don't use SELECT *).
- Use the Get accessor methods that return SqlTypes over the standard Get methods; the SqlTypes methods are faster because they don't have convert data types. They also support Null values.
- If you are returning multiple sets of records, as in the example, you should send over a batch of SQL commands or execute a stored procedure that returns a batch of recordsets and process the sets using the NextResult method. This keeps round trips to the server to a minimum and allows you to gather all the data for your report or Web page in one tight unit of work.
- From a security perspective, a best practice would be to always request data by calling a stored procedure, rather than querying the tables directly from the client. Using this approach, your DBA can disallow the SELECT permissions on the tables themselves, and govern all access through stored procedures that he or she writes.

Retrieving Schema Information from a DataReader

Knowing your schema is more and more important with ADO.NET. Not only is it a good idea to know the columns, data types, and constraints of all the columns in your results, but data in an ADO.NET DataSet is held together and even exported to XML by this schema. You can't always assume that your Database Administrator (DBA) got the structure exactly right. There are times when you may want to peek at the schema yourself, from your application. More likely, however, you'll need to query your schema to ask interesting questions like these:

- Which columns hold date values?
- Which columns are required and cannot be null?
- Which columns are my key columns and must be unique?

To build the truly data-driven killer app, you'll have to ask these kinds of questions at runtime and then provide alternative functionality or disallow functionality based on the answers.

Sample Code

```
Dim mySqlConnection As New System.Data.SqlClient.SqlConnection()
Dim mySqlDataReader As System.Data.SqlClient.SqlDataReader
Dim mySqlCommand As System.Data.SqlClient.SqlCommand
Dim myDataRow As System.Data.DataRow
' Establish Connection
mySqlConnection.ConnectionString = _
   "Server=(local);Integrated Security=SSPI;Database=Northwind"
mySqlConnection.Open()
' Create Command
mySqlCommand = mySqlConnection.CreateCommand
mySqlCommand.CommandText = "SELECT * FROM Employees"
' ExecuteReader
mySqlDataReader = mySqlCommand.ExecuteReader()
' Which columns are required?
For Each myDataRow In mySqlDataReader.GetSchemaTable.Rows
   If Not myDataRow.Item("AllowDBNull") Then
MessageBox.Show(myDataRow.Item("ColumnName"), "Required Field")
   End If
Next
' Browse entire schema in a DataGrid on your form
DataGrid1.DataSource = mySqlDataReader.GetSchemaTable()
' Done
mySqlDataReader.Close()   ' Always close the DataReader when you're done
mySqlConnection.Close()
mySqlConnection.Dispose()
mySqlConnection = Nothing
```

Best Practices

- You should always know your data before manipulating it. Querying the schema doesn't take any additional network traffic, as it accompanies your query results anyway.
- Not all of the columns in the schema table may be relevant. Make sure you are making your decisions on the correct columns.
- The SqlDataReader.GetSchemaTable method seems to work correctly, but expect some inconsistencies when calling the same method on the OleDb-DataReader.

Manipulating Data Manually Using a Command Object

The fastest way to make changes to your database, whether you're inserting, updating, or deleting, is to call a stored procedure or execute a SQL command directly. Sure, you could take the time to populate and update with a DataSet and then use your DataAdapter, with its Command objects populated by a CommandBuilder object. That's a lot of overhead if you simply want to insert a single, discrete record into a table.

As with prior versions of ADO, ADO.NET allows you to fire off any SQL statement or stored procedure that will execute at the data source via the command object. The single command batch will either fail or succeed. If you are making several method calls, either on the same Command object or on several on the same connection, then we recommend wrapping all of these commands or stored procedure calls into a transaction. This will ensure the state of the database, by disallowing any partial changes to be written unless the whole operation is a success. See the section titled *Executing Commands within a Transaction* in this chapter.

Sample Code

```
Dim mySqlConnection As New System.Data.SqlClient.SqlConnection()
Dim mySqlCommand As System.Data.SqlClient.SqlCommand
' Establish Connection
mySqlConnection.ConnectionString = _
   "Data Source=Omnibook;Integrated Security=SSPI;Database=Northwind"
mySqlConnection.Open()
' Create the command
mySqlCommand = New SqlCommand("INSERT Customers " & _
   "(CustomerID,CompanyName) VALUES ('WILEY','Wiley Publishing')", _
   mySqlConnection)
' Attempt to Execute
Try
   mySqlCommand.ExecuteNonQuery()
```

```
        MessageBox.Show("Success!", "Record was written")
    Catch ex As Exception
        MessageBox.Show(ex.ToString(), "No record was written")
    Finally
        mySqlConnection.Close()
        mySqlConnection.Dispose()
        mySqlConnection = Nothing
    End Try
```

Best Practices

- Because dozens of things could go wrong when you execute a command, be sure to use robust exception-handling techniques.
- Use Transactions to buffer multiple commands being executed.
- Ensure that your connection has the appropriate permissions to perform the operations.

Executing DDL Using a Command Object

Executing other types of SQL commands, such as ones that create database objects, are all in a day's work for the Command object. The tricky part is ensuring that your command syntax is correct. If you can, you should push all of this kind of work to a stored procedure, but if you must execute raw SQL from the client, then test the statements first by running them inside Microsoft Query Analyzer while wrapped inside a transaction. You will then learn if your SQL parses correctly and would execute correctly, without changing the state of the database.

Sample Code

```
Dim mySqlConnection As New System.Data.SqlClient.SqlConnection()
Dim mySqlCommand As System.Data.SqlClient.SqlCommand
' Establish Connection
mySqlConnection.ConnectionString = _
    "Data Source=Omnibook;Integrated Security=SSPI;Database=Northwind"
mySqlConnection.Open()
' Create Command
mySqlCommand = mySqlConnection.CreateCommand()
mySqlCommand.CommandText = _
    "CREATE TABLE CustomerOrderSummary (CustomerID nchar(10)," & _
    "TotalPurchase money CONSTRAINT [PK_CustomerOrderSummary] " & _
    "PRIMARY KEY CLUSTERED ( [CustomerID] ) ON [PRIMARY])"
' Attempt Execution(s)
Try
    mySqlCommand.ExecuteNonQuery()
    MessageBox.Show("Success!", "Table was created")
```

```
Catch ex As Exception
    MessageBox.Show(ex.ToString(), "No Table was created")
Finally
    mySqlConnection.Close()
    mySqlConnection.Dispose()
    mySqlConnection = Nothing
End Try
```

Best Practices

- Because dozens of things could go wrong when you execute a command, be sure to use robust exception-handling techniques.
- Use Transactions to buffer all of the commands being executed. Not all SQL commands, however, can be buffered inside of a transaction. SQL Server 2000 will buffer most DDL commands. See SQL Server Books Online for the specific commands which cannot be buffered by transactions.
- Ensure that your connection has the appropriate permissions to perform the operation(s). It is always best to create SQL Server database objects as SA or DBO, as this simplifies the naming of the objects and subsequent object requests.
- Create stored procedures for any lengthy or overly complicated SQL that must execute.

Returning Scalar Data Using a Command Object

Scalar data is data returned as a single value. This could be a quick count of records from a table, a property from the SQL Server itself, or the average price of coffee from a database table.

Sample Code

```
Dim mySqlConnection As New System.Data.SqlClient.SqlConnection()
Dim mySqlCommand As System.Data.SqlClient.SqlCommand
' Establish Connection
mySqlConnection.ConnectionString = _
    "Data Source=Omnibook;Integrated Security=SSPI;Database=Northwind"
mySqlConnection.Open()
' Create Command
mySqlCommand = mySqlConnection.CreateCommand
' Execute command to determine version and copyright information
mySqlCommand.CommandText = "SELECT @@Version"
MessageBox.Show(mySqlCommand.ExecuteScalar, "SQL Server @@Version")
' Execute command to determine the total count(*) of records
```

```
mySqlCommand.CommandText = "SELECT Count(*) FROM [Order Details]"
MessageBox.Show(mySqlCommand.ExecuteScalar, "Total Orders on File")'
Done
' Done
mySqlConnection.Close()
mySqlConnection.Dispose()
mySqlConnection = Nothing
```

Best Practices

- Because the ExecuteScalar returns only the first column of the first row, don't request more information than that.
- If you have several values to request, consider doing them all on a single SELECT statement or multiple SELECT statements in a batch and then using the ExecuteReader method instead.

Returning XML Data Using a Command Object

Typically, to get your ADO.NET data into XML form, you'll populate a dataset and then export to XML or an XMLDataDocument. The SqlCommand, however, has a handy method called ExecuteXMLReader that, when executed against a SQL Server 2000 or newer version, will return the results of the query as XML to an XmlReader object.

Once in the XmlReader object, you can access element or attribute information, but still only in a forward-only, read-only manner as with any of the .NET Reader classes.

Sample Code

```
Dim mySqlConnection As New System.Data.SqlClient.SqlConnection()
Dim mySqlCommand As System.Data.SqlClient.SqlCommand
Dim myXmlReader As System.Xml.XmlReader
Dim strAttributes As String
' Establish Connection
mySqlConnection.ConnectionString = _
   "Server=(local);Integrated Security=SSPI;Database=Northwind"
mySqlConnection.Open()
' Establish Command
mySqlCommand = mySqlConnection.CreateCommand()
mySqlCommand.CommandText = _
   "SELECT TOP 5 * FROM Products WHERE " & _
   "UnitPrice > 75 FOR XML AUTO"
' Assign results to XMLReader and Read
myXmlReader = mySqlCommand.ExecuteXmlReader()
```

```
While myXmlReader.Read()
    ' Display all attributes for current element
    strAttributes = ""
    While myXmlReader.MoveToNextAttribute()
        strAttributes = strAttributes & myXmlReader.Name & " : " & _
            myXmlReader.Value & ControlChars.CrLf
    End While
    MessageBox.Show(strAttributes, "Product Attributes")
End While
' Done
myXmlReader.Close()
mySqlConnection.Close()
mySqlConnection = Nothing
```

Best Practices

- Use the ExecuteXmlReader method for catching XML data returned from SQL Server.
- Use an XmlDataDocument to import XML data into .NET and eventually into an ADO.NET DataSet.
- By default, the XML returned by SQL Server 2000 maps the columns as attributes. If you desire them to be mapped as elements, append a ",ELEMENTS" after the FOR clause. Consult the SQL Server Books Online (BOL) for the other, various ways to use the FOR XML clause.

Using Parameters with a Command Object

When executing a SQL command or a stored procedure with parameters, you need to ensure that the Command object's parameters collection is populated before you execute it. With SQL commands, you need to create and populate the parameters only as input (which is the default). With stored procedures, however, it's more interesting because these parameters may carry information to the SQL Server, or they may carry information back from SQL Server, or both. If the stored procedure returns a return status code, you'll need to pick that up as a parameter, too.

Here is a simple stored procedure that demonstrates Input, Output, and Return parameters.

Sample Code

```
CREATE PROCEDURE RenewLicense
    @Company        Varchar(10),
    @CurrentYear    Int,
    @RenewalYear    Int OUTPUT
AS
```

```
    IF @Company = 'ACME'
      SET @RenewalYear = @CurrentYear + 10
    ELSE
      SET @RenewalYear = @CurrentYear + 5
    RETURN 1
GO
```

Now, take a look at the ADO.NET code to define the parameters, execute the command, and then query the Output and Return parameters.

Sample Code

```
Dim mySqlConnection As New System.Data.SqlClient.SqlConnection()
Dim mySqlParameter As System.Data.SqlClient.SqlParameter
Dim mySqlCommand As System.Data.SqlClient.SqlCommand
' Establish Connection
mySqlConnection.ConnectionString = _
   "Data Source=Omnibook;Integrated Security=SSPI;Database=Northwind"
mySqlConnection.Open()
' Create Command
mySqlCommand = mySqlConnection.CreateCommand
mySqlCommand.CommandText = "RenewLicense"
mySqlCommand.CommandType = CommandType.StoredProcedure
' Establish Parameters and Execute Command
mySqlParameter = mySqlCommand.CreateParameter
mySqlParameter.ParameterName = "@Company"
mySqlParameter.SqlDbType = SqlDbType.VarChar
mySqlParameter.Size = 10
mySqlParameter.Direction = ParameterDirection.Input
mySqlParameter.Value = "ACME"
mySqlCommand.Parameters.Add(mySqlParameter)
mySqlParameter = mySqlCommand.CreateParameter
mySqlParameter.ParameterName = "@CurrentYear"
mySqlParameter.SqlDbType = SqlDbType.Int
mySqlParameter.Direction = ParameterDirection.Input
mySqlParameter.Value = 2001
mySqlCommand.Parameters.Add(mySqlParameter)
mySqlParameter = mySqlCommand.CreateParameter
mySqlParameter.ParameterName = "@RenewalYear"
mySqlParameter.SqlDbType = SqlDbType.Int
mySqlParameter.Direction = ParameterDirection.Output
mySqlParameter.Value = 0
mySqlCommand.Parameters.Add(mySqlParameter)
mySqlParameter = mySqlCommand.CreateParameter
mySqlParameter.ParameterName = "@ReturnStatus"
mySqlParameter.SqlDbType = SqlDbType.Int
mySqlParameter.Direction = ParameterDirection.ReturnValue
mySqlParameter.Value = 0
mySqlCommand.Parameters.Add(mySqlParameter)
' Execute the Command
```

```
mySqlCommand.ExecuteNonQuery()
' Display the Output and Return Parameters
MessageBox.Show(mySqlCommand.Parameters("@RenewalYear").Value, _
    "@RenewalYear")
MessageBox.Show(mySqlCommand.Parameters("@ReturnStatus").Value, _
    "@ReturnStatus")
' Done
mySqlConnection.Close()
mySqlConnection.Dispose()
mySqlConnection = Nothing
```

Best Practices

- If all of your parameters are *Input* direction parameters, then you might consider concatenating all of the parameters and the appropriate delimiters into one string and executing it, without any accompanying parameters. This can be messy code, but it can result in a more efficient execution because neither SQL Server nor ADO.NET will have to marshal these parameter objects.
- A best practice to save "programmer time," would be to use the DeriveParameters method on a SqlCommandBuilder or OleDbCommandBuilder object to populate all of your parameters, data types, directions, etc. This code will not be as efficient as it could be as far as execution is concerned, because it will have to make a round-trip to the SQL Server at run-time to define those parameters.

Executing Commands within a Transaction

Whenever you are executing more than one command at a time and if those commands must execute as a unit of work such that none should succeed if any fail, then you must use transactions. Technically, you can continue to use transaction support built into the servers, such as embedding BEGIN, COMMIT, and ROLLBACK statements within stored procedures. This, however, should be avoided in lieu of using ADO.NET's transactional support on the Connection object, primarily because of the robust exception handling you get in .NET Framework.

Some pieces of ADO.NET transactions aren't up to speed yet, such as the lack of nested transaction (in most of the .NET data providers) or parallel transaction support (in all of the .NET data providers). The *Yukon* version of SQL Server promises many improvements, both to the SQL Server engine, as well as to ADO.NET. In fact, Microsoft will most likely use the Yukon release as a delivery vehicle for many improvements to the .NET Framework as a whole.

If your database application requires nested transactions today, then you're back to placing BEGIN, COMMIT, and ROLLBACK statements in your command text or stored procedures. In the example after this one, we demonstrate how to work around this limitation.

Sample Code

```
Dim mySqlConnection As New System.Data.SqlClient.SqlConnection()
Dim mySqlTransaction As System.Data.SqlClient.SqlTransaction
Dim mySqlCommand As System.Data.SqlClient.SqlCommand
' Establish Connection
mySqlConnection.ConnectionString = _
   "Data Source=Omnibook;Integrated Security=SSPI"
mySqlConnection.Open()
mySqlConnection.ChangeDatabase("Northwind")
' Establish Command
mySqlCommand = mySqlConnection.CreateCommand()
mySqlCommand.CommandText = "INSERT Customers " & _
   "(CustomerID,CompanyName) VALUES ('WILEY','Wiley Publishing')"
mySqlCommand.Connection = mySqlConnection
' Establish Transaction
mySqlTransaction = _
   mySqlConnection.BeginTransaction(IsolationLevel.ReadCommitted, _
   "NewCustomers")
mySqlCommand.Transaction = mySqlTransaction
' Attempt Execution(s)
mySqlCommand.ExecuteNonQuery()     ' INSERT succeeds
Try
   mySqlCommand.ExecuteNonQuery() ' INSERT fails on PK violation
   mySqlTransaction.Commit()
   MessageBox.Show("Success!", "Both records written")
Catch ex As Exception
   mySqlTransaction.Rollback("NewCustomers")
   MessageBox.Show(ex.ToString(), "No records written")
Finally
   mySqlConnection.Close()
   mySqlConnection.Dispose()
   mySqlConnection = Nothing
End Try
```

Best Practices

- Use transactions whenever you are issuing more than one INSERT, UPDATE, or DELETE in a batch to ensure that all of that work is executed together or none at all.
- Leverage ADO.NET's transaction support rather than issuing transaction commands directly.
- Exception handling and transaction rollback and commit were made for each other. You should make sure that your commit method is part of the Try block. Your rollback method will likely be a part of each and every exception that you catch.

Establish a Nested Transaction

Nested SQL Server transaction are not really supported in ADO.NET. Here's an example on how to nest transactions, using a blend of ADO.NET and Transact-SQL.

Sample Code

```
Dim mySqlConnection As New System.Data.SqlClient.SqlConnection()
Dim mySqlTransaction As System.Data.SqlClient.SqlTransaction
Dim mySqlCommand As System.Data.SqlClient.SqlCommand
' Establish Connection
mySqlConnection.ConnectionString = _
   "Data Source=Omnibook;Integrated Security=SSPI;Database=Northwind"
mySqlConnection.Open()
' Create ADO.NET Transaction with ReadCommitted Isolation level
mySqlTransaction = mySqlConnection.BeginTransaction()
' Create Command - notice the embedded Transact-SQL TRANSACTION
mySqlCommand = mySqlConnection.CreateCommand
mySqlCommand.Transaction = mySqlTransaction
mySqlCommand.CommandText = _
   "INSERT Customers (CustomerID,CompanyName) VALUES " & _
   "   ('ACME1','ACME District Office #1') " & _
   "BEGIN TRANSACTION TR2 " & _
   " INSERT Customers (CustomerID,CompanyName) VALUES " & _
   "    ('ACME2','ACME District Office #2') " & _
   "COMMIT TRANSACTION"
mySqlCommand.ExecuteNonQuery()
' At this point, the Inner INSERT was committed, but the ADO.NET
' transaction has not been. Any queries we execute with this same
' transaction handle will show that they've both been written.
' Verify both Customers were written
mySqlCommand = mySqlConnection.CreateCommand
mySqlCommand.CommandText = _
   "SELECT Count(*) FROM Customers WHERE CustomerID LIKE 'ACME%'"
mySqlCommand.Transaction = mySqlTransaction
MessageBox.Show(mySqlCommand.ExecuteScalar(), "ACME Customers") ' 2
' Now roll back the ADO.NET Transaction, which will roll back the
' inner Transact-SQL Transaction, even though it was committed.
mySqlTransaction.Rollback()
' Verify both Customers are gone
mySqlCommand = mySqlConnection.CreateCommand
mySqlCommand.CommandText = _
   "SELECT Count(*) FROM Customers WHERE CustomerID LIKE 'ACME%'"
mySqlCommand.Transaction = mySqlTransaction
MessageBox.Show(mySqlCommand.ExecuteScalar(), "ACME Customers") ' 0
' Done
```

```
mySqlConnection.Close()
mySqlConnection.Dispose()
mySqlConnection = Nothing
```

Best Practices

- Until ADO.NET matures to the point where it supports nested transactions on each of the .NET data providers, you must use a hybrid solution like this. Keep your eyes on the Microsoft Web site for new versions of the ADO.NET assemblies that will support this in the future.

Using a DataAdapter to Fill a DataSet

The DataAdapter has been described as the *glue* that holds the DataSet to its .NET data provider and the data source. The DataAdapter is responsible for populating the DataSet with the results of a Command's results as well as sending back any changes made to that DataSet since it was populated. The DataAdapter makes these changes with the use of its three Command objects, which contain SQL statements for making such changes.

The DataAdapter also has two events, the RowUpdating event and the RowUpdated event, which fire in that respective order. Business logic can be placed in these events to verify the data before the DataAdapter brokers the changes back to the data source (RowUpdating) and after the change has been made to the data source. This section, however, is about filling the DataSet.

Because the DataSet doesn't contain any information about connections, SQL statements, or other database states, it must rely on its associated DataAdapter(s) to provide this information. Once your DataAdapter has its SelectCommand property assigned, you can fill the DataSet with schema and/or data. We recommend always populating the schema information explicitly before reading data, as this defines all of the constraints.

First, you should call *FillSchema,* which adds a DataTable object to the DataSet and then populates the DataColumnCollection with columns and configures the PrimaryKey and Constraints properties. Once the schema has been loaded, you can be assured that data being loaded into your DataSet will not violate any of the basic constraint rules. Next, you would call Fill to actually place the data in the DataSet. Calling the Fill or FillSchema method will open and close the connection for you automatically, which can be a benefit or a nuisance. As a shortcut, you can also set the MissingSchemaAction property on your DataAdapter to AddWithKey, which will do an implicit FillSchema for you.

Sample Code

```
Dim mySqlDataAdapter As New System.Data.SqlClient.SqlDataAdapter()
Dim mySqlConnection As New System.Data.SqlClient.SqlConnection()
Dim mySqlCommand As System.Data.SqlClient.SqlCommand
```

```
Dim myDataSet As New System.Data.DataSet()
' Establish connection
mySqlConnection.ConnectionString = _
   "Server=(local);Integrated Security=SSPI;Database=Northwind"
mySqlConnection.Open()
' Create a Command
mySqlCommand = mySqlConnection.CreateCommand
mySqlCommand.CommandText = "SELECT * FROM Customers"
' Assign the SelectCommand to the DataAdapter
mySqlDataAdapter.SelectCommand = mySqlCommand
' Before filling a Dataset, you can specify SqlDataAdapter behaviors
mySqlDataAdapter.AcceptChangesDuringFill = True
mySqlDataAdapter.MissingMappingAction = MissingMappingAction.Passthrough
mySqlDataAdapter.MissingSchemaAction = MissingSchemaAction.Add
' Fill the DataSet schema (a good idea to do this explicitly)
mySqlDataAdapter.FillSchema(myDataSet, SchemaType.Mapped, "Customers")
' Fill the DataSet - "Customers" is an arbitrary name within the table
mySqlDataAdapter.Fill(myDataSet, "Customers")
' Done with the connection, but you can continue to use/edit the DataSet
mySqlDataAdapter.Dispose()
mySqlConnection.Close()
mySqlConnection.Dispose()
mySqlConnection = Nothing
```

Best Practices

- Establish a meaningful TableMappings collection, especially if your data source has illogical names.
- Caching entire databases into a DataSet may seem very appealing, but you must balance the time and memory required to populate the dataset with the benefits gained by having that data on the local machine in memory. Only cache those tables which you will be manipulating and any tables that you are constantly referencing. Foreign Key tables, for example, need only contain the key values for verification.
- If you are to be adding new records to a DataSet, you may not want to use Identity or AutoNumber columns as primary keys. Consider using a more globally unique identifier, such as a GUID, as it will avoid any collisions that might occur when you update the data source at a later time.
- Do not request more tables or columns than are necessary.

Defining SQL Commands Using a CommandBuilder Object

Visual Studio .NET protects its users with powerful wizards and graphical designers. When you're not using Visual Studio .NET, however, the CommandBuilder can be your best friend. Not only does it generate accurate INSERT, UPDATE, and DELETE SQL statements for you to use with your DataAdapter when reconciling any changes with a DataSet, but it will also generate your Parameters collection for you.

The SQL commands that the CommandBuilder object generates are good only for single table situations.

Sample Code

```
Dim mySqlDataAdapter As New System.Data.SqlClient.SqlDataAdapter()
Dim mySqlCommandBuilder As System.Data.SqlClient.SqlCommandBuilder
Dim mySqlConnection As New System.Data.SqlClient.SqlConnection()
' Establish Connection
mySqlConnection.ConnectionString = _
  "Server=(local);Integrated Security=SSPI;"
mySqlConnection.Open()
mySqlConnection.ChangeDatabase("NorthWind")
' Establish DataAdapter and CommandBuilder
mySqlDataAdapter.SelectCommand = New SqlCommand( _
   "SELECT * FROM Customers", mySqlConnection)
mySqlCommandBuilder = New SqlCommandBuilder()
mySqlCommandBuilder.DataAdapter = mySqlDataAdapter
' Assign the generated commands, so we can query the DataAdapter's SQL
mySqlDataAdapter.InsertCommand = mySqlCommandBuilder.GetInsertCommand()
mySqlDataAdapter.UpdateCommand = mySqlCommandBuilder.GetUpdateCommand()
mySqlDataAdapter.DeleteCommand = mySqlCommandBuilder.GetDeleteCommand()
' Test
MessageBox.Show(mySqlDataAdapter.InsertCommand.CommandText, "Insert")
MessageBox.Show(mySqlDataAdapter.UpdateCommand.CommandText, "Update")
MessageBox.Show(mySqlDataAdapter.DeleteCommand.CommandText, "Delete")
' Process Data using the DataAdapter Here
mySqlConnection.Close()
```

Best Practices

- Review and improve as necessary the SQL commands built by the Command-Builder object.
- Assign the Insert, Update, and Delete command objects to their respective properties on your DataAdapter, in order to be able to query the DataAdapter's CommandText directly.
- Use the CommandBuilder's DeriveParameters method sparingly. Although it is a time saver for developers, your users will pay that price as it will make a round-trip to the SQL Server for each execution of the code.

Conclusion

Unless you are working strictly with XML-based data, you will need to connect to a physical data store at least twice in the lifetime of a typical database application: once initially to load data and once later to update data. Typically, this cycle is repeated several times and in several different styles during the lifetime of a database application.

The physical connectivity to these data stores is handled through the respective .NET data provider. These providers may, in turn, use ODBC, OLE DB, or some other native .NET code to connect and operate with the data store. Opening connections, creating command parameters, selecting data, establishing transactions, executing commands, updating data, and listening for alerts are all concepts handled here, in this connected layer.

The next chapter will cover the tasks performed in the disconnected layer. Those classes are typically found in the System.Data namespace and are common across all of the .NET data providers.

CHAPTER

11

Manipulating Data in ADO.NET

This chapter will illustrate through sample code how to use the objects in the disconnected layer of ADO.NET. Although we will require the assistance of the data provider layer for retrieving and updating data, the majority of this chapter will focus on the objects found in the System.Data namespace.

The disconnected aspect of ADO.NET is one of its key features and is behind a large amount of the hype .NET has generated. Through the disconnected classes we can build an in-memory relational database, with all the associated tables, relationships, and constraints. In addition, there is sufficient XML meta data describing the data that updates can be easily made back to the data source.

The Disconnected Layer

One of the most important things to realize, when first learning to deal with the disconnected objects, is that they are independent of any data source implementation. Most readers will have likely dealt with data access technologies that were tightly coupled to their providers. Even previous versions of ADO, independent though they were of the data sources themselves, were tightly coupled to OLE DB and COM+. ADO.NET, on the other hand, maintains all of its meta data internally as XML and can be used to represent a wide variety of different types of data stores, including spreadsheet models, relational models, and many textual models as well. Its internal representation is a relational model, and it works best when provided with data in regular structures. When dealing with highly irregular or strongly hierarchical data, the System.Xml data access classes are likely a better solution.

Currently, however, the majority of electronic data in the world is still stored in relational databases, and it likely will continue to be for quite some time. (The authors, like many in the high-tech world, are a bit nervous about making concrete predictions about formats and technology timelines...) ADO.NET, with its relational structure and excellent XML interoperability, is uniquely suited to provide useful data access in an Internet-dominated world.

Structure of This Chapter

This chapter will walk the reader through the creation, filling, manipulation, merging, and update of a DataSet. We'll create some objects in the DataSet from information stored in a relational database and create others completely from scratch. Structurally, the example code will be a class, with a group of private variables holding the DataSet object and the supporting DataAdapter objects. A single public method, called DemoDisconnectedStructures, will be defined that will walk us through a series of private methods demonstrating various aspects of the data manipulation. A stubbed-out framework of the application is provided here.

```
Imports System.Data
Imports System.Data.SqlClient
Imports System.Data.SqlTypes
Public Class DemoDisconnectedDataManipulation
   Private WithEvents myConnection As SqlConnection
   Private WithEvents daCategory As SqlDataAdapter
   Private WithEvents daSupplier As SqlDataAdapter
   Private WithEvents daProduct As SqlDataAdapter
   Private WithEvents myDataSet As DataSet
   Public Sub DemoDisconnectedStructures()
      InitializeDataSetAndConnection()
      BuildSuppliersTableByHand()
      ImportCategoriesTableFromNorthwind()
      ImportProductsTableAndFillData()
      AddRelationships() 'fails
      myDataSet.EnforceConstraints = False
      AddRelationships() 'succeeds
      AddSupplierDataByHand()
      FillCategoriesTableWithExistingAdapter()
      AddDataToSupplierTableWithNewAdapter()
      myDataSet.EnforceConstraints = True
      UpdateNorthwind()
      Navigation_UsingFindAndSelect()
      Navigation_FollowingRelations()
      UpdateNorthwind()
      WriteDataSetToDisk()
      ReadDataSetFromDisk()
      MessageBox.Show("Demonstration Complete")
   'add private methods here.
End Class
```

As you can see, we have a relatively complete structure, minus all of the necessary code. As we progress through the chapter, we'll build each of these procedures in turn. Each method examines a small aspect of manipulating data using ADO.NET. Further methods build on the results of the previous methods, but the ideas are mostly independent, so if you're looking for a quick how-to, feel free to skip to the method that applies. You can download the complete code from the Web site, if you would like to see it in its entirety. It is available both as a text file and as a Visual Studio .NET project.

If you're new to ADO.NET and the .NET Framework, we recommend that you actually sit down and type out the code yourself. Computer programming, like skiing or tennis, can be most effectively learned by doing. But enough preaching—let's hit the code.

Building the Example Framework

First thing we need to do is build the framework class for the sample code. It's listed previously. You may want to make one modification if you're working in the Visual Studio .NET IDE. Instead of defining a class on your own, you may want to simply create a new Windows application and use Form1 as the class. Because forms are strict classes in the .NET Framework, you won't run into any unexpected problems using this method. In fact, you can sneak in a button on the form to trigger the DemoDisconnectedStructures method, a DataGrid to display intermediate results, and a TextBox to display the created schemas. If you use the defaults for the added Button, DataGrid, and TextBox, they'll be named Button1, DataGrid1, and TextBox1. Throughout the demo code you'll see commented-out references to DataGrid1 and TextBox1. If you wish to use these for visual display of results when running the code, simply uncomment them. If you decide to use Visual Studio .NET, you'll end up with something that looks like this code.

```
Public Class Form1
    Inherits System.Windows.Forms.Form
    Friend WithEvents DataGrid1 As System.Windows.Forms.DataGrid
    Friend WithEvents TextBox1 As System.Windows.Forms.TextBox
    Friend WithEvents Button1 As System.Windows.Forms.Button
    Private WithEvents myConnection As SqlConnection
    Private WithEvents daCategory As SqlDataAdapter
    Private WithEvents daSupplier As SqlDataAdapter
    Private WithEvents daProduct As SqlDataAdapter
    Private WithEvents myDataSet As DataSet
+   "Windows Form Designer generated code" 'Region not expanded
    Private Sub Button1_Click(ByVal sender As System.Object, _
          ByVal e As System.EventArgs) Handles Button1.Click
       DemoDisconnectedStructures
    End Sub
+   Public Sub DemoDisconnectedStructures() 'not expanded here
    'add private methods here.
End Class
```

From this code, we can see we've defined a Connection object as well as three DataAdapter objects. These all come from the SqlClient data provider, which seemed a natural choice for a demonstration due to the power and simplicity of the SQL Server provider. All of the examples here could easily be used against an Oracle database using the OleDb data provider by simply replacing the SqlClient objects with their equivalent OleDb objects. We'll use no special methods available only to SQL Server in this demonstration because we're focusing on the disconnected aspect.

In addition to the data provider object, you'll see one additional class-wide variable, myDataSet. This DataSet is the only object we need to define for common access across the class. All the other disconnected objects, such as the DataTable, DataColumn, DataRelation, and Constraint objects, will be contained in this one object. myDataSet will represent the entire disconnected, in-memory relational database used in this chapter.

Simple Utility Function

The first section of code we'll write will actually be a simple utility function that you can use to determine how the DataSet is progressing. The function allows an XML document describing the DataSet schema and data to be easily created and saved to the hard drive, where it can then be opened and viewed in any text reader (although Internet Explorer 5.0 and above looks better). Simply pass a complete filename and path and an optional Boolean value determining whether to include the schema in the output (default is True). There is no checking of the path, so ensure that a valid path is passed, or an exception will be raised. We recommend sprinkling this function liberally throughout the code as you create it, so that you get a feel for how the DataSet is changing. What you're seeing when you look at the output is an XML representation of the DataSet schema in XML Schema Description (XSD) format and the XML version of the data contained in the DataSet. (We'll see how to manipulate this in Chapter 12, "Integrating XML with ADO.NET.")

We'll actually be using the function later to save the DataSet to disk. We'll then use another function to read the file back from disk to populate an empty DataSet.

```
Public Sub WriteXmlToFile(ByVal fileName As String, _
      Optional ByVal withSchema As Boolean = True)
   ' Create the FileStream to write with.
   Dim myFileStream As New System.IO.FileStream _
         (fileName, System.IO.FileMode.Create)
   ' Create an XmlTextWriter with the fileStream.
   Dim myXmlWriter As New System.Xml.XmlTextWriter _
         (myFileStream, System.Text.Encoding.UTF8)
   ' Write to the file with the WriteXml method.
   If withSchema Then
      myDS.WriteXml(myXmlWriter, XmlWriteMode.WriteSchema)
   Else
      myDS.WriteXml(myXmlWriter, XmlWriteMode.IgnoreSchema)
   End If
   'clean up
   myXmlWriter.Close()
   myFileStream.Close()
End Sub
```

Creating the DataSet and Connection

The first step in the creation of an internal representation of data is the creation of the DataSet itself, which will hold all of the tables, relationships, and constraints. Despite its vast usefulness as a container, it is a remarkably simple object to build. We simply call the constructor, passing a name for the DataSet, and then set a few DataSet properties. We'll be setting all of them to their default values, right now, so the code is more an example of how to work with the properties than of any actual use for our example.

We'll also create a SqlConnection object, which we'll use when we need to access the Northwind database from which we'll be drawing much of our sample data. You may need to modify this connection, depending on the database you're using and its properties. If the default connection doesn't work for you, see Chapter 10, "Accessing Data Sources using ADO.NET," for complete information on how to connect to a data source.

```
Public Sub InitializeDataSetAndConnection()
    'initialize our DataSet
    myDataSet = New DataSet("DisconnectedDemoDataSet")
    myDataSet.CaseSensitive = False
    myDataSet.EnforceConstraints = True
    'initialize the Connection
    ' Establish connection
    mySqlConnection = New SqlConnection( _
       "Server=(local);Integrated Security=SSPI;Database=Northwind")
    Try
       mySqlConnection.Open()
    Catch e As Exception
       MessageBox.Show("Connection could not be opened.")
    End Try
End Sub
```

Best Practices

- See Chapter 10 for numerous tips on establishing connections to the data source.
- Use EnforceConstraints = True unless you must manipulate the data to ensure compliance with the constraints. In nearly all cases its more effective to mimic the constraints on the data source, rather than having conflicting constraints that must be reconciled every time you fill or update data.

Building the Suppliers DataTable Manually

Building a DataTable from nothing isn't much more difficult than building a DataSet, but it takes a little more thought on the constraints and column definitions. Because we're going to be importing data from the Northwind Suppliers table, we'll copy the schema from the Northwind Suppliers table directly. You can open up the definition of the Northwind table and create the DataTable schema on your own, or you can copy the code that follows. For comparison, you can use the next method we work on as a sample and import the schema for the Suppliers table directly from Northwind. By using the WriteXmlToFile function to export both of these to XML, you'll see that they are identical, with the exception that the automated schema import will name constraints "Constraint1" and such, instead of the more descriptive names we'll use.

Some important things to notice about the code. The code shows two different, but equivalent ways to create and add a DataColumn to a DataTable. The first uses the DataColumn constructor and generates a standalone DataColumn that is later added to the DataTable. This can be very useful for generating DataColumn objects automatically, in a loop of some nature. The second method uses the DataTable.Columns.Add method to create and add a column. This method is more readable and considerably shorter for adding columns by hand.

We've also called the first column in the Supplier column, SupplierKey, instead of SupplierID. This is merely to demonstrate later how to map differently named columns from a data source to a table in a DataSet. Then we create a unique constraint on the first column, and we declare it as the primary key. Finally, we add the DataTable to the DataSet and close all the objects we've used. Once the DataTable has been added to the DataSet, you can delete the table that you created without fear of losing it from the DataSet—the schema of the DataSet has been updated.

```
' Create our Suppliers table from nothing, using the
'   Northwind Suppliers table as an example.
Public Sub BuildSuppliersTableByHand()
   Dim tblSupplier As DataTable
   Dim myColumn As DataColumn
   ' Create the DataTable to use
   tblSupplier = New DataTable("Suppliers")
   ' Add Primary Key column (use the column constructor)
   myColumn = New DataColumn("SupplierKey", GetType(Int32))
   myColumn.AllowDBNull = False
   myColumn.AutoIncrement = True
   myColumn.AutoIncrementSeed = 100
   myColumn.ReadOnly = True
   tblSupplier.Columns.Add(myColumn)
   ' Add other columns (using the Add method)
   myColumn = tblSupplier.Columns.Add("CompanyName", GetType(String))
   myColumn.MaxLength = 40
   myColumn.AllowDBNull = False
   myColumn = tblSupplier.Columns.Add("ContactName", GetType(String))
   myColumn.MaxLength = 30
   myColumn = tblSupplier.Columns.Add("ContactTitle", GetType(String))
   myColumn.MaxLength = 30
   myColumn = tblSupplier.Columns.Add("Address", GetType(String))
   myColumn.MaxLength = 60
   myColumn = tblSupplier.Columns.Add("City", GetType(String))
   myColumn.MaxLength = 15
   myColumn = tblSupplier.Columns.Add("Region", GetType(String))
   myColumn.MaxLength = 15
   myColumn = tblSupplier.Columns.Add("PostalCode", GetType(String))
```

```
    myColumn.MaxLength = 10
    myColumn = tblSupplier.Columns.Add("Country", GetType(String))
    myColumn.MaxLength = 15
    myColumn = tblSupplier.Columns.Add("Phone", GetType(String))
    myColumn.MaxLength = 24
    myColumn = tblSupplier.Columns.Add("Fax", GetType(String))
    myColumn.MaxLength = 24
    myColumn = tblSupplier.Columns.Add("HomePage", GetType(String))
    myColumn.MaxLength = 1073741823
    ' Create the Primary Key on the first column
    tblSupplier.Constraints.Add("SupplierKey", _
          tblSupplier.Columns("SupplierKey"), True)
    ' Add the Supplier table to the DataSet
    myDataSet.Tables.Add(tblSupplier)
    ' Clean up
    myColumn = Nothing
    tblSupplier = Nothing
End Sub
```

Best Practices

- If using Visual Studio .NET, use the graphical builders and wizards. They are fast and efficient, and they produce remarkably good code. Manipulate this code if necessary for performance tuning.
- Avoid AutoIncrement fields if at all possible. Use GUIDs for DataSet primary keys. They will never, ever conflict, no matter how much manipulation is done when the DataSet is disconnected from the data source.
- Don't build DataTable or DataColumn objects manually if you're accessing a relational data source. Use GetSchema or set MissingSchemaAction to AddWithKey, to automatically import the data source schema into your DataSet tables and columns. (See later sections in this chapter.)

Importing the Categories Table from Northwind

Although creating the schema for a DataTable is a relatively simple task, it can be time consuming and error prone, especially for large tables. If you are using either the OleDb or SqlClient data providers, you can import the schema directly from the database. As well as reducing the chance of introducing hard-to-find schema errors, this can be a very important time saver.

You saw this method in action in Chapter 10, so we'll cover it only briefly here. Because we'll be using the DataAdapter object we define here again when updating the data source, we'll assign it to daCategory, a class-wide object. Notice that we must still define a Command object (in this case, SqlCommand) to retrieve the schema. In this case, we're selecting every column from the table, so we'll get the schema for the whole table. We could, however, select only the schema from a few of the columns in the source table. Two properties of the DataAdapter object bear special mention: MissingMappingAction and MissingSchemaAction. The MissingMappingAction property allows us to specify how the DataAdapter should respond when a mapping between the source table and the DataSet table cannot be found. Because we have not defined any mappings, we must set this to Passthrough, which will automatically add the table and column mappings to the DataAdapter. This will set the column names on the DataSet table to be identical to those from the data source, unless that would create a conflict, in which case a unique name is generated. The MissingSchemaAction determines what action the DataSet should take when the source table has a different schema definition than the DataSet. We must use Add or AddWithKey because our DataSet currently contains no schema for the Categories table.

Finally, we use the FillSchema method of the DataAdapter to retrieve the source database schema for the table and create it within the DataSet. By passing SchemaType. Mapped, we ensure that if there was already schema for the DataTable, it will be merged with the incoming mapping and not be deleted and replaced solely by the source schema.

```
' Import the schema for our Categories table from Northwind.
Private Sub ImportCategoriesTableFromNorthwind()
   Dim mySqlCommandBuilder As New SqlCommandBuilder()
   ' Create a DataAdapter and add the SelectCommand specifying
   '  where to get the data. The command need not return any
   '  actual data, since we're creating only the schema.
   daCategory = New SqlDataAdapter()
   daCategory.SelectCommand = _
         New SqlCommand("SELECT * FROM Categories", mySqlConnection)
   ' Use a SqlCommandBuilder to fill Insert, Update, Delete Commands
   '  (We'll be using these later for an update)
   mySqlCommandBuilder.DataAdapter = daCategory
   daCategory.InsertCommand = mySqlCommandBuilder.GetInsertCommand()
   daCategory.UpdateCommand = mySqlCommandBuilder.GetUpdateCommand()
   daCategory.DeleteCommand = mySqlCommandBuilder.GetDeleteCommand()
   ' Before filling a Dataset, you can specify SqlDataAdapter behaviors
   daCategory.AcceptChangesDuringFill = True
   daCategory.MissingMappingAction = MissingMappingAction.Passthrough
   daCategory.MissingSchemaAction = MissingSchemaAction.Add
   ' Fill the DataSet - "Categories" is an arbitrary name for the Table
   daCategory.FillSchema(myDataSet, SchemaType.Mapped, "Categories")
   ' Clean up
   mySqlCommandBuilder = Nothing
End Sub
```

Best Practices

- Edit the SQL Commands created by the SqlCommandBuilder to increase performance. By default, they return all columns to the data source when updating. This may not be necessary in your application.

Importing the Products Table with Data

We are not restricted to just loading the schema for the table. If we like, we can load the schema and data in one method call. This is virtually identical to the ImportCategoriesTableFromNorthwind method. Instead of calling the FillSchema method of the DataAdapter, we call the Fill method. In this method, we add a DataTable, filled with a selection of Products, to the DataSet. By setting the MissingSchemaAction to AddWithKey, we force the table's schema to be imported along with the data. The result is identical to first calling FillSchema and then Fill, both with the MissingSchemaAction set to Add.

WARNING Fill will also create a schema in the DataSet if the MissingSchemaAction is set to Add. However, the schema is not imported from the data source, but is inferred from the incoming stream of data. This generally results in a poor schema. More often than not, the primary key is not defined in the incoming schema.

```
' Import schema and data for the Products table
Private Sub ImportProductsTableAndFillData()
   Dim mySqlCommandBuilder As New SqlCommandBuilder()
   Dim mySqlCommand As SqlCommand
   ' Create a Command
   mySqlCommand = mySqlConnection.CreateCommand
   mySqlCommand.CommandText = "SELECT * FROM Products " + _
         "WHERE SupplierID < 3 AND CategoryID < 3"
   ' Assign the SelectCommand to the DataAdapter
   daProduct = New SqlDataAdapter()
   daProduct.SelectCommand = mySqlCommand
   ' Use a SqlCommandBuilder to fill Insert, Update, Delete Commands
   mySqlCommandBuilder.DataAdapter = daProduct
   daProduct.InsertCommand = mySqlCommandBuilder.GetInsertCommand()
   daProduct.UpdateCommand = mySqlCommandBuilder.GetUpdateCommand()
   daProduct.DeleteCommand = mySqlCommandBuilder.GetDeleteCommand()
   ' Before filling a Dataset, you can specify SqlDataAdapter behaviors
   daProduct.AcceptChangesDuringFill = True
   daProduct.MissingMappingAction = MissingMappingAction.Passthrough
   daProduct.MissingSchemaAction = MissingSchemaAction.AddWithKey
   ' Fill the DataSet - "Products" is an arbitrary name for the table
   daProduct.Fill(myDataSet, "Products")
   ' Clean up
   mySqlCommand = Nothing
   mySqlCommandBuilder = Nothing
End Sub
```

Best Practices

- Set MissingSchemaAction to AddWithKey. This forces any schema added to the DataSet to be pulled from the data source and not inferred from the incoming data.
- Edit the SQL Commands created by the SqlCommandBuilder to increase performance. By default, they return all columns to the data source when updating. This may not be necessary in your application.
- If filling an empty DataSet, set AcceptChangesDuringFill to True. This can drastically reduce the amount of network traffic when later updating the DataSet to the data store. When AcceptChangesDuringFill is set to False, every record is sent to the data source for update, even if no changes have been made (unless AcceptChanges has been called on the unchanged rows). (See *Add Data to Supplier Table from Northwind* later in this chapter for when to use AcceptChangesDuringFill = False.)

Form Parent-Child Relations between Tables

The next step in creating a useful DataSet is to relate the tables to one another, forming parent-child relationships and, in this case, related UniqueKeyConstraint and ForeignKeyConstraint objects. This is done with a DataRelation object. A DataRelation specifies a link between two tables, defining a parent-child relationship between them. Most commonly this is in the form of one or more unique columns in the parent table, being linked to a similarly typed column in the child table acting as a foreign key. This is often called a one-to-many relation. This allows relationships between the tables such as our Suppliers-Products relation. The primary key of the Suppliers table, SupplierKey, is related to the SupplierID column of the Products table. This allows us to easily find rows in the Products table that are supplied to our store by a given Supplier.

If you look closely at the DemoDisconnectedStructures method, you'll see that this method is called twice. This is done to illustrate the effect of the DataSet.EnforceConstraints property. We have intentionally, but unwisely, loaded the data for the Products table, but not for the Suppliers or Categories tables. We are attempting to establish a DataRelation with constraints between each of these tables and the Products table. In both relations the Products table serves as the child table. Thus, we will not be able to add the DataRelation and associated constraints without the current data violating the newly added constraint! Since the Suppliers table has no entries, there can be no supplier defined for any of the products. This will cause a ConstraintException to be thrown. We then set the EnforceConstraints property to False, and we call this method again, resulting in a set of relations and constraints being added to the DataSet. If we then set EnforceConstraints to True, without first filling the tables with the required rows, a ConstraintException will be thrown at that point.

This method demonstrates two ways to create a DataRelation. The first uses a DataRelation constructor to build an independent DataRelation object that is then added to the DataSet. The second uses the DataSet.Relations.Add method to create and add a relation in one step. By passing the Boolean value of True in the relation constructor, we are telling the .NET Framework to automatically generate the constraints that will make this a one-to-many relation. By passing a False, we don't automatically create the constraints allowing for the possibility of a parent-child relation that is a many-to-many relation.

WARNING **Creating a many-to-many relation is considered very poor relational design. Be very sure you know what you're doing when creating a DataRelation without the supporting constraints.**

```
' Relate the DataTable objects to one another
Private Sub AddRelationships()
    Dim myRelation As DataRelation
    ' Create a DataRelation between Suppliers and Products
    myRelation = New DataRelation("SupplierProductLink", _
          myDataSet.Tables("Suppliers").Columns("SupplierKey"), _
          myDataSet.Tables("Products").Columns("SupplierID"), True)
    Try
        ' Add pre-created DataRelation
        myDataSet.Relations.Add(myRelation)
        ' Create a relation between Categories and Products
        ' Add using the overloaded Add method
        myDataSet.Relations.Add("CategoryProductLink", _
              myDataSet.Tables("Categories").Columns("CategoryID"), _
              myDataSet.Tables("Products").Columns("CategoryID"), True)
    Catch e As Exception
        Dim strMessage As String
        strMessage = "Could not add relation" + ControlChars.CrLf
        strMessage += "Exception: " + e.ToString
        MessageBox.Show(strMessage)
        myDataSet.Relations.Clear()
    End Try
End Sub
```

Best Practices

- Add relations between your tables. Currently, you cannot import from the data source these relations, so they must be added manually.
- If you will be exporting your DataSet to XML, be sure to set the Nested property of the DataRelation. This will force the child tables in the XML output to be nested under their parent tables. (See Chapter 12 for more on using the Nested property.)
- Don't forget that when nesting tables, a child table may be nested under only one parent. This is a requirement of the way data is displayed hierarchically; however, it can be confusing for people used to dealing with relational data because a child table often has multiple parent tables.

Manually Add Data to the Suppliers Table

The next thing we'll do is manually add data to the Suppliers table. We'll establish two new Suppliers for our shop, which will later be merged with some of the data from the Northwind Suppliers table. As we've seen before, this code demonstrates two ways to add an object to a collection. In this case it's a DataRow. Using both the DataRow constructor and the DataTable.Rows.Add method, we'll add two suppliers to the Suppliers table. It bears repeating that the constructor method is nearly always the simplest when automatically building objects, whereas the Add method is more convenient and clearer when physically typing in the values in code yourself.

The secret to adding values to an auto-increment field is to not add a value to that column at all (in the case of the first method) or pass a null value (Nothing in Visual Basic .NET) in place of the column (in the second method). Because we've set our auto-increment to 100 (see BuildSuppliersTableByHand), the first supplier added will have SupplierKey = 100. This was somewhat of a cheat. Had we left the default, the next supplier added would have been SupplierKey = 1, which conflicts with data already in the Northwind Supplier table. In virtually every possible scenario when working with .NET, one or the other value will be overwritten and some of the products will then have the wrong supplier. This can easily be avoided by using a GUID in place of the AutoIncrement column for the Primary Key.

A short aside. Both of us feel that using an AutoIncrement column as a primary key is a very bad idea. The chance of having duplicated keys is simply too great. Using an AutoIncrement column as a primary key can be justified only when there is only one user of the database at a time, and the database is small, in-house, and will never be merge replicated across a cluster of databases. Basically, if you're using ADO.NET, you're building more than an Access database to track your pet names, so don't use an auto-increment column as a primary key. We recommend using GUIDs for all automatically generated primary key columns. GUIDs are unique across the universe, not just the globe; it's just that GUID is easier to say than UUID. Using a GUID guarantees you won't run into problems overwriting a valid row in a database with another, unrelated one. Sure, they're significantly uglier than a simple integer and a bit more awkward to deal with, but the benefits far outweigh the drawbacks.

NOTE Regarding duplicating GUIDs. The possibility of two generated GUIDs having the same value is virtually zero. Put it this way: If your employer is paying you $200 / hour, and a duplicated GUID would cost your employer $100 million in legal fees, you are not cost justified in spending more than one ten-billionth of a second thinking about the duplicate GUID problem.

HINT Using the Integer index values of DataColumn objects in a DataRow, instead of the String column name, can speed execution of the statement by up to three times. This makes the code less readable, though. Consider an enumeration for both readability and speed.

```
' Adds rows to the Supplier table manually
Private Sub AddSupplierDataByHand()
    Dim tblSuppliers As DataTable
    Dim myRow As DataRow
    ' Create a DataTable object for convenience
    tblSuppliers = myDataSet.Tables("Suppliers")
    ' Add a new row using the NewRow technique
    '  the AutoIncrement field will already be filled
    myRow = tblSuppliers.NewRow
    myRow.BeginEdit()
    myRow.Item("CompanyName") = "Marlene's Mosaics"
    myRow.Item("ContactName") = "Marlene Paulfranz"
    myRow.Item("ContactTitle") = "Chief Artisan"
    myRow.Item("Address") = "75 Satostr."
    myRow.Item("City") = "Wuerzburg"
    myRow.Item("Region") = "Bavaria"
    myRow.Item("PostalCode") = "97072"
    myRow.Item("Country") = "Germany"
    myRow.EndEdit()
    tblSuppliers.Rows.Add(myRow)
    ' Add a row using the Add method, and passing an
    '  array of objects (declared inline)
    tblSuppliers.Rows.Add(New Object() {Nothing, _
          "Bungle's Basement", _
          "Mike Patton", _
          "VP Sales", _
          "123 Faith Street", _
          "NoMore", _
          "CA", _
          "76589", _
          "USA", _
          "(888) 555-1212"})
End Sub
```

Best Practices

- To boost performance, pass an array of objects to the Rows.Add method, instead of creating a new DataRow and filling it with data first.
- Avoid AutoIncrement fields if at all possible. Use GUIDs for DataSet primary keys. They will never, ever conflict, no matter how much manipulation is done when the DataSet is disconnected from the data source.

Fill Categories Table from Northwind

In most applications, you'll likely retrieve your data directly from a data source. With ADO.NET this is very easy to do. In the example that follows, we'll use the already created daCategory data adapter to fill the table with selected data from the Northwind Categories table. (For information on how to create a data adapter to fill a table that already exists, see the next section, *Add Data to Supplier Table from Northwind*.)

First, we reset the CommandText to return only a subset of the Categories. This will make looking at the schema much easier. Because we are not modifying the columns returned from the SELECT command that was previously set, we don't need to reset the InsertCommand, UpdateCommand, or DeleteCommand values for the data adapter.

```
' Read data into a DataTable with an existing data adapter
Public Sub FillCategoriesTableWithExistingAdapter()
    ' Set the SelectCommand to return only a few Categories
    daCategory.SelectCommand.CommandText += " WHERE CategoryID < 3"
    ' Use the Fill command to fill the already created Categories table
    daCategory.Fill(myDataSet, "Categories")
End Sub
```

Add Data to Supplier Table from Northwind

Adding data from a data source to an existing, but unmapped, DataTable is not as easy as the other tasks we've done. First of all, a data adapter needs to be defined to pull the data from the data source. Then a mapping must be established that links the source table to the DataSet table, including mappings for each of the columns in the dataset. Luckily, some settings will allow much of this to be done automatically.

The first part of this method looks much like the previous methods because we're just establishing the DataAdapter. The key comes in our setting of the MissingMappingAction and MissingSchemaAction properties. By setting the MissingMappingAction to Passthrough, we are telling the data adapter to automatically add a mapping between columns of the source and destination tables. We're able to do this only because we have used identical names when creating our internal DataSet, except for one. Because we've named our primary key column "SupplierKey" instead of "SupplierID", we're forced to create our own mapping for this table. In this example, it was the exception, but it may be the rule for a DataSet deriving its schema from one table but updating to another.

HINT **You can define two data adapters for the same DataSet table. This can be useful if you need to update two data sources with the same data.**

We'll set the MissingSchemaAction property to Ignore. By using Ignore instead of Add, we're ensuring that our Suppliers table schema won't be updated with the HomePage column that we decided earlier to exclude from our table. Because we don't have the HomePage column defined in our schema, setting MissingSchemaAction to Error would cause an error to be raised.

Next we define a DataTableMapping between the Northwind Suppliers table and our DataSet Suppliers table. Even though they have the same name, we must define this mapping explicitly so that we can use it to define the mapping for its subordinate DataColumn objects. Now, we specify the mapping between the SupplierID column found in Northwind to the SupplierKey column found in our DataSet.

Finally, we use the Fill method to add the selected data from Northwind to our Suppliers table. Using Fill does not delete the columns that already exist in the Suppliers table, but it will overwrite any rows that have a matching primary key. This is the danger of using AutoIncrement columns as primary keys! Had we not known ahead of time that there were no current suppliers with SupplierID values of 100 and 101, we would have completely overwritten our additions to the DataSet. Worse, if we defined products that we're sold by the added supplier, the database would now show that these products were sold by someone completely different. In our case, we may end up requesting our edgy elevator music not from Bungle's Basement but from New Orleans Cajun Delights. Won't they be surprised? This can easily be solved by using GUIDs as primary keys, and we highly recommend them.

WARNING **Fill will overwrite any rows that have matching primary keys.**

HINT **Setting DataAdapter.AcceptChangesDuringFill to False allows you to compare rows that have been changed during the Fill operation. By comparing the updated row versions, you can decide to accept or reject the changes on a row-by-row basis. (Compare the row in the DataRowState.ModifiedCurrent version with the DataRowState.ModifiedOriginal version.) (See System.Data. DataRowState, in the reference section, for more information.)**

```
' Create a DataAdapter to fill a manually built table
Public Sub AddDataToSupplierTableWithNewAdapter()
   Dim mySqlCommandBuilder As New SqlCommandBuilder()
   Dim mySqlCommand As SqlCommand
   ' Create a Command
   mySqlCommand = mySqlConnection.CreateCommand
   mySqlCommand.CommandText = "SELECT * FROM Suppliers " + _
         "WHERE SupplierID < 4"
   ' Assign the SelectCommand to the DataAdapter
   daSupplier = New SqlDataAdapter()
   daSupplier.SelectCommand = mySqlCommand
   ' Use a SqlCommandBuilder to fill Insert, Update, Delete Commands
   mySqlCommandBuilder.DataAdapter = daSupplier
   daSupplier.InsertCommand = mySqlCommandBuilder.GetInsertCommand()
   daSupplier.UpdateCommand = mySqlCommandBuilder.GetUpdateCommand()
   daSupplier.DeleteCommand = mySqlCommandBuilder.GetDeleteCommand()
   ' Before filling a Dataset, you can specify SqlDataAdapter behaviors
   daSupplier.MissingMappingAction = MissingMappingAction.Passthrough
   daSupplier.MissingSchemaAction = MissingSchemaAction.Ignore
   ' Create a mapping between data source table and DataSet table.
   '   Then create a mapping between the SupplierID column from
   '   the Northwind Suppliers table to our SupplierKey column.
   daSupplier.TableMappings.Add("Suppliers", "Suppliers")
   daSupplier.TableMappings("Suppliers").ColumnMappings. _
         Add("SupplierID", "SupplierKey")
```

```
        ' Use Fill to append the imported data to our Suppliers table
        daSupplier.Fill(myDataSet, "Suppliers")
        '' Display resulting DataTable
        'DataGrid1.DataSource = myDataSet.Tables("Suppliers")
        'DataGrid1.Refresh()
        ' Clean up
        mySqlCommandBuilder = Nothing
        mySqlCommand = Nothing
    End Sub
```

Best Practices

- If calling Fill or Merge on a DataSet that already contains changed data, set AcceptChangesDuringFill to False. This will allow you to inspect any changes that were made at the data source and reconcile them with changes you've made at the DataSet.
- Never, unless you absolutely must, use AutoIncrement for a primary key on a table. Use GUIDs instead. You will save yourself countless hours of headaches when dealing with disconnected data.

Updating the Northwind Database

Once we've made some changes to the DataSet, we can use the various DataAdapter objects we've created to update the data source. We do this by simply calling the Update method on the various data adapter objects. There are several ways to do this. The simplest is to call the Update method and pass the DataTable that is being updated. The DataAdapter object will call the appropriate INSERT, UPDATE, or DELETE command based on the DataRowState value. In many cases, this is an appropriate procedure; however, you must be careful not to violate constraints on the data source. For instance, if you delete a row in a parent table, you may orphan child rows.

To get around this problem, you can issue several updates against a data source, each updating only a subset of the updates according to the table and the state of the rows. For instance, you can delete rows in a child table, before deleting rows in the parent table, and then add rows in the parent table, before adding rows to the child table. The preferred sequence of steps is as follows:

1. Delete rows from the child tables.
2. Insert, update, and delete rows from the parent tables.
3. Insert and update rows from the child tables.

Remember that some tables may be different roles in different relationships. This can increase the complexity of the update greatly. In later sections, we'll look at how to use DataRelation objects to navigate to child and parent rows. This technique can also be used to ensure that updates are done in the proper order.

The first update demonstration is commented out. To avoid violating constraints that may be in place on a database, we'll be sure to update the tables in the manner suggested previously.

Finally, we clear out all the data in the DataSet and reload it. This is normally not necessary, but Northwind uses AutoIncrement, Read-Only columns for primary keys. Thus, when we send the update to Northwind, the suppliers we've added will have different primary key values than the ones we've given them. We can see why when we look at the InsertCommand the CommandBuilder has generated for us:

```
INSERT INTO Suppliers(CompanyName, ContactName, ContactTitle, Address,
City, Region, PostalCode, Country, Phone, Fax, HomePage) VALUES (@p1,
@p2, @p3, @p4, @p5, @p6, @p7, @p8, @p9, @p10, @p11)
```

We can see the SupplierID column is left out completely. You cannot correct this by adding the SupplierID column to the InsertCommand because the column in Northwind is read only. Once again, we urge you to use GUIDs whenever you need auto-generated primary keys. GUIDs allow you to make primary key columns read-write, without sacrificing guaranteed uniqueness.

```
' Update the DataSet to Northwind
Private Sub UpdateNorthwind()
    Dim myTable As DataTable
    '' Simple Update method, which may cause problems
    'daSupplier.Update(myDataSet.Tables("Suppliers"))
    'daCategory.Update(myDataSet.Tables("Categories"))
    'daProduct.Update(myDataSet.Tables("Products"))
    ' Safe approach to Updating the data source
    ' Delete rows from the child table
    myTable = myDataSet.Tables("Products"). _
          GetChanges(DataRowState.Deleted)
    If Not myTable Is Nothing Then
       daProduct.Update(myTable)
    End If
    ' Insert, Update, and Delete from parent tables
    daSupplier.Update(myDataSet.Tables("Suppliers"))
    daCategory.Update(myDataSet.Tables("Categories"))
    ' Insert and Update rows from the child table
    myTable = myDataSet.Tables("Products"). _
          GetChanges(DataRowState.Added And DataRowState.Modified)
    If Not myTable Is Nothing Then
       daProduct.Update(myTable)
    End If
    ' Once the update has been made we can AcceptChanges
    myDataSet.AcceptChanges()
    ' Since we're dealing with AutoIncrement fields we really need
    '   to refresh all our data, so we'll clear it and reload
    myDataSet.Clear()
    daSupplier.Fill(myDataSet, "Suppliers")
    daCategory.Fill(myDataSet, "Categories")
    daProduct.Fill(myDataSet, "Products")
    '' Display the Suppliers Table to see the changes
    'DataGrid1.DataSource = myDataSet.Tables("Suppliers")
    'DataGrid1.Refresh()
End Sub
```

Best Practices

- Edit the SQL Commands created by the SqlCommandBuilder to increase performance. By default, they return all columns to the data source when updating. This may not be necessary in your application.
- Never, unless you absolutely must, use AutoIncrement for a primary key on a table. Use GUIDs instead. You will save yourself countless hours of headaches when dealing with disconnected data. (Despite the fact that they are longer than Integers, in the preceding example you would have reduced network traffic because you wouldn't have had to clear, then refill your DataSet.)
- Use GetChanges with the proper DataRowState to help you (1) delete rows from child tables, (2) update, insert, and delete rows from parent tables, and (3) update and insert rows to the child tables, in that order!

Simple Navigation Using Find and Select

Once a DataSet has been created and filled with data, the data needs to be found and manipulated. Two of the simplest methods are the DataTable.Rows.Find method and the DataTable.Select method. The Find method uses the primary key of the desired table to search through the DataRowCollection and return a single matching DataRow. The Select method, on the other hand, uses a SQL-like WHERE clause to return an array of DataRow objects that meet the passed criteria. These rows can then be manipulated.

WARNING **Setting a DataRow returned from a Find or Select method to null (**`Nothing` **in Visual Basic .NET) will not delete the row from the DataTable. You must use the Delete method of the returned DataRow.**

```
' Navigate and Modify Data in the DataSet
Private Sub Navigation_UsingFindAndSelect()
   Dim myRow As DataRow
   Dim myRows() As DataRow
   ' Find  row in the Products table with Primary Key = 1
   '   Set its supplier to Marlene's Mosaics (Supplier #100)
   myRow = myDataSet.Tables("Products").Rows.Find("1")
   myRow.Item("SupplierID") = 100
   ' Select UK suppliers, and append LLC to their names
   myRows = myDataSet.Tables("Suppliers").Select("Country = 'UK'")
   For Each myRow In myRows
      myRow.Item("CompanyName") += ", LLC"
   Next
   'delete a the first instance of Aniseed Syrup
   myRows = myDataSet.Tables("Products").Select("ProductName = " + _
         "'Aniseed Syrup' AND SupplierID = 1")
   If myRows.Length <> 0 Then
```

```
        myRows(0).Delete()
    End If
    ''Display the resulting Products
    'DataGrid1.DataSource = myDataSet.Tables("Products")
    'DataGrid1.Refresh()
End Sub
```

Best Practices

- If Find and Select clauses begin to get a bit bulky and you find yourself writing too much confusing logic, consider using XPath with an XmlDataDocument. Often this can considerably reduce the complexity of a query, especially when following multiple parent-child relations.

Navigation Using Relations

Often it's convenient to directly manipulate either the parents or children of a given row. To do this, use the DataRelation objects to return the desired rows. The examples that follow show how to find the children of a given row and the parent of another row. We also see here how to reject changes for one table, while accepting the changes made to another table.

```
    ' Navigate using Relations
Private Sub Navigation_FollowingRelations()
    Dim myRow As DataRow
    Dim myRows() As DataRow
    Dim myChildRows() As DataRow
    Dim myParentRow As DataRow
    ' Find all child products from New Orleans Cajun Delights
    '   and prefix their names with "Yummy "
    myRows = myDataSet.Tables("Suppliers"). _
        Select("CompanyName = 'New Orleans Cajun Delights'")
    If myRows.Length = 1 Then
        myChildRows = myRows(0).GetChildRows("SupplierProductLink")
        For Each myRow In myChildRows
            myRow.Item("ProductName") = "Yummy " + _
                    myRow.Item("ProductName")
        Next
    End If
    ' Find the Category of the Chai product, and change to Drinks
    myRows = myDataSet.Tables("Products").Select("ProductName = 'Chai'")
    If myRows.Length = 1 Then
        myParentRow = myRows(0).GetParentRow("CategoryProductLink")
        myParentRow.Item("CategoryName") = "Drinks" 'From Beverages
    End If
    ' Reject changes to the Products table
    myDataSet.Tables("Products").RejectChanges()
    ' Clean up
    myRow = Nothing
```

```
    myRows = Nothing
    myChildRows = Nothing
    myParentRow = Nothing
End Sub
```

Best Practices

- Because navigating using relations can be a bit clunky, consider using XPath in the XmlDataDocument that represents the DataSet data. (See Chapter 12 for more information.)

Writing the DataSet to Disk

We can write the DataSet to disk, completely delete our DataSet, and then reload it from disk, re-creating the DataSet. This method writes the DataSet to disk, along with its schema. It does not, however, write the current state of the DataSet. If any changes have been made to the data, the fact that they are changes will be lost when this method is used. There are ways around this by outputting the schema to disk and then outputting a DiffGram. We won't, however, explore that method here. There is a far simpler method using the System.Xml.Serializer class that we'll demonstrate in the next chapter. This method is used to demonstrate the disconnected nature of the DataSet.

In this method, we simply call the WriteXmlToFile method, passing True to indicate that we want to write out the DataSet schema as well. Then we reset the DataSet, eliminating all data and schema, and finally, for good measure, set the whole DataSet to Nothing. (Also, notice that we called the UpdateNorthwind method just prior to this method to ensure that all our data was updated to the database.)

```
' Write the Current DataSet to Disk
'   WARNING:  Do not use this function for full serialization
Private Sub WriteDataSetToDisk()
   ' Write the DataSet to disk using the WriteXmlToFile function
   WriteXmlToFile("C:\!DataSet_Disconnected.xml", True)
   'delete the DataSet
   myDataSet.Reset()
   myDataSet = Nothing
   If myDataSet Is Nothing Then
      MessageBox.Show("DataSet has been completely deleted.")
   End If
End Sub
```

Best Practices

- Use DataSet.WriteXml for high-performance XML output.
- Do not use any of the DataSet's internal XML methods for serialization. Although it can be done, using the XmlSerializer class is much simpler and far more robust. (See Chapter 12 for more information.)

Reading the DataSet from Disk

To complete the disconnected nature demonstration, this method reads the previously created file and rebuilds the DataSet in its entirety.

```
' Read the DataSet from disk and re-create it.
Private Sub ReadDataSetFromDisk()
   Dim fileName As String = "C:\!DataSet_Disconnected.xml"
   Dim strProof As String
   myDataSet = New DataSet()
   ' Create the FileStream to read with.
   Dim myFileStream As New System.IO.FileStream _
         (fileName, System.IO.FileMode.Open)
   ' Create an XmlTextReader with the fileStream.
   Dim myXmlReader As New System.Xml.XmlTextReader _
         (myFileStream)
   ' Read the file with the ReadXml method.
   myDataSet.ReadXml(myXmlReader, XmlReadMode.ReadSchema)
   'clean up
   myXmlReader.Close()
   myFileStream.Close()
   'display proof its been loaded
   strProof = "DataSet has been loaded." + ControlChars.CrLf
   strProof += "Loaded Tables are: " + ControlChars.CrLf
   Dim myObj As Object
   For Each myObj In myDataSet.Tables
      strProof += ControlChars.Tab + myObj.TableName + _
            ControlChars.CrLf
   Next
   MessageBox.Show(strProof)
End Sub
```

Best Practices

- Whenever possible, do not infer schema from an XML document. It tends to be geared toward a hierarchical view of data and will leave out many important relational aspects (such as primary keys).

Conclusion

The disconnected nature of the DataSet can throw programmers off at first. There's a certain mindset to dealing with disconnected database access. In many ways, it is similar to moving from a desktop GUI to Web design.

The disconnected portions of ADO.NET are some of the most powerful data manipulation tools available to you as a programmer. They scale well, are XML based, and help deal with concurrency and conflict resolution.

CHAPTER

12

Integrating XML with ADO.NET

Despite the power of ADO.NET, some tasks are better suited to other technologies. The primary example is hierarchical data. Although most regular hierarchies can be turned into a relational structure, often doing so is cumbersome and inefficient. Even a simple relational design can sometimes require complex SQL statements to return desired data. For instance, returning a set of rows that are related to a grandparent table (two parent-child relations) requires a fairly extensive, although not impossible, SQL query. The same query using XPath, an XML navigation technology, requires only a single, simple path statement.

On the other hand, some queries in SQL look downright trivial compared to their XML counterparts. Luckily, ADO.NET was built with XML in mind. The System.Xml namespace provides a specific type of XML document, the XmlDataDocument, that was designed to interoperate with an ADO.NET DataSet object. This allows you, the programmer, to link the two objects and use whichever one is most convenient for data manipulation. The data is automatically updated in the related object.

We'll take an introductory look at the XmlDataDocument in this chapter. We'll also look at the XML features that are built into the DataSet itself. These allow quick and easy import and export of various XML documents. We'll also have a brief look at the XmlSerializer class, which can be used to archive the complete state and data of a DataSet quickly and efficiently.

Like Chapter 11, "Manipulating Data in ADO.NET," the best way to demonstrate how XML interoperates with ADO.NET is to set up a framework within which to operate. Because we've already created a DataSet and supporting structures in Chapter 11, we'll use that code to build on for our demonstrations here. Basically, each of these functions can simply be added on to the same code that was developed in the previous chapter. This saves us from having to re-create code here to build and manipulate a DataSet, and we can focus on the primary mission of working with XML.

To tie this code to the other, simply place a call to the DemoXmlAdoInterop method after all of the other calls in the DemoDisconnectedStructures method. The DemoXml-AdoInterop method is provided in the code that follows. It simply calls the various methods we'll be defining in this chapter. We'll be using several methods to read and write XML using the DataSet, demonstrating an efficient way to serialize objects, and showing how the XmlDataDocument can provide a hierarchical view of the DataSet.

NOTE As in the last chapter, the code will contain several commented message boxes. By uncommenting these you can display the steps being followed.

```
Private Sub DemoXmlAdoInterop()

    ' Demo DataSet XML Features
    WritingDataSetInformationAsXml()
    ModifyDataSetXmlOutput()
    WritingDataSetInformationAsXml()
    ReadingXmlIntoDataSet()

    ' Demo XML Serialization
    VerifySerialization("C:\!SerializedDataSet.xml")

    ' Demo XmlDataDocument
    LinkingXmlDataDocumentToDataSet()
    LinkingDataSetToXmlDataDocument()
    UsingXPathToReturnDataRows()

    MessageBox.Show("Demonstration Complete")

End Sub
```

Using the DataSet XML Features

The DataSet class provides a great deal of XML functionality within itself. Often there is no need to go to the System.Xml namespace. In Chapter 11, we were introduced to the DataSet XML functionality by the DataSet.WriteXml method (in the WriteXmlTo-File function). However valuable this is for getting a feel for the structure of a DataSet, it is very limited. In this section, we'll look at using the internal XML features of the DataSet and contained classes in more detail.

Retrieving DataSet Information as XML Strings

Before learning how to tailor the XML output, it's important to know how to export the DataSet as XML in the first place. The DataSet has four sets of methods for generating XML information. They are the GetXml, GetXmlSchema, WriteXml, and WriteXmlSchema methods. The WriteXml methods are geared toward using Stream objects, so they are lighter weight and have a broader range of uses than the GetXml methods. They are not as easy to use, though, when merely trying to return a String value. In all cases, the XML returned is configured in much the same structure. We'll examine how to change the default structure in the next section.

The GetXml and GetXmlSchema methods are, by far, the simplest XML methods to use. They accept no parameters to configure the XML. They simply return the data as a String, in the case of GetXml, or the schema as a String, in the case of GetXmlSchema. To use the WriteXml and WriteXmlSchema methods, you either specify a file to write to as a String or pass one of the Stream objects (most likely a XmlTextWriter object). In addition, you can specify the desired output. By default, WriteXml does not include the schema with the data; however, by passing the XmlWriteMode.IncludeSchema the schema is output along with the data. Passing XmlWriteMode.IgnoreSchema produces an XML output document identical to the GetXml method. You can also force the WriteXml method to output an XML document in DiffGram format. This format is one of the most useful, and it is used for the serialization of the DataSet (see the *Serialization* section). It does not output the schema, but it does output both the current and original values of the DataRow objects in the DataSet. When coupled with the schema, this is all that is required to completely serialize a DataSet object. The DiffGram format is made up of three sections. The first provides for all of the current values of the data. The second contains all of the original values of rows that have been changed. The final section provides information on any errors that the DataSet may contain.

This procedure gives several examples of the XML output options available to you. Not all options are explicitly demonstrated; however, the key concepts are illustrated. One particular piece of information to note is that when defining an XmlTextWriter, you can define the text encoding. By specifying UTF8, we are using the most common Unicode format.

In the example that follows, the same WriteXml function is used, but through an XmlTestWriter and directly to a file. When writing directly to an XML file, the following line is output. (The standalone attribute specifies that this XML document doesn't refer to any external entities. It can speed document processing, in some cases, but it isn't necessary.)

```
<?xml version="1.0" standalone="yes" ?>
```

Because the XmlTextWriter can be used to join XML documents, output through it doesn't have the XML version line at the beginning of the document. Finally, we demonstrate the WriteXmlSchema by outputting the XML directly to an in-memory stream object.

```
' Outputing DataSet data and schema as Xml
Private Sub WritingDataSetInformationAsXml()

    Dim strXml As String

    ' Use GetXml to return the data as a String
    strXml = myDataSet.GetXml
    'MessageBox.Show(strXml)

    ' Use GetXmlSchema to return the schema as a String
    strXml = myDataSet.GetXmlSchema
    'MessageBox.Show(strXml)

    ' Write Xml data using an XmlTextWriter
    Dim myXmlTextWriter As New XmlTextWriter( _
          "C:\!XmlTextWriterOutput.xml", System.Text.Encoding.UTF8)
    myDataSet.WriteXml(myXmlTextWriter)

    ' Write the Xml data using only a filename
    myDataSet.WriteXml("C:\!WriteXmlOutput.xml")

    ' Write the Xml data with the Schema
    myDataSet.WriteXml("C:\!WriteXmlOutputWithSchema", _
          XmlWriteMode.WriteSchema)

    ' Write only the changed Xml data (can be used with SQL Server
    '    2000 UpdateGrams)
    myDataSet.WriteXml("C:\!WriteDiffGram.xml", XmlWriteMode.DiffGram)

    ' Write the DataSet schema to a Memory Stream & File
    Dim myMemoryStream As New System.IO.MemoryStream()
    myDataSet.WriteXmlSchema(myMemoryStream)
    myDataSet.WriteXmlSchema("C:\!WriteSchema.xml")

    ' Clean Up
    myXmlTextWriter.Close()
    myMemoryStream.Close()

End Sub
```

Best Practices

- Use the WriteXml method when speed is critical. It's faster. Don't use GetXml in loops that will be used extensively.
- Use GetXml for debugging and whenever you need a string representation with minimal fuss.
- You can use an ASP.NET Response object as the output stream when using WriteXml.
- Don't use the WriteXml method for DataSet serialization. Use the XmlSerializer class instead. (The XmlSerializer is optimized for serialization of .NET objects.)

Modifying the Default XML Output Format

Despite the usefulness of the default XML formats provided by the DataSet, there are times when it doesn't match the output desired. The default output format includes all data contained in element format. Often, data is better suited as an attribute. The default also specifies that each row in a table is output as an element of the same depth as all other rows. This is true even if a parent-child relationship has been established between the tables containing the rows. In most cases, a more natural representation would be to nest the child rows under the parent row element.

This is an example of what the default format of our DataSet looks like. We've chopped out quite a few of the elements to save space, but the idea should be clear. Notice here how the Supplier and Products elements have the same depth and that the SupplierKey is an element.

```
<?xml version="1.0" standalone="yes"?>
<DisconnectedDemoDataSet>
  <Suppliers>
    <SupplierKey>1</SupplierKey>
    <CompanyName>Exotic Liquids, LLC</CompanyName>
    <ContactName>Charlotte Cooper</ContactName>
  </Suppliers>
  <Suppliers>
    <SupplierKey>2</SupplierKey>
    <CompanyName>New Orleans Cajun Delights</CompanyName>
    <ContactName>Shelley Burke</ContactName>
  </Suppliers>
  <Products>
    <ProductID>1</ProductID>
    <ProductName>Chai</ProductName>
    <SupplierID>1</SupplierID>
    <CategoryID>1</CategoryID>
    <QuantityPerUnit>10 boxes x 20 bags</QuantityPerUnit>
    <UnitPrice>18</UnitPrice>
    <UnitsInStock>39</UnitsInStock>
    <UnitsOnOrder>0</UnitsOnOrder>
    <ReorderLevel>10</ReorderLevel>
    <Discontinued>false</Discontinued>
  </Products>
</DisconnectedDemoDataSet>
```

As you can see, the Suppliers and Products have the same depth in the document. This may be a good idea, but for our purposes, we're likely more interested in seeing the products tucked inside their supplier. In addition, the IDs should arguably be attributes included in their parent elements. Finally, for our current purposes, we don't care if the item has been discontinued, so we'd like to suppress the output of that column when creating XML.

A more appropriate output might look something like the document that follows. Notice that now the Products are nested under the appropriate Suppliers and the SupplierKey is an attribute.

```
<?xml version="1.0" standalone="yes"?>
<DisconnectedDemoDataSet>
  <Suppliers SupplierKey="1">
    <CompanyName>Exotic Liquids, LLC</CompanyName>
    <ContactName>Charlotte Cooper</ContactName>
    <Products ProductID="1" SupplierID="1" CategoryID="1">
      <ProductName>Chai</ProductName>
      <QuantityPerUnit>10 boxes x 20 bags</QuantityPerUnit>
      <UnitPrice>18</UnitPrice>
      <UnitsInStock>39</UnitsInStock>
      <UnitsOnOrder>0</UnitsOnOrder>
      <ReorderLevel>10</ReorderLevel>
    </Products>
    <Products ProductID="2" SupplierID="1" CategoryID="1">
      <ProductName>Chang</ProductName>
      <QuantityPerUnit>24 - 12 oz bottles</QuantityPerUnit>
      <UnitPrice>19</UnitPrice>
      <UnitsInStock>17</UnitsInStock>
      <UnitsOnOrder>40</UnitsOnOrder>
      <ReorderLevel>25</ReorderLevel>
    </Products>
  </Suppliers>
  <Suppliers SupplierKey="2">
    <CompanyName>New Orleans Cajun Delights</CompanyName>
    <ContactName>Shelley Burke</ContactName>
    <Products ProductID="4" SupplierID="2" CategoryID="2">
      <ProductName>Chef Anton's Cajun Seasoning</ProductName>
      <QuantityPerUnit>48 - 6 oz jars</QuantityPerUnit>
      <UnitPrice>22</UnitPrice>
      <UnitsInStock>53</UnitsInStock>
      <UnitsOnOrder>0</UnitsOnOrder>
      <ReorderLevel>0</ReorderLevel>
    </Products>
  </Suppliers>
</DisconnectedDemoDataSet>
```

This appears to be a much more appropriate representation of our data. The format we discussed earlier has been implemented in this output. But before we look at the code, there's something to think about. We've completely neglected looking at or mentioning the Categories table. Yet it is related to the Products table as a parent, just like the Supplier table. This dual parent relationship is very easy to express in a relational structure; in fact, it's completely natural. Try figuring out a way to smoothly express the same relationship in a nested hierarchical structure. Can't do it? Neither could we. Nor could Microsoft. Nor, we believe, could anyone, without seriously duplicating presented data. Thus you must decide which parent-child relation should be expressed in the XML output. And here we stress the singular. One table may be the child in only one relationship that is expressed as a nested relationship in XML. The same child, however, may be the parent in any number of nested relations—as long as the child tables have only one parent. Stated simply, a table can be nested under only one parent, but may contain multiple nested children.

The sample code that follows uses the DataRelation.Nested property to nest the Products table beneath the Suppliers table. If we were interested in looking at the Categories and their contained products, we could easily "unnest" the Products table from Suppliers and nest it under the Categories table instead. In the example that follows, the code to do just that is commented out. The code then demonstrates setting the DataColumn.ColumnMapping property to change the output format of the column. In most cases, we set the output to an attribute, but in the case of the Discontinued column, we suppress its output altogether.

Running the WritingDataSetInformationAsXml method, defined earlier, will result in an output roughly matching the example XML document presented previously.

```
' Modify the XML Output of a DataSet
Private Sub ModifyDataSetXmlOutput()

   ' Nest the Products under their Supplier
   '     (This produces the output seen above.)
   myDataSet.Relations("SupplierProductLink").Nested = True

   '' Unnest the Products table, and nest under Categories instead
   ''     (This nests the products under their catergories.)
   'myDataSet.Relations("SupplierProductLink").Nested = False
   'myDataSet.Relations("CategoryProductLink").Nested = True

   ' Set the ID columns as Attributes
   myDataSet.Tables("Suppliers").Columns("SupplierKey"). _
         ColumnMapping = MappingType.Attribute
   myDataSet.Tables("Products").Columns("ProductID"). _
         ColumnMapping = MappingType.Attribute
   myDataSet.Tables("Products").Columns("SupplierID"). _
         ColumnMapping = MappingType.Attribute
   myDataSet.Tables("Products").Columns("CategoryID"). _
         ColumnMapping = MappingType.Attribute

   myDataSet.Tables("Products").Columns("Discontinued"). _
         ColumnMapping = MappingType.Hidden

End Sub
```

Best Practices

- Use the Nested property and the ColumnMapping property liberally to ensure output XML meets your needs. It's easier and faster to ensure that you have the proper output the first time than it is to correct output using an XSLT afterward.
- Use MappingType.Hidden to prevent an XmlDataDocument from having access to that column. (See the text that follows for information on using the XmlDataDocument.)

Reading XML Data into a DataSet

Data in XML format can also be easily read into a DataSet. The cleanest imports come from data that was exported from a DataSet into XML format, but other formats can be handled as well. If a schema is not provided, it will be inferred from the structure of the incoming data. Be aware, though, that this process isn't foolproof, and you often end up with a structure that is entirely different from what you might have imagined.

The following code is a simple example of reading from an XmlTextReader and directly from a file. In the first instance, the schema is inferred from the data. Take a good look at the text in the message box. Notice the sequence in the output and the lack of a defined primary key. The inference engine placed a high priority on having the columns provided in proper order, but it completely missed the existence of a primary key (which is very hard to detect without meta data). The next example uses ReadXmlSchema to preload the DataSet with the proper schema, then reads the previously exported DiffGram to completely re-create the saved DataSet, including the DataRowState of each of the saved rows. (This successfully deserialized the DataSet, but it took two separate read operations. The section dealing with serialization shows how to do this more simply and with only one step.)

```
' Read XML documents into a DataSet
Private Sub ReadingXmlIntoDataSet()

   Dim myXmlTextReader As XmlTextReader

   Dim myNewDataSet As New DataSet("NewDataSet")

   'Read an XML document, inferring the schema
   myXmlTextReader = New XmlTextReader("C:\!WriteXmlOutput.xml")
   myNewDataSet.ReadXml(myXmlTextReader, XmlReadMode.InferSchema)
   MessageBox.Show(myNewDataSet.GetXmlSchema)

   ' Duplicate the previously saved DataSet
   myNewDataSet.Reset() 'delete all contents
   myNewDataSet.ReadXmlSchema("C:\!WriteSchema.xml")
   myNewDataSet.ReadXml("C:\!WriteDiffGram.xml", XmlReadMode.DiffGram)
   MessageBox.Show(myNewDataSet.GetXmlSchema)

End Sub
```

Best Practices

- Be suspicious of inferred schemas. The inference engine used is geared toward a hierarchical view, and it will miss many of the relational aspects of your data.
- Watch out for highly nonregular hierarchical data. It may map into an incredibly ugly, and completely useless, relational form.

XML Serialization Using XmlSerializer

Serialization is one of the most common requirements when building an application, especially when state must be saved between runs of the program. It is also useful when passing data across system boundaries, or over the Internet. XML serialization has become one of the most popular methods for serialization, since it is human readable and easily passes through virtually all firewalls. This section focuses on serialization of a DataSet using the XmlSerializer provided by the .NET Framework.

Serializing a DataSet Using XML

To begin with, let's go back to Chapter 11 and address one of the problems we had with storing the DataSet to disk and recovering it in the proper state at a later time. We had to be sure that we didn't have any changes to the DataSet that hadn't yet been updated to the data source. This is a very severe limitation. What would have happened, had we opened a DataSet and attempted to synchronize it with the data source? The DataSet would have treated all of the rows that were read (including ones originally retrieved from Northwind) as recent additions and would have called INSERT statements on all of them against the data source, wreaking havoc on our Supplier table (because it depended on AutoIncrement columns as a primary key). We would have created duplicates of every supplier that we had in the DataSet. This would be disastrous if repeated "SELECT *" statements are executed—geometric growth is pretty amazing!

The solution is to save the DataSet state with the data when it is saved to disk. This can be done using a combination of various parameters with the WriteXml and WriteXmlSchema methods, but it's very inelegant. (We saw an example of this in the last section, with the ReadXmlSchema method and ReadXml method using a DiffGram.) Instead we introduce serialization using the System.Xml.Serialization namespace. Serialization is the process of taking an object and saving to disk or stream all of the relevant properties, state, and data stored in that object. Later, the file or stream can be used to re-create the object in its entirety, including the proper state. In the past, most programmers designed proprietary algorithms and formats to archive their objects. With the popularity of XML and its associated tools, most serious programmers now use XML as a storage format for serialization of their objects. Thus, the System.Xml.Serialization namespace. This namespace was designed specifically for saving object state and data to XML. This provides the programmer with benefits outside of being able to store and retrieve object state. For instance, because XML is strictly a text format, it can stream, unhindered, through most firewalls, allowing objects to be re-created at another machine (possibly supporting a data-intensive XML Web service).

Although the System.Xml.Serialization namespace wasn't specifically designed for ADO.NET, it is very useful for serializing the DataSet. This simple method takes our DataSet and saves it to an XML file containing state as well as data. To perform the serialization, we use an XmlSerializer and XmlTextWriter. The XmlTextWriter provides access to the disk, and the XmlSerializer perfoms the serialization. The XmlTextWriter is set to use UTF8 as the text encoding. This is the Unicode format most often used for Unicode documents.

NOTE We have serialized the DataSet to disk using an XmlTextWriter. It can be just as easily serialized to any Stream object, including the Response object in ASP.NET or any number of other Streams.

```
' Serialize a DataSet using an XmlSerialize object
Private Sub SerializeDataSet(ByVal inDataSet As DataSet, _
                              ByVal fileName As String)

    Dim mySerializer As XmlSerializer
    Dim myWriter As XmlTextWriter

    mySerializer = New XmlSerializer(GetType(DataSet))
    myWriter = New XmlTextWriter(fileName, System.Text.Encoding.UTF8)

    mySerializer.Serialize(myWriter, myDataSet)

    myWriter.Close()

End Sub
```

Best Practices

- Use the XmlSerializer for all your serialization needs, not just the DataSet. It's fast and efficient, and it will prevent you from having to re-create serialization formats.
- If you're serializing a document for immediate use, don't serialize to disk, then reread. Simply use a stream object.

Deserializing a DataSet

Once a DataSet has been serialized, we're free to do any number of things; we can power down the computer, send it to a server on the Internet, or merely pass it from one object to another. Either way, the object is now saved in an XML textual format. To re-create the object in its original state, we need to create a new XmlSerializer specifying the type of object we're going to work with—in our case, a DataSet.

```
' Deserialize a DataSet using an XmlSerialize object
Private Function DeserializeDataSet(ByVal fileName As String) As DataSet

    Dim mySerializer As XmlSerializer
```

```
    Dim myReader As System.Xml.XmlTextReader

    mySerializer = New XmlSerializer(GetType(DataSet))
    myReader = New XmlTextReader(fileName)

    If mySerializer.CanDeserialize(myReader) Then
       DeserializeDataSet = mySerializer.Deserialize(myReader)
    Else
       DeserializeDataSet = Nothing
    End If

    myReader.Close()

End Function
```

Best Practices

- Use the CanDeserialize method to ensure that a stream can be deserialized.

Proving Serialization Works

The next method doesn't demonstrate any new functionality, but it does prove that the serialization/deserialization process maintained the state of DataSet. The state of a DataSet is basically in the states of the data rows. If a row has been changed, it maintains its original data as well as the changed data, and it sets its DataRowState to Modified. Using the DataSet.GetChanges method, we can return a DataSet containing only the data that has been changed since the last AcceptChanges was called. We can use this method to determine if the serialization was successful. We'll simply compare the DataSet returned from a GetChanges before the serialization to one returned after the deserialization. To compare the two DataSet objects, we'll use the GetXml method to return a String representation of the changes.

```
Private Sub VerifySerialization(ByVal fileName As String)

    Dim myChanges As DataSet
    Dim BeforeSerialization As String
    Dim AfterSerialization As String

    ' Get the records marked as Modified
    myChanges = myDataSet.GetChanges()
    BeforeSerialization = myChanges.GetXml

    'MessageBox.Show(BeforeSerialization)

    SerializeDataSet(myDataSet, fileName)

    ' Ensure our DataSet objects are completely gone.
    myDataSet = Nothing
```

```
        myChanges = Nothing

        If myDataSet Is Nothing Then
            MessageBox.Show("The DataSet is no longer with us.")
        End If

        ' Deserialze the DataSet from the file just saved
        myDataSet = DeserializeDataSet(fileName)

        ' Get the records marked as Modified
        myChanges = myDataSet.GetChanges()
        AfterSerialization = myChanges.GetXml

        'MessageBox.Show(AfterSerialization)

        If BeforeSerialization = AfterSerialization Then
            MessageBox.Show("The two recordsets have the same changes.", _
                    "Serialization Successful!")
        End If

    End Sub
```

Using the XmlDataDocument

In the past, data has been manipulated in either a relational or a hierarchical view. The introduction of the XmlDataDocument and DataSet changed that. You can manipulate data in either structure, and the changes to the underlying data are synchronized between the two documents. This opens up whole new areas of convenience and performance gains. Using XML-related technologies like XSL (XML Style Language) to quickly transform a DataSet into an HTML page and using SQL queries against an XML data source are just two ways that this integration will make your life easier. This section provides an introduction to using the XmlDataDocument to work with a hierarchical view of the data we've seen up to now, as hierarchical.

WARNING **Remember that XML is case sensitive. This means that you must be more cautious when working with XML data than with a DataSet.**

Linking an XmlDataDocument to a DataSet

The XmlDataDocument is an XML document class that was specifically designed to interoperate with the DataSet class. So, you'd expect linking an XmlDataDocument to be easy. It is. There's only one line that does the linking; the rest is there just to prove that it's actually happened. Simply create an XmlDataDocument, and pass the DataSet in the constructor. That's it. Here's the code:

```
Dim myXmlData As New XmlDataDocument(myDataSet)
```

The demonstration that follows points to an interesting effect. While iterating through the XmlNodeList, writing the names of the Products to the output string, we've used the ChildNodes property. This property returns the child node based on its ordinal position within the parent node. We're outputting the first child element (0), which is the product name. At least, now it's the product name. That assumes we've set our columns such that the ProductID column was set to an attribute, which we did earlier. If you comment out that piece of code and rerun the entire project, you'll find that a list of ProductID values is written, instead of a list of ProductName values. (We could have avoided this problem in a number of ways, primarily by using GetElementsByTagName("ProductNames") instead.)

TIP If a DataColumn has its ColumnMapping property set to MappingType.Hidden, that element will not be accessible from the XmlDataDocument. You can use this feature to hide columns from the XML representation of the data.

```
' Link a DataSet to an XmlDataDocument
Private Sub LinkingXmlDataDocumentToDataSet()

   Dim myNode As XmlNode
   Dim strOutput As String

   Dim myXmlData As New XmlDataDocument(myDataSet)

   ' Demonstrate the Data has been loaded.
   myNodeList = myXmlData.GetElementsByTagName("Products")
   strOutput = "Products: " + ControlChars.CrLf + ControlChars.CrLf
   For Each myNode In myXmlData.GetElementsByTagName("Products")
      strOutput += myNode.ChildNodes(0).InnerText + _
                   ControlChars.CrLf
   Next myNode
   MessageBox.Show(strOutput)

End Sub
```

Best Practices

- Use an XmlDataDocument when you want a hierarchical view of data or want to use XML technologies like XSLT, XPath, and XQuery.
- Don't confuse an XmlDocument with the XmlDataDocument. The XmlDataDocument extends the XmlDocument to provide tight integration with the DataSet. Both objects, however, fully support the W3C DOM Levels 1 and 2 and can be used as a source for an XslTransform object.

Linking a DataSet to an XmlDataDocument

As we've seen previously, linking an XmlDataDocument to a DataSet is very easy. The same applies for linking a DataSet to an existing XmlDataDocument. It's also just a few lines of code.

We are able to hide columns from the XmlDataDocument by setting the value of the DataColumn.ColumnMapping to Hidden. Similarly, we are able to hide the complexity of an XmlDataDocument from its associated DataSet. To do this, we create an XmlDataDocument without a linked DataSet. Then we retrieve a new DataSet, using the XmlDataDocument.DataSet property, and fill the returned DataSet with a schema that exposes only a portion of the data. This allows us to create a relational view of a small subset of the hierarchical data. By working with this small window, changes are made to the relevant pieces of data, while the remaining data is hidden. This can be very effective when data consumers or users have a need for only a small piece of the data, but all the data needs to be available for some other user or process. Several different data stores don't need to be created. Of course, if you want to expose all of the data in an XmlDataDocument, simply ensure that the schema in the DataSet covers all of the elements.

For our example, we'll create a DataSet able to view only the ProductID and ProductName columns of the list of products. Thus, the DataSet cannot be used to change any Supplier or Category information, nor to change any of the product columns besides the first two. Once the schema has been defined for the DataSet, the XmlDataDocument can be loaded. A list of product names is then produced, using the DataSet. Two message boxes have been commented out. Uncommenting these will show the severely limited data and schema provided by the DataSet.

WARNING **You cannot create or add to schema for a DataSet once the XmlDataDocument has been loaded with data.**

NOTE **Had we wished to load the entire schema, we could have used the ReadXmlSchema method to load a complete schema from an XML file.**

```
' Linking a DataSet to an XmlDataDocument
Private Sub LinkingDataSetToXmlDataDocument()

   Dim myXmlDoc As XmlDataDocument
   Dim myExampleDataSet As DataSet
   Dim myRow As DataRow
   Dim strOutput As String

   ' Create a
   myXmlDoc = New XmlDataDocument()

   ' Get a DataSet and build a very simple schema
   myExampleDataSet = myXmlDoc.DataSet
```

```
    myExampleDataSet.Tables.Add("Products")
    myExampleDataSet.Tables("Products").Columns.Add("ProductID", _
          Type(Int32))
    myExampleDataSet.Tables("Products").Columns.Add("ProductName", _
          Type(String))

    myXmlDoc.Load("C:\!WriteXmlOutput.xml")

    ' Prove the DataSet can access data in the XmlDataDocument
    For Each myRow In myExampleDataSet.Tables("Products").Rows
       strOutput += myRow.Item("ProductName") + _
                    ControlChars.CrLf
    Next
    MessageBox.Show(strOutput)
    'MessageBox.Show(myExampleDataSet.GetXml)
    'MessageBox.Show(myExampleDataSet.GetXmlSchema)

End Sub
```

Best Practices

- Use several DataSet objects on the same XmlDataDocument to create relational "windows" that are appropriate for different members of an organization.
- Ensure that your schema is complete before loading the XmlDataDocument with data.

Linking a DataSet to Existing XML Data

There's one more way to link a DataSet and XmlDataDocument. This is basically a combination of the two methods we've just seen, although it is more like the second approach. In this method, you load a DataSet with schema, create a new XmlDataDocument using the DataSet in the constructor, and finally load the XmlDataDocument with data from an XML file. Because this way of tying together a DataSet and XmlDataDocument is so similar to the other two, no example code will be provided. Simply be aware that this is one more approach to combining XML and ADO.NET.

Using XPath Statements to Return a DataRow

We've seen how to use ADO.NET methods for retrieving data from an XmlDataDocument. Exposing a hierarchical data source to relational manipulation can often be very useful. On the other side of the equation, we can use XPath not only to select and display XML nodes, but to return a set of DataRow objects. To demonstrate this functionality, we'll use an XPath statement to select a collection of nodes. These nodes are then converted to DataRow elements, using the XmlDataDocument.GetRowFromElement method. These DataRow objects are displayed and manipulated. To show that the XmlDataDocument has also been modified, the XPath statement is run again and the same nodes are returned. These are displayed, illustrating that the changes made to the DataRow objects have been reflected in the XmlDataDocument.

NOTE This book cannot serve as an introduction to XPath. The technology is simply too large. Please refer to an introductory XML book for information on XPath and other XML-based technologies.

```
' Demonstrate the use of XPath in navigating an XmlDataDocument
Private Sub UsingXPathToReturnDataRows()

   Dim myNodes As XmlNodeList
   Dim myNode As XmlNode
   Dim myRow As DataRow
   Dim strOutput As String

   Dim myXmlDoc As New XmlDataDocument(myDataSet)

   ' Select nodes from the XmlDataDocument using XPath
   myNodes = myXmlDoc.DocumentElement.SelectNodes( _
         "Suppliers[//Products/@CategoryID = 1]")

   strOutput = "Suppliers of Drinks: " + ControlChars.CrLf + _
            ControlChars.CrLf
   For Each myNode In myNodes
      If myNode.NodeType = XmlNodeType.Element Then
         ' Convert the Element to a DataRow
         myRow = myXmlDoc.GetRowFromElement(myNode)
         strOutput += myRow.Item("CompanyName") + ControlChars.CrLf
         ' Modify the DataRow
         myRow.Item("CompanyName") += " ***"
      End If
   Next
   MessageBox.Show(strOutput)

   ' Reselect show modifications were made to XmlDataDocument
   myNodes = myXmlDoc.DocumentElement.SelectNodes( _
         "Suppliers[//Products/@CategoryID = 1]")

   strOutput = "Suppliers of Drinks (Ver2): " + ControlChars.CrLf + _
            ControlChars.CrLf
   For Each myNode In myNodes
      If myNode.NodeType = XmlNodeType.Element Then
         ' Use XPath to select first child node named "CompanyName"
         strOutput += myNode.SelectSingleNode("CompanyName").InnerText + _
               ControlChars.CrLf
      End If
```

```
        Next
        MessageBox.Show(strOutput)

        ' Reject changes made to both DataSet and XmlDataDocument
        myDataSet.RejectChanges()

    End Sub
```

Best Practices

- Use XPath statements when querying for grandchildren of a record. This is both much clearer and faster than using the equivalent code in a relational DataSet.

Using ADO.NET with XML

The convenience of having two different views of the same data simplifies programming against that data. It allows you to use the right tool for the job. Sometimes using a relational view is awkward and time consuming. In this case, switch to the hierarchical view. Sometimes the inverse is true, in which case it makes sense to use the relational view.

Another consideration is your particular data manipulation skills. Now you can use the technologies you know well, regardless of the origin on the data. But don't use just the techniques you're comfortable with. Use the availability of the other methods to provide a gradual introduction to a new technology. If you're comfortable with relational data manipulation, use the XmlDataDocument for a gradual introduction to XML. On the other hand, if you're an XML expert, use the close ties with the DataSet to learn how to manipulate data in a relational data model. Either way, have fun, learn, and make money.

Using the XML features in these technologies is also a wonderful way to interact with operating systems and other programs that may not be compatible with yours. Using XML Web services is a key example of this use. With XML Web services, you can call methods on computers that are hosted on different operating systems or that are built using incompatible languages.

Index

A

D

E

F

G

H

I

J

K

L

M

T

U

V

W

X

Z